Praise for Joan

"Joanna Lipper's collection of exc

"There is nothing like the excitement of cracking open a new book, discovering talent, stumbling onto a fresh idea. It's what keeps us alert, trolling the endless shelves. . . . *Growing Up Fast*, the story of six teen mothers in a burnt-out rust-belt city (originally the subject of a documentary) reveals much about welfare reform, domestic violence, and the state of public education."

—*The Washington Post Fall Preview*

"This deserves a spot on the shelf near Robert Coles's similarly accessible investigations of contemporary social issues." —Stephanie Zuiren, *Booklist*

"Extraordinary reporting . . . clear, insightful prose . . . *Growing Up Fast* succeeds because of the author's evident respect for her subjects." —*Mother Jones*

"It is a Dickensian collection of tales. . . . Exhaustively researched . . . Lipper builds a detailed case against the systems—schools, welfare, the Department of Social Services—that repeatedly fail these girls."

—Lucinda Franks, *The New York Times Book Review*

"A searing, heartrending account . . . a strong argument for better state funding of teen pregnancy prevention programs that have seen cuts in recent state budgets. Somebody—an art teacher, a basketball coach, a pastor, a therapist—has to throw lifelines to these girls before they grow up too fast in a world in which premature sex and motherhood are rites of passage." —*The Boston Globe*

"What emerges is a detailed, brutally honest look at families broken, dreams shattered, crime rampant, and a once-bustling city rapidly dying. . . . Four years in the making, this excellent investigational study belongs in all academic libraries."

—*Library Journal*

"Compelling and important . . . this book adroitly illuminates a social crisis."

—*Publishers Weekly*

"A touching treatise on the role of individuality, responsibility, and luck in American society."

—*Salon.com*

"There are many reasons why Pittsfield, and similar struggling postindustrial communities, find it difficult to get at the problems that plague them, and one major reason is that those who suffer most from social and economic ills have no voice. Pittsfield's growing class of teenage mothers get that voice in the new book *Growing Up Fast*, and they should be listened to."

—*The Berkshire Eagle*

"What is society's role in this saga of young moms and dads continuing a legacy of unhappiness and dysfunction? Lipper does an excellent job of exploring how society in general and government in particular have failed to address the issue of single parenthood and its attendant issues of poverty, drug abuse, violence, and hopelessness."

—*Commonwealth* magazine

"Joanna Lipper's book works as a literary representation of the film *8 Mile*. Like the hit movie, Lipper's investigation of the young working class in a burnt-out, postindustrial, rust-belt city portrays lives of not-so-quiet desperation."

—Nelson George, author of *Hip Hop America*

"Writing in the tradition of *Winesburg, Ohio*, Joanna Lipper takes us into Pittsfield, Massachusetts. *Growing Up Fast* is an astonishing book combining arresting portraits of mothers and fathers who are themselves children with a devastating depiction of a community living on the edge of economic despair."

—Carol Gilligan, author of *In a Different Voice*

"America has been waiting for *Growing Up Fast* for too long. . . . In telling the stories of Jessica, Shayla, Amy, Sheri, Liz, and Colleen so sensitively, and often in the voices of the girls themselves, their families, friends, and partners, this landmark work of empathy and of oral history reads like a nineteenth-century novel of young women burdened by fates they did not choose. Everyone who works with young people and children should read this book; so should policy makers; so should parents; so should young people themselves."

—Naomi Wolf, author of *Promiscuities*

"Lipper writes with compassion and insight, is not judgmental, and accentuates subjects' strengths. I would recommend this book not only to health care professionals taking care of adolescent girls but. . . . to teenagers themselves, so that they can read firsthand about the struggles of these young parents."

—*JAMA (Journal of American Medical Association)*

GROWING UP FAST

Text and Photographs

by

Joanna Lipper

PICADOR NEW YORK

www.picadorusa.com

Picador® is a U.S. registered trademark and is used by St. Martin's Press under license from Pan Books Limited.

For information on Picador Reading Group Guides, as well as ordering, please contact the Trade Marketing department at St. Martin's Press.
Phone: 1-800-221-7945 extension 763
Fax: 212-677-7456
E-mail: trademarketing@stmartins.com

Design by Nick Wunder

Library of Congress Cataloging-in-Publication Data

Lipper, Joanna.
Growing up fast / Joanna Lipper.
p. cm.
ISBN 0-312-42222-9 (hc)
ISBN 0-312-42223-7 (pbk)
EAN 978-0312-42223-3
1. Teenage mothers—Massachusetts—Pittsfield—Social conditions. 2. Teenage mothers—Massachusetts—Pittsfield—Psychology. 3. Pittsfield (Mass.)—Social conditions. 4. Pittsfield (Mass.)—Economic conditions. I. Title.

HQ759.4.57 2003
306.874'3—dc21

2003049862

10 9 8 7 6 5 4 3 2

FOR MY MOTHER

Who Gave me Life and Showed me Strength

CONTENTS

AUTHOR'S NOTE

This is a work of nonfiction. All its characters are real, as are the places where they live and the details of their personal lives. Quotes from the subjects and dialogue I have used were taken directly from edited scenes I videotaped, as well as from edited transcripts of interviews I conducted and either videotaped or audiotaped.

All the teen parents seen in the photographs I took for this book are referred to by their real names. They embarked on this project knowing that their true stories would become public and that their identities and the identities of their children would not be hidden.

Their courage, their honesty, and their long-term commitment to sharing their stories over the course of four years made this book possible, and for that I shall always be extremely grateful.

Most of the other people who appear are referred to by their real names. Some names have been changed. Every instance in which a pseudonym is used is accounted for in the endnotes.

I was interested in presenting the subjective stories of these individuals, who spoke from the heart of their personal experiences and shared their unique perspectives on their lives and the world around them. I accepted what they said without judgment, not necessarily as the only truth, but as their genuine perception of the truth.

For the first and last chapters, I did substantial research and am greatly indebted to the work of experts, scholars, and writers in many fields. Details about the sources of the information and statistics in those chapters can also be found in the endnotes.

chapter one

PITTSFIELD

BILL AND DORIS WERE ADDICTED TO SKYDIVING. FALLING through space and time, their survival instincts kicked in. The adrenaline rush was pure and unparalleled. Parachutes snapping open, they surrendered to a blissful sensation of weightlessness, drinking in a bird's-eye view of the world, far above the burdens, frustrations, and disappointments that awaited them down on the ground back home, in Pittsfield, Massachusetts.

During the week, Doris drove a long yellow school bus. She had started this job when her two daughters were little, intending to move on to something else once they were older. Fifteen years later she was still driving the same bus, thankful for the benefits and paid vacations.

As Doris watched her daughters grow up, she felt her own youth slipping away. When she looked in the mirror, she saw barely any trace of the young woman who at nineteen had given birth to Jessica. Doris had subsequently divorced Jessica's father and married Bill, with whom she had her second daughter, Catherine, all before the age of twenty-three. All that seemed so long ago. As Doris studied the thin lines trailing out from the corners of her eyes, she worried that her life had been defined solely by the roles she played in relation to others. She was afraid that she hadn't done nearly enough for herself.

Skydiving was the only activity Doris indulged in solely for the purpose of her own enjoyment, but there was one hitch—each jump was wickedly expensive. Doris maneuvered her way around this obstacle by getting a weekend job at the drop zone, packing parachutes and videotaping other sky divers from a small camera strapped onto her head. In exchange for performing these duties, Doris was given a special pass that allowed her unlimited jumps at a huge discount.

Bill, a machinist, put extra money aside to support his skydiving habit, but as the years went by and jobs became more and more scarce, decent work was harder to come by. Starting out as an apprentice, Bill had worked his way up the ranks, taking time off to fight in Vietnam. His steadiest employment had been at a steel company that relied on subcontracts from General Electric. In the late 1980s, as GE pulled out of Pittsfield, that company went bankrupt and Bill found himself unemployed. He subsequently worked various jobs spinning steel, but none lasted very long or provided the steady income and security he longed for.

Bitter and disillusioned, Bill languished at the bar, passing long, uneventful hours reminiscing and joking around with his buddies while Doris, at home waiting up, covered his plate in Saran Wrap and stared out the window, watching as the trees in the backyard turned ashen and then disappeared, engulfed in darkness. The hours blurred into one another. Her eyes grew heavy. Sometimes she dozed off.

When the doorknob finally turned and Bill stumbled through the front door, Doris jolted herself awake and summoned up the last of her remaining strength. She fought and pleaded with her husband about his alcoholism. The sound of their arguing voices—his slurred, hers tired and high-pitched—wafted through the thin walls to where Jessica lay in her bed with a pillow over her head, doing her best to sleep through it all.

Bill acknowledged that his drinking and reckless spending put a tremendous strain on his marriage. "But guess what?" he remarked. "When you're screaming through the air at one hundred and twenty miles per hour, a bad day at home doesn't really come up!"

In the summertime, Bill and Doris crammed as many jumps as they could into a day, stopping reluctantly only when thunder crackled or the sun sank. Meanwhile, down below, fourteen-year-old Jessica and her younger sister spent lazy, humid afternoons in an overgrown field adjacent to the runway, listening to music, cooking hot dogs on the grill, bouncing on the trampoline, and stretching out on the hoods of cars in their bikinis, competing to see who could get the best suntan. When Jessica heard the plane's engine idling overhead, all she could do was hope for the best as she craned her neck upward and squinted into the glare of the sun, holding her breath, always terrified that her parents' next jump might be their last.

For the first few minutes Jessica often couldn't see her mother and stepfather at all. At such high altitudes, clusters of thick, fluffy white clouds usually obscured the rough contours of their bodies. With her heart pounding against her ribs, Jessica learned to force herself to imagine what she couldn't see—their canopies gracefully unfurling, creating the gentle tug of resistance that would cut the velocity of their steep, rapid descent.

Finally, after what seemed an eternity to Jessica, her parents would float into view, two small black specks on the distant horizon with nothing but thousands of feet of air between them and the hard, unforgiving earth. "No way would you ever catch me jumping out of a plane with a parachute," said Jessica. "A piece of cloth? No, no, no. I like my feet right on the ground, thank you very much!"

Blond, blue-eyed, willowy, and a stellar student to boot, Jessica entered high school with substantial potential. She rotated from one after-school job to another, unable to last long at places like Burger King, Pretzel Time, and Bonanza. Convinced that a good education would be her ticket out of Pittsfield, Jessica much preferred to spend her spare time working hard to get good grades.

Among her peers, Jessica hid her intelligence and ambition under a flippant, giggling, exaggeratedly feminine persona, often inviting comparisons with the character Phoebe on the hit television show *Friends*. Despite her widespread popularity and her movie-star looks, Jessica suffered from low self-esteem. She was unable to feel special unless she was the special girl in some guy's life. She explained, "I was one of those girls who just always had to have a boyfriend."

While Jessica steered clear of risks as extreme as skydiving, she was less careful when it came to sex. At the age of sixteen, she got pregnant. Too frightened to confide in anyone, Jessica hid her pregnancy for six months, hoping that the problem would just disappear so that her life could go on uninterrupted.

"I was in denial," she recalled. "I didn't want to be pregnant. All my friends would say, 'You're getting bigger. . . . Your stomach's getting bigger. . . .' I'd shrug and say, 'Oh, I'm just eating a lot.' "

Every day at school, Jessica felt sick and anxious. It was hard for her to concentrate on anything. Most nights she spent awake, tossing and turning in her bed, inhabiting the lonely, dark space carved out by insomnia as the clock beside her bed ticked and ticked. As she entered her third trimester, Jessica took a long, hard look in the mirror and saw a dramatically different body reflected back. She was enormous. None of her clothes fit. After one too many sleepless nights, she decided to break her silence. Too terrified to face her mother in person, Jessica chose to put her thoughts down on paper.

"I wrote a letter to my mom. It said, 'Please don't abandon me, I love you and I'm so sorry.' My mom was going skydiving, so I asked my sister to put it in her parachute bag, so she'd find it before she jumped!"

After reading Jessica's note on the plane, Doris floated down toward the ground. Airborne beneath her unfurled canopy, she had time to reflect on the sixteen years she had spent building up her hopes, dreams, and plans for her studious, spunky, beautiful daughter. Now all that would have to change, or at least be deferred indefinitely. In tears, she drove back to Pittsfield to confront Jessica.

"When my mom got home, she sat me down and said, 'Are you going to have this baby?' I said, 'Yeah.' I was already six months pregnant. There was nothing I could do. I wasn't gonna have an abortion. My parents—they weren't angry, but they were very disappointed. I had so much going for me, and it was all thrown in the garbage."

Jessica promptly transferred out of Taconic High School into the Teen Parent Program, affectionately dubbed "TPP" by its students. This alternative, nonresidential day school was located five minutes from the center of Pittsfield, in a small building attached to St. Teresa's Church. Upon enrolling, Jessica gained access to an array of special services, including one-on-one tutoring, child-development and parenting classes, medical care, counseling, and day care. Under the auspices of this support system, Jessica carried her fetus to term, gave birth, and nurtured her son through his first year of life while simultaneously completing the requirements she needed to graduate on time with her high school class.

Jessica was surrounded by many other pregnant and parenting teens. Between 1995 and 2000, an average of fifty-nine teenagers from Pittsfield gave birth each year. Approximately 81 percent of these teen mothers were white, reflecting the demographics of city's overall population, which the U.S. Census 2000 officially calculated as 92.6 percent white.

Prior to transferring into the Teen Parent Program, most teen mothers were registered at one of Pittsfield's two public high schools, which enrolled a combined total of approximately 1,570 students: 730 boys and 840 girls. Within these locker-lined corridors, every student had some exposure to teen pregnancy and parenthood, if not through their own direct experience, then through classmates or, in many cases, through elder siblings, cousins, and other family members. When Jessica was asked why she thought there were so many teen mothers in Pittsfield, she didn't mention the words "abortion," "adoption" or "choice."

"Pittsfield is very boring," she said. "There's nothing for us to do. I used to just drive around in my car with all my friends and hang out at the parks or hang out at some friend's house. We don't have anywhere to go. Nowhere . . . That's probably why there are so many pregnant people around here, because there's nothing else to do but have sex. I mean, there is nothing else to do!"

Jessica's negative impressions of her hometown were echoed by many of her contemporaries. When talking about Pittsfield, these teenagers often resorted to using words like "dead," "boring," "frustrating," and "hate." Many of their parents shared this extreme pessimism. Pittsfield's history illuminated the backdrop against which the dramas of these individual lives unfolded.

Located in western Massachusetts, approximately 150 miles from New York City and Boston, Pittsfield evolved throughout the nineteenth and twentieth centuries as one of several major pockets of industry. Imposing and strikingly urban, Pittsfield—with its towering smokestacks and gigantic, fortresslike factories—was always a bit of an anomaly, surrounded by the predominately mountainous and pastoral, picturesque terrain of Berkshire County, a region renowned for its sweeping open landscapes and the meticulously preserved elegance of its small Old New England towns with their Gilded Age mansions, world-class resorts, pristine spas, and thriving summer communities.

With its clear blue lakes, peaceful hiking trails, burnished autumn leaves, and necklace of cultural gems, Berkshire County never fails to attract throngs of tourists. Year after year visitors from all over the world are irrepressibly drawn to Tanglewood, the Williamstown Theater Festival, Shakespeare & Company, the Berkshire Theater Festival, Jacob's Pillow, and MASS MoCA. Adding to its allure is the fact that the region has been home to several major artists and intellectuals, including painter Norman Rockwell, psychoanalyst Erik Erikson, and legendary American authors Edith Wharton and Herman Melville.

Less often highlighted in Berkshire County's tourist brochures, but impossible to ignore in the context of teen parenthood, is Pittsfield's long, bittersweet industrial heritage, inextricably intertwined with the General Electric Company.

In its glory days, Pittsfield was endearingly referred to as "the Plastics Technology Center of the Nation." In addition, numerous industrial buildings housed GE's Power Transformer Division and its Ordnance Division, a major producer of armaments during World Wars I and II and the Cold War. GE's defense activities included contracts for the Polaris missile, naval ballistics missiles, and the Bradley Fighting Vehicle.

During the early postwar period, approximately three-fifths of Pittsfield's workforce was employed by General Electric. Then in 1960, Jack Welch joined GE's Plastics Division as a chemical engineer. For the next seventeen years Welch lived and worked in Pittsfield as he evolved into the legendary CEO whose leadership, vision, and strategy helped the corporation arrive at and maintain its enviable position as one of America's most profitable and valuable companies.

Throughout most of the twentieth century, GE maintained a vested interest in preventing other businesses from coming to Pittsfield, determined to control the workforce and the wages. The company's management exerted influence over the city council to ensure that protective measures were taken so that Pittsfield remained securely under GE's jurisdiction, conveniently isolated from competition. As anthropologist Max H. Kirsch explained: "The community was dependent on the corporation for the tax dollars that maintained the city's infrastructure developed to house its workers; workers were dependent on the corporation for jobs; families on wage earners; and secondary industries on the wages the workers generated."

Then, quite abruptly, GE's happy marriage to Pittsfield came to an end when Jack Welch led the corporation into a period of major downsizing and globalization, shifting the focus of U.S. operations from production to high technology and financial services, dramatically scaling back the blue-collar labor force; replacing thousands of U.S. workers with robots and cheaper nonunionized foreign labor; increasing efficiency, productivity, and profits while cutting costs. It was inevitable that high-tech solutions would eventually replace old-fashioned assembly lines, and as operations became more streamlined, jobs were tailored to those with higher education and expertise. Many blue-collar workers were laid off as GE edged its way toward the twenty-first century, wholeheartedly embracing the spirit of capitalism.

On Wall Street, shareholders' pockets jingled with profits. Jack Welch was hailed as a hero, and competitors around the world sought to emulate his strategies once they saw just how seductively lucrative they were. As globalization became more and more widespread, the purchasing power of the average American increased, thanks to the availability of goods that, because they cost less to manufacture, subsequently cost less to buy. Nevertheless, there are two sides to every coin, and as Janet Lowe, author of *Welch: An American Icon,* concedes: "As visionary as his leadership has been, Welch has also ushered in many ugly problems. Companies the size and scope of GE invariably raise questions about the way they affect lives everywhere, and though Welch has defended himself and the company, troubling conflicts still exist. . . . Nobody has figured out a way to build a world in which all people live in a just, humane society that rewards them adequately for the work they perform."

In 1986 GE announced the closing of the Power Transformer Division and began its withdrawal from Pittsfield. The city's unionized blue-collar jobs were sucked up into a vacuum. In 1988 defense production was sharply curtailed, and by the early nineties GE had sold many of its weapons businesses, cutting more jobs. GE Plastics' Global Headquarters housed the corporation's advanced Plastics Technology Center, which was the only division that remained in operation in Pittsfield, staffed primarily by a small number of highly educated, skilled employees who focused on research and development.

As GE stock shot way up, in Pittsfield the quality of life plummeted. The bottom fell out of the middle class. After being laid off, many former GE employees who had served the company loyally for decades were forced to take on lower-paying service and retail jobs that, in addition to being mostly unregulated by the unions, offered relatively meager compensation and few, if any, benefits. As a result of these dramatic economic shifts, society became increasingly polarized. The Pittsfield Economic Revitalization Corporation published a comprehensive report, warning that as the availability of "upwardly mobile types of jobs" quickly diminished, left behind were "a large group of single mothers, young people, and displaced blue collar workers for whom there is little hope for achieving a middle-class lifestyle."

At the time these unsettling economic changes took place, Jessica and her classmates at the Teen Parent Program were, for the most part, between the ages of five and eight. Their parents were in the prime of their working years. Quite suddenly, the manufacturing base of their region had virtually disappeared, with no prospect of recovery on the immediate horizon.

Bill described the traumatic time of transition that followed. "Pittsfield, once upon a time, was General Electric," he explained. "Thousands upon thousands of jobs were supplied by GE. Anybody that was anybody worked at GE. Everything else in town catered to the people who got their money from GE. Then, GE slowly but surely left town. When GE left, it wasn't that you were laid off; you weren't fired . . . your jobs just didn't exist anymore.

" 'Generous Electric' was the only union shop in town, and the company I worked at got a lot of the subcontracts from GE, so when GE went down the toilet, we were definitely affected. One Saturday morning I went in to do overtime, and there were padlocks on all the doors and NO TRESPASSING signs because the bank had just confiscated the building. The boss didn't see fit to tell anybody. We had no warning. Nothing. So everybody shows up at work to get the overtime, and you find out you don't even have a job!

"It leaves you in a strange predicament. Unemployment lasts only so long. And you're out of money. Basically, you have no skills because you've been a monkey and a button. You wind up working at McDonald's, a gas station, or whatever. After a while, even those jobs start petering out, because everybody and their brother is competing for those jobs."

In the wake of GE's departure, Pittsfield's shops, restaurants, and small businesses began shutting down as those families who once had money to spend left town in search of decent-paying jobs and healthier communities. "There is cause for alarm," warned the Berkshire County Development Commission in response to a study on Pittsfield's population, which rapidly dwindled from 57,020 in 1970 to 45,296 in 1999. The U.S. Census 2000 identified Pittsfield as one of the five metropolitan areas in America that on a percentage basis had experienced the steepest population drop during the 1990s. According to the census, only 12.4 percent of Pittsfield's remaining residents over twenty-five years of age held bachelor's degrees. Only 8.1 percent held graduate or professional degrees, and 79.5 percent had no college degrees at all.

Many of those who remained in Pittsfield could not afford to leave. North Street, once a bustling center of activity, quickly assumed the aura of a ghost town as this working-class community was thrown into an era of social and economic catastrophe. These sudden, pronounced demographic and economic shifts paved the way for the increasingly severe presence of a host of social ills, including drugs, crime, and teen parenthood.

Panic about a toxic-waste crisis compounded the economic disaster Pittsfield faced. In 1976 the federal government had banned PCBs (polychlorinated biphenyls) in light of substantial evidence that these synthetic chemicals posed an increased risk for cancer in humans, in addition to an array of other serious health problems. Manufacturing power transformers had traditionally been one of GE's core businesses in Pittsfield, and PCBs were part of a compound that comprised Pyranol, a fire-resistant insulating lubricant used in production and sealed inside of power transformers. These hazardous chemicals regularly spilled all over areas inside the factory buildings where the transformers were tested. "The Pittsfield Operations processed 140,000 pounds of PCB each week," reported Thomas F. O'Boyle, "several thousand pounds of which spilled on the floor, down the drain and into the Housatonic River."

Mickey Friedman, a local documentary filmmaker, interviewed many GE workers who were employed in the Power Transformer Division. "These guys spent their days slogging through this constant layer of liquid on the floor," he said. "The chemical was so potent that the boots GE would give them would be worn down if they stood in the liquid for too long—it would just eat the rubber right off the soles of their shoes.

"So because the floor was wet all the time, just drenched in chemicals, GE would use this absorbent dirt," explained Mickey. "It was a kitty-litter-like substance called Fuller's Earth, and they would throw it on the floor so that it would soak up the liquid. They were generating hundreds of barrels of this stuff. The first place they would take it was the old Pittsfield landfill. Two or three tractorloads would go out every single day into the city dump for years and years and years, to the point where they filled up the dump.

"Then in the 1940s," continued Mickey, "somebody at GE got the idea to create a fill giveaway program. They would encourage GE workers and local building contractors to come in and take away these barrels of contaminated Fuller's Earth to use on construction sites. GE also contracted with several local trucking companies to actually take the contaminated Fuller's Earth and deliver it to people's homes and, in fact, asked people to sign a waiver of liability when they received the fill, saying that they were, in fact, receiving 'clean-fill.' "

The contaminated fill looked just like regular dirt, so some people who had low spots in their backyards due to the river occasionally flooding used the fill to even out their land. Some workers used the fill to kill the unruly weeds that kept persistently nudging their way through cracks in the sidewalk. The fill was spread across dirt roads to keep the dust down and was suspected of being used to straighten out the oxbows in the Housatonic River, apparently in an effort to make the river more efficient, as it meandered through the center of the city. Over the years, truckloads of the fill were dumped at various sites in Pittsfield. By the time PCBs were declared to be a serious health hazard, there were pockets of contaminated soil all over the city, and the Housatonic River was horribly polluted.

In 1992 Mickey cofounded the Housatonic River Initiative, a coalition made up of activists from various walks of life, including GE workers, environmentalists, fishermen, scientists, sportsmen, and small-business owners whose commercial properties had been polluted by PCBs. All these people were united by their interest in protecting the environment and human health and by their desire to expose the truth about PCBs in Pittsfield. As this group became more vocal, public consciousness about the pollution grew. In 1997 members of the Housatonic River Initiative pressured the Massachusetts

Department of Environmental Protection to set up an anonymous tip line so that people could phone in and report whatever knowledge they had regarding where toxic waste had been dumped without fearing that GE would retaliate.

"Once we did that," said Mickey, "several people who had trucked toxic material called up and said, 'Listen, fifteen years ago, I took old transformers and barrels to what is now . . . this park . . . this children's park.' Slowly people started turning in sites, and that was the major breakthrough. It was a continuing battle because the state would say to us, 'You're just exaggerating. We don't necessarily believe this.' For years the environmental agencies were saying, 'Listen, this stuff did not really leave the factory.' We would have to convince them case by case that in fact—the unthinkable was true."

Pittsfield residents were alarmed when land was finally tested and PCBs were identified as the responsible agents in contamination of local sewer lines, residential basements, private gardens, an elementary school, the Housatonic River, and acres and acres of GE's former plant sites.

"First you have people coping with the fact that the jobs are leaving and then you have this added trauma," said Mickey. "These same people who worked very hard in the factory for years with enormous loyalty no longer have jobs and are now worried about their exposure. They are coming home to the house that they are so proud of and discovering that their backyard is contaminated. You have people discovering that the elementary school that their children go to was built on contaminated land. You have people on the west side of town whose kids have been playing basketball in Dorothy

Amos Park discovering that their kids have been exposed to unacceptable levels of PCBs. You have people who have beautiful homes along the Housatonic River who are now worried about the fact that their little children used to go down to the riverbank to play. So you add all that onto the first trauma of the economic engine of the community leaving and the burden of walking down the main street and seeing store after store that's been closed and seeing no vibrant downtown, and you're talking about an enormous psychological blow. It's hard enough when the economy crumbles around you, but then to fear for your public health? To worry about the air you're breathing? Psychologically, many people felt like they were living in a dying town."

Among certain circles of friends and neighbors, the incidence of cancer appeared to be rising at an alarming rate, and former GE employees who had worked in the Power Transformer Division found themselves frequently reaching into their closets to pull out the black suits they wore to funerals. Needless to say, the presence of PCBs made the already gloomy city an even less desirable destination for residents, tourists, and prospective new businesses.

The damage caused by this toxic-waste disaster was so extensive that it merited evaluation and federal intervention by the Environmental Protection Agency (EPA). Acres of GE's polluted plant sites and the Housatonic River with its PCB-laden sediment were the subjects of a legally binding consent decree involving the EPA, the Department of Justice, state officials, the city of Pittsfield, and General Electric. GE agreed to a $150–$200 million settlement of claims. They were required to pay for portions of the cleanup of the river and for the eventual redevelopment of the contaminated plant site.

Although they fought hard against it, GE was ultimately forced to dredge a polluted section of the Housatonic River. Beginning efforts have been made, but there is still a long way to go before the cleanup will be finished. The EPA estimated that the total price tag of resolving the toxic-waste crisis in Pittsfield would end up somewhere in the range of $300–$700 million, figures hotly contested by GE.

An EPA report warned that "teenagers growing up near portions of the river face a 1 in 1,000 cancer risk due to exposure to contaminated river soils. . . . Young children and teenagers playing in and near portions of the river face non-cancer risks that are 200 times greater than EPA considers safe. Non-cancer effects from PCBs may include liver and nervous system damage and developmental abnormalities including lower IQ's."

When asked for her theory about why teen parenthood had become such an epidemic in Pittsfield, Shayla, a teen mother who got pregnant in 1998, replied half jokingly, "It must be something in the water." Born to a fifteen-year-old mother and a seventeen-year-old father, Shayla was exposed to teen parenthood the moment she took her first breath. Sixteen years later, Shayla and her boyfriend, C.J., intentionally conceived a child together. "I really wanted to have a baby because all my friends had babies," explained Shayla. "I thought it would bring my popularity up because people would be like, 'Hey she's got a baby and that's cool.' I thought that C.J. and me and the baby would be a family."

A study conducted by the Alan Guttmacher Institute looked at a sample of teen mothers in California who, like Shayla, had *intended* to get pregnant:

> In the analyses including the father's intentions, young women who reported that their partner had wanted them to get pregnant were nearly fifteen times as likely as others to have intended the pregnancy (as opposed to having not intended it). In these young women's circles, early childbearing was not uncommon. Nearly seven in ten had close friends or teenage siblings who were pregnant or already had children. In addition, many respondents reported unhealthy past or present dating relationships. 47% had been in a controlling or abusive relationship, either prior to or with their baby's father.

"I definitely think my environment influenced me to get pregnant," said Shayla. "When you're around people that are constantly doing something, eventually, consciously or unconsciously, you're gonna pick that up. If I had hung out with people that were more school-oriented or more focused on the bigger picture, then I don't think I would have gotten pregnant. I really don't."

Framed by the majestic Berkshire Mountains, poverty in Pittsfield wore a prettier face than inner-city poverty but nevertheless was immediately visible. On residential streets, contemporary apartment complexes and public housing projects were interspersed with older single-family homes, many of which had been converted to house several families. Peeling paint, sliding shingles, cluttered porches, fractured windowpanes, and boarded-up storefronts silently reflected the reality that this city, home to one of the oldest minor-league ballparks in the United States, had definitely seen better days.

On North Street the once-spectacular Colonial Theatre remained the focus of a slow but steady restoration effort. After its construction in 1903, the theater was renowned throughout the country for its ornate interior and exceptional acoustics. Back in the theater's heyday, legendary performers including John Barrymore, Sarah Bernhardt, and Eubie Blake graced its stage. Sold-out shows included *The Ziegfeld Follies* and other hits of the era. The curtain closed for the last time in 1952, and when the property changed hands, the new owner converted it into an art-supply shop without making any major structural changes. Forty-six years later, in 1998, the city's determined efforts to salvage this run-down architectural jewel received a huge boost from the visit of then–First Lady Hillary Rodham Clinton. In association with the National Trust for Historical Preservation, she honored the theater by making it the first stop on the prestigious "Save America's Treasures" tour.

Sadly, other areas of Pittsfield were not the recipients of such special attention.

On the outskirts of town, giant abandoned manufacturing plants loomed ominously, weathering rain, sleet, snow, and the beating sun. Season after season, GE's former factory sites remained completely deserted, surrounded by tall chain-link fences emblazoned with imposing KEEP OUT and NO TRESPASSING signs. There was no need to enter. From the outside, the view through the cold, metal diamond-shaped slats was achingly clear: Pittsfield's most vital organs had died.

"When GE split, the heart and soul of Pittsfield pretty much went to shit," said Bill. "And when the money left town, all the supporting businesses went with it. So, you've got people losing their homes. You know, you worked for GE for twenty-six years, then you're out of work, you've still got five years left on your mortgage . . . bad news. You've got despair, depression—the whole nine yards. And, of course, the drug dealers come in. They start with the kids. And I hate to say it, but the parents follow suit. The kids see what's going on with their parents, and life can look pretty stinking grim. Kids get discouraged when they see their parents going down the toilet. They think, 'Is this what I have to look forward to?' "

In this morbid atmosphere, a thriving underground drug economy exploded, primed to exploit the unskilled labor force and the city's vulnerable youth.

"As General Electric left town and the population decreased, crime started to rise largely because of crack cocaine and the influx of drug dealers into this community," explained Captain Patrick Barry, a native of Pittsfield and the proud descendant of several generations of resilient police detectives. After joining the police force on Christmas Day in 1988, Barry became a narcotics investigator. By 1997 the raven-haired officer had impressed his superiors with his insight, diligence, and dedication. They promoted him to sergeant. Before long he was promoted to captain and given command of the Drug Unit and the Detective Bureau. He was subsequently named special operations commander, and his responsibilities expanded to encompass the Crime Scene Services Unit and the Anti-Terrorism Unit.

Divorced from his wife, who lived with their young daughter out of state, Captain Barry devoted himself to fighting Pittsfield's war on drugs. During his tiny slivers of leisure time he played golf, skied, and hiked up the Berkshire Mountains accompanied by his beloved beagles, Snoopy and Snoopy Two. However, as crime in Pittsfield escalated, those carefree moments of peace became increasingly rare and what little free time he had was spent visiting his daughter or catching up on sleep.

Usually Captain Barry was up all night on the midnight shift, patrolling the streets, often undercover. Most mornings he saw the sunrise with bleary eyes while breakfasting on an Egg McMuffin. On cold winter afternoons, when he had a moment to spare, he liked to warm up at the Elm Street Luncheonette, sipping hot coffee while thumbing through the newspaper, which often included articles about his department's latest arrests.

Throughout the 1990s, the drug scene in Pittsfield centered on crack cocaine. Starting in 1992, the Pittsfield Police Department's Drug Unit implemented an aggressive policy to win back the streets. Using undercover officers to purchase crack cocaine from street-level dealers, the unit made more than seven hundred arrests with a high rate of subsequent convictions.

"We would send a patrolman down and kick the dealers off the street corner, and then we would take over the street corner for that evening," said Captain Barry. "I had a beard and we'd wear different types of clothes to help disguise ourselves. We knew what the street-level dealers were like—what kind of clothing they wore and where they stood to deal. So we would try to be like them. People are desperate for the drug, and sometimes, even if they suspect you're a cop, if you're willing to sell it to them, they're willing to take it and they hope they'll get away.

"The population of users includes a vast range of people. They come from right here in the community in Pittsfield. We've had doctors out of Williamstown down here buying crack cocaine and well-to-do people out of South County as well.

"We've also encountered prostitution. That came along with the drug dealing. I worked as an undercover john to get hookers. I got several of them working the streets of the city of Pittsfield. Usually they're looking to buy crack cocaine and they don't have the money, so they want to turn a trick."

Captain Barry and his colleagues regularly apprehended drug dealers who conducted business in public places, including parking lots at McDonald's, Burger King, Big Y Supermarket, Harry's Supermarket, and the Pittsfield Plaza—all locations where many teenagers worked for minimum wage after school, during the summer, and on weekends. In these and other local settings, the culture of adolescence blended with the narcotic subculture. Thus, the social lives of some teenagers and some drug dealers began to merge. This was beneficial for the drug dealers because every new teenager they befriended or supplied could introduce them to more teenagers who were viewed as potential customers, potential runners, and potential girlfriends, who were valued because many helped dealers establish fronts in their apartments in exchange for money and the illusion of love.

Raised in Pittsfield, Nicole was always considered pretty. Her almond-shaped eyes defined her pale face and her long honey-blond hair cascaded down her back.

"My parents—they were into drug use," explained Nicole, "so I was around it pretty much all the time. As a young girl, I hung out with the older crowd. I was drinking at nine years old and smoking cigarettes. In sixth grade I started smoking pot, and basically it took off from there. I did cocaine, and then the higher high was crack. When I started getting into crack, everything went downhill.

"I was eighteen my senior year in high school and I went to my first rehab. I tried to stay clean and then I got back into it because I never changed the people I hung out with or the places I went. Every time I got back into it, I got in deeper and deeper. I couldn't function without crack. I had a couple of car crashes, and still nothing. I did some time in jail for my behavior. I knew nothing of life and how to live it without drugs."

Between 2000 and 2002, the drug trade in Pittsfield careened toward heroin with a velocity, intensity, and violence that stunned law enforcement and garnered headlines all across Berkshire County. Because of the widespread availability of extremely pure, potent heroin, users could now sniff or smoke the drug and still get a terrific high. The removal of the needle barrier made heroin more socially acceptable and increased its popularity among teenagers. The influx of drug dealers into the community was accompanied by an alarming surge in the numbers of vicious dogs that populated the city streets.

"Pit bulls are a status symbol for drug dealers and other young males," said Captain Barry. "So people want to have them just for that, but they're also used to intimidate people and to protect the drug houses."

Inside their mouths, often under their tongues, open street-level drug dealers hid small plastic bags containing a tenth of a gram of crack cocaine. These bags were sold on street corners for twenty dollars and could be swallowed easily if a guard dog's growl alerted the dealer to the approach of a cop. The dogs were equally vigilant indoors, where most heroin deals took place in the privacy of dank, musty apartments with the shades drawn.

"The drug dealers I knew would let their dogs fight for fun," said Nicole. "These dogs were very mean and very abused. By beating a dog, you're provoking them and they start going at it—and when pit bulls start going at it, they're really aggressive, especially when they're being beaten. They have no tolerance for anything, so it doesn't take much to get them to start fighting. If the dog got badly hurt, it became meaningless. They'd just let them go and not care for them. I seen two dogs left to die. It was horrible."

Just attending a dogfight is a felony in most states. The blood sport is widely condemned as a dehumanizing, criminal activity that frays the very threads of civilization. Such savagery demonstrates the power of two-legged monsters to create four-legged monsters by molding their minds and behavior through abusive, traumatic conditioning.

As dusk fell over Pittsfield's deserted alleys, slowly enshrouding abandoned industrial lots, it was not unusual to see a small group of youths goading and cheering on a pit bull as he leapt up to a low branch of a forlorn tree in an attempt to grab a sweatshirt that his owner had wrapped in fresh meat and hung as bait. Sometimes entire branches bent and snapped as they bore the brunt of one these "training sessions," during which, on command, the dog would do his best to jump as high as he could, pawing and clawing, sweating, drooling, and panting, until the sweatshirt, shredded like torn paper, dangled limp in the vise of his sharp teeth.

Terrified of incurring the wrath of their masters, these dogs stood alert, ready to pounce on command, discouraging nosy neighbors, inquisitive social services representatives, and law enforcement, making it safer for their owners to conduct business with maximum protection and minimal interference. Meanwhile, innocent members of the Pittsfield community lived in daily fear of being attacked. Numerous formal complaints were filed, including one from the U.S. Postal Service, whose representatives threatened to install cluster boxes so their employees wouldn't have to keep making door-to-door deliveries and risk being bitten. Policemen, firemen, paramedics, and postal workers took the extra precaution of arming themselves with Mace or pepper spray before leaving home to go to work.

The Berkshire Eagle featured headlines about the vicious dog problem. The city council responded to the community's widespread concern by approving an ordinance to identify and track vicious dogs and their owners. Owners of dogs designated as terrorizing dangers to others were forced to "pay for tattooing and/or implanting a microchip" and "to obtain liability insurance in the amount of at least $100,000, naming the city as an 'additional insured.' " They were also required to place large signs on their property, warning pedestrians to BEWARE.

Nicole doubted that the signs would do much good. She believed that the dogs and other persistent dangers would exist as long as Pittsfield remained infested with drugs. "Drug dealers just have no respect for themselves, so I think that they have no respect for humans or animals," she said. "Everybody out in the drug world—everything's abusive, no matter what it is."

"We have a lot of domestic-violence crime in Pittsfield," confirmed Captain Barry. "In fact, probably most arrests that we make are definitely for domestic violence. It's a problem here, and it's aggravated by drug and alcohol abuse. The chief and the district attorney's office take domestic violence very seriously. They have several victim advocates in the D.A.'s office for that, and the police department recently applied for a grant, which I believe we've been awarded, so that we could have a special domestic-violence officer just to work on reducing domestic-violence crime."

Colleen, a teen mother who attended the Teen Parent Program with Jessica and Shayla, described life with the abusive young heroin addict who was the father of her baby. "My boyfriend on heroin was like . . . he'd be quiet at times—or he'd be so nice to me. He could be this wonderful person, but yet it was the drug that was making him that happy. When he was down from the drugs, it was just awful. He was mean, terrible. He would say, 'Get me money, do *whatever* you have to!' He'd get so mad at me if I didn't give him any money for the drugs. He'd say I didn't love him and call me names. . . . Horrible verbal abuse. When I would get mad and want to leave, it would turn into physical abuse. The physical abuse at our apartment was really bad."

Sheri and Amy attended the Teen Parent Program the same year as Jessica, Shayla, and Colleen. At one point, several of these young women lived near one another with their children at the Dalton Apartments, a subsidized housing complex located on April Lane, near the border between Pittsfield and Dalton, ten minutes by car from a huge strip mall. For drug dealers, the fact that this housing project was slightly off the beaten path made it very seductive, as they were always on the lookout for places to temporarily shack up without attracting too much attention.

Amy got pregnant for the first time when she was fourteen. Unmoved by her mother's repeated attempts to convince her to put the baby up for adoption, Amy gave birth and kept her daughter. At seventeen, Amy gave birth to a son and moved to April Lane with the two kids and her son's father, Bernard. She hoped that this environment would be better than Riverview, the more urban project where they had previously lived, right beside the polluted Housatonic River. With its grassy communal lawns, rusty swing sets, and sparsely wooded play areas, April Lane did indeed initially seem quieter and more peaceful. But soon after moving there, Bernard, Amy, and her two young children discovered that life on April Lane wasn't always as peaceful as it appeared to be upon first glance.

One afternoon, in broad daylight, a gunman pulled into the parking lot behind Amy and Bernard's apartment and sprayed six bullets into the communal yard before backing out and zooming away. Luckily, no one was hurt, but a bullet was found in Amy and Bernard's apartment. The police dug it out of a wall not far from their son's bed. Thankfully, Amy, Bernard, and the kids had not been home at the time of the shooting. The perpetrator was never found, but a rumor circulated that the shooting was drug-related. When questioned by police, Amy and Bernard said that the bullets were not intended for their apartment. They insisted that the gunman's choice of where to shoot had been completely arbitrary.

"I was in charge of the Detective Bureau at the time," said Captain

Barry. "I remember interviewing people at the scene and seeing the bullet holes—you know, bullet holes, right in the house. We had nine shootings in 2002, and it's absolutely amazing that we haven't had a homicide as a result. My biggest fear is that an innocent bystander—someone just walking down the street—will be shot and killed."

After the shooting at April Lane, residents started a neighborhood watch in an effort to deter the drug dealers and related violence. Amy's father, James, doubted that such minor measures could even make a dent in Pittsfield's massive drug problem. A Pittsfield native and a second-generation GE employee, James realized that the city of his boyhood was long gone. He worried constantly about his grandchildren growing up in what had evolved into a considerably more dangerous environment.

"At one time April Lane was a project built for middle- to low-income working families," explained James. "I guess that's still what it's supposed to be, but people have to live in fear because there's guns. That comes along with the drug trade. Mayor Giuliani takes credit for cleaning up New York City, but my guess is that he drove the drug dealers into the small towns throughout New England and upstate New York. Instead of them dealing their drugs in the city, they're dealing them here now. We're easy pickings, which is not a very good thing."

The rapidly increasing migration of drug dealers from New York City to Pittsfield dates back to the early 1980s, coinciding with a short transitional period predating managed health care, when instead of being controlled by tightly regulated management on the insurance side, companies, organizations, and states were allowed to establish private contracts with various units of hospitals. In the arena of addiction services, this period of premanaged care was regarded as open season, in part because when it came to making money, detox units were relatively cheap to run and brought in a steady clientele—for some hospitals, these addiction units were cash cows.

Facing shrinking dollars and business in the local community, the McGee addiction unit at Hillcrest Hospital in Pittsfield reportedly took advantage of this friendly bureaucratic climate and allegedly set up lucrative contracts with New York Medicaid and a few other New York–based companies. The result was that hundreds of drug addicts from all boroughs of New York City were shipped straight to Pittsfield. Residents recall seeing busloads of addicts disembarking and entering the hospital, where they spent four weeks in detox. Many locals suspected that after being released, not all of the addicts hopped on the bus and went straight back to New York City. Many of those who did eventually returned to Pittsfield.

"I believe that the McGee unit worked hard to get contracts and established a contract with New York Medicaid," one doctor explained. "I still hear rumors that McGee was bringing bad characters into this community, and some were staying here and setting up shop. I am sure it happened. Drug dealers especially were causing disruptions. They found ways to get integrated into the system here, especially through the twelve-step programs. When they were in treatment, they met people and made connections."

"We had heard that the McGee unit was rehabilitating crack cocaine addicts that were being sent here from New York under their state Medicaid program," confirmed Captain Barry. "We heard that from a couple of different sources. Some of the people that were released into the community chose to stay here, and that began the demand for crack cocaine. There were a lot of other communities affected with crack cocaine in the 1990s, but because we're centrally located between New York City, Boston, and Springfield, we became a magnet."

"Here in Pittsfield, there's a much bigger profit, and dealers caught on to that," explained Nicole. "If you were to get a rock of crack around here, it's twenty dollars for a piece. That same piece would be five dollars in New York because of the fact that it's so much more readily available in New York than it is here. So they jack up the prices here."

As soon as Nicole was old enough to get her driver's license, she began transporting drug dealers back and forth to New York City. In exchange for acting as chauffeur and using her own car, Nicole was paid in cash or, more often, in grams of crack.

"A lot of the dealers that I know are actually users," she said. "A lot of their profit is their head money. They're supporting their own habit with the drugs that they're selling—that's like ninety percent of the drug dealers I hung out with."

Parked on street corners in Brooklyn and the Bronx, Nicole waited in her car while the drug dealers she was working for entered buildings and replenished their supplies. When they exited she had the motor running, ready to whisk them back to Pittsfield.

"When they go get drugs in New York City, lots of them don't want the same car traveling back and forth and they don't want to be the one driving back and forth. So they get someone like me to drive them," said Nicole. "A lot of them don't have a license when they come to Pittsfield and they don't pursue it," she explained. "They don't want to show their faces in the public eye, as far as like the Registry and police stations and that sort of thing."

Another major point of entry for out-of-town drug dealers was the local bus station. The Pittsfield Police Department's Drug Unit placed this location under tight surveillance. They regularly made arrests and seized large quantities of drugs from dealers arriving by bus from Springfield, Albany, and New York City.

"The drug dealers obviously have the money to have a vehicle, but they won't drive their own vehicles and flash them, because that would draw more attention to them," explained Nicole. "So once they got to Pittsfield, taxis were their means of transportation locally. Taxi drivers would support them with a ride, and the drug dealers would support the taxi driver with their drug habit, so it was an even trade-off."

Over the years, Nicole witnessed drug dealers flowing in from New York City, sometimes with relatives in tow. "The drug dealers let their brothers and their sisters know that in this area they made three times the profit, and the word kept being known through the families. The mothers of the families liked it in the Berkshires because they weren't in the high-rises and the whole city mode. They thought Pittsfield was like a vacation, so the whole family would move here. That's when it started getting really bad.

"In my experience," said Nicole, "about eighty percent of the drug dealers in Pittsfield are ethnic. I knew a lot of families that moved here from the Bronx because of the simple fact that their children were making more in Pittsfield. Dealing drugs is a way of life out there, and they were fine with that. That's their way of bringing in money for the mothers, for the babies. So they come here and make a life, and along with making a life, they make three times more money here and they start overpopulating different areas."

Pittsfield's crack cocaine and heroin epidemic had what law enforcement referred to as "an umbrella effect," spawning an array of spin-off crimes. "People need money for drugs," explained Captain Barry, "so there's theft and prostitution. Every hooker I bagged wanted the money for crack. People steal to get drugs. They'll ask a drug dealer, 'What do you want?' The drug dealer will pick out clothes. He might say, 'I want a size thirty-four-inch-waist pair of Tommy Hilfiger carpenter jeans and I want a green sweatshirt to go with it and a pair of Timberland work boots. The drug dealer will give an addict a shopping list, and they'll steal and trade the stolen goods for drugs. A guy was arrested a couple of weeks ago coming out of Price Chopper. He had stolen six hundred dollars' worth of steaks and lobsters. He tried to hide them with a couple of rolls of paper towels shoved over the top, and he got busted on his way to trade that food for drugs. People on public assistance abuse that and use that money for drugs. For example, they'll take food stamps and trade them for drugs."

Often drug dealers carried weapons, including guns, knives, box cutters, razor blades, and brass knuckles, ostensibly for protection in case someone tried to rip them off. Thus, innocent people lived in fear of being robbed and wounded, and children were surrounded by a culture of violence at an early age. Vulnerable, naive young girls in these environments were exposed to older males who were often sexual predators. Within the narcotics subculture, it was not uncommon for a drug dealer to father multiple children with several local teen mothers.

Once these young mothers got on welfare and got subsidized housing, their apartments were frequently used as fronts by the fathers of their babies. In exchange for cooperating, the girls often got money, gifts, and drugs. Many of these relationships were emotionally sadistic and addictive, and lots of girls found it hard to break free of them, especially after they had the dealer's baby. As Marjorie Cohan, the executive director of the Mental Health and Substance Abuse Services of the Berkshires, explained, "I think that these guys come to town and they can easily find somebody who will take them in because they have a lot of money and they can be very generous with their money and buy things—a nice new couch, a new this and a new that—and then the next thing we know, that apartment becomes a center for drug activity and as soon as the police hear about the drug traffic, the dealers move on. In the meantime, some nice young kid is pregnant and kind of left there. And that pattern repeats itself."

The idea behind a drug dealer's using a young woman's subsidized housing as a front is that in the event of a raid, if drugs are found on the premises tucked away in a drawer, buried beneath a pile of baby clothes, it is harder to tie the crime to the dealer whose name is not on the lease, and thus ultimately more difficult to prosecute the case and get a conviction. Pittsfield police have caught on to this strategy and cracked down. Before they make a raid, they gather information from informants who buy drugs from that particular apartment, so they know ahead of time exactly who the dealer is. If a drug raid takes place and drugs are found and the dealer is nowhere in sight, the young mother on the premises is often faced with a frightening choice: rat on your baby's daddy, or take the rap yourself.

"We tell the girl she could be charged with possession and with attempt to distribute," said Captain Barry. "We ask her to get on board and cooperate against the actual dealer so that in turn she won't face as much jail time and possibly won't even be charged in court. The girls usually cooperate," he said, nodding, as the corners of his mouth turned up in the slightest hint of a grin.

"The first offense for any drug possession is a misdemeanor, and you're probably not gonna go to jail," said Captain Barry. "They're probably gonna get you rehabilitation. But if you're caught selling, that's distribution—it's drug dealing, and the penalty for selling crack cocaine is a one-year mandatory minimum state prison term. The maximum is ten years. The penalties increase for multiple offenses and for larger quantities of the drug."

The state of Massachusetts is also tough when it comes to prosecuting assault and battery. Because of an avalanche of assault and drug-related charges, several of the teen mothers saw the fathers of their babies repeatedly going in and out of jail as if there were a revolving door. A few of their babies saw their fathers for the first time through the barrier of the glass partition that separates visitors from prisoners.

Incarceration is a legacy often passed down from one generation to the next, and compared with children born to older mothers, sons of teen mothers are at a higher risk of ending up in prison, and daughters are at a higher risk of becoming teen mothers themselves. Just as teen motherhood is a rite of passage for some girls in the absence of other valid landmarks and marked transitions, jail is a rite of passage for some boys. Jail culture offers inmates the structure, routine, rehabilitation, and predictability many never got from their broken homes, as well as a hiatus from a world driven by inequality and brutally divided between those who have money and power and those who have neither.

"Some people are incompetent to deal with society," said Nicole, speaking from own her experience as a young woman behind bars. "Some people get used to the jail world. It's almost like a form of retardation. Being in jail, you're a lot more accepted. You can deal with the mentality of the jail level, and you have a roof over your head, you have a meal, you have a bed, and some people are fine with that; but you put them out into society, and they're lost. They feel really out of control. To break a law is of no consequence to them. They don't mind going back in. So I think they don't think twice about it."

In jail, some young fathers feel liberated from the daunting adult responsibility of providing for themselves and their families. By the time they get out, many feel like survivors. Getting through their sentence is a tangible accomplishment and many view their time behind bars as a period of maturation and spiritual growth. In the real world with its laws, standards, and challenges, some of these young men experience little if any sense of achievement. More often there is just the daily grind, the escape route offered by drugs, the rage and shame associated with failure, and the constant need to prove one's manhood through repeated attempts to rebel against the perceived injustice of being stuck on the bottom rung of the ladder.

At the Teen Parent Program in Pittsfield, many infants born to teen mothers were of mixed race, which is interesting in light of the fact that according to the U.S. Census 2000, the city's officially registered total population was 3.5 percent black or African American, 2 percent Hispanic or Latino, and 91.6 percent white. Given that 81 percent of Pittsfield's teen mothers were white, the prevalence, significance, and implications of interracial relationships within this specific segment of the city's population cannot be underestimated.

Captain Barry said, "We've noticed a lot of interracial births among young white females from a lower socioeconomic background and young black males, many of whom are drug dealers from out of the area, many of whom have been convicted of using drugs."

"Interracial relationships are really well known in Pittsfield," confirmed Nicole. "The teen music is R&B and hip-hop, and that's the 'in' thing, and obviously most of the groups are ethnic groups, so for a white woman to be with a black guy . . . that's the fad, it's the thing to do, along with wearing the pants low and the whole thing. If you see something going on in the music world, it's usually going on in the teen world."

Sitting beside her daughter and son, whose brown skin contrasted with her own white skin, Amy said, "I know a lot of black people who don't like white and black couples, and I know a lot of white people that don't like black and white couples. They think biracial kids are wrong, but I don't see the difference. People who are racist learn from when they're young because their parents teach them that there is a difference between black and white, and then they just make stereotypes. My daughter doesn't have no problem with that 'cause she's not raised that way. She's four and she already asked me if she was brown or white. She came to me herself because she was wondering. I told her she was both. When she gets older, she'll understand."

Jessica talked openly about the strange experience of sometimes not being recognized as her son's mother, because she is fair and blond and he is brown with jet-black hair.

"My friend Tamika, she's black, and sometimes we'll go out and she'll be holding my son and people will go up to her and say, 'Oh, your son is so cute,' and I'll be like 'No, he's *mine!*' I don't really mind, because people don't really talk about mixed races anymore. It's not a big deal, because you see it everywhere. It's, like, not a new thing."

Shayla defied her father, who prior to his separation from her mother had ordered her never to date white guys. "I wasn't surprised that my baby came out very light because of his father's color," she said. "Sometimes when I walk around, people ask me whose baby he is because he doesn't look anything like me and because he's so light."

Liz grew up in a series of foster homes, and after several years of gang involvement, she ended up in Pittsfield at a juvenile lockup facility. Shortly after being released, she got pregnant at the age of sixteen and joined the other girls at the Teen Parent Program.

"My mother's ethnicity is Italian, and my dad's background is Hispanic," Liz explained. "My son is Puerto Rican and Chinese. We have a little nickname for him, 'Puerto-chink.' It's either 'Puerto-chink' or 'Chink-o-rican.' It's kinda cute, but I really don't want to say it that loud, because you say 'chink' and that's insulting Chinese people."

Liz's boyfriend, Peter, discussed the marriage of his Anglo-Saxon mother to his Chinese father, who, after being abandoned by his biological parents, grew up in a series of foster homes in Massachusetts.

Peter said, "I'm a mixed breed from my ethnic background. My son's background doesn't really make a difference. He's still human and he's mine. That's all that matters."

Bernard, the father of Amy's son, was raised in Africa. He immigrated to the U.S. as a young adult. "I think that issue of black and white should be over by now," he said. "We're living in the twenty-first century and this thing should stop. We had enough. People who have ideas of racism should learn more and teach their kids. I always think that people that hate black people end up being family with black people. I have seen a lot of white folks that hate blacks, and either their son or daughter becomes friends or family with black people. We are all equal. That's the way it's gonna be, and we should all move on."

The views and experiences of these young parents of multiracial children reflect some of the major developments and trends that are changing the face of America. The number of children who are multiracial is roughly double the percentage of adults and is likely to keep growing at an exponential rate. An article in *USA Today* cited the following projection made by demographers: "By the year 2050, 21% of Americans will be claiming mixed ancestry." In response to the release of the census data, national newspapers were flooded with scholars speculating that "as race fades as a basis for social distinctions and government policies, new lines may be based on socioeconomic class, geography, education and other factors."

As the significance of race diminishes as a basis of social distinction, many social disadvantages that go hand in hand with teen parenthood are coming into even sharper focus: most prominent is the sharp disparity between socioeconomic classes. Not since the Great Depression has America been so polarized between those who have access to money and resources and those who don't. The United States has the largest gap between rich and poor among industrialized nations—and also the highest teen pregnancy rate.

Sociologist Kristin Luker has done extensive research on the links between financial hardship and teen pregnancy. In stark contrast to teenagers from mid- and high-income backgrounds, who are much more likely to have abortions, *poor and low-income teenagers account for approximately 83 percent of adolescents who have a baby and become a parent and 85 percent of those who become an unwed parent*. Luker sees teen parenthood as "the province of those youngsters who are already disadvantaged by their position in our society. The major institutions of American life—families, schools, job markets, the medical system—are not working for them."

Luker identifies "early childbearing as a symptom—not a cause, but a marker of events, an indicator of the extent to which many young people have been excluded from the American dream." Reflecting on the statistic that almost three-quarters of all teen pregnancies are described as unintentional, Luker explains that "youngsters often drift into pregnancy and then into parenthood, not because they affirmatively choose pregnancy as a first choice among many options, but rather because they see so few satisfying alternatives. As Laurie Zabin, a Johns Hopkins researcher on teen pregnancy, put it, 'As long as people don't have a vision of the future which having a baby at a very early age will jeopardize, they won't go to all the lengths necessary to prevent pregnancy.' "

In light of the hard evidence that disadvantaged teenagers are much less inclined toward the options of abortion and adoption than girls from mid- and high-income families, Luker concludes that "the decision whether to terminate a pregnancy is powerfully affected by class, race and socioeconomic status. The more successful a young woman is—and more importantly, expects to be—the more likely she is to obtain an abortion."

Hope is the ingredient that is missing from the lives of so many young women who become teen mothers. In depressed communities such as Pittsfield, where positive role models, supportive mentors, fulfilling job prospects, decent incomes, happy marriages, and tangible achievements are hard to come by, the fantasy of motherhood promises unconditional love, an identity, and a sense of self-worth that comes from being vital to the survival of a tiny human being. Motherhood draws upon one of the few precious resources that a discouraged teenager may believe she has inside her: the capacity to nurture and give love to another human being. In some particularly dark environments, a girl's fantasy of finding comfort and intense intimacy through sex that results in a baby may be the only sparkle in her otherwise bleak vision of her own future.

Researchers have discovered strong links between childhood abuse and the sexual risk behaviors in young women that often culminate in teen parenthood. As head of the Department of Preventive Medicine at Kaiser Permanente, one of the largest HMOs in America, Dr. Vincent J. Felitti has been working in collaboration with epidemiologist Dr. Robert F. Anda from the Centers for Disease Control (CDC) on the ACE Study, a landmark, decade-long inquiry into the far-reaching, long-term medical and social consequences of Adverse Childhood Experiences and their link to self-destructive high-risk behaviors such as unprotected sex and addictions to food, cigarettes, drugs, and alcohol. These patterns of behavior frequently originate as coping devices used to deal with psychological stress stemming from severe family pathology. Dr. Felitti, Dr. Anda, and their colleagues have determined that over time and in excess, these self-destructive behaviors often trigger serious chronic health problems, many of which ultimately lead to the diseases that are the leading causes of death in adults.

For the purposes of their research, Dr. Felitti, Dr. Anda, and their colleagues created a seven-point checklist defining categories of Adverse Childhood Experiences. Three categories related to childhood abuse, including psychological abuse, physical abuse, and contact sexual abuse. Four categories related to childhood exposure to household dysfunction, including witnessing the violent treatment of a mother or stepmother, substance abuse, mental illness or suicide, and criminal behavior within the household.

One section of their study focused specifically on sexual risk behaviors in women. Based on information gathered from more than five thousand female participants, Dr. Felitti, Dr. Anda, and their researchers concluded that "each category of Adverse Childhood Experience was associated with an increased risk of sexual intercourse by age fifteen, and that the chances that a woman first had sex by age fifteen rose progressively with increasing numbers of such experiences from odds of 1.8 among those with one type of adverse childhood experience to 7.0 among those who had been exposed to six or seven categories."

Liz, Amy, Shayla, Jessica, Colleen, and Sheri were all sexually active by the age of fifteen. They conceived and gave birth with the determination that through their children, they would revise and rework the traumatic aspects of their childhood. Some of them viewed their babies as vessels for their own thwarted hopes, dreams, and ambitions. This attitude was reflected in the time and energy these girls spent altering conventional spellings of names, in an effort to ensure that their babies' would be special.

In a crib placed in one corner of the stuffed-animal-and-makeup-cluttered, half-adolescent, half-infant bedroom that Sheri shared with her daughter and her younger sister was a handmade pillow that had her baby's name and date of birth embroidered onto it. Instead of *Leah* being spelled with only one *e*, there were two *e*s stitched on, to spell *Leeah*. When asked about the unconventional spelling, Sheri explained that she wanted her daughter to have a name that no one else had. She had seen the name "Leah" in a "what to name the baby" book, and although it was not a common name in Pittsfield, she had wanted to add the extra *e* to make the name unique.

Jessica named her son Ezakeil, a name that appears in the Bible with the spelling Ezekiel. Jessica purposely changed the *e* to an *a* and reversed the *ie* to *ei* in order to create a more original spelling. Jessica's friend Mary Ann had named her daughter Karesse after meeting her friend's daughter whose name was Caressa. Mary Ann explained that she thought the name she chose for her daughter was unusual and liked the way it sounded but had changed the spelling because she, like Sheri and Jessica, wanted her baby to be one of a kind. For the exact same reason, Amy named her daughter Kaliegh, after seeing the name spelled as Kaylie and as Caleigh in a name book. For these young mothers, the act of naming was weighted with power. They shared a strong, conscious desire for their babies' names to be unusual and somewhat exotic, which could be interpreted as an expression of their collective wish that the lives of their children would transcend the ordinary, surpassing the boundaries and limitations they perceived within themselves and their environment.

Robert Coles has written poignantly about encountering a similar mind-set while interviewing a pregnant fourteen-year-old girl in a Boston ghetto. Coles found "a conviction on her part that the word 'success' belonged to others. Yet she considered her baby, still inside her, as quite possibly one of those 'others.' He or she would grow up to be 'different.' He or she would 'escape.' "

At age sixteen, Shayla, like many of her peers in Pittsfield, didn't clearly see other possible ways of doing something that even came close to the magnitude of bringing another life into the world. For Shayla, having a baby was the only dream that at that particular moment seemed to be remotely within reach. Conceiving a child was a way of bringing drama and significance and purpose into her life; it was one definite way of taking control of her destiny.

"I felt that if I had a baby, it would change things," Shayla sighed. "I thought it would make my life a lot better."

David Simon and Edward Burns encountered a similar mind-set when writing their book, *The Corner,* which chronicles the lives of people living in a drug-infested neighborhood in West Baltimore, a city that has one of the highest teen pregnancy rates in the country. On the subject of teen parenthood in that particular community, they wrote: "These children have concluded that bringing about life—any life whatsoever—is a legitimate, plausible ambition in a world where plausible ambitions are hard to come by. This they can do."

Robert Coles encountered a similar point of view when he interviewed a teen mother who recounted the following mother-daughter dialogue: "My mother said, 'Don't you have a child until you're good and ready.' When I got pregnant I told her, I said, 'It may be early for me, but to tell you the truth, I'm good and ready.' Then I told her why: because I wasn't getting any place any other way, and so this was the way for me."

Education might appear at first glance to be one of the few accessible routes out of a place like Pittsfield. For some students it was, but for many others it most certainly was not. After expensive structural renovations and modernization of Pittsfield's school buildings, the two public high schools were so stretched for costs that in 2002 there was talk of merging them under one roof to save money. Students were acutely aware of the lack of resources. They organized bake sales in order to help fund sports and extracurricular activities and did what they could to stave off the threat that at any moment, these too could be slashed.

Their teachers lived with the same uneasiness and precarious instability. In May of 2002, *The Berkshire Eagle* reported that "the School Department issued layoff notices to fifty-eight teachers, and put them on a recall list. Those teachers could be recalled based on their seniority in the areas in which they are certified to teach if funding for those positions becomes available. The remaining thirty-eight teachers were given termination notices, based on classroom performance and certification issues." These ups and downs ensured a reasonably high turnover of faculty and made many teachers feel that they and their services were undervalued.

Mary arrived fresh from out of town to teach in Pittsfield's public school system. Youthful, energetic, and idealistic, she entered the classroom on the first day fully prepared to give the sixth grade her very best effort. She had many ideas about what she wanted to teach, but as her enthusiasm was dealt one heavy blow after another, she was forced to rein in her objectives.

"I've never done anything as challenging as teaching at Reid Middle School in Pittsfield," she said. "I was asked to get the kids to write creatively and also to teach them punctuation and grammar and spelling. I would be given a certain amount of pencils and paper, and sometimes if we ran out I'd be told, 'There's no more.' We would have to wait or the kids would have to provide their own; and some of them couldn't really provide their own materials, because they didn't have the resources to do it. So if a school can't provide a pencil and paper for a kid, then that kid doesn't have the basic tools to even begin to write.

"For my class, there were no materials for them to read in school or to take home, and I think you can't really learn to write unless you read other writers. Grammar lessons are really boring for kids—practicing where to put commas and that kind of thing—it's just not interesting unless you can put it in context and show the kids why it's useful. So here's what I tried to do. I went and photocopied excerpts from Anne Frank's diary and from Frederick Douglass's autobiography. I wanted to give the kids the idea that like Anne Frank, kids their age write and express themselves, so that it wasn't such a foreign idea.

"I handed those excerpts out at the beginning of the semester and then I was told, 'You have to stop doing that, because you're going to exceed your photocopying limit.' This happened during the first six weeks of the semester. So I then realized, okay, I can't provide them the materials that I need to help inspire them to start journals. So what am I supposed to do?

"I decided I'd try to make up really simple exercises that only required pencils and paper and their imagination. Some days it would just be my saying, 'I want you to go look out the window for two minutes and I want you to remember whatever you see and write about it. . . .' I thought to myself, *I'm failing these kids, every day.*

"I observed a group of very dedicated teachers. Many of them had been there for twenty-five years and they wanted to help. But they had reached a point, they sort of . . . their behavior was . . . Well, the message I got was 'Don't rock the boat. You're breaking the code by questioning the fact that we can't have glitter for Christmas decorations. We can't afford that stuff!' To question that and complain about it? I really felt like I had stepped out of line when I did that.

"The thing that has to be said over and over again until anybody who cares about education feels like a broken record is that the public school system has got to be supported. It has to have resources, and it has to be reorganized so that it functions. Right now, at least judging from my own experience, that system is completely dysfunctional. It just doesn't work. It doesn't serve the educators or the children. People should be able to have an education so that they can achieve their full potential. That should be a right, but that's completely gone. I don't think that right exists."

A year after Mary taught at Reid Middle School, President Bush signed the historic No Child Left Behind Act of 2001. Among its many provisions, this bold new federal law promises to hold public schools more accountable for the performance of students; promises to give parents of children from disadvantaged backgrounds the option to transfer a child out of a failing school into a better public or charter school; and, where failure persists, allows federal funds to provide supplemental education services, including tutoring, after-school services, and summer school programs.

This sweeping educational reform occurred a year or two after Jessica, Colleen, Amy, Shayla, Liz, and Sheri had gotten their high school diplomas or their GEDs, so they did not have a chance to reap any of its benefits. Instead, they were stuck scrambling to comply with the stringent demands of the 1996 welfare reform bill, which had replaced Aid to Families with Dependent Children (AFDC) with Temporary Assistance to Needy Families (TANF), ending sixty years of welfare entitlement, limiting each person's eligibility for federal assistance to a maximum of five years per lifetime and requiring with very few exceptions that teen parents who were minors live with a parent or responsible adult in a supervised setting. It became mandatory for teen mothers with children over a year old to attend school or college or professional training full-time and/or work—in some cases, up to forty hours a week. Failure to abide by these and a host of other strict rules raised the possibility of sanctions that potentially included the abrupt suspension of benefits.

This shift in policy rendered the myth of the welfare-incentive argument obsolete. It no longer made sense for disgruntled taxpayers to accuse adolescent girls and young women of having children on purpose out of sheer laziness in order to milk the government for free money and housing rather than going to school or getting a job. After welfare reform, the system was anything but user-friendly, especially when it came to teen mothers.

Although Jessica, Colleen, Amy, Shayla, Liz, and Sheri worked and went to high school and longed to be independent and self-sufficient, they confessed that they had never taken the SAT, nor did they remember ever being told that this test was required for application to most four-year colleges. They had never been told about the different ways of financing a college education and were not aware of the existence of need-blind admissions. Most just assumed that if they continued their education, they would choose between two local institutions: Berkshire Community College or the Mildred Elly Business School, which was located a few minutes away from North Street, in a strip mall next to the Misty Moonlight Diner. To these teenagers, life began to look more and more like a one-way dead-end street that ended not far from where it began . . . in Pittsfield.

chapter two

AMY & BERNARD

"When I met my first boyfriend, it wasn't really about the sex part. It was the fact that I had a boyfriend that was so great. My friends kind of looked up to me because my boyfriend was in high school. I was hanging out with the popular clique. I wanted to be friends with everybody who was cool. I ended up getting pregnant around the end of my eighth-grade year."

CONTINUITY AND TRADITION WERE THE CORNERSTONES of Amy's family history. She grew up on a quiet street in a neighborhood populated almost exclusively by white married couples with children. Her parents owned a three-bedroom ranch house just two doors down from her mother's nearly identical childhood home.

Born in Italy, Amy's maternal grandfather came to Pittsfield at the age of ten. In his early twenties, he married an Irish woman with whom he had five children, including Amy's mother, Donna. While making a living painting houses and factories, Amy's grandfather was exposed to high levels of asbestos. During a routine health examination administered by his labor union, he tested positive for high levels of chemical poisoning. He was subsequently diagnosed with a rare, fatal form of lung cancer. He received several small settlements from some of the companies responsible for manufacturing the products that had made him so gravely ill. When he died at the age of sixty-one, he bequeathed his business to his son.

Amy's paternal grandfather was of Irish Catholic descent. He devoted the prime years of his life to General Electric. He and his wife had thirteen children, including Amy's father, James. In 1973, at the age of nineteen, James followed in his father's footsteps and reported for his first day of work at GE. He was assigned to the Power Transformer Division. Several years later, he was transferred to the Ordnance Division, where he served as a cog in the giant machine that orchestrated the complex multistep process of manufacturing guidance systems for missiles launched from submarines.

During his years at GE, James was called upon to fulfill a variety of functions: welder, fabricator, burner, and assembler. Proficient at wiring, he often built circuit boards. After putting in a grueling forty-hour week at the plant, James liked to spend his leisure time hunting and fishing with his buddies. He also enjoyed relaxing with his family and tending to the pale pink roses that bloomed in his spacious backyard.

Calm and reserved, with gray hair and a thin mustache, James was a man who appreciated what he had. He took pride in his home and was content with his solid marriage to his wife. Donna stayed home during the week with their three kids, until they were all old enough to go to school; then she worked part-time, driving for a local transportation company and waiting tables at a local restaurant on weekends. Secure in their daily routine, James and Donna divided their time between their respective jobs and raising their three beautiful children—Shalene, Michael, and Amy, who was the youngest.

Amy and her siblings attended catechism at St. Mark's and maintained strong ties to the local Catholic Youth Center. Under the umbrella of this organization, they participated in a variety of sports and extracurricular activities. Michael was a star basketball player, and his parents proudly videotaped his games. Amy and Shalene were cheerleaders. On Saturday afternoons, as Donna and James relaxed on the deck above the backyard, they could see their daughters enthusiastically practicing their routines. On Sundays, the family went to church. Every Christmas Eve, Donna and James stuffed stockings full of small gifts for the children and placed larger gifts under a glittering tree. There were Little League games, barbecues, birthday parties, and hearty Thanksgiving dinners. Overall, life was good.

James had expected to work at GE until he was old enough to retire and get his pension, just as his father had done. He was alarmed in 1988 when GE shut down the Power Transformer Division. Many of his friends were among the thousands of workers who lost their jobs.

James continued working at the Ordnance Division, anxious about his fate. He felt as if he were sitting on a time bomb. The amount of his retirement package would be contingent upon his years of service and his salary at the time he stopped working for GE. He was only thirty-seven, and he worried that if he was laid off, he might have to wait until he was sixty in order to receive his pension. He wondered how he would support his wife and his three school-aged children if he lost his job. As GE scaled back its Pittsfield operations, James feared that Jack Welch's strategy of downsizing and globalization might end up costing him and his family their security and the way of life they had until then taken for granted.

"GE is a union shop, so the pay is pretty high," James explained. "It's probably double of what most workers make around here. Fifty, sixty, even seventy thousand dollars a year: for a factory worker, that's pretty good. You can make a decent living. It's enough to support a family and send your kids to college. That's what you want to do now, because they're not gonna have the factories anymore. You always want better for your kids. You want to be able to send them to college."

In the early 1990s, when GE sold most of its weapons businesses, James's worst fears were realized. Nearing forty, with almost two decades of service under his belt, he was laid off, and the lifestyle he and his family had became accustomed to was thrown into jeopardy. Uncertainty crept into their lives, spreading its tendrils in every direction.

Amy was ten when her father lost his job at GE. Stress in the family escalated. Her mother began working longer hours for the transportation company, sometimes chauffeuring clients as far as New York City, Boston, and Albany.

Included in the severance package GE had given James were funds earmarked for education and job training. James left his family in Pittsfield and temporarily moved to Vermont to attend a trade school. He took courses on how to be a professional wallpaper applier. James hoped that GE would recall him to another plant, but as a backup plan, he made tentative arrangements to join forces with his brother-in-law who had inherited his father's painting business. Since wallpapering often went hand in hand with painting, the idea was that when James got back to Pittsfield armed with a new set of skills, he and his brother-in-law would share clients.

In the wake of GE's departure, the city James had grown up in was evolving in ways he had never dreamed of. During his childhood, there had seemed to be a public school on every other block. Back then each school reflected the character of its distinct neighborhood and offered both parents and children a sense of cohesion and community spirit. Now many local neighborhood schools had shut down, and instead of walking a few blocks to school, students were packed onto buses and transported to a handful of public schools near the center of town. As James observed the modern world of fractured single-parent families encroaching on his old-world values, he worried about his kids.

After completing his course at the trade school in Vermont, James returned to Pittsfield, where he was forced to come to terms with the fact that locally there was no work that would offer him wages and benefits that were comparable to what he had gotten from GE. After a year, his hope of being recalled by GE gave out. One afternoon James found himself behind the wheel, driving to the local stationery store to place an order for business cards for the wallpapering company he intended to run out of his home. His backup plan was now his game plan.

James remembered that among his coworkers at GE there had been a saying: "Last one in, first one out!" This adage and the seventeen years of service James had racked up proved to be his salvation. After wallpapering houses for six months, he was one of the chosen few who were recalled to the GE plant in Schenectady, New York. Ecstatic after hearing the good news, James tossed his wallpapering business cards into the garbage, grateful to his union for coming through for him.

At the Schenectady plant, James was assigned to a team that manufactured generators. His relative seniority in Pittsfield meant very little at this new job, where he was regarded as both a newcomer and an outsider. There had been massive layoffs in Schenectady, and many native workers deeply resented that a handful of Pittsfield workers had been imported to take over a few of the remaining scarce, coveted positions. Hostile coworkers dubbed James and his Pittsfield colleagues "the Massholes."

James was given the undesirable night shift, where he subsequently spent the next six years. Back when he was a young man just starting out, he had worked nights in Pittsfield until he had enough seniority to be transferred to days and could have a life again. With his new schedule in Schenectady, James was on his way out or already gone by the time his kids came home from school, and he was either fast asleep or just waking up when they left for school in the morning. Donna worked during the day, so the couple's time together was sharply reduced. After sundown James was on the road, alone amid the glare of headlights, coasting along the interstate beneath the sleek, black, often starless sky.

The new job in Schenectady made James feel that he was being forced to start all over again at the bottom, largely surrounded by younger guys who were less experienced. Very few of his old pals had been rehired. The camaraderie that had brought humor, friendship, and team spirit to the job was gone. Despite his many reservations, James resigned himself to the monotonous labor, the nocturnal hours, and the sixty-mile commute, determined to work the fifteen years he had left until he would be eligible for his pension. After all, GE had given him a "good-paying job," and good-paying jobs were few and far between.

Burdened by her husband's frequent absence, Donna struggled to shepherd her three children through adolescence. Amy's friends made jokes about her father never being home. They teased her, saying that her father probably had a secret life that she knew nothing about—maybe he even had another family. Amy insisted that that wasn't the case and explained that her father had to work all the time. But when asked, she had to admit that she wasn't quite sure about what he did, for although Amy had attended several family nights at GE, she had never been allowed to actually watch her father work. Her imagination ran wild as she wondered what his all-consuming, important job really was and concocted outlandish stories to appease the curiosity of her friends.

"My dad is very busy and very important and he's not allowed to talk about his work," Amy explained to a circle of rapt eleven-year-old girls. "I think he's an FBI agent," she would whisper. "He works part-time as a private eye. That's why he drives that long detective's car and gets home so late."

Later that same year, when Amy had her first period, she locked herself in the bathroom and cried. Donna knocked on the door and then handed her a worn-out old book her own mother had given her at the same point in her life. The book contained diagrams about menstruation and reproduction. Donna assumed the book contained all the information Amy needed to know at that early juncture. Amy barely even glanced at it.

Eager for more adult company and additional income, Donna started working at a shop that sold arts and crafts. She did her best to help the kids through the painful transition to puberty. The two elder children were self-motivated and functioned well independently, excelling at school and remaining focused on grades, sports, and college, but Amy had a hard time academically and failed to find her niche. In the congested hallways of her school, she often felt that aside from her beauty and popularity, she was interchangeable, just one of the crowd. It seemed as if the teachers gave most of their attention to the tiny group of "star" students who got their pictures printed in the newspaper when they won awards.

Amy had a hard time just passing her tests, let alone acing them. She longed for some defining talent or special attribute that would distinguish her, something that would shift the spotlight away from her siblings onto her, something that would make the teachers and her parents reach out and pay more attention to her. Feeling outshone by her siblings and overlooked by her teachers, Amy became disenchanted with school. She gave up on her classes and diverted her energy to her social life. Failing to find support or direction or goals to anchor her, in seventh grade Amy began smoking and drinking at parties with her friends.

"When Amy went to middle school, she got tied in with some other girls," said James. "I think every single one of them was from single-parent families with, like, no control whatsoever. Those girls got ahold of Amy and kinda took control of her life. That's the way I see it."

Strongly susceptible to peer pressure, Amy was prepared to do whatever it took to be part of the popular clique, no matter how risky. She enjoyed the thrill of walking the tightrope of adolescence without a safety net, boldly putting one foot in front of the other, showing off, and never thinking for a moment that with one false move she might come tumbling down.

Amy didn't know how to say no to her friends. Despite her

mother's protests, the family home became a late-night hangout for a horde of wild teenagers. At thirteen, Amy was dying to be older than she was. She viewed her mother as an adversary, envied her elder siblings, and yearned for the extra privileges that were bestowed upon them as a result of their perceived maturity. She became enraged when her mother denied her these same privileges, insisting that she was still too young.

Amy's rebellious behavior far exceeded what James and Donna had gone through with their other children. They adopted a strict, no-nonsense attitude, set more rules, and tried to monitor their teenage daughter's every move. Whenever Amy went out at night, they called other parents to verify her whereabouts and grounded her when she broke her curfew and lied about whom she was with or where she went. Amy was infuriated by her parents' surveillance. Determined to break loose from their jurisdiction, she became sly, sneaky, and secretive about her social activities.

Behind her parents' back, she began dating Trevor, a senior at the local high school. Amy's romantic link to a black guy who was seventeen raised her status immeasurably within the competitive social hierarchy of the eighth-grade girls who occupied coveted positions in the "popular" clique. This social circle included girls from various ethnic backgrounds who wholeheartedly embraced hip-hop fashion and music and interracial relationships, which were considered to be extremely cool and in vogue.

Having Trevor as her boyfriend gave Amy a false sense of superiority over other girls her own age. Her advancement in the arena of dating compensated for her lack of distinction in academics, art, music, and sports. Amy wanted to be among the first of her friends to go all the way with a guy. When she achieved this goal, her friends showered her with questions, congratulations, and admiration.

"The fact that I had a boyfriend was so great," explained Amy. "All my friends looked up to me."

While on a superficial level being part of a couple validated Amy's insecurities about being attractive and desirable, on a deeper level her relationship with Trevor was immature and emotionally unrewarding. Their interactions revolved around public displays of affection intended to maintain an appearance of being sexy, cool, popular, and in love. This role-playing mimicked behavior they saw in movies and on television shows, but behind all their posturing, Amy and Trevor's relationship was characterized by a total lack of communication. They rarely discussed their thoughts or emotions, and during their many sexual encounters, the question of contraception was never raised.

Amy described Trevor as "extremely quiet," terms similar to those she used to describe her father. According to Amy, she and her father rarely had conversations or connected in a significant way that made her feel whole and recognized. She interpreted her father's frequent absences and silence as a lack of interest in her. At night, while her father was away at work, Amy made life miserable for her mother. She was rude, disrespectful, and provocative. When no one was looking, she would sneak out of the house and meet her older friends around the corner. They would whisk Amy away in their cars, leaving her mother to discover an empty bed when she opened the door to Amy's room.

Amy quit catechism and refused to abide by any of her mother's rules. Donna resented the fact that her husband wasn't there to help discipline their teenage daughter. After working the night shift, he'd come home to find the entire household fighting. James got caught between Amy and Donna. Amy complained to her father that her mother was exaggerating and being unreasonable. Donna was put in the awkward position of having to defend herself. She insisted to her husband that Amy's behavior was indeed inappropriate and out of control, and demanded that he intervene. When he tried, Amy argued and did her best to drive a wedge between her parents. She often succeeded in turning her father against her mother. Donna deeply resented that her husband allowed their adolescent daughter to poison the tiny slivers of time they shared together as a couple. It wasn't long before Amy's rebellious, manipulative, attention-seeking behavior began to shake the very foundation of her parents' marriage.

Finally, after the police came to the house and found Amy and her underage friends with booze, Donna told James she had had enough.

"My wife—she actually moved out of the house," he recalled. "She couldn't handle Amy. They couldn't be in the same room together. Donna came to me and said, 'That's it, you deal with it, I can't take it anymore,' and she left. I was shocked. I kept asking her to come back, but she was firm on it. She said, 'No. I'm not coming back until Amy straightens out.' "

Donna moved in with one of her friends. James requested to be transferred off the night shift, citing family problems. His request was denied. He was reminded that shifts were allocated on the basis of seniority and was told to wait his turn.

James resorted to putting his son, Michael, who was in the tenth grade, in charge of keeping Amy out of trouble. Amy continually disobeyed her elder brother. Fed up with screaming matches that sometimes escalated into knock-down-drag-out fistfights, Michael threw up his hands and told his father that, short of calling the police, he knew no way of preventing his crazy little sister from having friends over on weeknights when she was supposed to be doing her homework and going to bed early.

"Amy would have people over," James recalled, "and I'd get home at midnight and tell them all to get out, but they never wanted to leave."

One night, after arguing with a group of Amy's friends who refused to depart, James exploded.

"You know what you're doing," he shouted at Amy, hoping to elicit a confession.

Amy played dumb.

"I'm working second shift, I come home at midnight, and you got all these guys in here, sitting on the couch with you and your girlfriends and . . ."

James paused awkwardly, wishing his wife were there to help him through this delicate moment. He took a deep breath.

"If you keep this up, you're gonna get pregnant," he told Amy. "It's gonna happen."

Silent and mortified, Amy remained seated, hugging her knees as she rolled her eyes. James stared at his daughter, waiting for her to respond. Averting her gaze, Amy got up, stomped into her bedroom, and slammed the door.

James took a few steps toward Amy's closed door. When he

opened it and peered in, he saw her curled up on her bed, facing the wall. Strains of blaring rap music spilled out of her headphones as she deliberately ignored her father's presence.

Feeling very tired, James left the room and shut the door behind him. What James did not know was that he had initiated the right conversation at the wrong time. As another month went by, Amy continued to hide her pregnancy.

Eventually, Amy decided to confide in her best friend. Unbeknownst to Amy, her best friend's mother had picked up the extension to make a call and had heard the girls chattering away about Amy's pregnancy. After eavesdropping on the rest of the call, her best friend's mother then telephoned her good friend, Amy's aunt.

Donna was ringing up a sale at the crafts store when the call came.

"It's your sister," shouted her coworker.

Donna picked up the receiver.

"Hello?"

"Donna, I think you'd better come home," her sister said.

"Why?" Donna asked. "Is something wrong?"

"I don't know how else to put this to you, but Amy is five and a half months pregnant."

"She's *what?*"

Despite their problems, Donna hadn't expected this. Images of Amy as a little girl scrolled through her mind. She remembered how all her friends used to compliment Amy and say that she was such an angel.

"It was a big shock," said Amy. She giggled. "Everyone thought I was still a virgin."

Since Donna had left home she had not noticed that Amy had been gaining weight. For the first three months Amy had been tiny and had even dared to wear a bikini on several occasions without anyone's noticing her condition. The biggest hint had been Amy's irritability, which both parents had interpreted as her standard belligerence.

"My mother was really upset," Amy recalled. "She was over having babies. She didn't want any more babies in the house. It was too late to have an abortion, but she didn't want me to keep the baby. She thought it was going to ruin my life."

"I was the last to know," said James, "and I was *pissed—real* pissed. My question to Amy was, *Why?* Why would you do something like this?"

"I think my pregnancy happened because I was so young," said Amy. "I didn't think something like that could happen to me. I didn't think I could get pregnant. It was just something that never crossed my mind. I never really talked to my parents about sex. I had it in health class, but it really didn't faze me."

Amy paused, allowing herself a rare moment of introspection.

"I also think the fact that me and my parents weren't that close contributed to the fact that I got pregnant," she said. "I didn't think they had any expectations of me. They didn't really tell me how to do things. They never gave me a path to go toward."

The moment Amy's pregnancy was out in the open, the question of what path she would take became the central topic of every family discussion. All other issues in her parents' lives paled compared with Amy's present condition and her questionable future.

At Donna's insistence, Amy made her first visit to the doctor, who confirmed that she was almost six months pregnant. Abortion was no longer an option. At that juncture, James and Donna made their expectations clear: They wanted Amy to continue with school, go on to college, and make something of herself. They did not feel it was feasible for her to raise a child at fourteen. They wanted her to put the baby up for adoption.

Donna viewed Amy as a wild child who could barely take care of herself. She knew that a baby wouldn't change Amy's nature and could see that on top of battling over curfew, unwanted visitors, homework, and her own job at the crafts store, she would become a full-time baby-sitter. Whatever little free time she and James might have together would be devoured. Raising another infant was not something Donna was willing to take on after having raised three children. She wanted to be the kind of grandmother that grandchildren visited once or twice a week, and had no intention of becoming a primary caregiver.

Donna contacted adoption agencies. Feeling guilty for all the stress she was causing her family, Amy went through the motions with the adoption agency that her mother selected. Several weeks later, Amy received a photograph of the couple who wanted to adopt her baby as soon as it was born. As her pregnancy continued into its final weeks, Amy agonized over her decision to give up the baby. Finally she decided that there was no way she could go through with the adoption. She mustered up the courage to stand up to her mother.

"Mom, I'm keeping the baby," she announced.

"What do you mean? You can't back out now," Donna said. "What about that lovely couple who have their heart set on adopting the baby?"

Amy could see her mother's lower lip trembling. She took a deep breath and stuck to her guns.

"Mom, I can't carry a baby in me for nine months and then give it away to somebody. That just isn't me."

Though Amy had the authority and right to defy her mother with her decision to keep her baby and could refuse to sign the adoption papers, she lacked the power to make Trevor take full responsibility for the pregnancy.

"My daughter's father was seventeen," Amy recalled. "When I brought up the situation, he didn't really say anything. He didn't know what to make of it. I didn't really know what to make of it. I went through a phase where I was screaming and yelling at him. Telling him that he needs to do something with his life, telling him to get off his butt and take care of me. It was just too much pressure for him.

"I thought that maybe we could be together and everything, but as the pregnancy went along, we were in school and he was, like, hiding under the stairwells from me because I was walking around pregnant and I was humongous. He and his friends were into cheerleaders and stuff like that, so he didn't want anything to do with me. Behind closed doors, it was fine and he was supportive and everything. But when it came to his friends . . . he just didn't want to be around it near his friends. I didn't think it was going to be like that. I didn't picture going to my first year of high school pregnant and having my boyfriend *ignore* me . . . but that's what happened."

Amy gave birth to a beautiful baby girl. With her pale brown skin, almond-shaped eyes, and jet-black wavy hair, Kaliegh was a perfect combination of both her parents.

"Donna came back when Kaliegh was born," recalled James. "Things were okay for a while. Amy and Donna were getting along better. Then all of a sudden, it got worse. Amy saw us as instant baby-sitters, so she'd say, 'Oh, I'm going out.' And we were left watching the kid."

Amy thought that because she was now a mother herself, she was automatically an adult and her mother no longer had any right to tell her what to do. Donna disagreed. As long as Amy was fifteen and living under her roof, she had to abide by whatever rules were set, regardless of whether or not she had a child.

One chilly winter night, Amy wanted to go to a party. Her mother forbade her from leaving the house, saying that she didn't want to baby-sit. Amy picked up her daughter, who was several months old, and said, "Fine. Then I'll take Kaliegh with me," and headed out the door.

Donna grabbed Amy and dragged her back inside. Amy started yelling and screaming at her mother. Donna picked up the phone and called the police.

"I've got a fifteen-year-old thinking she's an adult," she said, then begged the officer to stop Amy from leaving the house with the baby. "It's way too cold and she's in no condition to go anywhere alone with the baby," Donna explained.

The policeman went to the house. Donna was shocked when he greeted Amy by name. He had encountered Amy on other occasions during parties that had been busted. In an effort to break the tension in the household, the policeman took Amy to a friend's house, leaving Kaliegh in the warmth with her grandmother. The next morning, Donna decided to file a CHINS petition against Amy. She called the

Department of Social Services (DSS) and announced that she had a Child in Need of Services.

"Me and my mother had a lot of arguments about how to raise my daughter," recalled Amy. "I was still young. I still wanted to go out with my friends. I wanted to party like regular teenagers do once in a while. My mother really didn't know how to control me. She wanted somebody to be able to come in and have more authority over what I was doing, so she called DSS and got them involved. I needed guidance, and they were more stern—you know, straight down to the point with me. I had to listen to them. There were consequences if I didn't."

"It was no joke," was James's view. "DSS—they take control of your life. They tell you what you're gonna do and how you're gonna raise your kids. If you don't like it and you don't do it, they'll take your kids away from you."

Faced with the threat of having her daughter removed from her custody and placed in foster care, Amy got her act together. She enrolled in the Teen Parent Program and moved forward with her studies. She began working part-time as a waitress at Friendly's.

"Having a baby turns your life around," Amy said. "You have to grow up so fast."

Trevor went off to the army, leaving Amy to raise their child on her own. Right after Trevor signed up, Amy's father went to talk to the recruiters. He wanted to make sure they knew that Trevor had a daughter and was obliged to pay child support. As James had suspected, Trevor hadn't written anything on the forms about being a father, nor had he mentioned it in his interview.

James presented Kaliegh's birth certificate to the recruiting officer on duty. The officer suggested that James contact his local congressman, John Olver, who was widely respected in the county for being a strong advocate for working families, youth, child care, and affordable health care. James called the congressman's office and spoke to a page who helped him file the necessary paperwork so that child-support payments would be automatically deducted from Trevor's monthly salary. They also made sure that Kaliegh was placed on the army's health insurance plan. Soon after being recruited, Trevor was stationed in Colorado. He called Amy and told her that he'd be spending only a few weeks a year in Massachusetts. He said he hoped to see his daughter for a few days at Christmas.

While attending the Teen Parent Program, Amy was separated from most of her friends at Pittsfield High School. Her life was boring compared with what it used to be. She did her best to prove herself a fit mother, and after a year of relatively good behavior, she succeeded in convincing DSS that she could handle the responsibility of raising a child.

"They dismissed my case because they thought I was doing good," she said.

Amy left the Teen Parent Program and went back to Pittsfield High School. With DSS out of her life, Amy, now sixteen, felt it was time to find a way to escape from her parents' house. She felt trapped living at home and longed to be free of her mother and father's watchful, critical eyes. She had rapidly lost the weight she had gained during her pregnancy, and with her long, luxurious brown hair, her perfectly applied makeup, her stylish clothes, and her long painted fingernails, she was a magnet for the opposite sex. When Kaliegh was one and a half, Amy's friend introduced her to Bernard, a young African who was working in Pittsfield and taking classes at Berkshire Community College.

"The first time I met Amy, she had a little girl with her," Bernard recalled, "and I was like, 'Who is she?' She said, 'My daughter.' Well, I didn't believe it. I was, like, 'Oh no, I don't think so.' I said to myself, 'It's probably her sister or something, her little sister.' "

Amy was immediately captivated by Bernard's exotic, thick French accent. She was intrigued to learn that he had recently

come to America from Ivory Coast to live with relatives and pursue his studies, in fulfillment of his parents' dream. Bernard's mother and father wanted their son to become rich and successful in America.

Amy had not traveled far from Pittsfield and had never been outside the United States. She loved the idea of spending time with a man who had grown up in Africa, in the midst of a different culture and with a set of values and experiences that were so completely fresh and unlike anything she was familiar with. Compared with other guys Amy knew, Bernard seemed more serious about his education, more ambitious, more idealistic, and more conscious and appreciative of the opportunities America offered. He adored his part-time job at the Center for Disabled Children and spoke enthusiastically about the children he worked with.

"Bernard's an intelligent guy," said James, "but he was older, so I wasn't too hip on the situation. Bernard was, like, at least twenty-two years old. I don't know. I think he was attracted to Amy 'cause she's good-looking."

Amy was extremely impressed by the fact that Bernard had his own car, his own apartment, and a steady flow of income. She told Bernard that because of a medical condition, she couldn't get pregnant again. They had sex and never used any contraception. After they had been dating for three months, Amy missed her period.

"I ended up getting pregnant again," she said. "It was just another mistake. People make mistakes."

"Amy told me that she couldn't get pregnant," said Bernard. "I was so stupid. I didn't even think about it."

"I was on the Pill and then I was off," Amy explained, "but I didn't think I could get pregnant. I thought that . . . I don't know what I thought . . . I just wasn't thinking!"

Amy's father had a different theory about what motivated his daughter's second pregnancy.

"Amy was living here at home, and she was still battling all the time and fighting with everybody. So I think she got pregnant on purpose, just to get out of the situation she was in here."

Amy didn't hide her second pregnancy. She told Bernard right away.

Bernard recalled, "When Amy told me she was pregnant, I said, 'Amy, the baby is not a baby yet. It's just a development. It's just a little egg that is growing inside you. If you do an abortion, it would be so fast. If you let the baby grow inside you, the process will be so much harder.' I said, 'Please, Amy, let's do an abortion.' "

Bernard shook his head. "She said, 'No!' "

"When I was pregnant with my daughter, I didn't want to get an abortion," explained Amy. "Being pregnant the second time around, I looked at my daughter and I figured that I couldn't kill a baby. That's all."

The decision about what to do with the fetus was ultimately up to Amy. The appropriate time for Bernard to make a clear, definitive statement about not being ready to become a father had long passed. Now that the situation had progressed to this stage, Bernard was forced to live with Amy's decision, whether he agreed with it or not.

Amy went to the doctor. After checking the results of the tests, the doctor put her hands on her hips and asked Amy, "So, what are you going to do?"

The condescending tone of the doctor's voice caused Amy to

shrink away from the cold metal of the stirrups around her feet. The rough white paper crackled beneath her back as she sat up and stared into the cold, hard eyes of the forty-something, instrument-wielding female gynecologist. In a clear voice, Amy stated her wish to have the baby and raise it herself. There was a palpable current of silent condemnation in the stark, white institutional room. Amy felt it settle on her like a cloud of dust. She felt dirty, ashamed, and defiant. She hated the doctor for making her feel that it was expected she would want an abortion, given her age and circumstances.

Rather than having a conversation about her options and emotions and her relationship with Bernard, Amy remained silent and furious throughout the rest of the examination. This encounter sealed Amy's dislike and mistrust of doctors. They didn't respect her, so she didn't respect them. She would show them she was capable of raising two children. They'd see. She would prove to everyone that she could be a good mother.

"No, not again!" James and Donna screamed when they heard that Amy was planning on keeping the second baby. They reminded their daughter of the enormous additional responsibility of clothing, feeding, and educating another child, not to mention the extra time, love, emotional energy, and attention a second child required. Amy told them that she had made up her mind and that nothing anyone said would change it. She packed up her and her daughter's belongings and moved in with Bernard. James and Donna disapproved.

"Bernard had an apartment at this place called Riverview," James recalled. Located at the bottom of a ravine behind shrubs and foliage, the river was barely visible from the high-rise building; it was the contaminated Housatonic River, where PCBs from GE had been dumped. "It was kinda a low-middle-income project," said James. "There were drug dealers in there. It's not a place I would want to live."

Amy didn't like the project, either, but she did her best to make it as nice as she possibly could, decorating it with pretty curtains and other knickknacks. She was relieved to have escaped her parents' house. She desperately wanted Kaliegh to have a father figure in her life, and Bernard seemed willing to take on that role, at least initially. Since her life already revolved around motherhood, Amy thought a second baby would solidify her life with Bernard. It wasn't quite that simple.

Bernard was in turmoil about the impending arrival of the baby. For months, he couldn't bring himself to tell his parents that he was going to be a father. They had worked hard to be able to send their son to America and harbored high hopes for what he would be able to accomplish, armed with a degree from an American college. The last thing Bernard wanted to do was dash their expectations and wound their pride. Yet in order to help support Amy, the baby, and Kaliegh, Bernard would have to work full-time, which would entail postponing his studies indefinitely.

Not wanting to break his parents' hearts, Bernard kept finding excuses to avoid telling them. Finally, toward the end of Amy's pregnancy, he picked up the phone and made the international call to Ivory Coast. As expected, his parents were devastated. When Bernard recalled the telephone conversation that transpired, he bowed his head and fixed his eyes on the ground. His voice sank into his throat, weighed down by a sense of shame and failure.

"My father, he sent me to America to go to school," he explained.

"For my father—seeing his son having a baby and dropping out of school . . . It was a big disappointment for him."

While Bernard and Amy were adjusting their lives to accommodate parenthood, Amy's brother and sister were on a completely different track. They left Pittsfield and enrolled in college. Amy's sister majored in environmental science. Her brother studied communications in the hopes of someday fulfilling his dream of becoming a sportscaster.

College was not in the cards for Amy. After giving birth to her healthy son, Marcus, she struggled to balance the demands of being a teen mother of two children with the challenge of completing her high school education. She transferred back into the Teen Parent Program and continued working part-time as a waitress at Friendly's.

Marcus was admitted to the Teen Parent Program's nursery, but Kaliegh, now three, had to attend different day care. The rule at the Teen Parent Program was that once kids were old enough to walk, their mothers had to find alternative day-care facilities for them. Amy found private home day care that would accept her vouchers. On weekdays, when school let out at three o'clock, Amy strapped Marcus into his car seat and drove to the place where Kaliegh spent most afternoons.

It took Amy ten minutes to get to the street that led to the gravel driveway of the run-down private home that doubled as a day-care center. As Amy turned the knob, the screen door swung open into a dusty room that was dingy and poorly lit. Children lay strewn around on the floor, looking bored and lethargic.

Kaliegh ambled over in a daze and threw her arms around her mother in a prolonged embrace, glad to be picked up. The gaunt middle-aged woman who looked after the children didn't say much more than hello and good-bye. Her mind was elsewhere. She moved as if caught in slow motion. Kaliegh ran outside, eager to breathe some fresh air. She hopped into the car beside her little brother, who gurgled a warm greeting. Amy drove through Pittsfield, past the Friendly's where she worked. She turned the corner and pulled into the parking lot of the tall subsidized apartment building that she, Bernard, and the kids called home.

For Amy, getting her daughter and infant son out of the car and up three flights of stairs to their apartment was a major daily ordeal. That afternoon Kaliegh bounded up the stairs, way ahead of her mother, who yelled out to her to be careful and slow down. Nervous about Kaliegh's being way ahead of her and out of sight in the unsafe drug-infested apartment building, Amy fought to balance her son in one arm and his carriage in the other, along with her school bag, which was casually slung over her shoulder. It was a heavy load to carry up three long flights of stairs, and when she got to her front door, she was panting and out of breath. As Kaliegh wailed impatiently, Amy set everything down and fumbled for her keys. She heaved a deep sigh of relief as the door swung open. Once the kids were safely inside, Amy finally had a chance to catch her breath.

Without any help, Amy faced these and other practical challenges every single day. Even the simplest, most mundane tasks that most people take for granted were rendered exponentially more difficult by the presence of two young children. Complicating matters, Amy and Bernard's relationship remained strained. The birth of their son had increased the tension between them rather than alleviating it, as Amy had hoped.

Although Amy deeply appreciated Bernard's presence and the fact that he fulfilled his duties as a father to both her daughter and their son, they were constantly fighting. Bernard resented not being able to go to college because of his obligation to work to support his family. He came from a home where the male was the sole bread-winner, and he was uncomfortable with Amy's working and making as much money as he did. Amy didn't like being told what to do by her boyfriend. She became extremely frustrated and upset when Bernard criticized her friends and tried to exert control over how she spent her free time.

Amy and Bernard's shared sense of responsibility for the two kids was the glue that held their fragile relationship together. Although all relationships require compromise, the longer two people know each other, the more aware they become of exactly what those compromises are going to be. Then when they make a decision to commit to a relationship for the long term, the choice is ideally an informed decision. Amy and Bernard went about it the opposite way, committing to a person each barely knew and then slowly learning about the other as they went along, balancing their personal conflicts with the added pressure of raising two children and the challenge of living together in a small apartment while struggling to make ends meet.

When Marcus was a few months old, Amy heard some ugly rumors. She had good reason to believe that Bernard was being unfaithful to her. Her fears came to the surface at the Teen Parent Program in May, when for an hour each week she attended a series of writing workshops conducted by visiting psychologist Carol Gilligan and her colleague Normi Noel.

Carol and Normi used Edith Wharton's novel *Summer* as a starting point for discussions and writing exercises. Set in the early 1900s in North Dormer, a bleak fictional town believed to be a composite of Pittsfield and surrounding areas of Berkshire County, Wharton's novel describes the plight of a teenager named Charity Royall. Following a passionate love affair with Lucius Harney, a rich architect from out of town, Charity finds herself pregnant. Just as she is wondering how and when she should break the news to her lover, she hears some upsetting gossip: Harney is, in fact, already engaged to a rich socialite from one of the city's finest families.

Amy sat very still as she listened to Carol Gilligan read the following passage aloud:

> Sometimes as Charity lay sleepless . . . she planned many things. . . . It was then she wrote to Harney. But the letters were never put on paper, for she did not know how to express what she wanted to tell him. So she waited. . . . Since her talk with Ally she had felt sure that Harney was engaged to Annabel Balch. . . . She was still sure that Harney would come back, and she was equally sure that, for the moment at least, it was she whom he loved and not Miss Balch. Yet the girl, no less, remained a rival since she represented all the things that Charity felt herself most incapable of understanding or achieving. . . . The more she thought of these things, the more a sense of fatality weighed on her:

> She felt the uselessness of struggling against the circumstances.

After reading the passage, Carol described how Charity subsequently feels unworthy of getting what she wants, so she writes a short, self-effacing letter to Harney that completely misrepresents her true feelings, hides the reality of her pregnancy, and masks her desire. She pointed out how Charity's options shrink and her future darkens as a result of her silence and fear of speaking the truth.

Carol then set the novel down and asked Amy and the other teen mothers in the workshop to write two letters to the fathers of their babies: one that they would be willing to send, and another that they wouldn't dare send, for fear of the implications of expressing their real thoughts and feelings. When it came time for the teen mothers to read their letters out loud, Amy adjusted her glasses and began:

> *Dear Bernard,*
>
> *I wanted to let you know I am very happy. But I am also very unhappy. I wish we could take this relationship to another level. I am tired of the rumors. I am tired of the lies. I want a picture-perfect relationship. I want so much more than I have at this point.*

Smiling nervously, Amy paused and picked up the letter that she *wouldn't* send.

"Okay," she warned her attentive peers. "This is the bad one. This is the one I wanted to write to him."

Dear Bernard,

I hope you did not sleep with my friend. I don't understand why my friend would say such things to me. I'm not sure what to believe. But I hope to God that you care too much for me to be so stupid.

Amy took off her glasses, wiped the tears from her eyes, and fought to compose herself.

"This just makes me really mad," she said. "Because I want to kill somebody right now."

Later, when asked to respond to Amy's worries about his infidelity, Bernard was evasive. He addressed the issue in an indirect, inconclusive way that neither affirmed nor denied Amy's fears about his cheating on her. He shrugged his shoulders, squirmed on the couch, took a deep breath, and tried to justify himself.

"I would consider myself like Bill Clinton," said Bernard. "He's got a family. He got a job, I have a family, I have a job, and I would do the same thing, too. He's raising his family, and I have to do the same. Everybody should do the same."

"That letter that I wrote to Bernard was kind of nasty," Amy acknowledged a few weeks later. "But I guess things are working out right now; they're going really good. Bernard supports me really well. He helps me. He pays bills. He takes my daughter to the doctor. He watches my daughter. He's really supportive."

"I have to support my family," said Bernard. "That's the way my father raised me. My mom was a teenager, too, when she met my father. My father never ran away. He stayed there for my mother. They were both young. He stayed there, stayed there, worked, worked, worked. . . . Now things are getting better."

Refusing to be held back, Amy graduated from Pittsfield High School with the rest of her class. The ceremony was held in the neighboring town of Lenox. Cloaked in purple caps and gowns, the class of 1999 filed into the spectacular Seiji Ozawa Hall at Tanglewood, home of the world-renowned music festival.

When Amy's name was called, she ascended the podium. Onstage, the mayor of Pittsfield handed her a white rose and her diploma. Later that afternoon, James and Donna hosted a big party at their home. While Amy and her friends celebrated, a group of small children congregated on the lawn and had a party of their own. The young sons and daughters of the class of '99 drove their plastic cars in circles, admired one another's balloons, and devoured hot dogs drenched in ketchup.

After graduation, Amy enrolled in a cosmetology course offered at the vocational school attached to Pittsfield High School. For two years, she trained to get her license, focusing on hairdressing. She was required to put in one thousand hours of training before she could take her state boards and be certified. Amy started out cutting hair on mannequins and then moved on to real people. She was taught how to do manicures, facials, and waxing. On days when she didn't have class, she continued waiting tables at Friendly's.

"My hours are from as early as six-thirty in the morning until six o'clock in the afternoon," she said. "I don't work nights anymore because nights are too much."

"Welfare's a little different now," James explained, " 'cause the federal government clamped down on that. Before, it was like you could be on welfare all your life and they'd just send you a check every month plus food stamps, free medical, and all that. They're a little tougher on that now. Amy works full-time so her income is up to a point where she doesn't get any money.

"When I say Amy doesn't get any money—her rent is subsidized, so welfare's probably paying five hundred dollars a month toward her rent. Her health insurance is MassHealth, so if she goes to the hospital, she don't pay anything for that. The state pays that. I guess if you're working, you can get health insurance, rent subsidies, and food stamps, but lots of times nowadays, they don't give out money."

Bernard continued to work at the Center for Disabled Children. He structured his schedule to complement Amy's. In order to make it possible for him to spend time with the kids during the week while Amy was working, Bernard worked thirteen- or sixteen-hour shifts on Fridays, Saturdays, and Sundays. He regretted that he had to work on weekends because that's when most of his friends were going out and having fun.

Although the pay was minimal, Bernard got tremendous satisfaction out of working with handicapped children and seeing them learn and progress. His work experience gave him insight into children's thoughts and behavior. Bernard felt strongly that this insight made him a better parent. He used many of the concepts and techniques he learned on the job at home to guide him in his attempts at understanding and teaching his son. While Bernard enjoyed his work, he remained troubled by a sense that he was failing to achieve his full potential.

"I love the job that I do, but it's not something I want to do for the rest of my life. It's a beginning," he stated emphatically. "I do what I have to do to have my family live under a roof and eat something."

Amy and Bernard were alarmed when the rent for their apartment skyrocketed. James explained what had caused the sudden increase.

"These subsidized housing projects were built by the state, but these large corporations own them, and they're always buying and selling them. This one company bought the project where Amy and Bernard lived and then went in there and renovated it and then jacked the rents up, double or triple. The low-income people who were living in there were asked to pay eight or nine hundred dollars a month. That's outrageous for this area, so Amy and Bernard moved out to another housing complex on April Lane.

"In subsidized housing," said James, "the state has a formula based on what you can afford to pay for rent, and they figure out what you can afford. So Amy—she hardly makes anything. At April Lane it's probably six hundred a month, but because it's subsidized, Amy probably pays eighty dollars a month. Taxpayers pay the rest."

Amy and Bernard and the two kids settled in to a duplex apartment on April Lane. Although drugs were still a concern, as was the rare drive-by shooting, these apartments were on the whole more child-friendly, surrounded by grass and trees and swing sets. The doorways were all at ground level, so Amy was spared the hassle of hiking up three flights of stairs.

Wanting to increase her income beyond what she was making at Friendly's, Amy began looking for a second job. When a position opened up at the Teen Parent Program, she called and submitted her name for consideration. She was hired to take care of babies while their mothers were being tutored. Amy returned to the grueling night shift at Friendly's so that she could be free to work at TPP during the day.

On a typical day, Amy woke up at seven and dropped the two kids off at day care on her way to work.

"My job was really tiring," she said. " 'Cause I just watched babies all day and then I'd come home to my own babies. And it was just—ugh . . . sometimes I just . . . I would just go home and fall asleep."

Amy had a few hours off in the late afternoon, and when she could keep her eyes open, she used this time to run errands, shower, change into her uniform, and make dinner for the kids. She would then drive to Friendly's, where she worked until midnight.

Bernard had mornings to himself. Usually he relaxed, did errands, watched TV, and caught up with his pals during his daily workout at the gym. After lunch he would head out to pick up the kids from day care. He spent most weekday afternoons playing with the children in the park or at home.

Bernard felt that his role as a father combined teaching with discipline. He did his best to teach the children to respect adults and avoid violence. He believed that children should have "less toys and more books."

"I want my kids to be wise," he said. "One day, I want to be proud of them. To teach kids to love books, you have to start from a young age. The more reading they do, the more they learn—the smarter they get."

Overloaded with the dual responsibility of being a mother of two and providing for her family, Amy had absolutely no time to herself. Going to and from work, she and Bernard passed each other like ships in the night. Most days she felt physically, emotionally, and spiritually drained.

"I'm nineteen going on twenty, and I feel like I'm fifty," she said. "I'm just so tired. I do what people are supposed to do when they're thirty, or in their late twenties. I'm running around all the time, getting up early, working, and chasing kids. A lot of people my age don't get up early and get two kids ready. I have to get them dressed and feed them breakfast and take them to school. It's frustrating that I can't work every day because I have to work around the kids' schedules, so I'm not free to make as much money as I want to. It's hard. I feel like I'm old."

Amy shook her head in wonder, remembering how naive she was back at the beginning of eighth grade, before she got pregnant for the first time.

"I never thought I'd be in the situation I'm in now," she said. "I was just a normal teenage girl who thought that nothing could faze me, that nothing bad would ever happen to me—that nothing bad *could* ever happen to me."

Kaliegh, nearly five years old, entered the room, dressed up as a bride. The little girl had used bobby pins to attach a piece of white lace to her hair. The lace draped across Kaliegh's face like a veil, as she put one foot in front of the other, pointing her toes, making every effort to walk gracefully in a perfectly straight line. Holding her son, Marcus, Amy turned to look at her daughter.

"What are you doing, Kaliegh? Getting married?"

Kaliegh broke into a huge smile, nodded, and continued her walk down an imaginary aisle.

Amy laughed at her daughter's pretend game, and shook her head. For Amy, marriage seemed far off in the distant horizon. "I want to get married someday," she said, "but Bernard and I are both still young, and we have a lot ahead of us. When I get married, I want to be settled down, having a house, doing the right thing, making lots of money. . . . I don't see that happening in the next two years, but eventually . . ."

Bernard agreed that marriage was not something he was ready to dive into.

"You don't say, 'I want to get married,' because it's fun," he said. "I've seen people that got married and got divorced in less than two weeks. I want to get married eventually, but right now I'm just waiting. Right now there is commitment between Amy and I. We act like we're married. Because of the kids we have, we each fulfill a parent's life. Once in a while I tease Amy and say, 'Oh, I wanna marry you,' you know, stuff like that. She knows I do that just to tease her, and we laugh about it."

"I know he's kidding me," Amy snapped, "because he knows not to come to me without a ring."

"How much does a ring cost? Thirty dollars?" Amy frowned as Bernard shrugged his shoulders, a wide grin on his face. To him, it was all a big joke.

"Thirty dollars?" Amy glared at him. "An engagement ring better be way more than thirty dollars, or I'll return it."

"I can go to New York and buy you a fake one. You know, those crystals."

"Yeah, right," said Amy. "If you ever buy me a ring to get married, I'll bring it to the jeweler and make sure it costs way more than thirty dollars."

Eighteen months after graduating from high school, Amy looked pale and haggard. She had chopped off almost all her hair and covered what remained with a bandanna. Working two jobs was getting to her. At home she could be found curled up on a chair, lost in a deep sleep, oblivious to the sounds of the kids playing, undisturbed by the drone of a game show on TV.

In spite of their initial resistance to Amy's having children at such a young age, James and Donna had fallen deeply in love with their grandchildren. They often stepped in to help Amy, appreciating that she was doing her very best to stay afloat under extremely difficult circumstances.

"I see Kaliegh and Marcus three or four times a week," said James. "Kaliegh learned how to use the phone and she's constantly calling here saying, 'Grandpa, I wanna sleep over your house tonight.' I always say, 'Okay, come on over.' They're here all the time."

"My parents have taken my kids to Disney World, the Jersey Shore, and the Bahamas. At age six, my daughter has gone more places than I have in twenty years," said Amy, her voice tinged with envy, her eyes brimming with gratitude.

On Halloween, rather than trick-or-treating around April Lane, Amy and Bernard decided to take the kids to James and Donna's neighborhood, which they felt was much safer. While Amy and her mother stayed at home and offered hungry ghosts and goblins handfuls of candy, Kaliegh dressed up as an angel and set out on her own candy-hunting mission, accompanied by her little brother, who was trick-or-treating for the first time. James and Bernard led the kids from house to house, laughing as Marcus unabashedly ran straight inside every door with his arms outstretched and palms open, eager to grasp the next Tootsie Roll, Starburst, or lollipop.

Having lived in the neighborhood for more than twenty years, James was on familiar terms with his neighbors. Their houses and yards were decorated with all sorts of ghoulish displays, including plastic skeletons and gigantic spiderwebs dangling from trees, as well as glowing, grinning pumpkins of all shapes and sizes. They appeared to enjoy the annual ritual almost as much as the kids did.

As each door opened, James introduced Bernard and his grandchildren to the mostly white neighbors who lived on his street. Some of them were meeting Bernard and the children for the first time. Their eyes traveled from James to Bernard to the children, mentally inserting Amy, the missing piece of the family portrait.

As November swept through the Berkshires, the trees lost the last of their leaves and the temperature plummeted. Amy bundled up to face the bitterly cold New England mornings. Back on the breakfast shift at Friendly's, she poured coffee and took orders for eggs over easy, occasionally glancing out the steamed-up windows into the parking lot, where snowflakes fell onto windshields as customers hurried inside, shivering as they removed their hats, gloves, and parkas. Amy was always ready with her pad and pencil. She took pride in her work and always tried to be at her best for the people she served.

Amy's fluctuating hairstyles provided the best indication as to what was really going on behind her pretty smile. The novelty of having two kids had worn off, and Amy was looking for new ways to captivate and startle people. In efforts reminiscent of her old need to get attention from her preoccupied family, Amy changed her hair length, color, and style several times a month. It went from brown to red to blond to a different shade of brown. On one occasion, she braided straw-blond extensions into her short brown hair to make two-tone cornrows. Though it was easy for Amy to change her hairstyle or her nail polish, it was much harder to change other aspects of her life.

Amy finished her one thousand hours of training and passed her state boards for her cosmetology license. During the exam, she used her mother as a model and gave her a haircut. Now certified, Amy longed to get a job as a hairdresser so that she could give up her job at Friendly's. She enjoyed hairdressing because it allowed her some creativity, unlike waitressing.

"I've gone out looking for jobs for hairdressing, but a lot of the hours that people want me to work are hours that are impossible for me because I have kids. I can basically work thirty hours a week during day-care times. I can't work weekends, 'cause Bernard works weekends."

The division of labor between Bernard and Amy meant that there wasn't a single day of the week that the entire family could spend together. The time each spent with the kids became increasingly stressful.

"Money is a big problem," Amy said. "We fight over bills, and bills, and more bills. Neither one of us has jobs that we make tons of money at. We both have a limit. Bernard's okay because he pays for a lot. It's hard for me to pay for a lot because my job isn't that good."

Bernard's eyes narrowed as he chastised Amy.

"Don't sit down and talk about how we fight for money, we fight for this, we fight for that! We have arguments. We don't fight! We talk. When we don't compromise, I go my way, she goes her way."

Amy sat absolutely still, saying nothing, looking weary and slightly embarrassed by Bernard's harsh rebuke. Exasperated, Bernard sighed and shook his head.

"My stress—my stress is not money. My stress is that I'm not accomplishing the things that I wished for. I will accomplish something. It has to be with school. I hope I go back. I want to finish what I started. Right now we're at a young age and we're raising two kids. It's not easy."

Like many immigrants, Bernard came to America with high expectations based on fairy-tale impressions of a culture he knew only from TV shows such as *Beverly Hills 90210* or *Friends*. Bernard dreamt that the education he would receive in America would open door after door, eventually empowering him to ascend the ranks and make lots of money. He envisioned himself living a lifestyle not unlike those he had seen night after night on television in his parents' modest home in Ivory Coast.

After several years of living in Pittsfield, Bernard had become much more jaded. He recognized his lost innocence in the hopeful faces of his friends who remained in Africa, clinging to their dreams of someday going to America and transforming their lives.

"A lot of my friends in Africa think that America is the country of opportunity," Bernard explained. "Why? Because they know that by coming here, they can do better than back home. It's not easy back home, and by seeing stuff on TV all the time, they wish to be here; they think America is paradise. I went home this summer and I told them, 'You think America is a paradise, but it's not easy to live there. It's a lot of struggle, and you gotta work through your whole entire life. You get a job, and your whole paycheck could be gone in less than a minute. You work to pay bills. You work, and they take your money. You work and you pay insurance for your car. You pay rent. Even food is expensive. It's not easy.' I tell them that. I tell them, 'The people you see on American TV shows, they're doing well. But many of us are suffering. It's not only me.'

"It's not easy, but my dream will come," promised Bernard. "My dream is to be somebody one of these days, to be able to have a house. . . . I don't want to be a millionaire, but I need something for my family to be happy. I don't want my kids to struggle."

Bernard paused, deep in thought. Suddenly his face lit up and his mood shifted. He sat up straight, his shoulders back, his head held high.

"I brought my son to work today, and everybody was saying, 'Oh my God, I can't believe it. Look how fast Marcus can talk. He's only two. He's so active. He's learning so quick.' It makes me feel good when my coworkers talk about how good my son is. It makes me feel like I'm raising him the right way. I'm gonna see it go further," said Bernard. "I'm gonna do a lot with my son."

The tension between Amy and Bernard escalated as Bernard tried to assert more control over Amy's life. He complained about her choice of friends and made it clear that he didn't approve of her going out and partying. Amy was furious. She had moved in with Bernard to get away from her parents, and now she felt that Bernard was acting as if he were her father. She told him that she wouldn't tolerate his behavior and that she would do what she wanted, when she wanted, with her own money.

Bernard and Amy usually made about the same amount of money per week but occasionally Amy made more, because of tips. Bernard was uncomfortable with Amy's role as a breadwinner who made all her own decisions, spent her money as she pleased, and had no qualms about running out to bars and nightclubs with her friends whenever she felt the urge to party.

"You can't do that," protested Bernard as Amy ran out of the apartment, jumped into the car, and drove off, dressed for a night out on the town. "You have children!" he yelled. "It's your job to stay home and take care of the children!"

Bernard's words fell on deaf ears. Amy wanted her freedom and balked at Bernard's efforts to rein her in. Since Bernard was so far away from his own family, he sometimes turned to Amy's father for advice on how to deal with Amy.

"Bernard, this is America," James told him. "Women aren't slaves in this country. If they want to go out, they get a night out."

"But she goes out with those bad kids," Bernard complained.

"That's a different story," said James, knowing from his own experience exactly what Bernard was up against. "I hate to tell you, Bernard, but Amy chooses the people she hangs around and there's nothing you're gonna be able to do about that. If you think you're gonna keep her tied down in the kitchen, barefoot and pregnant—that's not gonna happen." James chuckled. "Bernard, if you think you're gonna control Amy's life, you might as well forget it."

Seeking peace and a bit of a break from the tumultuous situation with Amy, Bernard made plans to go back to Ivory Coast to visit his family. He stayed in Africa for a month, during which time Amy and the kids stayed behind in Pittsfield. Unbeknownst to Bernard, Amy viewed that time as a trial separation. She was surprised at how well she managed taking care of the two kids on her own.

"Amy and Bernard's relationship is pretty stormy," said James, his face graying in the rapidly fading winter light. He paused for a moment, looking out the window, gathering his thoughts. "I think a lot of it could be their age difference. Bernard seems like a calm, mature guy, but Amy—she's kinda immature and stubborn. I know Bernard wants to continue his education. I told him, 'Well, if that's what you want to do, go ahead and do it.' If he thinks that having a child and Amy are holding him down, I don't know, maybe he's gotta choose. . . .

"Bernard comes from a different culture," explained James. "He says to me, 'In Africa a woman doesn't do this or that.' I tell him, 'You're not in Africa. This is America and I don't know if you guys are ever gonna make it.' "

"We broke up," reported Amy shortly after Bernard's return from Ivory Coast. "Bernard's a jerk and I don't want to be with him anymore. We fight all the time. I'm sick of him, and he's sick of me. We shouldn't be together. We have absolutely nothing in common at all. All Bernard does is bitch at me for everything I do. He doesn't like me to go out, and I like to go out a lot. He don't let me do nothing. He acts like he's my father. He's not my father, and I will not be pushed around like that. I don't like to be stepped all over, so I'm moving out. My kids are gonna live with me. I'm gonna be raising them.

"I applied for Section Eight housing. For some people, it takes up to a year to two years to get it, but there was an opening on the list and they ended up sending me a letter that I got it. I don't have any furniture yet. I got money back after I paid my taxes from working all year. I'm gonna use that to get some furniture."

"If you make under a certain amount of money," explained James, "then, I believe it's the federal government, they give you fifteen hundred dollars per child. You don't claim it against your income. So Amy, she gets a big tax return, twice as big as I get. She's got two children, so that's three thousand dollars. They just give it to her."

James and Donna helped Amy get the bare essentials for her new apartment, a duplex in the April Lane housing project, less than a minute's walk across the parking lot from Bernard's front door. As Amy settled in with the two kids, Bernard sharply reduced the amount of time he spent with them. He told Amy that he didn't feel he had any responsibility to Kaliegh, since she wasn't his daughter.

He saw his son much less than Amy had expected, given that he lived practically next door.

One night a week, Marcus slept over across the yard at his father's apartment. The rest of the week the family rarely saw Bernard, not even in passing. Often when Amy was overwhelmed with work and exhausted after looking after the two kids, she would call Bernard and ask him if they could work out a schedule where they shared custody of Marcus; she would take care of the little boy four nights a week, and Bernard would take him the other three nights. Bernard refused, claiming he was too busy to make that commitment.

Bernard continued working at the Center for Disabled Children and enrolled in a course at the Mildred Elly Business School. After completing the course, he got a job designing websites for a local company. He loved this job. Trained by his coworkers, Bernard was constantly expanding his capabilities and learning new skills. His bosses were very pleased with his progress. When the company traveled to New York City for trade shows and conferences, Bernard was one of the employees chosen to attend.

Amy started working at a hair salon at the mall in Great Barrington. It was the job she had been hoping for. Her boss adored her, and she had many regular customers. She worked forty hours a week but remained financially strained because despite the success Bernard was enjoying at his new job, he didn't regularly pay child support and, aside from a few small gifts here and there, he left Amy with the responsibility of providing for their son.

"Bernard throws a few bucks here and there," said James, "but as far as a monthly payment? No, he don't pay. I'm trying to encourage Amy to take him to court."

Amy was amazed at how fast the kids were growing up. Kaliegh attended summer camp at the Girls Club. Marcus celebrated his fourth birthday at a pizza parlor. Bernard attended the party with some of his friends. He, Amy, Kaliegh, and Marcus posed for a rare family snapshot.

Amy turned twenty-one and began to outgrow her hard-partying ways as she saw more and more of her friends from high school succumbing to serious drug addictions. She began saying no when her friends asked her to do things that she thought might be unsafe. Gradually Amy began figuring out which of her friends were worth keeping.

"Amy had a couple of girls come over, and I think they were drinking," said James. "They wanted Amy to give them a ride home, and Amy couldn't because of the kids. So she let the girls take her car. One girl got dropped off, and the other girl went to another party, got loaded, and ended up upside down in a river with a fractured skull. Somehow she survived it. Amy was out of a car, but dear old dad took care of it."

James bought Amy a new car. He sensed that although Amy still had a long way to go, she was starting to make some real progress. He knew life wasn't easy for her, and he did whatever he could to help out with the kids.

When Amy wanted to go on a vacation, Donna and James assured her that they would look after the kids while she went away. Amy

collected travel brochures about Florida. For months, she saved up tips from work, stuffing her cash into an empty champagne bottle that she kept hidden in her closet.

One night, Amy's childhood friend Bridget stopped by for a drink. Once a member of the popular clique in high school, Bridget had become a teen mother and, like Amy, had given birth to two children at a very young age. Whereas Amy had buckled down and was devoted to her career as a hairdresser, Bridget had become addicted to crack. When she visited Amy, she talked about how the Department of Social Services had removed both her children from her custody. They were now in foster homes.

After spending roughly an hour at Amy's apartment, Bridget gave Amy a hug and departed. The next morning as Amy was getting dressed, she looked into her closet and realized that her champagne bottle stuffed with cash was gone. Convinced that Bridget had stolen it, she drove over to the apartment where Bridget was staying and confronted her boyfriend. He said that Bridget was gone and claimed to know nothing about a champagne bottle.

That same day, Bridget skipped out of town. There were rumors that she had gone down South. Most people suspected that she was holed up somewhere on a binge. Amy never heard from her again.

Months later Bridget's former boyfriend confessed to Amy that he had indeed seen broken glass all over the floor of their bedroom. Amy had no doubt that the shards were from her shattered champagne bottle. She knew that her former best friend had stolen her hard-earned savings, probably to buy more crack.

Amy started saving up her tips again. When James and Donna celebrated their twenty-fifth anniversary, Amy, her sister, and her brother all chipped in to buy them tickets to Ireland. James was thrilled. He had always dreamed of traveling to the country where his ancestors had lived. A rare smile illuminated his face, and Amy was delighted to see her father looking so happy.

chapter three

LIZ & PETER

"When I was seven I got molested by my mom's boyfriend. Charges were pressed. He was put in jail for two years. After that, he came out on parole and it was sort of weird because I knew he was out there somewhere still and I just didn't feel too comfortable. After that, life was just sort of about trying to get my life back together."

LIZ WAS BORN IN SPRINGFIELD, AN HOUR AWAY FROM Pittsfield, where she ended up at the age of fourteen when the Department of Social Services placed her in a juvenile correctional facility. Between stints in lockup, Liz lived in a series of foster homes. She became pregnant at the age of seventeen and enrolled in the Teen Parent Program. Her luminous brown eyes traversed the cracks in the ceiling as she searched for the right words to describe the jagged shards of the years that had constituted her childhood.

"My childhood? I got deprived. That's how I'd put it. I grew up in a violent home, so it wasn't easy. There were a lot of beatings in my house, other than me. My dad would always beat up my mom and yell at her and throw stuff. My mom would do the same. Since I was born this was happening.

"In my neighborhood there were shootings, stabbings, rapes, murders, hit-and-runs. . . . I had to deal with it," said Liz, "because I lived there no matter what. Everyone there was—you can't say poor—but you could say that it was hard to get money. People would do dumb things to get cash. You'd see hookers, drug dealers, people robbing other people, that kind of stuff. There were lots of gangs, too."

Liz could not remember a time when her mother, Paula, wasn't dependent on welfare. Paula worked sporadically at an array of fast-food restaurants and went through long periods of unemployment. Liz shrugged her shoulders as she rattled off a few adjectives that described her mom:

"White, Italian, about three hundred pounds, long hair, wears glasses . . ." Liz sighed and collected her thoughts. "I don't know how to explain my mom any more than that," she concluded. "She's got five different people all inside one person, so it's hard to describe her personality. It's easier to describe what she looks like."

When she was an infant and toddler, Liz stayed home with her biological father, who had come to the United States from Puerto Rico. He spoke Spanish to his daughter and could not read to her because he was illiterate.

"When I was five years old, my dad left me to be on his own," Liz explained. "He got tired of my mom and tired of me, I guess, from what my mom tells me. I really haven't seen him that much since then.

"As a kid, I saw him once in a blue moon, whenever he felt like stepping in. It kinda bothered me that my dad would come in and out of my life whenever he wanted, but my mom let it happen. It was like everything was okay, but it really wasn't. I couldn't say 'I love you, Dad,' and really mean it, 'cause I didn't know the guy."

Enraged after Liz's father walked out, Paula redirected her anger toward the one thing he had left behind: their daughter. In what became a pattern throughout Liz's childhood and adolescence, her mother frequently beat her. Paula once explained this violence by saying that she couldn't look at Liz without being reminded of her father. As the blows were falling, Liz recalled crying out, "How can you see my father in me? I am so different from him!"

Liz looked Hispanic like her dad, not white like her mom. Her identity as a child of mixed race was a huge issue in her life.

"The kids, they'd point at me and say, 'Oh, look at that, eeww. . . .' They'd call me a 'Gringo,' which in Hispanic slang means 'white girl.' People would also call me a half-breed because I'm Spanish and Italian. I didn't like being called those things. It was rude. I liked the fact that I wasn't all one person; I was white, I was Hispanic and a couple of other things, a whole bunch of breeds."

In conversations with Liz, it was impossible not to notice her high level of self-awareness and her excellent ability to express herself verbally. It was hard to believe that this spirited, alert, observant, articulate teenager had been held back in first grade and had subsequently failed many of her classes from that point on. The reason for her bad grades was not her aptitude or her lack of intelligence: it was her chronic absenteeism, a warning flag of child abuse.

The obstacles between Liz and an education did not originate within her. They were rooted in her unstable home environment. Teachers failed to effectively intervene, despite strong clues that this young child was living in a destructive, malignant home environment. Liz associated her early years with a sense of resignation, powerlessness, and loss. She described being held as a virtual prisoner in her own home, isolated from other children, forced to cater to her demanding mother's every need.

"I almost never went to school, because my mom preferred me to stay home and take care of her. She wanted me to be her 'duty girl,' fixing her things to eat, bringing her coffee. . . . It was just

'Liz, can you do this for me? Liz, can you get that for me? Can you light my cigarette for me?' I was like her slave girl. When kids in my class made fun of me, sometimes they would actually call me a slave because they knew why I was home. I don't know how they knew, but they knew.

"I had no friends. I was basically on my own. It was me, Liz, and Liz. That was all I could focus on because none of the kids at school ever wanted to get along with me. They used to laugh at me because of the way I looked. I had bowl haircuts and I looked like a boy. I dressed funny, in corduroys and butterfly collars, always in very funky colors—you know, pink with green. Very stupid-looking colors that I would never choose. My mom put that stuff on me 'cause that was all she could afford. So I can't get mad at that. All the other kids at school had the name-brand clothes on. I used to go to school and they'd say, 'What did you get at the Salvation Army yesterday?' I don't know how they knew, but they knew I went to the Salvation Army.

"My mother wasn't an alcoholic or a drug user, but she was a very lazy person. Not to be rude, but she really was the lazy kind. People say I should've focused on myself more, but it was kinda hard when you have one person like your teacher telling you that you should be in school and your mom saying, 'You should be home, listening to me and doing what I'm telling you.' As a child, I was really confused."

Liz was very self-conscious about the fact that her mother was obese. Paula's imposing three-hundred-pound frame often prompted nasty jeers and jibes from kids as well as from random people on the street, rude phrases along the lines of "Hey, fat lady walking down the street, how you doin'?" Liz felt guilty for not being able to defend her mother against these verbal assaults, but as a small child, she was too scared and too shy to open her mouth about anything to anyone.

Soon after Liz turned six, her mother gave birth again. According to Liz, her half sister's paternity remains a mystery. Now struggling to support two children on welfare, Paula pulled herself out of unemployment and started a new part-time job several nights a week.

Liz was too young to look after her baby sister, so her mother would often leave her daughters in the care of her boyfriend at the time, a man by the name of Ted. During Paula's extended absences, Ted began physically abusing Liz and her infant sister. This violence was conducted under the guise of discipline. It increased in severity as time went on.

One night Ted kicked open the door to Liz's bedroom and molested her, brutally forcing his hands inside her vagina as she sobbed. After sexually assaulting Liz, he went on to the infant. When Liz tried to intervene, Ted pushed her away. Liz was forced to watch helplessly as this man inappropriately fondled her little sister. Ted threatened Liz, telling her in no uncertain terms that he would kill her and her mother if she ever told anyone what had happened.

Midway through the evening, Vivian, a friend of Paula's, came in to check on the kids. She was greeted by the sight of Liz crouched in a corner, holding her body, clutching her nightgown, tears streaming down her face. When she asked Liz what on earth had happened, Liz tried to explain but was interrupted by Ted, who stormed in and began arguing with Vivian, denying everything and saying that Liz was lying. Unsure of whom to believe and not wanting to get involved, Vivian took the children to the home of Liz's biological father and left them in his custody. Ted insisted on accompanying them. He would not let Liz out of his sight. In addition to being her mother's boyfriend, Ted was a close friend of Liz's biological father, and to Liz's utter horror, her father welcomed this man into his home.

Later that night when Paula came to pick up the kids, Ted told her that Liz had misbehaved terribly. Liz's mother spanked her as punishment for her supposed misconduct. Then her father took her into the bathroom and spanked her again, even harder.

In the days that followed, Ted kept threatening Liz, assuring her that if she told anyone about the molestation, he would kill her mother. He further terrorized the little girl with threats of vague, dark, unspeakable things he would do to her, things that would be more terrible than anything she could possibly imagine, more terrible even than death. Liz could barely imagine what could be worse than what he had already done to her and certainly didn't want to find out.

In the wake of being molested, Liz shut down emotionally and spiritually. She continued to be absent from school and was forced to repeat first grade. By law, teachers must report sexual abuse if a child discloses it. However, some teachers neglect to pursue clues less overt than disclosure, such as extensive and unexplained absence, impaired social skills, and poor academic performance. Liz was exhibiting all these indicators of sexual abuse, but the teachers, possibly overwhelmed trying to control the rambunctious students in their classrooms, failed to question the child and did not launch a detailed investigation into her home environment before or after the molestation took place. At the young age of seven, Liz felt invisible, isolated, and fearful, trapped in her mother's tight grasp, victimized in her own home, and forgotten by those who might have helped her.

Liz's grandmother and friends of the family began to comment on the little girl's strange, withdrawn behavior. After observing her over the course of the year, her mother's friend Vivian became convinced that Liz had been telling the truth. After struggling internally about what to do, she confronted Paula with her suspicion that Ted had molested Liz. Paula went ballistic, chased Vivian out of her apartment, followed her home, and proceeded to smash through the terrified woman's front door with a baseball bat, leaving a gaping hole.

Next, Paula confronted her eight-year-old daughter. When Liz confirmed what Vivian had said, her mother demanded to know why she had never been told about the molestation a year ago, when it happened. Crying, Liz told her mother that she had tried to tell her many, many times. She vividly described moments when she had been trying to get her mother's attention and recalled fragments of the numerous conversations she had tried to interrupt as she searched for a way to confide in her mother, who had always been dismissive—too busy, too frazzled, or too distracted to listen.

After hearing Liz's detailed account, her mother finally began to piece together the truncated sentences her daughter had uttered over the past year, along with the very strange, worrisome behavior that many people had noticed and commented on when in the presence of the little girl. The truth was staring Paula in the face. Her child's agonized eyes were unwavering and unforgiving.

Paula contacted Vivian, who agreed to help her press charges. Liz was taken to a doctor, who examined her and confirmed that the molestation had taken place. The doctor completed the necessary paperwork for the courts. Liz courageously made a statement to the authorities describing the sexual abuse that had occurred. Ted pleaded guilty. The result? He was sent to jail for two years and was served with a restraining order prohibiting him from going near Liz for the rest of his life.

Although Paula was initially furious with Ted, her anger soon subsided. She confessed to Liz that she was still head over heels in love with him, in spite of the molestation. Paula made it clear to Liz that she resented her for coming forward. She held her eight-year-old daughter responsible for the fact that she was now separated from her lover, and blamed her for ruining her romantic relationship. Her mother's bitter accusations only added to the guilt and self-loathing Liz already felt. Bombarded with memories of the sound of her mother's harsh, reproachful voice, Liz cringed and shrugged her shoulders, justifiably incredulous after all these years.

"I don't know how a mother could love a guy that molested her daughter. I don't understand my mom's thinking," sighed Liz. "She just—it's like her mind slipped somewhere. . . . I don't know where. She always told me that she loved him. I got confused. I'd be, like, 'Why would you want him still here, knowing what he did to me? Would he do that again?' "

To Liz, Ted's jail sentence seemed much too short. Before she knew it, he was out on parole, back on the streets of Springfield, haunting her neighborhood. The ten-year-old lived in constant fear of running into the man who had molested her.

Liz rarely visited her biological father, except when she got into huge fights with her mother or when her mother was with a guy and didn't want her around, but one afternoon when she was at his apartment, she heard a knock at the door. When her father asked who was there in Spanish, Liz froze at the sound of an eerie, familiar voice. It was Ted.

Her father walked to the door and, without a second thought, turned the knob and let Ted in. Liz was in shock. Her own father was allowing this sexual predator to be under the same roof as her, in blatant defiance of the court's restraining order. Liz panicked and looked for a place to hide. Queasy with fear and repulsion, she cowered in the bedroom, pressing her full weight against the closed door in a forlorn protective gesture. But even as she covered her ears with both hands, she could not block out the sound of the men's voices.

She overheard Ted confronting her dad, telling him that she was a liar. Ted told her father that the only reason he had pleaded guilty to Liz's charge of sexual abuse was to spare her mother the agony of a long, drawn-out trial. Liz's father chose to believe Ted instead of his daughter. To Liz's disgust, the two men remained friends.

Overcome by feelings of seething rage, guilt, and resentment, Liz felt utterly betrayed by both her parents. Her self-esteem was already low, but her spirit sank even further, weighed down by her disappointment in their failure to protect her in the most basic, vital way. All through her tainted childhood, Liz internalized her mother's lack of concern for her daughter's physical and emotional safety and incorporated this maternal recklessness and negligence into her own view of herself. As a result of being convinced that no one gave a damn about how she was treated or cared whether she lived or died, Liz failed to develop either a strong sense of ownership or boundaries in relation to her own body. As she entered an extremely turbulent adolescence, she carried her precariously damaged body image with her.

By the age of ten, Liz was already making out with boys. At age eleven, she hit puberty and became confused, embarrassed, self-conscious, and alarmed over the changes she observed in her body. To Liz, it seemed as if her mother was in denial about the implications of her maturing body and emerging sexuality.

"I was developing different and that was hard because my mom never wanted to talk me about it. She never wanted to help explain what was going on. So, I had to figure it out for myself," Liz recalled. "I had to go to school and ask teachers what this meant, why this had to happen, why my breasts were growing, that kind of stuff."

By the time she entered the sixth grade, Liz was dating lots of different guys, most of whom were fifteen or sixteen years old. By engaging in this precocious, sexualized behavior, Liz cut short what ideally should have been a period of latency, a developmental phase that takes place roughly between the ages of eight and twelve, during which girls generally tend to turn away from boys and have mostly female peers. Ideally, it should be a time when girls develop skills and assert themselves in sports, academics, and the arts—learning about the world and building up confidence in their own abilities, laying the foundation for a strong sense of self defined independently of the opposite sex.

Having leapfrogged over this essential developmental phase, Liz struggled to fill her inner void by acting out "adult" roles, dressing provocatively and precociously, mimicking the sexualized behaviors that she saw in music videos, movies, and magazines—and at home. Her mother never drew any clear lines regarding what kinds of boys were appropriate or inappropriate for Liz to date, nor did she set a good example for her daughters when it came to relationships and the kind of men she associated with.

"My mom was dating all sorts of men," said Liz. "Every week there was a new guy I was introduced to. I thought that was her focus, to have these guys in her life to take care of her, which was wrong. One week this guy would try to be my father, and the next week some other guy would try to be my father. It was awful. I had all these guys trying to be my dad and I knew they weren't, so I defied them. That caused more problems between me and my mom. The fact of all these guys trying to be something they weren't for me, or to me . . . I didn't want to be around that situation and I didn't want my little sister to be around it, either. But I couldn't take my little sister, 'cause back then I didn't even know how to take care of myself."

Instead of reaching within and building up reservoirs of strength, conviction, and self-confidence, Liz searched outside herself for affirmation of her identity. She desperately craved acceptance, love, and validation. Her self-esteem was a completely unstable entity—dependent upon male attention of a sexual nature.

Liz's early re-initiation to sex occurred with a series of predatory adult male partners. Beginning at age thirteen, the sexual situations she found herself in were unquestionably defined by the same features as her molestation at age seven: a tremendous inequality in power, strength, and age, and her own objectification and exploitation.

"After I got molested at the age of seven, the next time I had sex was at the age of thirteen, which is quite young, now that I think about it. It was hard because I kinda went crazy. I liked the feeling of being near people. Being near a man, to me, was great. I thought I was being loved. I ran away after I first had intercourse. I stayed with the guy I slept with because I was scared to go home. I didn't want my mom to hit me or anything, because she was quite violent.

"The guy I was with when I was thirteen, he was twenty years old, he was Hispanic. He was a gang member, one of the Latin Kings. To me, he was good-looking at the time. Probably right now I wouldn't say that anymore. I felt like I was loved, so that's why I did it.

"I stayed at his house. I didn't go to school. I had to worry about cops. I had to worry about seeing my mom because I was only three buildings down from my own home. After that I ran away like thirty more times within two years. I never wanted to be home.

"It wasn't fun being on the run. You had to hide all the time. You were always scared. Like, if you saw a police officer, you ran the other direction because you didn't want him to take you back home. When I ran away, I felt more grown-up. I didn't feel like this little thirteen-year-old girl."

Liz was quickly exposed to the seedy underworld of hookers and drug dealers. Although Liz deluded herself into thinking that the older men who offered her shelter loved her and cared for her, the reality was that they were exploiting her. During many of these early sexual encounters, Liz didn't use any contraception.

"I was always trying to get pregnant," she recalled. "I always wanted to have a baby." Liz cited two primary motives for this unrelenting desire for a child: a deep sense of loneliness and the desire to have something that no one could ever take away from her.

Following the advice of some of her friends on the street, Liz started using condoms at least some of the time. It was only because of sheer luck that her high-risk unprotected sex with older men did not result in an earlier pregnancy, infertility due to a chronic STD, or AIDS. One night, exhausted, frightened, and tired of prostituting herself, Liz reached out for help. She called the hotline of a local organization for children in need. When they bluntly and unsympathetically advised her to turn herself in to the police, she hung up on them.

Unlike some less fortunate runaways who link up with pimps who drug them, kidnap them, and transport them across state lines, where they often meet with ugly fates, Liz never left the immediate vicinity of her hometown. She would run away for a while and then return to her mother's apartment, where she faced physical and verbal abuse. It was a vicious cycle. When Liz finally left home for good, it wasn't to go to a shelter where there was support and guidance. Instead, at age fourteen, she was sent to court in shackles and handcuffs.

"The violence between me and my mother got to the point where my mom would slap me a lot. She'd just start hitting me," said Liz. "One day I came home . . . I was like fourteen years old, and I was staying at my mom's house again. She told me I could go with my friends to the mall. So I did. She said to be back by eight o'clock. I was back two minutes after eight. I was slammed in the corner when I walked in the door. I was getting slapped in my face. Getting yelled at . . . 'Where were you for the two minutes?' She really flipped out on me. I had no other defense other than pushing my mom off me. So I slapped my mom, and that's when everything really changed.

"The cops got called. I got arrested for the first time. Charges were pressed on me from my mother. She accused me of assault and battery, which I don't think was right, because she was really hitting me hard. She was abusing me, literally abusing me. Physically, mentally, verbally, it was just all there.

"I went to court after my mom pressed charges. The first time was to be before the judge, and the second time was—they call it a sentencing. In the courtroom, I had handcuffs and shackles on. If I tried running, I'd fall on my face. You only have enough space with the chains so that you could walk. Then you had a chain coming up from your feet to your hands, so you were hooked that way. You felt like you were already in prison.

"The choices were either to be put in a foster home, stay at home with a zero curfew, or go into a lockup facility for juvenile delinquents. At this time, because it was my first offense, they chose for me to go to a foster home because they felt it was unsafe for me to be at home because of my mom's temper and because of my temper. The fact that all the men were coming in and out of the home—

they felt it was unsafe. I didn't feel right, either. So they took the handcuffs and shackles off me and they sent me with my DSS worker to my first foster home.

"At first I lived with Hispanic people, and that foster home was really crowded," recalled Liz. "There was three little rooms for foster kids, and every room had, like, five or six kids in it. It was the worst place for them to send me to, because the lady didn't care what time I came in or what time I came home. She didn't care what time I got up, as long as I went to school. She didn't care, as long as she got her check. That's what most of the foster homes I was in were like.

"The foster parents get paid to have foster kids there. I felt that the reason why I was there was so they could get a paycheck. A lot of the foster homes were crowded with, like, five foster kids, and when you needed something, most of these foster homes would say they never had any money—when you know they did. You'd see that check come in every week, and they'd have that smile on their face.

"I started hanging out with people ten years older than me, like twenty and twenty-four years old. I got into drugs, alcohol, and stealing. I stole my first car, which was scary because I didn't know how to drive and I worried that the police were going to see that and pull me over and send me to jail.

"After a month I begged to go home, and DSS worked out an agreement between me and my mom. It didn't work out. Two weeks after I moved back home, I ran away again.

"I would run away to people who had things to offer me," said Liz, "not just to some house that had nothing in it. I ran away to people who had food, people who had money to help support me, people who would care for me, people I wished I lived with rather than my mother.

"Every time I ran away, DSS put me in a different foster home. The social workers would try to set goals for me to achieve by certain dates, like achieving a certain amount of days in school. I had a chore chart. I had a checkoff chart. If I earned a certain amount of stars or checks, I'd earn a grab bag. I really didn't have myself focused on any goal, because I really didn't know what I wanted.

"I wasn't stuck in one neighborhood. I went from a poor section of town to rich people. I went to one foster home where it was like one of those fantasy-type houses. Like you would think about it, but you thought it would never come true. It was a real nice house. I had my own room, my own TV, basically my own everything. I could eat whatever I wanted. They had two dining rooms, one for the grown-ups, one for the foster kids. At the time there were only two foster kids, me and this other girl. There was a good-size living room with chandeliers. . . . The kitchen was humongous with a counter in the middle. The bathroom alone was humongous. There was a toilet and you'd walk five steps and then get to the toilet and then another ten steps to the shower. The place was awesome. I felt like I was rich, but I really wasn't. We were in the quiet section of Springfield, which I didn't like, 'cause I didn't know anything about it. I ran away from that home. I don't know why I did it, but I did. That was my problem—I didn't want to have rules. So I totally trashed that house, I just ran. I just forgot about it. I just put it aside. I didn't want to be there no more."

By the time Liz got to this foster home, where the living conditions were relatively good, she was already a veteran of many negative experiences. Her view of herself was so damaged, her self-esteem so fragile, her expectations for her life so shrunken that she could not bear the idea of becoming accustomed to a more comfortable lifestyle that might, without warning, be taken away from her. Unlike an adopted child who would have the security and permanence of a new family, as a foster child, Liz sensed the transience of her situation. She knew that nothing was forever and that she would eventually be back where she started. She felt unworthy and out of place in this house of dreams. Thus, she acted out in a destructive way and instigated her own departure. After this incident, Liz was put on probation. She intensified her gang associations in a desperate search for a sense of belonging that was otherwise absent from her life.

"The reason why I felt comfortable with the gang is that they actually respected me," explained Liz. "They were there for me—at least, I thought they were. They gave me that feeling like I was supposed to be there. I didn't get any of that feeling at home. I'd go home and everyone would be screaming and hollering at me, saying things like 'I hate you!' the minute I walked through the door. I felt like the devil was in my house. But when I was with the gang, it was, like, 'Oh, what's up, how you doing?' There was a general respect for someone. I was more respected in the gang than I was at home."

One of the gang members started giving Liz assignments to go beat up certain girls. Liz would do as she was told. She built up an intimidating reputation as someone to be afraid of. She hated fighting and hurting people. Looking into the frightened, tearful eyes of a girl she had beaten black and blue made Liz feel horribly about herself. That one moment of searing self-loathing was enough to halt her foray into violence.

Liz kept running away from foster homes and cutting school. Between the ages of fourteen and sixteen, she was placed in a lockup detention center on three separate occasions. After being admitted to lockup for the first time, Liz demanded to see a doctor and stated that she wanted to be tested for STDs. She had been having discolored vaginal discharge and feared she had AIDS. She was not HIV-positive but did test positive for gonorrhea. The doctor commended Liz for seeking treatment right away and explained that untreated gonorrhea could increase a person's risk of catching HIV and could also cause PID, an infection of the reproductive organs that sometimes leads to serious, potentially fatal complications during pregnancy. Liz was treated with a single dose of antibiotics. Much to her relief, the infection went away. After serving several terms in lockup, Liz was placed in the Key Program, which was more tightly regulated and regimented than any place she had ever been.

"The Key Program is a place for adolescents eleven and up," said Liz, "who have problems at home and who run away all the time, like I did. It was for people who were considered problem people with gang issues and other stuff like that. It was a really strict place. You shared your room with about three other people. You had to ask permission to go to the bathroom. You had to ask permission to brush your teeth and to get up from your seat. They had control over you. You couldn't do anything unless they said it. It was kind of like a jail. I was there for three or four months. Then they let me out."

Liz was fifteen and a half when she was let out of the Key Program. She was placed in a foster home in Pittsfield. She began dating a local gang member named Ricardo. Eventually she found out he already had three kids and a wife. While Liz was still involved in this relationship, she met a nineteen-year-old named Peter, who treated her with a level of kindness and decency that she was completely unaccustomed to. After years of accepting abuse and disrespect from the adults who had brought her up and the men she had subsequently subjected herself to, Peter was a blast of fresh air, a ray of hope. He empathized with Liz's vulnerability and was able to sense the fragility beneath her tough exterior.

"I first met Liz through my good friend's brother," explained Peter. "My friends would tease me because I was white and Chinese but I hung out with nothing but Puerto Rican or Spanish people. Pittsfield had a Latin dance group. I ended up doing that to do something besides working. One night after dancing, I heard my friend's brother and Liz arguing over their relationship. We all went to the arcade, and he kept bad-mouthing her, not treating her right, not showing her any kind of respect as a female, just none whatsoever. I went up to her while she was playing a video game. She was almost in tears, but she was holding them back, like 'I can't cry, I'm strong.' I rubbed her back and I told her, 'It's okay.' I said I'd bring her home if she wanted to be brought home. She said no and gave me a funny look. I went back and finished playing pool. When it came time to leave, my friend's brother told me, 'Leave her. Don't put her in your car.'

"I'm not like that," said Peter, shaking his head, "I'm not like that at all. I brought Liz home. While I was driving I just kept looking at her, thinking to myself, *Damn, she's a pretty girl!* How could she have a relationship like that? How could a guy not respect her? I believe women should be treated with utmost respect. That's how my grandmother and my mother raised me. When I dropped Liz off, I told her if she needed anybody to talk to, she could give me a call. With me growing up the way I did, I always try to be everybody's big brother. I told her, 'You can always have my shoulder to cry on. My ear is always there to listen to you.' That's how I met Liz."

Peter understood what Liz had gone through. His Asian American father had been raised in a foster home. While Peter was growing up, his parents worked "hell hours" to provide for their six kids. His father had put in eighty hours a week as a general manager at McDonald's, and his mother had worked nights as a security guard for fifteen years.

"My dad would probably work anywhere from eleven o'clock in the morning until midnight. My mother would work from three in the afternoon to seven o'clock the next morning. That was the kinda life that I lived growing up, taking care of my brothers and sisters. It really wasn't much different than being their parent, except I was their older brother."

"When I met Peter, he was a virgin," Liz recalled. "When he told me that, it shocked me. I never had a guy who hadn't been with anybody else. When it comes to a virgin-to-nonvirgin deal, it's usually the guy that's not the virgin and the girl who is. It felt weird to have the role reversed. I felt guilty because I wasn't a virgin, but then I didn't feel so bad because we talked about it and I told him everything about my past. I thought that if I was gonna be with a guy who gave his virginity up for me, it wasn't just a one-night stand—it obviously meant that we'd be together forever—or at least for a long period of time.

"That first night that Peter and I shared together—I think that's the night I got pregnant. We were at my foster home and we were supposed to be watching a movie Peter had rented. It was funny because we watched part of the movie and he kept talking about how he liked me and I kept talking about how I liked him. All of the emotions started happening, and it sort of went from there. I wanted the sex to be more natural, so I wasn't thinking about using condoms and I don't know if Peter was thinking about it, 'cause he didn't ask me and I didn't ask him, either. I didn't say, 'Wait a minute, shouldn't we think about this?' like everybody says you're supposed to. I didn't think before I did it."

Two and a half months later Liz was at a party and she had stomach cramps. She sat hunched over with her arms crossed over her chest. Her friend took a good look at her and shook her head. She told Liz she suspected she was pregnant. The two girls drove to a drugstore in a nearby strip mall. While Liz waited in the parking lot, her friend ran inside and stole a box of home-pregnancy tests. After two pregnancy tests came out positive, Liz went to Peter's job site and broke the news.

Peter was shocked. He stared at Liz, speechless. Becoming a father at such a young age was not part of his plan. He had been hoping not to have a child until he was at least twenty-five. He had wanted his career to be more in order before he started a family.

Peter's parents had divorced several years earlier, and with his father out of the picture, Peter had become the man of the house, responsible for looking after his five younger siblings and his mother. Fatherhood seemed like an impossibly difficult challenge to add to his already full load. All these thoughts swirled through his head as he looked at Liz standing there, gazing at him, awaiting his response.

"I decided to grow up then and there," Peter recalled. "I decided not to be like so many of the men out there these days. When the female tells them they're pregnant, they bounce! They get up and they leave or they tough it out in the beginning and then when they realize how hard it's going to be, they just take off. I decided not to be one of those men.

"Any person can make a child or conceive one," said Peter, "but when it comes down to the nitty-gritty, it takes a man to raise one. The only time I can consider myself a man is when my son is raised. When he's doing well for himself, then I know my job is done."

Liz enrolled in the Teen Parent Program but found it hard to keep up with her schoolwork. "When I was pregnant, I was sick a lot. I was sore a lot. You know . . . typical pregnancy things. It affected my attendance. To try to be in school all the time was hard. I wanted to get my diploma, but it didn't happen. I chose to go for my GED instead, because they don't go based on how many days you've been absent. They go based on how much you've learned."

Peter and Liz rented a walk-up apartment near the center of Pittsfield and started living together. Summer arrived and Liz gave birth to a son, whom she named Pete, after his father.

"Pete's birth gave me a sense of unconditional love," said Peter. "The responsibilities that were bestowed upon me were getting up in the middle of the night, changing his diapers, calming him down

when he was crying, waking his mother up to get ready to breast-feed him, or getting his bottles together. Being a father is basically another full-time job. My twenty-four-hour-a-day job."

Peter had to take little Pete to the emergency room on several occasions. Once Peter found the baby in the kitchen, gagging on Pine-Sol, which was all over his lips. Luckily Peter had stepped into the room moments before the baby could swallow the potentially fatal poison.

During his first summer the baby broke out with hives all over his body and was having trouble breathing. The doctors said it wasn't asthma and concluded that the respiratory difficulties were probably related to the hives. After a month of being sick, the baby recovered.

When Peter's mother and younger siblings were forced to leave the place where they had been living, Peter graciously allowed them to move in with him and Liz. This crowded situation was supposed to be temporary, but it went on for months. The downside was the total lack of privacy. The upside as Liz and Peter saw it was that while they worked long, late hours at Kentucky Fried Chicken and McDonald's, Peter's family members could fill in as built-in live-in baby-sitters.

For Liz, the problem with being employed at McDonald's and Kentucky Fried Chicken was that aside from having no benefits or health care, she had to work nights and there were no child-care facilities in the vicinity that were open late. In the absence of other affordable options, Liz and Peter were not at all concerned about leaving the task of caring for their infant son in the hands of Irene, Peter's eleven-year-old sister. They felt that Irene was more than up to the task of watching the baby on her own several nights a week. On the few nights that Peter's mother and his other siblings weren't working late at McDonald's, they helped baby-sit. Liz depended on their assistance because her days and her nights were long and grueling.

"I get up at nine-thirty," she said. "Then I work at KFC from ten o'clock in the morning until about four in the afternoon. Between four and six-thirty, I take a shower, clean the apartment, and try to get ready for my other job. I try to spend as much time as I can with my son. From seven o'clock on, I'm at my other job at McDonald's. The end of the night is basically cleaning wherever they need me to clean. By then I'm really tired and my legs are ready to give out 'cause I'm on my feet all day. I'm usually done by midnight. When I get home, I look at everyone sleeping and check to make sure everything's okay. I'm pretty dead by then. I just want to die in my bed. That's basically my day, every day except for Sundays and Wednesdays, when I'm off."

Peter was an assistant manager at Kentucky Fried Chicken, in training to be a general manager. He was Liz's boss, which at times added pressure and increased the friction in their already stressful relationship. With Liz working two jobs, Peter worked fewer hours, so it was he rather than she who spent the most time with the baby.

"My day starts whenever the baby wakes up," he said. "When Liz is at work, I feed the baby his lunch or give him his bath, or take a walk. By two o'clock I'm back in the house, showering and getting ready for my job."

Peter was making $500 per week while Liz was bringing home between $165 and $180 per week. Peter accounted for the disparity in their incomes by citing the fact that he had a higher rank at KFC; as an assistant manager he was on salary, whereas Liz was part of the regular crew staff and therefore got paid minimum wage. Peter usually worked from three in the afternoon until midnight, but more often than not his boss phoned him on weekends and on his days off, asking him to fill in for other people. Eager to ascend the ranks to general manager of KFC, Peter almost always said yes to his boss, which annoyed Liz, who wished he would say, "I'm sorry, I can't come in. Today's a day I have to spend with my family."

Like most adolescents, Liz experienced huge swings in her behavior, moods, and emotions. Sometimes she acted immaturely and lost her temper; other times she was wise beyond her years. When people who didn't know Liz looked at her, often they assumed that she was thirteen or fourteen. Sometimes she felt that young inside. Other times she felt much, much older.

"Certain days I'll feel like I'm ninety-five 'cause that's the way my body feels, and then other days I'll feel like I'm twelve because of the way my attitude is. I vary," explained Liz.

In hindsight, Liz wished that she had waited and had her baby when she was financially and emotionally more stable. Her dreams for the future revolved around money, love, and security. Someday Liz wanted to be able to buy a house and get married. In the immediate future, she hoped to save up enough money to buy a white oak bedroom set for her son so that his room could look more like those she had seen displayed in mail-order catalogs.

"My hopes are for us to financially get our act together, you know, where we're not just gonna be broke. I would like to go to college. I don't know what I want to study yet, but I wanna get a degree. I wanna get higher. I don't want to be at these six thirty-five or seven-dollar-per-hour jobs. I want to get a nine- or ten-dollar-per-hour job."

Peter's goal was to become a general manager of a chain restaurant or a hotel. He took his job at KFC seriously, took pride in his work, and saw each day as a step toward a higher position. His identity and sense of self-worth remained rooted in his dedication to work and his devotion to his family.

"I've got two separate lives," he explained. "I live KFC when I'm in the uniform. When I'm in regular clothes, I'm this little guy's dad and Liz's boyfriend. The thing that makes me the most happy is coming home to my family. I like waking up knowing I still have them with me."

"The thing that makes me happiest is being with Peter," said Liz. "Because of the way my past was, I didn't expect my life to be in

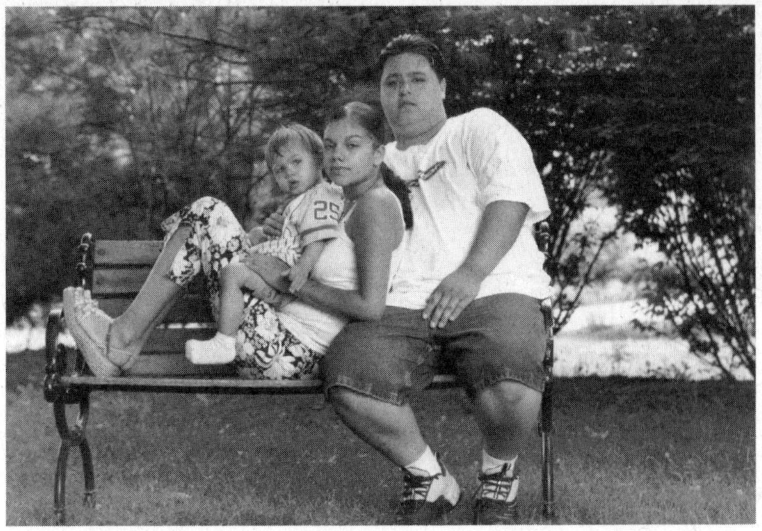

such good order. I'm so grateful for Peter and so grateful for my son. It makes me feel good inside to know that I have a family, to know that I have people to be around, to know that they're not just going to up and leave. . . . That trust is really there. That's a good feeling. I'm grateful for what I've done. Waking up in the morning and knowing that you've accomplished a lot more than what you expected yourself to accomplish is great."

chapter four

COLLEEN

"The other mothers at the Teen Parent Program would be telling me, 'Oh, my baby's doing this, my baby's doing that. . . .' Jonathan was older than they were and he wasn't doing anything at all with his right arm or leg. His right hand would always be clenched right up to his chest. He couldn't hold his own bottle. He never crawled. He used to just scoot across the floor and drag his feet the whole way. You know your child. I mean, you might not know exactly what they have, but you know when something is wrong. The guilt . . . You always feel it's your fault."

COLLEEN GREW UP IN A CATHOLIC HOUSEHOLD. SHE lived with her parents and her elder brother on a quiet tree-lined street in Dalton, a small suburban New England town bordering Pittsfield. Dalton serves as the headquarters for the Crane Paper Company. In addition to its renowned stationery, Crane manufactures the currency paper for the U.S Bureau of Engraving and Printing.

Colleen's father did not work at Crane. He worked alone from a home office adjacent to his dining room, designing machinery on his computer. He printed out his plans and then sent them off to factories. Colleen's mother, Maureen, was a medical assistant in a pediatric unit. Both of Colleen's parents were satisfied with their jobs, but behind the facade of their stable working-class existence, the family lived in turmoil.

"My childhood was hard," said Colleen. "My parents fought a lot because my dad had an alcohol problem and my mom has depression and she's fighting anorexia. Their fighting would just make me so sick. My father—he never wanted to listen to me about his alcoholism. I always felt I had to protect my mom. So, basically, I never really had a childhood. It was all taken away. I never wanted to go out or anything. I just wanted to stay home."

When Colleen was eleven, her grandmother died, leaving Maureen in a state of profound mourning. Her sadness escalated into a full-blown clinical depression.

"My mom being sick was just like this quiet moment in my house," said Colleen. "No one wanted to talk, no one wanted to do anything with each other. We all knew she was quiet. Her attempting suicide—that was really hard. Depression is just something that runs in my family."

More hardship was in store for this already overburdened family. When Colleen was thirteen, her cousin was killed in Florida, the victim of an accidental shooting at a fraternity. Colleen became silent and withdrawn. She could not make up for the loss of her cousin. She could not convince her mother to eat. Nor could she convince her father to stop drinking. Colleen felt powerless. She watched helplessly as her mother suffered in the clutches of deep, black mood swings and was hospitalized several times. Maureen had to be hooked up to IV needles that dripped nourishment into her emaciated body. Colleen plummeted into despair.

Whenever Colleen looked in the mirror, she was filled with self-loathing. She worried that she would never be smart enough, attractive enough, or thin enough to gain the acceptance and respect of others. She became reclusive and spent long hours alone in her bedroom, listening to music and mulling over the problems that were afflicting her family. None of Colleen's teachers reached out to inquire about her quiet, withdrawn, antisocial behavior. Ignored, Colleen retreated further into her shell.

Although she didn't say much at school, Colleen always listened closely to the other kids and kept tabs on what was going on around her. In the seventh grade, she overheard some girls bragging that sex was just the greatest thing they had ever done. Colleen decided that she wanted to find out for herself. She lost her virginity to a boy she befriended at school. Colleen had hoped that the experience would be amazing, magical, loving, and healing. Disappointed, she concluded, "Sex isn't everything it's cracked up to be."

A few months later, Colleen's relationship with her first boyfriend ended. Her next romantic relationship was a secret: at the age of fourteen, she fell in love with a girl from school. Colleen worried about her sexual identity and felt tremendous guilt. She hoped that her passionate interest in girls was just a phase that she'd grow out of.

Colleen started working a full shift after school at Burger King. Work was a welcome distraction from her dark ruminations. Her schedule maximized her time away from home, and when she was on duty, her mind was completely occupied with the task at hand. Meanwhile, at home, Colleen's family problems persisted. She worried that her father was drinking himself into oblivion while her mother was starving herself to death. Whenever her parents fought, Colleen repeatedly tried to intervene in defense of her mother. She continued using every tactic she could think of to get her dad to stop drinking, but all her efforts met with failure. Over and over again, Colleen kept reenacting the drama of confrontation, disappointment, and defeat. Her thwarted desire to play the role of the savior remained strong throughout her adolescence.

Ryan entered Colleen's life on a picturesque winter day. Snowflakes cascaded down from a sky cloaked in thick layers of fog. The streets wore a slick coat of ice. The sidewalks had not yet been shoveled. Colleen trudged through soft snowdrifts on her way home from her driver's ed. A car glided over to the curb. Colleen heard someone call out her name. She stopped and turned around. A girl she knew from school rolled down the window and said hello. Colleen walked over to the car and was introduced to Ryan, who sat in the backseat with some other guys. After sizing Colleen up, Ryan asked for her number. He said half jokingly that he wasn't going home without it.

A few hours later Colleen's phone rang. It was Ryan. The teenagers got to know each other over the course of several long phone calls. As they began spending more and more time together, Ryan opened up to Colleen about his traumatic upbringing.

Colleen recalled Ryan telling her that he had grown up believing that his stepfather was his real father. At the age of nine he found out that this wasn't true, when his mother admitted that she had lied about his paternity and bluntly told him that he would probably never get to meet his biological father. For years Ryan watched in helpless agony as his drug-addicted stepfather abused his mother. Ultimately, Ryan's stepfather was arrested for domestic violence and sent to jail.

Colleen was determined to save Ryan from his own demons. She believed that if she gave Ryan enough love, his childhood wounds would eventually heal. Colleen made excuses whenever Ryan treated her poorly. The harsh truth was that Ryan repeatedly acted in an abusive manner, reinforcing the worst of Colleen's familiar feelings of low self-esteem. In Ryan's presence, Colleen felt helpless, powerless, anxious, and worthless. The pattern of her emotions within the relationship re-created a template that was in many aspects a facsimile of her childhood experience.

The first time Ryan and Colleen had sex, they used a condom but then stopped after Ryan assured Colleen that he knew how to have unprotected sex without getting a girl pregnant. Disregarding the possibility of contracting HIV or other STDs, Colleen gave Ryan her blind trust.

One night Ryan assaulted his mother's boyfriend. This was not Ryan's first violent outburst and proved to be the final straw for his mother. She kicked Ryan out of the house. Colleen asked her mother if Ryan could move in with them temporarily, just until he found a new place to live. Initially, Maureen found Ryan charming. She understood how tempestuous family life could be and was happy to help out this young man who seemed to be one of her lonely daughter's few close friends. Colleen's parents agreed to let Ryan sleep in the den until he made peace with his mother. They offered him meals and did their best to make his stay as comfortable as possible.

Ryan made himself right at home and immediately began to take advantage of the family's hospitality. Late at night, when Colleen's parents were fast asleep upstairs, Ryan would sneak his friends in and party with them into the early hours of the morning. He tried to hide his drug problem from Colleen, who chose to keep quiet and look the other way. She didn't want her parents ever to find out.

Ryan's life revolved around heroin. He made a habit of pocketing cash he saw lying around and stole odds and ends every time he had a chance. As Ryan became more and more desperate for money, his trips to the local pawnshop became more frequent.

For a while, Colleen's parents were unaware of Ryan's nocturnal visitors and hadn't the faintest inkling about the illicit activities that were going on under their roof. Gradually Maureen began to notice that some of her things were out of place; others were mysteriously missing. When confronted, Colleen played dumb and pretended she had no idea what was going on. Unconvinced, Maureen began to monitor Ryan's behavior more closely. At first he had seemed like a nice guy. Now she wasn't so sure.

One evening on the way home from work, Maureen stopped at an ATM and got the cash she needed for her weekly errands. The next morning she woke up early and went grocery shopping. As the cashier rung up her purchases, Maureen reached into her wallet and was greeted with an unpleasant surprise: bare leather, no bills. All her money was gone.

Enraged, Maureen stormed out of the store without her purchases and drove straight to Burger King, where Colleen was working. In a loud, angry voice, Maureen told her daughter about the missing money. Colleen was speechless. A few of her nosy coworkers stared at her, wondering how she would respond. Colleen took a deep breath and told her mother that she had to get back to work.

Disgusted with her daughter and with Ryan, Maureen drove home. Ryan had expected Maureen to be at work, so her stormy entrance took him by surprise. He was caught red-handed in Colleen's bedroom, rummaging through her belongings. Maureen told him in no uncertain terms that he was no longer welcome in her house.

Ryan got defensive and denied Maureen's accusations, but she held fast to her convictions and ordered him to pack his bags. Ryan mumbled that he didn't have anything to pack his stuff in. Maureen handed him a garbage bag.

When Ryan left, he vowed to keep seeing Colleen, no matter what. Maureen subsequently forbade Colleen from seeing Ryan, but to no avail. The teenagers continued to meet regularly.

Colleen's obsession with Ryan intensified. She shut herself off from friends and family and walked around in a daze with a deadened, blank look in her eyes. Ryan was the only thing she focused on or cared about. Like a vacuum, he sucked up all her energy.

Shortly after Colleen's sixteenth birthday, Maureen came home from work to find her daughter lying prostrate on the dining-room table in a state of utter despair. In between wrenching sobs, Colleen told her mother that she didn't want to live anymore. She wanted to die. She said that the family problems were too much to bear and then stammered through tears that Ryan had been cheating on her.

What Colleen withheld from her mother was that when she confronted Ryan about his betrayal, he had responded with verbal and physical abuse, causing her fear, pain, and humiliation. It was not the first time Ryan had been violent and threatening toward her. Colleen was terrified. She was too embarrassed to confide in anyone. Her victimization was her own dark, shameful, secret.

Using a calm, soothing voice, Maureen tried to talk some sense into Colleen, who remained curled up in a fetal position on the dining-room table. Colleen couldn't stop crying. Over and over she repeated the words "I want to die!" Alarmed by Colleen's morbid thoughts, Maureen persuaded her daughter to sit up and gently helped her down from the table. She put Colleen in the car and drove her straight to the emergency room.

"I went into the hospital when I was sixteen," recalled Colleen, "because everything was all adding up: my mom's depression, I knew I was pregnant, and the fact that Ryan had cheated on me. So the nurse took my blood to find out if I was pregnant, and I was. I found out about an hour before my parents found out. We had a meeting with the doctor. My parents weren't too happy, because it was with Ryan's baby, and at that time they weren't really wanting me to have a baby with Ryan, because of other problems that were going on."

After an evaluation, Colleen was admitted to the hospital's psychiatric unit. According to the *Physicians Assistant's Guide,* roughly 26 percent of female suicide attempts presented to a hospital are preceded by abuse. Somehow the abuse element of Colleen's story did not emerge during the evaluation, a fact that would come back to haunt Colleen and her family further down the road.

Colleen's parents did not believe in abortion. In an effort to overcome their reservations about Colleen having Ryan's baby, they turned to God and attributed the pregnancy to His Divine Plan. As the months went by, Colleen and her parents became convinced that the fetus she was carrying was the long-awaited answer to their prayers, a growing, healing force of salvation that would endow their lives with joy, significance, a higher purpose, and the spirit of life.

"I'm Catholic and I just made my confirmation," said Colleen. "My religion set in when I got pregnant. I had the choice of adoption or abortion or keeping the baby. I went to church and they talked about abortion and how wrong it was. You know all the Bibles—they all say abortion is against our religion, so I respected that enough to keep Jonathan. I would just feel so guilty thinking, *Oh, you know, I killed a child.* People say it's just a seed, but it's really not. It's a human being that hasn't fully grown yet. I didn't want to worry about my religion and the jeopardy I was putting myself in. So abortion wasn't my choice.

"When I was younger, I had a lot of doubts about my religion," confessed Colleen. "Because of the way my life was going, I kind of didn't think there was a God. There were the problems with my parents, I wasn't smart enough, I wasn't pretty enough. God had certain people die in my family. Then finally when I was a few months pregnant, I felt Jonathan moving in me, and that made me realize that there was a God."

After being released from the psychiatric ward, Colleen transferred into the Teen Parent Program. She noticed a marked difference in Ryan's behavior toward her. He was not happy about the news that he was going to be a father.

"When he found out I was pregnant, everything went downhill," said Colleen. "Ryan's drug problem went out of control."

Over the next few months, Ryan was repeatedly arrested on various charges, including larceny and shoplifting. One day, while on probation, he got into a massive fight with Colleen. Maureen's eyes filled with tears as she recounted the incident.

"Colleen called me at work one day. She was crying hysterically. Ryan had assaulted her. I called the police and when I came home, there were three police cruisers outside. They were interviewing Colleen and her friend, who had witnessed the attack. Apparently,

Ryan had gotten angry and thrown a phone at Colleen. Then he had kicked her in the stomach, not once but several times. The police were very worried about Colleen. They were especially worried about the baby, since she was several months pregnant at the time."

Ryan fled. The cops put out a warrant for his arrest. Several squad cars were sent out to scour the neighborhood. Later in the day the cops found their suspect. They immediately snapped handcuffs around Ryan's wrists and hauled him off to jail.

Like so many abused women, Colleen was trapped in a web of fear and ambivalence. She decided not to press charges. The state of Massachusetts was less forgiving. Ryan was sentenced to a year in jail.

As Colleen's pregnancy advanced, her father weaned himself off alcohol. Over the past few years he had cut back significantly on his drinking. The forthcoming baby was his main incentive to stop completely. With Ryan behind bars, he knew that Colleen would need all the help she could get from both him and his wife. By the time the baby was born, Colleen's father was sober. Maureen had gained some weight. Colleen was no longer depressed and suicidal.

"Giving birth to Jonathan was the happiest moment of my life," she said. "I gave birth naturally, four and a half hours of labor. I loved him from the first moment I saw him. Jonathan is my world. I thank God every day for my son. He brought everyone in my family together. I feel like God sent him down here to make me happy."

Soon after Colleen brought Jonathan home from the hospital, she resumed her studies at the Teen Parent Program. When Colleen was in tutoring sessions, her tiny baby spent his day in a crib in the nursery, one floor below her classroom. During meals and recess Colleen visited her son and fed him. When Jonathan was done feeding, Colleen held him on her lap, fidgeting with him incessantly: tugging at his shirt, diapers, and socks; smoothing his hair down with the palm of her hand; shifting him from one side of her lap to the other. Colleen's hands were hardly ever still. In contrast to his mother, Jonathan was incredibly immobile. Most of the time he stared straight ahead with his right fist clenched tightly by his chest and his body slightly slumped over into the crook of his mother's arm.

At the end of each school day, Colleen drove home to her parents' house, where she peeled off her clothes and took a brief shower. After putting on her uncomfortable uniform and pulling her hair back

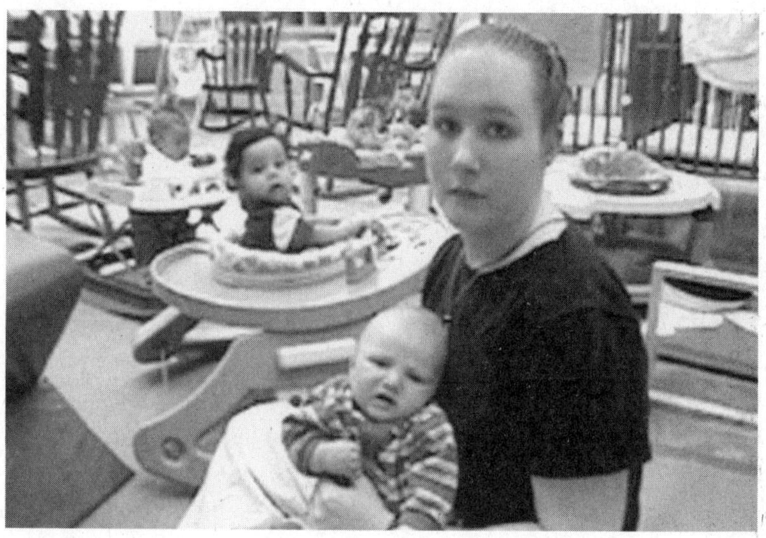

into a tight bun, she waved good-bye to her parents, planted a kiss on Jonathan's forehead, got back into her car, and drove ten minutes to Burger King. On her feet for six hours straight, Colleen stuffed bags for the drive-through, worked the register, and sorted through change as car after car came and went, the faces of the customers a complete blur, their voices amplified and distorted through the speakers as they shouted out their orders, one after another in what sometimes seemed like a never-ending, monotonous cycle.

"It's really hard going to school, going to work, and raising a baby," Colleen lamented. "I know that I'm only seventeen and people do look at me as, like, you know, a teenage mom, so they think we're all on welfare or whatever, but I'm not. I work every day. I only have Sundays off. I don't see Jonathan a lot, and when I'm at school, he's taken care of by the day care. I go to work at four and get off at nine, so it's really hard finding time for him."

Three days a week, Colleen took Jonathan to visit his father in jail. Jonathan's first sight of his father was through the strong glass barrier that separates prisoners from everyone else. Colleen described their weekly mother-father-son ritual:

"Visiting hours start at two o'clock. You have to go into a cagelike room to check in. Then you sit down at tables and he comes out and there's a counter between you. He can hold the baby for five minutes and then he has to give him back. And usually we're getting along, but just sometimes you argue about things, like him being in there. It just gets really hard to think that I'm sitting out here eleven months waiting for him. He loves Jonathan, I can see that, but I don't know if he'll change."

Colleen deluded herself with comforting fantasies of how great things would be when Ryan got out of jail, completely disassociating herself from memories of the physical and verbal abuse she had suffered before Ryan's incarceration. She remained optimistic that Ryan would get off drugs and turn over a new leaf. But even while incarcerated, Ryan managed to have drugs smuggled in to him.

"Jail was like a vacation for Ryan," said Colleen. "He still did drugs and he had free rent and free food to eat every night."

Undeterred by being locked up, Ryan worked hard to maintain psychological control over Colleen. He continued his pattern of abusive, manipulative, sadistic behavior, sending wonderful letters that never failed to raise Colleen's hopes, followed by cruel, obscene letters full of horrible threats and accusations. Often when Colleen showed up for visiting hours, Ryan showered her with insulting, degrading comments and accused her of cheating on him, using the crudest terms he could think of.

In the wake of these incidents, which left her in tears, Colleen became more and more enmeshed in the relationship, in part because, like so many daughters of alcoholics, she experienced love intertwined with erratic behavior, denial, disappointment, anger, and shame. Because her father had finally become sober after a lifelong struggle, Colleen believed that Ryan, too, could and would eventually conquer his drug addiction. She attributed Ryan's bad behavior to the influence of drugs and held on to her belief that apart from the drugs, Ryan was essentially good and loving.

Colleen went to elaborate lengths to convince herself that the cruel Ryan wasn't "the real" Ryan. To counteract her devastation and loneliness, she escaped into a world of fantasy. Here, Ryan loved her passionately and unequivocally and was the man of her dreams, not the incarcerated brute who had kicked her in the stomach when she was pregnant. In her dream world, Colleen was beautiful and beloved, not abused and disrespected.

As the months went by, Colleen fell deeper and deeper into an abyss of idealization and delusion. Gradually, fantasy and reality merged completely. In the same way that Ryan depended on heroin, Colleen fed off her fantasies of a fairy-tale romance and relied on them to transport her far away from an acutely painful reality.

While Ryan was in jail, Colleen began attending Carol Gilligan and Normi Noel's writing workshops at the Teen Parent Program. In these seminars, Colleen nourished her sugarcoated fantasies by writing dramatic, impassioned letters to Ryan, which she read aloud to her classmates.

> *Dear Ryan,*
>
> *I would like to thank you for our beautiful son. I see the sun every morning, but it never shines because we're not together. I always look forward to the days I see you. I'm mad that you have totally vanished out of my life, but the day that you return to me my sun will shine. I will feel safe again. We can be the family we should have been a long time ago. You are my best friend, my lover, and most of all, my baby's father. Thank you so much. I love you until the day I pass on to my next life. I could never imagine my life without you.*
>
> *Love always,*
> *Colleen*

When asked to explain why she was so convinced that Ryan would be a good father once he got out of jail, Colleen said, "Ryan knows how important it is for a child to have a father because of everything he went through not knowing his real father." She then paused for a moment, realizing that besides this one idea, she couldn't come up with any good reason or solid evidence that might even faintly suggest that Ryan would be an adequate—let alone "good"—father. At that point, Colleen confronted reality.

"If Ryan and I don't end up together, then fine," she concluded dejectedly, "but I don't want Jonathan not to have a good mom and a dad." Colleen took a deep breath. "One thing I regret is that maybe he won't."

When Colleen navigated the depths of her despair, she occasionally heard a thin voice rising up from deep within her, struggling to be heard.

"If I listened to the little girl in me, she would say not to take this crap from Ryan," Colleen confessed. "She would say that I should move on. She would say that I can leave Ryan. She would tell me that I won't be alone forever. She would say that one day I'll find someone else."

Despite all the conflicts and the strong, obvious negatives, Colleen's amorous investment in her troubled relationship with Ryan remained disturbingly unwavering. When Ryan got out on parole, she told her parents that she wanted to take the baby and move in with him. Colleen's parents were against the idea. They thought that Colleen and the baby should continue living at home.

Colleen argued that Ryan had reformed his old ways. She told her parents in no uncertain terms that they were not to interfere with her wish to raise her baby in the presence of his biological father. They had no choice but to let Colleen do as she pleased. The situation was beyond their control.

For Colleen, setting up a household with Ryan was a rite of passage. She put her pride on the line, determined to prove that she was a mature, self-sufficient, independent adult and a competent caretaker, capable of living in her own household with her boyfriend and baby.

"The day Ryan got out of jail, we got engaged," said Colleen. "Then two weeks after we moved in together, he started doing heroin again. It started off once a week and then became an everyday thing. Ryan on heroin was like . . . he'd be quiet at times—or he'd be so nice to me. He could be this wonderful person, but yet it was the drug that was making him that happy. When he was down from the drugs, it was just awful. He was mean, terrible. He would say, 'Get me money, do *whatever* you have to!'

"He'd get so mad at me if I didn't give him any money for the drugs. He'd say I didn't love him and call me names. . . . Horrible verbal abuse. When I would get mad and want to leave, it would turn into physical abuse. The physical abuse at our apartment was really bad. The cops were called on us. I never pressed charges 'cause I knew he'd just keep doing it anyway.

"Ryan would hit me on my body but not on my face, so when the police came, they couldn't see the bruises. I would be crying, but I had to pretend that nothing was going on, that we were fighting, just arguing. I think I was more scared of my life than anything."

Like many abusers, Ryan worked hard to make Colleen feel as though she deserved to be punished. Using manipulative mind games, he brainwashed Colleen and distorted reality to the point where she believed that she was provoking him to abuse her. Ryan persuaded Colleen that his violence was a justifiable reaction to her negligence and that he had every right to be enraged by her failures as a girlfriend and as a mother to their son.

Colleen internalized Ryan's accusations and felt stupid, inferior, and powerless in his presence. When questioned by the police, Colleen denied being abused because she was frightened that Ryan would be arrested. Colleen knew that ultimately Ryan would blame her and hold her responsible for his jail time. She worried that as soon as he got out, he would retaliate by beating her even more severely. She feared he might attack her family. As devastating as the abuse itself were the paralyzing terror and the blanket of silence that enshrouded her.

Colleen's parents had no idea what was going within the four walls of the young couple's apartment. Whenever they called to ask how she and Jonathan and Ryan were doing, Colleen always told them that everything was just fine. Meanwhile, Ryan hovered menacingly in the background, hanging on her every word. Colleen always had to have an excuse prepared in case her parents asked to see her and the baby. Perhaps Colleen's parents should have been more suspicious, given Ryan's history, but they themselves were no strangers to fighting, addiction, and its companion, denial. When Colleen insisted that everything was "fine," her mother and father chose to believe her.

Ryan kept the apartment stocked with a rotating supply of stolen

TVs, VCRs, and car stereos. When he was low on cash, he bartered these items for heroin. During the day, he stayed home with Jonathan while Colleen worked double shifts at Burger King in order to pay the rent. Every minute she was away, Colleen was gripped by the fear of coming home from work and finding her son dead or injured on account of Ryan's drug-induced negligence.

After several months filled with fighting and repeated episodes of domestic violence, Colleen's fear began to outweigh her tolerance. It took time for her to come to terms with the fact that her efforts to be autonomous had failed miserably. She was reluctant to relinquish her dreamlike hold on the idealized, romantic adult life she had aspired to. It was humiliating to acknowledge her feelings of worthlessness and dependence after having rebelled so strongly to win freedom and independence. That her parents had been right about Ryan all along was a bitter pill to swallow, but to her credit, concerned about her own survival and determined to get her baby out of harm's way, Colleen put her pride aside and asked her parents if she could move back home.

"Just because a teenager has had a child and is shouldering the responsibility, that doesn't mean that she's an adult," explained Maureen. "Teenagers don't have the mental capacity and the experience that adults have to make their decisions. They are new at it and they do need the support of their mothers, fathers, family, and friends. Colleen was very fortunate that she had all that. When she found out that she did indeed make a mistake, we were all here for her."

Colleen's parents were relieved to have their daughter and their grandson back under their roof but were worried about Colleen, who appeared to be severely traumatized by events she refused to discuss.

Maureen decided not to push her daughter. She realized that when Colleen was ready, she would talk about what was bothering her. Meanwhile, both parents did their best to make Colleen and Jonathan feel safe, comfortable, and loved.

Colleen's self-esteem was in shreds. Recovery was a painstakingly slow process. Gradually she established a threshold of trust and began to open up to her mother about the devastating abuse she had suffered. Maureen was shocked.

"While Colleen was living with Ryan, she never mentioned anything to her father or myself about the daily beatings that she was getting. After she moved back home with us, she finally told me everything that had happened. I asked her one question. I said, 'Colleen, why? Why did you take it from him?' She said, because she was afraid, afraid for herself, for me, for her father, and for the baby. She said that she thought the abuse was all her fault. For months after she moved back home, I had to keep reassuring her. I had to keep telling her, 'It's not your fault. It's not your fault.' "

Ryan's troubles with the police induced him to leave Pittsfield. After crossing the Massachusetts state line, he continued south, finally stopping in Florida. He never sent any child-support payments. Ryan occasionally called Colleen long-distance and harassed her. Maureen advised her to hang up on him the moment the conversation took an ugly turn. Colleen followed her mother's advice. Eventually, she stopped taking Ryan's calls.

With the help of her therapist, the support of her family, and her own hard work, Colleen was gradually able to understand her self-destructive pattern of embracing the dual roles of rescuer and caretaker. When Colleen looked back at the past, instead of blaming herself for not being good enough or loving enough, she began to hold Ryan responsible for all his actions. Colleen finally accepted that Ryan wasn't separate from the drugs; when the drugs were in his system, they were part of him.

"I guess I was just naive about Ryan," she said in retrospect. "I didn't realize that people were telling me the truth about his drug addiction and about how mean he is. I didn't want to believe it, because I saw a different side of him. I saw, like, two different sides: the really nice part of him and the really mean side. The mean side just didn't mix with me. That's why we're not together right now. And I don't see myself going back with him, either. Yeah, I did love him at one point, but the love that I did have for him is not in me anymore. I have no desire to even speak to him at this time because I have so much anger—that's about all I have for him.

"If a teenage girl were to ask me what she should do if her boyfriend has a drug problem, I would give her the following advice: He won't change. If drug addicts want to change, they have to change for themselves. They're not gonna change for you—they're not gonna change for your child. That fact is a pretty hard thing to accept. People told me all the time, 'You need to get out of this relationship.' I regret not listening to them sooner, but I had to learn for myself."

Relieved of the burden and stress of Ryan's dark presence in her life, Colleen blossomed with the passing of each month. She lost a great deal of extra weight she had wanted to shed for some time. Her acne all but disappeared. She stopped speaking in a flat monotone. Her eyes regained their luster. She found herself able to laugh again.

After graduating from the Teen Parent Program, Colleen left her job at Burger King and got a job making grinders at Angelina's sub shop. After a few months there, she quit and got a job at Wal-Mart as a supervisor and customer service manager.

"I take care of customers," she explained. "If they need a certain item or a price check, I help them out. I also supervise my cashiers. If they have a problem with a customer, I take care of them. I help them answer any questions that they have."

At Wal-Mart, Colleen made three hundred dollars per week. This was just enough money to cover her car payments as well as toys and supplies for Jonathan. Colleen was proud that she was doing everything within her power to make ends meet.

"I've never been on welfare or any kind of assistance," she said. "If I'm capable of working, then I'm gonna work. I'm not out to get free money. I have family to help me watch Jonathan."

In addition to her job at Wal-Mart, Colleen enrolled in several classes at Berkshire Community College. She was studying to be a respiratory therapist but soon became unhappy with her jam-packed schedule.

"My time with Jonathan was very limited," she explained. "I was going to school every day and working every day. I was only seeing my son for about an hour, and during that hour he was taking his nap. So I decided to put school off for a little while. It may be a bad decision, but it's the decision that I've made."

Colleen's decision was strongly influenced by her concern about her son, who appeared to be lagging alarmingly behind in his development.

"The other mothers at the Teen Parent Program would be telling me, 'Oh, my baby's doing this, my baby's doing that. . . .' Jonathan was older than they were, and he wasn't doing anything at all with his right arm or leg. His right hand would always be clenched right up to his chest. He couldn't hold his own bottle. He never crawled. He used to just scoot across the floor and drag his feet the whole way. You know your child. I mean, you might not know exactly what they have, but you know when something is wrong. You always feel it's your fault."

Although Colleen had a bad feeling that something was wrong, for months she was too afraid to take Jonathan to the doctor to see exactly what the problem was. Encouraged for nearly a year by staff members at the Teen Parent Program, Colleen finally mustered up the courage to overcome her terror and denial. She gave up her fantasy that Jonathan's symptoms would miraculously disappear and went to her local pediatrician, seeking a diagnosis.

"It took me three months to get a referral to a neurologist," said Colleen. "The doctor kept putting me off, which made me angry. Finally I walked into his office crying and told him that I wanted a referral. I got one, and that made me happy because I felt like I accomplished something. I overpowered a doctor by telling him that there was something wrong with my son. I just had this instinct about it."

A neurologist at Bay State Hospital in Springfield examined Jonathan and administered an MRI, after which he immediately diagnosed Jonathan with two serious medical disorders: cerebral palsy, caused by defects in the brain and spinal column, and polymicrogyria, a rare brain disorder.

When Colleen looked up *polymicrogyria* on the Internet, she found the following description of how it can affect those who suffer from it: "Most children with polymicrogyria, but not all, have some degree of global developmental disabilities or delays, seizures, feeding difficulties, respiratory problems, motor dysfunction and mental retardation. It is difficult to make a predictable prognosis for children with the diagnosis of PMG because each child is very unique in their presentation of this disorder."

Maureen cringed as she recalled the moment when the doctor

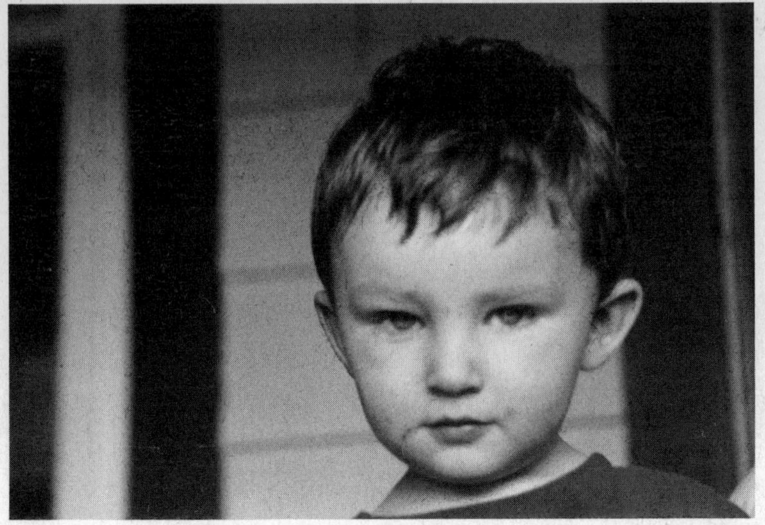

came out and said that her grandson was mentally retarded. "We use the word disability," she explained. "That's a much kinder word. It doesn't put such a label on a child."

Children with cerebral palsy have a hard time controlling movement and posture. The doctor told Colleen that Jonathan would need a leg brace in order to walk. The doctor warned Colleen that because the left side of Jonathan's brain was underdeveloped, there was a high chance that his cognitive and verbal abilities would be permanently and significantly impaired.

"I was wicked upset when Jonathan was diagnosed," recalled Colleen. "The guilt . . . When something's wrong with your child, you always feel it's your fault."

Many of the causes for cerebral palsy remain unknown, but known reasons include injuries during pregnancy or birth that cause prolonged oxygen deprivation, leading to a stroke in utero; an infection in the mother during pregnancy that spreads to the baby and the uterus; chromosomal abnormalities; and meningitis during infancy or childhood.

After looking at the results of Jonathan's MRI and a battery of other tests, the neurologist asked Colleen if she had experienced any severe trauma during her pregnancy, such as a fall, an illness, or an infection of any kind. Colleen answered with a firm no. Maureen challenged her daughter's claim and could not shake her gnawing suspicion that Jonathan's cerebral palsy was a direct result of the trauma that was inflicted when Ryan kicked Colleen in the stomach several months into her pregnancy.

Colleen was determined not to give up on her son just because he was disabled, so she restructured her entire life around his need for special attention and intensive medical care. As part of an early-intervention program, a pediatric worker began coming to Colleen's house once a week to do exercises with Jonathan. At first, Colleen had no idea how she could possibly afford these kinds of treatments. She was assured that doctors' bills, medication, physical therapy, and eventually leg braces would all be covered by Social Security and medical insurance, both of which offered special benefits for disabled children.

Colleen and her family rallied around the baby and showered him with affection and support. The adorable red-haired toddler loved all the attention. He frequently wore a huge smile on his face. He made eye contact with the adults around him and played with his huge pile of toys. He had no fear of strangers and gradually became bold enough to attempt to balance upright on his own. When Jonathan was about eighteen months old, much to everyone's surprise, he started taking tentative steps, holding on to railings, tables, and the arms of chairs for support. Then one afternoon, according to Maureen, Jonathan let go of the table and "just took off by himself and started to walk across the room. Every time that he would walk across the room, all of us would clap. My husband and I would clap. We'd say, 'You did a good job.' And Jonathan thought this was great. He realized that the more he did this, the more we would clap. To see this child walk, and to think that he was never gonna walk without a brace . . . It just filled us with so much happiness. It's almost like a miracle. We prayed and prayed that he would do this. He's still got a way to go yet. He's kinda behind on his speech, but we're working on that with pediatric development."

Colleen was delighted with Jonathan's progress but was careful not to elevate her hopes to unrealistic heights. "So far, my son walked without a brace and he's learning to do things with just one hand," she said, "but he is going to need a leg brace eventually. We'll be getting that for him soon."

From time to time, Colleen mourned the death of her dream of a strong, intelligent, healthy, athletic child. Occasionally her thoughts would be dominated by worries about how Jonathan's life would be affected by his multiple disabilities. Despite moments of bottomless pain and sorrow, Colleen and her parents refused to allow themselves to be paralyzed by anger, regret, and disappointment. Instead, they maintained the highest expectations for Jonathan. They focused on the best possible prognosis and tried not to think about the worst possible outcome.

Colleen kept her heart set on eventually being able to mainstream Jonathan into a school with children who were not disabled. She and her parents believed in Jonathan, and every day they encouraged him to defy the dire predictions of his doctors. They didn't treat him like a damaged child, nor did they protect him as if he were a piece of glass that they feared might shatter upon the slightest impact. Not wanting Jonathan to feel stigmatized or rejected by his own family, they interacted and played with him as if there were no limitations on his abilities. This approach proved to be very beneficial for the child. Rather than withdrawing and dislocating like some handicapped children do, Jonathan began to develop a playful sense of self-confidence.

Many handicapped children often appear more disabled than they really are because they internalize the pity and horror of people around them and ultimately evolve into receptacles for shock, grief, disgust, and disappointment. Like sponges, these children soak up the negativity around them, adding intense emotional handicaps, such as self-pity and self-hatred to existing organic handicaps. Colleen and her family were determined not to let that happen to Jonathan. They provided him with support, admiration, and positive reinforcement. When it came to caring for the little red-haired boy, there was never a shortage of love.

Colleen had started to keep a journal when Jonathan was diagnosed. She was very proud of her writing. Articulating her thoughts and feelings on paper gave them weight and durability. In her journal she wrote about her mother and her son, and she wrote about the new object of her affections, an artistic young woman. Colleen's love for this woman was deep. It inspired her to write several romantic poems. The two women found an apartment in Pittsfield and began living together and sharing the responsibility of raising Colleen's son.

Colleen found the courage to open up to her parents about her bisexuality. Although they were upset at first, both her mother and father ultimately accepted her choice of lifestyle and continued to love her and their grandson unconditionally.

In her journal, Colleen wrote:

In my dreams I never would have imagined my life this way. I would want nothing to be wrong with my son. Could it be that my dreams are not meant to be? Could I work harder at my dreams? Is it possible? Will anyone really know why this was brought upon us? Do I blame myself? In some ways, yes. I don't understand why life is the way it is. Why can't people accept what they are and accept what others are like? Will kids realize that Jonathan has a disability? Will they be able to look beyond that? I could sit here and blame myself, but I'm not going to anymore. Jonathan will be brought up strong enough to the point that no matter what someone may say or do to him, he will know that his life is important.

I am a young mother trying to be stronger for her son.

chapter five

SHAYLA & C.J.

"When I was sixteen years old, I really wanted to have a baby because all my friends had babies. I wanted a baby so I'd have a friend twenty-four hours a day, and because I thought they were really cute. I sort of planned it because I didn't take any birth control, so I knew it was going to happen."

SHAYLA GREW UP BELIEVING THAT SOMEDAY HER GOOD looks would be her ticket out of Pittsfield. She fantasized about being a model and practiced strutting down an imaginary catwalk like the tall, skinny girls she saw on TV. Shayla also dreamt about being a cheerleader for the Dallas Cowboys. She pictured herself wearing their official uniform: knee-high white cowboy boots, short white shorts, a navel-baring shirt knotted at the sternum, and a crystal-studded, star-spangled vest that sparkled in the sunlight.

On winter afternoons when temperatures hovered close to zero, Shayla could often be found curled up on the sofa, poring over the latest edition of the sizzling-hot Dallas Cowboys Cheerleaders swimsuit calendar. Impressed and intrigued, she flipped through photographs of scantily clad, nubile young cheerleaders frolicking on the sandy shores of some distant tropical paradise. With their perfect bodies, pearly teeth, and gigantic smiles, these cheerleaders were magnets for the adoration of millions. Shayla longed for a similar level of attention, approval, affirmation, and appreciation and wondered what it would feel like to perform in Texas Stadium in front of television cameras and thousands of fans.

By the age of sixteen, Shayla was pregnant, and instead of cheering for heroes at Texas Stadium, she was making them at the local Subway. That summer the heat was stifling, but the humidity didn't deter any of the hungry customers who crowded into the sandwich shop, forming a lunchtime line that snaked around in a semicircle. Behind the counter, Shayla pulled a steaming loaf of bread out of the oven, pausing to wipe the sweat off her brow before satisfying a customer's demand for bologna with extra cheese, lettuce, mayonnaise, mustard, pickles, salt and pepper. Her body ached from exhaustion. Her feet were swollen. She felt faint. She wondered if her friends were swimming down at the lake at that very moment.

Shayla had once thought that someday she would be able to invent a life as lavish as those she saw depicted on her TV screen, but as each month passed, the worlds of the characters she admired on *Sex and the City* seemed more and more distant and inaccessible. Wal-Mart didn't carry anything even closely resembling the Jimmy Choo shoes on Carrie Bradshaw's feet, and Pittsfield had no equivalent of Bungalow 8, the hot spot Carrie frequented with her friends. The food court at the local mall just didn't compare, and though Shayla could place her hand flat against the television screen, there was always that unsurpassable glass barrier.

Mired in a state of frustration and despair, Shayla redirected the mental energy she had once devoted to her own goals toward her relationship with her nineteen-year-old boyfriend, C.J. From the outset, Shayla's relationship with C.J. had been laced with tension. She attributed some of the stress and fighting to the fact that they both lacked parental role models and therefore had no positive examples to emulate. Perpetuating the familiar was automatic. Shayla noticed herself repeating patterns of behavior she had witnessed growing up as the daughter of teen parents.

When Shayla was born, her mother, Kelly, was fifteen and her father, Alan, was seventeen. Kelly and Alan went through numerous separations and subsequent reconciliations. They never married. Kelly got a job working with the elderly in a home care program, and Alan worked in a home for delinquent boys and took classes at the community college.

Shayla suffered at the center of her parents' explosive relationship. Some nights she cowered in her room, her hands pressed hard against her ears, muffling the sounds of screaming and yelling and "stuff being broken." When things got really rough, Shayla was shuttled off to the home of her maternal grandparents.

Shayla's grandmother worked in the produce department at Stop & Shop, and her grandfather had retired from GE. Now working as a carpenter, he made extra money building furniture for people in the neighborhood. Their home was a haven compared with the chaos Shayla faced living with her parents.

When Shayla was six, her little sister, Ashley, was born. Soon afterward, Alan was arrested on drug-related charges and sentenced to two years in prison. While incarcerated, he completed a special-educational program that helped him qualify for a scholarship at a state college. The fact that his college tuition was completely funded shocked and upset Kelly, who had to struggle to raise their two daughters while getting a GED and working three jobs without any help from the state. Kelly found it unjust that the father of her two children got more opportunities as a result of going to prison than she got as a young mother forced to juggle all her responsibilities.

Neither Kelly nor the girls visited Alan in prison. When he was released, he was a stranger. "He was a different man when he came home," said Kelly, "harder to deal with and harder to understand." Alan had converted to Islam in prison. He went out of his way to impose his newly adopted religion on his family. Behind bars, his beliefs, rules, and rituals had been enthusiastically shared by a host of other inmates. At home, his entreaties were met with steadfast resistance.

Alan cracked down on the girls. He insisted on keeping Shayla cooped up in the house even on sunny days when most kids in the neighborhood were outside playing. Alan made sure that his daughter understood that her education was his number one priority. When Shayla finished her homework early, he assigned her extra reading. Boys were completely off-limits.

Alan was adamant about disciplining his daughters. Shayla feared the belt whenever she disobeyed him. Anticipating punishment, Shayla's judgment was often clouded by feelings of panic, dread, and gnawing anxiety. She had trouble making decisions, especially under pressure, and grew up questioning her ability to do the right thing. Too often her fear of failure prevented her from taking on new challenges.

Soon after entering middle school, Shayla began cheerleading for the football, soccer, and basketball teams. She adored the dance, the music, and the acrobatics. With her long brown legs kicking higher than those of the girls beside her, Shayla effortlessly exuded the grace and agility that came naturally to her. After her fifteenth birthday, Shayla's dedication to cheerleading wavered. Science, once her favorite subject, suddenly lost its allure. She began to devote most of her attention to her appearance, and to boys.

These pronounced shifts in Shayla's priorities coincided with her parents' decision to permanently end their relationship. Shayla's father moved away to another town to attend college and medical school. Shayla and her little sister stayed behind with their mother in Pittsfield.

"Before her dad left home to go to UMass, Shayla had been an A student and a cheerleader," recalled Kelly. "She wanted to go to college. But after her dad left the home, I could see her start to change. When her father stopped coming back and forth to pick the kids up for weekends and started breaking promises, I could see Shayla start going after all the wrong things. She started dating. She was very secretive and for a while she was seeing lots of different guys. Her first year of high school, she met C.J. He was her idea of a 'bad boy,' I guess: tattooed, a rock-and-roller type, really rough around the edges. Shayla's father was always telling her, 'Don't you ever date any white boys!' Knowing how her dad felt about her dating white guys, I think Shayla's relationship with C.J. was her way of striking out at him.

"I think Shayla's anger wasn't so much because of what her father had said to her—it was the abandonment. Her father broke so many promises. He used to call her and say, 'I'm gonna pick you up, be ready! We'll go out to dinner, we'll do this, we'll do that. . . .' Then he'd be a no-show. Shayla would put herself out there time and time again, and her father just kept on disappointing her. It got to a point, I think, when she just really wanted to get back at him."

As Shayla got closer to C.J., he gradually opened up to her about his difficult childhood. When angry and upset, C.J. sometimes resorted to violent outbursts as a means of self-expression. On one occasion, his mother called the police and asked to have her son forcibly removed from the family home. She claimed that he was a disruptive presence. Outside the home, C.J. exhibited threatening behavior toward his ex-girlfriend and her new boyfriend, prompting police to serve him with a trespass notice for violating a restraining order the ex-girlfriend had obtained against him.

Shayla was fully aware of C.J.'s short temper, lack of self-control, depression, drinking problem, and violent streak. Whereas some young women might have been deterred from pursuing a romance, Shayla dismissed such behavior, convinced that it was part of C.J.'s past, not part of the future she was going to build with him. The two teenagers bonded over the inner darkness they sometimes felt. During late-night conversations, they shared their dreams, fears, and insecurities. After several months of dating, their relationship became more intimate.

"C.J. was the first person I had sex with," said Shayla. "We were together for a couple of months before I had sex with him. It was really embarrassing. It was like little-kid sex. It was bad. I mean, it wasn't bad . . . it was different. It was kinda weird. We weren't open with our bodies. It was a pretty middle-school type of thing. We didn't plan it. It just happened."

Kelly expressed her disapproval of the relationship. Shayla found her mother intrusive and chose to ignore her. In Shayla's mind, certain topics were completely off limits to her mother. Sex was one of them. Shayla was determined to guard her idealized vision of her relationship with C.J., even if that meant hiding troubling aspects of their turbulent romance.

C.J. tended to be possessive and controlling. He was verbally abusive, especially when he drank. He soon learned that in Shayla, he had met his match. She quickly proved herself more than capable of dishing out her share of insults and profanity. But beneath her tough exterior, Shayla's self-esteem was achingly low. She craved love more than anything and was willing to go to great lengths to transform C.J.'s abusive behavior into something that felt more like affection. Terrible clashes were followed by passionate reconciliations. After one altercation, the two teenagers got their tongues pierced.

They began sporting matching tongue studs as a sign of their commitment to each other.

C.J. dropped out of high school and began working at a small flooring company run by his mother. He went from client to client, installing tiles, carpets, and linoleum floors. His goal was to save up enough money to realize one of his biggest dreams: owning a tattoo parlor. C.J.'s other big dream was to become a father—the father he had never had—and Shayla was eager to become a mother. Together, the two teenagers made a conscious decision to become teen parents. Shayla began trying to conceive.

"I felt that if I had a baby, it would change things," she said. "I thought it would make my life a lot better, not only in my relationship with C.J. but with my friends. I thought it would bring my popularity up because people would be like 'Hey, she's got a baby, and that's cool.' "

For Shayla, gaining the admiration of her friends was paramount. Her peer group exerted enormous influence and set standards for acceptance at a time when she, like many adolescents, was at her most vulnerable, insecure, and malleable. Because Shayla feared rejection and was desperate to belong, she tended to go with the flow and was easily influenced by others. When the first few girls in her class started to have babies, they enjoyed their fifteen minutes of fame. Shayla wanted hers, too.

The skewed values of Shayla and her peers reflected the widespread lack of role models, support, guidance, and resources either at home or in school and the community at large. Shayla had neither a solid sense of herself nor a robust vision of her future. She felt what she described as "a void" deepening within her. Rather than looking ahead to a future filled with choices, transitions, and different opportunities, she looked around and saw a lot of poor, unhappy, frustrated people, struggling and stagnating, so she adjusted her expectations, lowering the bar to avoid disappointment and the all-too-real possibility of failure.

"I love to learn," she said. "I always wanted to go to college but I never sat down and said, 'I want to try to get good grades because I need good grades to get into a nice college.' I don't like to make long-term plans, because they always seem to get broken. They always do."

In the absence of clearly defined goals, Shayla began to rely exclusively on her peers for a sense of direction. She copied their behavior and adjusted her standards to match theirs. Buddies since kindergarten, Shayla and her best friend, Sheri, had sleepovers, partied together, got into trouble together, and stayed out late together, drinking and missing curfew. The two girls seemed to be on parallel roads, egging each other on, sharing experiences, breaking rules, and commiserating when their boyfriends cheated on them. One afternoon Sheri called Shayla and announced that she was pregnant. Shayla could hear the mixture of fear and elation in her friend's voice. Sheri now had something definitive and real to look forward to, something that would be completely hers. It wasn't long before all that was standing between Shayla and teen motherhood was nine months.

Too frightened to tell her mother that she was pregnant, Shayla sought help from her grandparents. Initially, she didn't confide in them and just said that she couldn't bear living at home anymore because she and her mother were always fighting.

Shayla's grandparents were concerned about her. They welcomed her into the sanctuary of their immaculate home. In their custody, Shayla felt safe with her secret. Life with her grandparents was calm and predictable. Her grandmother hosted barbecues every Sunday and invited all her relatives. Her grandfather devoted a good portion of his spare time to keeping his spacious backyard in tip-top shape. Intent on making the half acre of grassy space a fun environment for his grandchildren, he hung a tire from a thick rope and tied the rope to the strongest branch of a giant elm tree. When Shayla's little sister came to visit, she loved spinning around and around on the tire, tilting her head back to catch glimpses of greens, blues, browns, and yellows blurring together into a kaleidoscope of brilliant color.

As Shayla sat on the back deck, watching her little sister carousing in the yard, her own childhood seemed far away. As she looked at her sister's skinny body and flat chest, she touched her own rounding stomach that no one apart from C.J. knew about.

"My reactions to Shayla telling me she was pregnant were very good," C.J. recalled. "I was happy, smiling, you know, my life started all over again. I didn't have a father. I didn't have a very good childhood. I wanted to have a child so I could give him a good childhood and teach him to be a better man than I could be, 'cause I didn't have a father to teach me. I was raised by my mother, and by my brother's father. And it's just . . . there was always an emptiness."

Shayla described similar feelings of worthlessness. At a very young age, partially as a result of frequently being punished by her father, Shayla had started to believe that she was a "bad" person. She blamed herself for every mistake she made and often felt that she couldn't do anything right. With a fractured sense of logic, she believed that somehow having a baby would resolve all her problems and erase her self-doubt because at least in the baby's eyes she would be a "good" person. She craved the intense unconditional love that only a speechless, dependent infant was capable of giving.

Shayla's pregnancy was the perfect antidote to her fear of abandonment. She wanted to believe that C.J. would never leave her the way her father had, but if he did, having his baby ensured that she would hold on to at least a part of him. By making a conscious decision to get pregnant at age sixteen, Shayla actively turned the tables on her father, so that instead of her being disappointed in him, he was disappointed in her. She succeeded in creating a situation that allowed her to take an active rather than a passive role in the dissolution of the father-daughter relationship.

"My dad warned me my whole life not to get pregnant because it was so hard," she explained, "but I'm the type of person that does whatever I want to do because I have to learn on my own. So when I got pregnant, he didn't accept me at all. He totally disowned me, and to this day he doesn't want anything to do with me. He thinks I don't deserve to have a father, because I didn't listen to him. He was supposed to be there to protect me, and I went ahead and did it anyway, so it's my own fault."

So, instead of being overwhelmed with boundless sadness, Shayla could accept blame, take responsibility, and point to a concrete explanation of why her father was no longer in her life. This justification lent Shayla an illusion of power over her father's abandonment. It was easier for her to bear the thought that her father had disappeared from her life because she had disobeyed him by getting pregnant than to think that he just simply didn't give a damn.

A small part of Shayla had dared hope that her pregnancy, an act of blatant defiance, would attract her father's attention and reawaken his capacity to give unconditional love—if not to her, then to her baby. This hope was dashed the moment Shayla called him to share the news.

"Her father basically told her, 'You no longer exist,' " Kelly recalled. "He just dismissed her. He hung up on her, and she's never talked to him since."

"My mother couldn't handle the news, either," said Shayla. "She was bawling. It was hard for her to take. She talked to my grandfather and my grandmother. They said, 'Kelly, we went through this same thing with you. We're not gonna turn our backs on Shayla. You just need to understand that she's gonna have a baby.' It was really hard for my mom to understand. She wanted me to have an abortion."

Shayla's fantasy of having a baby had been wonderful, but almost immediately after getting pregnant, she became ambivalent about the grave reality of her predicament. Overwhelmed by the extremely negative reactions of her parents, she began to reconsider her decision to become a teen mother. After a few weeks of deliberation and heartache, Shayla made a doctor's appointment to find out about the option of having an abortion, allegedly in an effort to appease her mother. She got to the hospital and was examined by a doctor. C.J. followed Shayla to the hospital, and while she was having her ultrasound to see how far advanced her pregnancy was, he came in and said, "No! You're not getting an abortion!"

Shayla decided not to terminate the pregnancy. She didn't feel comfortable going against C.J.'s wishes, and when it came down to making the decision, she realized that, like C.J., she wanted the baby, despite her mother's incessant warnings about how hard it would be to raise the child. Incredibly conflicted over her decision and debilitated from repeatedly arguing with C.J., Shayla enrolled in the Teen Parent Program. She was frequently absent because of stress, exhaustion, illness, and crippling depression. Her grades suffered.

Members of the staff were fully aware of the difficulties Shayla was facing. They made a concerted effort to prevent her from dropping out of school. If Shayla was late in the morning, Helen, the wonderful and dedicated headmistress, would get in her car, drive to Shayla's house, drag her out of bed if necessary, and make sure that she made it to her tutoring sessions. B.J., the social worker in residence, drove Shayla and the other pregnant teenagers to their doctors' appointments, wanting to be sure that they didn't miss out on prenatal care. Even in her incapacitated state, Shayla could see that the staff at the Teen Parent Program really cared about her. These unfalteringly committed individuals gave Shayla the strength and support she needed to continue with her studies.

During the first few months of her pregnancy, Shayla had dropped out of gym class at Pittsfield High School, citing medical problems as her excuse. As a substitute assignment, her gym teacher asked her to write an essay on the subject of women in sports. Shayla never finished the essay because a few days before it was due, she was rushed to the hospital.

"Shayla went into false labor six times," recalled Kelly. "Her son was underdeveloped. She almost lost him several times during the pregnancy. I think it was due to all the stress and all the arguing with C.J."

Shayla winced as she recounted the excruciating agony she endured her last trimester. "When I was about five months pregnant, I found out I had kidney stones. I was in the hospital two or three times a week because the kidney stones would bring on preterm labor. So from the time I was five months pregnant to the time I delivered my son, I was in the hospital in unbearable pain, on medication and IVs to keep the fluids in me. I couldn't really eat or drink anything, because everything I was eating was coming back up. The doctors said the complications were caused by a calcium buildup from my prenatal vitamins, which happened because I wasn't really a milk drinker and I didn't really have a lot of dairy products, so my body wasn't used to processing the calcium. They told me to start putting calcium in my regular diet."

Having completed all her required academic work, Shayla was eagerly looking forward to graduating with her class at Pittsfield High School. During the many long hours she spent in the hospital, the thought of this exciting day was like a light at the end of a long, dark tunnel. Sadly, however, she was denied her diploma because her gym teacher flunked her for failing to turn in her "Women in Sports" paper, leaving her one credit short. He refused to accept the complications with Shayla's pregnancy as a medical excuse, citing her for "not completing the assignment" and for "having a bad attitude."

Both Shayla and her mother pleaded with the principal for leniency, but to no avail. Brutally disappointed, Shayla deeply resented that her diploma had been denied her on the basis of such a small technicality. She was furious about having to enroll in yet another semester of the Teen Parent Program, where she had to take more classes in preparation for her GED. Shayla made a promise to herself: First she would get her GED as soon as possible. Then she would enroll in a course at cosmetology school. If she couldn't be a model, at least maybe she could be a model's hairdresser. She hoped that once she got licensed, she'd be able to do hair for the fashion shows they had several times a year down at the Berkshire Mall. But before she could even think about doing any of that, she had a baby to deliver.

Shayla gave birth to a son, whom she named Jaiden. This baby was living proof of her power to conjure up a human being who, by nature of his infantile dependence, would be "a friend twenty-four hours a day." Back when she had first gotten pregnant, Shayla had only thought about how great it would be to have a baby. She hadn't given any thought to the painful, draining birthing process and its aftermath and was shocked to discover the rigorous aspects of this experience, which the women she knew had kept to themselves.

"After you have your baby, there's so much trauma that goes on in your body," Shayla explained. "You really don't want to be touched. When your milk comes in, your breasts start leaking. They're, like, rock hard. It's really uncomfortable. You don't want nobody to touch you. For a while, sex wasn't really an option."

C.J. had thought that the baby's birth would transform him into the ideal father he had always dreamed of but had never known. In theory, C.J. "wanted" to be a good father, but in practice he left Shayla with the bulk of parental duties. C.J. had expected that fatherhood would make him feel stronger, more confident, and more capable. Instead, when it came to caring for his son, he felt terribly inadequate whenever he failed to live up to Shayla's and his own expectations.

"In terms of responsibility for the baby, I'd have to say that

Shayla takes care of him most of the time," admitted C.J. "Because I'm either working all week or . . ." His voice trailed off as he fumbled for an excuse. "Or . . . I'm usually doing something."

Listening to C.J., Shayla rolled her eyes, knowing all too well that his all-important "something" was usually partying, lifting weights, or playing video games with his friends.

Shayla made it clear that she wanted C.J. to take on a more equal share of child-care responsibilities, both financially and in terms of parenting. C.J. found this arrangement unacceptable. He had no qualms about asserting his extremely rigid, old-fashioned views of gender roles. He told Shayla that a woman's place was in the home, cooking, cleaning, doing laundry, and taking care of the children, while her man was out working and spending time with his friends. To drive his point home, C.J. added, "That's what women are supposed to do and that's what the man does, and if you don't like it, that's tough."

Furious and frustrated, Shayla resorted to relentlessly nagging C.J. to do things like changing the baby's diapers. When that tactic got her nowhere, she started yelling at the top of her lungs. When pestered, C.J. would retaliate with vicious rounds of verbal abuse that left Shayla feeling withered, crushed, despondent, disgusted, underappreciated, and even more enraged.

After a few miserable months of living with Shayla and the baby, C.J. moved out. He got a couple of his buddies together and rented an apartment. One of C.J.'s best friends was an obese youth nicknamed Pills, after the Pillsbury Doughboy. This young man was a self-cutter who mutilated his own skin on a regular basis, leaving scars and open sores. C.J.'s other friend had enormous tattoos all over his back and arms. These guys all partied hard and kept late hours. Their apartment was a filthy maze of beer cans and dirty laundry. C.J. made no secret of the problems he was having with his baby's mother.

"If it were up to Shayla, our son would be dead," said C.J. "He'd be dead, he wouldn't be here right now." C.J. paused and looked over at his buddies, who sat beside him on the couch, nodding in silent acquiescence. C.J. took a moment to reflect. "You know," he said, "not to be bad or nothin', but maybe I should have just let her do it. If it was gonna be all this hard to be a freakin' parent, then I should have."

Shayla was uncomfortable around C.J.'s friends. She did not feel safe leaving her son alone with his father in this unpredictable environment. C.J. resented Shayla for not trusting him. They had hideous fights about how to parent Jaiden. When Jaiden cried, Shayla would always want to pick him up. C.J. argued that if Shayla picked Jaiden up every time he cried, he'd never become independent. The last thing C.J. wanted was a son who was a spoiled, sissy crybaby and a mama's boy. Loud altercations repeatedly escalated into fights, ending with Shayla storming out, taking the baby with her.

Seeing C.J. living in a pigsty, spending his time playing video games with his dazed and hungover friends, did not exactly inspire Shayla's confidence in his ability to be a responsible caretaker. She did not want her son exposed to that seedy environment. Fed up with listening to C.J. hurl insults at her, she stopped taking Jaiden to visit his father. C.J. was livid.

"Everybody thinks I'm such a bad father because I never see Jaiden," he raged. "I never see him because Shayla never brings him over here! If I could take him and raise him all by myself, I'd do it in a heartbeat. I'd take him for weeks—I'd take him for weekends. . . . I could do it all by myself. I know I could."

C.J.'s frustration was very real, as was his genuine desire to be a good father. Although he may have had the best intentions, they bore no relationship to the practical reality of his immediate environment and lifestyle. C.J. rarely went out of his way to visit the baby at Shayla's mother's or her grandmother's house, both of which were nearby. He accused Shayla of restricting access to their son. As Jaiden's father, C.J. felt he was entitled to authority and respect. He was resentful of the control Shayla had over their son. His anger grew as he felt more and more trapped in this unsatisfactory relationship.

"If I break up with Shayla, then she's gonna use the kid to get back at me," he lamented. "She's gonna say, 'No. You can't see him.' Or she's gonna say, 'You can see him, but only when your mother's around for supervision.' If I needed supervision, I wouldn't have had him! If I didn't have a baby with Shayla, I wouldn't be with her right now. I really wouldn't. There ain't no point in us being together if we can't get along."

As the baby got older, Shayla and C.J. tried living together again. The problems between them intensified.

"C.J. definitely has a problem with alcohol," Shayla explained. "When he starts drinking and he's around his friends, he's fine. But when he starts drinking and he's around me, he just flies off the handle. He doesn't know how to control himself."

After several brushes with the police, C.J. was put on probation for offenses that included drunk driving. A few days after Christmas, C.J.'s explosive behavior got him in trouble with the law again. This time it was on a charge of domestic assault and battery.

"Me and C.J. got into a huge fight," said Shayla. "I asked him to do something, and he criticized the way that I raise Jaiden. I went over to him and I decked him; I punched him right in his face. He grabbed me and was shaking me, calling me all types of names, telling me, 'I can't believe you just did that!' He said, 'I'm done with you! I'm leaving! We're not going to be together no more!'

"Every time he said that, I took it to heart," said Shayla, "so I started beating him up and he started shaking me around. The cops came. I was sitting there, crying, saying, 'C.J. hit me in my ear—I can't hear!' I was making myself be the abused one that night. I just wanted attention.

"I was going through a bad time and I wanted everybody to hate him, so I said a lot of things that weren't true. I just said a whole lot of things and never really understood what the outcome would be. And, yeah, he shouldn't have even been putting his hands on me, but people don't understand. I mean, I went over there and I decked him right in his face. If anybody had any marks, it was him. He had scratches all down his neck and his chest."

Shayla's contradictory account of events encompassed accusations, denials, self-recrimination, repression, and confession. She portrayed herself in a derogatory light and made it sound as if she had instigated and manipulated the entire incident. By sharing responsibility for the violence, Shayla was able to protect her love for C.J. and her positive feelings toward him, which the reality of being abused by him would have undermined.

In the picture Shayla painted of that night, the truth remained slippery. In her mind, the roles of victim and aggressor swung back and forth like a pendulum. Shayla had trouble distinguishing one from the other. She blamed herself and she blamed C.J. Her distorted, jumbled thinking served an important purpose: it offered a solid defense against the inherent disappointment and devastation of fully acknowledging that the man she loved and had a child with was damaging and hurtful toward her, compromising her equilibrium and the well-being of their child. When the police arrived on the scene, they evaluated the situation and made an immediate judgment call: they took C.J. to jail, where he was booked and fingerprinted. Shayla was taken to the hospital.

After depositing C.J. in the local jail, the policeman who made the arrest went to Berkshire Medical Center to see how Shayla was doing. He spoke with her and her grandmother. Shayla agreed to file a report. She took out a restraining order against C.J. and was given a domestic-abuse card.

"I told my family that C.J. kicked me in the ear, but the thing was, we were wrestling and I hit my ear. I thought he hit me. . . . I don't know. . . . I know he didn't come out and punch me," said Shayla, still trying to protect C.J. and her lingering romantic feelings for him. "I can't really remember what happened that night," Shayla said, her eyes going completely blank. "I block that stuff out. I don't know. . . . I can't explain."

"I don't know" and "I can't explain" were much more efficient shields than "I know" and "I can explain." In order to justify her love and her overriding self-destructive desire to reunite with C.J., Shayla needed to see reality through her own distorted lens. She wanted to live in complete denial about the abusive nature of her relationship with C.J.

Shayla longed for C.J. to live up to her idealized image of him as her lover and her baby's father. She preferred to focus exclusively on the parts of C.J. she loved, and to pretend that the negatives didn't exist. Shayla attempted to warp reality just enough to bend C.J. into a shape that would fit into her cookie-cutter dream of a stable, intact family. Maintaining the fantasy of a happy future together became more difficult in the aftermath of C.J.'s arrest.

"Because of that night we fought, my family believes that C.J. hit me," said Shayla. "They don't want nothing to do with me and him together, which makes things a lot harder for me now because we want to work things out. We're trying to be a family now. I can't share that with my family, because they have such a strong hate toward C.J. because of all the pain that he put me through.

"All the times that I cried when I was pregnant—I was all upset and having to go to the hospital because of stress. . . . My family witnessed that. They seen how many times I cried and how angry I got when C.J. did things to me. C.J. really took a toll on me, and my family noticed that. They noticed that a lot. They put a temporary restraining order on the house. His mom bailed him out of jail, and he started living with her."

A few months later, the police were called to the residence of Shayla's grandmother, who at the time was baby-sitting for Jaiden. C.J. had tried to kick in her front door, with the intention of taking the baby. By the time the police got to the house, C.J. had fled. The police searched for him all over Pittsfield; when they finally found him, they served him with a trespass notice.

"Even though Shayla didn't want to press charges, the state did," Kelly recalled. "They took over the case and C.J. ended up leaving the state of Massachusetts to get away from the police and the court."

Fearing prosecution, C.J. took what little money he had, packed his bags, and drove out of town. He had been threatening to leave for a while. Shayla had never believed that he would actually go through with it.

"When I first left Pittsfield, I was on my way to California to be an actor," C.J. explained. "I wanted to try something new, but I stopped in Arizona to see my brother and I ended up just staying there. I got my GED and I'm going to school to be an accountant, then hopefully I'm going to go to a four-year college. I'm doing everything just for my son. That's the whole reason I came out West: to make myself a better father for Jaiden. Before I left, things were real bad between me and Shayla. Everything was always her way or the highway. So I finally packed up and hit the road. Shayla needed a reality check, and I needed to get out of Pittsfield.

"Lately things have been okay over the phone, but it's long-distance. Shayla says she's changed, but I'll see. I just want her to grow up. We had an immature boyfriend-girlfriend relationship. I want trust. I don't want to fight about every little thing. All she used to say was 'You can't do this, you can't do that,' like I was her kid or something. I hope maybe now she's starting to realize that we don't own each other, we just love each other.

"In Pittsfield, I was just doing the same thing every day, hangin' out, partying, makin' no money, so I decided to punish myself by taking my family away. When I left Shayla and Jaiden, I said to myself, 'You don't deserve them. You gotta do something to win them back.'

"I've matured these past months. Now I'm not partying no more, I got more responsibility. I really don't do the bad things I used to do. I don't want to get back to my old ways. I don't have any friends over. No partying. No distractions. I just work and go to school. If I do good enough, maybe I'll earn my family back."

When she heard that, Kelly, Shayla's mother, was incredulous.

"Earn his family back? To this day, C.J. has never paid one dime for no Pampers, no formula, no clothing, nothing."

According to Kelly, it would be virtually impossible for law enforcement to do anything about the fact that C.J. was a deadbeat dad, given that he was out of state and didn't have a steady job.

"If C.J. worked, they could do something," explained Kelly, "but C.J. doesn't work. This past year, I doubt he kept a job for more than two weeks. C.J. doesn't know how to continue. He starts something, decides it's not for him, then says, 'I'm done,' and quits. He doesn't realize that this is not something you can do when you have a son."

Shayla consistently attended her classes at cosmetology school and got licensed. Without any help from C.J., she supported herself and Jaiden with the one hundred dollars a week she got from working in a hair salon at the Berkshire Mall, plus the money she received from welfare, which totaled roughly four hundred dollars per month. Although Shayla was grateful for the money she so desperately needed, she hated being dependent on the system and wished that she could earn enough money to break free from all its rules, regulations, inquiries, and constraints.

"If you get a job while you're on welfare, you have to report every paycheck stub," said Shayla. "You have to get a letter from your employer saying that you work there. You have to report any kind of income you have—your bank accounts, whether you have a car, whether you have money on the side, if you make tips. . . . You have to get a letter from your day-care provider so that in return they can give you a voucher for day care, because you can't pay for full-time day care on your own because it's really expensive.

"It's hard because I was sixteen years old and trying to have a baby somewhat on my own. But welfare is just not letting yourself be independent because you have them in your face 24/7. They want to know everything about everything you do. They get really personal and ask questions like 'When did you have sex? What day? What time? Did you have sex with multiple people?' You have to put up with a lot of hassle and a lot of stress. They're so involved in your life, and you don't even get that much money.

"You have to report your child's doctor's appointments and hand in his immunization charts, and if you're missing one little piece of information, they cut you off. If you're not there for your appointment with the social worker, then your money doesn't come in. If your money doesn't come in, you're not getting diapers and you're not getting food." Shayla sighed. "I've had repeated times where my welfare was cut off."

Shayla and Jaiden moved into subsidized housing on April Lane. They lived right across the street from Shayla's best friend, Sheri, and Amy, whom she knew from the Teen Parent Program. Shayla couldn't afford to buy a car and had to rely on the Job Access Program, which provided her with transportation to and from the workplace. On her way to work, Shayla usually dropped Jaiden off at day care.

"When I first started working after Jaiden was born, I put him into a home day care because I wanted him in a smaller setting where there weren't so many kids around where he could get enough attention. I noticed a lot of times when I picked Jaiden up from day care he had bruises on him, like this one time he had a black eye. But I never asked any questions because he's a hyper kid. He does jump around a lot and fall down and stuff, so I never really put two and two together.

"But now people are saying the lady who ran that day care died of a drug overdose. It bothers me because a lot of times things weren't always a hundred percent, and I never put two and two together. How do I know she wasn't a hostile person? How do I know she wasn't spanking my kid or neglecting my kid?

"A few times when I took Jaiden home from day care, he was acting strange. He was different, more drawn away from people, more sad. When I used to discipline him, he'd come over and kick me back and yell in my face, 'No, Mommy, you don't tell me!' Then when I yelled at him, he'd curl up in a ball and say, 'I'm so sorry, Mommy.' I look back and I see all of these things that I should have asked questions about. But how was I supposed to know that the lady who ran that day care was on drugs?"

Shayla switched Jaiden to a new day-care facility and did her best to reduce the amount of time he spent there. Whenever possible, she preferred to leave him with her grandmother, and on her days off she kept him at home with her. Shayla found that taking care of Jaiden was much more exhausting and stressful than her job.

Jaiden grew into an extremely demanding, hyper, energetic, and adventurous toddler. He was constantly asking questions. Shayla found that he never wanted to sit still and was always pestering her to play with him and always wanting to run around outside. Since he couldn't play outdoors unsupervised, often she would have to stop whatever she was doing and take him out—or listen to him throw a tantrum if he didn't get his way. Shayla rarely had a moment of peace and quiet. She longed to sleep late on Sunday mornings and resented never being able to enjoy that luxury.

"On days when I'm not working, Jaiden wakes up at eight and he's a total terror until he takes his nap at noon. He likes to stick stuff in outlets, stuff like that. If he touches something that could hurt him, I usually just say no and talk him through it. He likes to tell me no all the time, and he likes to bang his toys around. Sometimes he breaks lamps and dishes. Lately, he's been hitting and spitting and saying 'bullshit' a lot. I try to discipline him by saying no in a loud, firm voice, and if he keeps on hitting me, I slap his hand. If he's really having one of his days when he's not listening, then I spank him. Then he starts to understand.

"I definitely think that if you were brought up being spanked, then that's how you bring your child up. I don't feel being spanked had a bad influence on me. I don't think that I was abused or anything like that. I just think that it was enough that I knew my limits. That's the way I intend to raise Jaiden."

Though Shayla blamed her son's acting-out on the terrible situation at his former day care, her mother offered a different theory about the origins of her grandson's aggressive behavioral problems.

"I think Jaiden started hitting people when he seen his father hitting his mother," said Kelly. "Now that's his way of greeting you. You open your arms to him and he hits you. That's his way of his saying hi to his mom now. He doesn't know how to love her; he just wants to hit her. We can't seem to break those habits. So, you can see, the damage has already been done."

As Shayla struggled to teach her son right from wrong, C.J. remained in Arizona and had no contact with them other than by telephone. Gradually Jaiden's behavior began to improve. Shayla was proud to see him coming home from day care singing songs and reciting the alphabet. At night she often took him across the street to play with her friend Sheri's daughter, Leeah.

While the kids entertained themselves, Sheri and Shayla cooked dinner together and watched television. They enjoyed each other's company and took solace in being able to talk frankly about what they were going through. Before they had become mothers, their conversations had centered on lipstick colors, unrequited crushes, the latest awesome song on the radio, grueling homework assignments, nasty teachers, petty arguments with other girls, fights with their mothers, and agonizing decisions about which outfit to wear to so-and-so's party on Friday night. Now all those concerns seemed trivial. On languid summer nights, as Jaiden and Leeah prattled in the background, Sheri and Shayla's conversations centered on two subjects: raising their children and the challenges of maintaining their relationships with their boyfriends.

Lonely in C.J.'s absence, Shayla spent a tremendous amount of mental energy obsessing over how to get him back. The distance between Pittsfield and Arizona and C.J.'s extended absence both served as safeguards, enabling Shayla to sink into a quicksand of idealized romantic fantasies about how great things would be when they saw each other again after such a long separation.

Sheri gently gave Shayla a reality check. She reminded her how rough things had been with C.J. and suggested that she consider dating other guys. Shayla refused to even consider dating someone new. Convinced that C.J. would come back for her and Jaiden, she held on tight to her hope that they would soon be reunited as one happy family. When months went by and it didn't happen, Shayla came up with a plan. She decided to hunt down C.J. in Arizona. She envisioned one of two outcomes: either C.J. would come back to Pittsfield or he would ask her and Jaiden to live with him in Phoenix.

One payday, Shayla realized to her delight that she had finally earned enough money to make the trip to Arizona. She grabbed her week of vacation and proudly bought two Greyhound bus tickets to Phoenix. Having never ventured far from Pittsfield, Shayla was apprehensive about making such a long journey all alone with her toddler, but she was propelled by her intense desire to see C.J.

Aboard the bus, Shayla and Jaiden stared out the window at long stretches of seemingly endless highways. By the third day, they were both impatient and exhausted. Fearing a temper tantrum, Shayla held Jaiden in her lap, stroking his forehead, doing her best to keep him calm. To her surprise, the little boy behaved well during the entire bus ride, as if somehow he sensed that the trip was vital to his mother.

Finally, mother and son arrived at their destination, their exhaustion mixed with excitement. C.J. met them at the station. Within minutes, he told Shayla that he wished she had not come.

During her short stay in Phoenix, Shayla telephoned Sheri long-distance four times, sobbing uncontrollably. Through her tears she told Sheri that C.J. was being really mean to her. He wanted her to go home, and he told her that though he wanted to be friends for the sake of the baby, he didn't want to continue any kind of romantic relationship. Shayla made a similarly desperate call to her grandmother, who immediately purchased two airplane tickets, eager to get her granddaughter and great-grandson home quickly and safely.

For the first time in both their lives, Shayla and Jaiden got on an airplane. As the plane took off and climbed toward the sky, Shayla stared out the window, mesmerized by the view. She had always dreamed of flying to some faraway place where she could build a new life for herself, but instead, a few hours after the plane's wheels bumped down on the runway, she was back in Pittsfield, sitting on the sofa in her apartment on April Lane, watching TV.

Shayla was devastated. She couldn't accept what had happened in Arizona, so she began reinventing the events of the disastrous trip, transforming the upsetting facts into a fairy tale. When family and friends asked how the visit went, Shayla pretended that it had been a blast and that everything with C.J. was just fine and dandy. She told people how gorgeous C.J.'s apartment was. These stories wore thin a few days later when C.J.'s phone in Arizona got disconnected and he was kicked out of his gorgeous apartment for not paying rent.

Despite these developments, Shayla continued to conjure up images of a rosy, romantic future with C.J., while sinking deeper into depression. She lived in a state of denial, caught up in a web of unrealistic ideas and longings, unwilling to confront her disappointment, despair, and terrifying uncertainty about her future. In addition to Jaiden, the one thing that kept Shayla going was her job at Hair Express. She found the atmosphere at the mall socially stimulating and enjoyed the distinction of being regarded a professional hairdresser. She managed to cross the six-month threshold, marking the longest period she had consistently held one job.

Then without warning, Shayla was abruptly fired after being accused of handling a customer rudely and unprofessionally. Shayla insisted that the charges weren't true, but her boss chose to believe her coworker's account. She told Shayla in no uncertain terms that she was no longer welcome at the salon.

"I was really, really upset," said Shayla, shivering at the memory of those bitterly cold winter months. "I had picked out all types of stuff to get Jaiden for Christmas and I couldn't get that stuff, because my boss fired me over something that I didn't even do."

Shayla did her best to bounce back. She landed another job at Filene's. She quickly moved on to a resort, where she worked in housekeeping, cleaning rooms for ten dollars an hour. When that didn't work out, Shayla asked Sheri if she could help her get a job cleaning rooms at the bed-and-breakfast where she worked. Sheri spoke to her boss, and Shayla was hired. For a few months the two friends worked side by side, doing laundry, vacuuming floors, dusting tables, scrubbing toilets, and changing sheets. Shayla often thought of C.J. and wondered what he was up to in Arizona. She told Sheri that she hoped C.J. was "growing up" and "getting his act together." Sheri was skeptical and encouraged Shayla to consider dating other guys.

C.J.'s prolonged absence combined with her own life experience as a single mother gave Shayla some necessary distance from her high-school years as well as a new perspective on all that had transpired since then. With the enhanced self-awareness, Shayla reflected on her decision to get pregnant at such a young age. Looking back on her younger self, Shayla saw "a very immature sixteen-year-old." She acknowledged that her relationship with C.J. had been overburdened with problems from day one. Having a baby hadn't magically resolved these issues, as she had hoped—instead, it had complicated them.

"I thought having a baby would work out all corners of my life, but it really hasn't," said Shayla. "It stressed my life out and it made everything much more difficult."

"I think we should have waited," agreed C.J., "because there's a lot more to life than just hurrying up. I feel like I'm already, I don't know, thirty or forty. I feel like I'm grown up and there's not much left to do in the world."

As Shayla matured, she got used to being a single mother. She realized she was capable of dealing with the challenge of raising her son.

"Six months ago, if you had asked me if I was prepared to be on

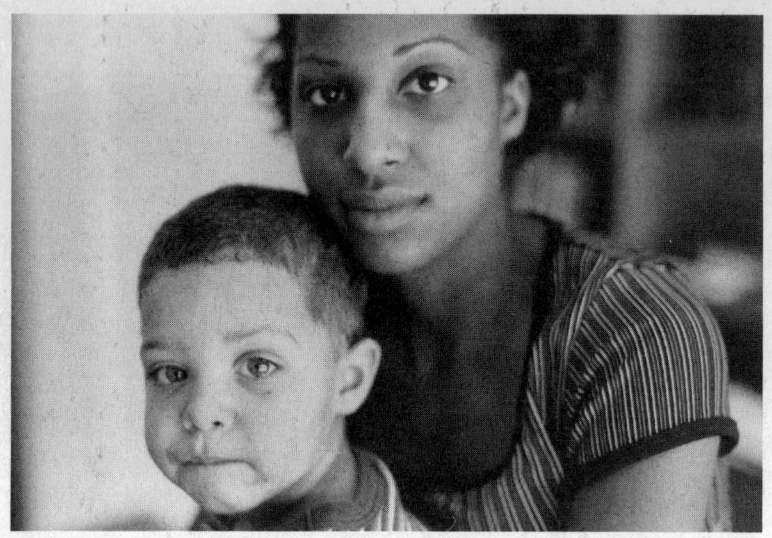

my own, I would've told you straight up, 'No!' " said Shayla. "I would have said that because I was so dependent on C.J. But now I'm starting to grow up and I realize, it's true: I am definitely prepared. Nothing really matters but Jaiden. My whole focus goes toward him. I'm just gonna work on making things right for him. If C.J. decides that we can be a family and things are gonna work out so that Jaiden is happy, that's fine. But Jaiden comes first."

Shayla finally got over C.J. and started dating Ian, whom she had known since elementary school. Ian had recently gotten out of jail and needed a place to stay, so he moved in with Shayla and Jaiden. Ian already had a daughter with another teen mother. He complained to Shayla that his ex-girlfriend wouldn't let him see the child and had taken out a restraining order against him. After Shayla found several items missing from her apartment, she kicked Ian out.

When things didn't work out in Arizona, C.J. returned to Pittsfield. He had to keep a low profile because there was still a warrant out for his arrest. Shayla gave C.J. a chance to prove that he had changed. He quickly failed to persuade her.

"At first, we were gonna try to be together," said Shayla, "but after five years putting up with all the arguing and fighting, I decided I didn't want to be with him, so he moved back in with his mom. He takes Jaiden once a week. We get along as friends for Jaiden's sake.

"C.J. used to make me feel really insecure about myself. He used to tell me all the time that he was the only one who wanted me and that I was ugly to everybody else. All that crap wasn't true. I thought me and C.J. were gonna be together for . . . I wouldn't say forever, but I'd say for a long time. I thought we'd stick it out—but I wasn't happy with him. Jaiden knew I wasn't happy. He could tell. I couldn't take care of him being all sad and depressed every day. I take care of him a lot better now because I'm a happier person."

Soon after breaking up with C.J., Shayla began dating Jay. He was white, tattooed, and roughly the same height and physical type as C.J. He had dropped out of high school in tenth grade and worked as a butcher at a grocery store. He and his friends all wore their pants down super low so that their boxer shorts stuck out jailhouse-style, between their long T-shirts and their belt buckles.

At eighteen, Jay was younger than Shayla. He was content to let her be the dominant one in the relationship. On his days off he hung out at Shayla's apartment, watching TV, or wandered around the neighborhood with his buddies.

"Jay treats me with respect and makes me feel a lot better than C.J. made me feel," said Shayla. "I really like him a lot and he really, really likes me a lot. Jaiden loves him to death. He doesn't look at him like he's his father because he knows who his dad is, but they're getting along real well."

Three months into their relationship, Shayla got pregnant. She offered contradictory explanations for how and why this second pregnancy occurred. Sometimes she made it sound as though she and Jay had planned the pregnancy, other times she indicated that she had been taking the Depo-Provera shot and had combined it with muscle-relaxing medication, which she claimed had caused this method of contraception to fail. In either case, once she was pregnant, she decided to carry the baby to term.

Jaiden was already three years old. He was becoming independent, and Shayla missed having a baby in the house. Also motivating Shayla to have the second child was her feeling that with Jaiden, she had missed out on the relaxing, wonderful, bonding moments a mother and infant were supposed to have together. Two weeks after Jaiden was born, she had rushed back to school. After a long day at school she had worked at Friendly's, and then there had been all the stress with C.J. Shayla felt that Jaiden's infancy had gone by way too fast, and she longed for the chance to mother an infant all over again, this time the right way. She wanted to stay home with her second baby without any other demands on her time and energy. She also desperately wanted a baby girl. Jay was pretty relaxed about the idea of becoming a father. Many of his friends had kids, and he felt ready to do the same thing.

"At first, my mom and my grams were a little upset about me

being pregnant again," said Shayla, "but within the same day they were fine about it. I already have to wake up in the morning with Jaiden. I'll have to wake up in the morning with the baby. I give Jaiden a bath. I'll give the baby a bath. It's the same thing. I'm a little nervous because I don't know how Jaiden will react to a baby coming home. I worry about if he's gonna be jealous, but other than that, I'm fine about it."

Shayla knew that she would need more money when the second baby arrived. She and Sheri enrolled in a computer class at the Mildred Elly Business School. They learned how to enter data and how to make spreadsheets in Excel. Shayla hoped that her newly acquired skills would help her get a better job.

As her pregnancy continued, Shayla became determined to make C.J. pay child support for Jaiden. Whenever she broached the subject with him, he would verbally attack her and refuse to pay. Absolutely furious that Shayla was carrying Jay's baby, C.J. was eager to make life hell for both of them. Although fear of the warrant for his arrest made him circumspect about where he went and with whom, it didn't stop him from using the telephone as a weapon.

"I was three or four months pregnant, and Jay was working full-time. I was home and C.J. would call me all day and he'd threaten. . . . He'd call me a bad person because I had a new boyfriend and I was starting a new family, and he'd harass Jay and threaten to beat him up and strangle him and stuff. . . . I told him, if you keep calling my house, harassing me, I'm going to call the police on you."

C.J. disregarded Shayla's warning. When the phone rang again, Shayla picked up, hung up on C.J., and called the police. She told them exactly where to find their man.

"C.J. was arrested immediately, and he went to jail," recalled Shayla. "He had to serve four months in a correctional institution, and he had to do a month of rehab for his alcohol and drug abuse because he was smoking marijuana and he drank uncontrollably."

Jaiden didn't visit his father behind bars. "C.J. wanted him to come," said Shayla, "but I don't think they allow children in that jail anymore."

C.J. was surprised to find that the months he spent in jail did him a lot of good. Most of the other prisoners in the local jail were incarcerated on charges related to drugs, stealing, domestic violence, alcohol-related brawls, or drunk-driving incidents. Behind bars, C.J. worked out, ate three regular meals, and put on thirty pounds. He started reading the Bible, searching for the meaning and purpose of his life. The months flew by. C.J. got sober, got rest, and matured. Jail was his rite of passage into manhood.

When C.J. was released from jail, another court date awaited him. Shayla, six months pregnant, faced him in front of a judge and demanded child support. The judge made it clear that if C.J. didn't get a job and support his son, he'd go straight back to jail. Soon after, Shayla received the first of what would be regular child-support payments. They were small at first but gradually increased when C.J. got a better job painting houses.

All the stress of these traumatic, emotional events took a toll on Shayla's pregnancy. One afternoon while she was attending her computer class, she went into labor. She panicked. It was way too early. Shayla's voice trembled as she called Jay. He rushed over, picked her up, and took her to the local hospital. The doctors there made arrangements for her to be transported to a bigger hospital in Springfield.

"When I first started going into labor, I was only twenty-four weeks pregnant, and in Pittsfield they can't take you into labor if you're before thirty-four weeks, so I had to go to Springfield, which is about an hour and a half away by ambulance. The doctor gave me some medication through an IV, and it stopped my labor. I stayed in the hospital for a week and a half to be monitored so that they could make sure that the labor was stopped. Then they sent me home on total bed rest. They told me to take sponge baths because they didn't want me standing up in the shower. But I had a three year old at home and I had a house to take care of, so I couldn't stay on total bed rest. I was up walkin' around, and that put me back into labor at thirty-two weeks. They brought me into Springfield for an emergency C-section because the baby was in breach position. The umbilical cord was wrapped around his neck, so they were really worried about his breathing."

Shayla gave birth prematurely to Caleb, a baby boy who weighed only three pounds. He spent the first week of his life hooked up to life-support machines in the intensive care unit for newborns at the hospital in Springfield. After only five days, he was taken back to Pittsfield by ambulance. The infant spent another three weeks in an incubator at a hospital there. Shayla, Jay, and Jaiden visited every day. Jaiden was extremely worried about his little brother being in what he referred to as "that little box."

"After almost four weeks in the incubator, the doctor said Caleb had gained enough weight," said Shayla, "so we brought him home. He seemed absolutely fine until Jay woke up at two in the morning to feed him and suddenly he just stopped breathing and started coughing up blood."

Jay called out for Shayla. She leapt out of bed, alarmed by the sheer terror in his trembling voice. After one glimpse at the baby, Shayla switched into full gear.

"I snatched the baby. I was trying to get him to breathe," said Shayla. "I was shaking him a little bit, shaking his little arms to get him going, and he kept breathing very faintly but he had a lot of mucus stuck in his throat. So it was like three in the morning. I wrapped him up in a blanket, and it was freezing outside. I put him in the car. My whole windshield was glazed thick with ice, so I couldn't see. I had to roll my window down and look out the driver's side window all the way to the hospital.

"When I got to the emergency room, I was frantic. I said to the nurse, 'You need to help my baby out! He's not breathing!'

"The doctors were so worried about taking Caleb's temperature, and they were just poking at him. That frustrated me a lot because it was really serious to me, and they were saying, 'Well, we have to take his temperature, we have to do this, we have to do that. . . .'

"To me it was like 'He's not breathing! Can't you help him out a little bit?' It was really frustrating. Although he made it through the night, I wanted to switch him to a better hospital, so we went to Bay State in Springfield. As soon as I got him down there, they told me exactly what he had and within five minutes they took care of him."

Caleb was diagnosed with respiratory syncytial virus (RSV), a common condition that affects nearly all adults and children in the form of a common cold. The doctor told Shayla that premature babies such as Caleb were at much higher risk of developing an acute, potentially fatal form of the contagious virus, which strikes mostly during autumn, winter, and early spring. Caleb remained in the hospital in Springfield for two weeks. While he was being treated for his illness, the hospital allowed Shayla and Jay to stay a block away at the Ronald McDonald House, a residential facility that offered rooms free of charge to parents of hospitalized children.

"You could live there for two days or two months," explained Shayla. "It's absolutely free. They offer you a kitchen. They have a huge basement playroom in case you have any other children you have to bring with you. It was really nice. The hospital was right down the street, so me and Jay would walk there. The baby's feedings were, like, every three hours, so every single night we'd switch, every other feeding, so that we could go up there and sit with him and feed him. We stayed there for hours."

After several weeks, the doctors pronounced Caleb healthy enough to leave the hospital, ending the long ordeal. Shayla spent six months at home taking care of him. This time around, the welfare caseworker was much more understanding and tolerant. Shayla was pleasantly surprised to learn that as an adult in possession of her GED, she was governed by a different set of rules. She managed to get through Caleb's infancy without ever having her welfare cut off, which had been a constant worry when Jaiden was younger. Shayla cherished the time she spent with Caleb. It was a luxury to be able to be a mother for six months without having to worry about work and school.

While holding and feeding her baby, Shayla spent hours watching MTV. She particularly liked the reality shows. Her favorite show was called *MADE,* which took real teenagers who had a dream and gave them the means to realize that dream.

"They had two shows," recalled Shayla, "one where a girl got to become a model and one where she got to become a professional cheerleader. That really interested me because I want to be either one of those things. The one that I liked the most was about a girl who became a model. I think her name was Nadia, and she didn't look that special. She just looked like a normal black girl, and when I was watching the show, when I was looking at her doing the shopping and getting her makeup done, I thought it was something I could do. She just looked like an average person, and I know I could do the same thing. They set her up with a coach who taught her how to walk and how to be a model, and while she was being trained, they set her up with a place to live in New York City and they helped her get a job as a waitress at The Coffee Shop. Her coach took her to all the different modeling agencies until she finally got a contract. She went to, like, twenty agencies and got offered a contract by six of them.

"It was easier for that girl than it would be for me," said Shayla, "because she was in college and didn't have any kids, so she could just move to New York for two months while she was being trained. She could just quit school and quit her job and just up and leave—but for me, I wouldn't be able to do the same thing because I have two kids.

"But I was just wondering if there's some way that I'd still be able to be on that show. If MTV says the rules are that you have to dedicate all your time twenty-four hours a day to training and going after your dream, then it would be something I wouldn't be able to

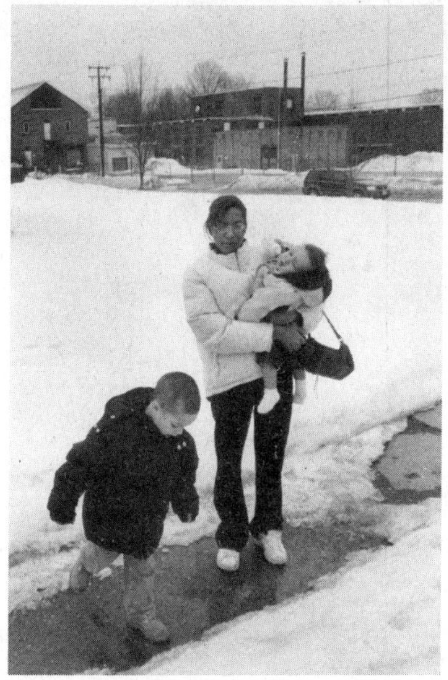

do. But I know that a lot of the girls who are Dallas Cowboys Cheerleaders have kids. So they must be able to do both. They make their schedules for dance classes and their exercising fit in with being a mom. It just seems like when you're a singer, or you become a model or a cheerleader—people start when they're like sixteen and actually get into it by the time they're twenty. I'm gonna be trying to start something when I'm twenty-one or twenty-two," Shayla lamented.

C.J. and Shayla went back to court to define the terms of his rights as Jaiden's father. Jaiden was now four years old, and Shayla had

matured to a point where she recognized that it was important for him to have a relationship with C.J. Her son often asked about his dad. Shayla decided to put her negative feelings aside and do what was best for the child.

"I started to allow C.J. to visit Jaiden for an hour a week under outside supervision," she explained. "During these supervised visits Jaiden really got to know his dad. They started spending a lot of time together."

After a few months of supervised visits, C.J. was allowed to take his son by himself on weekends. He had rented a studio apartment on a quiet residential block, eager to provide a peaceful, positive environment for his son. Continuing the search for purpose and meaning in his life that had begun while he was incarcerated, C.J. read a book that made a huge impact on him. It was titled *SQ: Connecting with Your Spiritual Intelligence,* and was cowritten by Danah Zohar, a professor at Oxford University, and Dr. Ian Marshall, a psychiatrist and psychotherapist. Their ideas offered C.J. a new way of appreciating himself and gave him a sense of value and direction, helping him begin to fill the inner void he had described so vividly when reflecting on his life at about the time he and Shayla had conceived Jaiden. C.J. began doing yoga every morning, copying the movements from a class taught on television. He mellowed out, got a steady job as a waiter at a local restaurant, and held on to it. Jaiden's overall behavior improved significantly as he spent more time with his dad, adhering to a consistent, predictable schedule.

"C.J. told me that he's not angry anymore about the whole situation," said Shayla, "but when he first went to jail, he was so mad at me for calling the cops. Now he thanks me, because he's a lot more mature now, so he's happy with the outcome. Going to jail helped C.J. grow up. It helped him learn to take care of Jaiden responsibly, the way he's supposed to."

When Caleb was seven months old, Shayla got a part-time job in telemarketing. At malls across the country, people were given the opportunity to enter a raffle to win a Jeep. On the raffle ticket they had to put down their telephone numbers in case they won. These phone numbers were then assigned to Shayla. She was instructed to try to sell these people time-share vacation homes. Irritated at being bothered and having no idea how she got their home numbers, people

usually spoke to her rudely and then hung up on her. Shayla hated the job and eventually quit.

Jay was also temporarily out of work. He and Shayla sat home together with the two kids, watching television. Their phone was cut off because they didn't pay the bill. People who wanted to get in touch with them had to go to their apartment in person.

"My relationship with Jay is a lot different than what I had with C.J.," said Shayla. "Jay and I get along. We like a lot of the same things. I don't really go out that much. I'm kinda a homebody. I like to stay at home and keep to myself, and Jay doesn't mind that. He doesn't mind sitting at home with me, watching a movie. He's not the type of person who needs to be out all the time. One of the big problems I had with C.J. was that he never liked to stay home and help. Now, whenever I need any help, Jay is right there. He's there all the time. It's a lot easier to get along with him and have a better relationship when he's always here. He doesn't give me a hard time about having to get up in the middle of the night with the baby. He just sucks it up and he does it."

Jay adopted a pit bull puppy from a friend who didn't want the dog anymore. He named the dog Tigger. Shayla hated having the dog in the house with the two kids. The dog kept getting out and jumping over the fence. It tore open garbage bags and whatever else it could sink its teeth into. Shayla wanted to get rid of the dog, but Jay wanted to keep him. Jaiden grew very attached to the dog. The little boy often tried to hug Tigger, but usually the pit bull just growled and scared him away.

When Jaiden was four, Shayla noticed that his upper front teeth were growing abnormally sharp, yellow, and rotten. The doctor diagnosed him with "milk rot," a dental condition that occurs when infants and toddlers sleep with bottles in their mouth, leaving milk or, worse, high-sugar juices or soda in contact with the teeth for extended periods of time, causing decay. Jaiden had to have his front teeth pulled and his back teeth filed down.

As the baby got older, Shayla needed to get a full-time job. In an effort to help her out with the two kids, her grandmother took a course offered by an organization called Resources for Child Care. Upon completion, she received accreditation as a home day-care provider. With this certification, she could take care of her great-grandchildren and get paid for it with vouchers that she could trade in for cash.

Now that Shayla didn't have to structure her work hours around the hours of a day-care center, she could work longer hours and had more options and flexibility in terms of shifts. There was an opening at Dunkin' Donuts a block away from where she lived. Shayla was hired. The branch where Shayla worked was always busy, frequented by a broad array of characters, ranging from tourists to locals to homeless vagrants who wandered in, clutching a few coins in their hands, begging for a cup of coffee.

Shayla liked the hustle and bustle and the fast turnover. She became friendly with her coworkers. The pace, the energy, and the camaraderie stimulated her and made the hours go by faster.

On most days, Shayla wore her hair pulled straight back in a simple ponytail. The hair extensions she had once been so enamored with sat unused in a drawer. Shayla wore glasses all the time and rarely wore makeup. When she wasn't in her uniform for work, usually she hung around in jeans, T-shirts, and baggy sweatpants. Her days of dressing glamorously and daydreaming about modeling bikinis were long gone.

Shayla's younger sister, Ashley, was now in junior high. She and her friends sometimes passed by Dunkin' Donuts when Shayla was working her shift. Witnessing her elder sister's struggles, Ashley did what she could to help out with her nephews. She doted on Jaiden and took tremendous delight in playing with the baby. Whereas Shayla was always exhausted, Ashley had boundless energy and could easily keep the baby engaged and entertained when Shayla nodded off for a nap. Shayla saw how much her sister enjoyed spending time with the baby and made sure that Ashley participated in the drudgery of childrearing as well as its pleasures.

"My sister and I are two very different people," said Shayla pointedly. "She sees how hard it is to have a baby because I give her things to do. I don't think she'll end up like I did. She's into a totally different direction.

"Right now my little sister sees a lot of stuff on TV and in the movies with the young girls doing a whole bunch of things," said Shayla, "and that kind of inspires her. She's fourteen, and she's seeing all these girls on TV actually doing something and not just sitting around, having a boyfriend or having a kid. So she actually is inspired to do something else. Like on MTV, there was one show called *Sorority Life,* and it was just them following these college girls who wanted to be in a sorority. You follow them partying and hanging out and trying to get their homework done, just stuff that happens in their real lives. My sister watches that and she's like 'Oh, I want to go to college. . . . I can't wait to go to college!' "

Ashley was a talented cheerleader. She devoted most of her energy to rigorous practice sessions and participated in competitions. At night and on weekends, when she was bored at home, she would visit Shayla and the kids, often dressed in short miniskirts that showed off her unbelievably long legs. An array of camisoles and colorful tank tops accentuated her lacy bras and her developing cleavage.

"That's exactly what Shayla used to look like," said Sheri nostalgically as she watched Ashley walk down the street and disappear around the corner.

chapter six

SHERI

"You just didn't know what was gonna happen at my mom's. You just took it minute by minute. You didn't know if there was gonna be a fight. You didn't know who was gonna show up or at what time. There were always people there who I didn't like. My mom's friends were lowlifes. They didn't have nothing goin' for 'em. I don't know exactly what kind of drugs they were into, but I didn't want to be a part of that."

SHERI'S MOTHER, PAT, WAS FIFTEEN THE FIRST TIME SHE got pregnant. She lost the baby not long after being beaten up by her boyfriend and was unable to put the guilt and bereavement behind her. Every year on what would have been her baby's birthday, Pat's spirits plummeted and she entered a state of profound mourning.

At the age of seventeen, Pat was pregnant again. She dropped out of high school and married her new boyfriend, Greg, who already had a two-year-old son. Pat gave birth to a baby boy and devoted the remainder of her teenage years to raising this child and her stepson. Several years later, Sheri was born.

"Sheri's dad was an alcoholic," Pat recalled, "and when he'd have his hangovers, he'd be verbally abusive and he'd make me go out and mow the lawn, pregnant. The lawn mower would break down and he would tell me where the parts were to repair it. He wasn't a very loving husband. He did a lot of running around. In fact, when I went into labor with Sheri, he unplugged his phone. So I had Sheri all by myself that night."

As a toddler, Sheri witnessed wild fights between her parents. Fists flew, plates were shattered, furniture was broken, and liquor bottles were smashed. By the time Sheri was three years old, she had a large, wide, half-moon-shaped scar on one of her cheeks but no memory of how the injury occurred. Her mother told her she had fallen while running, carrying a glass of water. According to Pat, the glass had shattered and one of the fragments slashed Sheri in the face, leaving a deeply etched mark that measured nearly two inches. The injury nearly cost the child one of her eyes and required several operations. Finally, when Sheri was a teenager, plastic surgery resulted in a dramatic improvement, but even as the scar on her face faded, the internal scars she incurred growing up remained raw.

"While I was pregnant with Sheri's little sister, Nadine, my husband just got up and left," Pat recalled. "He never gave us any child support. . . . He was gone for ten years, without a trace."

Sheri, nearly four, waited and waited for some word of her daddy's whereabouts—an address, a phone number, a letter, a birthday card, a message—but there was nothing. By the time Nadine was born, Sheri and her elder brother had adjusted to their father's absence. They no longer expected him to show up at the front door, begging Pat to take him back, as he had done so many times before.

Four years later, when Sheri was seven and Nadine three, Pat married her boyfriend, Steve, a truck driver. Nadine grew up mistaking Steve for her biological father. Pat and Steve's marriage was strained by financial hardship and loud arguments. Pat was frequently tired, irritable, depressed, and strung out. She chain-smoked nonstop and suffered from recurring anxiety attacks. Because of a severe cocaine addiction and an eating disorder, Pat was dangerously underweight and incredibly volatile.

"My mom's mood—it was always changing," Sheri recalled. "One minute she'd be nice and caring and loving, and the next she'd be kind of on the edge. There was times when I felt like she didn't want me around. I would sometimes ask myself, 'Why am I even here? Should I be doing something different for my mom to want me here?' " Sheri took a deep breath and shook her head. "I shouldn't have had to feel like that," she said.

Echoing her elder sister's perceptions, Nadine explained, "My mom has many different personalities. She can be really nice. One minute she'll be laughing, next minute she'll be throwing things at you, next minute she'll be crying, and the next minute she'll be going psycho, just screaming and breaking things. Her moods change like that!" Nadine said, snapping her fingers to illustrate the rapid shifts.

As the girls were growing up, Pat and Steve were each arrested more than a dozen times on charges related to drugs, assault and battery, and disturbing the peace.

"Cops were always showing up," said Nadine. "Watching that every day—fighting, drugs, drinking, drug dealers coming in and out—it got a little crazy. It was hard. I dealt with a lot of abuse," she said quietly, raising her finger to touch her forehead. "It ruined me up here—and everywhere else.

"When I was about five years old, there was fighting," recalled Nadine. "Pans were flying and I got hit with hot grease. I went to school and they wound up seeing that I was burned from grease and I wound up telling them what had happened and the cops wound up coming and taking us away. Sheri and I got put in a foster home because of the drugs."

After a few months, the girls were returned to the custody of their mother and stepfather. Pat took Sheri out of school for several months, which resulted in her having to repeat a grade. One afternoon when Sheri was seven years old, she and another little girl were dropped off at the house of a family friend. Sheri had never met this man who was supposed to "baby-sit" for the day while her mother and aunt were both at work. As soon as Sheri's aunt drove away, the man locked the two girls in the bathroom, where they were surrounded by sex toys, lewd photographs, and S&M costumes. They were held hostage for several hours.

When he finally let the girls out, the man forced them to watch pornographic videotapes featuring children performing sexual acts on various adults. One of the children they saw was a six-year-old boy they knew. Sheri was terrified. She and her friend were asked to dress up in costumes. They refused. Trembling, Sheri kept quiet and watched the videos, praying that her aunt would come to pick her up.

In the late afternoon, Sheri's aunt arrived to retrieve the girls. As soon as she got home, Sheri told her mother everything that had happened. Pat took her to the police station. A report was filed. A week later the police raided the man's house. He was found dead in his garage. He had committed suicide.

Sheri was haunted by this death. She felt guilty, sensing that people blamed her for the suicide. She worried that by telling her mother what had happened, she had caused this man to kill himself. From that point on, when bad things happened behind closed doors, Sheri embraced silence. To this little girl, silence seemed much safer than causing someone's death.

One night Sheri and her little sister were awakened by sounds of yelling and screaming. They opened their eyes and saw strangers standing in their bedroom. They were urged to get dressed and pack their suitcases. Frightened, Sheri went downstairs and asked her mother and stepfather what was going on. She was told that she was being taken to a foster home. No further explanation was given.

"Sheri and I went in and out of a few foster homes together, but we didn't stay long," recalled Nadine. "We just wound up going in and out of them and then back to my mom's."

Sheri and Nadine loved their mother in spite of her shortcomings. Each time the Department of Social Services intervened and put them into foster care, Pat blamed the girls "for causing trouble." From a safe distance, the girls worried about betraying their mother by telling the truth about some of the things that went on inside the four walls of their small wood cabin. They felt immensely ambivalent about being separated from their mother, and thus had great difficulty settling in to the foster homes where they were placed. Deep down, they didn't want new families to take them in—they just wanted their own family to be different.

"A lot of foster parents, they're really mean people," Nadine said. "They're not nice at all, and you can tell for a fact they're just doing it for the money. If you try to talk to them, pretty much all they say to you is 'Go to bed' or 'It's time to eat' or 'It's time for you to do a bath.' They don't sit down and really talk to you. They just tell you what to do and then say good night or good-bye."

As a result of these failed foster care placements and the girls' intense ambivalence, Pat was given many second chances to take care of her children. She knew that her daughters loved her. Not wanting them to be taken away from her for good, she made a conscious effort.

"I went to the adult learning center and got my high school diploma," Pat recalled. "Then I got a housecleaning job at an inn. That didn't last too long, so I got my hairdressing license and did hairdressing for a couple of years. Then I needed benefits, so I went to got my certified nurse's assistant license. It was hard living on welfare like we did all those years. It was a long, hard struggle."

When Sheri turned sixteen, she was eligible for her working papers. Her aunt worked as a housekeeper at Canyon Ranch, a world-class spa and resort located in Lenox, fifteen minutes from Pittsfield. She helped Sheri get a job there.

"I worked long hours and cleaned lots of rooms," Sheri remembered. "After school I'd go in from three o'clock until nine, almost every day, because I needed the money." The rooms at Canyon Ranch were usually empty when Sheri cleaned them. The hours she spent at work passed quietly. No one bothered her. She had been cleaning her mom's house for as long as she could remember, so the skills she needed came naturally. Sheri found the atmosphere of the resort soothing compared with her frazzled family life. Between going to work and school, her goal was to spend as little time at home as humanly possible.

At sixteen, Sheri was old enough to distance herself somewhat from the chaos at home. She chose to steer clear of substance abuse and devoted her time and energy to her job and to maintaining her close relationship with her boyfriend, Jon, whom she had met at school. With his calm voice and quiet, relaxed manner, Jon became Sheri's anchor.

Nadine had no anchor. At twelve, she was sensitive, vulnerable, and very impressionable. Trapped with her mother and stepfather, she was at sea in a culture of violence, crime, and addiction.

"I first partied when I was eleven," she recalled. "Already back then, I had a problem with alcohol."

The existing stress in the household was exacerbated when Sheri and Nadine's stepfather, Steve, took a leave of absence from work because of a back injury. At the same time, their elder brother was recovering from surgery following a car accident. With the two men incapacitated and hanging around the house all day, the burden of supporting the family fell squarely on Pat's shoulders.

In order to pay the bills and keep food on the table, Pat, then employed as a nursing assistant, had to increase her workload to fifty or sixty hours per week. Most days, she arrived at work exhausted, pale, weak; by then she was emaciated. It was all she could do to summon up the strength to push the elderly around in their wheelchairs. During the limited hours she spent at home, Pat divided most of her time between sleeping and arguing with her husband. She had to curtail her partying habits because she couldn't afford to lose her job. She had very little patience with her children.

Most days when Sheri came home from school, Steve was waiting to greet her. Sheri had very little privacy, and as the tension between her and her stepfather escalated, she felt safer and more at ease outside the home, working or hanging out with friends. Faced with Sheri's emerging femininity and youthfulness, Pat was intensely competitive and envious. She accused Sheri of acting inappropriately and of being provocative at home. She screamed, shouted, intimidated, and grounded Sheri—but all her efforts to rein her eldest daughter in failed miserably.

Seeking attention, Sheri tested her mother by disobeying rules and staying out past her curfew. Any reaction was better than nothing. Any show of emotion, including anger, was seen as a sign that her mother did indeed care about her. Instead of asking Sheri what was bothering her and trying to create a safe line of communication, when faced with Sheri's blatant defiance and lack of respect, Pat became more and more explosive. Pat had more than enough problems of her own and couldn't tolerate Sheri's adding to them.

Sheri had an equally hard time tolerating her mother's behavior. She saw the example Pat set in the house with her own friends, partying into the early hours of the morning, and couldn't understand how she could then turn around and forbid her daughter from doing whatever she wanted. Sheri was too embarrassed to bring friends home, because her mother and stepfather were usually drinking, fighting, and doing drugs.

Sheri continued acting out and spent less and less time at home. Her reluctance to stay home was due to much more than simple teenage rebellion. She didn't like being around her stepfather. Pat refused to acknowledge what made life at home so unbearable for both her daughters.

"When I was in eighth grade at Reid Middle School, I wound up talking to a counselor about the situation in my household," said Nadine. "DSS wound up coming for a meeting, and my mom said I was lying about everything, and I knew I wasn't. So one day I flipped out and screamed and yelled at my stepdad, 'Get the fuck outta my house!' He wound up leaving, but then my mom took him back and threw my sister out."

Sheri confided in Jon, who by then had been her steady boyfriend for three years. She told him that a string of bitter fights had made life at home impossible for her and her mother. Jon had witnessed the friction and upheaval in Sheri's household. He couldn't stand seeing his girlfriend so miserable all the time, so he asked his parents to let Sheri come live with them.

Aware of Sheri's toxic home environment, Jon's parents agreed to allow her to move in to their home. Several days later, Sheri arrived at their front door, suitcase in hand. She stayed with Jon and his family for six months while Nadine remained with her mother and stepfather.

"The fighting in our household was out of control," said Pat. "I thought Sheri would run away. I didn't want to see her out on the streets. I didn't want to see anything happen to her. That's why I agreed for her to go to Jon's house and stay with him and his parents. They had a very nice home. They were very good people.

"I was kinda afraid that maybe Sheri would get pregnant," Pat confessed. "The thought crossed my mind several times. I took her to the doctor, and it was her decision to take the Pill or practice safe sex."

Sheri went on the Pill. She was Jon's first serious girlfriend, so it was a special time for them.

"When I was living with Jon's family, it was great," Sheri recalled. "They made me feel really comfortable. I loved it. I really did. Jon's parents made me feel like they cared more about me. They cared more about my feelings. They just made me feel good. They made me feel like they were my parents. My mom, on the other hand . . . I mean, I don't know . . . see, it was different. It was hectic at my mom's. At Jon's parents house it was nice and calm."

Sheri enjoyed being a guest in Jon's home, but as the months passed and the winter holiday season approached, she felt guilty about being estranged from her family. She knew that she couldn't impose on Jon's family forever. Not wanting to wear out their goodwill toward her, she moved back to her mother's house.

"It's just not the same around Christmas without your own family," she explained.

The small two-bedroom wood cabin with its thin walls and low ceilings was exactly how Sheri had left it six months before. Nadine was thrilled to have her elder sister back. She quickly cleared her stuff out of Sheri's half of their room. Upon settling in, Sheri did her best to make peace with her mother.

"When I moved back in, things got a lot better," Sheri said, " 'cause my mom was glad I was home, and I was glad. We sat down and talked, and I told her what was really bothering me. I said, 'Mom, I don't like the friends of yours that come in and out of the house. They come here at two o'clock in the morning. . . . I don't like that. That's not a home to me.' My mom said, 'I do want you back, and things will change.' "

A tired grin spread across Sheri's face as she shook her head, all too familiar with her mother's broken promises. Deep down, she knew it was just a matter of time before her mother and stepfather reverted back to their old ways.

One afternoon the following spring, Nadine, now thirteen, came home from school and found the house deserted. She knocked on her parents' bedroom door. There was no answer. She knocked again.

Silence. Pat and Steve had told the kids that they were planning a trip, but Nadine hadn't expected them to leave so soon. She wandered into the kitchen and saw that the sink was stacked with dirty dishes. A crumpled note lay on the counter. Pat had scrawled a quick message in black ink:

> *We'll see you sometime. . . . We're in Florida.*
>
> *Love, Mom and Dad*

"They took off on us," Nadine explained. "It was me and Sheri and our brother. While my parents were away, Jon wound up sleeping over a lot, and that's when Sheri got pregnant. When my parents came back from Florida, a lot happened. More drugs were coming in. It was real bad."

Sheri first realized she might be pregnant when she missed her period. She took a home-pregnancy test, which came out negative. Wanting to make sure that she wasn't pregnant, Sheri took another test, just in case the previous result had been false. The second pregnancy test came out negative. Sheri didn't consider the possibility that maybe she wasn't administering the home pregnancy test correctly. She was relieved about the negative results—until she missed another period.

Sheri woke up with morning sickness. She dragged herself out of bed, staggered to the bathroom, and vomited. Still worried that she might be pregnant and confused about why the home-pregnancy tests kept coming up negative, Sheri decided to confide in her mother. Pat took her to the see a doctor, who determined that Sheri was indeed nine weeks pregnant.

Sheri was shocked. She had been taking birth control pills regularly—well, almost. Going back and forth between her mother's house and Jon's house, she had misplaced a packet of pills and hadn't gotten around to replacing them for four days.

"And in those four days, I got pregnant," she explained.

Sheri was seventeen: the thought of having a baby at that point in her life was overwhelming and terrifying. She didn't feel ready. Tears streamed down her face as her skinny legs dangled over the edge of the doctor's examining table. Across the room, Pat was crying tears of joy.

"I was happy," Pat recalled. "We were gonna have a new life in the family, and I was gonna be a grandma! I can't believe I had such an excited feeling about that. I told Sheri that there was nothing we could do to change things, so we might as well accept the facts and be happy and make the best of what was to come."

In Pat's experience, destiny was something one surrendered to and survived, as opposed to something one tried to shape or control. Having been a teen mother herself, Pat knew the ropes. She didn't feel it necessary to discuss abortion or adoption, nor did she address any hopes, plans, or opportunities Sheri might have had other than motherhood.

"I'm Catholic," Pat declared, "and I don't believe in abortion. We've made it, struggling all our lives. What's one more mouth to feed? I knew we'd make it. We'd do whatever we had to, to make it."

Sheri's stepfather had a dramatically different reaction.

"When Sheri got pregnant, my husband was very upset," said Pat. "He wanted Sheri to finish high school. He thought her having a baby so young would interfere with her future. His opinions created a lot of problems in the home."

Pat and her husband continued to fight bitterly over Sheri's pregnancy. Pat remained stubborn and unyielding when it came to discussing options other than Sheri's giving birth and raising the baby herself. The violence in the house escalated.

"My dad took a picnic bench and put it through my ma's car window. That really shocked me," said Nadine, "so I went to school and I called DSS on myself this time. I said, 'Listen . . . I can't be at home.' "

The Department of Social Services sent a social worker to talk to Nadine's parents. Pat and her husband assured the worker that everything was just fine. Nadine's complaints were dismissed.

The next morning, while looking through a calendar, Pat told Nadine that she thought Sheri's baby would be born close to February 28, the day that would have been the birthday of Shannon Marie, the fetus Pat had lost, years earlier at the age of fifteen. Pat became intensely focused on how closely Sheri's predicament resembled her own experience at a younger age. The sense that Sheri was heading down a familiar, well-trodden path made Pat feel much more validated than she would have felt if Sheri had rejected her lifestyle. The line that separated Pat's identity from Sheri's was blurred so that one bled into the other. At a certain point, Pat's image of her daughter became a self-fulfilling prophecy.

"I kinda wasn't surprised when Sheri told me that she was pregnant," Pat finally admitted. "I kinda thought that that would happen, 'cause I was a teen mom.' "

Although Pat was pleased about the news that she was going to be a grandmother, Jon had mixed feelings about Sheri's pregnancy and his becoming a teen father. Still a junior in high school, Jon was an extremely laid-back, quiet fellow with modest ambitions. A slacker when it came to schoolwork, Jon's favorite pastime was shooting hoops and hanging out with his friends. Several nights a week he worked in the kitchen of a local restaurant. Enmeshed in his life as a regular teenager, Jon was afraid to even contemplate shouldering the responsibility of caring for a child and providing for a family. From the outset, Sheri was honest, open, and direct about her condition.

"I told Jon right away, as soon as I found out. I said, 'Jon, I'm pregnant.'

"He started crying. He hugged me. He said, 'Everything will be fine. I'll be there for you, Sheri. We're gonna raise this baby together.' "

Throughout Sheri's pregnancy, Jon remained at Pittsfield High School. His day-to-day life remained much the same as it had been before, but Sheri's life was turned upside down. When she transferred into the Teen Parent Program, many of her so-called friends from her old school stopped calling her up to see if she wanted to hang out. She got the impression that they had written her off, assuming that she wanted to be left alone to deal with the pregnancy in complete privacy.

Nothing could have been further from the truth. Sheri longed for the support of her friends, more so than ever, but most of them were self-absorbed and busy with their own lives. It seemed Sheri had gone from being popular to being forgotten overnight.

Soon after entering her second trimester, Sheri suffered from severe abdominal pain. She was rushed to the emergency room, where the doctors diagnosed her with acute appendicitis and announced that they had to remove her appendix immediately. Before she went under the knife, she was warned that there was a chance that she could lose the baby. Terrified, she went into surgery. The operation went smoothly and Sheri didn't have a miscarriage. However, her problems were far from over. While she was recovering from the surgery, her phone rang. It was Jon.

"Sheri, I think we should just be friends," he said. When Sheri asked why, he replied, "Because I don't want to be with you. I'll take care of my baby, I'll take on that responsibility—but I don't want to be with you."

Sheri, now five months pregnant, was totally crushed. But worse was to follow when she discovered that Jon was spreading rumors about her. He accused Sheri of cheating on him and convinced his parents that he wasn't the father of her unborn baby. When Sheri invited Jon and his family to the baby shower, they refused to go. They said they had no business there because the baby wasn't Jon's.

Sheri was sure both that the baby was Jon's and that he knew that abandoning his pregnant girlfriend for selfish reasons would make him look like a bad guy. Thus he had come up with a convenient lie that allowed him to turn the tables and blame Sheri for wrongdoing while at the same time exonerating himself. She was devastated that someone she had loved was capable of hurting her so deeply and so dishonestly with no regard for her reputation or dignity. Jon stopped taking her calls.

"When Jon broke up with me, it was like the world was on my

shoulders," Sheri recalled. "I had to deal with it. I cried all the time. I never heard from him. . . ."

Jon's lack of communication and his denial of their relationship was particularly heartbreaking to Sheri because it created a scenario that replicated her father's abandonment of her at the age of three, when he disappeared without warning, offering no explanation.

The closer Sheri got to giving birth, the more desperate she became for Jon to acknowledge paternity. When Jon refused to even discuss the issue, Sheri cried for hours at the thought of her baby growing up as she herself had, without a biological father. Sheri suffered severe depression but emerged from it determined to do everything in her power to reverse the circumstances.

"When I was eight months pregnant, I called Jon and said, 'We have to work things out. We have to be a family.' "

Jon was unresponsive. Sheri kept calling him, emphasizing how important it was for them to get back together, if only for the sake of the child. Jon would just listen without saying much. Then he would say he had to go. What little communication they had was always on his terms.

When Sheri went into labor, she called Jon, who finally broke down and cried. Realizing that his false accusations would soon be exposed, he raced over to the hospital, arriving just in time to see Sheri give birth to a baby girl. Sheri named her daughter Leeah. She was not surprised to see that the newborn looked exactly like Jon. A paternity test showed that Jon was definitely the baby's father.

At Jon's suggestion, they went for counseling, where Sheri made it clear that despite how badly Jon had treated her when she was pregnant, she was willing to bury her anger. She was prepared to make any sacrifice necessary to keep him involved in her daughter's life.

"As a child, I would wake up every day and know that my real dad was not there or around," she said. "I don't want Leeah to feel the same way that I felt. I want her to wake up and be able to be happy and know that both parents are there for her."

Although Sheri and Jon got back together after the baby was born, they decided not to live together. Jon continued living with his parents, and Sheri remained living with her mother, her stepfather, and Nadine. Jon visited Sheri and the baby regularly and tried to make amends. Sheri was thrilled. They began the slow process of trying to repair their fractured relationship.

"Jon apologizes every day for what he did to me when I was

pregnant and for how he hurt me," Sheri reported. "I mean, he looks at the baby every day, and he even apologizes to her. It's so funny, but he does. He's a great dad. He's the best dad. I couldn't ask for a better dad for Leeah."

After Leeah's birth, Sheri quickly returned to the Teen Parent Program, desperate for companionship, mentorship, advice, and some familiar faces. When Leeah was a few months old, Sheri confided in Jon about how cut off she was feeling from the world and began an effort to get back into the loop with some of her old friends. Together, Sheri and Jon made a pact to keep doing most of the things that teenagers without babies did. Sheri was ecstatic when Jon asked her to the prom. She rushed to the mall and purchased an elegant black gown.

On the afternoon of the prom, Sheri went to the hairdresser and had her hair styled in a chignon, studded with baby's breath held in place by bobby pins. After carefully applying her makeup, Sheri asked her mother for help zipping up the sexy tight-fitting dress, which flattered every inch of her slender frame. A wistful look crossed Pat's face as she watched her daughter posing in front of the mirror, studying her reflection and examining how the dress looked from every possible angle.

"I didn't get to go to my prom," she sighed. "I was home with the kids and married." Pat tried to smile but her eyes filled with tears, which she quickly brushed away, not wanting to ruin Sheri's big night.

Out on the back deck, Sheri paced back and forth nervously as she waited for Jon to come pick her up. She was unhappy with how her hair looked, but it was too late to do anything about it other than worry. Her mother and stepfather came out to check on her.

"Do I look okay?" Sheri asked them, trembling with insecurity.

"You look like a movie star," her stepfather reassured her. "Can you walk like one?"

"No."

"Can you act like one?" Pat asked.

"Probably not," Sheri murmured sheepishly.

"Well, have fun," Sheri's stepfather said, grinning from ear to ear. Sheri grimaced and squirmed as he took her in his arms and gave her an affectionate hug and kissed her good-bye as Pat watched, a few feet away, leaning against the railing of the back porch, smoking a cigarette.

Nadine came out to the deck to let Sheri know that Jon had arrived. The family walked around to the front of the house, and everyone watched as Jon presented Sheri with her corsage. Pat proceeded to take pictures of the beautifully dressed young couple and their daughter. Sheri handed Leeah to her mother and got into Jon's car. Nadine and Steve wished the couple well and went inside. Pat remained on the sidewalk, holding the baby, following the car with her eyes until it disappeared around the corner. Suddenly the street seemed quiet and very empty. Pat carried the baby back into the small wood cabin. The screen door slammed shut. Inside, Pat finally let out the tears she had struggled all afternoon to contain.

The prom was without question *the* social event of the year for the entire town of Pittsfield. Every year families, friends, and teachers lined up outside the entrance of the building where the prom was held, creating a human corridor that stretched across the entire length of the huge parking lot. Flashbulbs popped relentlessly as Sheri, Jon, and their peers paraded down the red carpet, the emphasis on looking the part of the perfect couple. The onlookers acted out the role of the paparazzi, making sure that these teenagers had their fifteen minutes of fame, or at least the illusion of it.

In imitation of the Hollywood celebrities they saw on TV and in magazines, the boys wore tuxedos and sunglasses and the girls wore gowns that were as tight, skimpy, and glamorous as possible. The Goth kids were the exception: white-faced, heavily made-up, garbed in black from head to toe, and carrying the occasional riding crop, this striking group looked ready to party with vampires.

For a few hours Sheri and Jon were able to lose themselves in the myth of carefree adolescent romance. On the dance floor, Sheri and Jon's physical contact appeared inhibited, stiff, and somewhat reserved. This was most apparent during the slow dances. Sheri later acknowledged this discomfort and attributed it to their need for time to slowly rebuild the trust in their relationship.

"We have a little bit of trust now, but it's not like it was in the beginning, when we had all the trust in the world. Our trust will come back, it just takes time, that's all."

As Sheri voiced these thoughts, she sounded more like a jaded forty-year-old than a romantic teenager. In fact, Sheri was somewhere in between these two extremes: less optimistic than she should have been at her young age but unusually and precociously pragmatic and realistic about the need for compromise, particularly when it came to maintaining her relationship with Jon. Sheri understood the stark difference between her dreams and the reality of having to settle for less in order to keep her baby's father involved in her life.

As Sheri and Jon left the prom early, music spilled into the night. Couples stood outside, leaning against the railing of the ramp, smoking, making out, and lingering in the cool breeze before returning to the crush of the dance floor. Drivers sat in stretch limos talking among themselves in the parking lot. As Sheri and Jon walked toward Jon's car, one of their friends yelled, "Sheri, Jon, hey! Where are you guys going? To a motel?"

Sheri shook her head and kept walking.

A few weeks after the prom, Sheri and Jon brought Leeah to their high school graduation ceremony. Leeah stood out in Sheri's arms, her pink hat and matching pink outfit, a stark contrast to the purple and white gowns worn by graduating seniors. Prior to the ceremony, many of Sheri's old friends gathered around the couple to admire the baby for the first time. One girl looked at Leeah and then at Jon, and then back at Leeah, comparing the baby's features with those of her father.

"Oh my God!" she squealed. "She looks *just* like him!"

Sheri nodded and exchanged a knowing look with Jon. Music began to play. The seniors lined up in single file. Sheri followed her fellow students into the auditorium and took her seat next to Jon. When her name was called, she marched onto the stage and received her diploma and a white rose from the mayor of Pittsfield. As Sheri returned to her seat, she looked around the theater filled with hundreds of students and their families. Her eyes were shining.

"I'm so proud I did it," Sheri said. "Without the Teen Parent Program, I never would have gotten this far."

"We never had a Parent Teen Program," retorted Pat. "So there was no going back to school for me."

Right after graduation, Pat made it very clear that she no longer wanted Sheri and the baby living under her roof.

"There was a lot . . . a lot of stress in the family," Pat explained. "I was working a tremendous amount of hours, basically taking care of the whole household, and that gave me awful anxiety. I couldn't eat. I lost an awful lot of weight and became very ill through the whole ordeal. Especially when it was prom time. I was overwhelmed. I think I was overwhelmed with the whole situation.

"It's not that I didn't want Leeah in my house, or that I didn't love Leeah, or that I wasn't happy about her being born . . . it was just, with the stress and everything—I got ill—and the fighting between my husband and myself was just ridiculous. I felt it would be better if Sheri got her own place with Leeah so that she could be more relaxed, so that she wouldn't have to hear us fighting all the time. I felt it wasn't healthy for a baby to be around so much anxiety."

After months of witnessing the decline of her mother's mental and physical health, as well as the constant drug-related traffic within the house, Sheri was eager to find her own apartment—a small, quiet place where she and Leeah could live in peace. She found a two-bedroom duplex apartment in the same low-income housing project on April Lane where Amy and Bernard and her best friend, Shayla, lived. When Sheri packed her bags and said good-bye to her family, fifteen-year-old Nadine had to face Pat and her stepfather alone. Before long, she was back in foster care.

"The foster home I was sent to was really bad," she said. "I couldn't use the phone. I couldn't watch TV. I felt like I was behind bars all day, every day. I was there for about a month. Then I went back home, and it was like a repeat of my life, you know what I mean? Going in and out, and back and forth for the same reasons—but they still let me go back home, which is what I don't understand."

By then, Nadine knew the drill as well as she knew the alphabet. When things went terribly wrong at home, she could complain to the counselor at school, who would promptly issue a report to the Department of Social Services, causing social workers to confront her mother, who would inevitably claim her daughter was lying, at which point either they would dismiss the case and leave Nadine to her own devices or they would attempt to temporarily remove her from the home and place her in a foster home where she didn't feel comfortable. Nobody took the time to get to know her well enough to make an appropriate foster care placement. She was passed from counseling to DSS to foster care like a baton changing hands in a relay race. There was no continuity or permanent support. Sometimes Nadine would run away and stay with a friend or neighbor, but she never got very far; inevitably, the cycle would end up where it started—at Pat's house. Shortly before her sixteenth birthday, Nadine dropped out of school—this time for good.

"School just wasn't working out for me," said Nadine. "I wasn't getting up. I wasn't going to bed at the right hours. It just got real tough."

Nadine would visit Sheri at her apartment on April Lane. Sheri was grateful to see her sister's familiar face, but as she listened to Nadine's tale of woe, she felt immensely relieved to be out of her mother's house once and for all. Nevertheless, living all alone with the baby without any help whatsoever was proving to be an intensely lonely, isolating experience. The April Lane housing project was located several miles away from town and the nearest shopping mall, so there was really no place for Sheri to go without a car, other than the swing set in the communal yard behind her apartment and the mailbox in the parking lot.

"I didn't have no car or no day care or no baby-sitter," Sheri explained. "I wanted to go back to work, but I really couldn't."

For the first year of Leeah's life, Sheri relied on the monthly $485 welfare check to help pay the rent. Rent alone was $418 per month. The rest of the money went toward food, clothing, diapers, toys, and other supplies for the baby.

Jon received a promotion and became a cook at the restaurant where he had worked steadily for several years. He frequently visited Sheri and Leeah but continued living at his mother's house. Sheri accepted this arrangement with Jon but found it difficult to be alone in a room for hours on end with no one to talk to but her baby. Frustrated, bored, and craving human companionship, Sheri sank into a state of gloomy depression. She registered for an educational program in accounting but dropped out after just two weeks because she wasn't interested in the subject.

When winter came with its short days and slivers of sunlight collapsing into darkness undercut by freezing cold, Sheri spent day after day inside her apartment with the baby. She began to go stir-crazy. At times when Leeah would cry, it was a struggle for Sheri to stay calm, but she soon realized that if she lost her temper or burst into tears herself, it only made Leeah more upset.

Sheri became anxious as her "free" time on welfare started to run out. She knew she had to find a job or enroll in school or a vocational training program but she didn't want to rely on the welfare-to-work transportation service. Sheri wanted to be able to come and go whenever she pleased and she wanted privacy and flexibility in case there was an emergency with her daughter, but she simply couldn't afford to buy a car.

When Sheri's elder brother received a settlement from an insurance claim he had made three years earlier after being injured in a car accident, the money was enough to buy three used cars: one for himself, one for Pat, and one for Sheri. Having a car changed Sheri's life. With the help of her aunt, she immediately got a job in housekeeping at a small bed-and-breakfast, a twenty-minute drive from her April Lane apartment.

As soon as Sheri started working during the day, Jon began to share the responsibility of taking care of Leeah. Because he worked the night shift at the restaurant, he was free during the day while Sheri was at work. Their schedules complemented each other, and as a result, both parents were able to spend large chunks of time with their daughter. This new arrangement brought Sheri and Jon closer. Jon started staying at Sheri's place several nights a week. They began talking about living together full-time.

Pat insisted that her daughter's life was a dream compared with what she had to go through. "When I was on welfare, it was harder for me," she said, raising her eyebrows so that the lines in her forehead became more pronounced. "I had three kids. I had no transportation. I had no education at all. It was very difficult for me to find day care or employment to support three children. We were living in foundations and places nowhere near as nice as where Sheri lives. So, the difference between me and Sheri is . . . I don't know . . . she's just so far advanced from where I was at her age."

Though Sheri's life may have been somewhat easier than her mother's, it was by no means easy.

"Leeah wakes me and Jon up between eight and nine in the morning," Sheri said, describing a typical day. "We go downstairs and change her diaper. I give her a glass of milk and some vitamins, and then I make her breakfast. While Leeah's eating her breakfast, she watches her cartoons and I clean the house and do the dishes. Then me and Leeah go upstairs and wake Jon up so I can get ready for work. While I'm in the shower, Jon watches Leeah. Then I go to work at the bed-and-breakfast in Lee where I work as a housekeeper.

"I get to work at about ten. I make sure all the laundry is done. I make sure the sheets and towels are folded up and put away. There are ten rooms. Like room one maybe gets a 'turnover.' That means the guests are checking out, so we have to do the whole room—change the bed, clean the bathroom, dust, and just make sure that it looks really nice. Then sometimes we have a 'change,' which means to just change the bed and put fresh towels in, 'cause the guests are staying another night. Or we have a 'make.' That means that we don't change the bed. We just give the guests fresh towels and make sure the room's nice and neat when they come back. It's an all right job. I make about ten dollars an hour. It's good pay. I don't really mind doing that kind of work right now because my pay is pretty good, but I know I don't want to do it forever.

"Jon pays thirty dollars for child support a week, but I only see fifty dollars a month because I'm on welfare, so they take the other half. My rent right now is four hundred and thirty-five dollars a month. I pay all my own utilities. It gets high, so I need to work every day.

"While I'm at work, Jon watches Leeah and takes her outside. Before lunch Leeah takes a nap for about an hour. When Leeah wakes up from her nap, Jon feeds her lunch. After lunch, Jon plays with Leeah until I get home. When I get home from work at two o'clock, Jon goes to work at the restaurant. Me and Leeah drop him off. Then we visit my mom, go for a ride, or get an ice cream.

"After that I come home, and most of the time Shayla comes over with her son, Jaiden, and we let the two kids play together. At five o'clock I make dinner for me and Leeah. While I'm making dinner, Leeah is running around the house. We sit down and eat. Me and Leeah always eat dinner together.

"After dinner, Leeah takes a bath. While she is in the bath, I sit in the bathroom with her until she's done. After her bath we come back downstairs and I clean up the after-dinner mess. After that me and Leeah sit down and watch TV and just relax. By that time she's tired and I'm beat.

"We usually watch movies on Lifetime. I love Lifetime. Leeah goes to bed between eight-thirty and nine. Then I come back downstairs and make myself a cup of tea and I just watch TV. After Leeah's asleep, I have nothing else to do. I watch the nine o'clock movie and go to bed at eleven, when the movie ends. Jon gets home around midnight."

Sheri's routine remained constant throughout the second year of Leeah's life. During this period, the biggest change in her life involved

Pat, who finally separated from her husband. Living on her own, Pat gained forty pounds and cut down on her chain-smoking.

"I'm much more relaxed now," Pat said. "Right now I'm doing an introduction to basic computers, learning the keyboard. I'm on the Internet, which is fun. I like the computer. It's interesting. I want an office job. I know it's gonna take me a little time, but I know I'll do it. I'll do it."

"My mom is doing really good for herself," remarked Sheri, who then admitted, "I never thought I would see this day. It makes me so happy to see my mom like this. I'm glad Leeah gets to see her like this, too."

In sharp contrast to Pat's round cheeks and new curves, Sheri's face was gaunt. Her arms and legs were like toothpicks and when she looked in the mirror, her hungry eyes and protruding bones reminded her of how her mother used to look. The resemblance wasn't just physical—the roles of mother and daughter had effectively been reversed.

While Sheri embraced her identity as a mother and assumed the adult responsibilities that such a role entailed, Pat attempted to resume her life where she had left off at age seventeen, when she first got pregnant. Pat saw an office job as a step up from the more menial labor she had done in the past. Initially, she was excited to have the chance to obtain the skills she needed to be considered for this type of work.

Nearing forty, Pat had to start at the bottom rung. Her skill level, even after weeks of computer training, was lower than that of many teenagers straight out of high school. Pat soon realized that in the job market, even for entry-level positions, she would have to compete against some kids and young adults who had grown up in the Internet age, for whom computers were second nature. Despite these harsh realities, Pat swallowed her pride and continued her classes. After years of what she perceived to be self-sacrifice, she was content finally to be able to do something for herself.

Sheri, on the other hand, was leading a completely selfless existence. Her life was structured around Jon and her daughter, yet she dared dream of a future that was very different from her mother's life. In Sheri's fantasy, enduring love, strong family values, and financial stability were central themes.

"What would make me happiest is me and Jon getting married, hopefully soon," Sheri said. "I've asked him if he wants to get married

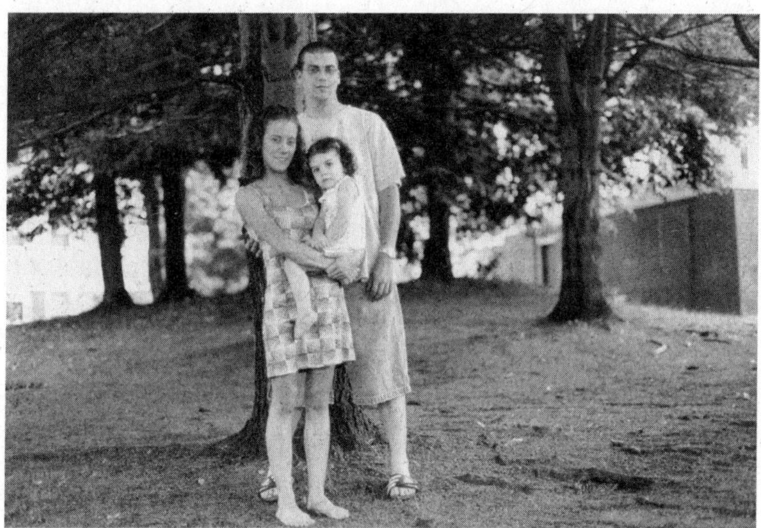

and he said yes, but we know we can't get married right now. We both want a big wedding, we want a lot of people there, and we can't afford it. We figure if we save up, in about four years we can have a nice big wedding.

"I would love to grow old with Jon. I would love to buy a new car, buy a house, and be able to give Leeah whatever she needs and more. Within a couple of years, I would love to have another baby, when we can afford it, when we don't need welfare.

"Jon told me he wants to be with me forever. I feel the same way about him. He and Leeah are my life."

Pat had a less romantic outlook when it came to predicting what lay ahead for Sheri. "I think that Sheri's future is gonna be going back to cosmetology and being a hairdresser," she said. "I think that's really what her dream is. As a matter of fact, we talked about it the other day. She gave me a haircut. She definitely wants to get back in the profession. I can see Sheri getting her cosmetology license and staying in town."

Sheri agreed that she would probably remain in Pittsfield, but she definitely did not see herself becoming a hairdresser. Her close friend, Shayla, had completed the full-year cosmetology course required for entry-level certification as a hairdresser, but as Sheri pointed out, Shayla had already been fired from Hair Express and wasn't able to find another opening in a hair salon. A few months later, when Shayla's new job at a chain store didn't work out, she asked Sheri for help getting a housekeeping job. For a while, the two friends cleaned rooms together at the same bed-and-breakfast. Judging from Shayla's experience, Sheri didn't see the point in wasting a year of hard work on a cosmetology course if when all was said and done, she was likely to end up right back where she started, cleaning rooms.

Sheri's goal was to get off welfare. She was prepared to do what she had to in order to get by. She saw her job not as a way of finding fulfillment, satisfaction, and happiness, but as a necessary step she had to take in order to provide the essentials for herself and her daughter. Her first priority was to make sure that Leeah was given the opportunities that she had missed out on. Sheri was thrilled when Jon's father gave Leeah an old computer. Eager to know enough to at least teach Leeah something about computers, and hopefully to get a better job, Sheri enrolled in a computer course at the local Mildred Elly Business School. She learned how to enter data using the program Excel.

In order to make time for school, Sheri had to adjust her hours at the bed-and-breakfast, where she had worked steadily for two years. Without warning, her boss replaced her with "a girl who was more available." Sheri was disappointed, but she couldn't afford to be picky. She immediately found a new job cleaning rooms at a sprawling hotel in Lee, which was more than four times the size of where she used to work. Her new position required her to clean rooms for forty hours each week. Working on weekends and holidays was mandatory. Sheri was forced to withdraw from her computer class mid-session.

"I know I should be in school," she explained, "but I'm not, because I need to work."

At this hotel, Sheri was one of many employees. She felt anonymous, interchangeable, and unappreciated. She had one thirty-minute lunch break in the middle of her eight-hour workday. The housekeeping staff wasn't invited to eat food prepared in the hotel kitchen, and there was no staff dining room where prepared meals were available. Half an hour was barely enough time for Sheri to drive into town, get something to eat, and drive back, so usually she brought food from home, a sandwich wrapped in tinfoil or a container of cold ravioli.

Sheri saved more than a thousand dollars. The more money she made, the closer she came to being able to realize her dreams for herself, Jon, and Leeah. Soon after Leeah's third birthday, Sheri's welfare counselor told her that she made too much money to continue on welfare. Sheri regarded her independence from the system as a marker of success and a rite of passage. She considered getting off welfare to be her biggest achievement in her adult life.

Armed with new confidence and strengthened self-esteem, Sheri set out to find a job that she would enjoy more than being a housekeeper. She no longer wanted to work weekends and holidays, because day cares were closed then and it was much more difficult and expensive to find baby-sitters who were available. Sheri longed for a regular nine-to-five job in a stimulating environment where she would have a chance to meet some new, interesting people.

In response to an ad in the newspaper, Sheri dropped off her résumé at a local bank. When she called a week later to schedule an interview, her call was not returned. She phoned the bank several times to inquire about the status of her job application but never received any response.

Cleaning rooms forty hours a week was physically exhausting, and Sheri was dangerously thin. She thought about trying to get a job as a waitress at the end of the summer when all the college kids who worked in the fancier restaurants went back to school. When September approached, Sheri changed her mind, deciding that she didn't want to commute to the neighboring towns where those upscale restaurants were located. She preferred to be closer to her daughter and wanted to work weekdays, as opposed to nights and weekends.

Sheri asked for a job at Leeah's day care. During her interview with the woman who ran the center, she admitted that she didn't have any formal credentials but stressed that she had plenty of experience raising her own daughter. To her surprise, Sheri was given a job taking care of infants in the day care's nursery. She was delighted. The pay was a bit less than it had been at her previous job, but she got benefits and the hours were longer and more consistent.

Sheri was thrilled to be working in the same building where her daughter spent her days, right down the hall in the toddlers' room. At her previous jobs, Sheri had always been preoccupied and concerned about whether or not Leeah was safe and being cared for properly. It was extremely comforting to be able to check up on Leeah anytime she wanted.

This job at Leeah's day care improved Sheri's life dramatically. The hours were decent, her coworkers respected her and treated her like a human being, she had weekends and holidays off, and she could see her daughter as often as she liked.

"I finally have a life," said Sheri, her voice brimming with pride.

Though Sheri maintained her momentum, her mother's energy waned. Her positive attitude toward finding a new job that "had something to do with computers" was short-lived. Frustrated with her lack of progress and no longer wanting to put in the effort, Pat quit school and remained unemployed. She took up with a new boyfriend and succumbed to her old addictions.

Nadine was sixteen and still living at home after another failed foster care placement. Her stepfather was finally out of the picture, but now she had to contend with her mother's new boyfriend, who had a criminal record and a history of drug abuse.

"My mom was in the other room, drunk, passed out on the floor," Nadine recalled. "I was in my room sleeping, and her boyfriend came into my room and wound up leaving me a hickey. When I felt him, I ran into my mom's room and I woke her up."

"You better get out of my house," Pat drawled in a daze.

Nadine stared at her mother, incredulous.

"Get out now!" hollered Pat. "Go find your own boyfriend!"

"I wound up having to leave there at four o'clock in the morning. I went to a neighbor's house up the street and slept there. The next day my mom wound up blaming it on me. Telling me I just wanted him, and that ain't even true. I don't need to go out with her boyfriends. I can find my own."

Nadine found a tough white guy named Brad.

"Brad was twenty-five when I met him. I was sixteen, just turning seventeen. We met down by Pontoosuc Lake. We started hanging out. He had his own apartment, so I started staying with him. He seemed really nice. I was going through a lot with my mom, and he helped me, he was really there for me. I could talk to him about anything, and he'd just sit down and listen to me. I felt like he was the only person I had at that time."

Brad had already fathered a son with another teenage girl. He made quick cash dealing drugs, and when he wasn't dealing, he was using. His vicious rottweiler dog accompanied him wherever he went. On command, the dog was trained to inflict maximum damage on his victims. Most people knew better than to mess with Brad.

"About five months into our relationship, Brad just snapped," Nadine recalled. "He beat me every day. I got so scared that sometimes I wouldn't even get out of bed. I was too scared to leave.

"Brad's rottweiler got put to sleep for tearing skin off legs of cops in Lenox, but then he got another mean dog. One day when I ran out the front door, Brad pointed to me and said, 'Get her!' The dog went wild. I got away, but he ate the curtains.

"I was always puking. I was always sick. I was always stressing. I didn't know if I was gonna live."

Following one of Brad's beatings, a friend of Nadine's called the cops. They came and picked up Nadine and dropped her off at her mother's house. Nadine limped in to her mom's living room, wearing sunglasses and a baggy sweatshirt. Sheri and Leeah had stopped by for a visit. They were outside on the back porch with Pat. Nadine could hear them talking, but depressed and exhausted, she didn't feel like joining them. Without telling anybody that she was home, Nadine slumped over on a faded beige sofa, unable to think of anything outside of her own pain. As she recalled, "Leeah came in and said, 'Take those sunglasses off, Aunt Nadine.' I said no, and she took them off me and I had two black eyes. She started crying—she didn't know what it was. She was shocked. I told her it was makeup. She kept crying and she said, 'Aunt Nadine, please, go wash your face, 'cause it's everywhere.'

"I had bruises all over my arms. That's why I had a sweatshirt on. My mom came in and said, 'Let me see, because I know you have more bruises than that.' I was bruised from my eyes to my legs. That's when my mom and sister found out what Brad was doing to me."

A week later, Nadine returned to Brad and suffered more abuse. He continued to violently assault her and eventually he was arrested and sent to jail. By the time Brad went behind bars, Nadine knew that she was pregnant with his baby. She tried to figure out exactly when the baby had been conceived.

"I was on the Pill and I missed three days and that's how I wound up getting pregnant. Brad flushed my pills down the toilet, but I thought I misplaced them. But when we broke up, he wound up telling me, 'I flushed your pills. . . . I cut the condom, and I hope you're pregnant.' I guess he thought if he got me pregnant, I'd stay," she murmured.

The doctor asked Nadine if she would consider having an abortion, in light of the horrible circumstances and the violent beatings she had endured during the first month of pregnancy. Nadine's mind filled with thoughts of her mother and her unborn sister. Instead of distancing herself and viewing her mother in a critical light, Nadine identified with her and adopted her views on abortion.

She looked the doctor in the eye and said, "I'm having the baby."

Soon after Brad's arrest, Colleen's ex-boyfriend, Ryan, was partying with Pat and her friends. He went into the kitchen for a drink and

saw a photograph of Nadine adorning a magnet stuck to Pat's refrigerator.

"Your daughter is so pretty," he said. "When can I meet her?"

Pat explained that Nadine had been in a violent relationship for months and had suffered terrible abuse. Ryan decided to wait at Pat's house until Nadine came home. He told Pat that he already had a disabled son with Colleen, a teen mother who had attended the Teen Parent Program with Sheri. He didn't tell Pat that his relationship with Colleen had collapsed when she could no longer tolerate his heroin binges and violent abuse. After a stint in jail and a sojourn in Florida to avoid a warrant for his arrest, Ryan was back in Pittsfield, eager to find a new girlfriend who would meet his needs. He stayed in Pat's living room for several days, until Nadine, who had been staying at a friend's house, finally showed up.

Nadine and Ryan formed an intense, obsessive, codependent relationship. Most people mistakenly assumed that the baby Nadine was carrying was Ryan's. As Nadine's pregnancy progressed, she witnessed her mother's deterioration.

"My mom was abusing her psych meds and drinking while she was on them, so she wound up going into seizures. She'd start flopping everywhere and foaming. . . . Her tongue was going back in her throat. It got to the point where we couldn't stop it and had to call an ambulance."

Nadine went into early labor during her first trimester, and again when she was six months pregnant. Both times she was rushed to the hospital, where they gave her medication to stop the contractions. Nadine kept quiet about her traumatic home situation and did not tell her doctor about the crippling depression that was slowing down her thinking and enhancing her fear that her life was hopeless.

Nadine spent most of her last trimester hanging out with Ryan, who was still heavily involved with drugs. She worried constantly about the fact that soon after her baby was born, Brad would be out of jail. Extremely troubled and upset throughout her pregnancy, Nadine made a big mistake. Toward the end of her pregnancy, she did cocaine. The stimulant immediately put her into labor.

"At the hospital I hemorrhaged in labor and they thought something was weird because I hemorrhaged really bad. Real bad. Blood clots the size of watermelons were coming outta me. They almost had to put more blood into me. And my water was a funny color. It was a brownish green because the baby pooped inside me because the drugs got him worked up. They knew something was weird about that."

Nadine gave birth and named her son Dylan. The hospital immediately contacted the Department of Social Services. As the umbilical cord was cut, Nadine felt dread rather than relief. She feared that she wouldn't be allowed to keep her baby.

Sheri was in the delivery room when her nephew was born. She watched helplessly in horror as the doctors discovered drugs in his system. Her sister was forbidden to leave the hospital. The doctors kept a close watch over the baby to make sure that he had adequate medical support as he went through the difficult symptoms associated with cocaine withdrawal. Nadine was told that her baby would have to be placed in foster care until she could prove to DSS that she was fit to be a mother.

"That's when I flipped out," recalled Nadine. "I threw things. I broke the phone. I told them my baby wasn't going home with them. They told me when I find a good environment for my son—then I'll get him back. The cocaine did show up in his system, so I was screwed."

The Department of Social Services took custody of the baby when he was one day old. It was devastating for the entire family. Sheri considered trying to get permission to have the baby and her sister live with her but realized that with work and her own daughter, it would just be too much for her. Sheri and Nadine were allowed to visit Dylan. They were impressed by how big and grand the baby's foster home was compared with where they lived, and were relieved that the baby was being well looked after.

"I became good friends with my son's foster parent," Nadine said. "Really good friends. She's the one who got me through all of this. If it wasn't for her, I don't know what I would've done. When we went to court, I told the judge the truth—I didn't lie. I told them that I hated my lifestyle . . . hated it. I said that I didn't want my son having the life or the environment that we had when we were younger. I told the judge how I never wanted my life like that, and how I always, always wanted it to change."

Nadine's pleas for a second chance were ultimately successful. After nearly two months, it was decided that Nadine would be allowed to have her son back, but only if she moved to Redfield House, a high-security subsidized housing project for single mothers and their children. This residence had its own nursery, day care, and playground on site, as well as a trained professional staff on hand to advise the young women on issues related to health care, safety, welfare, and childrearing issues. Many residents were coregistered at the Teen

Parent Program, which was located within walking distance from Redfield House. In order to get her son back, Nadine had to agree to frequent randomly administered drug tests.

Every area of Nadine's life was tightly supervised by the Department of Social Services. She had to agree to begin treatment with a psychiatrist, who put her on Zoloft for her depression. She had to attend counseling regularly. Social workers and investigators routinely visited the apartment to check up on her and the baby. There was tight security at the front door of Redfield House. The guard asked Nadine for a photograph of Brad. He was out of jail, and just in case he happened to show up, the guard wanted to know what he looked like so that he could be prepared. All Nadine's visitors had to be approved by the social worker in charge of her case and were closely monitored.

"My mom can see my son," said Nadine, "but it has to be visitation rights with DSS at the Y. She has to get drug-screened and she told me she don't think she's gonna be able to see him because she knows she can't pass 'em. That hurts me—knowing that she ain't there for me when I need her because the drugs are more important."

Nadine paused. Her baby was crying. She rocked him gently and tried to soothe him.

"I've been involved with DSS since I was born," she said. "At first I was really mad that I had to work with them when I had my son, but now it's not bad with them being in my life. They help you a lot. They're really getting me on the right road I need to be on with my son."

After all Nadine's terrible experiences as a child with counselors

who couldn't seem to get her out of the room fast enough, she was understandably wary about trusting a new counselor. Like Sheri, Nadine had learned from experience that remaining silent was much safer than voicing the truth. She struggled to come to terms with her fears about talking about her problems.

"Last time I got involved with counseling, I wound up getting taken away from my ma," she said. "So now I know what to say and what not to say. But my son—I don't want him to get taken away if I say the wrong thing."

Nadine was assigned to a counselor who seemed legitimately concerned and dedicated to helping her. As Nadine realized that this counselor might actually stick around for a while instead of passing her on to someone else, she began to look forward to her weekly sessions.

"My counselor—she just sits there and I tell her everything so I don't blow up. I tell her what bothers me . . . just stupid shit like that. She's, like, in her late thirties or early forties. She just talks to me and tries to help me through my problems.

"They want me to take Zoloft and keep going on it until I prove better with my depression, because I cry a lot and I stress out a lot. They referred me to go see a—I can't say it . . ." Nadine fumbled with the syllables. "A psy-chi-a-trist. Because of my past, when I was younger and the fact that I did try cocaine, they're gonna work with me to get off it and make sure I don't go back."

As Pat deteriorated even further, Sheri and Nadine's estranged biological father, Greg, reappeared in Pittsfield and did what he could to help both girls, in an effort to make up for all the lost years.

"Since I had my son and he got taken away from me, my real

dad, Greg, he's been really helping me out a lot, because I'm not getting any income. Nothing," said Nadine. "So my dad's been supplying me with baby diapers and wipes. He brings me to all my appointments when it's cold and I can't walk. He's there. He's the only one I really talk to now besides my sister."

It was agonizing for Sheri and Nadine to see their mother self-destructing. At times, Sheri cut off all but the most basic, essential communication. The relationship became too emotionally taxing, and Sheri needed to stay strong for her own daughter. She had chosen a drug-free life for herself and didn't want Leeah exposed to her grandmother's world. Like Sheri, Nadine also felt that in order to protect herself and her son, it was necessary to disengage emotionally from the strong ties that bound her to her mother.

"I can't deal with my mom no more," said Nadine. "I just can't watch it. I can't do it no more. I don't think she's gonna make it. Nope. My mom is very, very sick. The doctors say that she's doing really bad. She has meningitis and she has pneumonia. Every other day she's puking blood. Sometimes she can't even get out of bed. And she's only forty-five years old. She's not even old. Her bones ache. They're killing her. She can't walk. She has very bad arthritis. Her body is just shutting down.

"I've been trying to help her for eighteen years now, and I know when she goes, I'm gonna . . . I'm gonna flip, really. But there's nothing I can do now. I have a baby of my own now. I just worry about him. My mom's forty-something years old. She should know better. I don't want her to go, but everybody goes sooner or later, and I think her time is almost here. Ain't nothing I can do about that."

Under all the stress of dealing with her mother and her sister's troubles, Sheri continued losing weight at an alarming rate. Her head began to look too big for her frail body. Referring to Sheri's arm, which was blocking the TV screen, Leeah, now three and a half and very talkative, leaned over and said, "Mommy, can you move your bone?"

Sheri wanted to gain weight. She drank special milkshakes that were supposed to help people put on weight, but worried about the cost of these drinks—six bucks for a pack of six. Eventually she stopped buying them. Sheri grew smaller and smaller.

The one part of her life that Sheri was content with was her relationship with Jon. She was extremely grateful that he was there for her and Leeah. He was her rock of stability, and besides her daughter, he was the one person who made her feel valued and appreciated. Sheri was saving up money and working hard to build a solid future with Jon. Her intact family was the center of all her hopes and dreams. She was excited about the possibility of getting married in the very near future.

One night while Sheri was home alone with Leeah, her phone rang. It was Jon on the line, calling from the restaurant where he worked.

He told Sheri he wasn't coming home. Ever.

"I'm not happy," he said.

The fact that Jon was unhappy was news to Sheri. When Jon

came by to pack up his things, he refused to discuss his abrupt decision to break off their seven-year relationship.

"I would respect Jon more if he would've came to me and sat down and said, 'Listen, Sheri, these are the things bothering me; if they don't change, I'm gonna have to leave.' I'd respect him more for talking it through instead of just getting up and walking out. Which is exactly what he did. It's funny, because the week before Jon left, he wanted to have another baby with me. We were even trying. And then a week later he leaves. When I call him and ask him to explain why he wasn't happy, he says, 'I don't want to talk about this right now.'

"See, I was Jon's first girlfriend and I think he wants to go see what's out there. I wish he would just tell me, but he can't. And the restaurant business does not help. He sees all these young people with no kids, no responsibility, going out every night, doing what they want, not answering to anybody, and I think that's what he wants right now.

"I did ask him, I said, 'Don't you want to come home to your family?'

"He said, 'I would love to come home to my family, but I can't.'

"That's all he says. . . . He don't explain why he can't. . . . So I've got to figure it out for myself. I just wish he would sit down and talk to me. You know . . . And just say . . . you know, Sheri, this is what I want, this is what I don't want. If he would just let me know. . . .

"I think Jon just wants me to hang on, so that if he does plan on coming back, I'll be there. I don't even want to go out and find another boyfriend and date—at least not right now. I still hope he's coming back. I mean, if it comes down to it and months down the road I definitely know he's not coming back, I'll go out—but not right now. Right now it's just me and Leeah. Hopefully Jon will come back soon because I'm not gonna sit around and wait forever. I'm not gonna be alone forever.

"If Jon were to come back right now, I wouldn't take him back right away. He'd have to go to counseling with me. He'd have to sit down and talk to me. He'd have to prove to me that he wants to be with me and Leeah.

"Right now I don't receive any child support. Jon said that his employers are taking it out of his checks, but I still have not received child-support checks. I don't know if he's lying, or what. I tried to call the child-support unit, but I can't get through to them. They have an 800 number, but you can't talk to a representative unless you punch in your PIN number and I don't have one. I guess I'll have to go to the courthouse.

"Since Jon moved out, he don't see Leeah very often, not nearly as much as I'd like him to see her. They had a really close relationship, but now it just seems like they're separating quick. I want their relationship to be close and I know Leeah does, too, but I think Jon's just pulling away from a lot of things and not thinking.

"Leeah's hurt that Jon just got up and left. You know, how do you explain to a three-year-old that Daddy's not gonna be here no more? It's hard. A couple of nights ago I walked out of the room and she called me back in and said, 'Mommy, you're not gonna leave, right?'

"I just lost it. My daughter shouldn't have to feel like that."

Nadine tried her best to be supportive of her elder sister. She wanted Sheri to get Jon out of her system so that she could move on with her life, but Sheri just couldn't let go. She started stalking Jon, and when she found him and his new girlfriend making out in a parking lot, she took her umbrella and scratched up their car, then dragged the girl out of the car by her hair and started punching her.

"Sheri's just so hurt, she don't know how to react to it," said Nadine. "This girl knew Jon had a family. The girl knew that he had a kid. She knew that they were together for seven years 'cause Sheri used to go to school with her. But I think that Sheri was Jon's first. And I think Jon just wants to experiment. He's still young. She's still young. Yes, they might have a kid together, but there's more men out there—she don't need to be chasing this one down."

Sheri finally convinced Jon to come to her apartment and talk things over. Once Jon was there, Sheri told him over and over again how much she and Leeah loved him and needed him. Reluctantly he agreed to move back in with Sheri and said he was willing to give their relationship another try. Sheri forced him to call his girlfriend and break up with her. Wanting to make sure that there were no misunderstandings, Sheri listened in on the phone as Jon told his girlfriend that their relationship was over and made it clear that he had decided to go back to his family.

Jon played house with Sheri. He read to Leeah, fed her, gave her baths, tucked her into bed at night, and sat with her until she fell asleep. For three straight days Sheri's apartment was a portrait of domestic bliss. Then Jon left and moved into his new girlfriend's apartment.

"Sheri's crushed," said Nadine. "She cries to me every night. Leeah's always talking about her dad to her mom, saying 'When's he coming home? Why ain't he home? I miss him!' She keeps thinking her daddy's coming home to pick her up, but he ain't."

Sheri broke down, immobilized by acute depression. She missed a week of work and kept Leeah at home with her. She lost her job at the day-care center, the one job she had loved so much.

Nadine wasn't able to stick to the program at Redfield House. She took the baby off the premises after hours and continued seeing her boyfriend, Ryan, who was eventually sent back to jail. DSS removed Dylan from Nadine's custody and put him into another foster home. This time around, his foster mother was interested in possibly adopting him. Nadine checked herself into rehab, determined to try again to reclaim custody of her son.

"I'm only eighteen and it's just been . . . it's just been too much," she said. "Drugs, alcohol, abuse; it's just been goin' down generation to generation. I wish I had been in a foster home my whole life." Nadine paused, full of emotion. A moment later she swore, "I'm gonna get my son back. I've got to get him back."

While Nadine was in rehab, Sheri got back on her feet. She got a job at Rent-A-Wreck. Sheri was bored stiff at this job. She had to sit in a tiny office all day. Business was slow. She was lucky if she leased three used cars in a day. After several weeks she quit.

Sheri found a new job at a shop at the mall. Finally she gave up on Jon and began dating one of his relatives, Ian, who had briefly lived with her best friend, Shayla. Times were tough, but Sheri remained steadfast in her commitment to steer clear of drugs.

"Believe it or not, I've never touched drugs," she said. "I don't see my life going that way, because I don't want my daughter to see the things I've seen or to live the life I've lived."

chapter seven

JESSICA

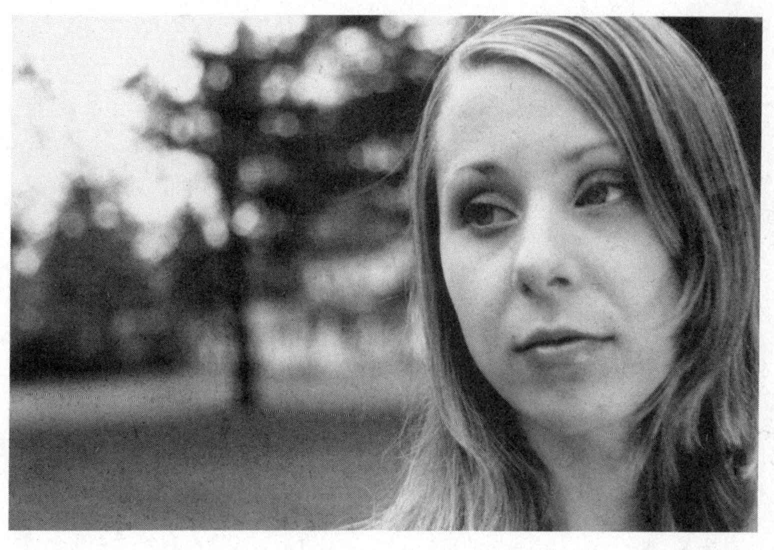

"I had so much going for me before I got pregnant. I was doing everything. I was doing great. I was getting really good grades. I was someone to look up to."

JESSICA DREADED THE LONG INTERSTATE DRIVE FROM Pittsfield to the drop zone. She much preferred spending weekends hanging out with her friends. Jessica begged her mother, Doris, and her stepfather, Bill, to let her stay home alone while they went skydiving.

Bill's mother lived in a small apartment at the front of their house. The old lady agreed to poke her head in every now and then to check up on Jessica. With this safeguard in place, Bill and Doris had no qualms about letting their fifteen-year-old spend weekends in Pittsfield while they went out of town. They trusted Jessica and thought she was exceptionally mature and reliable for her age.

Bill endearingly referred to Jessica by her childhood nickname, the Little Princess, because unlike most teenagers he and Doris knew, Jessica showed no outward signs of rebellion. The Jessica that Bill and Doris saw every day was charming and good-humored. She hung out with a crowd of respectable, well-behaved kids, took school seriously, got good grades, earned her own money at an after-school job, and didn't even have a boyfriend. She planned on going away to college and was smart enough to understand that a good education could be a key that opened many doors.

Although Jessica lived with her mother and stepfather, she remained extremely close to her biological father, Robert, who lived in an old mill in Pittsfield, where he worked as an artist and sign painter. Like Doris and Bill, Robert had high hopes for his beautiful daughter. Jessica longed to live up to his expectations.

Jessica's mother and father had married as teenagers. They had Jessica a year later and divorced when she was two years old. Robert remained in Pittsfield and saw Jessica a few days a week. He and the little girl developed a close bond. Jessica was his sunshine, the one bright light that made his life worth living.

When Jessica was seven, her father was sentenced to a year in jail on charges of marijuana possession. Robert didn't want to lose touch with Jessica and was adamant about having Doris bring her to visiting hours. While holed up in his cell, Robert spent a great deal of time drawing. He gave the pictures he made to his daughter as gifts. After each visit, Jessica took her father's artwork home and hung it on the wall by her bed. Whenever she missed him, looking at his pictures gave her tremendous comfort.

When Robert got out of jail, he found an old, abandoned, ramshackle school bus. He fixed it up and began living there. When Jessica went to see him, he took her on hikes and to the lake. He taught her to appreciate the beauty of nature and to have respect for all forms of life. Together they rescued injured dogs and scooped up birds with broken wings. During their frequent visits to the vet, they made every effort to save these suffering animals.

Jessica enjoyed the visits, but as she grew older she began to worry about her father's dramatic mood swings. She was troubled by the fact that he often seemed sad. Robert struggled against depression but refused to speak to Jessica about the violent abuse that had indelibly marred his childhood. He was determined that the trauma he had experienced as a child would not repeat itself. He longed to protect Jessica from the pain that he, his mother, and his eight siblings had endured. He was convinced that silence regarding that subject was the best way to shield his daughter from the agonizing truth.

From snatches of conversations that Jessica overheard throughout her childhood, she guessed that her father's secrets had something to do with her paternal grandparents, but for years their absence remained an unexplained gap in her life. One day when Jessica was ten years old, she saw her grandparents featured as fugitives on the television program *America's Most Wanted*. Jessica watched the show in the company of her mother and stepfather, who assumed that the disturbing content went way over their little girl's head and therefore did not discuss it with her. Although Jessica was indeed young and too scared to ask questions, she understood much more than Bill and Doris gave her credit for.

"The story was about how my grandfather used to sexually abuse my aunts and how he abused my uncles, and how my grandma didn't do anything about it," explained Jessica. "He and my grandma went running from the law and changed their names."

John Walsh, the host of *America's Most Wanted,* reported the story of how Jessica's grandmother and grandfather had slipped under the radar and evaded justice. Back when Jessica was a toddler, her two eldest aunts had finally summoned up the courage to break the silence that had enshrouded their family's tangled web of physical, sexual, and emotional abuse. At the time they pressed charges against their father, Jessica's aunts were young adults. They had moved out of the family home but were certain that their father was continuing to beat and rape their three younger sisters the same way he had for years beaten and raped them. Their mother had always known about the violent abuse and had also been subjected to it. Nevertheless, she allowed herself to continue being victimized and did nothing to protect her children from their father.

Longing to save their family members from more torture, Jessica's aunts finally reported the abuse. Their younger siblings were taken out of school and into safety by a social worker and were later placed in foster homes. Jessica's grandparents were arrested and put on trial.

Newspapers in Pittsfield and Springfield covered the case. Jessica's aunts went through the painful process of testifying in public against their own father. Then a day before the verdict was to be announced, Jessica's grandparents abruptly vanished without a trace. For more than ten long years, they lived hidden lives, under assumed names, while their sons and daughters were left to live in constant fear and suffering, without any closure or resolution.

With the help of one of Jessica's aunts, John Walsh began a thorough investigation, determined to bring this fugitive pedophile and his wife to justice. Between 1990 and 1992, *America's Most Wanted* aired three programs about the case. The first two broadcasts yielded no solid leads, but minutes after the third show aired, a woman from California called in and gave the operator a crucial tip: the couple they were looking for had left her house a few hours ago. The woman had cleaned her house and the man did odd jobs and had fixed her car. The caller told the operator that the couple lived on a boat. She gave the operator directions to where the boat was docked. An FBI agent was dispatched, and Jessica's grandparents were promptly arrested, extradited to Massachusetts, and sentenced.

John Walsh was outraged and disgusted by this case—so outraged and so disgusted that he ultimately included Jessica's grandparents among "America's Worst Criminals" in his book on true crime, *No Mercy*. In his book, Walsh reported that Jessica's grandfather "was charged with nine counts of incest and rape of a child . . . and given a sentence of thirty-six to fifty-four years in prison. He will be eligible for parole in the year 2016, when he is eighty-five years old—although with his list of crimes it's unlikely that he'll get out even then, if he lives that long." Jessica's grandmother "was charged with three counts of failure to provide care and protection. . . . She got two years."

The sentencing was a formal resolution, but the residual trauma lingered and affected family members in different ways. For some family members, there was ambivalence and guilt over the fate of Jessica's grandmother, a masochistic, brainwashed woman who had herself been viciously abused by her husband all through their marriage. Others felt little if any mercy for her and blamed her for allowing her own children to be abused for so many years. After Jessica's grandmother had served her two years and was released from prison, she moved to a town close to the prison where her husband was incarcerated. When John Walsh followed up on the case, he discovered a bizarre twist: Jessica's grandmother visited her husband in prison nearly every day and remained "totally devoted" to him.

Not long after Jessica's grandparents were apprehended, one of her aunts drank herself into a stupor and wandered deep into the woods on a bitterly cold night. Her body was found the next day in a creek. She had frozen to death. Some labeled the death an accident. Others suspected that, like the death of Jessica's uncle several years before (he had gotten on his motorcycle with no shoes or helmet on and had zoomed ahead at full speed straight into a Mack truck), the death of Jessica's aunt might very well have been a suicide.

Jessica was disturbed by the untimely deaths of these relatives. She felt shocked, uncomfortable, dirty, and ashamed of the crimes her grandparents had perpetrated. Yet she never discussed these feelings with anyone.

"This was supposed to be a family secret," Jessica murmured. "My dad really doesn't like to talk about it, because it hurts him inside. He just doesn't want to think about it. I never really wanted to know about it. I've never straight-out asked him, 'Why did Grandpa do that?' It scared me. I didn't want to know."

As Jessica was growing up, she felt tremendous pressure to right the wrongs of the past. She wanted to replace sadness with happiness and was desperate to please her father, her mother, and her stepfather. Eager to make her parents proud, she painstakingly cultivated and maintained her reputation as a model child. Yet just beneath the surface, Jessica hid her own mountain of secrets. In retrospect, her stepfather said, "Jessica was too perfect." He shook his head. "Way too perfect."

When her mother and stepfather were away, Jessica's house became known as the place to party. Jessica quickly got caught up in a fast crowd. Unbeknownst to her parents, she lost her virginity at age fourteen. By tenth grade, she had been in and out of four sexual relationships, driven not by love but by her craving for attention and validation.

Jessica found that she was attracted only to black men. Her friends didn't bother setting her up with white guys, because they knew she probably wouldn't be interested. Halfway through her junior year, a friend introduced Jessica to Dwayne, a high school dropout who wasn't part of their usual crowd. At nineteen, Dwayne was three years older and slicker and more street-smart than the guys Jessica had dated. He was known to be a drug dealer. Jessica didn't let that faze her. Tired of what she perceived to be her bland, monotonous daily routine, Jessica welcomed Dwayne's aura of danger, adventure, and transgression.

"When I met Dwayne," Jessica recalled, "I thought that he was gorgeous. I looked at him like 'Oh my God, he is *fine!*' Me and Dwayne started sleeping together after a couple of weeks. It felt like we'd known each other forever. . . . I think I got pregnant the first time we had sex."

The night that ended with Jessica's getting pregnant began with a group of teenagers driving around in search of a good time. Jessica and Dwayne were part of the group, along with another young couple. Shortly after midnight the teenagers headed out of town to pick up some liquor because the stores in Pittsfield shut down early on weekends. After driving around aimlessly for several hours and getting trashed, the teenagers somehow found their way back to Pittsfield at about five in the morning.

Jessica had made plans to sleep over at her friend's house, so no one was waiting up for her at home. She was buzzed, groggy, and completely exhausted. More than anything, she wanted to curl up on a comfortable bed, lay her head down on a soft pillow, and drift off into a deep, deep sleep. However, because she didn't have her own transportation, Jessica was at the mercy of her friends, who weren't ready to call it a night.

The teenagers decided to hang out at the home of one of Dwayne's friends. Upon entering, Jessica's friend rapidly vanished behind closed doors to make out with her date. Jessica found herself alone in a room with Dwayne. He kissed her, and one thing led to another. Jessica made it clear that she didn't want to have sex. She said no several times but eventually surrendered, too tired to fight about it. The moment she caved in, a thought flashed across her mind, *I might as well just get it over with.*

Jessica didn't want to deal with Dwayne being angry with her. She placed conflict avoidance at a premium. At that particular moment, she wasn't confident that she had the physical and mental strength to assert her will. Getting out of this bad situation seemed difficult, complicated, and messy. Surrendering to Dwayne's desire seemed much easier. In her previous sexual encounters, the boys Jessica had been with had used condoms. Dwayne didn't offer to use any protection. Not wanting to make a big deal out of it, Jessica went ahead and had unprotected sex, ignoring the risk of sexually transmitted diseases and never for a moment dreaming that she would be unlucky enough to get pregnant the very first time she had sex with a new partner.

In the weeks following her sexual encounter with Dwayne, Jessica remained convinced of her good luck, her immunity to risk, and her own invincibility. When she missed her period, she quickly repressed her worry that she might be pregnant. Three more months went by and despite missing a second, third, and fourth period, Jessica went on with her life as if everything were completely normal.

Jessica's father suspected something was very wrong when one afternoon, after a routine visit, his daughter asked him to drop her off at a friend's place instead of at her mother's house. Robert followed Jessica's directions and they ended up at a decrepit apartment complex. Rap music was blasting. Drug dealers were lounging around. Robert flat-out refused to stop the car. Enraged, he screeched out of the parking lot. A huge fight between father and daughter ensued. Robert told Jessica that she was crazy if she thought he would ever let her off at a place like that. Jessica insisted that her "friends" lived there and that it was perfectly safe. Later that night Robert got a call from Doris, who suggested that he had overreacted and had upset Jessica. Robert reminded Doris how much he cared about their daughter and said that he wasn't sure if he had been overprotective or if there was indeed serious cause to worry. Doris insisted that their daughter was doing just fine.

In hindsight, Jessica's stepfather offered the following explanation for his wife's failure to see the warning signs that suggested something was terribly wrong.

"I think Doris had got that ostrich thing going on," said Bill. "You know, stick your head in the sand and if you don't know it's happening, then basically it's not happening—until it comes up and slaps you dead in the kisser!"

For six months, despite seeing Jessica nearly every day, not a single member of the family suspected that she might be pregnant. Robert worried that Jessica might be at risk for teen pregnancy but didn't think it had already happened. Bill and Doris were preoccupied with problems in their marriage. Adding to the stress in their home, their younger daughter, Catherine, had been acting out, stealing and failing tests at school. She was the one they were anxious about, not Jessica. As time passed, Jessica became more and more stressed-out about hiding her pregnancy. Her family's living quarters were cramped, and privacy was virtually nonexistent. She was terrified of being discovered.

Seeking refuge in secrecy and denial, Jessica hid under baggy sweatshirts, ashamed of her condition and fearful of disappointing her family. She longed to rewind her life back to the day before she got pregnant and fantasized that somehow by ignoring the pregnancy, she could magically turn back time and reverse the consequences of unsafe sex with Dwayne. Resisting the impulse to confide in a relative, teacher, doctor, nurse, or friend, Jessica clung to her unrealistic wish for her stomach to shrink so that her old jeans would zip right up without a hassle. But as the months passed, her pregnancy didn't disappear. All that disappeared were her choices.

Jessica's silence was a time bomb. By not speaking up for so long, she deprived herself of medical care, psychological support, and advice that could have benefited her during the first two trimesters. She also missed the opportunity to seriously consider and discuss one major alternative: a safe, early abortion.

When Jessica was six months pregnant, she broke down and wrote a note to her mother. As word spread quickly through Pittsfield that Doris and Bill's "Little Princess" was pregnant, Jessica was barraged with an unpleasant assortment of facts about Dwayne that she had previously been unaware of. Jessica realized that although it had felt to her as though she and Dwayne had "known each other forever," they had dated for only just over a month. In fact, she knew astonishingly little about the father of her baby.

People in the community came forward and told Jessica that hers would not be Dwayne's first child. Jessica was shocked to discover that he had already fathered three children with two other young mothers. Dwayne was arrested and jailed for assault and battery of one of his other girlfriends and was behind bars, far from the delivery room, on the day Jessica gave birth to their son, whom she named Ezakeil.

Inside the stark, white hospital room, as Jessica stared at Ezakeil's brown face, black hair, and dark, shining eyes, she felt the weight of Dwayne's absence bearing down on her. Disappointed by his irresponsible behavior, no one in her family had ever even met Dwayne. At the mention of Dwayne's name, Bill would clench his fist, tensing up his whole body, as his face reddened with anger.

"If I were to meet the father of Jessica's baby, I don't think I'd say a whole lot," he fumed. "He's older and he's got three other kids with as many girls. . . . I don't think there'd be anything for me to talk about! I think I'd just go straight to physical. That's why it's best that I haven't met him, because assault is a terrible thing, and I'm already on probation for drunk driving!"

Single motherhood at such a young age destroyed Jessica's autonomy. Suddenly she couldn't even consider going away to college, because she needed her family around her to help care for the baby. The little money she made had to go toward supporting the baby, and in order to remain eligible for welfare while she was still a minor, she was required to remain in a supervised setting with a parent or responsible adult—for the near future, that meant living with Doris and Bill.

"Since I was fourteen, I've always been working," Jessica said matter-of-factly. "I've always wanted to make my own money. I don't like taking money from other people, like my mom, or anything, 'cause then I gotta pay her back. Might as well make my own money. Then I don't got to pay anyone back."

More than anything, what Jessica wanted out of a job was a sense of personal fulfillment and the knowledge that her work made a difference. The money was important, but a sense of satisfaction and being able to take pride in her work was more important—and much, much harder to find. Her work history was long, varied, and littered with a string of disappointments.

"My first job was at McFarlane Office Products," Jessica explained. "It was a desk job, boring, didn't like it. Moved to Burger King. I got sick of that and went to Rave, the clothing store. I didn't get along with my boss, so I moved on to Pretzel Time. It was just a quick little job in the wintertime just to make some extra money. Then I went to Bonanza. I had to wear a stupid outfit and a stupid hat and I looked corny. I got out of there smelling like meat and potatoes. So then I got a job at Edgecombe Nursing Home. I love the elderly, they're wonderful, and Alzheimer patients, I mean, you can just sit there and listen to all their stories because they'll come up with anything."

During the first year of her son's life, Jessica felt inadequate because the money she was making working at the nursing home after school and on weekends wasn't enough to provide her son with all the things she wanted him to have. She devised a plan with a friend who worked behind the counter at a store in the mall. This girl agreed to let Jessica through the checkout line without ringing her up on the register. As Jessica tried to leave the store with a bagful of merchandise she hadn't paid for, a security guard grabbed her. Within minutes the police were on the scene and she was arrested for shoplifting.

"I had stolen this really nice baby mobile, some baby clothes, a child's car seat, a baby monitor . . . just stupid stuff," said Jessica, shaking her head in disbelief over her own impulsive actions. "The police slapped handcuffs on me. I had to go to jail and get fingerprinted. The police took my picture. It wasn't a pleasant experience. What I did was so stupid and immature. I shouldn't have done it. I had money in my pocket, and my son was only a couple of weeks old."

Jessica's father contacted a friend of the family who was a lawyer, and he succeeded in getting Jessica out of the mess with a clear criminal record and a serious warning. Frightened by what had happened, Jessica realized that as a single mother, she could not flirt with danger or take any unnecessary risks. She suddenly understood that she had to be extraordinarily responsible in every area of her life because if anything happened to her—be it illness or injury or trouble with the law—there was no father to step in and take care of her son. Jessica accepted that with Dwayne still in jail, all the pressure of raising their son and supporting him fell squarely on her shoulders. As Jessica's parents drove her away from the police station, she resolved that rather than crack under the weight of such enormous responsibility, she would become strong enough to deal with it.

Despite Dwayne's absence and his failure to pay any child support, Jessica continued to make efforts to get him involved in her son's life. She took Ezakeil to visit his father in jail, hoping that Dwayne would bond with the infant. When Ezakeil was six months old, Dwayne got out of jail.

"He didn't call or show up to see how his son was doing," Jessica reported.

Anguished and reeling from Dwayne's neglect, Jessica temporarily cut off all contact with him. A few months later she heard from friends that he was back in jail. For several months Jessica decided not to take Ezakeil during visiting hours. That was her way of punishing Dwayne for being a bad father.

"I have no contact with my son's father," she explained. "I prefer it this way because I don't want him floating in and out of my son's life, messing his head up."

At the Teen Parent Program, Jessica was able to work through some of her disappointment with her son's father when she attended the writing workshops conducted by Carol Gilligan and Normi Noel. Considering that teen mothers such as Jessica stored up massive reservoirs of pent-up stress and rage with few available constructive outlets, Carol and Normi made every effort to create a safe haven that could contain and support the release of these ragged emotions so that rather than being turned inward in a silent, self-destructive way, these feelings could be discussed.

Carol and Normi discussed Charity Royall, the teenage character in Edith Wharton's novel *Summer*, who is constantly in conflict over how to express her seething rage. When Charity, knowing she is pregnant, sees her friend Ally mending an extravagant lace blouse for Annabel Balch, the rich socialite who is her rival for her lover's affections, she explodes, rips the garment out of her friend's hands, and tears it to shreds: "She had never known how to adapt herself; she could only break, tear and destroy. The scene with Ally left her stricken with shame at her own childish savagery. . . . But when she turned the incident over in her puzzled mind, she could not imagine what a civilized person would have done in her place."

When Carol asked the teen mothers in the workshop to write two letters to the fathers of their babies—one conventional, safe letter that they would be willing to send, and the other one that they would hide in the back of their minds, unwritten and unsent because it contained seeds of rebellion—Jessica seized the moment, put her thoughts down on paper, and read the letter she would not send out loud to a rapt audience:

> *Dwayne, I hate you! You are the most horrible man I have ever met. I never wanted to have sex with you in the first place! When I look at you, you make me sick. I don't understand how you can take care of your other three children but pay no mind to mine. I would really like to punch you in the head. Maybe that would knock some sense into you. When we first met, you were so kind. But you changed so quickly. Why couldn't you have stayed the same? Maybe we could have raised our son together—if you weren't such an asshole!*

The act of writing the letter entailed confronting the origins of the strong feelings of sadness and rage that had driven away words in the first place. Rather than splitting off into denial and justification for being treated badly, the girls were encouraged to venture into territory they felt was dangerous and provocative. They were encouraged to have higher expectations of themselves and to take more control over their relationships with the men in their lives.

Jessica's line "I never wanted to have sex with you in the first place" was one of several comments she made that implied the first time she and Dwayne had intercourse, resulting in her pregnancy, was not totally voluntary. Jessica made it clear that she did not view the experience with Dwayne as rape: she saw it as her own failure to enforce what she wanted, and felt that her ambivalent silence and passive submission had constituted consent. She therefore took full responsibility for her involvement in the encounter and for the fact that she had been drinking that night; nevertheless, she wished in hindsight that she had handled the situation differently.

Though Jessica had regrets about the night her son was conceived, she had no regrets about keeping her baby. "I could never give my baby up for adoption," she said tenderly. "Every day I would wonder where he was, how he looked, what he was doing. . . . I love my son to death. He is my love."

Preoccupied with Ezakeil, work, and studying for final exams, Jessica steered clear of dating and sex, consoling herself with the thought that "dating isn't worth it 'cause men are nothing but trouble."

Her attitude changed when tickets went on sale for the senior prom. Jessica longed to go. She went to the Berkshire Mall and tried on elegant floor-length strapless dresses and glamorous high-heeled shoes. She experimented with different makeup and hairstyles, and imagined herself walking down the red carpet on the big night. Jessica had saved up enough money to buy the gown of her dreams and two tickets to the prom, but there was one big problem: she didn't have a date. After much deliberation, she finally mustered up the courage to ask friends to help her find someone to escort her. They found a guy who said he was up for it. Jessica was ecstatic. Her fantasy had morphed into reality—or so she thought.

"The prom in Pittsfield is supposed to be a fun thing, but it wasn't fun for me," said Jessica. "I found a guy to go with but he backed out, so I didn't get to go. He told me the day before that he wasn't going, so I didn't have any time to find someone else to go with. I had a brand-new dress that was altered to fit me, and nowhere to go in it."

Jessica shook her head in despair as her memories transported her back to the disappointing night.

"I stood outside and watched people going into the prom, what fun! But I didn't get to go in 'cause I didn't have anyone to go with. I sat home with my son and did nothing. All because of that freakin' idiot."

For weeks Jessica's brand-new ethereal peach ball gown hung forlorn on a wire hanger, covered in plastic, gathering dust. It had been painstakingly altered to fit every curve of her slender body, so she could not return it to the store. Jessica was sure she would never have another opportunity to wear such a fancy, exquisite dress. She saw herself as a Cinderella-like character: the prom had been her ball, the one magic occasion in her otherwise uneventful life. When family and friends tried to console her with the idea that surely she would have other special events in the future, Jessica shook her head mournfully.

"Where am I gonna go?" she asked, her humor barely masking the despondency beneath it. "If only I hadn't had the dress altered," she bemoaned. "Then at least I could have returned it and gotten my money back."

Jessica's stepfather wore a pained expression on his face as he witnessed Jessica's crushing disappointment and deflated spirits. He blamed her pregnancy for causing her to become isolated from what he referred to as "the mainstream." He felt that her social life had suffered immensely on account of having a baby and that while the Teen Parent Program had its benefits, being surrounded by teen mothers day after day hadn't exactly increased her chances of meeting a cool, nice guy who might be reliable and fun to date. Bill drew attention to the fact that in the two years since Jessica had gotten pregnant, she hadn't been asked out on any dates. Not a single one.

As Bill talked about time lost, a very subdued Jessica listened. Her characteristic sharp wit, warm laughter, vibrant energy, and boundless enthusiasm had deserted her. Unafraid to speak the truth, Bill had hit on two of Jessica's vulnerable points. Beneath her cheerful optimism and tenacious resilience lay her gnawing worry that she was missing out on the joys of being a young, attractive, sexy single woman. She worried that lots of guys would never want to seriously date, let alone marry, a teenager who already had another guy's baby. Jessica took a deep breath and gathered her strength to respond to Bill's comments about her lack of a social life.

"It's true, but so what! Men are nothing but trouble. Maybe someday I'll find one who will change my mind, but for now I'm too busy goin' to school, goin' to work, and being a mom. I don't have time for anything else."

While raising Ezakeil was hard work, the baby was Jessica's main source of joy. Days went by when she felt unappreciated by her employers, exasperated by her family, frustrated by school, and trapped in Pittsfield, but her son never failed to surprise her with unexpected demonstrations of love, affection, and appreciation.

"My favorite moments are when Ez gives me big hugs out of the blue. When I'm lucky, he'll come up to me and squeeze me tight and give me a big kiss. I love that."

A few weeks after the prom, Jessica graduated from Taconic High School with honors. Ezakeil sat in the bleachers of the gymnasium with his grandparents, watching the ceremony with a huge smile on his face. He loved the way his mommy looked in her bright yellow cap and gown, holding a red rose. Out of the blue, he gave her a big hug.

Jessica's father was immensely proud of his daughter. He constantly reminded her how crucial it was for her to continue her education and develop a trade. His dream was for her to become a nurse. Jessica adopted her father's goals and enrolled in the nursing program at Berkshire Community College, a ten-minute drive from the house where she still lived with her son, Bill, Doris, and Catherine. Initially, Jessica was worried about how she would pay for a college education, but the issue was resolved with the assistance of her welfare worker and the financial-aid advisor at the college.

"College was offered to me for free. For having a kid, I get a grant each semester for two thousand dollars and that's plenty for what I need. I don't use the whole two thousand. I usually get a thousand back, so it's like they're paying me to go to school.

"When I meet with my welfare worker, I always ask what programs are available—if you don't ask, no one's gonna tell you. An organization called Berkshire Works pays for my books, and they pay for my uniforms for nursing. They're going to pay for my testing when I get my RN licensing. Every time I call them I say, 'Thank you so much.' Day care is offered to me for free through an organization called Resources for Child Care. They offer my son good meals, every day. It seems like everywhere you turn, people are willing to help you. That's one of the reasons why I'm still in Pittsfield."

Despite having these services at her fingertips, Jessica had her hands full keeping up with college and her part-time job at the nursing home. However, all these challenges paled compared with the challenge of learning how to adapt and evolve as a single mother in order to keep up with the different phases of her child's development, each with its own demands, challenges, and pitfalls.

"Ezakeil is now eighteen months old and he's a very active eighteen-month-old. I'm glad I'm young," said Jessica, "or I wouldn't be able to keep up with him! I never get a full night's sleep! Never! Ezakeil goes to bed at eight-thirty and wakes up once or twice in the middle of the night. He usually cries and wants to sleep in my bed. I get up and get him something to drink. Sometimes I have to change his diaper. For a while he was having night terrors. He would scream and cry, and if you touched him, he would just get worse. It was like he was in the middle of a nightmare and he looked awake, but he was really asleep. He just had no idea what was going on. There was nothing I could do to make him feel better. All I could do was make sure he didn't fall out of his bed or hurt himself somehow. Every day I get so tired. People told me that Ezakeil waking up at all hours of the night would end when he turned one, but it hasn't ended. He still does it. Every single night."

Because of the lack of space in her parents' house, Jessica and her son had to sleep under the eaves of the roof in a windowless corridor that connected Bill and Doris's room to Catherine's. Whenever the baby cried, it was hard, if not impossible, for anyone in the house to sleep.

Catherine complained, "Ez doesn't sleep through the night because you baby him too much!" Stung by her sister's criticism, Jessica's eyes narrowed defensively.

She fired back, "You try having a baby, Catherine. It's not as easy as people think!"

Jessica persevered through her first two years at Berkshire Community College, where she pursued a degree in nursing while continuing to work part-time with the elderly at a local nursing home for an hourly wage of $7.25.

"Welfare gives me five hundred dollars a month," Jessica explained. "I work one day a week because I go to school full-time, so I can't work any other days. So welfare takes that thirty-four dollars I get from working those hours and subtracts it from the five hundred dollars, and then I'll get the remainder. If I work a couple of extra hours they'll take those extra hours out of the five hundred, so no matter what, I'm only getting five hundred dollars a month. And five hundred dollars is nothing . . . you can't live on five hundred dollars a month. I mean, I obviously live on five hundred dollars a month, but you can't get things that you want. You have to pay your bills and just get regular household stuff like dish detergent and clothes, if you need clothes. My rent is a hundred and forty-three dollars. My cable is usually like forty dollars. My phone bill is usually like eighty or ninety. My electric bill is like fifty-four dollars. My car insurance is sixty dollars. There's other stuff, and it all adds up to a lot; and by the end of the month, I'm broke. I don't have any more money to save.

"I hate being on welfare," said Jessica, "but I have to, there's no way around it. I can't work full-time and go to school—it's impossible. If I could, I would; I don't want to be on welfare. I'm trying to do what I have to do to get off of it. I don't want to be stuck in the system, but thank God for the system.

"Welfare does help me. It really does. I don't know what I'd do . . . I mean, 'cause Dwayne was in jail . . . I never could've . . . I mean, I'm only . . . I'm young. I can't get a full-time job with college and a two-year-old. So welfare was the only thing I could do. I'm so thankful for it, for real, I really am. I don't know what I'd do without it—I mean, of course I know what I'm gonna do without it in the future. That's why I'm going to college. So I don't have to be on welfare. So I can have a good life and make my own money.

"Once I get my registered nursing license, I'll probably work in a hospital for a while, in the ER or pediatrics. I have to get my bachelor's after I get my RN, and then I'll work in delivery. My income is going to increase a lot once I get my registered nursing license. By the time I get up there, it'll probably be like twenty-four dollars an hour."

During Jessica's first two years at Berkshire Community College, her home life became more difficult. Her stepfather's drinking got out of hand, and the cops had to be called to break up a violent fight he had with her mother. Doris began to spend more and more time skydiving by herself at a new drop zone. One afternoon Bill followed Doris to a trailer park and spied on her. He caught her having an affair with one of her fellow sky divers.

"I was a basket case," recalled Bill. "I went between suicidal and homicidal. . . . You know, back and forth, back and forth, back and forth. Kill myself, kill her, kill myself, kill her, ah, fuck it—I'll kill her, then I'll kill myself!"

In the wake of this event, Doris shocked her daughters by announcing that she was moving out. Enough was enough. A teen mother and the veteran of two marriages, Doris longed for time to herself. She was sick of being tied down, and tired of all her responsibilities. Most of all, she was fed up with Bill's drinking.

"There were good times and bad times," said Doris, her voice tinged with sadness. "It was like a cycle with Bill. He would go months and months and months and not drink, and it would be good. When he got sent away the first time, after he got out, he went for two years without drinking, and that time was great. But then it started again. It was 'Oh . . . I'll just have one.' That lasted for a little while and then it was 'Oh, I'll just have two,' and of course he started again.

"I tried not to let the kids see it, but I think the mood that it put me in affected them more than him actually drinking himself.

"When he would drink, he would do it late at night when the kids were sleeping. He wouldn't come home. I wouldn't know where he was. He'd be spending a ton of money, so I was on edge all the time and I didn't have the patience I should have had with the kids because I was upset with Bill."

As her marriage collapsed, Doris reflected on the consequences of becoming a teen mother before having the chance to define herself independently as an adult.

"I felt that I was always Bill's wife or the girls' mother, it was never just me. When I started skydiving—that's part of what broke

Bill and I up. I mean, there was definitely troubles before that . . . lots of troubles . . . but skydiving made me more independent, and he didn't like that. He used to say, 'It always used to be "Bill and Doris," and now it's not anymore.' I couldn't make him understand that it wasn't that I didn't need him or that I didn't want him . . . I just realized that I could do stuff for myself."

Doris told Jessica, Catherine, and Bill that she had signed a lease on an apartment a few blocks away. She made it clear that she expected the girls to remain at the house, living with Bill. She pulled out a stack of boxes and started packing up her belongings.

The day before Doris was scheduled to move in to her new apartment, Bill went to a drop zone in New York, got hammered with his friends, and then tried to drive home. He drove about fifty yards from the bar before being busted by the cops for DUI. The cops discovered that Bill had been arrested on similar charges before and that his license had been taken away. At the time this incident occurred, Bill was on probation and was explicitly forbidden from getting behind the wheel. By driving without a license and being outside the state of Massachusetts, Bill was violating his probation—and on top of that, he was driving while intoxicated. In the courtroom, the judge was not sympathetic when Bill tried to explain that his car had swerved because he bent down to pick up a CD case that had fallen on the floor. The gavel came down hard. Bill was sentenced to six months in jail.

"Actually, going to jail was probably the best thing that happened to me because it gave me time to sit back, it definitely took me out of the loop. I had no dealings with Doris and her boyfriend. I just got totally out of it," Bill said, winding his fingers together and bending them backward until his knuckles cracked.

In spite of Bill's unexpected incarceration, Doris felt compelled to move in to her new apartment. Never mind that it meant leaving her two teenage daughters to their own devices. After all, she had signed the lease and put down the deposit. Claiming her independence had been a big step for Doris, and she wasn't going to be diverted by what she considered to be Bill's childish antics. Seated on a sofa in her own apartment, Doris talked about how much her life had changed since leaving Bill.

"When you're young and you have kids, you're tied down, that's it," she explained. "You have no life until they're grown. Now I can enjoy the freedom that I have. I can come and go as I please."

Bill's incarceration, compounded by Doris's abandonment, left Jessica, at nineteen, completely in charge of Ezakeil, who was just a toddler, and Catherine, who was sixteen. In addition, she had to shoulder the added burden of handling all the household affairs. Bill's aging mother still lived in the front apartment and checked up on the girls from time to time, and Doris, living nearby, had them over for dinner a few nights a week and poked her head in regularly to make sure everyone had enough to eat and that the house wasn't falling to pieces. Her affair with her fellow sky diver was going well, and to the girls, she seemed happier and more relaxed than she'd ever been.

In contrast, Jessica was extremely stressed-out. Pounds began dropping off her. Exhausted, pale, and emaciated, she attributed her significant weight loss to the fact that she was anxious all the time and, as a result, was suffering from terrible stomach cramps. She described a typical day, which began with her waking up at four in the morning to the sound of Ezakeil crying because he was hungry, and then consisted of her running from day care to college classes to a welfare meeting to the grocery store and then back to day care before going home to clean the house and pay a stack of bills. The pressure of her everyday life was killing her appetite.

Jessica had never imagined that she would get stuck managing a household while being a surrogate parent for her sixteen-year-old sister and dealing with what she referred to as her son's "terrible twos," on top of attending Berkshire Community College as a full-time student. As if that weren't already a heavy enough load, Jessica was also working part-time as an activities assistant at a nursing home, supervising games, arts and crafts, and other projects for Alzheimer's patients.

"Living with Catherine and Ezakeil without my parents is totally different than what I thought it would be," said Jessica. "I thought it would be easier and that I wouldn't have to worry about my mom saying stuff like 'Don't you think you should give Ezakeil a bath now?' I just thought that I'd be able to do what I want to do, but it is so not fun. I feel like a thirty-year-old woman. It's hard. And my sister, she doesn't have a job or anything, and her friends come over and I buy the groceries and I come home and everything is gone."

Jessica applied for subsidized housing, eager to be on her own with Ezakeil. She was put at the end of a long waiting list. She had no idea when there would be an opening. She waited and waited. In the dead of winter, the heating suddenly stopped working. Jessica couldn't afford to buy a new heating system, so she, Ezakeil, and Catherine moved in with Doris. Jessica slept on the couch until finally she received a letter in the mail saying there was an apartment available for her at the Wilson projects, near the center of Pittsfield. She was given a duplex, and for the first time, she had privacy and a space she and Ezakeil could call their own.

Jessica got very worried about Ezakeil when she observed that he couldn't play with other kids for long periods of time because he was allergic to dust and had trouble breathing. After a few minutes of play, his eyes became itchy and watery. He tired easily and often had to sit down in the grass and catch his breath. One day Jessica took him to a store and after a few minutes of excited exploration, he started coughing, choking, and vomiting. Similar episodes kept oc-

curring, and when Jessica took Ezakeil to the doctor, he was diagnosed with severe asthma. Jessica was given prescriptions for Claritin and Singulair as well as a nebulizer, a device that uses pressurized air to turn liquid medication into a fine mist for inhalation. Ezakeil relied on his nebulizer two or three times a day.

Jessica had her hands full balancing work, school, and taking care of her son. She became friendly with Dwayne's mother and sister, who often stayed in her apartment, sometimes for days at a time. They looked after Ezakeil when Jessica had to go out. Robert helped her as often as he could. Some days Ezakeil went to day care, other days he went to his grandfather's art studio. Robert taught the little boy how to paint and draw. He was amazed by the toddler's intelligence, curiosity, and wide-eyed innocence. Grandfather and grandson developed a close attachment. The adoration was mutual. As soon as he could talk, Ezakeil called his grandfather "Pa."

"Ez and my dad are best friends," said Jessica. "My dad taught him how to ride a bike and taught him how to swim. They go hiking in the woods. My dad means the world to me and to Ezakeil. The world."

Jessica was extremely grateful for her father's help and involvement; her main regret was the continued absence of her son's biological father.

"Dwayne's been in jail mostly all Ezakeil's life. I was pregnant, he was in jail; I had the baby, he was in jail. Now he's back in jail. But Ezakeil knows his father. We visit him in jail, so he knows him from going to see him there, and Ezakeil has seen him for a few months in between. Like on Halloween, we went trick-or-treating together."

When Dwayne got out of jail, he approached Jessica about rekindling their relationship. Jessica wavered, tempted to get back together with him. After several failed attempts to woo Jessica back sexually, Dwayne abruptly curtailed his visits to Ezakeil. Despite the temptation and her desire for Ezakeil to have a father in his life, Jessica resisted.

"After Dwayne got out of jail the last time, he got back with his baby's mother, the one who has his other son. They got in a fight and he hit her and now he's back in jail for a year and a half because he can't keep his hands off his girlfriends. He just can't stay out of jail. I don't know why he keeps hitting people."

At the Pittsfield police station, a computer search of the names of the fathers of the six teen mothers' babies revealed more than sixty police reports. The policeman who conducted the search explained that certain basic reports were available to any American citizen under the Freedom of Information Act, provided that the names of victims and witnesses are blacked out. Many of these reports documented arrests for assault and battery, restraining orders, and larceny charges, in addition to describing altercations or incidents involving harassment.

Jessica knew that Dwayne had a violent streak but was shocked when she was presented with copies of page after page of police reports that featured the name of her son's father. There had been many more arrests than even she had suspected. The majority of them were for assault and battery of other women—particularly the mothers of his other children.

Previously, Jessica had disassociated herself from what she knew about Dwayne's violence. She preferred not to know about it and was eager to minimize its implications. Because of the brevity of their relationship and Dwayne's having been behind bars for most of the time they had known each other, Jessica had thankfully never been a target of his assaults.

"I've never been hit by any of my boyfriends, even though they've hit their other girlfriends. I would never stand for a man hitting me," Jessica insisted. "I would do everything in my power, if a man hit me, to hit him back. I just wouldn't be with them. But it doesn't matter if you're in jail or not. I mean, a man can be a lawyer and beat the crap out of you. Or a man can be in for attempted murder and not beat the crap out of you."

Jessica couldn't pretend that the stack of police records sitting in front of her didn't exist. No longer able to deny the reality of the violent nature of the man whom she was dealing with, Jessica acknowledged how painful and difficult it was going to be to explain to Ezakeil why his father kept going to jail.

"Ez just loves his dad. I know he loves his dad. Every day he says, 'Daddy,' every day he wants to know where his father is. It's just really hard not knowing what to say. I mean, what am I supposed to say to a two-year-old? And when he gets older, what am I supposed to say? 'Your dad's working,' or 'Your dad doesn't care about you, Ez, and he doesn't want anything to do with you'? I can't imagine how Ezakeil's gonna grow up not having a father figure. A child needs a father."

Jessica was also upset that Dwayne never contributed a dime of child support. As he kept screwing up every chance to make a difference in Ezakeil's life, her disappointment slowly fermented into rage.

"He didn't even give me . . ." Jessica's voice broke. She slowed down and gathered her thoughts. "I asked Dwayne for ten dollars for Ezakeil's birthday cake. His birthday cake cost twenty dollars, I asked him for ten. He wouldn't even give me ten dollars and he didn't even call on Ezakeil's birthday. He's not gonna live that down. I am through with him. Ezakeil is better off. It's hard to say that, though, because he needs his father. But not like he is now. I'm through with people that go to jail. I mean, I'm not really through with people that go to jail, I'm just through with having to go and visit, and having to bring my son there. I just don't like going."

Sensing that the past was colliding with the present, she paused for a moment, overwhelmed with emotion.

"I remember ever since I was, like, seven years old, visiting a family member in jail. And now, it's still the same thing. Everyone that I love just keeps going to jail, everyone that I care about. I'm just tired of it. It's really depressing. Here one minute and gone the next for a long time. I just . . . It's just too much for me. I don't like seeing people I love locked up. Just the thought of people being in there . . . You just wish they didn't do what they did. But, I mean, if they're gonna go do that, then they have to suffer the consequences. Sometimes I don't really mind bringing Ezakeil to jail. It's the real world."

Jessica rationalized that because so many of her friends and family had been in and out of jail, it couldn't be possible that everyone who was incarcerated was a bad influence or in fact dangerous. She often sympathized with the inmate's side of the story, regardless of whether it was the truth or lies. As a result, her judgment suffered and she often underestimated the negative influence of the people she continued to surround herself with.

Rather than meeting new friends at college or at one of the hospitals or nursing homes where she worked, Jessica remained loyal to her old peer group, many of whom went in and out of jail and were involved with drugs. Within this peer group, Jessica had to hide her intelligence. Her kindness and generosity were taken advantage of. Jessica admitted that she was "too nice" but continued to associate with friends who had less going for them than she did.

Jessica felt ambivalent about her pursuit of a higher education and her aspirations for a steady job and a better life—as if somehow her choice to chase these dreams meant that she was indirectly criticizing and rejecting the circle of friends she had grown up with. She didn't want to feel that she was "better" than they were. Jessica wanted to fit in and feel accepted, terrified that outside this small circle she might not have a place in the world. At times she realized that her allegiance to this old peer group might be holding her back from reaching her full potential, but she found it difficult to break away.

Jessica was apprehensive about entering new social circles. She worried that guys she met in the college environment would be critical of her being a single mother with a son of mixed race. Sadly, her experience proved that her fears were well founded.

"The men in college—I'm just not attracted to them. I have not met . . . oh my God . . . yes I did—I met this guy named Eric. Oh my God, he's so sexy. He is the finest man in the entire world. He's white and he is so fly. He wanted me to go out to dinner with him. One time he asked me to just go sit out and watch the stars and just relax and talk. I said, "I can't. . . . My son is here.' And he said, 'Your son?' That screwed everything up."

A friend invited Jessica on a road trip, telling her that she and her boyfriend were going to visit his brother, Wes, who was incarcerated at Bridgewater Prison. Jessica snapped her son into his car seat, and they went along for what turned out to be the first of many visits.

"Jess let it slip one day that she was going to Bridgewater," recalled Doris. "I said, 'What are you going there for?' She said, 'To see Wes.' I said, 'Jess, why are you bringing Ez there?' She said, 'Oh, well, Wes is there, he's all by himself. We're friends, we're just gonna go and visit him.' I wasn't thrilled with her going that far and taking Ez there," said Doris, shaking her head. "It's a good two hours at least."

"I met Wes a long time ago," explained Jessica. "He was friends with my son's father and my best friend's boyfriend. So I just knew him from around town. I knew him from seeing him from when I was even younger, like sixteen and seventeen. He used to call me Blue Eyes. I'd be walking down the street and he'd be, like, 'Hey, Blue Eyes!' I never knew who he was, so I'd just keep walking.

"Nothing really serious happened then because I wasn't really interested in him, but when he went to jail, we started corresponding through letters. Finally we just decided to form a relationship. We committed ourselves to each other, and everything just evolved from there."

For reasons Jessica didn't understand, she equated sexual attraction with violence and repeatedly found herself drawn to men with criminal records.

"Wes was convicted of rape," said Jessica, "but he says he didn't do it. In jail they have this rape class you can take if you're convicted of that sort of crime, and he won't take it.

"Wes said he would die for me. I mean, that's probably what every man says and I just . . . I don't know . . . I like how he talks. I like how he acts. I just . . . He just attracted me. I thought it was kinda crazy.

"My friends were like 'That man has got six to nine years left in jail. You're gonna wait for him? You've never been with him before! You never had a relationship with him before! You don't even know what it's like to live with the man!'

"I said, 'I know . . . but I love him. . . .' It'll work out. We're meant for each other."

Jessica visited Wes regularly, taking three-year-old Ezakeil with her.

"When you go to visit—every jail is different," Jessica explained, "but at the prison Wes is in right now, you have to wait in this long line to give your paperwork to the people. You have to give your license and your birth certificate to prove who you are. Then you go into another room, where the lockers are, and you put all your valuables in the lockers. Then you wait until they call who you're going to see and you stand up and they search you. They feel your body to see if you have anything on you, and they ask you to stick out your tongue, take off your shoes, take off your belt, unroll your pants, and undo your hair—you can't have anything in your hair and you can't wear any jewelry. You go through a metal detector. You have to get buzzed into the visiting area through two doors, and once you get into the room you have to give your paperwork to the officers—there's like six of them bad boys!

"The chairs are lined up facing toward you, so you pick a chair and you wait another fifteen minutes and then your visitor comes out. You can stand up and hug and kiss at first, for the initial greeting, then when you sit down you have to sit knee to knee. There's a lot of people visiting and there's like six or seven guards and they just go up and down the rows and make sure you're knee to knee. You can't lean over. That's against the rules. If you do it twice, they'll terminate your visit. That's pretty much how the visit is, and it can last three or four hours.

"When Ezakeil visits Wes, he says, 'We're going to the big one?' He's used to seeing his dad in the little one. At Wes's prison, they have a playroom. Ezakeil and the other kids have a designated person in there that watches them. The guards search the kids. They have them stand with their hands wide open. They go around them with the handheld metal detector. If the kids have their cuffs rolled up, they'll undo the cuffs. Sometimes they'll check the babies' diapers. So they do pretty much the same search on the little kids as they do for us."

Because of the distance and her busy schedule, Jessica didn't visit Wes more than once a month. However, the two maintained a constant correspondence via letters and phone calls. Jessica regarded Wes as her boyfriend, and for more than a year she didn't date anyone else, convinced they would end up living together as soon as he got out.

"I love him to death," Jessica said, lost in reverie. "He calls me his queen and he's my king."

Wes told Jessica he would give her a little girl as soon as he got out of jail. The obvious irony, as Jessica's friends were quick to point out, was that iron bars protected her from actually having anything even remotely resembling a real relationship. The distance allowed Jessica to inhabit a safe, idealized fantasy world, where violent, dangerous predators were magically transformed into gentle, charming, valiant kings. Carrying on this rigidly regulated relationship with Wes under the watchful eye of prison guards who monitored their every move gave Jessica an illusion of power and control over the romance and allowed her to hold on to the hope that love could heal the legacy of violence that, in her mind, was inextricably connected to sex—it allowed her to be in a romantic relationship that had firm boundaries and could not, by its very nature, involve a sexual component.

The fairy tale that Jessica had concocted didn't last. Wes became verbally abusive and started arguments with Jessica during visits and phone calls. Determined to exert power and control, Wes told Jessica that he didn't want her going out with her friends and that he didn't want her having any friends over to the apartment. He started referring to himself as her "husband" and kept asking her to marry him in jail.

Jessica managed to keep the relationship a secret from her dad until one evening Robert recognized the sketches she had posted on the walls of her apartment—they were prison drawings. Jessica told him that her friend, Wes, had paid other guys in prison to draw these pictures for her. Robert shivered, eerily reminded of the drawings of

Care Bears he used to lovingly make for his daughter when he was in jail. Jessica had saved all of Wes's letters and had propped up her favorites on the television stand. When his daughter wasn't looking, Robert stuffed some of the letters underneath his shirt and smuggled them home. A few days later he managed to steal a few more letters. By the time Jessica caught him red-handed, he had managed to skim through most of the correspondence and was in a deep panic.

The sinister letters Wes wrote to Jessica were full of romance, promises, sweet talk, manipulation, and commands. Within months, Wes had convinced Jessica to assume power of attorney for him and to open a joint bank account in both their names. Even from the confines of his cell, he managed to control Jessica, telling her what errands to run for him, what letters to type on his behalf, and whom to see. Jessica did whatever he told her to do, including filing his medical and legal records in her apartment.

Robert asked Jessica if she was naive enough to think that she was the only girl Wes was brainwashing and manipulating. Jessica refused to accept this interpretation of her relationship with Wes and continued her regular visits and phone calls. Deeply alarmed and worried, Robert begged Jessica to cut all ties to Wes, for the sake of her son. For months his pleas fell upon deaf ears.

The situation exploded when Wes wrote to Robert—a letter that opened with insults and ended threateningly with Wes demanding Jessica's hand in marriage.

"Over my dead body," Robert told his daughter.

Doris sat down with Jessica and told her in no uncertain terms that she wanted her to break up with Wes immediately. Then she dared ask her daughter a pressing question that had been on her mind for years.

"What do you have against white guys?" she inquired.

"I've just never dated a white guy before," said Jessica. "I'm not objecting to them. I mean, if I find the right white man, so be it, but I'm more attracted to black men. God knows why, but I just am attracted to the bad ones that are in jail, who don't know how to work. It is so weird, but I always do it. I like rough guys. I don't know why."

Robert became more and more hysterical about Jessica's relationship with Wes. He interrogated Jessica and expressed his disapproval, certain that her relationship with Wes would lead to disaster. Robert knew his daughter was an adult, and although he feared losing her by interfering in her personal life, he could not remain on the sidelines and watch his precious daughter being subjected to a life full of pain, trauma, and abuse—a life he was all too familiar with.

"My dad said that if I kept having a relationship with Wes, I was gonna be pregnant and barefoot as soon as he got out of prison. He said that I'd be poor forever and that I'd have eight kids and that Wes would beat me. And he said that I'd never have Christmas because Wes believes in the Muslim faith."

Robert and Jessica had screaming matches that often pushed their relationship to its breaking point before ending in tears and reconciliation. Finally, Jessica began to see that beneath her father's rage was deep, genuine love and concern for her and Ezakeil. Robert's emotional demonstration of his love and his assertion of paternal protective instincts gave Jessica the strength and conviction to end her relationship with Wes. Jessica's phone rang for weeks as Wes repeatedly called her collect from jail, eager to win her back. Jessica refused to accept his calls and stopped responding to his letters.

"The last letter I got was an angry letter," she reported. "Wes is mad at me because I broke up with him. He wrote, 'See you in 2006! I'm gonna cause you even more pain than you caused me.' "

Jessica's mother shook her head when Wes's name came up. She had seen all of Wes's letters posted around Jessica's apartment, and there was no doubt in her mind that he was dangerous. Though she was relieved that the relationship had ended, she still worried about Jessica and was critical of the decisions her daughter had made.

"Jessica's life is very hard because of having Ez," observed Doris, "and, you know, if she hadn't had him, she probably wouldn't even be around here. She was talking about going to college down in Georgia, where her aunt lives. I know Jess doesn't want to stay in this area, so I'm hoping she'll be done with school and have a good job, making good money by the time Wes gets out of prison. I'm really hoping she'll be far away from this area before there's any chance of him getting out."

Doris complained that "Jessica just makes choices that make her life so much harder than it needs to be. I mean, look at her, she's not even twenty-two years old and she's got a kid who's nearly four, and she's working three jobs and trying to get through nursing school. She's got a car that's falling apart around her ears, and that alone is hard enough, and then she keeps letting these men in her life that add even more stress to it."

When Dwayne got out of jail, he began seeing Ezakeil from time to time. Although he and Jessica didn't get back together, Dwayne felt he had a right to enter her apartment whenever he pleased, and Jessica didn't feel it was necessary to get a restraining order.

"I'm his baby's momma," she said in a resigned effort to explain their renewed contact. One day Jessica refused to give Dwayne the keys to her car. He demanded that she drive him to the store.

"Dwayne threw a fit," said Jessica. "He went ballistic with Ezakeil right in front of him. He smashed a glass against the wall and cut himself. He got blood everywhere, blood all over my nice couch and blood all over my nice rug. The glass went everywhere. I'm still finding glass to this day underneath the couch and underneath the cushions. And then Dwayne kicked in my front door. It's still broken. He's just ridiculous. He's got some serious malfunctions."

Soon after that incident, Jessica's father gave Ezakeil a radio as a gift. At nearly four years of age, the little boy was articulate, sensitive, and perceptive. He told his grandfather that he could listen to the radio at the art studio but that he didn't want to take it home. He was terrified that his daddy would come over and break it.

The relationship between Ezakeil and Dwayne continued to be problematic. Jessica had wanted her son to have his father involved in his life, but she began to see that it just wasn't going to work out—she began to accept that Dwayne's presence hurt rather than helped Ezakeil. He routinely taunted the little boy, calling him a punk and a sissy.

"Ez can ride a bike without training wheels," said Jessica. "My dad taught him how. He does wheelies and everything, and he wanted to show his dad. So Dwayne walks outside and looks for two seconds and then walks back in the house. Ezakeil yelled for him to come back, and Dwayne was, like, 'Uh, hold on, Ezakeil, um . . . uh . . . I seen you, man, I seen you.'

"I said, 'Dwayne, you're ridiculous! Ezakeil is proud of himself that he learned to ride a bike. Why can't you be, like, 'Ezakeil, that is so good, I am so proud of you'? That makes a person feel good. . . . I don't think Dwayne ever had that.

"Dwayne just makes me sick about the things he does," Jessica continued. "Like, he cannot get a job. He's got four kids and don't take care of one of them. I never filed for child support myself because I just—I'm too nice. I just didn't, so welfare had to do it. I mean, thank God they did. I mean, how can someone like Dwayne have four children and not even give a damn? I had to change my whole life around for one child, and he hasn't changed anything for four!

"I just can't stand Dwayne. I let him get away with everything, but I've had about enough. I've said it about a thousand times that I've had enough with him, but this time I really and truly have had enough. I will see him in court. If he doesn't get a job, he goes to jail, and if he tries to run away and doesn't check in with his probation officer, they'll issue a warrant and if they find him, they'll arrest him for child support."

Jessica was particularly concerned about getting her son's father to start paying child support because she would soon no longer be eligible for federal assistance under the terms of the 1996 welfare reform bill, which had replaced AFDC with TANF, restricting people to five years maximum on welfare.

"I got on welfare before I got into college," Jessica explained, "and the RN program is a four-year program when you add up all the prerequisites—English, math, science, sociology, psychology—so I'm not gonna make the whole four years on welfare. I had to take some summer months off from welfare so that I could work and then add the welfare time onto my school months. Right now, I'm taking a semester off and working three jobs so that I can save up money so that it will all work out.

"When I'm in school I want to be able to be dedicated to school and to only have to work a couple of days a week. When I go back next semester, my program is going to be very intensive; three days a week you have in-class studying, where they teach you about medications and about everything you need to know about being an RN. The other two days you go into a hospital and you take care of patients for the day and report back to the RN on how the patients are doing. You have to write in a journal and do all kinds of paperwork.

"Right now, I'm a certified nursing assistant and I work at an agency where they tell you what nursing home to go to. When I have elderly clients, I go to their homes and get them ready for the day. I get them in the shower, make breakfast, and clean their houses. I make sure everything is neat and tidy so that they don't trip on anything. I also work at a nursing home as an activities assistant.

"I will finish school. I will become a registered nurse. There's no doubt about that. I will get a car that doesn't need its door held closed with a bungee cord, and I'll have a nice house someday. As for romance—I don't know. I'm gonna try to find a man that will treat me nice and give me something in return for what I give.

"Ezakeil will be starting school in September. When I brought him in, the teachers were just amazed because he is so intelligent. It's amazing. I mean, he's tiny, really small for his age, but I always encourage him to do everything. He gets along with other kids really well. No matter if they're older, younger, girls, boys—he makes friends wherever we go. I really encourage him to do that because you have to be able to socialize with all different people of all different races."

Ezakeil loved listening to music. Rap was his favorite. Jessica was astounded that her four-year-old knew almost every word of most Eminem songs that played on the radio.

One morning while Jessica was driving Ezakeil to school, her cell phone rang. There was bad news. Dwayne had been arrested again in relation to a shooting incident that had occurred the night before. Jessica turned the radio down. Ezakeil turned it back up. Jessica turned it off.

"Daddy's in big trouble," she said. Ez didn't say a word. He just stared out the window at the rows of worn houses. His faith in his father had run out a long time ago. Nothing his mother said surprised him.

A few days later the story of Dwayne's arrest appeared in the local newspaper. Dwayne had gone to a man's house after midnight. The two had gotten into a drug-related argument. Worried about being robbed and fearing for his life, the man had fired shots at Dwayne, apparently in self-defense. With Dwayne momentarily distracted, the man had then fled from his own apartment. He sought refuge at the home of Sheri's mother, Pat, who was known to be heavily involved in the neighborhood drug scene.

Dwayne pursued the man to Pat's house and bashed a hole right through the front door with his head. Pat hid in a closet, terrified. Dwayne pointed a handgun through the hole in the door, but before he could fire, the man inside Pat's apartment fired at him. The stray bullet hit the door. Dwayne ran away but then returned to Pat's house a few hours later, threatening to kill the man if he found him. He was promptly arrested.

The assistant district attorney asked that a high amount of bail be set for Dwayne "because he has a criminal record that includes six convictions for assault and battery, as well as threatening to commit a crime, operating a motor vehicle to endanger, and operating a motor vehicle after his license has been revoked. . . . His New York state record also includes using a different last name."

Dwayne was charged with two counts of armed home invasion, carrying a firearm without a license, and attempting to break and enter in the nighttime with the intent to commit a felony. Bail was set at $100,000. Jessica expected that her son's father would be put away for a long time. Her little boy might be a man by the time his father got out of jail. If the sentence wasn't that long, Jessica had no doubt that the next one would be. Back at the Wilson projects, Jessica watched Ezakeil playing animatedly with his toy cars. She walked over and pulled him toward her in a gentle, firm, protective embrace.

"Wanna go outside?" she asked him. He nodded. Jessica pulled a hat over her son's ears. As the sun lingered overhead, they played together in the last of the dying autumn leaves.

When Jessica's stepfather, Bill, got out of jail, he moved back into the house where he and Doris had raised the girls. The once

noisy rooms were now silent. No arguing voices, no giggling teenagers, no loud rap music, no crying infants. It was just Bill, a beer in one hand and a cigarette in the other, screening calls to avoid the creditors who kept harassing him.

"After my mother passes, I'm gonna sell this mausoleum," he said. "My ass is going to Belize, because I don't know anyone there. . . . No one knows me. . . . I know there are places to skydive and a warm ocean and I know I can turn a dollar down there. God knows I'm a handy kinda guy . . . just gotta get the hell out of here. Pittsfield leaves nothing to offer, and if the girls were smart, they'd get the hell out of here, too."

"I am not living in Pittsfield all my life," Jessica vowed. "When I get my RN, I am not staying here. Ezakeil will not grow up in this town. There's nothing here. You get stuck. There's nowhere to go. You go to freakin' Berkshire Community College, so what? No, no, no. We're leaving. . . .

"My son—he's gonna be something special. He is something special. He amazes me every day. He's the best thing I could have ever wished for. He is precious."

chapter eight

COMMUNITY

"I wish I could think of you as happier, less lonely. . . . Things are sure to change for you, by and by."

"Things don't change at North Dormer: people just get used to them."

The answer seemed to break up the order of his prearranged consolations, and he sat looking at her uncertainly. Then he said, with his sweet smile: "That's not true of you. It can't be."

The smile was like a knife-thrust through her heart: everything in her began to tremble and break loose. She felt her tears run over, and stood up.

"Well, good-bye," she said.

She was aware of his taking her hand, and of feeling that his touch was lifeless.

—*Edith Wharton,* Summer

TEEN MOTHERS WERE ON TINA PACKER'S MIND. HER husband, Dennis Krausnik, was adapting Edith Wharton's novel *Summer* for the stage, and during their frequent conversations about the book, Tina found herself marveling at just how contemporary the book's themes remained despite the passage of more than eighty years since its publication back in 1917. Tina knew that minutes from her home in Stockbridge, numerous unwed pregnant teenagers throughout Berkshire County shared the predicament of Wharton's tragic heroine, Charity Royall. She wondered how she could make a difference in their lives.

Sixty and still pulsing with the passion and exuberance of her British youth, Tina was dedicated to her role as artistic director of Shakespeare & Company, the theater group she had cofounded in 1978 with renowned voice teacher Kristin Linklater. Based in Lenox, Massachusetts, Shakespeare & Company was headquartered fifteen minutes from Pittsfield, on the grounds of Edith Wharton's former estate, The Mount. Tina had rescued this beautiful historic property from neglect after happening upon it by chance and discovering that the once-grand mansion had fallen into dilapidated disrepair.

Over the years, as Shakespeare & Company established strong roots in Berkshire County, an outdoor main stage was constructed near the imposing mansion. Every year the company presented two full seasons of plays by a variety of authors, focusing on but not limited to their two natural favorites, Shakespeare and Edith Wharton. Wharton's former stables were converted into theater space, and her parlor became the setting for more intimate productions. Many student performances took place at a lovely Greek theater hidden in a clearing sheltered by the woods bordering the property.

The breadth of Shakespeare & Company's activities quickly expanded far beyond professional performances, into the realm of educational outreach and teacher training. For more than two decades, Tina Packer, Dennis Krausnik, and the company's directors of education, Kevin Coleman and Mary Hartman, have remained steadfast in their devotion to administering the educational outreach program that has brought Shakespeare to more than one hundred public elementary, middle, and high schools.

"Right now we're working in ten high schools, four middle schools, and four elementary schools," said Tina. "We also work in the juvenile justice system, and the kids can choose: they can either do community service if they've done something which is against the law or they can come to us. The children who are in foster care, mostly because their parents are drug addicts and have neglected them or deserted them, come to us and we act out the Shakespeare plays with them using Shakespearean language, but sometimes we actually go to their life stories as well. The themes in Shakespeare often help inspire kids to articulate things that they're thinking and feeling but haven't previously had the words to say."

Teaching the kids to read and act Shakespeare entailed shepherding them through a process of socialization, collaboration, and self-exploration. Researchers from Harvard's Project Zero evaluated the effectiveness of Shakespeare & Company's educational outreach program and gave it rave reviews, concluding that mentors with experience as actors and directors nurtured the imagination, self-awareness, confidence, communication skills, judgment, knowledge base, intellectual curiosity, and emotional growth of the students who participated.

In support of its educational outreach efforts, Shakespeare & Company has been awarded many prestigious grants, including several from the GE Fund totaling more than $600,000. The philanthropic foundation of the General Electric Company "invests in improving educational quality and access, and in strengthening community organizations in GE communities around the world." One of the foundation's programs aims to "double the rate of college attendance in low-income, inner city schools in GE communities." It is precisely this kind of partnership between a mammoth corporation and a dynamic artistic organization that promotes a sense of hope, providing joy, innovation, the satisfaction of accomplishment, and a valuable opportunity for thousands of children, all very much in keeping with the spirit of GE's new slogan, "Imagination at Work."

"When kids are being creative, they're much more capable of dealing with the problems of their life, rather than just receiving the blows of fortune," explained Tina. "They are able to think creatively about how they can change their circumstances, and able to think creatively about how it feels to interact with other people and make a difference. The plays are an art form that spiritually transports the kids to another place and gives them a bigger palette to work with other than just 'I hate school' or 'I hate my family.' Through performing these plays, kids can actually acquire the tools to think in a bigger way about what's going on, and that to me is a godsend, it's a lifeline."

In March 1999 Tina contacted Helen Berube, the director of the Teen Parent Program in Pittsfield, and asked if she would be interested in hosting a Shakespeare & Company residency. Helen responded with hesitation, explaining to Tina that the teen mothers were very secretive and reticent and very stressed-out and overburdened with responsibilities. She wasn't sure that they would be interested in or, for that matter, willing to perform Shakespeare.

Tina suggested a writing workshop that incorporated some theater training as an alternative to the time-intensive process of mounting a full-scale student production. She explained that her theater company was doing a production of Edith Wharton's *Summer,* which dealt with the story of a teenager in Berkshire County who got pregnant, and that the workshops she envisioned would meet one hour a week for a period of six weeks during school hours, using the text of Wharton's novel to inspire writing, reading, and discussion, perhaps culminating in a staged reading. The director agreed to Tina's proposal, and tentative dates for the workshop were set.

Tina then approached her close friend psychologist Carol Gilligan, who lived twenty minutes from Pittsfield, in West Stockbridge. Renowned for her seminal writing about adolescent girls, she was, in Tina's mind, the perfect person to lead the seminars. Over the course of three years, Carol had conducted workshops with girls ages nine through eleven as part of a Harvard research project called Strengthening Healthy Resistance and Courage in Girls. Accompanied by

Normi Noel, a Linklater voice teacher and theater director, and by Annie Rogers, a colleague from Harvard, Carol had worked within the public school system in the Boston metropolitan area. Using voice exercises, writing exercises, and improvisational theater games, they had developed a method of working to empower young girls.

Carol and her colleagues sought to help each girl they worked with to establish a stronger, more active, articulate presence in her own life. The alternative they had observed and were trying to counter was the adolescent girl's retreat into passivity, repression, dissociation, and silence. Their work with the girls in Boston focused on strengthening three different levels of relationships: the girls' relationships to one another, which involved their sharing thoughts and feelings with a group, resulting in the realization that they were rarely isolated or alone when it came to their perceptions and experiences; the girls' relationships to nonjudgmental mentors who acted as guides and facilitators along their paths of self-discovery, without limiting or constraining them to conventionally accepted thoughts, behaviors, or emotions; and finally, the girls' relationships to the community at large, a connection that was established at the end of the workshop, through a publicly staged reading of the girls' own writing.

When Tina asked Carol and Normi if they would adapt their approach to fit the special needs of students at the Teen Parent Program in Pittsfield, they enthusiastically agreed. Their workshops with the teen mothers in Pittsfield were funded in part by a grant to prevent repeat pregnancies, which represent more than 20 percent of teen births. One of the biggest risks for teen pregnancy is a previous pregnancy. Almost one out of every three young women whose first birth occurs before the age of seventeen has a second child within twenty-four months. Thus, the population of teen mothers with one child is a group for whom successful intervention can be key in preventing the compounded economic and social risks that are intensified by having two children at such a young age.

Carol and Normi's objectives included enhancing the teen mothers' access to their own voices and improving their grasp of language as a means of self-expression so that when it came time for them to communicate their needs for respect and protection within a relationship, they would be more likely to have the confidence and conviction to assert themselves, to stand up for what they valued, and to be present in an active, influential way, shaping their destiny instead of just passively letting events unfold.

As soon as Carol and Normi started working with the teen mothers, they realized that many of these girls had been wounded by society's negative reaction to their predicament and deeply affected by the labels and stereotypes that defined them as "bad girls" solely on the basis of their being young, visibly pregnant out of wedlock, and determined to keep their babies. When Carol read parts of Edith Wharton's novel *Summer* aloud, she made a point of stressing that a prominent, prolific American author had written an entire novel about a girl in their situation, demonstrating that empathy and compassion were indeed possible responses.

"Charity Royall wasn't just condemned and humiliated," said Carol. "Wharton described her as a girl with a lot of integrity. My hope was that reading the book would give the girls a sense that language, culture, and art were capable of holding complicated truths, and would help them to understand that not everything needed to be defined in black-and-white terms as either 'good' or 'bad.' "

The workshops also aimed at helping the teen mothers feel more connected to the community by including them in cultural events. In addition to Shakespeare & Company's *Summer,* the Berkshire Opera Company was presenting its own production of Wharton's novel. Affiliated with both organizations, Carol made arrangements to reserve some complimentary tickets for the teen mothers. However, when the staged reading of the teen mothers' writing was scheduled and publicized, some people in the community voiced their opposition to the prospect of this particular group performing.

"Initially," recalled Carol, "when we announced that we were going to involve the girls in the community celebration of Wharton's novel *Summer,* the response of some people was 'You can't do this. The community doesn't want to see these girls.' I remember reading letters that criticized us for giving these girls special attention, and more or less implied that instead of being put onstage as if they were heroes, these teen mothers should be covered with shame and hidden from sight as if they didn't exist.

"If teen mothers get that message from society, their voices recede and they feel that they have nothing to say and that they're not of value," said Carol. "To encourage the voice that in fact would work against teen pregnancy, you have to first start by creating a place or an atmosphere that invites their voices. You have to want to hear what they have to say."

Too young to vote, most teenage girls have no political voice, and when it comes to important debates about the very circumstances that define their lives, to a large extent they remain silent and excluded. Whenever teen parenthood is filtered through the media, so often the national spotlight remains fixed on the moral and theoretical battles waged between liberals and conservatives. Each side comes to the table armed with competing agendas regarding sex education, contraception, abortion, family values, and the relationship between church and state. In contrast, most pregnant and parenting teens remain sequestered on the fringes of society, represented as statistics, deprived of a forum to refute those who stereotype them, positioned helplessly as scapegoats, and powerless to contradict those who have written them off as ignorant, irresponsible youngsters with doomed futures.

"Prior to Carol and Normi's workshops using Edith Wharton's *Summer,* we had never ever done a program specifically for young girls who were in the predicament of teen pregnancy or motherhood," explained Tina Packer, "but I actually think theater is one of the ways out of a predicament like that, because it entails articulating what you think and feel and presenting yourself and being able to say to a large group of people what you think is going on. It strengthens your voice, and the voice is the most important thing. One of the primary functions of theater is to articulate what is not being said within a society. Within a community, if you don't hear what teenagers are saying and if they sense they are not being heard, it's difficult to make progress in getting them out of that cycle."

Reflecting on her work with the teen mothers, Carol said, "That very brief experience in the Berkshires with our very short program suggests that a program that is coherent and focused on voice and relationships, and that uses the arts to give girls a vehicle for discovering what in fact they think and feel, can help girls to be present with one another in an honest way and can help them to see themselves as connected with the world, rather than shunned by the world. I think that integrating those particular concepts into a larger teen pregnancy program would be another step forward for prevention. What I've found in all my work with girls is that they are constantly underestimated."

Six weeks after beginning the writing workshop, Jessica, Liz, Colleen, Sheri, and Amy sat on chairs staggered along the stage of Shakespeare & Company's marvelously austere, naturalistic Greek theater. As the warm June sun danced upon the slim, gnarled branches of the trees, creating soft shadows, each teen mother read her own writing out loud to an attentive audience composed of Shayla and other classmates from the Teen Parent Program, as well as friends, teachers, affiliates of Shakespeare & Company, and a few parents. Carol Gilligan and Normi Noel beamed with pride as each teen mother read her own writing aloud in a clear, confident voice.

"What I've learned from my work with these girls," said Normi, "is that with whomever it is you are mentoring, you better know how to show up yourself, and you better be able to find your own humility in that position because it requires you to have the courage to stand openly with another person and to be in the presence of the currents of truth that they are looking for.

"I once saw a street sign pasted up on a window of an abandoned building," Normi recalled. "It said, 'The greatest teachers of all are ice cubes.' What I interpreted that to mean is that as a teacher, you need to be able to melt in the water, you need to be able to disappear. You're with the kids, and then in the end you need to gracefully let go of that position when you have supplied something for them that other people have done for you, which is simply being there and listening."

A week after their staged reading, several of the teen mothers attended Shakespeare & Company's production of *Summer.* As the houselights dimmed and the curtain lifted, they sat back and watched, captivated, as Charity Royall's destiny played itself out right before their eyes. The story was one that by then they knew well:

Charity Royall hates her life, has a tense relationship with her foster father, and dreams of escaping North Dormer. She pins her hopes on a handsome young architect from the city who visits the library where she works to do research on old houses in the area. Before long, Charity and this seductive stranger are romantically entangled. After a few months of reckless passion and exquisite pleasure, Charity discovers that she is pregnant. Before she even has a chance to share this news with her lover, she learns of his grievous betrayal. Too proud, too heartbroken, and too bewildered to confide in anyone, Charity decides to hide her pregnancy while she explores her options. Her own parents are not around to advise her. Her biological father is in jail for murder, and she has long been estranged from her mother, an impoverished alcoholic and former prostitute who lives in a decrepit shantytown on the peak of a foreboding mountain.

Removed from her mother's home at age four, Charity has been raised by her foster father, Mr. Royall. After the premature death of his wife, Royall disgusts Charity with his drunken binges and his inappropriate sexual advances. There is no one Charity trusts, no one she feels she can turn to for guidance. She feels totally alone in the world. Determined to keep her pregnancy a secret, she struggles for months, until the changes in her body begin to make the truth visible. At that point, she is forced to make a difficult decision about her destiny and the future of her unborn child.

When *Summer* was first published, it was viewed as scandalous and incendiary. People were taken aback by Charity's raw eroticism and disgusted by the incestuous undertones of her relationship with her foster father. Readers were stunned that Edith Wharton, a woman so cushioned by wealth all her life, had dared step away from familiar terrain to take a hard, critical, unflinching look at the sharp divisions between social classes, zeroing in on the darkest of subject matter: hopelessness, despair, crime, alcoholism, prostitution, incest, abortion, absent parenting, and premarital sex.

In the novel, Edith Wharton contrasts the beautiful freedom of nature and the transcendence of unbridled passion with the unrelenting constraints of Charity's life in an oppressive, stifling small town, spiraling downward, bereft of hope and opportunity. The profound inequality inherent to American society is personified by Charity and her rival for her lover's affections, the fabulously wealthy, elegant, refined, city-born-and-bred, blond-haired, blue-eyed Annabel Balch.

Incisive and unrelenting, Edith Wharton's social conscience was ahead of its time and remains to this day at the center of her indelible legacy. Perhaps most notable is Wharton's blatant refusal to whitewash her perceptions of what went on "behind the paintless wooden house-fronts of the long village street or in the isolated farm-houses on the neighboring hills."

In her memoir, *A Backward Glance,* Wharton offered the following response to critics of her stark, brutal realism:

> *Summer* . . . was received with indignant denial by many reviewers and readers; not the least vociferous were the New Englanders who had for years sought the reflection of local

> life in the rose-and-lavender pages of their favourite authoresses—and had forgotten to look into Hawthorne's.

"Here in Pittsfield, we're heavily involved in dealing with sexual abuse," said Captain Patrick Barry, speaking from a dimly lit room at the police station where old records were stored. "One of our day detectives handles sex crimes and he focuses almost exclusively on child abuse sex cases. The Department of Social Services reports information to the district attorney's office and then it comes to us. We also get some reports directly in cases where a child may disclose something to the other parent or a friend or relative or a teacher or a doctor. There are certain mandated reporters. Under the law they have to report suspected abuse. Priests, by the way, were never mandated but now they will be after that scandal."

In a discussion of the results of the ACE (Adverse Childhood Experience) study, Dr. Felitti, Dr. Anda, and their colleagues raised several questions, including the issue of "whether sexual abuse during childhood is the primary destructive force or simply a dramatic marker for a severely dysfunctional family." Statistics show that a significant number of teen mothers such as Liz have painful histories indelibly marked by sexual trauma. In July 1998 the *Journal of the American Medical Association* published a review of several of the most conclusive research studies to date regarding the significant links between sexual abuse and teen pregnancy:

> Child and adolescent sexual abuse is a risk factor for teen pregnancy on two levels. First, sexual abuse is a common

> antecedent of adolescent pregnancy, with up to 66% of pregnant teens reporting histories of abuse. Conversely, sexually abused adolescent girls are significantly more likely to have been pregnant than teens without abuse histories. A history of sexual abuse has been linked to high-risk behaviors that may account for increased risk of early unplanned pregnancy, including young age at initiation of sexual intercourse, failure to use contraception, prostitution, engagement in relationships involving physical assault, and abuse of alcohol and other drugs. Moreover, girls with histories of sexual abuse have been found to have a greater desire to conceive and increased concerns about infertility than girls without abuse histories.

At age eight, Liz found a way to tell the story of her molestation to a judge, but how many young girls and teenagers remain silent, repressing, suffering, and disassociating as the abuse goes on, sometimes for years, as it did in the traumatic case of Jessica's grandparents and their children? How many doctors neglect to ask pregnant teenagers if they have ever been sexually abused? Every day in this country, how many sex education classes are taught in which the phrase *sexual abuse* is never even mentioned? Can sex education classes that promote "abstinence only," give teenagers and preteens the knowledge, comfort level, and negotiation skills to defend themselves against molestation, incest, date rape, and sex described as "voluntary but not really wanted"?

For years a cloak of silence, denial, and discomfort has covered sexual abuse in medical and educational settings and within American society at large, preventing the public from clearly seeing key factors that are inextricably entwined with the roots of teen pregnancy. The scandal within the Catholic Church has opened up a dialogue about sexual abuse, but perhaps even more difficult for society to stomach is the thought of sexual abuse occurring with alarming frequency within the four walls of the family home. Without widespread acknowledgment of the prevalence of childhood sexual abuse in all its forms and a strategy to address this particular risk factor, plans for significantly reducing teen pregnancy remain incomplete, like a puzzle missing a crucial, central piece.

After years of experience counseling teen mothers, Joann Oliver accepted the position of clinical coordinator at Berkshire County Kids' Place, a child-advocacy center in Pittsfield that specializes in treating children who have disclosed sexual abuse. Within the comfortable, homelike environment of Kids' Place, young victims of sexual abuse receive services from a multidisciplinary team that includes trained clinicians, police officers and detectives, the district attorney's office, and pediatricians. Kids' Place coordinates and unites these separate organizations so that they can act as a team to represent the best interests of each child.

In her mid-thirties and a mother of two, Joann is passionately committed to counseling and mentoring the children who are referred to her. She estimates that approximately one hundred new sexual-abuse cases are referred for treatment every year. The vast majority of the children and adolescents are residents of Pittsfield.

Although Joann counsels some teenagers and small children, most of her clients are between the ages of eight and eleven. In addition to all the new referrals, there are roughly 175 children in ongoing treatment for traumas such as sexual abuse, physical abuse, and witnessing domestic violence.

"I don't think that once the damage occurs, that's it," said Joann. "I think education is a big part of recovery. I think if the child has a good support system, that's very important. If there's just one person in their life who believes their account of the abuse and takes them seriously, that can be very helpful."

One of the biggest challenges Joann faces in her job is explaining the family dynamics within which sexual abuse occurs. Often these dynamics are either not well known or are misunderstood.

"We're often asked by the police or the D.A.'s office, 'Why didn't this kid tell, if the abuse has been going on for five years?' I have to explain that maybe a young girl didn't disclose because the perpetrator said that her family would fall apart and her mother would kick her out. And, in fact, when she does tell, that's exactly what happens."

Joann is familiar with the varying degrees of household dysfunction and abuse described by Sheri, Nadine, Colleen, Shayla, Jessica, and Liz. In her line of work, she comes across similar stories every day.

"In households where there's sexual abuse and/or domestic violence, there are not good boundaries in place," Joann explained. "There's a lot of sexual innuendo and a lot of situations where boundaries just are not defined. If a young girl is in the bathroom taking a shower and her father or stepfather or brother comes in to go to the bathroom, even if they don't look at her, they are showing no regard for boundaries and no respect for her space.

"Then when these girls grow up and they end up in a relationship where the other person is possessive and likes to know where they're going and what they're doing all the time, they actually see that as loving and caring rather than as controlling. They often think, 'Oh, this person cares so much about me. He doesn't want me to see my friends, he only wants me to be with him.' I don't even think these young women see their bodies as their own. They find love by physical contact and they end up in these relationships where they're not able to say, 'Stop!' or, 'We need to use protection!' "

Over the years, Joann has closely observed and documented the symptoms exhibited by teenagers who have been sexually abused. Suffering immensely, these troubled adolescents often engaged in high-risk, self-destructive behaviors such as self-cutting, drug use, excessive drinking, promiscuity, and running away. As Joann astutely pointed out, these symptoms were identical to the high-risk behaviors that resulted in their getting into situations in which they faced a huge risk of getting pregnant. When Liz ran away at thirteen to escape her abusive, promiscuous mother and the host of boyfriends drifting in and out of the family home, she subsequently sought food and shelter in the apartments of adult men who were able to convince her that they "loved" her.

Joann has seen numerous cases like Nadine's, in which adolescents' accounts of intolerable home situations were contradicted by their parents and simply not believed by the Department of Social Services or the police, resulting in the teenagers being shuttled from one foster home to another in between repetitious stints in their original malignant home environments.

"A lot of the struggles we have with the different professions and agencies we have to work with relate to the problem that sometimes the high-risk self-destructive behaviors ruin the girl's credibility," explained Joann, "so then when she comes forward and says that she has been sexually abused, oftentimes a parent or family member may say, 'Well, she's always running away, or she's always lying to me. Now she's lying about this, too.' It's a double-edged sword because the very symptoms that are due to the sexual abuse often confuse people into thinking that the girl is not credible.

"Most of the time if a child or teen discloses and the mother does not support them or believe them, the chances of them recanting are pretty high," said Joann. "We've had a number of cases with teen girls where they've disclosed and the perpetrator has been the mother's boyfriend or their stepfather. What happens then is that the mother doesn't believe the girl partly because of those acting-out behaviors I spoke about earlier. So she's forced to make a decision to kick the father out or to put the child in foster care. Oftentimes the girl goes to foster care and the mom continues living with the perpetrator. In those situations, those girls are at a much higher risk for teen parenthood."

Compounding the problems that abused girls face in their own homes is a foster care system that is often extremely impersonal. Liz, Sheri, and Nadine reported being extremely unhappy with their foster home placements; yet instead of someone helping them adjust and find their way into a more stable situation, often anonymous workers within the bureaucratic system actualized the girls' fears of upheaval and transience by arbitrarily returning them to their original home environments and then reassigning them to a new foster home when trouble inevitably arose again. None of these girls ever had a sense that one mentor within the system was consistently concerned and looking out for them and making sure to place them in a supportive, nurturing foster home where they might thrive. Where they ended up just seemed to be the luck of the draw, reinforcing their sense that they had no control over their own lives.

Between 1995 and 2000, while Liz estimates that she was in and out of twelve foster homes, the number of children in America's foster care system doubled, from 250,000 to roughly 560,000. In November 2000 *Time* magazine ran a cover story titled "The Crisis of Foster Care." The article addressed several key factors that were responsible for the bureaucratic system's failure to ensure the welfare of the children it was supposed to protect. The list included poor, archaic recordkeeping (hardcover binders as opposed to a centralized national computer database), inadequate monitoring of individual cases (missed visits, bad decisions about placements), and a huge turnover of social workers (close to 70 percent in some states). One lawyer the journalists interviewed remarked dryly, "You can't even run a Burger King with a seventy percent turnover!"

At Kids' Place, Joann Oliver made sure she maintained a consistent, relatively long-term presence in the lives of the children she treated. Girls whom Joann had treated when they were nine were encouraged to stop in to see her as teenagers. She tried to maintain her connections with these kids and made it clear that if at any point in their lives they needed advice, guidance, or services, they could count on her being a phone call away. Joann realized that her steady, predictable presence in their lives was vital, particularly in cases where a girl's disclosure of sexual abuse had severely impaired her relationship with her mother and splintered her family, leaving her with few if any sympathetic, receptive elders to turn to.

"We've had situations where even though the case has gone to court and the stepfather has been found guilty and sentenced to jail for fifteen or twenty years, the mother still will not make reparations with the girl," said Joann. "That kind of mother-daughter relationship is really damaging to the young girl's development. Those teenagers are much more at risk of ending up in really bad relationships and becoming pregnant."

Joann frequently talked to teenage girls who believed that giving their mothers grandchildren might be the first step toward mending their fractured relationships. All too often, this was proven to be true, at least in the short term. Sheri and Liz both reconciled with their mothers temporarily during their pregnancies, and the arrival of Colleen's baby, Jonathan, did indeed bring joy and cohesion to a depressed household.

In addition to treating children who had disclosed sexual abuse, Joann treated boys and girls who had witnessed domestic violence. She found that when very young children witnessed their mothers being battered, it was as detrimental to them psychologically as if they themselves were the victims because at that age, they had not yet separated from their primary caretaker, so watching their mother being abused was just as damaging as it would be if the pain were inflicted directly upon them.

"There's a lot of research that has indicated that boys who have witnessed domestic violence are much more likely to become sexual perpetrators," said Joann. "The element in common seems to be power. When young sexual offenders perpetrate sexually, they feel powerful and don't have that feeling of helplessness that they had when they stood by and witnessed their mothers being battered."

The numerous arrests, prosecutions, and subsequent incarcerations of the fathers of Shayla's, Jessica's, Colleen's, and Nadine's babies on charges of assault and battery reflected the police department's hard-core approach to addressing the problem of domestic and dating violence, particularly in households where young children were living with young mothers. Some of these perpetrators, who had fathered children with one or more teen mothers, had reportedly witnessed their own mothers being battered at some point during their childhood. These were not isolated, unusual cases.

Domestic and dating violence among teenagers is a nightmare that America is slowly waking up to. According to estimates from the U.S. Centers for Disease Control and Prevention, 22 percent of high school students are victims of nonsexual dating violence, with girls slightly more likely to report being victims. Even more teens experience verbal or emotional abuse. A similarly disturbing statistic surfaced in an article published in the July 2001 issue of the *Journal of the American Medical Association* featuring a study led by Jay G. Silverman of Harvard University's School of Public Health. Silverman's research sample was composed of 4,163 students who attended public schools in the state of Massachusetts. More than 70 percent of the girls who participated in the study were white. Participants were asked if they'd ever been shoved, slapped, hit, or forced into any sexual activity, including rape, by a date. They were also asked about recent risky behavior. The results indicated that "one in five high school girls had been physically or sexually abused by a dating partner, significantly increasing their risk of drug abuse, suicide and other harmful behavior. Victimized girls were about eight to nine times more likely to have attempted suicide in the previous year and four to six times more likely to have ever been pregnant."

Colleen's and Nadine's brutal victimization during their pregnancies was sadly and alarmingly a common thread that connected their experience to those of other pregnant teenagers across the country. Violence expert James Makepeace explained that "because teenagers are lacking in the developmental maturity and self-control that ideally should accompany sexual intimacy, there is a greater risk that they will use violence to vent frustration, punish their partner, or in an attempt to terminate an unwanted pregnancy." A survey administered to pregnant adolescents in metropolitan areas yielded the following results: "Of the more than two hundred pregnant teens surveyed, twenty-six percent reported they were in a relationship with a male partner who was physically abusive. Of those females being abused, forty to sixty percent stated that the battering had either begun or escalated since discovery of the pregnancy. Even more alarming was the fact that sixty-five percent of those abused had not talked with anyone about the abuse, and no one had reported the abuse to the law enforcement agencies." The study concluded that "battering during teen pregnancy is potentially a major adolescent health problem, jeopardizing adolescent and infant health. Women abused during pregnancy are at greater risk for medical complications of pregnancy, delivery of low birth-weight babies and homicide."

As director of the Berkshire Violence Prevention Center in Pittsfield, Katrina Mattson-Brown chose to dedicate herself to teaching high school students. Whenever she guest-lectured health classes, her goal was to teach teenagers how to identify the components of abusive relationships, and to then explain why it was essential for them to get out of such situations. Limited by funding constraints, Katrina could spend only two days at each high school. She made the most of what little time she had.

Katrina devoted one day to gender identity. She led discussions that explored how kids felt about the ways in which the media, popular culture, and their own friends and families defined the roles and expectations for male and female behavior. Her perception was that as patterns of abusive relationships observed during childhood repeated themselves from one generation to the next, they were often characterized by heavy gender-stereotyping: women were more likely to assume the passive role of victim, and men were more likely to assume the active role of perpetrator.

Katrina observed that as many teenagers struggled to define themselves and sought status and popularity within their peer groups, they often experimented and role-played, trying on new "adult" identities, often going to extreme caricatures of masculine "macho" and feminine "submissive" behaviors in their efforts to conform to distorted, archaic gender stereotypes. Sometimes adolescents who felt the desperate need to boldly assert their masculinity or femininity resorted to using teen parenthood to bolster their efforts, assuming the generic roles of "mother" and "father" while searching for authority and self-esteem somewhere within the fragile narcissistic grandiosity they felt when relating to a helpless, dependent child.

However, because developing a mature, integrated identity is by its very nature a long-term process entailing a period of psychological growth that stretches into young adulthood and often beyond, the expectation that teen parenthood could provide a shortcut to self-definition usually turned out to be a fleeting illusion that quickly soured into bitter disappointment. As in the case of C.J. and Shayla, the reality was that more often than not, the strain of teen parenthood produced feelings of profound inferiority, particularly in the young fathers who found themselves incapable of meeting the needs of their girlfriends and children. Physical aggression was a last resort, a desperate attempt to assert power, enforce control, and prove one's masculinity.

"When we talk to teenagers about the different types of abuse," said Katrina, "one of the things we talk a lot about is sexual assault and rape and another kind of sexual violence—being pressured to have sex. With teen pregnancy, what sometimes happens is that the girls are in an abusive relationship and don't feel powerful enough to say no."

During her presentations Katrina always discussed the controversial issue of sex when a female is intoxicated. "We explain to the kids that if a girl is drunk, sex may be considered rape. We tell them that the law is quite clear that if someone is drunk, it's very questionable as to whether or not they are capable of consenting. Most kids are pretty surprised about that. When they leave, they're asked to fill out evaluation forms and there's a section of fill-in-the-blanks. Almost all the boys and girls write: *One thing I didn't know before this course was . . . the law about rape and alcohol and consent.*"

In classrooms all over Berkshire County, Katrina ventured beyond the physical, concrete aspects of violence to address the more complex psychological characteristics of abusive relationships. Wherever she lectured, she brought along a large piece of white fabric on which the forlorn life-size outline of a person was traced. This "person" appeared completely empty and expressionless, devoid of any defining features and characteristics. Katrina hung this dull, lifeless, limp "person" up on the blackboard and wrote five haunting words above its head: "Could This Happen to Me?"

A few boys usually tittered nervously before silence descended upon the class and all eyes gravitated toward the front of the room where the empty "person" hung. When she was confident that she had captured everyone's attention, Katrina proceeded to hand out pads of Post-it notes in a rainbow of colors and asked each teenager to write down words that represented something about themselves and their lives that was very personal, very important, and very precious—something that they would never allow anyone to take away from them.

Pens scribbled and a few minutes later Katrina asked the students to share with the class what they had written. Some teenagers who had answered with the words "my family" explained that their parents and grandparents and siblings provided unconditional love, confidence, and positive reinforcement. Some who had written "being good at soccer" or "basketball" explained that they liked being part of a team and that they liked games and competitions because those events gave them something exciting to work toward and look forward to. Others who had written "doing well in school" said that getting good grades gave them hope and a sense of pride and accomplishment. Others wrote "friends" because they valued the support of their peers.

After listening to all the responses, Katrina asked the students to stick their Post-it notes on the "person," who was suddenly transformed from a blank, depressing canvas into a colorful, vibrant, multilayered figure adorned with all the words that described the things that were most precious and most important to the students. Katrina then began a discussion that centered on how the items the teenagers had written down and posted fed "the person's" self-esteem. Then using an interactive question-and-answer method that involved the kids' ideas and participation, Katrina proceeded to construct a story in which she demonstrated how an abuser could strip these positive attributes away from the "person."

"Your family doesn't like your boyfriend," Katrina said. "They think he treats you badly and they tell you to stop dating him. What do you do?" she asked.

"Keep dating him anyway," agreed a few girls, giggling.

"So the abuser has already created a wedge between you and your family," said Katrina, removing the fluorescent yellow Post-it upon which the words "my family" were written.

"Your boyfriend says that he loves you and that he's jealous of the time you spend with other people. He makes it clear that he wants you to spend all your free time with him and says that if you really loved him, you would. So you want to make him happy . . . What do you have to give up in order to do that?"

The classroom was quiet.

"Well, if you're spending all your free time with your boyfriend, how are you gonna keep up with your other friends? And what about soccer practice?"

Katrina removed the lime green Post-it notes upon which the words "my two best friends" and "soccer" were written. She proceeded with this line of thought until every single Post-it note—fluorescent yellow, lime green, orange, turquoise, and hot pink—had been removed, leaving the "person" blank and colorless.

"So what's left to fuel this 'person's' self-esteem?" Katrina asked before explaining that because "the person" had allowed the abuser to make her give up all the other sources of pride, accomplishment, companionship, and support in her life, she was now dependent on him for all those things, so it became that much harder to leave him, because the connection with her abuser was the only thing sustaining her. Now she would go to great lengths and tolerate more abuse in her repeated attempts to win back the love and approval of the abuser who had suddenly become the most important person in her life. Why? Because she had allowed the abuser to become the sole provider of her self-esteem, validation, and sense of identity, all of which she craved desperately and felt empty without.

"This is what it feels like to be trapped in addictive, abusive relationship," Katrina concluded, pointing to the blank, lifeless outline of a person hanging limply from the blackboard at the front of the classroom.

In another visually captivating classroom demonstration, Katrina drew a giant heart up on the blackboard. She asked the teenagers to identify things they felt were healthy in a relationship and things they felt were unhealthy. As each student named behaviors, situations, and feelings, Katrina wrote their words inside the perimeter of the heart. On the left side of the heart she wrote things that were positive and healthy, and she wrote things that were negative and unhealthy on the right side. She explained that abusive relationships don't always start out with violence, that at first there was usually a honeymoon period in which the couple fell in love and everything went smoothly. Then one day that honeymoon period was shattered by a seemingly spontaneous episode of physical or verbal abuse, followed by more romantic, loving moments. The problem was that over time the abuse often overshadowed the romantic, loving moments, yet the two still coexisted within the relationship, which made it all the more difficult to walk away.

"Most women stay with their abusers because they keep wishing and hoping and believing that things will go back to being great again," said Katrina, "but more often than not, once violence makes itself known, it doesn't just go away even though there are still some good times."

Like Shayla and Colleen, many teenagers tended to think of relationships as either good or bad, and it was hard for them to comprehend how a relationship could be good and bad at the same time. Within their relationships with the fathers of their babies, Colleen and Shayla defensively split off from the negatives, pushing the abuse out of their consciousness and denying its implications while romanticizing and magnifying the small embers of love they stoked as they clung to their increasingly unrealistic hopes that their boyfriends would morph into the idealized men they fantasized about. Both teenagers suffered the consequences of remaining trapped in abusive relationships for too long. Katrina's objective was ideally to intervene in the lives of teenagers such as Shayla and Colleen before they got trapped in abusive relationships that rendered them powerless and at risk for pregnancy.

"Every time I finish a presentation a few kids come up to me," said Katrina. "They usually say something like 'This really hit home' or 'Can I talk to you about my relationship?' In some schools we used to provide office hours. We would be on-site one day a week so that if our presentation triggered something and the kids needed to talk to us privately, they could come see us. We're not able to do that anymore because of funding. We just can't afford to. Our program used to receive state funds from the Department of Education, but then one Friday, last September, when the governor was on her way out, all of a sudden we heard that all our funding had been completely cut. We knew budget cuts were coming, but we mistakenly thought that our program to prevent teen dating violence was safe."

Worse lay ahead for Katrina and other dedicated workers. In January of 2003, Mitt Romney was sworn in as governor of Massachusetts. Facing a $650 million budget gap, he promptly resorted to using emergency budget-balancing powers and announced plans for enormous cuts, including $114 million from local aid, $41 million from education, and $133 million from social and health-care programs. Programs to prevent teen pregnancy suffered.

Statewide, anxious administrators of these and other youth-oriented programs racked their brains for ways to slash costs, determined to keep their doors open so that their young people would not be shortchanged. Months went by, and with America in a recession and billions going toward national defense and the war in Iraq, many wondered how, where, when—and if—their country would be able to find the resources necessary to ensure the welfare of its many children at risk.

Despite falling upon hard times, Katrina refused to sacrifice her idealistic objectives.

"We're committed to continuing our work," she insisted. "We're still going into almost every school in Berkshire County. We always leave the kids making sure they understand how to access services at Kids' Place and at the Elizabeth Freeman Center, which is Pittsfield's shelter for battered women. We give the kids these telephone numbers and we tell them, 'This is where you can call, this is what you can do.' We remind them that the school counselor is there to listen to them and we stress that if kids disclose anything, they will be sure to get access to the right services."

At Pittsfield High School, guidance counselors have caseloads of 250 to 260 students each, and as much as they try to stay involved in the lives of students, the reality is that they are spread too thin. *The Berkshire Eagle* featured an article titled "Mission Impossible?" in which the director of guidance at the high school bemoaned that "counselors spend most of their time on problems like why kids are running away from home or won't do their homework rather then on what colleges they should apply to. 'We are trying to find out why a lot of kids seem to have no connection to what's going on,' she said. 'They are living day-to-day and I am living six months in their future. I can see the consequences of not doing something today and they are struggling with things at home.' "

"Our schools are conscious of the fact that a lot of the things parents and families used to do for children, schools are now expected to do," said Pittsfield's mayor, Sara Hathaway. "Unbelievable demands are being placed on the community and on the school system, and on the after-school programs, too. We have a great Boys and Girls Club, we have Boy Scouts, Girl Scouts, and Cub Scouts. We have team sports and organized sports outside of the schools and leagues. We have all kinds of activities available for young people, and I think that all of the adults that are affiliated with these groups are reaching out constantly. But I think a lot depends on the parents. Did they read to their kids? Did they talk to their kids about drugs? Do they sit down around the table and eat dinner and ask their kid how their day was? What kind of rapport do they have with their children? Where do they take up the responsibility of paying attention to their kids? There's only so much the schools can do."

During the past decade, many factors have contributed to this increasingly relevant and controversial issue of the widening gap between where a parent's responsibility ends and a school's begins. The number of households headed by single women who have children grew nearly five times faster in the 1990s compared with the number of married couples with children. Less than a quarter of American households are made up of married couples living with their children, and more than 40 percent of female-headed families live below the poverty line. Six years after the 1996 national welfare reform law went into effect, it was declared by many to be an unequivocal success, with advocates pointing to data showing that "welfare rolls have plummeted by more than 50% and child poverty is at its lowest point in more than twenty years."

But behind these new and improved statistics were many single mothers such as Liz, Sheri, Amy, and Shayla who worked long hours at grueling, monotonous, low-wage jobs, and Jessica, who went to college and worked part-time. While these young single mothers attended work or school, their small children spent most of their waking hours in day-care centers that varied enormously in terms of quality and reliability of personnel, as was evidenced in Katherine Boo's shocking investigation of Washington, D.C., day-care centers and by Shayla's terrible experience of seeing her son coming home with mysterious bruises, thinking he must have gotten them while playing, and then finding out that the woman who ran his day-care center had overdosed on heroin and died.

It won't be long before Jaiden, Kaliegh, Marcus, Peter, Ezakeil, Caleb, Jonathan, and Leeah and other children like them start turning to their schools in search of the guidance, nurturing, and adult mentorship that was so sparingly rationed to them by their hardworking parents during their early years. The growing void when it comes to the social and emotional nurturing of young children across the country presents an enormous challenge, and many schools have not yet begun to adjust their curriculums because they lack either the inclination or the resources, or both. Nobel laureate economist James Heckman believes that earlier intervention costs less and is more effective and that as children become teenagers and teenagers become

adults, the cost of intervention goes up as the rate of intervention success goes down. Thus, says Heckman, "It pays to invest in the young."

Heckman questions the prevalent tendency among American educators to overemphasize cognitive skills as measured by academic achievement or IQ tests while virtually ignoring "the critical importance of social skills, self-discipline and a variety of non-cognitive skills that are known to determine success in life." He believes that "one can make a bigger difference and have more of an impact with children during the early years because the social skills they learn in the very early years set a pattern for acquiring life skills later."

Some of the very same issues of emotional maturity, social skills, and life skills are at the core of President George W. Bush's Marriage-Incentive Program. Eager to increase success rates of marriages and to restore the shattered institution of America's nuclear family so that

more children can grow up in loving two-parent homes, the current administration has allocated funding for marital counseling, mentoring, and educational programs that aim to help married couples stay together. Following the logic of James Heckman, wouldn't some of this money be better spent nurturing the emotional, social, and life skills of the very young?

Across the country, a handful of bold educators familiar with Howard Gardner's theory of multiple intelligences and Daniel Goleman's theory of emotional intelligence have pioneered innovative new programs that place a premium on what James Heckman calls "noncognitive skills." Within galvanized curriculums, these educators are actively addressing the enormous importance of their students' emotional competence, motivation, and stress management. They are prioritizing the development of the ability to relate to others effectively and with empathy, and they are recognizing the need for activities that serve as rites of passage for adolescents as they approach the transition to adulthood. Rather than lamenting or evading their students' growing need for guidance and mentorship in all areas of their lives, these educators are confronting it and attempting to offer leadership and counsel.

One of the most impressive curriculums created to address the social, emotional, and spiritual needs of adolescents is the Council Program, founded in 1980 by Jack Zimmerman, educator, therapist, and president of the Ojai Foundation.

"Inspired by the Native American tradition of council, the program is based on the belief that respectful listening and speaking from the heart are central to creating a sense of community," explained Zimmerman. "These concepts are represented by the form of the circle, within which close, sustained, open interaction between elders and the younger generation is possible."

After its initiation at a small experimental school in the early 1980s, the Council Program was incorporated into the curriculum at the Crossroads School in Santa Monica, California. At this private school, the course was nicknamed "Mysteries" because in each group the teachers asked the teenagers to share their deepest questions, thoughts, fears, and feelings. Every year, the course retains a degree of flexibility and can be broadened and enhanced to address the issues that are of greatest concern to the students in any given group. One of the reasons adolescents love "Mysteries" so much is because they actively collaborate with their teachers to help create the curriculum, thus playing a central role in determining, shaping, and influencing what they learn.

Back in 1982, Jack Zimmerman and his colleague, Ruthann Saphier, wrote in their mission statement:

> We have discovered that our young people have unspeakable fears about the future and that they yearn for a sense of *meaning* or *purpose*, which they don't know how to find.

> These young people long to connect to something larger than themselves. They long to find their place in creating and participating in a new, more hopeful paradigm. We must dare to create in our schools a place to begin to meet those needs. "Mysteries" arose from and thrives from a bold re-envisioning of the meaning of education, health, and citizenship for the twenty-first century. . . . "Mysteries" aims to help teenagers from all walks of life come to terms with matters such as the erosion of family and community, a changing economy, the changes in the American workplace, a mass media wildly at odds with traditional values, the destruction of our biosphere, the untenable balance of resources in our country and our world, and the threat of more immediate destruction still posed by nuclear weapons.

In the more than twenty years that have elapsed since this mission statement was first written, American society has endured many destabilizing shifts: an increase in single-mother families; constantly evolving definitions of gender roles; the pressing moral and ethical questions posed by corporate corruption; the pollution of the natural environment; the widening income gap; the recession; the stressful, heightened presence of chemical and biological warfare; terrorism's encroachment on daily life; and the threat of weapons of mass destruction. All have intensified the sense of anxiety, alienation, emptiness, and confusion about the future that so many teenagers experience, making the Council Program and its "Mysteries" curriculum more compelling, relevant, and vital than ever before.

At the Crossroads School, the Council Program is integrated into life-skills seminars administered by the Human Development Department. These seminars convene for roughly ninety minutes once a week, during which time the comprehensive "Mysteries" curriculum sets out to reduce stress and self-destructive behaviors among adolescents in grades six through twelve by "building identity definition and self-esteem; setting goals and strengthening the will; creating and instituting rites of passage, both on the school premises and on multiday retreats that bring the kids closer to nature; developing communication and decision-making skills, as well as nonviolent exploration and resolution of conflicts; nurturing imagination, intuition, and a mind-body connection; offering preventive health education about sexuality, drugs, and gender identity; fostering access to feelings of playfulness and joy; celebrating human diversity; discussing the importance of self and group validation; encouraging divergent thinking; exploring group problem solving; discussing the meanings of friendship and intimacy; teaching personal and social responsibility; and enhancing spiritual education that stems from developing a sense of meaning and purpose through storytelling about one's own life in a way that evokes a sense of personal myth."

The program at the Crossroads School culminates in a five-day rite-of-passage ceremony for seniors. This retreat takes place on the grounds of the Ojai Foundation. From start to finish, the program provides a form and context within which each teenager can engage in a process of self-definition that occurs internally and through the experience of being witnessed by others.

The curriculum and teaching methods Zimmerman and Saphier pioneered have since been expanded and refined by several innovative and dedicated educators, including Maureen Murdock, Rachael Kessler, and Peggy O'Brien. Kessler has written extensively about her work in the area of social and emotional learning in a book titled *The Soul of Education: Helping Students Find Connection, Compassion, and Character at School*. Following the years she spent as chair of the Department of Human Development at the Crossroads School, Kessler became director of the Institute for Social and Emotional Learning. She provides workshops for educators all over the country and consults with schools that want to develop curricula like the Council Program. Kessler emphasizes the importance of "Passages," which she defines as the series of transitions that characterize the adolescent's journey into adulthood.

"What distinguishes the 'Mysteries' and 'Passages' curriculum from many of the other programs in social and emotional learning," writes Kessler, "is that it also recognizes spiritual development in the adolescent and provides an opportunity for students to explore meaning and purpose in life, to experience stillness, silence, and solitude, to express their yearning for transcendence, joy, and creativity, and to experience a deep connection to themselves, others, and the wholeness of life. Thus 'health education' is returned to the original meaning of health, 'to make whole.' Health from this perspective is defined as the integration of mind, body, community, spirit, and heart."

The Palms Middle School is one of several public schools in the Los Angeles Unified School District that have adopted the Council Program. Jack Zimmerman estimates that the cost of delivering the program to the twelve hundred Palms sixth and eighth graders is about $125 per student per year and can run up to $250 per student for some programs depending on their size and scope. Not a huge price to pay for enhancing the development of the next generation, who will inherit the responsibility of nurturing and sustaining a very diverse, very complex America.

"We just got a grant from the Annenberg Foundation," Zimmerman reported jubilantly. "It's to help the Palms Middle School become an Institute for Council Training so that more teachers can come and learn how to replicate the Council Program in their schools."

Like the Council Program, the Children's Aid Society-Carrera Program, created by Dr. Michael Carrera, takes a comprehensive, long-term approach to youth development. Unlike the Council Program, which has been integrated directly into the school curriculum at private and public schools, the Carrera Program meets after school at different sites in indigent neighborhoods across the country and is geared toward adolescents who are at high risk for teen pregnancy and parenthood. The program's curriculum aims to fill the frequently unsupervised hours between late afternoon, when school ends, and evening, when parents get off from work, provided that they only have one job and work the day shift. The curriculum is designed to work with eleven- to twelve-year-olds who meet five or six days a week, twelve months a year, for five to seven years, until they graduate from high school.

An intensive evaluation of the Carrera Program conducted by Douglas Kirby for the National Campaign to Prevent Teen Pregnancy "demonstrated that, amongst girls, it significantly delayed the onset of sex, increased the use of condoms and other effective methods of contraception, and reduced pregnancy and birth rates." Supported over the years by the Robin Hood Foundation, the Bernice and Milton Stern Foundation, and the Charles Stewart Mott Foundation, the

Carrera Program costs $4,000 per child per year and encompasses "family life and sex education, individual academic assessment, tutoring, help with homework, preparation for standardized exams, and assistance with college entrance. It provides opportunities for self-expression through the arts and participation in sports activities. It makes available comprehensive health care, including mental health and reproductive health services and contraception. In addition, it offers work-related activities, including a job club, stipends, individual bank accounts, employment, and career awareness."

When it comes to sex education, the current administration has been strident about allocating federal support to "abstinence only" programs. The success of the Carrera Program shifts the spotlight away from the government and illuminates the vital, pivotal philanthropic role that can be played by private, family, and corporate foundations that take the initiative and follow their own independent agendas. According to the Charles Stewart Mott Foundation newsletter: "The Carrera program, which currently serves more than 2,000 adolescents annually, is considerably less expensive than the public cost of teenage pregnancies, estimated by the National Campaign to Prevent Teen Pregnancy at more than $7 billion each year for health care and financial assistance to teen mothers and their children."

A five-year replication project costing about $10 million is currently under way to bring the Carrera Program into even more communities. Five regional training centers have been established across the United States, and each will manage seven Carrera-based teen pregnancy prevention programs.

No plans or funding are yet in place to open a Carrera-based program in Pittsfield. In 2001 the city faced a budget deficit of $8–

$10 million. A state oversight board was closely monitoring its finances. In city council meetings that addressed how to reduce Pittsfield's expenditures, several people suggested turning off the streetlights.

Mayor Sara Hathaway was elected in 2002. She faces many obstacles in her quest to help Pittsfield and its citizens into a phase of recovery, renewal, and self-definition, yet like the creators of the Council Program and the Carrera Program, she embodies a spirit of courage, optimism, idealism, and innovation. A native of Michigan, Sara Hathaway upset Pittsfield's entrenched old boys' network when she defeated nine male opponents to win the election. To many citizens of Pittsfield, the swearing-in of this bright, focused, strong, compassionate, energetic woman in her late thirties symbolized their ability to initiate change in their community through participation in the democratic process.

With a degree in urban planning and previous experience as senior planner of the Berkshire Regional Planning Commission and as State Senator Andrea Nuciforo's chief of staff and district director, Mayor Hathaway brought expertise to the table. She formulated a detailed plan to revitalize Pittsfield's downtown using funds from a settlement with GE and has expressed her dedication to improving educational opportunities and vocational training. She dreams of starting a performing arts magnet school in Pittsfield that would draw on the region's wealth of talent and train a new generation of actors, musicians, filmmakers, composers, dancers, theater directors, and production designers.

Mayor Hathaway remains committed to ensuring that all citizens of Pittsfield have direct access to her and are allowed to have their say when it comes to determining how their city should be run. In her inauguration speech she vowed, "While I am your mayor, no one person, no one business, no one group, no single elected official, no single special interest, will decide how we will do things in this city." Right after being elected, true to her word, Mayor Hathaway began hosting coffee hours at locations across the city, including the library and the local bagel shop. These events were open to the public, and the mayor made sure that people knew she was approachable, eager to hear their thoughts and opinions, and very open about sharing her own.

During her first year in office, Mayor Hathaway made a special visit to the Teen Parent Program. "I sat in the chair at the front of the room, and each one of the teen mothers talked a bit about their lives. They all said that they were tired. Whether they were pregnant or they had already given birth—they were very tired. I asked them about the things they had to give up. One of the girls had been a great basketball player and she couldn't do it anymore. I asked them what their boyfriends were like—that was a sore subject. None of them were happy with the men who had participated in the situation. I tried to draw them out a little bit about what their hopes were for the future. It was clear that these lives were being drastically affected by pregnancy and parenthood. On the other hand, one of the girls said, 'I'm getting the best education I've ever gotten out of being in this program because it's individually geared to the level I'm at, and that's what I needed. I wish I could have had tutoring before I was pregnant.' There were some strange ironies that my visit to the Teen

Parent Program raised, like how sad it is that we had to wait until this child was in crisis before this level of individual attention was made available to her."

"I think Mayor Hathaway's burden is to translate her good intentions into a large, community-organizing process," observed local documentary filmmaker Mickey Friedman. "Many, many people are exceedingly cynical that anything can be done in Pittsfield. You've got to convince them that there's a reason for them to get involved. The older people are tired and worn down, and the younger people don't have an awful lot of hope."

Captain Barry sat at his desk at the Pittsfield police station, surrounded by photographs of his ancestors. "I like helping people," he said. "I enjoy making a difference in their lives. I always wanted to do this. It's in my blood. My dad wanted to be a police officer, but at the time they had a height requirement and he was a quarter inch too short. My grandfather was a vice squad detective during Prohibition and his father, Daniel Barry, was a detective here in the 1800s. Now it's my job to serve and protect, and I take it very seriously. I want Pittsfield to be a good, safe community for the people that live here."

Years ago when Captain Barry was in the Air Force and the Air National Guard, he had the chance to travel extensively. Occasionally he found himself wondering what it would be like to live somewhere else, somewhere far away from Pittsfield. But every time he contemplated moving, he ended up appreciating where he was.

"Recently," he said, "I took a train to Albuquerque to see a friend of mine who was in the Air Force, and the most beautiful scenery I saw was in South County on my way out of Pittsfield. I realized that Berkshire County is a beautiful place to live and that although I like the warmer climate as I get older, I still like it here. I like going out with my dogs, Snoopy and Snoopy Two. Those beagles are my best buddies. I got Snoopy when I got out of the Police Academy. She'll be fourteen in March. I picked up Snoopy Two when I was in charge of the city dog pound a couple of years ago. I felt sorry for him because he had been living there for about four months and because he was such a menace to society, nobody wanted him. So I took him."

Captain Barry paused and looked out the window. The sky was gray. Snowflakes were falling. "I like it here in Pittsfield, and I want to stay here," he murmured. "There are beautiful mountain views and I like the four seasons. We have a lovely autumn and I like that. . . . This is the path I chose, so I'll be here for the long haul."

Although Carol Gilligan commuted to New York City several days a week to teach and traveled all over the world for conferences, home was Berkshire County. "The community is going to live with the consequences of what happens here," she said, "and in spite of all efforts to prevent it, some girls do get pregnant and it seems very shortsighted to pull resources away from these girls or to condemn them. The fact about these girls is that they have become pregnant and they have given birth to babies and they are still very young, so you have their lives and you also have the lives of their children, so it's a very good place to put community resources to try to prevent this cycle from going on into the next generation.

"When you look at a teen mother like Jessica—she made some good decisions, like going back to school, and she made some bad decisions—but all people make good decisions and bad decisions," said Carol. "The problem with these girls is that there is no safety net. The absence of resources really needs to be addressed. I remember being shocked that they were going to school and taking care of their babies and working and earning so little money and staying up all night with their babies, ratcheting up the stress level to the point where the consequences would be borne by them and by their children. If you don't put resources behind this—it's like not having prenatal care—then you have trouble."

Back in her apartment on April Lane, Sheri stood in her kitchen, heating up some macaroni and cheese for Leeah's dinner. She set the steaming bowl down in front of her daughter and sat beside her while she ate.

"When I was pregnant," said Sheri, "lots of people told me, 'You're gonna be a teen mom—your life is over.' Whoever says that to teen mothers is lying. My life is just beginning."

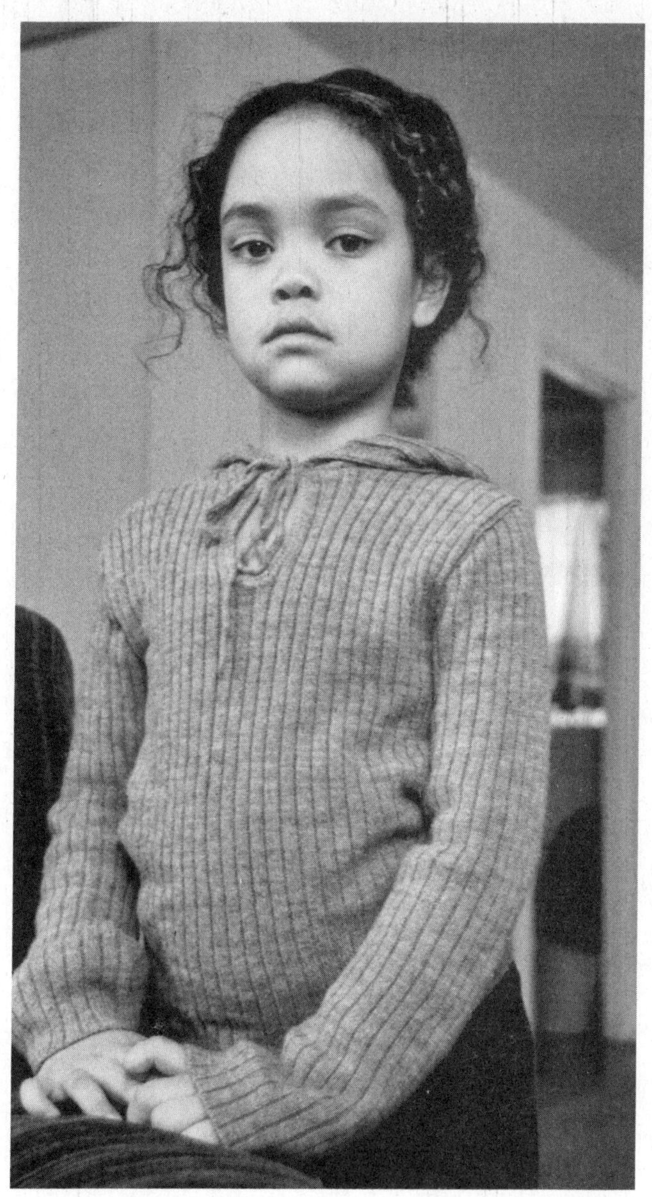

NOTE ON METHOD

It was Carol Gilligan who first invited me to come to Pittsfield to videotape the workshops she taught with Normi Noel at the Teen Parent Program and offered to allocate some grant money she had received toward this purpose. Our relationship dated back to the Boston Festival of Women's Cinema, where in 1998 she had moderated a discussion following a screening of a documentary film I had produced and directed, *Inside Out: Portraits of Children*. That particular screening happened to be a benefit for the Guidance Center, a multicultural nonprofit organization in Cambridge that addresses the needs of economically and socially challenged families. Their mission is "to provide innovative prevention, intervention, and educational programs that empower families to confront challenge and crisis proactively."

Carol was deeply moved by my film about the imaginary worlds of children. She encouraged me to consider making a documentary film about teen motherhood. A year later, I joined her in Pittsfield to explore this possibility.

During the first workshop session I attended, Carol showed the teen mothers a section of my previous film, which was narrated exclusively by its subjects, children between the ages of five and twelve. After the screening, I asked the teen mothers how they would feel about being in a documentary and explained what this endeavor would entail. First and foremost, they had to want to be seen and heard. They had to believe that what they had to say was valuable and important. They had to have the courage to place their thoughts, feelings, emotions, and intimate family histories and relationships under a microscope in front of a judgmental public. They had to be strong enough to confront their own vulnerability and live with it. Each girl had to be driven by the desire to shatter what up until now had been her own private silence.

A few members of the group were interested and felt strong enough to attempt it. Those who were game tested the waters and allowed me to interview them. Those who felt comfortable being videotaped identified themselves as being interested in participating as subjects. Aware of the level of intimacy, involvement, scrutiny, and commitment that the project required, they agreed to let me into their world.

Recognizing that their lives were incredibly stressful and busy, I made myself available to meet with them completely on their terms, at home, at work, at school, and at social gatherings. We caught up with one another during their fifteen-minute lunch breaks, between classes, late at night after their kids were fast asleep, early on bitterly cold days when their early-morning shifts were slow, in between customers at the drive-through if the manager happened to be on break, and on weekends, if and when they were lucky enough to have half a Saturday or Sunday off from work.

Occasionally the teenagers would lose track of time and forget to call to cancel scheduled meetings when excursions to the lake or the mall lasted longer than expected or when they were overwhelmed with errands or doctor's appointments or when they had to work late unexpectedly or if transportation got tricky. In those instances when they were late or didn't show up at all, I would wait in my car, often for hours, parked on street corners or in the parking lots of housing projects, staring out my window, watching children playing, mail being retrieved from mailboxes, snowflakes falling, leaves burning, raindrops splattering on the windshield, and people coming and going.

Ultimately, this patience and unwavering dedication constituted the foundation upon which our relationships were built. As the teen mothers witnessed my respect for them, and my commitment, I was rewarded with their trust and raw honesty.

Not too far removed from the ups and downs of my own adolescence, I empathized with their fluctuating moods and their many conflicting obligations. I was sensitive to the crushingly high levels of stress that saturated their daily lives. We shared good days, bad days, and many ordinary days. I witnessed private and public moments. As they introduced me to the fathers of their babies and to their parents, slowly I began to get a sense of their romantic relationships, their friends, and their family histories. What initially had been a blank canvas began to take on color, shape, and dimension as I learned more and more about the different layers of their lives.

The short documentary we made during the first few months we worked together was screened at venues ranging from the Museum of Tolerance in Los Angeles to Harvard's Graduate School of Education in Cambridge, HBO's Frame by Frame Film Festival in New York City, and the health class at Reid Middle School in Pittsfield. The film was distinguished as one of the outstanding short documentaries of 1999 by the Academy of Motion Picture Arts and Sciences and was screened in its annual documentary series at UCLA.

This documentary covered the teenagers' lives through their last months of high school. After the documentary film was completed, the teen parents and I agreed to continue videotaping interviews with the objective of creating a book. Over the course of four years I continued to interview them and their families while simultaneously operating a handheld Sony VX-1000 mini-DV camera, relying on natural light and trying to be as unobtrusive as possible. I also continued to photograph and videotape them as they went through their days, visiting them at home, at work, at their parents' homes, and, in the case of Jessica, at Berkshire Community College.

I attended children's birthday parties, the senior prom, graduation, family barbecues, and other special events. We spent a substantial amount of time hanging out, driving around, and talking when the camera wasn't running. In addition to all the videotaped material, some interviews were audiotaped, conducted over the telephone or in person. All the interviews were transcribed and edited, with an emphasis on maintaining the integrity of each voice while trying to extract the most clear, vivid story from hours of material.

I began this project without any agenda other than curiosity about the lives of teen mothers, which at the outset, I knew very little about. All my subsequent research was motivated and spurred on by the content of the oral histories I collected. The interviews with the teenagers and their families left me with many questions. As a voracious reader, I began my search for answers in books and gradually expanded the scope of my interviews to include people like Captain Patrick Barry, Mayor Sara Hathaway, Nicole, Katrina, Joann, Mary, Jack Zimmerman, and Dr. Vincent J. Felitti.

The one book that inspired me most and galvanized me every day was

Dorothy's Allison's stark, incisive, courageous, gripping memoir, *Two or Three Things I Know for Sure*:

> Behind the story I tell is the one I don't. Behind the story you hear is the one I wish I could make you hear. Behind my carefully buttoned collar is my nakedness, the struggle to find clean clothes, food, meaning and money. Behind sex is rage, behind anger is love, behind this moment is silence, years of silence.
>
> *Two or three things I know for sure, and one is that I would rather go naked than wear the clothes the world has made for me.*

NOTES

Many excellent works influenced this book and are referenced in the notes below. Among them, Kristin Luker's *Dubious Conceptions: The Politics of Teenage Pregnancy* provided me with an essential conceptual framework for understanding the complex construct of teen parenthood. Positioned somewhere between the liberal and conservative perspectives, Luker views teenagers as capable of making their own decisions but emphasizes that often these decisions are strongly influenced by environmental factors. For facts about the General Electric Company's history in Pittsfield, I am indebted to Thomas F. O'Boyle's book, *At Any Cost: Jack Welch, General Electric, and the Pursuit of Profit*, and to two professors of anthropology, each of whom wrote incredibly detailed books set entirely in Pittsfield: June C. Nash, author of *From Tank Town to High Tech: The Clash of Community and Industrial Cycles*, and Max H. Kirsch, author of *In the Wake of the Giant: Multinational Restructuring and Uneven Development in a New England Community*. I am also indebted to Mickey Friedman, who spent ten years making the documentary *Good Things to Life: GE, PCBs and Our Town*, and to *The Berkshire Eagle*, for their outstanding coverage of local events. I have identified direct quotations from printed sources. Other quotations are from personal interviews conducted between 1999 and 2003.

Chapter 1: Pittsfield

3 Catherine—not her real name.

7 The Alan Guttmacher Institute regularly publishes outstanding reports on teen pregnancy and parenthood. For detailed information about the history of adolescent health services under the umbrella of what is now the

Department of Health and Human Services (DHHS) and for details about the legislation enacted to support institutions like the Teen Parent Program in Pittsfield, refer to the Guttmacher Report on Public Policy 3, no. 3 (June 2000).

8 While the number of national teen pregnancies, abortions, and births began to decrease about 1991 and have continued to decline every year since, in certain economically depressed communities, such as Pittsfield, teen birthrates have remained persistently high and are not showing as much improvement when it comes to prevention.

In his report *Emerging Answers: New Research Findings on Programs to Reduce Teen Pregnancy,* Douglas Kirby writes:

> Teen birth rates are now at their lowest recorded level ever. But even with recent declines the United States still has the highest teen pregnancy and birth rates among comparable industrialized nations. More than four in ten teen girls still get pregnant once before the age of 20 which translates into nearly 900,000 teen pregnancies a year. In addition, between 2000–2010 the population of teen girls aged 15–19 is expected to increase by nearly 10%—which means that even declining rates may not necessarily mean fewer numbers of teen pregnancies and births (pp. 1–4).

This report can be viewed on the National Campaign to Prevent Teen Pregnancy website, www.teenpregnancy.org.

8 *Adolescent Births: A Statistical Profile,* Massachusetts, 2000. Massachusetts Department of Public Health: Bureau of Family and Community, Office of Statistics and Evaluation; Bureau of Health Statistics, Research and Evaluation. Refer to Table 24, "Trends in Birth Rates Among Women Ages 15–19 for Selected Communities, Ranked by Teen Birth Rate, Massachusetts: 2000." See also 1995, Table 24, "Births by Mother's Age and Race/Hispanic Ethnicity for Selected Communities, Massachusetts: 1995." Both tables are available at www.state.ma.us/dph.

8 Including Nadine, five out of the seven teen mothers in this book are white; one is black; and the other is half white, half Hispanic. Often when the American public and media discuss teen motherhood, they tend to associate it with the African American and Hispanic populations, feeding stereotypes connecting poverty and social adversity to minorities while turning a blind eye to the fact that while the teen parenthood rates are indeed significantly higher within these populations—more than twice as high as that of white teenagers (a fact that merits major attention, resources, and targeted intervention), in sheer numbers, white births account for the largest proportion of teen births. In other words, most American teen mothers are indigent and white.

In *Dubious Conceptions,* Kristin Luker addresses this issue:

> Although African Americans do account for a disproportionate share of births to teenagers and unmarried women, unmarried African American teenage mothers are not, statistically speaking, typical unwed teenage mothers. . . . In 1992, for example, about 60% of all babies born to unmarried teenage mothers were born to whites. Some commentators, among them, Charles Murray, say that the rising birthrates among white unmarried teenagers presage the growth of a white underclass, which will take its place alongside historically disadvantaged African Americans. In essence, Murray argues that as racial differences become less important in the life of the country, Americans will separate into two nations—no longer black and white, but married and affluent on the one hand, and unmarried and poor on the other (p. 7).

Bell Hooks raises the issue of the racial stereotyping of poverty, welfare, and teen parenthood in her startling chapter "White Poverty: The Politics of Invisibility" in *Where We Stand: Class Matters:*

> Today most people who comment on class acknowledge that poverty is seen as having a black face, but they rarely point to the fact that this representation has been created and sustained by mass media. Concurrently, reports using statis-

> tics that show a huge percentage of black folks in the ranks of the poor compared to a small percentage of whites make it seem that blacks are the majority group in the ranks of the poor. Rarely do these reports emphasize that these percentages are based on population size. The reality they mask is that blacks are a small percentage of the population. While black folks disproportionate to our numbers are among the poor, the vast majority of the poor continue to be white. The hidden face of poverty in the United States is the untold stories of millions of poor white people (p. 117).

Similarly, the stories of white teen mothers more often than not remain obscured from the public eye, leaving millions of young mothers silenced, disenfranchised, isolated, and unrecognized—apart from their inclusion in mass, depersonalized national and state statistics.

8 Census 2000, Redistricting Data (Public Law 94-171) Summary File. Geographic Area: Pittsfield city, Massachusetts, available at http://factfinder.census.gov.

9 June C. Nash, *From Tank Town to High Tech,* pp. 29–92. Traces industrial evolution of Pittsfield throughout nineteenth and twentieth centuries.

10 Ibid., p. 27. For details about GE's defense contracts.

10 Ibid. During the postwar period three-fifths of Pittsfield's workforce was employed by GE. See pages 100–104 for a discussion of Pittsfield's economic vulnerability and dependency on GE.

10 Thomas F. O'Boyle, *At Any Cost: Jack Welch, General Electric, and the Pursuit of Profit*, pp. 48, 57–66. For an account of Welch's arrival and seventeen years spent in Pittsfield, see Chapter 2, "Passing the Baton."

10 Nash, p. 104. "Eight of eleven city council members worked for GE."

11 Max Kirsch, *In the Wake of the Giant*. For an analysis of the structure of Pittsfield's economic dependency, see page 4. See also pages 59–60:

"When the umbrella of the corporation started to break down during the 1970s, Pittsfield became analogous to a small colonial state that had just been granted independence: it had no mechanisms in place to deal with its new status."

11 Nash, pp. 232–33. Nash describes GE's "shift in production from blue-collar assembly work to steel collar robots," and discusses GE's entry into and prioritization of high-tech and financial operations.

11 Janet Lowe, *Welch: An American Icon*, pp. 240–41.

12 Nash, p. 5. In 1986 GE announced the closing of its Power Transformer Division, "downsizing" its electrical machinery plant in Pittsfield.

12 Lowe, pp. 88–89. "The Companies General Electric Dumped: No More Weapons of War." In 1993 GE sold its aerospace division to Martin Marietta for $4 billion in cash and preferred stock. In 1995 Martin Marietta merged with Lockheed Corporation to become Lockheed Martin.

12 Nash, pp. 9, 235. GE Plastics Worldwide Headquarters housed the corporation's Advanced Plastics Technology Center "in a new facility that employs around 700 people, for the most part highly skilled and educated engineers, designers and managers, and despite high sales in the first few years of its development, it is not expected to increase employment by more than 30%, since there will be no production work on the site. . . . Production might be done in one of the dozen plastics injection and mold businesses that have grown in the city."

12 Pittsfield Economic Revitalization Corporation, *An Economic Base Study of Pittsfield and Berkshire County* (Pittsfield, Mass., 1988).

14 R. Calahan and S. Watson, *A Strategy for Economic Development in Berkshire County*. See also Max Kirsch's discussion of this report in his chapter "Development Strategies," pp. 54–55.

14 Educational attainment: Pittsfield city, Massachusetts Data Set: Census 2000 Summary File 3 (SF 3)—Sample Data DP-2. Profile of Selected Social Characteristics: 2000, available at http://factfinder.census.gov.

14 In *At Any Cost,* Thomas F. O'Boyle chronicles other casualties that were once "pillars of the GE Empire." His list includes "Schenectady, which has twenty-two thousand fewer GE jobs than it did in 1978; Erie, Pennsylvania, six thousand fewer; Lynn, Massachusetts, seven thousand fewer; Fort Wayne, Indiana, four thousand fewer; Louisville, Kentucky, thirteen thousand fewer; Evandale, Ohio, twelve thousand fewer. . . . All these communities have the same worn, dazed look that puts one in the mind of a losing prizefighter about to answer the bell for the fifteenth round."

What happened in Pittsfield is, according to O'Boyle, "a story that's repeated a thousand times in cities across the once vibrant industrial heartland, repeated with such frequency that America has become inured to it, much like stepping over a drunk in the street" (p. 32).

Max Kirsch's *In the Wake of the Giant* cites other corporations that through downsizing have dramatically transformed industrial communities: the Sunbeam Corporation in Biddeford, Maine, and the Thunderbird plant in Lorain, Ohio, and Youngstown, Ohio, formerly a thriving auto-producing community, are situations he uses as comparisons to the situation in Pittsfield with GE (pp. 111–12).

15 O'Boyle's chapter "Great River of the Mountains" contains a detailed discussion of the history of synthetic chemicals, the mixing of PCBs to create Pyranol, and the use of this fluid in three plants, two on the Hudson River and one in Pittsfield, and describes the increased incidence of cancer and premature mortality in workers who worked in Building 12 at the Pittsfield Plant (pp. 183–209).

15 I interviewed Mickey Friedman, the producer, director, and editor of a ninety-minute documentary film titled *Good Things to Life: GE, PCBs and Our Town.* Mickey spent ten years interviewing GE workers and following the progression of the toxic-waste disaster in Pittsfield. His documentary is ex-

tremely thorough and includes interviews, footage of the land testing and former dump sites, footage of the river being dredged, scenes of meetings and negotiations between GE and the EPA and the people of Pittsfield, as well as presentation, analysis, and discussion of many documents—including articles from *The Wall Street Journal* and *The Boston Globe,* results of the EPA's studies regarding levels of PCBs in Pittsfield, and a few pieces of GE's internal correspondence throughout the twentieth century on the subject of PCBs. In addition, Mickey was a co-founder of the environmental activist group Housatonic River Initiative. To view further information related to PCBs in Pittsfield and the efforts of this group to hold GE accountable for the contamination, go to www.housatonic-river.com.

To order a copy of the video, contact Mickey Friedman at Mfried@bcn.net.

17 In late 1997, *Inside Edition,* television's longest-running nationally syndicated newsmagazine show, aired an investigative report questioning whether GE had for years, knowingly and deliberately, covered up the fact that it was dumping dangerous PCBs in Pittsfield. This episode aired on CBS and was titled "Living with Danger." It was produced by Scott Rappoport and James Bogdanoff. For information on how to purchase this video, visit www.insideedition.com.

18 David Stout, "G.E. Agrees to Clean Part of Tainted River in Massachusetts," *The New York Times,* Sept. 25, 1998; Scott Allen and Peter Howe, "GE Accepts $150M Plan to Clean Pittsfield Sites," *The Boston Globe,* Sept. 25, 1998; "Pittsfield Officials, GE Tout Cleanup Plan Seen as a Key to Revitalizing City," *The Boston Globe,* Oct. 15, 1998; Associated Press, "GE to Pay $150 Million to $200 Million to Clean Up New England River," *The Washington Post,* Sept. 25, 1998; Jack Dew, "GE Challenges Cleanup Cost Complaint Targets New Method of Accounting," *The Berkshire Eagle,* Feb. 5, 2002.

19 This EPA report on PCB-related health hazards in Pittsfield was dated June 4, 1998, and appears in Friedman's documentary.

19 Alan Guttmacher Institute, "Occidental Report—Teenagers' Pregnancy, Intentions and Decisions, 1999."

20 The issue of the environment and peer pressure is key when it comes to at-risk girls such as Shayla who get pregnant on purpose. There are many who believe that taking an at-risk child out of one environment and putting her in a different school could help reduce the risk of her becoming a teen parent.

In *Dubious Conceptions,* Kristin Luker writes: "A young black or white woman who is poor, having trouble academically, and becoming convinced that she is unlikely to get ahead is better off—whatever her individual risk factors—if she is in a good suburban school where a majority of her peers view pregnancy as an obstacle to achievement" (p. 116).

Reading the above passage, I am reminded of Francie, the ebullient thirteen-year-old who is the central character in Betty Smith's classic, *A Tree Grows in Brooklyn*, later turned into a terrific movie directed by Elia Kazan (1945). Like the small tree near her tenement, Francie seeks out the light as she struggles against poverty and a life overshadowed by her father's alcoholism and her parents' strained relationship. One day while walking outside the periphery of her destitute neighborhood, Francie wanders into a wealthier area and sees a beautiful school. She longs to go there instead of to the grim one she attends. Her father comes up with a scheme. They take down a random address of a house in the wealthy neighborhood near the school, and her father writes a letter requesting a transfer, claiming that he's moved there. The request is granted, and Francie's life changes.

The No Child Left Behind Bill offers parents the option of transferring their children out of failing schools. In addition, through their foundations, philanthropists such as Theodore J. Forstmann, John T. Walton, and Bill and Melinda Gates have allocated substantial grants to help parents in need with tuition so that they can transfer kids into private elementary schools (in the case of the Children's Scholarship Fund) and to support parents in sending their kids to smaller, alternative schools (in the case of the Gates Foundation).

For more information, see www.scholarshipfund.org and www.gatesfoundation.org.

21 Jim Bouton, *Foul Ball: My Life and Hard Times Trying to Save an Old Ballpark.* A former major-league pitcher for the New York Yankees recounts "the battle waged in Pittsfield over whether to build a new stadium to replace 83-year-old Wahconah Park, a contentious struggle that pitted the wishes of the people against those of the local power elite."

In light of the budget deficit Pittsfield faced in 2001 (which was in the realm of $8–10 million), residents voted by a narrow margin not to establish a new $18.5 million stadium to lure a new minor-league baseball team.

21 See website for the Colonial Theatre, www.colonialtheater.org.

23 In addition to interviewing Captain Barry at the police headquarters, I referred to a document he provided me, a research report he had commissioned internally on the subject of the history of the drug trade in Pittsfield.

25 Tony Dobrowolski, "Heroin Rears Its Ugly Head in Pittsfield," *The Berkshire Eagle,* Nov. 10, 2002.

25 Ibid. See also D. R. Bahlman, "City Ordinance Aims to Leash Vicious Dogs," *The Berkshire Eagle,* Oct. 14, 2002, and "Vicious Dog Rule Endorsed," *The Berkshire Eagle,* Oct. 24, 2002.

36 Rebecca Maynard, ed., *Kids Having Kids: Economic Costs and Social Consequences of Teen Pregnancy.*

> Early childbearing and youth crimes are linked. . . . If young teens delayed their first childbirth until ages 20 or 21, their child's risk of incarceration would fall by an estimated 12% and the correction costs incurred by more than $900 million. . . . The age of the mother has less of an effect on delinquency than other differences in the circum-

> stances facing the children of young teen versus non-teen mothers (pp. 16, 252).

See also Jeffrey Grogger, "Incarceration-Related Costs of Early Childbearing," in ibid.

> Children of young teen mothers are almost three times as likely to be behind bars at some point in their adolescence or early 20's in comparison to the children of mothers who delayed childbearing.

36 According to statistics compiled by Adolescent Pregnancy Prevention, Inc. (APPI), a nonprofit service agency in Fort Worth, Texas, children born to teen mothers are:

> More likely to be low-birth weight and have developmental problems
> More likely to be victims of abuse
> More likely to repeat a grade
> Males are more likely to be incarcerated, and females are more likely to become teen parents themselves.

The APPI website, www.appifw.org, lists a compilation of data from a variety of sources, including the Alan Guttmacher Institute; National Center for Health Statistics; Texas Department of Health; National Campaign to Prevent Teen Pregnancy; Annie E. Casey Foundation, 2000 Kids Count Report; Youth Risk Behavior Survey, 1995; Centers for Disease Control; Time/CNN poll, 1999; Kaiser Family Foundation; Sexuality Education and Information Council of the United States; Advocates for Youth; *Pediatrics*, Feb. 2001; *Men's Health,* June 2001; APPI independent surveys.

38 James Gilligan, *Violence: Reflections on a National Epidemic*. An eloquent explanation of the theory that violence often arises out of a deep desire to correct/counter a perceived injustice.

38 For demographics of Pittsfield by race, see U.S. Census 2000 at www.census.gov.

40 Martin Kasindorf and Haya El Nasser, "Impact of Census' Race Data Debated: Some Say It Will Divide Country; Others Say Unite," *USA Today,* March 13, 2001.

> By 2050, 21% of Americans will be claiming mixed ancestry, according to projections in 1999 by demographers Jeffrey Passel of the Urban Institute and Barry Edmonston of Portland State University in Oregon. . . . More and more of us will look like singer Mariah Carey, who has a half-Venezuelan, half African-American father and an Irish mother. Or like golfer Tiger Woods, who describes himself as "Cablinasian," an amalgam of Caucasian, black, American Indian—from his father, Earl Woods—and Asian from his mother, Kultida Woods, a Thai, partly of Chinese origin.

Michael Lind of the New America Foundation, based in Washington, D.C., is one of several scholars who believe that "with race due to fade as a basis of social distinctions and government policies, new lines may be based on socioeconomic class, geography, education or other factors."

41 Paul Krugman, "For Richer: How the Permissive Capitalism of the Boom Destroyed American Equality," *The New York Times Magazine,* Oct. 20, 2002, compares the wide income gap that defines contemporary American society and draws a parallel with the era of the Great Depression.

See also Edward N. Wolff, *Top Heavy: The Increasing Inequality of Wealth in America and What Can Be Done About It.*

41 Marc L. Miringoff, *The Social Health of the Nation: How America Is Really Doing*, p. 104.

In a comparative study of teen parenthood rates (1991–95) in six industrialized countries conducted by the Alan Guttmacher Institute, the U.S. ranked highest with a teen parenthood rate of 9 percent, Great Britain second with 6 percent, then France with 2 percent, and Germany, Poland, and Japan with 1 percent.

41 Kristen Luker, *Dubious Conceptions,* pp. 107-108.

For detailed statistics on what percentage of teen mothers come from low-income or poor families, see the Alan Guttmacher Institute's *Teen Pregnancy and Welfare Reform Debate* and *The Politics of Blame: Family Planning, Abortion, and the Poor.*

> Poor and low-income teenagers, whose prospects for a good education, a decent job and marriage are dim or nonexistent, often have little incentive to delay childbearing. As a result of differences in pregnancy and abortion rates, *poor and low-income teenagers account for 83% of adolescents who have a baby and become a parent and 85% of those who become an unwed parent.* By contrast, higher income teenagers who make up 62% of all women aged 15–19 represent only 17% of those who give birth. . . . Many teenagers who become mothers would have been poor later in life even if they had not had a baby.
>
> Almost three-quarters (70%) of higher income teenagers who become pregnant have abortions; they choose to postpone childbearing so they can complete their education, get a good job, establish their financial independence and get married before they can start a family.

41 Kristin Luker, "Dubious Conceptions: The Controversy Over Teen Pregnancy," in Andrew Cherlin's *Public and Private Families.*

41 Luker, *Dubious Conceptions,* p. 182. She sees teen parenthood as a symptom of "the toll that a bifurcating economy is taking on Americans" and asserts that young, poor women have babies in a search for meaning and purpose, desperately seeking the right to make some kind of claim on society that is achieved in small but meaningful ways when they have babies.

42 Ibid., p. 154. Luker discusses the various factors that influence whether a teenage girl has an abortion. In addition to class, race, and socioeconomic status, she comments on the roles of significant others in the girl's

life. She then goes into a detailed analysis of the legislation and policy surrounding teenage abortions in various states, and she addresses the issues of access, funding, and parental consent.

43 Vincent J. Felitti, Robert F. Anda, Dale Nordenberg, and David F. Williamson, "Relationship of Childhood Abuse and Household Dysfunction to Many of the Leading Causes of Death in Adults," The Adverse Childhood Experiences (ACE) Study, *American Journal of Preventive Medicine* 14, no. 4 (May 1998), pp. 245–58. See also Vincent J. Felitti, "Adverse Childhood Experiences and Adult Health: Turning Lead into Gold," *Permanente Journal* 6, no. 1 (Winter 2002), available at www.drfelitti.com.

When I met with Dr. Felitti in San Diego, where he heads the Department of Preventive Medicine at Kaiser Permanente, we discussed his work with patients who have experienced childhood sexual abuse, which is one of the areas the ACE Study has pinpointed as a category of risk. Felitti's view is that although it is uncomfortable for physicians to integrate questions regarding sexual abuse into their routine evaluations of patients, it is necessary for them to be trained to overcome this reluctance. He feels strongly that a direct, open, clinical approach is essential when it comes to patients who present the psychosomatic symptoms often seen in people with histories of childhood sexual abuse, symptoms that include but are not limited to chronic depression, obesity, gastrointestinal distress, chronic headaches, and chronic sleep disturbance.

Dr. Felitti has found that a significant number of patients who come to him with these complaints have kept memories of childhood sexual abuse secret for decades and that often once they disclose them and discuss them and deal with the trauma, some of their symptoms begin to disappear. This was most visually apparent in his work with obese female patients, many of whom lost weight rapidly after disclosing memories of child abuse and discussing them in the open, supportive environment of the clinical setting.

43 Vincent J. Felitti, Susan D. Hillis, Robert F. Anda, and Polly A. Marchbanks, "Adverse Childhood Experiences and Sexual Risk Behaviors in

Women: A Retrospective Cohort Study," *Family Planning Perspectives* 33, no. 5 (Sept.–Oct. 2001).

45 Robert Coles, *The Youngest Parents,* pp. 6–7.

45 Shayla's comment regarding her fantasy that having a baby would "change things" made me think of a metaphor used by Kristin Luker in *Dubious Conceptions.* She compares a disadvantaged teenager's fantasy of having a baby to a lottery ticket: "It brings with it at least the dream of something better, and if the dream fails, not much is lost" (p. 182).

46 David Simon and Edward Burns, *The Corner: A Year in the Life of an Inner-City Neighborhood*, p. 235.

46 Coles, *The Youngest Parents*, pp. 78–79.

47 Tony Dobrowolski, "Pittsfield Lays Off 96 Teachers," *The Berkshire Eagle*, May 2, 2002.

49 No Child Left Behind website at www.nclb.gov.

50 Katherine Boo, "Welfare Reform Series" from *The Washington Post,* Dec. 15, 1996–Dec. 21, 1997. Portraits of individuals and institutions engaged in the daily struggle of coping with various aspects of welfare reform.

50 Martha Matthews, "Teens and TANF: Welfare Reform Could Have Major Impact on Youth," *Youth Law News* 14, no. 5 (1998). This article provides a thorough review of the impact of welfare reform on pregnant and parenting teens. Although parents under eighteen are only a small percentage of all welfare recipients, teen mothers tend to be blamed for numerous social problems. These youths are specifically targeted by a number of recent changes in federal and state welfare laws—particularly the requirement that to receive federally funded TANF ben-

efits, teen parents must live in adult-supervised settings and attend school or work. The article discusses the need for safe and stable living environments, meeting adolescent educational needs, and advocacy efforts.

Chapter 2: Amy & Bernard

63 Trevor—not his real name.

82 Edith Wharton, *Summer,* pp. 156–57.

102 Bridget—not her real name.

Chapter 3: Liz & Peter

108 Paula—not her real name.

111 Ted—not his real name.

111 Vivian—not her real name.

118 For a discussion of the role of predatory adult men in teenage childbearing, refer to: Joycelyn Elders and Alexa E. Albert, "Adolescent Pregnancy and Sexual Abuse," *Journal of American Medical Association* 280, no. 7 (Aug. 19, 1998):

> Gov. Pete Wilson's Statutory Rape Vertical Prosecution Program and the Teenage Pregnancy Prevention Act of 1995 are two pieces of legislation enacted in California to more aggressively prosecute adult men sexually involved with adolescent girls. Several other states, including Delaware, Georgia, Florida, Pennsylvania, and Texas, have taken steps to punish these "male predators."

125 Ricardo—not his real name.

130 Irene—not her real name.

131 Eric Schlosser, *Fast Food Nation*. In his investigative report on America's fast-food industry, Schlosser highlights the way in which teenagers such as Liz are integral to the operation of places like McDonald's and KFC. He noted that because these teenagers are for the most part unskilled, part-time, willing to accept low pay, and unlikely to start or join a union, they are perfect fodder for these routine assembly-line-style jobs with unorthodox hours. Teenagers such as Liz, Amy, Shayla, Jessica, and Colleen (all of whom have worked at fast-food restaurants) accepted these less-than-ideal circumstances at various points in their lives when they were absolutely desperate to work because they needed the money to support their babies.

Schlosser offers the following critique of what he asserts is the fast-food industry's meticulous plan to exploit adolescent workers in subtle, seemingly benign ways:

> No other industry in the United States has a workforce so dominated by adolescents. About two thirds of the nation's fast food workers are under twenty. Roughly 90% of the nation's fast food workers are paid an hourly wage, provided no benefits, and scheduled to work only as needed. Crew Members are employed "at will" and managers try to make sure that each worker is employed less than forty hours a week, thereby avoiding overtime payments (p. 68).

Chapter 4: Colleen

140 Ryan—not his real name.

144 *Physicians Assistant's Guide to Health Promotion and Disease Prevention,* Emory Medical School, 1996.

149 Mary Pipher, *Reviving Ophelia*. She discusses the case of a teenager named Rita whose upbringing with an alcoholic father conditioned her to be drawn into chaotic relationships with unpredictable men, a pattern that may be observed between Colleen and Ryan. "The familiar was comfortable" (p. 192).

163 Valerie Sinason, *Mental Handicap and the Human Condition*. When I did my M.Sc. at the Anna Freud Centre/University College London, I had the pleasure of meeting and working with Valerie Sinason, who was based a block away at the Tavistock Clinic. Her book permanently altered and enhanced my understanding of primary and secondary handicap and helped me understand how organic disability can often appear much more serious and acute when compounded by emotional disability. A crucial, compassionate book for all parents of mentally and physically handicapped children.

See also Valerie Sinason, *Understanding Your Handicapped Child*.

Chapter 5: Shayla & C.J.

171 Alan—not his real name.

179 For more on how a father's abandonment of his daughter can have lasting effects, including the precipitation of teen pregnancy, see Jonetta Rose Barras, *Whatever Happened to Daddy's Little Girl?: The Impact of Fatherlessness on Black Women*. Barras writes that teen girls who grow up without their fathers tend to have sex earlier than girls who grow up with their fathers; a fifteen-year-old with just a mom is three times more likely to lose her virginity before her sixteenth birthday than one living with both her parents. Based on her personal experience, Barras offers the following explanation for why the idea of getting pregnant is often so alluring to this potentially more vulnerable segment of the female population:

> In our fantasies we try to believe that the man we have chosen to love will not leave—as our fathers did. But we half expect him to; we program ourselves for his inevitable departure. The baby is a feature of that programming. At least when he leaves we will have someone—we won't be alone. In fact we'll still have him, because we have his baby. It's ludicrous, but nevertheless, we cling to this reasoning; it is our life-preserver (p. 70).

188 In roughly 92 percent of all domestic-violence incidents, men commit the crimes against women, and according to a study conducted by the

U.S. Department of Justice, women are five to eight times more likely than men to be victimized by an intimate partner. Because of these statistics, police are much more likely to arrest the male than the female, even if both parties have suffered injuries.

For the National Domestic Violence Fact Sheet and Statistics re: Incidence of Partner Abuse, go to the website www.ndvh.org.

200 Ian—not his real name.

211 Danah Zohar and Ian Marshall, *SQ: Connecting with Your Spiritual Intelligence.*

Chapter 6: Sheri

219 Greg—not his real name.

220 Nadine—not her real name.

220 Steve—not his real name.

224 Steven Greenhouse, "Problems Seen for Teenagers Who Hold Jobs," *The New York Times,* Jan. 29, 2001.

The issues Greenhouse raises brought to mind images of Sheri working from 3 to 9 P.M. as a housekeeper every day after school at age sixteen, and Colleen working long hours after school at Burger King. The article refers to a study conducted by two arms of the National Academy of Sciences—the National Research Council and the Institute of Medicine. This study found that when teenagers work more than twenty hours a week, the work often leads to lower grades, higher alcohol use, and too little time with their parents and families. The article discusses efforts in Massachusetts to enact legislation limiting the maximum hours teenagers are allowed to work:

> In Massachusetts, several lawmakers are seeking to limit the maximum amount of time 16-year-olds and 17-year-olds can work during school weeks to 30 hours, down from the cur-

> rent maximum of 48 hours. "We have 16- and 17-year-olds working 40 hours a week on top of 30 hours in the classroom," said Peter J. Larkin, the Massachusetts state representative sponsoring the bill to reduce the number of hours teenagers can work. "Something has to give, and academics seems to be taking a back seat. Sure there is pressure against the bill from employers who need teenage workers to help in a full-employment economy, but many other employers are complaining that the graduates of our high schools are not up to par."

For the complete article, go to the *New York Times* archives at www.nytimes.com.

231 In her book *Of Woman Born,* Adrienne Rich has a wonderful passage that gave me insight into the immense impact of the mother-daughter relationship, specifically when it comes to teen motherhood and relationships like the one between Pat and Sheri and now between Sheri and her daughter, Leeah. In the passage below, Rich takes on the idea of the baby as a wish—and makes the point that in addition to investing their own hopes and dreams in children, mothers need to serve as examples of individuals who are in some way chasing their own dreams, who have not given up on their own lives, and who have not sacrificed their own identities completely and become entirely consumed in their roles as mothers at the expense of their own freedom:

> Only when we can wish imaginatively and courageously for ourselves can we wish unfetteredly for our daughters. But finally, a child is not a wish, nor a product of wishing. Women's lives—in all levels of society—have been lived too long in both depression and fantasy, while our active energies have been trained and absorbed into caring for others. It is essential now, to begin breaking that cycle. . . . As daughters we need mothers who want their own freedom and ours. We need not be the vessels of another woman's self-denial and frustration.

> The quality of the mother's life is her primary bequest to her daughter, because a woman who can believe in herself, who is a fighter and who continues to struggle to create livable space around her, is demonstrating to her daughter that these possibilities exist. Because the conditions of life for so many poor women demand a fighting spirit for sheer physical survival, such mothers have sometimes been able to give their daughters something to be valued far more highly than full-time mothering (pp. 246–47).

252 Brad—not his real name.

256 Dylan—not his real name.

265 At various times, the teen mothers in this book were incapacitated by depression. In *The Noonday Demon: An Atlas of Depression,* Andrew Solomon writes: "Depression cuts across class boundaries, but depression treatments do not. This means that most people who are poor and depressed stay poor and depressed; in fact, the longer they stay poor and depressed, the more poor and depressed they become. Poverty is depressing and depression is impoverishing, leading as it does to dysfunction and isolation" (p. 335).

Chapter 7: Jessica

271 John Walsh, *No Mercy: The Host of* America's Most Wanted *Hunts the Worst Criminals of Our Time,* pp. 154–216. Although I incorporated some of Jessica's recollections about her grandparents as well as the recollections from one of her aunts whom I met, I relied on John Walsh's book for the details about her grandparents' trial, the years they spent as fugitives, and the story of how they were ultimately apprehended and sentenced to prison.

275 Dwayne—not his real name.

282 Edith Wharton, *Summer,* p. 157.

283 Jessica's remark "I never wanted to have sex with you in the first place" points to another problem area: the difficulty of a teenage girl asserting to a man that she isn't ready for sex, doesn't want it, and will not do it. This is a serious problem because its roots lie not in the sexual situation but at the heart of the relationship. Has the teenager chosen to date a guy whose behavior in other areas demonstrates that he cares about her, values her feelings, and will respect her wishes? If not, she is already in trouble and at risk by the time she enters a sexual situation. In one large survey, 31 percent of teen girls ages fifteen to nineteen said their first sexual experience was either nonvoluntary or voluntary but not really wanted. See www.appifw.org/statistics.html.

Joycelyn Elders and Alexa E. Albert refer to the same issue in their *JAMA* article, "Adolescent Pregnancy and Sexual Abuse." They report that:

> [T]he incidence of non-voluntary sexual experiences that occur in adolescence, and thus, could lead to teen pregnancy, appears greater than previously assumed: One study of a mixed-ethnic sample of almost 2,000 middle and high school students in Los Angeles, Calif., found that 20% had unwanted sexual experiences, with 51% of adolescent girls having their first coercive sexual act between the ages of 13 and 16 years.

284 Some teenagers share Jessica's misconception that all adoptions are closed and require complete separation and anonymity between birth mother and child. These teenagers are not informed about the option of an open, private adoption. Justifiably, they fear surrendering their children to what they believe to be the utter unknown and are unwilling to agree to terms that they expect will require complete confidentiality and a severance of all ties with their babies.

The battle between secrecy and disclosure of adoption records is still being waged in state legislatures and on the federal level, but significant progress has been made. Laws have been rewritten and revised, broadening the spectrum of parents who are eligible to adopt and making it easier for children to find permanent homes. The tide has shifted dramatically over the past twenty years, and the majority of infant adoptions that occur in America are private and open to varying degrees. The Internet has played a huge role in the move toward open adoptions, and all a teenager has to do is log on to websites such as www.birthmother.com or www.adoption.com to get complete information about attorneys and agencies in various states.

Attorneys representing clients who are desperate to adopt will pay to fly a teenager in Jessica's situation all the way across the country, if necessary, to hold interviews in the hopes of arriving at an agreement. In an open, private adoption, a birth mother is often allowed to maintain a relationship with the adoptive parents, who agree to pay for all her medical costs during the pregnancy. The birth mother is free to say yes or no to the prospective adoptive parents after meeting them and getting information about their lives, families, and financial profiles. Similarly, the adoptive parents can interview the birth mother to ascertain that they feel comfortable with the idea of adopting her baby. Although it varies, depending on the specific contracts, often letters, phone calls, and photographs can be exchanged so that a teenager such as Jessica wouldn't have to live a life full of unanswered questions about her son. She'd be able to maintain some level of connection to the child she relinquished. She would be able to know "where he was, how he looked, what he was doing."

For more on how adoption laws are being revised and the expanding role of the Internet, see Adam Pertman, *Adoption Nation: How the Adoption Revolution Is Transforming America*, pp. 1–26, 103–28.

Another issue that cannot be ignored is that most adoptive parents are white and are looking to adopt white children, which could potentially make it more challenging for a baby of mixed race, like Jessica's son, to find a home. In his book *Interracial Intimacies,* Randall Kennedy writes:

> In the 1980s a federal government investigation found that a healthy black infant waited about four times as long for placement as a healthy white infant. By the 1990s the dis-

> parity had remained the same or widened. . . . Racial preference for white children remains a decisive and pervasive influence within the adoption system (pp. 448–49).

Racial issues aside, it cannot be denied that giving up one's child is a gut-wrenching process, no matter how great the adoptive parents are. Making that particular decision requires an unmarried teen mother to place a higher value on money, security, marriage, a stable two-parent home, and other environmental comforts she might not be able to provide, as opposed to maternal love, which is one of the few priceless resources she is capable of offering a child.

In the cases of teen mothers like Liz, who themselves spent time in foster care, there is the fear that if they put their child up for adoption, the child could end up unwanted by adoptive parents and be forced to spend his or her childhood moving from one foster home to another. That is not a risk many teen mothers are willing to take.

For more on why so few teen mothers choose to put their children up for adoption, see Kristin Luker, *Dubious Conceptions,* pp. 161–64.

302 Wes—not his real name

Chapter 8: Community

317 Edith Wharton, *Summer,* p. 84.

321 Steve Seidel, "*Stand and Unfold Yourself: A Monograph of the Shakespeare & Company Research Study.*"

321 For more information about the GE Fund, visit www.ge.com/community/fund.

323 Kristin Linklater, *Freeing the Natural Voice.* Kristin Linklater's theories and approach to the human voice are central to the work of Tina Packer, Carol Gilligan, and Normi Noel. Linklater explains:

> The basic assumption of the work is that everyone possesses

a voice capable of expressing through a two-to-four-octave natural pitch range whatever gamut of emotion, complexity of mood, and subtlety of thought he or she experiences. The second assumption is that the tensions acquired through living in this world, as well as defenses, inhibitions, and negative reactions to environmental influences, often diminish the efficiency of the natural voice to the point of distorted communication. Hence, the emphasis is on the removal of the blocks that inhibit the human instrument as distinct from the development of a skilled musical instrument. The object is a voice in direct contact with emotional impulse, shaped by intellect, not inhibited by it.

323 For more on the work of Carol Gilligan and her colleagues, see Carol Gilligan, *In a Different Voice: Psychological Theory and Women's Development*, and "Joining the Resistance: Psychology, Politics, Girls and Women," *Michigan Quarterly Review* 24 no. 4, pp. 501–36 (presented as the Tanner Lecture on Human Values, University of Michigan, March 16, 1990); C. Gilligan, J. V. Ward, and J. M. Taylor, eds., *Mapping the Moral Domain;* C. Gilligan, T. J. Hanmer, and N. P. Lyons, eds., *Making Connections: The Relational Worlds of Adolescent Girls at Emma Willard School;* and C. Gilligan, A. Rogers, and D. Tolman, eds., *Women and Therapy* (special issue on adolescence), also published as *Women, Girls, and Psychotherapy: Reframing Resistance*.

323 The Alan Guttmacher Institute published statistics on the risk of repeat teen pregnancies in the Guttmacher Report on Public Policy 3, no. 3 (June 2000). This report also addresses the increased number of teenagers who are switching from birth control pills to the contraceptive implant Norplant and, to an even greater extent, the three-month injectible, Depo-Provera. Several of the teen mothers in this book tried "the Shot" as a form of birth control after having their first child. Shayla reported uncomfortable side effects, including chronic migrane headaches, that discouraged her from continuing with this mode of birth control.

324 When I interviewed Carol Gilligan, she mentioned several classics in addition to *Summer* that she thought could be used effectively by mentors working to strengthen the voices and psychological awareness of adolescent girls. All of the books she mentioned have one thing in common: each features an intense, complicated, highly perceptive girl or young woman as narrator and/or central figure, and addresses trauma and painful emotions in an honest way: *To Kill a Mockingbird* by Harper Lee, *The Bluest Eye* and *Sula* by Toni Morrison, *Jane Eyre* by Charlotte Brontë, *Annie John* and *Lucy* by Jamaica Kincaid, and *Harriet the Spy* by Louise Fitzhugh.

329 Regarding the critical reception of Edith Wharton's *Summer* in 1917: in her introduction to the Scribner paperback edition, Marilyn French writes:

> *Summer*'s excellence was recognized at the time it was published by readers like Joseph Conrad, Howard Sturgis, and Percy Lubbock, the latter two of whom compared it not unfavorably to *Madame Bovary*. But most Americans were scandalized by the book's subject matter, and Wharton was reproached for it (p. 41).

In her introduction to the Bantam paperback, Susan Minot wrote the following about the critical reception of *Summer* in 1917:

> The chapter about a drunken funeral on the Mountain was according to Wharton, "received with indignant denial by many reviewers and readers," and while she was not required to defend her fictional choices, she did reveal that the scene was taken directly from an account given to her by the rector of the church in Lenox (p. xiii).

329 Edith Wharton, *A Backward Glance,* p. 294:

> In those days the snow-bound villages of Western Massachusetts were still grim places, morally and physically: insanity, incest and slow mental starvation were hidden away behind the paintless wooden house-fronts of the long village street, or in the isolated farm-houses on the neighbouring

hills; and Emily Bronte would have found as savage tragedies in our remoter valleys as on her Yorkshire Moors.

330 Joycelyn Elders and Alexa E. Albert, "Adolescent Pregnancy and Sexual Abuse," *Journal of the American Medical Association* 280 (Aug. 19, 1998), pp. 648–49. This article discusses teen pregnancy as an all-too-common scenario for 800,000 U.S. adolescent girls each year and examines the prevalence of sexual abuse among this population, citing data from numerous studies: A 1992 Washington State study of 535 teen mothers revealed that the first pregnancies of 62 percent of the participants were preceded by experiences of molestation, rape, or attempted rape. The mean age of their offenders was 27.4 years (D. Boyer and D. Fine, "Sexual Abuse as a Factor in Adolescent Pregnancy and Child Maltreatment," *Family Planning Perspectives* 4, 24, no.1 [Jan./Feb. 1992], pp. 9–11, 19). A 1986 study of 445 teen mothers in Chicago reported that 60 percent claimed they had been forced to have an unwanted sexual experience, with a mean age for the first incidence of abuse being eleven. (H. P. Gershenson et al., "The Prevalence of Coercive Sexual Experiences Among Teenage Mothers," *Journal of Interpersonal Violence* 4 [1989], pp. 204–9).

Jacqualine Stock et al., "Adolescent Pregnancy and Sexual Risk-Taking Among Sexually Abused Girls," *Family Planning Perspectives* 29, no. 4 (1997). Data on 3,128 girls in grades eight, ten, and twelve who participated in the 1992 Washington State Survey of Adolescent Health Behaviors were used to analyze the association of a self-reported history of sexual abuse with teenage pregnancy and with sexual behavior that increases the risk of teen pregnancy. An association between sexual abuse and teenage pregnancy appears to be the result of high-risk behavior exhibited by adolescent girls who have been abused.

332 Valerie Sinason, ed., *Memory in Dispute*. Composed of articles by British psychoanalysts and psychotherapists, this book explores the many levels of complexity involved in acknowledgment of child abuse and its consequences, and addresses the clinical challenges these issues present. Chapter 2, "Children Are Liars, Aren't They? An Exploration of Denial Processes in

Child Abuse," by Arnon Bentovim, looks at issues such as children's statements, psychological denial, social denial, denial and the court system, and trauma-organized systems as an exploratory model for denial processes.

332 Judith Herman, M.D., is clinical professor of psychiatry at Harvard Medical School and director of training at the Victims of Violence Program at Cambridge Hospital in Cambridge, Massachusetts. She first published *Father-Daughter Incest* in 1981. When it was reprinted in 2000, she included a new afterword in which she discussed the findings of Andrea J. Sedlak and Dianne D. Broadhurst, who wrote the *Executive Summary of the Third National Incidence Study of Child Abuse and Neglect* (Washington, D.C.: United States Department of Health and Human Services, 1996):

> The most recent survey, conducted in 1996, arrived at a conservative estimate that 217,000 children were sexually abused in that year. Roughly half of these children were abused by their fathers, stepfathers, or other father figures. . . . Unfortunately, the capacity of state authorities to intervene on behalf of abused children has not kept pace with the professional capacity to identify children at risk. As reporting has soared, the number of case investigations has remained static, resulting in a declining percentage of investigated cases. By 1996, only 28 percent of the cases identified by sentinels were officially investigated, even when the children had serious physical injuries. . . . Back in 1990, the National Advisory Board on Child Abuse and Neglect was describing the situation in child protection as a "national emergency." Since then, matters appear to have gotten worse. . . . This crisis in child protective services is but one example of a larger conflict between public concern about the welfare of children and reluctance to intervene or to commit resources on a scale that might realistically be necessary to provide all children with adequate care and protection (pp. 222–23).

333 For more on the complexity of sexual abuse and disclosure, see Herman, *Father-Daughter Incest,* pp. 129ff.

336 Timothy Roche, "The Crisis of Foster Care," *Time,* Nov. 13, 2000.

338 J. G. Silverman and Anita Raj, "Dating Violence and Sexual Risk Behavior Among a Representative Sample of High School Females," *Harvard Children's Initiative,* Harvard University, in *Journal of the American Medical Association* 286 (Dec. 12, 2001), p. 2813.

339 Barrie Levy, ed., *Dating Violence: Young Women in Danger*. The chapter by Judith McFarlane, "Violence During Teen Pregnancy: Health Consequences for Mother and Child," relates directly to Colleen's and Nadine's stories.

339 James M. Makepeace, "Courtship Violence as Process: A Developmental Theory" in Albert Cardarelli, ed., *Violence Between Intimate Partners: Patterns, Causes, and Effects,* p. 33. In this chapter, Makepeace discusses how a high school dating culture that revolves around cars, sex, and alcohol contributes to "terrible and epidemic consequences." For more on interpersonal violence and adolescent pregnancy, go to www.noappp.org.

339 L. Bullock and McFarlane conducted a 1988 survey of pregnant teens in several large metropolitan areas. Of the more than two hundred pregnant teens surveyed, 26 percent reported physical abuse, 40–60 percent stated that the battering had either begun or escalated since the discovery of the pregnancy, and 65 percent of those abused had not talked to anyone about the abuse.

340 For more on extreme stereotyped gender roles and their relation to dating violence within the adolescent population, see Levy, ed., *Dating Violence* pp. 4–5. This book also includes an outstanding, very detailed section on education and prevention projects (pp. 223–78).

346 Rick Klein, "Romney Team Spreads Its Cuts," *The Boston Globe*, Jan. 31, 2003.

346 Erik Arvidson, "Romney Aide: Budget Cuts Spare 'Muscle and Bone'" *The Berkshire Eagle*, Jan. 31. 2003.

347 Pat Nichols, "Mission Impossible?" *Berkshire Eagle,* Oct. 27, 2002.

348 For more on absent parenting and the aloneness of many of today's teenagers, see Patricia Hersch, *A Tribe Apart: A Journey into the Heart of American Adolescence*. Hersch spent several years documenting the lives of teenagers in Reston, Virginia.

348 Eric Schmidt, "For the First Time, Nuclear Families Drop Below 25% of Households," *The New York Times,* May 15, 2001:

> For the first time, less than a quarter of the households in the United States are made up of married couples with their children, new census data show. That results from a number of factors, like many men and women delaying both marriage and having children, more couples living longer after their adult children leave home and the number of single-parent families growing much faster than the number of married couples. *Indeed, the number of families headed by women who have children, which are typically poorer than two-parent families, grew nearly five times faster in the 1990's than the number of married couples with children* (italics mine).

348 Marc L. Miringoff, *The Social Health of the Nation:*

> In 1996, female single-parent households had a median income of $16, 389 per year, compared to $51,768 for married couples with children. More than 40% of all female-headed families had incomes below the poverty line (p. 128).

349 William J. Bennett and Jack Kemp, "Keep Reforming Welfare," *The Wall Street Journal,* Aug. 1, 2002. Bennett, a former secretary of education, and Kemp, a former secretary of housing and urban development, cite the 1996 welfare reform bill as "one of the most significant and successful

pieces of social policy enacted in the last half century. Welfare rolls have plummeted by 50%, child poverty is at its lowest point in 20 years, poverty levels of black children are at their lowest recorded level ever."

349 Katherine Boo, "Welfare Reform Series," *The Washington Post,* Dec. 15, 1996–Dec. 21, 1997. See Part 4, "Day Care Centers in Trouble."

350 James J. Heckman, *Invest in the Very Young,* published by the Ounce of Prevention Fund, available at www.ounceofprevention.org.

351 See Howard Gardner, *Intelligence Reframed: Multiple Intelligences for the 21st Century* and *The Unschooled Mind: How Children Think and How Schools Should Teach*.

351 Daniel Goleman, *Emotional Intelligence: Why It Can Matter More than IQ.* Goleman makes the case for emotional intelligence being the strongest indicator of human success.

352 Jack Zimmerman and Virginia Coyle, in *The Way of Council*, describe the roots of the Council Program and its application to family life and adult groups, including business organizations, as well as to teenagers in a school setting. Influences discussed include Native American traditions, Quaker Meetings, extended family gatherings, and many contemporary techniques of group dynamics.

352 Jack Zimmerman and Ruthann Sapphier, *The Mysteries Sourcebook and Lesson Plan*. This program was developed with the support of the Ojai Foundation and initiated in 1983 at the Crossroads School in Santa Monica, California, and was expanded to a variety of schools, including the Palms Middle School in the Los Angeles Unified School District. All descriptions of the course were taken from this highly detailed booklet, which contains the course program broken down on a week-by-week basis and lists discussion topics, educational philosophy, assignments, and teaching methodologies.

For information about teacher training and to order this outstanding course book complete with lesson plans, visit the resources section of the website www.counciltraining.org.

355 Rachael Kessler, *The Soul of Education: Helping Students Find Connection, Compassion, and Character at School* and "Passages: Fostering Community, Heart, and Spirit in Adolescent Education." This article is available at www.newhorizons.org.

For information on Kessler's workshops, consultation, and materials, go to www.mediatorsfoundation.org or contact:

The Passageways Institute for Social and Emotional Learning
3822 North 57th Street
Boulder, CO 80301

More thoughts regarding the importance of rites of passage:

In her book *Promiscuities* Naomi Wolf devotes a section to this topic:

> Anthropologists who look at adolescent rites of passage agree that their importance cannot be overstated, not only for the sake of the developing adolescent, but for the sake of the coherence of a society.

Wolf goes on to argue that in the absence of other rites of passage that are present in other cultures, the transition from girlhood to womanhood has for many American adolescents become defined by sexual availability, and often young girls misinterpret teen pregnancy and motherhood as a confirmation of adulthood in the absence of other indicators (pp. 143–46).

While doing research for this book, I made several visits to Raw Arts Works (RAW), a nonprofit art-therapy organization in the depressed city of Lynn, Massachusetts. This outstanding program offers adolescents two groups that are dedicated to rites of passage, Men 2 Be and Women 2 Be. Through field trips, overnight camping trips, and artistic group projects, this nonprofit organization takes kids at risk who live in nearby public housing projects through steps toward maturation that involve cooperation, exploration of identity, reliability, persistence, and courage. They have seen hardly any teen pregnancies among kids who have participated in their program.

Of particular interest is their exceptional work with middle-school and high-school boys in the Men 2 Be group, led by gifted art therapist Jason Cruz. Below is an example of one of Jason's assignments for the boys:

> *Breaking Broken Records:* Write down on the record the places where you feel stuck, where the "needle keeps skipping," and then smash the record. Take the pieces and create a sculpture that describes changes you want to make in your life. Define how you will change the "Broken Record."

For more on RAW programs, see their website, www.rawarts.org.

355 Jack Zimmerman is currently editing and co-writing a new book with educators who have implemented the Council Program in several schools in different parts of the country. This book will include information about how to implement the Council Program at public and private schools and will be available in 2004.

For updates about Zimmerman's forthcoming book and for information about teacher training, go to www.counciltraining.org.

356 Douglas Kirby, *Emerging Answers: New Research Findings on Programs to Reduce Teen Pregnancy,* the National Campaign to Prevent Teen Pregnancy, May 2001. For a summary of his study of programs with both sexuality and youth-development components and his specific comments on the success of the Children's Aid Society-Carrera Program, see pages 15–17. Kirby's study is available at www.teenpregnancy.org.

357 Tamar Lewin, "Program Finds Success in Reducing Teenage Pregnancy," *The New York Times,* May 20, 2001.

357 "The Carrera Model: A Success in Pregnancy Prevention" was published in the newsletter of the Charles Stewart Mott Foundation, April 2, 2002.

358 I met Mayor Hathaway for the first time at one of the coffee hours she held at the Berkshire Athenaeum in Pittsfield. True to her campaign

promises, in person she was warm, accessible and receptive. She granted me an interview the following day.

362 Alexander Stille, "Grounded by an Income Gap," *The New York Times,* Dec. 15, 2001. Economist James Heckman is quoted in this article expressing a view similar to that of psychologist Carol Gilligan:

> Never has the accident of birth mattered more," he asserts. "If I am born to educated, supportive parents, my chances of doing well are totally different than if I were born to a single parent or abusive parents. I am a University of Chicago libertarian, but this is a case of market failure: Children don't get to 'buy' their parents and so there has to be some kind of intervention to make up for these environmental differences."

BIBLIOGRAPHY

Adolescent Pregnancy Prevention, Inc. *Facts About Teen Pregnancy*. April 1999, from www.appifw.org.

Alan Guttmacher Institute. The Guttmacher Report on Public Policy. *Teenagers' Pregnancy, Intentions and Decisions*. 1999.

———. *Teen Pregnancy and the Welfare Reform Debate*. 1998.

———. *The Politics of Blame: Family Planning, Abortion, and the Poor*. 1995.

———. *Public Policy* 3, no. 3 (June 2000).

———. *Teen Sex and Pregnancy*. September 1999.

———. *U.S. Teenage Pregnancy Statistics*. March 2001.

These reports are all available at www.guttmacher.org.

Allison, Dorothy. *Bastard Out of Carolina*. New York: Plume, 1993.

———. *Trash*. New York: Plume, 2002.

———. *Two or Three Things I Know for Sure*. New York: Plume, 1996.

Alonso-Zaldivar, Ricardo, and Robin Fields. "Latino, Asian Populations Rise Sharply in Census: New Multiracial Figures Find a Substantial Growth of Immigrants in Nontraditional Regions." *The New York Times*, July 31, 2001.

Anda, R. F., and D. P. Chapman, V. J. Felitti, V. E. Edward, D. F. Williamson, J. P. Croft, and W. H. Giles. "Adverse Childhood Experiences and Risk of Paternity in Teen Pregnancy." *Obstetrics and Gynecology* 100, no. 1 (2002), pp. 37–45.

Anda, R. F., and V. J. Felitti, D. P. Chapman, J. B. Croft et al. "Abused Boys, Battered Mothers, and Male Involvement in Teen Pregnancy: New Insights for Pediatricians." *Pediatrics* 107, no. 2 (2001), p. e19.

Anderson, Sherwood. *Winesburg, Ohio*. New York: Bantam Classic, 1995.

Barras, Jonetta Rose. *Whatever Happened to Daddy's Little Girl? The Impact of Fatherlessness on Black Women*. New York: Ballantine, 2000.

Bentovim, Arnon. "Children Are Liars Aren't They?—An Exploration of Denial Processes in Child Abuse," in Valerie Sinason, ed. *Memory in Dispute*. London: Karnac Books, 1998.

The Berkshire Eagle.

Arvidson, Erik. "Romney Aide: Budget Cuts Spare 'Muscle and Bone.'" January 31, 2003.

Bahlman, D. R. "City Ordinance Aims to Leash Vicious Dogs." October 14, 2002.

———. "Vicious Dog Rule Endorsed." October 24, 2002.

Carey, Bill. "Crane Wins $336M Currency Paper Contract." October 16, 2002

Dew, Jack. "Pittsfield, N.A., See Big Drops in Census." October 24, 2000.

Dew, Jack. "GE Challenges Cleanup Cost, Complaint Targets New Method of Accounting." February 5, 2002.

———. "PCB Contamination Experts to Meet for Panel Discussion." February 9, 2002.

———. "Coffee Talks Cover the Same Ground; Hathaway Touts Solutions to Pittsfield's Many Woes." October 8, 2002.

Gosselin, Lisa. "1 Man Nabbed, 1 Man Sought in City Shooting." November 13, 2002.

———. "Shooting Incident Suspect Ordered Held on High Bail." November 14, 2002.

Mehegan, Julie. "Heroin Abuse in Mass. Called an Epidemic." December 18, 2002.

Nichols, Pat. "Mission Impossible?" October 27, 2002.
The above articles are all available at www.berkshireeagle.com.

Bernstein, Nina. "Side Effect of Welfare Law: The No-Parent Family." *The New York Times,* July 2, 2002.

Boo, Katherine. "Welfare Reform Series" from *The Washington Post,* December 15, 1996–December 21, 1997.

Bouton, Jim. *Foul Ball: My Life and Hard Times Trying to Save an Old Ballpark.* North Egremont, Mass.: Bulldog Publishing, 2003.

Bragg, Rick. *All Over But The Shoutin'.* New York: Vintage, 1998.

Brown, L., and C. Gilligan. "Meeting at the Crossroads: Women's Psychology and Girls' Development." *Feminism and Psychology* 3, no. 1, pp. 11–35.

Calahan, R., and S. Watson. *A Strategy for Economic Development in Berkshire County.* Cambridge, Mass.: John F. Kennedy School of Government, Harvard University, 1984.

Cherlin, Andrew J. *Public and Private Families: A Reader.* 2d ed. Boston: McGraw-Hill, 2000.

Coles, Robert. *The Youngest Parents.* New York: Center for Documentary Studies in association with W. W. Norton, 1997.

Dash, Leon. *When Children Want Children: An Inside Look at the Crisis of Teenage Parenthood.* New York: Penguin, 1996.

Dietz, P. M., and A. M. Spitz, R. F. Anda, D. F. Williamson, P. M. McMahon, J. S. Santelli, D. F. Nordenberg, V. J. Felitti, and J. S. Kendrick. "Unintended Pregnancy Among Adult Women Exposed to Abuse or Household Dysfunction During Their Childhood." *Journal of the American Medical Association* 282 (1999), pp. 1359–64.

Ehrenreich, Barbara. *Nickel and Dimed: On (Not) Getting By in America*. New York: Metropolitan Books, 2001.

Elders, Joycelyn, and Alexa E. Albert. "Adolescent Pregnancy and Sexual Abuse." *Journal of the American Medical Association* 280, no. 7 (Aug. 19, 1998), pp. 648–49.

Erikson, Erik H. *Identity: Youth and Crisis*. New York: W. W. Norton, 1968.

Felitti, V. J. "The Relationship Between Adverse Childhood Experiences and Adult Health: Turning Gold into Lead." *The Permanente Journal* 6 (2002), pp. 44–47. Available at www.drfelitti.com.

Felitti, V. J., R. F. Anda, D. Nordenberg, D. F. Williamson, A. M. Spitz, V. Edwards, M. P. Koss, et al. "The Relationship of Adult Health Status to Childhood Abuse and Household Dysfunction." *American Journal of Preventive Medicine* 14 (1998), pp. 245–58.

Friedman, Mickey. *Good Things to Life: GE, PCBs and Our Town*. A feature-length digital video documentary about General Electric and its use and misuse of the toxic chemicals, PCBs. Blue Hill Films, 32 Rosseter Street, Great Barrington, MA 01230. Mfried@bcn.net.

Froomkin, Dan. "Welfare's Changing Face." *The Washington Post,* July 23, 1998.

Gardner, Howard. *Intelligence Reframed: Multiple Intelligences for the 21st Century*. New York: Basic Books, 2000.

———. *The Unschooled Mind: How Children Think and How Schools Should Teach*. New York: Basic Books, 1993.

Gilligan, Carol. *In a Different Voice: Psychological Theory and Women's Development*. Cambridge, Mass.: Harvard University Press, 1982.

———. "Joining the Resistance: Psychology, Politics, Girls and Women." *Michigan Quarterly Review* 24, no. 4, pp. 501–36. Presented as the Tanner Lecture on Human Values, University of Michigan, March 16, 1990.

Gilligan, C., J. V. Ward, and J. M. Taylor, eds. *Mapping the Moral Domain*. Cambridge, Mass.: Harvard University Press, 1988.

Gilligan, C., T. J. Hanmer, and N. P. Lyons, eds. *Making Connections: The Relational Worlds of Adolescent Girls at Emma Willard School*. Cambridge, Mass.: Harvard University Press, 1989.

Gilligan, C., A. Rogers, and D. Tolman, eds. *Women and Therapy*. Special issue on adolescence (1991). Published also as *Women, Girls, and Psychotherapy: Reframing Resistance*. New York: Hayworth Press, 1991.

Gilligan, James. *Violence: Reflections on a National Epidemic*. New York: Vintage Books, 1997.

Goleman, Daniel. *Emotional Intelligence: Why It Can Matter More than IQ*. New York: Bantam Books, 1997.

Goodnough, Abby. "Policy Eases the Way Out of Bad Schools." *The New York Times*, December 9, 2002.

Greenhouse, Steven. "Problems Seen for Teenagers Who Hold Jobs." *The New York Times*, January 29, 2001.

Hathaway, Sara. Mayoral Inaugural Address, Pittsfield, Mass. January 7, 2002.

Heckman, James J. *Invest in the Very Young*. The Ounce of Prevention Fund, from www.ounceofprevention.org/publications/pubindex.html.

Herman, Judith Lewis. *Father-Daughter Incest*. Cambridge, Mass.: Harvard University Press, 1981.

Hersch, Patricia. *A Tribe Apart: A Journey into the Heart of American Adolescence.* New York: Ballantine, 1998.

Hillis, S. D., R. F. Anda, V. J. Felitti, and P. A. Marchbanks. "Adverse Childhood Experiences and Sexual Risk Behaviors in Women: A Retrospective Cohort Study." *Family Planning Perspectives* 33 (2001), pp. 206–11.

Hooks, Bell. *Where We Stand: Class Matters*. New York: Routledge, 2000.

Hymowitz, Kay S. *Ready or Not: Why Treating Children as Small Adults Endangers Their Future—and Ours*. New York: Free Press, 1999.

Jencks, Christopher. *Rethinking Social Policy: Race, Poverty, and the Underclass.* Cambridge, Mass.: Harvard University Press, 1992.

Kagan, Jerome, and Robert Coles, eds. *Twelve to Sixteen: Early Adolescence.* New York: W. W. Norton, 1972.

Kasindorf, Martin, and Haya El Nasser. "Impact of Census' Race Data Debated: Some Say It Will Divide Country; Others Say Unite." *USA Today,* March 13, 2001.

Kennedy, Randall. *Interracial Intimacies: Sex, Marriage, Identity, and Adoption.* New York: Pantheon, 2003.

Kessler, Rachael. *The Soul of Education: Helping Students Find Connection, Compassion, and Character at School*. Alexandria, Va.: Association for Supervision and Curriculum Development, 2003.

———. "Passages: Fostering Community, Heart, and Spirit in Adolescent Education," from www.newhorizons.org.

Kirsch, Max H. *In the Wake of the Giant: Multinational Restructuring and Uneven Development in a New England Community*. Albany: SUNY Press, 1998.

Klein, Rick. "Romney Team Spreads Its Cuts." *The Boston Globe*, January 31, 2003.

Kotlowitz, Alex. *There Are No Children Here: The Story of Two Boys Growing Up in the Other America*. New York: Doubleday, 1991.

Krugman, Paul. "For Richer: How the Permissive Capitalism of the Boom Destroyed American Equality." *The New York Times Magazine,* October 20, 2002.

Levy, Barrie. "Abusive Teen Dating Relationships: An Emerging Issue for the '90s." *Response to the Victimization of Women and Children* 13 (1990).

Levy, Barrie, ed. *Dating Violence: Young Women in Danger*. Seattle: Seal Press, 1991.

Lewin, Tamar. "Program Finds Success in Reducing Teenage Pregnancy." *The New York Times,* May 20, 2001.

———. "Zero-Tolerance Policy Is Challenged." *The New York Times,* July 11, 2001.

Linklater, Kristin. *Freeing the Natural Voice*. New York: Drama Book Specialists, 1976.

Lipper, Joanna. *Inside Out: Portraits of Children*. New York: Ruby Slipper Productions, 1996. www.rubyslipper.net.

———. *Growing Up Fast* (the documentary). New York: Ruby Slipper Productions, 1999. www.rubyslipper.net.

Lowe, Janet. *Welch: An American Icon*. New York: John Wiley & Sons, 2001.

Lukas, Anthony J. *Common Ground. A Turbulent Decade in the Lives of Three American Families.* New York: Vintage Books, 1986.

Luker, Kristin. *Dubious Conceptions: The Politics of Teenage Pregnancy*. Cambridge, Mass.: Harvard University Press, 1996.

———. "Dubious Conceptions: The Controversy Over Teen Pregnancy" in Andrew Cherlin, ed., *Public and Private Families*. New York: McGraw-Hill, 1996.

Makepeace, James M. "Courtship Violence as Process: A Developmental Theory" in Albert Cardarelli, ed., *Violence Between Intimate Partners: Patterns, Causes, and Effects*. Boston: Allyn & Bacon, 1997.

Maynard, Rebecca A., ed. *Kids Having Kids: Economic Costs and Social Consequences of Teen Pregnancy*. Washington, D.C.: Urban Institute Press, 1997.

Miringoff, Marc L. *The Social Health of the Nation: How America Is Really Doing*. New York: Oxford University Press, 1999.

Morrison, Toni. *The Bluest Eye*. New York: Penguin, 2000.

———. *Sula*. New York: Knopf, 2002.

Musick, J. S. *Young, Poor, and Pregnant: The Psychology of Teenage Motherhood*. New Haven: Yale University Press, 1993.

Nash, June C. *From Tank Town to High Tech: The Clash of Community and Industrial Cycles*. Albany: SUNY Press, 1989.

National Campaign to Prevent Teen Pregnancy. *"Just the Facts": Data on Teen Pregnancy, Childbearing, Sexual Activity and Contraceptive Use*. 2000.

O'Boyle, Thomas F. *At Any Cost: Jack Welch, General Electric, and the Pursuit of Profit*. New York: Vintage, 1998.

Ounce of Prevention Publications. *Heart to Heart: An Innovative Approach to Preventing Childhood Sexual Abuse*, from www.ounceofprevention.org/publications/pubindex.html.

Pertman, Adam. *Adoption Nation: How the Adoption Revolution Is Transforming America*. New York: Basic Books, 2001.

Pipher, Mary. *Reviving Ophelia*. New York: Ballantine Books, 1995.

Rich, Adrienne. *Of Woman Born: Motherhood as Experience and Institution*. New York: W. W. Norton, 1976.

Roche, Timothy. "The Crisis of Foster Care." *Time*, November 13, 2000.

Sander, Joelle. *Before Their Time: Four Generations of Teenage Mothers*. New York: Harcourt Brace Jovanovich, 1991.

Schlosser, Eric. *Fast Food Nation: The Dark Side of the All-American Meal*. Boston: Houghton Mifflin, 2001.

Schmidt, Eric. "For the First Time, Nuclear Families Drop Below 25% of Households." *The New York Times,* May 15, 2001.

Seidel, Steve. *Stand and Unfold Yourself: A Monograph on the Shakespeare & Company Research Study*. Project Zero, Harvard Graduate School of Education, 1998.

Silverman, J. G., and Anita Raj. "Dating Violence and Sexual Risk Behavior Among a Representative Sample of High School Females." *Journal of the American Medical Association* 286 (Dec. 12, 2001), p. 2813.

Simon, David, and Edward Burns. *The Corner: A Year in the Life of an Inner-City Neighborhood*. New York: Broadway Books, 1997.

Sinason, Valerie. *Mental Handicap and the Human Condition*. London: Free Association Books, 1992.

———. *Understanding Your Handicapped Child*. Toronto, Ontario: Warwick Publishing, 1997.

Smith, Betty. *A Tree Grows in Brooklyn*. New York: Perennial Books, 1998.

Solomon, Andrew. *The Noonday Demon: An Atlas of Depression*. New York: Scribner, 2001.

Stille, Alexander. "Grounded by an Income Gap." *The New York Times*, December 15, 2001.

Tanner, Lindsey. "Study: Girls Victimized by Dates." Associated Press, July 31, 2001.

Taylor, J., C. Gilligan, and A. Sullivan. *Between Voice and Silence: Women and Girls, Race and Relationships.* Cambridge, Mass.: Harvard University Press, 1995.

Terkel, Studs. *Working*. New York: The New Press, 1974.

U.S. Department of Health and Human Services. *A National Strategy to Prevent Teen Pregnancy*. Annual Report 1999.

U.S. Department of Labor. *About Welfare—Myths, Facts, Challenges and Solutions*. 1998.

Walsh, John. *No Mercy: The Host of* America's Most Wanted *Hunts the Worst Criminals of Our Time*. New York: Pocket Books, 1998.

Wharton, Edith. *Summer*. New York: Bantam, 1993.

———. *A Backward Glance*. New York: Touchstone, 1998.

Wolf, Naomi, *Promiscuities: The Secret Struggle for Womanhood*. New York: Fawcett, 1998.

Wolff, Edward N. *Top Heavy: The Increasing Inequality of Wealth in America and What Can Be Done About It*. New York: New Press, 2002.

Zimmerman, Jack, and Virginia Coyle. *The Way of Council*. Las Vegas: Bramble Books, 1996.

Zimmerman, Jack, and Ruthann Saphier. *The Mysteries Sourcebook and Lesson Plan*, from www.counciltraining.org/resources.html.

Zohar, Danah, and Ian Marshall. *SQ: Connecting with Your Spiritual Intelligence*. New York: Bloomsbury, 2001.

Selected Websites

www.appifw.org—*Adolescent Pregnancy Prevention, Inc.*

www.cdc.gov/nchs—*National Center for Health Statistics of the Centers for Disease Control and Prevention*

www.childstats.gov—*Federal Interagency Forum on Child and Family Statistics*

www.counciltraining.org—*Mysteries Program, council training, and resources*

www.drfelitti.com—*information on the ACE (Adverse Childhood Experience) Study*

www.drugfreeamerica.org—*Partnership for a Drug-Free America*

www.etr.org/recapp/index.htm—*Resource Center for Adolescent Pregnancy Prevention* www.growingupfast.com—*book website with photo galleries*

www.guidancecenterinc.org—*Guidance Center Inc.*

www.housatonic-river.com—*Housatonic River Initiative*

www.jama.ama-assn.org—Journal of the American Medical Association

www.mediatorsfoundation.org—*Passageways Institute Connection, Compassion and Character in Learning the Soul of Education*

www.molt.org—*The Charles Stewart Molt Foundation*

www.ndvh.org—*National Domestic Violence Hotline*

www.noappp.org—*National Organization on Adolescent Pregnancy, Parenting and Prevention*

www.nochildleftbehind.gov—*U.S. Department of Education*

www.ounceofprevention.org—*Ounce of Prevention Fund, James Heckman*

www.plannedparenthood.org—*Planned Parenthood Federation of America*

www.pzweb.harvard.edu—*Project Zero, Harvard Graduate School of Education*

www.rawart.org—*Raw Arts, art therapy for youth at risk*

www.rubyslipper.net—*Ruby Slipper Productions*

www.safehorizon.org—*Domestic and dating violence prevention*

www.scholarshipfund.org—*Children's Scholarship Fund*

www.shakespeare.org—*Shakespeare & Company, Lenox, Mass.*

www.state.ma.us/dhcd/—*Massachusetts Department of Housing and Community Development*

www.state.ma.us/dph/—*Massachusetts Department of Public Health*

www.stopteenpregnancy.com—*Carrera Program*

www.teenpregnancy.org—*National Campaign to Prevent Teen Pregnancy*

www.teenweb.org—*Berkshire Coalition to Prevent Teen Pregnancy*

www.wroc.org—*Welfare Rights Organizing Coalition*

ACKNOWLEDGMENTS

I would like to extend my deepest gratitude to all the people who spoke from their hearts and shared their stories for this book. Thanks to Amy, Bernard, James, Donna, Colleen, Maureen, Shayla, Kelly, Ashley, C.J., Sheri, Jon, Pat, Nadine, Liz, Peter, Jessica, Doris, Bill, Robert, Mary Ann, Captain Patrick Barry, Mary, Nicole, Mayor Sara Hathaway, Jack Zimmerman, Marjorie Cohan, Mickey Friedman, Joann Oliver, Katrina Mattson-Brown, Dr. Scherling, and Dr. Vincent J. Felitti. Thanks also to the late Helen Berube, the former director of the Teen Parent Program, and to B. J. Mancari, who was the social worker in residence the year the documentary film was made. My gratitude also extends to the children I had the privilege of observing from infancy on: Ezakeil, Kaliegh, Marcus, Leeah, Jonathan, Jaiden, Caleb, and Peter.

Without the participation of these young parents and the adults in Pittsfield who shared their unique perspectives, this book would never have come into existence. I would like to thank them for everything they have taught me, and for giving me a collection of special moments and poignant memories that I will always treasure. Being a vessel for their words and a mirror for their emotions was an enormous honor and an immense responsibility. I can only hope that I have risen to the occasion and done an adequate job of reflecting the character, strength, eloquence, humor, insight, and courage of these young parents, their families, and the people in their community.

I never dreamt that I would be so fortunate as to have an editor like Frances Coady enter my life. Her energy, brilliance, and dedication to this book have been nothing short of phenomenal. With her imagination, empathy, boundless energy, and vivid social conscience, she helped extract, structure, and shape the panorama that became this book—regarding every aspect of the process, from the photography to the videotaped interviews to the writing, with equal respect and meticulous attention, offering strong input while also giving me the freedom to explore and determine my ultimate destination. I thank Frances and all her colleagues at Picador—including Josh Kendall, Christine Preston, Tanya Farrell, and Leia Vandersnick—for making the process of writing my first book such an intense, challenging, joyful experience.

Thanks to my agent, Jennifer Rudolph Walsh at William Morris, to Xanthe Tabor, also at William Morris, and to my lawyer, Michael Schenkman, at Bloom, Hergott. Their counsel and expertise have been invaluable.

I would like to thank Carol Gilligan for believing in my work, for inviting me to Pittsfield, for making it possible for me to start this project, and for encouraging me and inspiring me along the way. Similarly, I would like to thank Tina Packer, Jane Fonda, Normi Noel, Kirsty Gunn, and Margaret Mahoney. With their sheer strength, intellect, power, insight, and sensitivity, these trailblazers continue to give me much to aspire to. Special thanks to James Atlas for his support, enthusiasm, encouragement, and guidance.

While an undergraduate at Harvard, I took courses taught by professors who profoundly influenced my thinking and encouraged me to approach subjects from a rigorous, passionate, interdisciplinary perspective. I extend my gratitude to Elaine Scarry, Philip Fisher, Stanley Cavell, Sacvan Bercovitch, Susan Suleiman, Jerome Kagan, Svetlana Boym, and Patrice Higonnet.

While a graduate student at the Anna Freud Centre and University College London, I attended insightful seminars led by the late Joseph Sandler, Anne-Marie Sandler, Peter Fonagy, and Pauline Cohen. Their emphasis on child development from infancy through adolescence, their focus on observation, and their exploration of the evolution of psychoanalysis from the time of its inception through the present provided me with a rigorous conceptual and historical framework. This background, along with the monumental work of Erik Erikson, helped shape my many questions about an individual's relationship to family and society at various phases of the life cycle.

I would like to thank the Woodhull Institute for Women and Ethical Leadership and three of its board members, Dr. Robin Stern, Erica Jong, and Naomi Wolf, for their support and friendship throughout the writing process, and for hosting the teen mothers at a screening of our documentary followed by an inspiring discussion at Makor. Thanks to Raj Guru at Manhattan Color Lab. Gratitude also to Garth Thomas and Barrington Pheloung for their support, friendship, and invaluable contributions to both my documentaries.

Thanks and much love to my family and friends for their love, support, humor, and encouragement. Special thanks to Frederick, Laura, Clara, Catherine, Ezra, Anne, Jenny Lyn, David B., Jeffrianne, Chris, Nelson, Noga, Peter, Katie, and Zooey.

Walter Ramin took time to assist me at every step of this project, painstakingly transcribing every single interview I conducted, accompanying me on many trips to Pittsfield, and wearing many hats, including that of production coordinator and sound recordist. His efforts were vital in helping bring this endeavor to fruition. For his wonderful friendship and for the warmth and kindness he displayed toward all the subjects in this book and their children, I am extremely grateful. In between trips to Pittsfield and long hours devoted to this project, Walter, a talented musician and the guitarist of the rock band RPC, opened for Ozzy Osbourne and Tool in Prague. I feel so fortunate to have had such a talented, driven, kind, patient, amusing, entertaining comrade on this adventure.

My mother has always been an inspiration to me, both personally and professionally. With love and admiration, I have dedicated this book to her.

J.H.L.
New York City
March 11, 2003

$hitcoin.

HAYDN WILKS

deadbirdpress.com

ISBN (PB): 978-1-8380831-0-6
ISBN (E): 978-1-8380831-1-3

CONTENTS

LEGAL DISCLAIMER

SHITCOIN is a work of satirical fiction written by Haydn Wilks. All names and situations within the novel that follows are purely imaginative, except in cases when real public figures have been used in a satirical manner. Nothing any public figure or celebrity does in this novel is any way intended to reflect on their real life character or any real actions or events. All such events within this novel are so obviously not based on reality than no one with intellect enough to read a book could possibly be stupid enough to confuse what happens within these pages with things that have happened or could possibly happen in real life. So please don't sue me. Or do – I guess I could use the publicity.

$HITCOIN.

Extract from Graham Jones, THE DEATH OF A SHITCOIN BILLIONAIRE (FletcherWilliams, 2022):

Guus van Hooijdink's body was discovered in his Hillsborough, California home on June 29, 2020. It is believed he may have died sometime in April or May. The only other living being thought to have been in Guus van Hooijdink's home at the time of his death was his pet chimpanzee, Raskolnikoff.

Raskolnikoff escaped from the home after Guus van Hooijdink's death. Several of Hillsoborough's affluent residents reported seeing the chimpanzee on their property while living under a stay at home order made by the state's governor in response to the COVID-19 global pandemic. The chimpanzee was captured and identified after breaking into a locked down restaurant on Primrose Road in the neighboring community of Burlingame.

Guus van Hooijdink's body was cremated at a ceremony in the Silicon Valley community of Mountain View on July 6, 2020. His parents and elder brother were unable to travel to the funeral due to sweeping travel restrictions enacted in response to the pandemic. Leading figures from the cryptocurrency community posted truncated tributes to various social media platforms, generally fitting within the confines of a 140 character tweet or Instagram image overlay. The home in which van Hooijdink died was purchased in February 2018 for a reported $50 million. At the time of his death, Guus van Hooijdink was worth somewhere in the region of $500 million.

Conspiracy theories filled internet forums in the immediate aftermath of the discovery of Guus van Hooijdink's body. Many focused on the seemingly insincere nature of an R.I.P. tweet sent by actor Olly Tulip, who won an Academy Award for his portrayal of Guus van Hooijdink in the 2019 film

Moon Boys. Others looked to the various shady underworld characters with whom Guus van Hooijdink is believed to have interacted, or his one-time girlfriend Alicia Huang, who is believed to have left Guus van Hooijdink to begin a relationship with Tulip. Many theories pointed to one or both of the two co-founders of the cryptocurrency coin which provided Guus van Hooijdink with his tremendous wealth. This is the story of that coin.

</extract.>

August 2017.

London, England.

12 years. 2005 to 2017 = 12 years. And a 6 hour bus. £35, Liverpool to London Victoria. Departing bleary-eyed 7.30am, arriving half-past 1. *7:30 to 13:30 = 6 hours.* A train - Liverpool Lime Street to London Euston - would've been £235 & taken 2 hours. But they wouldn't reimburse Graham for that. Nor pay for a hotel. No – after 12 years, all Dead Bird Press were willing to give Graham was £50 in travel expenses.

"Your fault for living up North!" Terrance Kant, Editor-in-Chief at Dead Bird Press, had said when Graham suggested Dead Bird cover the cost of his rail fare.

"Twelve years, and they make you to take a fucking bus?!" Graham's wife Melina had snapped in an explosion of stereotypical Latina temperament.

As Graham disembarks the bus & moves through Victoria Coach Station to the flow of foot traffic on the street outside, the London rush hits him like cocaine inflaming the brain of a City Boy; the buzz & bluster of Britain's great asset: a city like no other.

No place to raise a kid though, Graham reminds myself, thinking of little Luis as he ignores the tourists waiting for a green light & crosses the street to Victoria rail station.

Even if he & Melina could afford to live in London, there are compelling reasons for them to carry on living in Liverpool.

Graham moves through the manic station, business-suited blokes in immense hurries side-stepping bewildered tourists trundling suitcases, flashing back through his London years as he moves towards the Underground.

2002/03 – the big move, King's College, studying English & Film, big dreams of being a filmmaker/journalist; Halls at Denmark Hill, constant evading of security staff to smoke weed in the rooms & rob from the fully-stocked refrigerators of the international students' pantries; the buzzing London music scene, the long boozy evenings of Fresher's Week soon blossoming into wild city-wide exploratory odysseys: taking his first E in Central after being refused entry to a club, he & Joe & Sadiq dancing circles around the roundabout Monument outside Buckingham Palace, bloated black pupils swelling up & swallowing the iris as they came up, then on through the city, Houses of Parliament, Big Ben, Westminster Bridge, London Eye, sitting on swings at the base of it, swinging up & toward it, the big Eye bloating bigger, reflected in the blacks of their own bloated eyes, & Joe's comical use of the adjective 'ethereal' to describe it, & the endless quoting of that phrase throughout the entirety of their 3 years at uni…

Graham reaches the Tube as he reminisces, descending into the city's bowels, that old familiar sense of all that makes London London: a city of sprawl & imperial grandeur, now set in stone, literally carved into the Earth, so that while new skyscrapers pop-up & high-money luxury apartment complexes appear as investment vehicles for Arab & Chinese & Russian billionaires, & gentrification rampages through the city's periphery, torching long-worn communities with a kindling that starts with artists & hipster cafes & cool cocktail lounges & students, burning until all sense of danger has been eradicated from the area, & rents rise, & the cool escapes into ethereal London expansion with it, &

Graham reaches the Victoria Line platform & awaits his train & thinks of the million-strong march that moved through the city in 2003, protesting the Iraq War, the wild hedonism & abandon that captured the spirit of a nation united long into the night, & that first rush of real journalistic intent he'd felt, inebriated on the zeitgeist of the times – Libertines, New Labour, London: sprawling, manic London;

& as Graham boards the train, he thinks of the endless East London gigs & clubs & squat parties, of Bloc Party, Foals, & the ascension of dubstep;

& as he boards the Walthamstow-bound Victoria Line train, he thinks of all the clubs & venues lost to the city's evolution into a money pit for the jet-set international elite: Herbal, Passing Clouds, Plastic People, & The End.

& the first thing he got accepted into Dead Bird, a gig review for a band poised on the cusp of cool called Crystal Castles, & how he quickly got into the wild-night write-up business throughout his last year of uni, barely managing to get a 2:1 for a shite dissertation written on the treatment of gender in the works of Charles Bukowski & Jack Kerouac;

remembering, as he changes trains & makes the long walk between platforms at King's Cross St. Pancras, how the grading professor had furiously underlined a paragraph that said Kerouac couldn't be a homophobe as he had gay friends like Allen Ginsberg;

& the Northern Line, to Old Street, old memories flooding back ever-quicker as the stops pass by the window, flickers of a thousand recollections racing to reach him before he runs out of opening doors & accompanying 'Mind the Gap' announcements;

& he reaches Old Street, & lets old thoughts fall away, leaving himself with Melina: meeting her at The Roxy, 2009, they both a little too old for the studenty crowd; falling in love, travelling South America, keeping the Dead Bird job long-distance, constantly finding something interesting of the world to keep the word-count up;

proposing in Bangalore;

a double wedding, Medellin & Liverpool;

a year in Bonn, to bypass ludicrous British visa regulations;

& then Liverpool, & the birth of Luis, & the scope for articles falling away, & no other publication seeming open to him, he having spent too long in the studenty atmosphere of Dead Bird Press, he becoming progressively less hip as all he knew of London & the cool night spots of the world beyond crumbling as life revolved around the little one.

Graham reaches the Dead Bird Press offices as all thoughts reach their natural conclusion: that he should've branched out & left this place years ago, but didn't, while his global gallivanting let others push ahead of him into Editorial positions, then move on to more respectable publications, he & Terrance Kant the only two left from the mid-2000s Hoxton glory days.

Graham takes a breath before pushing the button for the intercom, then he's buzzed straight in.

An unknown attractive black girl on reception tells him that Terrance is expecting him, & will be with him in a minute, & has barely got her sentence out before Terrance is out, all slaps of hands & 'mate!'s & his usual bullshit routine of camaraderie, until he leads Graham into his office, sits Graham down across the desk from him, takes his own seat, & lets the pretence fall away & the inner Kunt take control.

"So, yeah, mate, been a while since we touched base, yeah? How's life in Liverpool?"

"It's good, yeah. Y'know, keeping busy."

"With the little one?"

"Yeah."

"What was it, Hugh?"

"No. Luis."

"Luis? Not Hugh?"

"Yeah. Luis."

"Maybe I'm thinking of Hugh Laurie… y'know, Fry & Laurie, House, that guy… you reckon that might be it?"

"Yeah, maybe."

"And little Laurie's how old now?"

"Four."

"Fucking hell, mate! It's been that long? He'll be on staff with us 'fore we know it! Yeah, so, look, I ain't got long, busy man, doing busy man t'ings, and what I'd suggest is for you to just give it to me straight, like a cider that's made with 100% pear: what's in the pipeline? What you got for us? What's Liverpool Graham got to offer Big City London?"

"Well, I was thinking, what with the trouble with the government and Brexit and all that, it might be neat to do a bit on Boris Johnson, and how he pissed off all Liverpool, and the general—"

"Nah, mate. Absolutely not. You know Murdoch's media enterprise owns us now, yeah? And they'd have my head stuck on a pike on Tower Bridge if I went after Bo Jo. Nah, mate, absolutely not happening. Next."

"Well, apart from that, there's a general state-of-the-nation thing that I think we could go for, y'know, post-Brexit vote, I think there's a lot of mileage in looking at how people feel a year on from the Referendum."

Terrance sighs dramatically. He's developed more stubble than he had in his early-20s, when they would sink pints together in The Macbeth or Old Blue Last, but otherwise is still chasing the same East London hipster look, today wearing a grey beret & red-and-white striped shirt.

"Fucking Brexit, mate? Jesus. I've literally just commissioned six articles on it this week. C'mon. Give me something a bit juicier than that."

"Well… I was thinking I could maybe go over to Berlin, or somewhere like that, and take a look at Brexit from the European point-of-view?"

Graham's waited as long as possible to pitch something based on Berlin. His younger brother Robbie is currently living there, doing his Master's in Psychology, & Graham's been hoping for a long while to go out & see him, but with money tight, he's had no chance yet; a Dead Bird-sponsored trip would be the magic bullet.

He sees the cogs whirring in Terrance's tiny hipster monkey brain; Graham decides to pile on while he's primed.

"And I was thinking of a few more things I could do while I'm over there, squeeze a few articles out of it, maybe do something about the Berlin club scene, and I know you've commissioned a lot on that, but I could maybe do a piece on Berghain, how its atmosphere's changed since becoming a tourist attraction, or maybe something on the Berlin fashion scene, whatever's trend-setting and new, or maybe a tour of chic boutique hotels, I heard there's a lot of real creative ones, or maybe a piece on how they're feeling in the lead-up to next year's World Cup, y'know, especially after Brexit, because Germans are typically not that nationalistic, especially in Berlin, and you'll tend to see more European Union flags flying there than German tricolours, or I could maybe do something on Syrian refugees, their day-to-day plight, how they're struggling to survive out there—"

"Graham. Mate. Please. Shut the fuck up a minute. That's a thousand fucking ideas there, mate, and let me just run back through and unpick them one-by-one. Syrian refugees? Fuck that. No-one's interested. That's something The Guardian would write about. Not for us. And then the nationalism… football… thing… nah, not for me, man, I think I'll hold off on all that bollocks til next spring when the World Cup's coming up. And what did you say before that, boutique hotels? Boutique fucking hotels, mate? I'd be more likely to send you to do a piece on fucking youth hostels. But I think you're a bit beyond the age limit of them nowadays! Haha, just kidding, just fucking with you, bro. But that's a shit idea. And the fashion scene? The fucking fashion scene? You want me to fly you out to Berlin to write about the fucking fashion scene? When you're sitting across from me today dressed like Alan Partridge's grandad? Fucking jog on, mate. Ha! That's a joke, that. And what was before that? Berghain? Mate, dressed like that? No chance of you getting in fucking Berghain. And at your advanced years, you're the last staff writer I'd sent to do a piece on the non-stop 24-hour Berlin party scene. And… what was the first thing you said?"

"About Brexit. Looking at it from different perspectives—"

"Nah, yeah, that's shit as well, but I have had an idea though. You spreken a bit of Deutsche, right?"

"Yeah. I was in Bonn for—"

"There's actually something I was just thinking about this morning that I'd like to get someone over to Berlin for. We've got a few peeps over there, of course, but one lad's on holiday, and the other girl's exclusively doing articles on Berlin drug experiences these days, so I didn't think she'd be right for it… but you… nah, yeah, you'd be fucking perfect."

"What is it?"

"Cryptocurrency."

Graham pauses, processes the word, then nods: "Right. Yeah. Cryptocurrency."

"What do you know about cryptocurrency?"

"Well… I mean… yeah… it's… I dunno, it's a bit of a weird one to explain, innit? I mean…"

"It's, like, fucking Bitcoin and that. You know what Bitcoin is, yeah?"

"Yeah. Right. Yeah. Bitcoin. Digital money."

"Precisely."

Graham's heard of it in passing before, but 'digital money' about covers everything he knows on the topic.

"We're starting to see mad click-through rates on anything we publish which is cryptocurrency-related. And Berlin is always a big click driver. Next month there's a big crypto meetup over there. And since you speak German, and since you know what Bitcoin is…"

Graham spends the coach ride back to Liverpool reading all he can on cryptocurrency, beginning with wikipedia.org/bitcoin: Bitcoin – created 2009 by Satoshi Nakamoto, the pseudonym of an otherwise anonymous individual/group, largely in response to the 2007~2008 global financial meltdown stemming from the American subprime mortgage crisis, conceptualised as a global digital currency beyond the control of any central bank, transactions completed peer-to-peer & verified by a decentralised network of nodes…

Graham re-reads the last part, struggling to understand it: *verified by a decentralised network of nodes;* stored cryptographically in a decentralised distributed ledger: this distributed ledger = blockchain.

He looks away from the phone screen & out the window, at the flat fields of England flanking the motorway. He thinks of Berlin, its dense squat-chic Gothic architecture, a chance to meet his younger brother, to get away from England…

Keep reading, he implores himself. *You'll understand at least some of this shit eventually.*

Bitcoins are created by computers solving complex mathematical problems, a process known as 'mining.' In the early days, any idiot with a laptop could mine Bitcoin, but it was designed to become progressively harder, so that today, giant farms of Bitcoin mining rigs exist. The process is massively energy-intensive, and is consequently focused on countries where electricity is cheap, like China.

No chance of profitably mining Bitcoin here in Britain, then, Graham thinks, recalling his & Melina's extortionate EDF energy bill.

Bitcoins were initially worth pennies, but with a limited number of 21 million ever to be produced, and the production of these coins becoming progressively more difficult, the price of each Bitcoin inevitably rose. In 2013, the price of a single Bitcoin soared above $1000. Then came a massive hack of the world's largest Bitcoin exchange, Japan's Mt. Gox: 850,000 Bitcoin were stolen, the price plummeted, & it didn't hit $1000 again until this January. The price has been climbing steadily since the start of the year & is currently edging towards $3000, with no sign of slowing down.

So that's why Terrance is suddenly interested in it.

Bitcoin's growth inspired other cryptocurrencies. Initially these were novelties, with names like Dogecoin, KanyeCoin, & PutinCoin. Over the past two years, these 'alt-coins' have become more serious. The most successful alt-coin, Ethereum, was launched in 2015 by a programmer using his real name, Vitalik Buterin. Buterin was a Bitcoin enthusiast who was frustrated by the inflexibility of Bitcoin. Ethereum allows for the execution of scripts on a Turing decentralized virtual machine operating across the Ethereum network of public nodes.

Graham re-reads that last sentence a dozen times & still has no clue what-the-fuck it means, even after poring over the linked Wikipedia page on Turing virtual machines. After scanning back & forth between the Ethereum Wikipedia page & several online articles, the best he can understand is that Ethereum is a kind of app platform, a bit like the software that's used as an operating system on a computer or mobile phone; & this platform allows for all new kinds of crazy technology to be implemented over 'the blockchain';

& whatever the fuck all of that means, companies like IBM, Microsoft, & Samsung are currently developing Ethereum-related things, & the price of a single Ethereum has risen from less than $0.01 at launch to just under $10 at the start of the year, & is today at over $250 & still increasing.

"Fuck me," Graham whispers.

He reads until the battery's almost drained, then plugs in the charger & reads more, delving ever deeper into this subterranean world of unknown fortune, familiarising himself with names like Litecoin – like Bitcoin, but 4x faster – & NEO – like Ethereum, but Chinese – & then the crazy burgeoning money pit of ICOs – Initial Coin Offerings: new coins promising to utilise blockchain tech to revolutionise everything from air travel to real estate, generating tens of millions in funding, promising investors huge near-term Return on Investment (ROI).

He doesn't stop reading until Liverpool, even staying on the bus during the service stop, & once he's home & reunited with Melina & Luis, he continues reading on long into the night.

CHPTR 02.00 : GENESIS.

@location: ***Groningen, Netherlands.***

02.01.

"NEO?"

"It's like the Chinese Ethereum. Except it isn't really anything like Ethereum."

Wesley enters & interrupts: "What the fuck, guys?"

Guus & Aart are sitting together on the middle of the huge quad sofas in the kitchen/living room's corner-nook, Guus on his laptop & Aart tapping at his phone screen. A Honey Badger music video is playing on the 60-plus inch plasma screen affixed to the nook's dark green wall.

Aart: "Then how is it the Chinese Ethereum?"

Guus: "It's a Chinese dApps platform."

Aart: "What's the price at?"

"Guys!" Guus & Aart turn from the ever-fluctuating prices on CoinMarketCap to look at Wesley, who's standing beside the huge table that takes up half of the spacious room's kitchen area. "Look at this place."

Aart scans a room decorated with clusters of bottles & cans – debris from the previous night's party: "What's wrong with it?"

"The girl is gonna be here in, like, twenty minutes," Wesley says, sweeping bottles from the table into a black plastic bin liner. "You said you'd clean up."

"We did clean up," Aart protests. "This place was really fucked up when you left us."

"What girl?" Guus asks.

"The girl who's here to take on Rick's room," Wesley says, moving about the room and hurrying bottles & cans into the bin liner.

Guus: "No girl's gonna wanna live in a frat house. I don't know why you don't just get a guy in."

"Nah, man," Aart says, standing up & moving to the kitchen area, "he can't join the fraternity, and you know he'll want to."

"But what kind of girl's gonna wanna live in this place?" Guus says, returning his attention to the laptop.

"Where's Federico?" Wesley asks, bin liner fully loaded.

"I don't know," Guus says. "I think he's still in bed. Yo, Aart, the price is at twenty dollars right now. It was, like, thirty dollars less than a week ago."

Wesley: "He's sleeping? It's almost 15:00."

Aart unrolls a bin liner: "He's Italian, what do you expect? Guus, what price did you buy at?"

Wesley moves to the hallway: "Federico!"

Guus: "I got in before it rebranded from AntShares. It's up about 600% on then. But now's the time to get in, man, this dip won't last. A year from now, it'll be two hundred dollars, minimum."

Wesley: "FREDDY!"

Federico groans inside his bedroom: "What?"

"I don't know, man," Aart says, slowly picking up & crushing Hertog Jan cans & placing them in his bin liner. "I think Bitcoin's about done dropping. It'll probably be worth like six thousand dollars in a couple of months."

"It'll be back to zero before the semester's finished," Wesley snaps, returning to the room. "Guus! Get the fuck off the sofa and grab a bin liner."

Guus sighs dramatically & closes his laptop.

"I thought you said Bitcoin was already six thousand dollars," Wesley says, unrolling another bin liner.

Aart casually smooths out the crinkles in a Hertog Jan can before bagging it: "I said I had six thousand dollars' worth of Bitcoin. But that's before the price dropped."

Wesley side-steps Guus to tackle an accumulation of bottles surrounding the quad sofa: "So how many Bitcoin do you have now?"

Aart: "I've still got 1.5 bitcoins, but the price dropped."

Wesley: "So what's that in real money?"

Guus stops at the door to the hallway, intrigued by the sound of Federico conversing with a female: "Is that the girl you're talking about?"

"I don't know," Aart says, picking up an ash-covered Hertog Jan bottle that's stuffed half-full of cigarettes, contemplating whether such a thing is fit to be thrown in with the recycling. "Today, it's a little less than five thousand."

Wesley: "Five thousand Euros?"

Aart: "Five thousand dollars."

Guus: "Wes, I think the girl's here."

"Fuck." Wesley drops the bin liner at the side of the sofa & moves to the doorway, turning back briefly to admonish Aart: "Why do you measure everything in dollars? You're not fucking American." Wesley stares down the hallway, where Federico has just turned away from a closed front door: "Did she leave?"

Federico: "Yeah."

Wesley: "What the fuck?! Why?"

Federico stares at Wesley, Federico's handsome Italian features as befuddled as his tousled just-out-of-bed black hair. "She had to go home."

They stare at each other for a moment before Wesley speaks: "Ciara?"

Federico: "Who's Ciara?"

Wesley: "The girl."

Federico: "What girl?"

Wesley: "The girl who's looking at Rick's room."

There's a long pause before Federico makes sense of things: "Oh, that girl. No, that was Lina."

Wesley: "Who's Lina?"

Federico: "The German girl."

Wesley: "What German girl?"

"The German girl I fucked last night." Federico opens the bathroom door & flicks a light switch; Honey Badger's hit 'Fuck Me (Like a Badger in Heat)' plays automatically as the cupboard-small bathroom's walls covered with pics of big-titted blonde models are illuminated.

02.02.

Ciara locks her bicycle among the scores of similar bicycles lining the pavement outside the JUMBO supermarket on Oosterstraat, a bustling single-lane street lined with bars, shops, & restaurants running up to the medieval Dutch city's Grote Markt central square. She looks up at the apartments above the street's businesses, wondering which is the place, & whether she has enough time to smoke a cigarette before heading inside. She takes her phone from her pocket: 14:57. She taps at Google Maps and then starts walking towards her destination.

02.03.

"Hey," Wesley says, smiling as he opens the door to her. "You must be Ciara."

She's as pretty as he'd hoped: fair hair, pale freckled complexion, a very London beige overcoat underscoring her Britishness.

Ciara smiles back at Wesley: he's equally all that she'd expected of a Dutch frat bro – tall, blonde, with a baggy Rijksuniversiteit Groningen sweatshirt hanging off his sports-honed frame.

Introductions are exchanged and Wesley leads Ciara through the hallway, pointing out the bathroom door & hoping that Federico doesn't open it &

potentially scare her away with the garish array of big tits inside. He stops along the hallway at Rick's room: she looks at the cosy desk & double-bed & nods approvingly: "Yeah, this looks alright."

It would have to be pretty bad to stop her accepting the place. She's spent the summer travelling the continent – Munich, Prague, Bratislava, Budapest, Zagreb, Split, Sarajevo – & returned to Groningen just a day before the semester started, expecting no problem finding a place to stay in a city that must be 50% short-term student accommodation. But she hadn't reckoned on the scores of students doing the same as her, and with a few perfect places being snatched away when on the cusp of signing a contract, and having spent the past two weeks on her friend Jurate's sofa, she's more than willing to take on the wild novelty of a year as the sole girl in a frat house.

The tour continues through to the kitchen/living room, Wesley explaining that Rick's spending a year's exchange in Pittsburgh, & stopping to introduce Ciara to Guus & Aart: "Ciara, this is Guus—" – a slightly-pimpled and awkwardly skinny guy with an oddly intense demeanour & almost-shaved short hair that protrudes into a ridiculous '90s-style gelled spiked fringe – "and Aart." – a far more attractive though equally odd frat member, with hair matted into dreadlocks along the centre of an otherwise completely shaved head.

Aart: "Nice to meet you."

Ciara looks around approvingly at the bar-style central living space, with dartboards & beer advertisements & basketball hoops & other paraphernalia covering almost every inch of wall space, more than a dozen framed photographs of past iterations of the fraternity being the most intriguing item.

"And this is the patio," Wesley says, leading Ciara outside.

"What do you think of her?" Aart asks Guus in hushed conspiratorial tones upon the sofa.

"Yeah, she seems okay," Guus says, fully engrossed by his laptop. "This project sounds really interesting. They want to create a bridge between blockchains, a kind of go-between interface for interconnecting pre-existing cryptocurrencies. It's $3.51, down from $4.10 yesterday, with a four-hundred-million-dollar market cap. It might be worth buying a few hundred bucks worth."

Aart: "I don't know why you screw around with all these alt-coins, man. You know Bitcoin is gonna outperform all of them."

"How much money do you think I made on Ethereum?"

"Yeah, but there's a limit, man. No way all these coins can survive long-term."

"They don't have to. They just need to survive long enough for me to make Lamborghini money."

"If you want a Lambo, bro, buy more Bitcoin. It'll be ten thousand dollars by next spring, man, I'm telling you."

"Yeah, which is like a 350% return on investment. The stuff I'm looking at is like a 10,000% return on investment."

"But anyone can make a coin, man. Slap some code together, get it listed on an exchange – boom. Make a quick buck off idiots looking to get rich quick, and disappear forever to an island somewhere."

"That's why you've gotta do your own research."

"But, like, me and you could probably make a coin."

"I probably could. You couldn't even set your own wallet up."

"Well why don't you then?"

"Maybe I should."

Aart stares at the television screen. Honey Badger is in some tropical island paradise, dancing at the poolside in a suit, surrounded by big-titted bikini babes and chimpanzee butlers. Still a little stoned from his hangover-staving wake-up spliff, Aart is mesmerised by the jiggling girl bits and chimps in bowties for a few moments before speaking: "How much money do you think Honey Badger's worth?"

"Probably a few million dollars."

"A few million dollars," Aart mutters, a thought forming. "And how much did you say that coin you're looking at's market cap is?"

"Four hundred million dollars."

"Four hundred million dollars…" Honey Badger is on the deck of a yacht now, at night, pouring what looks like an extremely expensive bottle of alcohol over some woman's cleavage. "And the people who made that coin probably kept a couple for themselves, right?"

"Probably."

"They probably kept a lot for themselves, right?"

"Probably."

"And right now they don't even have a working product or anything, do they?"

"This one does… I think. But a lot of them don't."

"And you think you could probably code your own cryptocurrency?"

"Probably." Guus looks up from the laptop at the television; Honey Badger is in the yacht's master bedroom, fanning himself with a wad of hundred-dollar bills as two girls in lingerie dry-hump his legs.

"We should do it, man."

Honey Badger is now in the yacht's dining hall, using diamond-encrusted platinum chopsticks to delicately remove a piece of sushi from the crotch of a fully-naked big-titted blonde who lays splayed upon the tablecloth.

"Maybe we should, man. Maybe we should."

Wesley leads Ciara back into the kitchen area: "What do you think?"

She struggles not to gush too much enthusiasm: "Yeah, it's great."

02.04.

The cycle back to Jurate's place is blissful, the beauty of canal-bisected Groningen's centuries-old buildings & crispness of Dutch autumn overwhelming all Ciara's earlier fear, uncertainty & doubt. As her bike flows with the thousands of other cyclists traversing the city's narrow streets, she knows that all is right & well in her life, & that this year will be even better than the last.

When she enters Jurate's house, Jurate is drinking coffee at the kitchen table with her housemate Vallya, who is considerably less blissful: "…and so I cannot work without the Dutch citizen number, this BSN, and they cannot process this without the official document from the university in Moscow, and the university in Moscow only can give this in Russian, and the City Hall here will only accept this in Dutch or in English, unless that I get a legalised translation, which it has to be legalised by the Russian Consulate, which is wanting to charge maybe one hundred Euros, and maybe taking more than three weeks, which is time I cannot do working during…"

Jurate briefly disengages to greet Ciara: "Hey."

"Hey."

The interlude leads a frustrated Vallya to bring her story to its end: "…and it's just *nyet, nyet, nyet* from every direction, and my parents say it is now too much to send me more money, and I do not even know what in the fuck I should do about everything."

Hearing Vallya's bureaucratically-inflicted agony, & being reminded similar pain may yet await her whenever Britain finally leaves the European Union, Ciara again dampens her enthusiasm when Jurate asks her how the place was: "Yeah, it was great – well, the best I'll get at this point," & she answers Jurate's follow-up question about how the guys were with an emphasis on Wesley's tall Dutch jockishness, & Jurate says, "You'll have to invite us to one of their frat parties," & asks Ciara what she's doing tonight, with Vallya & Jurate having plans to go out; "I'm working at Mountain at nine."

Vallya: "*Oy!* All I want is to work while I study. I do not know why must it be so difficult."

02.05.

The overnight shift at Mountain Bar isn't something Ciara would recommend to anyone, though €7 per hour & free alcohol through the night is enough to make it bearable. She parks her bicycle among the ever-expanding sea of bicycles beside the Grote Markt, the streets beginning to fill up with the first of the student-city's night-time revellers. Ciara walks the narrow bar-lined side street to Mountain. Inside, Ibrahim is at the counter & a few young Dutch guys are knocking back 1 Euro Heinekens. A few others trickle in to order 1 Euro beers & shots during the first hour, European EDM blaring & echoing off the walls of the almost-empty room. The population swells at 10pm & gets bigger as the night progresses, Ciara becoming busier & busier behind the bar. By 11, she's in constant movement, racking up beers & Jaeger Bombs & tequila shots, knocking back the few that are bought for her by drunk guys trying to hit on her. Every hour, she slips into the crowded smoking room at the back of the bar to roll & smoke a cigarette. As the time creeps closer to midnight, more & more groups are asking for NOS-filled balloons to huff, falling into dizzy drunken laughing fits after each bout of inhalation. When Ciara next enters the smoking area, a clearly-underaged guy is stumbling about, annoying everyone. Ciara ignores his presence, a stance she regrets fifteen minutes later when an irritated German student comes to the bar and says: "Somebody has been sicked up all over in the smoking area."

Ibrahim is conveniently dealing with a large drinks order: "Do you mind cleaning it up?"

With a sigh & a shrug, Ciara takes a mop to the smoking area, where the idiot teenager is slumped in a chair. "Where are your friends?" she asks him, sloshing his vomit over the floor with the mop.

"I think they left already," says a Dutch guy smoking a joint. "You want some of this?"

She accepts the spliff & after a few tokes continues mopping, the strong Dutch high-grade inoculating her to the grossness of her task.

And then the lads from the frat enter.

Wesley: "Oh, hey, Ciara!"

Fuck.

She laughs & talks with them, fully preoccupied with trying to overcome her stoned inoculation & the embarrassment of her puke-mopping predicament.

Ciara then returns to the bar, FMLing, as Wesley, Guus, & Aart re-join Federico & their other friends Jako, Wander, & Max on the packed dancefloor.

The Honey Badger & Cheap Ho song 'All Fucked Up from Fucking You' hits & the lads spill Heineken as they raise their glasses & shout along to the lyrics. Guus is deep in the throes of inebriation, having huffed a NOS balloon just before the song hit. He closes his eyes as he sings & sways & spills beer, picturing Honey Badger in the dining hall of the yacht in his music video, eating sushi off the genitals of a beautiful big-titted blonde with diamond-encrusted platinum chopsticks.

"We gotta make the coin, man," Guus says, spilling beer onto Aart's shirt as he leans toward him.

"WHAT?!"

"We gotta make the coin," Guus shouts over the booming music. "We can be richer than Honey Badger."

Aart: "Fucking A!"

The ratio of guys to girls on the dancefloor at Mountain Bar is decidedly harming the lads' chances, so after bidding adieu to Ciara & having a final Jaeger Bomb for the road, they're out onto narrow student-swarmed streets, weaving between Wednesday-night revellers, Wesley & Federico & Jako arguing over whether they should go to Twister or Kokomo or Ocean 41. Wesley wins the debate & the gang take a right at De Negende Cirkel & enter the small bar-rammed square containing Twister.

"That's Nguyen!" Guus shouts, the Vietnamese name sounding garbled & incomprehensible to Aart, who follows Guus to the bemused Asian guy standing in the street swigging from a bottle of premium Belgian beer, as the rest of the gang continue on into Twister.

"This man's a genius," Guus gushes. "Nguyen, I was telling you about the coin, right? We have to make the coin, man. We can be richer than Honey Badger, man. Yachts and boats and chimpanzees and eating sushi from model's pussies with fucking diamond-encrusted chopsticks, man. Helicopters and big piles of cocaine and fucking everything, man. Lamborghinis. Two Lamborghinis, man." Guus is rambling & swaying, eyes focused on nothing, the intensity of his slurred speech being met with a confused & slightly nervous smile from his Asian classmate. "Hey, Nguyen, where are you going tonight?"

Nguyen: "I don't know, I was just—"

Guus: "Come to Twister with us!"

Minutes later they're inside, the trio shoving their way through the densely packed crowd in search of the rest of the frat lads.

Jurate & Vallya are at the bar awaiting service. Federico leads Jako & Welsey toward them: "Hey." Federico leans in to Jurate, talking quickly, his Italian charm producing schoolgirl giggles, as Wesley & Jako stand either side of Vallya, trying & failing to say something to bring a smile to her unmoved Russian face.

Once drinks have been served, all five move into the swell of the dancefloor. Federico's hands are at Jurate's waist as 'Despacito' blasts through the club, the many Spanish students dotted throughout the crowd belting the lyrics out. As the second chorus hits, Federico leans his face towards Jurate, who closes her eyes and thrusts her lips at his, & their tongues cascade in & out of each other's mouths while Wesley & Jako jerk their bodies to the song at either side of Vallya, who's looking alternately at the floor & ceiling & rest of the crowd, trying to focus her eyes anywhere but on her potential Dutch suitors.

Guus, Aart & Nguyen push their way past another group to reach Wesley, shouting something about having been looking for him, creating a distraction that Jako seizes upon to offer a hand to Vallya, which she reluctantly accepts.

When Wesley turns back to face them, Jako & Vallya are dancing an awkward semi-tango. He turns to Guus & Aart, irritated, though he smiles on seeing two girls approach who were at the previous night's party – a German & a Spanish girl, Lina & something – *Lina* – and as Wesley greets them both, he realises Lina is the girl Federico fucked, & when Federico pulls his lips free of Jurate's & gazes dreamily into her eyes, Lina spots him, & her mouth drops open, & Federico glances at her, & instinctively thrusts his hands away from Jurate's waist, &

02.06.

Sometime later, Guus, Aart, Nguyen, & Wesley are in the smoke-filled Dees coffee shop, on a narrow alleyway running between the bar-filled backstreets and Oosterstraat.

"I don't know how he does it, man," Aart says, forming his words slowly, bloodshot eyes staring into the middle-distance.

"He's Italian," Guus says, the words bubbling up from his throat in a way that renders them incomprehensible.

Aart: "What?"

"He's Italian," Guus repeats, with force; the force tickles his cannabinoid-coated respiratory tract & sends him into a coughing fit.

Wesley's watching Nguyen toke on the spliff with great interest. Their short & unthreatening Asian companion sucks deeply upon the spliff for as long as ten seconds at a time, filling his lungs completely with smoke. Nguyen then half-chokes on the smoke & half-swallows it, turning his head to the side & lifting his right arm across his mouth to block the cough. Then he returns the spliff to his mouth with his left hand & repeats the entire process.

"Hey, Bogart," Wesley says, "you wanna share some of that joint?"

Nguyen stares at Wesley for a few moments, face completely red, understanding none of what was just said to him. The silence & stares of Guus & Aart fill Nguyen with dread. Smoke rises from the joint & wafts across his field of vision, & it suddenly clicks. He hands Wesley the spliff, then turns his head & returns his right arm to his mouth & coughs & coughs & coughs.

"Bogart," Guus repeats, toying with a frayed piece of roach material on the tobacco-strewn tabletop. "That's an old reference."

"It's a classic," Wesley says, before inhaling deeply.

All are silent for a moment. Then Aart speaks: "Do you think Federico's fucking that girl right now?"

Wesley: "Of course."

Guus: "Which girl even went home with him?"

Wesley: "The German one, I think."

Guus: "Which was the German one?"

Wesley: "The one from last night."

Guus: "Where was the other girl from?"

Aart carefully ponders all the memories & knowledge of Federico he can summon as Guus & Wesley speak. He thinks of the shape of Federico's nose – prominent, Romanesque; the tan complexion of his skin; his height – reasonable, but unremarkable, particularly here in the Netherlands; his easy-going personality, which is surely a factor in Federico's seeming irresistibility to women. Aart then begins wondering how he could be more like Federico. Each point seems an impossibility: a nose job is possible, but might make him uglier than before; fake tan and sunbeds exist, but they might make him look ridiculous; Aart's tall enough already – he might even have a few centimetres over Federico; and the personality… he ponders for a moment, & concludes he's already reasonably easy-going…

Aart: "Do you think I should try a different hairstyle?"

Guus & Wesley stop speaking and stare at Aart. They're struck first by the question's weirdness, then they both take the time to really examine his odd shaved-sides & dreads-on-top look.

"I think it looks cool," Wesley concludes.

Guus: "It's distinctive."

"Thanks," Aart says, accepting the spliff from Guus.

Wesley: "I think your friend's passed out."

Guus looks at Nguyen, who's hunched over the table, resting his heads on top of folded arms.

Guus: "Hey, Nguyen, you okay man?"

"…yeah…"

"You want a Coke or something?"

"…imalright…"

Nguyen's condition is quickly forgotten as the others fall back into conversation about Federico's effectiveness with women.

"He talks to girls," Wesley says, sweeping aside Guus & Aart's focus on the superficial. "It's that simple."

"You talk to girls," Guus says. "I don't see you fucking anyone."

Wesley: "I got a phone number."

Guus: "You think it's a real one?"

"Yeah," Wesley says, tapping at his phone & thrusting it in front of Guus's face. "I got her on WhatsApp."

Guus looks at the profile pic of the smiling brunette: "She looks okay."

"But Nguyen was approaching everyone," Aart says, confident Nguyen's too inebriated to hear him. "He must've talked to six different girls, and every time they just laughed at him, or told him to go away."

"That's because they're racist," Guus says, scowling. "Dutch bitches are the worst for that."

"You're Dutch," Wesley laughs.

"I'm Friesian," Guus says. "And that's all the more reason to know what Dutch bitches are like. They're the most superficial cunts in Europe."

"Woah," Aart laughs. "Fucking chill on the red pill, man."

"I'm just being serious," Guus says. "Real talk. They want a tall man first, a white man second, maybe a black dude if they think no-one's watching. Asian guys fall pretty far down their list. Unless they're rich. If you're rich, you can be a 90 year-old Chinese midget, and every 20 year-old blonde in Twister's gonna suck your cock."

"Fuck, man," Aart says, choking on smoke as he falls into a laughing fit.

"See, this is why you don't get women," Wesley says, taking the spliff off Aart.

Guus: "Because I'm honest?"

Wesley: "Because you're a fucking sociopath."

It takes Aart a while to calm down, while Guus sits & stews over Wesley's appraisal of him. Once Aart's stopped laughing, Wesley holds the nub of a spliff that remains up for the group: "Anyone want BLTs?"

Guus snatches the nub of spliff from him & sucks on its scorching end.

"Come on, let's wake Nguyen up and go to Warhol," Wesley says, standing up.

"Hey, Nguyen," Aart says, shaking Nguyen's arm.

Nguyen doesn't respond.

Aart shakes his arm harder.

"Come on, wake up."

Nguyen meekly raises his reddened face, eyes lolling in their sockets: "Ithinkimgonnathrowup."

"You're alright, man," Aart says, almost at the exact moment Nguyen throws his head to the side & cascades vomit all over himself.

02.07.

"Goodnight."

Ciara lights her rollie as she walks away from Ibrahim & Mountain Bar, the previously busy bar-lined streets eerily quiet in the gently rising early morning light. The only person in the street is some junky in a tracksuit, who immediately stops fiddling with some random bicycle & eyes Ciara suspiciously as she passes. The scent of long-roasting meat hits Ciara as she passes a kebab shop at the end of the street. She thinks of ending her night/starting her day with some greasy sustenance. She pauses & watches the hacked-at lamb spin slowly against the grill through the window & decides to hold on for home & something healthier. She drops her rollie to the floor

& continues on to the huge bike parking area at the edge of the Grote Markt, with about a dozen bikes now dotted around it. She heads to the spot she left her bike at, but doesn't see it. She walks slowly around the parking area, scanning each bicycle carefully. When she's finished, she circles around back to the start. She does this three times, each time suppressing a growing fear, a developing sinking feeling in her stomach. After the third search, she admits defeat.

"FUCK'S SAKE!" Ciara yells, startling a bumbling old bloke & some pigeons.

Her bike's been stolen.

02.08.

Statistical modelling that should be second nature to him is somehow leaving Nguyen completely confused; he checks variables, consults Google, but still keeps returning results that make no sense whatsoever.

"Why in shit isn't this result significant?" Nguyen moans, the effort of pushing the words out in English making him aware of the thick-cloud of the-night-before cloaking his every thought & action.

Guus takes a quick look at Nguyen's screen & tuts loudly: "You are mixing the European and English decimals."

"What?"

"Here." Guus highlights an entire column of data on Nguyen's computer, opens Excel, copies & pastes the offending digits into a new spreadsheet, then performs a quick search & replace, changing every '.' English-style decimal into a ',' European one. "We use commas for decimals," Guus says, copying the altered data & pasting it back into the SPSS data modelling software. "Now try."

With a few quick button presses, Nguyen returns the statistically-significant result he was looking for. "Damn," Nguyen mumbles. "I knew that."

"You're still fucked up from last night, huh?"

"Mmm."

"You remember puking all over that coffee shop?"

"No."

"I don't think you can go back to there."

"Ugh."

They sit in silence for a few moments, each working their way through their data analysis homework, as Guus thinks of more ways to annoy Nguyen. He thinks of teasing Nguyen about the many Dutch girls Nguyen threw himself at, but then remembers the hope-filled conversations he had with Aart about the potential of making their own cryptocurrency: "Hey, remember I told you that me and Aart are thinking about making our own coin?"

Nguyen doesn't answer, frowning in concentration at some difficult-to-decipher English-language sentence on his problem sheet.

"Do you know how to make one?" Guus continues. "You're usually pretty good with that stuff."

"What, making a cryptocurrency?" Nguyen asks. "What makes you think I'm good at that?"

Guus: "I don't know, just making things in general. You made your own phone apps, right? iOS and Android. And computer software."

Nguyen: "Yeah, but I never set up an entire blockchain."

"I don't know if you need to create an entire blockchain. I thought you can make it like an app on Ethereum? Same as making an app for a phone or something."

"What, you mean like setting up an ERC-20 token?"

"Uh… yeah…"

"Sure. That's easy."

"Yeah?"

"Yeah. I've set a few up on testnet just to play around with it. It takes like twenty minutes."

"Really?"

"Yeah. You've just got to copy and paste a pre-existing smart contract and swap the variables out to meet your specifications."

"…yeah?"

"It's super easy. It couldn't be easier." The fog of the previous night is lifting, Nguyen's spirits rising now he's found something pure to distract himself from the garbled English grammar of his data analysis problem sheet. "What do you want your token to do?"

"I don't know… it doesn't really need to do anything. We just thought we could maybe make a lot of money."

"Well then it's super easy. Incredibly easy. A baby could do it."

"Yeah?"

"Yeah. Look, watch this…"

02.09.

It's already passed 4pm when Ciara's dragged her tired self from the university to the Grote Markt & on to the bar-filled streets beyond, and the bike hire shop at the far end of the boozing district, facing the canal.

She's at the counter, rummaging through her pockets, in a panic: "What happens if I can't find the key?"

The women at the counter's previously-friendly face grows suddenly serious: "Then you must pay us for the cost of the bicycle."

The repairman at her side, fiddling with some disc-shaped bike part, adds gravely: "We'll take it from the bank account you registered with."

Ciara: "And I still have to keep paying the rental fee each month?"

The woman: "Of course. You signed a contract."

Fuck's sake.

Back out on the square, stumbling in a half-awake sleep-deprived daze. Ciara's thoughts tumble over themselves, until she stops outside a bar & takes her phone from her pocket & connects to wifi.

"Hiya, Mam," Ciara says, once her Facebook Messenger call's connected. "I've got a bit of a problem."

"Oh, you don't need to borrow more money, do you?" Ciara's Mam asks, sounding worried.

"Well… last night I went to work at that bar I'm working at, and I was working until early in the morning, nine til six, then when I got out, I went to where I'd parked my bike, and…"

"…because I just lent your brother two hundred quid, and we've just had to get the double-glazing done on the windows, and I'm down to my last pennies now…"

"Yeah, it's just that I can't find the bike key, and they say without it, I have to keep paying every month, and I still need to get a new bike for getting around, and it's a few weeks until I get paid again…"

"Can't you ask your father?"

Ciara sighs: "You know what's he like. And he's already lending me the money for the deposit on the house, he's not gonna give me any more than that."

"And I thought you were working?"

"I am, but I'm only making, like, six hundred Euros a month, which after rent is barely fifty Euros a week to live off…"

"…and I thought you were getting money back off the Dutch government?"

"I am, but like one-hundred sixty Euros a month…"

"So can't you buy a bike with that? It doesn't have to be a fancy one, does it?"

"…no, yeah, but… I mean…" She sighs, defeated, deciding to steel her mind for the final ordeal of the long walk back to Jurate's, & the long walks from there to & from university until a new bike's sorted. "Alright… I'll figure something out."

02.10.

"Hey, Aart, check this out," Guus says, bringing his laptop into Aart's room, cold autumn rain lashing the streets outside the frat house.

"What're you doing?" Aart asks, as Guus sits upon his bed and starts tapping at the laptop.

"Here." Guus places the laptop beside him on the bed & motions for Aart to use it.

Aart sits & stares at a line of zeroes on the laptop screen: "What's this?"

"Move the mouse around."

Aart drags his finger across the laptop's touchpad; the zeroes are replaced with a string of random letters and numbers.

"Write the number down."

"What is it?"

"Your private key."

"For what?"

"For Pussy Sushi."

Aart stares at Guus in confusion; Guus stares back, bearing yellowed teeth with an enormous grin: "Pussy Sushi?"

"Like the Honey Badger video," Guus explains. "This is our ticket, man. Lambos, yachts, and banquets of sushi served on the bare bodies of beautiful big-titted blondes. Write the key down."

Aart stands up, grabs a sheet of paper, & jots the key down: *5xBee23aZc41nErd1AsddDNeXfg543009ah18EfnM*. He clicks continue. "You made this yourself?"

"Nguyen helped me."

"So I've got a wallet," Aart says. "What happens now?"

"What's your public address?"

Aart reads the numbers out, Guus meticulously tapping each onto his phone screen. "Okay, now wait a minute… wait… wait… anything happening?"

"Nothing…" Aart hits refresh. "Nothing… nothing… nothing… oh, sweet."

The zero balance on the wallet has suddenly become 15 followed by six zeroes.

Guus: "You are now the owner of fifteen billion Pussy Sushi coins."

02.11.

"This place is crazy," Jurate says, twirling in the frat's bar-like main living space.

"It's cool, yeah?" Ciara's enthusiastic, & happy her friend shares her enthusiasm.

"It looks like a bar," Vallya says, betraying no emotion.

"Can I get you a drink?" Wesley asks. "We've got beer, vodka, gin, whiskey, bourbon, white rum, dark rum, tequila, sambuca, ouzo, Aftersock, absinthe—"

Jurate: "Beer's fine."

"But what are you supposed to do with it?" Jako asks, sitting on one of the corner-nook sofas.

"This exactly what I say to them," Federico says. "Is fucking useless."

Guus: "It's a proof of concept."

Jako: "But what concept have you proved?"

Guus: "That we can make a coin."

Federico: "That you can make a fucking shit coin! The coin you've got is no use to anyone!"

"So we've got the proof of concept," Guus says, ignoring Federico. "Now we just need a use case."

Jako: "That's, like – how you say? Carriage in front of the horse. You're doing it backward."

Federico: "Exactly!"

Jako: "Surely you find a problem first and then design a solution for it?"

Federico: "That's what I tell him!"

"Think about mouthwash," Aart says, knowing Jako, Wander & Max are much more likely to be convinced by marketing-focused explanations than technological ones. "Mouthwash had no obvious use case; in fact, the guys who made it thought it might be used for floor cleaner, or toilet cleaner: they had no idea it would take off as an oral hygiene product until the marketing guys got hold of it."

"And that's where you guys come in," Guus says, smiling smugly.

Jako: "Well, my opinion is you need to change the fucking name first!"

"What, you don't like Pussy Sushi?" Guus asks. "It's like in the Honey Badger video…"

"Just call it Fucking Shit Coin," Federico says, sharing an awkward half-second of eye-contact with Jurate as Wesley brings the girls over.

"Hey, guys, this is…"

Introductions follow, bottles of Hertog Jan are clanged together, & space is made for Wesley & the girls on the sofa. Time passes, conversation flowing, the rate at which beers are sunk increasing.

"I'm sorry about the time before," Federico says to Jurate. They fall into drunken forgiveness & flirting.

"I heard Putin's really into blockchain," Guus tells Vallya, who tells him: "I don't know anything about it."

& so on, empty beer bottles accumulating, cigarettes being smoked, joints rolled, harder drink turned to – beginning with tequila shots – , the night getting progressively messier, the chatter getting louder, music videos playing on the television, & then the Honey Badger one comes on – the one which inspired Guus & Aart in the first place, where's he's on the yacht eating sushi off a model with the diamond-encrusted platinum chopsticks.

"And so tomorrow I have to go again to the place," Vallya pouts. *"Oy."*

"That sucks," Ciara says, though she's honestly fed up of hearing about Vallya's endless bureaucratic issues getting Russian documents approved in the Netherlands.

Guus: "You know, that could all be solved instantly with blockchain."

"Really?" Vallya asks, showing genuine interest for the first time all evening.

"Yeah," Guus says, one eye on the television, awaiting the triumphal moment when Honey Badger brings out the diamond-encrusted platinum chopsticks. Guus launches into an in-depth explanation of the transformative power of decentralised distributed ledger technology for all manner of cross-border record keeping, Vallya rapidly losing interest as it becomes apparent he's offering no immediate-term solutions.

"Would you shut up about the Fucking Shit Coin?" Federico says, arm now around Jurate a couple of seats away.

Everyone laughs, & Federico leans back in to talk seductively to Jurate, who's very much into it, Federico playing up his accent for maximum effectiveness; & Jako & Wesley both draw Vallya's attention away from Guus; & Guus stares at the television, as the Honey Badger music video gives away to Gucci Mane living the high life in some lush tropical island mansion; & Guus keeps pinging the two mantras off each other – Vallya's issues with the Russian documents, & Federico's repeated denigration of "your Fucking Shit Coin," & Guus' mind swirls as more alcohol's sunk – a double berth of sambuca & ouzo shots – & the night wears on, much booze drank & weed smoked, & Ciara & Aart & Guus & Max & maybe one other one who's too fucked to say much are in Aart's room, smoking another joint & drinking Jack & Coke, & Guus is ranting about blockchain & the potential use case for the Coin Formerly Known as Pussy Sushi, & how they need a high-quality whitepaper written in English, & Ciara would maybe be perfect for it, & everyone else is too fucked to say much, so Ciara's indulging him, & trying to comprehend Guus' jargon-laden rant, & Aart's getting tired of listening to him, & when Ciara says for the fifth or sixth time "I don't really get it though," and this time asks after "How can you stop other people stealing your coins from you?", Aart pushes past Guus (who's still ranting) to open a desk drawer & pull out his paper with the private key for his Ethereum wallet on it, & he's excitedly explaining to Ciara how "this key is completely unique, and as long as nobody else sees it, nobody can access anything, and your public key is a totally different number that you can send money to," & now that he's interrupted from his rant, Guus is left to rock back & forth in his stoned drunkeness, & he suddenly blurts out what he'd been looking for: "I'VE FUCKING GOT IT!"

& Max stirs on the bed, & whoever's lying beside him's woken from their slumber by Guus's cry, & those two & Aart & Ciara stare at Guus in half-comprehension as he bring his rant to the climax he's been looking for:

"Fucking Shit Coin! FSC! Federico's a fucking idiot, but he's got a thing for marketing, right? FSC! Got a good ring to it! So we use it to sync the documents, so Vallya's situation's solved on the blockchain, right? So her Future's secured on the blockchain. So there's Synergy between the documents issued in Russia and Nederlands. So there's Synergy from past to present to Future. So that's what we call it, right?"

Guus stares at the others, awaiting their enthusiasm.

"…sorry…" Ciara mumbles, "I'm don't get it…"

"Future Synergy Coin!" Guus shouts. "FSC! It's fucking *gezellig!* A decentralised blockchain platform for the secure cross-border storage and access of the important documents of the citizens of all the world's nations!"

Max opens & closes his mouth a few times, too fucked up to say anything.

Ciara stares at Guus, then at Aart, still utterly confused.

Guus looks at Aart, eyes pleading with him to be the first to understand him.

"Yeah, I get it," Aart says, mostly out of sympathy. "Future Synergy Coin… because it synergies with your future…"

"Exactly!"

& the rant continues, & all rapidly interest, but Guus is enthused through the next ten drinks, & as the others pass out & disappear into the night around him, he becomes the last person awake in the frat house, sitting on the quad sofas beside a passed-out Wander, furiously scribbling a rough abstract for the Future Synergy Coin whitepaper across a bunch of McDonald's napkins found in a kitchen drawer.

02.12.

"…and we can pay you," Guus says.

Ciara's trying to listen to Guus, she hungover, barely able to focus, until he says those magic words: *we can pay you…*

"Yeah?"

"Of course. I've made a bunch of money from crypto already, but I'm sure this idea's gold. Future Synergy Coin is gonna make a thousand times more than whatever I've made buying other people's coins."

"But… a whitepaper?" Ciara leans forward in her seat, between Aart & Guus on the quad-sofa in the party-ravaged frat's main living space. "I don't even know what that is…"

"It's like a research paper explaining what the coin does," Aart says. "It's not much different than an essay you'd have to write for your course."

Ciara's relieved that Aart's stepped in: he explains everything so much more calmly & understandably than Guus.

"You just have to look at some other whitepapers from successful cryptos," Aart says. "You can pretty much just copy their background sections, take a few bits and pieces from different papers, and put it into your own words."

"But I don't get why you want me to do it," Ciara says. "Surely you both know a lot more about this crypto thing than I do?"

"Because the English needs to be perfection," Guus says. "The whitepaper is everything. The whitepaper is what convinces people this isn't just some new Fucking Shit Coin; this is Future Synergy Coin. This is something world changing. Something they have to invest in."

"Yeah? Well… I suppose I could write something like that…"

"Of course you can," Guus grins. "And as I say, we'll pay you. We can pay you in cash – say, 500 Euros?"

Fuck. Ciara imagines the bike that €500 could buy.

Aart stares at Guus, shocked he's offering so much.

"Or we can pay you some part in cash, some part in Future Synergy Coins," Guus says. "I can almost guarantee the price will rocket. Every coin's going up at the moment."

"500 Euros is fine."

"Excellent." Guus leans back on the sofa, clasping his hands behind his head, triumphant. "I'll tell Nguyen to start working on the website."

ICO.

Ciara completes the whitepaper in a few days' rush, desperate for the €500 & a new bicycle, pulling together sections & strands & diagrams from a dozen pillaged & semi-plagiarised pre-existing professional efforts, rejigging sentence structures & paragraph orders to avoid plagiarism-detecting algorithms – a skill her university course has taught her well – while Nguyen rustles up a rudimentary website, then makes adjustments & adds swirling graphics of blockchain-signifying spiderwebs of interconnected nodes under Aart's direction, while Guus suggests a few slight changes to both the whitepaper & the website, feeding Ciara & Nguyen the details to make the whole thing a success: giving the coin a total supply of 10 trillion, a high enough figure to make each coin seem unbelievably cheap compared to the likes of Bitcoin & Ethereum, even if FSC's marketcap was to soar into the tens-of-millions-of-dollars range (a goal Aart laughs at the impossibility of), with 50% of coins available to the crypto investors via the Initial Coin Offering (ICO) crowd sale, 25% split between Aart, Guus, & Nguyen, & the last 25% allocated to the Future Synergy Coin development budget; fluffing the resumes of the team to be listed on the website, vastly overinflating the success of Nguyen's previous coding projects, making Aart out to be an elite Dutch business bastard & an expert in every topic touched upon in any of his university modules, while Guus depicts himself as the genius at the center of it all, an incomparable fusion of tech & business savvy, a hip young master of the future tokenised economy; & the hard-cap on the ICO is set at 15,000 ETH, a figure roughly equal to $4.5 million, & at this point Aart & Ciara are convinced this bold project will come to nothing, that they'll never find enough people stupid enough to fund a project with such ambitions from a group with such little track record: & because of this, Aart balks when Guus asks him to contribute his 1.5 bitcoin, with Guus adding 1.5 of his own, to bribe a leading ICO review website into giving their project a 4-star rating (a 5-star rating cost far more Bitcoin than either possess or can afford); but Guus promises Aart the potential returns are astronomical, far outstripping anything he could get by simply hodling & hoping for Bitcoin to increase in value: & against his better judgement, Aart gives in to Guus, & transfers his 1.5 BTC to the ICO review website; & the 4-star rating appears, & on 17th October 2017, the Future Synergy Coin ICO goes live.

3. LISTING.

Genoa, Italy.

"Hey, Giovanni."

Paolo stands in the doorway & awaits a response; hunched over his computer, his flatmate says nothing. The only sound Paolo hears is the tapping of keys & low hum of server cooling fans.

"Hey, Giovanni," Paolo says, louder. *"Vaffafanculo! Coglione! Testa di cazzo! Figlio di putana!"*

"WHAT?!" Giovanni snaps, turning from the computer to the doorway.

Paolo flicks the light switch & illuminates his housemate's pallid face within the darkened digital-humming room.

"Manchester City versus Napoli," Paolo says. "We can go to Santino's bar to watch it. The Portuguese guys are going. And maybe Natalia will be there, huh?"

"I'm busy," Giovanni grunts, returning to the computer.

"Hey, *vaffanculo,* you've been sat in front of that computer for days. Did you even eat?"

"I ate pizza."

"That was last night. *Coglione."*

Giovanni flips the greasy lid of a pizza box at the side of his computer monitor & removes a thin slice of room-temperature pepperoni: "There's still some left."

"Hey, *putana,* the fuck are you doing there anyway? Semester just started. We ain't got any project due for, like, three months at least."

"BitBucks," Giovanni grunts, staring at the computer screen.

"Che due coglioni! I don't understand you. Hey, *testa di cazzo,* what the fuck did you say?"

"BITBUCKS!!" Giovanni screams.

"The fucking crypto thing?"

"Yeah."

"How's it going?"

"Good."

Paolo waits for a more elaborate response. When he doesn't get one, he gives up: "Okay, then. *Porca Guida! Fottiti!*"

Paolo storms out of the apartment, slamming the door as he leaves. Giovanni barely notices, fully engrossed with the clicking of keys & reassuring hum of server fans. He's clicking back & forth between support tickets & withdrawal approvals; he sends 15 ETH to a customer's external wallet after a brief check that all seems legit, then does the same with 4 BTC; then he's reading support tickets, wishing he could address these fucking morons with the same kind of language Paolo just used against him. There's some idiot American asking why his 0.05 BTC deposit wasn't approved yet: 'We have no control over when miners confirm & sign Bitcoin transactions,' Giovanni types. 'Try paying a higher transaction fee next time.'

There are ID documents to verify from customers looking to increase their 0.5 BTC daily withdrawal limit; Giovanni clicks through these quickly, approving scanned passports from the USA, Canada, Australia, Germany, France, Venezuela, etc., etc., just checking if the country & name on the scanned passports matches the country & name the users signed-up with.

There are support tickets to deal with – endless support tickets – some days old, most probably resolved already, assuming the idiots sending them pulled their heads out of their asses long enough to google the most basic information about cryptocurrency trading.

And then there's Giovanni's main project of the evening, which everything else is simply distracting him from: adding three more coins to BitBucks' 12-strong offering of Bitcoin & Ethereum trading pairs. There's GUM, a global oral health blockchain solution from a team based out of Belarus; TRAP, a coin that seeks to celebrate the popular American hip-hop 'trap' sub-genre, created by two Iowa State University students; & GLUM, an ambitious project from some Argentinian researchers who aim to defeat depression by integrating blockchain-based psychoanalysis via yet-to-be-created decentralized Internet-of-Things connected apps which continuously monitor the user's mental health.

Giovanni, like BitBucks' customers, knows little about these projects, or the teams behind them; but he knows that most of these coins haven't been listed anywhere else yet. The small exchange he runs out of this small shared apartment above a cheap pizzeria on a backstreet in Genoa is the first place these coins will ever be available to trade. While some coins will surely stall & falter & disappear, others will flourish & pump & rocket to the moon. For those lucky few, BitBucks will be the first step towards getting listed on major exchanges, & getting in early on those few rare coins will result in a 5 times, or 10x, or 20x, multiplying of the dollar value of BitBucks' customers' investments. And BitBucks – Giovanni – will take a big chunk of those price increases through fees for listing & trading & withdrawal.

So Giovanni remains slumped in front of his computer screen through the night, tapping away at the JavaScript console, integrating these three new coins. He works without stopping to drink water or piss or to eat more than a half-slice of stale pizza, until Paolo returns, drunk, from Santino's. Giovanni works as Paolo sways in the doorway, retelling the story of his night, explaining the missed chances & misfortunes & amateur-league defending that led Napoli to lose 4-2 to Manchester City. And Giovanni continues as Paolo disappears into his bedroom. He continues as his phone vibrates upon the desk beside him, even though he can hear the phone's rattling over the constant server hum, even though he correctly guesses that Natalia's calling, & she's one of the rare truly attractive girls on his & Paolo's Computer Science course. He pauses & considers calling her back at just after 2am, maybe half an hour after the phone's stopped vibrating, once GUM trading is active & TRAP is getting there, but then looks at the €12,465 in trading fees BitBucks has taken already this week, & quickly calculates that he might double the €18,962 BitBucks made the week before, & reminds himself that if he spends a year or two generating this kind of income, he'll have a hundred girls a thousand times hotter than Natalia drunk calling him late at night.

So Giovanni works until dawn, a flurry of typing & clicking resolving around 50% of support tickets, approving numerous large withdrawal requests, verifying scores of ID documents, & activating trading on all three of BitBucks' new coins.

Giovanni's hunched over the keyboard, light beating against the curtains, the clock in the corner of the screen telling him it's 5:07, but his work is done. He opens his Gmail tab, ignores the handful of new support tickets & large withdrawal requests, & opens an email with the subject: "Exciting new project seeks listing on BitBucks – FUTURE SYNERGY COIN."

He scrolls through the usual blurb about how great & revolutionary this coin will be, & smiles when he reaches the end of the email & sees FSC has yet to be listed on any other exchanges. He checks the time again – now 5:09. He has class at 11, but he could skip it. He fires back a quick email in sleep-deprived broken English, promising that FSC trading will go live within the next four hours, as long as the team can send 0.25% of the total coin supply as a listing fee. He checks the FSC ICO website, runs a quick mental calculation, & laughs to himself deliriously over the server fans as another $11,250 is added to BitBucks' weekly earnings.

4. A VIEW TO A SHILL.

Berlin, Germany.

04.01.

"So a key thing is banking the unbanked in countries where traditional banking services are inaccessible," the guy says.

"…and unbanking the banked in countries where trust in traditional banking services has been eroded," says the girl.

Graham nods sagely & scribbles the phrase into his notebook: *bank the unbanked / unbank the banked.* "Could you elaborate on that a little bit?" Graham says, sipping from his pint of weissbier. "I'm not sure I fully understand it."

The guy & the girl exchange a knowing look; this is not the first time they've encountered blockchain non-believers.

"So if you look at countries that are experiencing hyperinflation," the guy explains, in perfectly measured Southern Estuary English that betrays only the slightest hint of a German accent, "Venezuela, Zimbabwe, countries like that, these provide a real-world test case for the transformative power of cryptocurrencies."

"Around 95% of the population in sub-Saharan Africa lack access to traditional banking services," the girl adds.

Her accent is pure Home Counties – from Kent, maybe. The couple look every bit the Berlin crypto evangelists: style caught somewhere between Yuppie banker & squat-dwelling hipster chic; her thick frizzed black hair pulled into a bunch at the back; his sleek black hair twisted into a slender ponytail; she wearing an oversized mustard sweater; he a T-shirt with the logo of the Ethereum cryptocurrency on it beneath a vintage corduroy blazer.

"What I don't get though," Graham says, "is why something like Bitcoin would be any sort of solution to hyperinflation? I mean, the value of Bitcoin has increased about 7000% so far this year."

"It isn't the dollar value that's important," the guy explains. "It's an issue of trust."

"Bitcoin's decentralised," the girl says.

Guy: "Exactly. There is no central bank exerting control over it. There's no entity that can print more Bitcoin whenever the economy tanks. There will only ever be 21 million Bitcoin in existence."

Girl: "And so it serves the same purpose for unbanking the banked in developed countries."

Guy: "2007."

Girl: "2007, the subprime mortgage crisis in America…"

Guy: "…global financial crisis…"

Girl: "…the Credit Crunch…"

Guy: "…bailing out the banks…"

Girl: "…the biggest transfer of wealth in human history…"

Guy: "…austerity…"

Girl: "…Greece…"

Guy: "…Cyprus…"

Girl: "…the Cypriot central bank seized something like 10% of everyone's assets…"

Guy: "…every bank account given a 10% haircut…"

Girl: "…maybe 20%, something like that…"

Guy: "…and Bitcoin's decentralised…"

Girl: "…and it isn't just Bitcoin…"

Guy: "…Bitcoin was the start of it…"

Girl: "…this is revolutionary tech…"

Guy: "…the next Internet…"

Girl: "…it's like the Internet was in 1995…"

Guy: "…decentralised applications, run on the Ethereum protocol…"

Girl: "…Internet-enabled devices, freely exchanging data, through the IOTA direct acyclic graph tangle…"

Guy: "…completely decentralised…"

Girl: "…an immutable ledger…"

Guy: "…impossible to censor…"

Girl: "…an uneditable record of transactions…"

Guy: "…a permanent store of value…"

Girl: "…and of data, ideas…"

Guy: "…almost limitless possibilities…"

Girl: "…it's like looking at Angelfire or Geocities in 1995 and trying to imagine Facebook…"

Guy: "…or Netflix…"

Girl: "…or Uber…"

Guy: "…or online banking…"

Girl:"…decentralised communities, global communities…"

Guy: "…free of all oversight and interference from any centralised entity…"

Girl: "…is that Vitalik Buterin?"

The guy & the girl break off building on each other's sentence fragments to stare across the Kreuzberg pub at a stick-thin pale East European or Russian looking guy in a bright white Ethereum logo T-shirt.

"No," the guy concludes. "I think Vitalik must be taller than that."

"I'm sorry," the girl says to Graham. "Are we going too fast for you? It's all a bit much to take in at first."

"No, I think I got everything," Graham lies, staring at the jumbled mess of buzzwords decorating his notebook.

"I think that's David Sontesebo," the girl says.

Guy: "From IOTA?"

Girl: "Yeah."

Guy: "Maybe we should go say 'hallo.'"

The guy & the girl say ciao to Graham & walk over to a figure hidden by a mob of excited crypto geeks. Graham stares at his mess of buzzwords, then frowns. The last month was a lean one, & he'll be cutting deep into his savings to pay rent if he doesn't get at least one article sold out of this Berlin jaunt. But despite talking to a half-dozen groups & individuals at 'The 27th Krypto in Kreuzberg Monthly Meet-Up,' he doesn't have any idea of how to turn this into a readable article. He flips back through the near-incomprehensible jumble of jargon filling the last few pages of his notebook, thinking that the best thing would probably be to adopt Dead Bird's typical house style & snidely dismiss everything about the event in a sarcastic we-are-cooler-than-thou way. But as Graham sighs & glugs back weissbier, he thinks of how enthusiastic everyone back in Shoreditch seems to be about this cryptocurrency bullshit. And given that he's now ten years' older than everyone in the office except Terrance Kant, the snide approach would probably have him labelled out of touch & kicked out of his job.

I'm getting too old for this shit, Graham's forced to admit to himself, as he taps at his iPhone & sends a Whatsapp message to Melina: 'How's everything going at the Immigration Office?'

"Y'alright, la?"

Graham looks up upon hearing the unmistakable nasal Scouse voice of his younger brother. Graham's straight to his feet, gripping his brother in a tight bear-hug, & switching from the softened London-twinged accent he's been using on the crypto folks to an authentically full-force Liverpudlian patois: "Fucking hell, soft lad, you're looking well. How's it going?"

Robbie gets a pint & joins his brother at the table, listening to Graham whinge about how he can't understand anything about the crypto scene & has no idea what kind of article he's going to write about it.

"I tell you what, la, here's a real-world use case for ya," Robbie says, "I know a bloke, Eritrean guy, here on asylum, can't get no work until he gets the visa sorted, gets like a hundred Euros a month stipend off the government to survive off, and obviously the lad's turned to selling gear to get by, like, and making a tidy profit off it, as you would, selling gear in fucking Berlin, like, and, well, the interesting thing for you is that he prefers to get paid in crypto."

Graham: "But ain't it supposed to be fully traceable now? Like the government have cracked Bitcoin or whatever, and they've closed down most of the darknet drug markets?"

"Yeah, that's why you don't use fucking Bitcoin to buy drugs, la," Robbie says, taking his phone from his pocket. "You use Monero. I'll give him a buzz now. What you after? I'm sure he'll throw in a complimentary interview."

Graham pauses for a moment & thinks of Melina at the Immigration Office, with little Luis. *I really am getting to old for this shite,* he thinks, but that thought is instantly countered with a barrage of other ones – *ah, come on, you're in Berlin, la, and it'll probably help you write your article, and you ain't seen your little bro in months, and once you've done this piece, you can start working on your exit strategy, moving to a more legitimate publication…*

Graham: "Yeah, go on, la, let's get a gram of whizz in."

04.02.

"Ah, fucking hell," Graham says, reading Melina's message.

Robbie: "What's happened?"

"There's been a problem at the Immigration Office," Graham says, re-reading the message as he walks. "Melina's forgotten a form or something. She's gonna have to take another day off work to go back again." Graham thinks of another day's lost salary & his own dim prospects of returning from Berlin with something Dead Bird will pay to publish. "Do you know how fucking ridiculous our country's immigration policy is?"

Robbie: "You had to live here in Germany six months first or something before she could move over, yeah?"

The brothers are walking from the Krypto Meet-up to a huge sunken garden that runs along the edge of the Kreuzberg district, Graham explaining to Robbie the tangled legal loophole he & Melina & thousands of similar couples have exploited: whereby the UK requires an income of £50,000 per year per person (no option of splitting the difference) or a savings account loaded with £500,000 cash to issue a UK spousal visa to the wife of a British citizen, even with kids involved; but how this contravenes the laws of most

EU member states, & how he & Melina had relocated to Bonn for 6 months – he still doing freelance stuff for London-based Dead Bird, she working in a Mexican restaurant – & then slipped in through Britain's legal back door after 6 months residency in an EU member state, she then ironically recognised by the British government as the spouse of an EU citizen, but how this solution is temporary, & she's now required to acquire on-going 6-month visa extensions.

"That's fucked, la," Robbie says, pulling a pack of cigarettes from his jeans' pocket.

"You're fucking right it is, la," Graham agrees, pulling out his e-cigarette. "And it's not gonna get any easier, with this Brexit shite going on. Those Tory cunts'll doing anything to keep the headline immigration figure down."

"You want a proper one, la?" Robbie asks, holding his cigarettes out.

Graham hesitates, then thinks of the soon-to-be-delivered cocaine: *In for a penny, in for a pound:* "Go on then, kiddo, I'll rob one of y'us."

A sharp inhalation of smoke grates on Graham's throat, prompting instant regret, but within a drag or two it's like he never stopped smoking. Robbie explains the concept of Monero, with it's completely anonymised ledger, & how all transactions on the Monero ledger will be completely hidden from government & all other institutions until the eventual advent of quantum computing: "and that'll be mad, that will, la, almost infinitely powerful computers, like, you set them the problem of curing cancer or something, and it'll run a billion calculations in a nano-second, and you'll have the cure right then and there, and it'll be able to crack the most uncrackable security, hack into North Korean nuclear plants or whatever, it'll change the world, la, for the better or worse…"

"Yo."

A gruff voice announces the arrival of Robbie's guy, a dark-skinned guy with a slender build, wearing a nondescript black jacket & red Bayern München baseball cap.

Robbie fist bumps his guy & introduces his brother. The dealer starts shuffling through bags in his pocket as Robbie opens the Monero wallet on his phone.

"One G, yeah?" the Eritrean asks, eyes bulging wide as he scans an elderly man in a coat across the long narrow garden taking a dog for a walk.

Robbie: "You wanted one, didn't you, Graham, la? Yeah, better make it two, mate."

"Cool, I got you, man."

"So my brother's a journalist, working for Dead Bird, the hipster London magazine, you know it?"

"I don't read no London hipster magazines, boss."

"Well he's doing a piece on crypto, and we've been at this crypto meet-up round the corner from here, but it was all a bit fucking dull to be honest with ya, and I was wondering if maybe you'd mind giving him a quick interview?"

"What do you wanna know?" the Eritrean asks, holding his phone out for Robbie to scan the QR code.

"Well…" Graham begins, taking a deep final drag on the cigarette to help crystallise his thoughts. "I've been wondering why you'd want to get paid in crypto? Surely cash is already completely untraceable?"

"Yeah, but where am I gonna keep it?" the Eritrean says, stuffing two plastic wraps into Robbie's jeans' pocket. "I still got family back home that I want to help out, help them get over here. What am I gonna do, walk into Western Union with a bag full of Euros?"

"Do you even get Western Union in Eritrea?" Robbie says, squeezing the two wraps in his pocket to check they're of a decent size.

"Of course, man. How you think we send money before crypto come along?"

Graham: "Eritrea's kind of like the North Korea of Africa, right?"

"Something like that," the Eritrean says. "The government control everything."

Graham: "But they can't control crypto."

"No they can't," the Eritrean says, opening CoinMarketCap on his phone's web browser. "So today Monero is $94.58, so €80 a G is…"

Robbie & the Eritrean race to be the first to check the US Dollar/Euro conversion rate on XE.com: "About $185 for two," Robbie says.

Both open their calculator apps, tap out a quick formula, & arrive at the same conclusion: "1.956 Monero for both."

"Yeah, that's exactly it," Robbie says, tapping out the required figure into his Monero wallet. "It were 2 Monero each G last time we met, yeah?"

"True fact," the Eritrean says. "You getting a good discount today. Monero pumping hard. Any other coin you recommend?"

"Ethereum's on the rise, mate, trust me."

"I got enough Ethereum. I wanna diversify my portfolio."

"How about NEO?"

"NEO?"

"It's the Chinese Ethereum."

"I don't know, man, can you trust? I heard China wanna ban crypto."

"They won't ban it. 90% of the world's Bitcoin mining happens in China."

"Yeah, but they government want to control currency outflow, yeah? Big deal in China. They don't want situation like here, where citizen send money anywhere."

"It's up to you, man, but I reckon it'll be a big gainer in the next few months."

"I'll look into. What you been doing here so far?" the Eritrean asks Graham.

"Well, I got in last night, just had a beer and some bratwurst at a restaurant near my hotel."

"Where you staying?"

"Mitte."

The Eritrean smiles: "You balling, man. Where you stay there, Hilton? Sofitel? Regent?"

"The Amano."

"Nice place. What you boys doing now?"

Robbie: "Did you wanna go back to the crypto meet-up?"

Graham drops his cigarette to the floor, it already having burned down to the nub. An idea strikes him: "You know, my magazine are big into these kind of in-depth gonzo journalism pieces. If you're not too busy, maybe we could go grab a pint somewhere and have a chat about stuff? I'll buy you one."

04.03.

"So Eritrea's the east coast, across water from Yemen…"

Graham: "Yemen… that's a fucked up place right now…"

"Yeah, man. Saudi Arabian bomb them like American bomb Afghanistan. It's crazy. You go to coast in Eritrea, you see them bombs light up sky in distance."

Robbie: "It's almost as bad as Syria there, yeah?"

"Worse," Graham says. "Maybe." His mind's working super-quick from the line he just sniffed off his iPhone in the traditional wood-panelled German pub's toilets. He stumbles back over his words, correcting himself: "I don't, like, Syria's pretty bad, but there you've got Russia backing the Assad regime, and ISIS are the main existential threat to Western global hegemony or whatever these days, so you get a ton of media coverage on it, whereas in Yemen it's Saudi Arabia doing the bombing, and despite the US admitting a Saudi prince funded 9/11, we're their allies, so you don't get nearly as much critical media coverage, even though what they're doing there's probably worse than what anyone can get away with in Syria… So where you from in Eritrea?"

"You probably don't know my place – Ghinda. Is not so big, but near capital city, Asmara. I think Eritrea's maybe not like how you imagine; many beautiful building. You know we was colony of Italia? Italian make many nice building. Our capital look maybe like Firenze or Venezia. And my town, we grow many fruits. It maybe be not so bad place, but it very poor, and the government is rule with the iron fist, so Eritrea very difficult place to survive and make some good life for yourself."

Graham: "So how'd you get to Berlin?"

"It took long time. Too long. First, I go to border with Sudan, with group of other guy like me, walking across desert. Very dangerous. Many people die there. We lucky, our whole group live to tell tale. Across Sudan, we go Egypt, then to coast, then we meet we people smuggler. We each pay him $500. That very hard money to get in Eritrea, took me long time of working hard to get. And that's why me family stay behind. My brother come, he stay in Italia now. But my mother, my brother wife, he children, all them stay Eritrea. That's why me send money back, maybe they can come more safe path to Europe."

"And where'd you go from Egypt?" Graham asks, enthralled.

"Egypt maybe more dangerous than Sudan. Desert border to Gaza, so there many terrorist, bandit, and desert is desert. Many dangers just from that. But we lucky, we get to coast, we meet we people smuggler, he have us raft. Maybe one thousand people, one raft, floating on Mediterranean. When we close Italia, coastguard pick we up. Me stay some time Genoa, sleep on streets. Many man try sell trinkets to get by, or try connect tourist with weed or something. My brother, he do okay there, but it very difficult. Many African same situation as we, so not easy to make some success. And Italian no so happy about we be there, and I hear Germany very welcoming, so I come here in Berlin."

"How'd you get from Genoa to Berlin?" Graham asks. "Exactly? You take a bus, a train…"

The Eritrean laughs: "They no let African board train or bus with Eritrea passport. No, me get to Berlin by foot."

"You walked?" Graham asks, surprised.

"Mate, he fucking walked from Eritrea to Egypt," Robbie laughs. "Italy to Germany's the easy part."

"No so easy, man. Desert and Sudan and Egypt all very dangerous, but Europe too fucking cold."

04.04.

Some bar somewhere in the city, loud & crowded, each beer & gummed or snorted dab of powder – gummed discreetly at the table, or lifted to alternating nostrils with a key in a toilet cubicle – brings Graham more excitement about his mission, Negassi the Eritrean's wild journey & Robbie's enthusiasm all making this thing so much clearer, so much more essential…

"But don't you think this is all a bubble?" says some beautiful blue-eyed blonde German girl – *Erika?* Graham thinks, trying to remember her name & wondering whether his brother's shagging her, & thinking if he is, good on him; & he tries to speak, to add a coke-amplified opinion, but the others are speaking so loudly & quickly that whatever he says is lost in the mess of voices:

"…like Tulipmania, in Nederlands, or Ty Beanie Babies," Robbie's wild-haired German mate Luther's saying, "all will go to nothing, and you'll be left with nothing but some shitty computer code that…"

Robbie: "…yeah, nah, but with all them though, they were functionless, had no purpose…"

Negassi: "…send money outside Europe in a minute, man, and the fees is…"

Erika (?): "…cannot keep going up forever, surely, the bubble most pop sometime…"

Robbie: "…decentralized apps, la, dApps…"

Luther: "…but it's a nonsense, why in the fuck anyone needs this…"

Negassi: "…and no one but you can know, man, control your own banking…"

Robbie: "…a decentralized fucking internet, la, imagine the repercussions on that for China…"

& as the conversation rages, Graham zones out & thinks of Melina, & her trouble at the Immigration Office, & the permanent precariousness of their situation, & whether it'll ever be resolved, or if Luis will grow to be a teenager with his mother's visa status still subject to the whims of clueless cowardly Conservative governments & racist foreign newspaper owners feeding the idiot 52% of the British electorate a brainwashing diet of racially-charged rhetoric & sensationalist anti-immigration headlines; until Graham's thoughts & the conversation coalesce, Robbie saying something:

"—Future Synergy Coin, it's this project from this elite team of programmers in Amsterdam, where they want to keep a record of all official documents on the blockchain, and you pay a small fraction of FSC whenever you need to access them, instead of spending a fortune on notaries and legalisation or whatever, and carrying a thousand different documents around with you; like Negassi, if you needed to prove you're an Eritrean and a legit asylum seeker, instead of some fucking Nigerian opportunist or whatever, you could use FSC without having to carry your passport around with you, or Graham, when Melina went to visit the Immigration Office, she could've just—"

04.05.

Graham recoils from the baggie's final line & stares at the laptop screen: he's at the desk of his room at the Amaro, ready to unleash all he's heard through the night; and he slams it out, taking sips of Edelweiss snow weissbier every few hundred words, until he's crafted a near-perfect distillation of Negassi's insane journey through Northeast Africa to Central Europe; then he sits back, looks at the word count – a healthy 2,565 – & thinks of Melina, her troubles at the Immigration Office – & wants to message her, but he checks the time in the corner of the laptop screen – 4:52am – & realises the UK's only an hour behind, 3:52, & remembers what Robbie said of that mythical coin produced by elite programmers from Amsterdam – FSC; Future Synergy Coin – that coin that promises to solve all immigration issues eternally & forever, & sparks a cigarette, drains his Edelweiss, realises he's got a second can in the spätie bag, & residue on the coke baggie, so he smokes 2 or 3 more fags, sups beer & licks the baggie out, then rapid-fires a passionate piece on how world-changing FSC could be, cryptically referencing Melina & Negassi's situations, imagining as he pounds the laptop keyboard a world where blockchain obliterates borders, a world fit for Luis to grow up in.

04.06.

Graham shuffles with the rest of the deplaned passengers through the 'Nothing to Declare' customs check at John Lennon Airport & briefly wonders whether he could squeeze in a final cigarette before Melina meets him, after which he's made a firm promise to never stray from the e-cig again, but Melina & Luis are already at the gate, smiling, & Graham scoops Luis up & hugs Melina & feels a rush of endorphins his brain sorely needs after following the high of the night before with the low of low-budget air travel.

"Y'alright?"

"Yeah. How was Berlin?"

They walk out to the car park as Graham gives a sanitised version of events, telling Melina that Robbie's doing well, & there might really be something to this cryptocurrency stuff. He explains Future Synergy Coin to her on the drive from the Airport to the Wirral, but reminding Melina of her trouble with the Immigration Office only irritates her, so Graham changes the subject & asks Luis if he saw Liverpool smash Southampton 3-0.

At home that afternoon, Graham drinks coffee & tidies the articles up, his later-written one on Future Synergy Coin being particularly full of overwrought prose & bizarre grammatical errors. Once they're done, & he's happy with them, & Melina's scanned them & said they're great – as she always does – Graham emails both articles to Terrence Kant, editor @ Dead Bird Press. Then he takes Luis to the park & gets an email on his phone saying that Dead Bird will publish the wild tale of Negassi the Monero-accepting Eritrean coke dealer but they've no interest in the piece on Future Synergy Coin. After dinner, & once Luis' been put to bed, & Graham & Melina are on the sofa in front of an episode of Narcos, Graham's searching for more info on the wild world of cryptocurrency on his phone, pouring over Medium articles & Reddit comments, & the thought strikes him not to let his article on Future Synergy Coin go to waste, so he uploads it to Medium himself, then shares the link to reddit.com/r/cryptocurrency & forgets about it until the following morning, when he checks his phone's Reddit app with surprise: 1608 upvotes, 275 comments, far outperforming any Dead Bird article he ever shared on Reddit. And then he googles Future Synergy Coin, and sees the price has increased from .0013 cents to .0046 cents per coin.

"Bollocks," he says out loud, startling Luis & drawing admonishment from Melina. *If only I'd bought some of the pissing coins before publishing that thing & pumping the price up.* But as thoughts whir through his mind, he moves from annoyance to calculation; if you can pump the price 350% without even trying, then…

5. THE MAN ON THE MOON.

Isla de Joven Belleza, El Salvador.

"Senor McAvoy."

Jack McAvoy doesn't look up, engrossed in the Graham Jones-penned article he's reading on Medium: *How Future Synergy Coin Could Change the Shape of International Borders.*

"Senor McAvoy," Tiny repeats, louder.

Jack McAvoy looks at Tiny, the M16-carrying head of his personal security force. As the name suggests, Tiny's short – maybe 5'5"/165cm – but even without the gun, he cuts a commanding figure; muscular, to the point his dirty-grey tank-top barely fits him; shaved head & crazy eyes, with an inch-thick scar running from the corner of his right eye almost to his mouth.

"Good morning, Tiny," McAvoy says. "How are you today?"

"Is fine, but Senor McAvoy, there is man come to see you."

"Who?"

"He say he journalist. He work from Financial Weekly."

"Show him in."

"Si."

McAvoy returns his attention to the article as Tiny leaves the massive open-plan kitchen, its perfectly white surfaces stretching out to floor-to-ceiling windows providing a magnificent sweeping view of a white sand beach dotted with towering palm trees, rolling out to the shimmering clear azure waters of the Pacific Ocean. McAvoy's young girlfriend, Manuela, is beside him, idly playing with her thick black hair as she sits cross-legged upon a gleaming chrome bar stool.

"Manuela, eat your breakfast," McAvoy says without looking up from his laptop.

"I eat."

"You *ate* what?"

"Some grape."

"Manuela, 'some grape' is not breakfast. Breakfast is the most important meal of the day." Eyes still fixed on the screen, McAvoy pushes a large bowl of mixed nuts along the kitchen counter toward her. "Eat some."

Without saying anything, she picks out a single Brazil nut & eats it.

"Manuela, one nut does not a breakfast make. Eat more, por favor."

She does as instructed, scooping a handful of nuts from the bowl & munching on them noisily.

"Senor McAvoy," Tiny says, returning to the kitchen, worn knuckles clenched tight around the M16's barrel. "Here is journalist."

"Hola," McAvoy says, standing up & offering a handshake to the frazzled gringo from Finance Weekly.

"Mr. McAvoy, it's a pleasure to meet you," the journalist gushes, glad to have the chill of air conditioning to replenish him from the sweat-drawing tropical heat. He tells McAvoy his name – Matthew Cooper – & a brief rundown of what Finance Weekly's intentions are in sending him all the way from New York to an island off the coast of El Salvador for this in-person interview. McAvoy will be the magazine's cover star, with an in-depth profile of the fascinating tech billionaire filling at least a half-dozen pages inside. McAvoy's not particularly interested in what Matthew Cooper tells him; instead, he's checking the pot of coffee, then instructing Manuela to make a fresh one, & to serve some fruit for the journalist, then insisting that she eat a bowl of yogurt.

Matthew Cooper stops speaking once it's clear that McAvoy isn't really listening to him. Cooper sits on one of the chrome barstools surrounding the kitchen island & looks at the breathtaking opulence of Casa McAvoy, with its stunning view of the pristine Salvadoran sands outside: "This is quite the place you've got here."

"This is a magnificent country, Sir," McAvoy says, returning to his own stool. "Quite simply, this is the most beautiful country on Earth. The most beautiful country, with the most beautiful people." McAvoy looks longingly at Manuela's ass, cheeks hanging out either side of undersized tight shorts, as she prepares the requested fruit, yogurt, & coffee.

"Is this… your girlfriend?" Matthew Cooper asks, hesitating as he does so; because of her age, he'd assumed her some sort of live-in housekeeper; but his research on the maverick billionaire Jack McAvoy tells him he's likely to have a girlfriend some years his junior.

"Yes, Sir," McAvoy says, still staring at Manuela's ass. "And you should let your Finance Weekly readers know she is of legal age!" McAvoy lets out a roaring laugh, the kind of full-of-life laugh that wealthy expats in tropical paradises are wont to burst into at a moment's notice. "She celebrated her eighteenth birthday just a week ago, as a matter of fact. And I do not mind you printing that, Sir, if that's what you think your readers might be interested in. No, I know why you're here; you find me fascinating, is that correct?"

"Well…"

"I mean, who wouldn't? The billionaire seventy-two-year-old playboy, living in a tropical island paradise, with his teenage girlfriend. It's fascinating shit, right? Titillating stuff, to put between your serious financial analysis and business news and all the rest of the dry grey Wall Street fluff that fills the pages of Finance Weekly."

"Well, you are an… interesting individual…" Cooper says diplomatically, mentally composing notes on how he'll physically describe McAvoy & Manuela in his Finance Weekly article: *McAvoy insists his girlfriend just turned 18, but I can't shake off the suspicion she may be a few years younger… just as McAvoy himself is 72 years old, but looks as slender, toned, & stylish as a man less than half his age…*

"We should all strive to be interesting, Sir. We have but one life to live, and if you're not striving to make it interesting, then what the heck are you doing with the limited time that's been allotted to you?

"Yes…" *…whether it's the gorgeous sun-kissed El Salvador climate, or the love of a much younger woman, or simply the blond frosted-tips in his hair that harken back to the 1990s – the decade in which software pioneer Jack McAvoy made his fortune – or some other age-evading secrets known only to the planet's wealthiest individuals, Jack McAvoy appears as youthful & vibrant as… as…*

McAvoy continues rambling, a little too fast for Matthew Cooper to make sense of, his mind still adjusting from the heat outside to the cool air inside the McAvoy mansion. Manuela lays out a large spread of all manner of tropical fruits, then two bowls of yogurt, and two cups of coffee; "Manuela, please, eat some yogurt! And drink some coffee!" McAvoy says, grasping her slender wrist & looking into her deep hazel eyes. "It's good for your digestive system."

Without a word, Manuela returns to her earlier position, sitting cross-legged atop a barstool, & pours out a third cup of coffee, this one for herself. She then delicately spoons yogurt into her mouth as McAvoy & Cooper talk.

"This place really is magnificent," Cooper says, once there's a lull in the conversation.

"Absolutely it is. The most beautiful God-damn country on Earth. It's beautiful, but it's not without its problems."

"What kind of problems?"

"How did you get here?"

Cooper exhales, wondering how much detail to go into: "I flew from New York to Atlanta, then from there to San Salvador, then I took a four-hour cab ride to the coast, and a forty-minute cruise out to the island."

"Uh-huh. And how long were you waiting at the ferry terminal?"

"About half an hour."

McAvoy laughs. "When I first arrived here, there were two ferries a day. 10am and 4pm. That was the schedule. But every God-damn time I flew in from somewhere or other, I'd be sat at that ferry terminal with my thumb up my ass for hours before the damn boat would show up. So you know what I did? I made my own ferry company. I created the McAvoy Island Express. Twelve journeys a day, never more than ten minutes late, at half the price of the pre-existing ferry company, with concessions for local residents on low wages, and with double the salary of that God-damn floating turd of a ferry that connected this island to the world before I got here. And within six months, I put those sons of bitches that ran the old ferry line out of business. And the people of this island love me for it! They get the most reliable ferry service in the Southern Hemisphere, and my employees receive a benefits package that is the envy of the Western world. Full healthcare coverage, a living wage – the people working on my ferry live a better life than an United States Senator! But you know something, Sir? Not everybody is as concerned with the welfare of the people of this island as I am."

Cooper lets silence hang heavy in the air for a moment before he's compelled to ask: "Who do you mean?"

"The sons of bitches that ran the old ferry company, for one. Those God-damn corrupt pig bastards. But, I mean, they've got to a make a living, right? I have a lot of sympathy for them. I've got a lot of sympathy for everyone in this country. I love this country! But it is a God-damn festering Third World shithole, Sir." McAvoy's eyes grow wilder as he talks, to the point that looking at them makes Cooper feel uncomfortable. The journalist shifts his focus to Manuela instead, innocently spooning yogurt into her mouth. "Eat some more nuts," McAvoy tells her, his rant on Salvadoran corruption & the establishment of the ferry company over. Manuela dips her spoon into the bowl of nuts & scoops an assortment into her mouth. "But, anyway," McAvoy says, smiling calmly, eyes no longer ablaze with madness, "I don't expect Finance Weekly has sent you all the way out here just to do a piece on Central American water-based transportation networks."

"Well, as you're well aware, one of the topics that is fascinating our readers right now is cryptocurrency—"

McAvoy laughs at the mention of it, eyes gleaming again with that mischievous glow known only to those with enough money to command their own heavily-armed personal security force.

"You've certainly been a very active and outspoken advocate for cryptocurrency," Cooper says, feeling the foreplay's over & he's now getting to the main action of the interview. "I was wondering how you see this space developing in the future?"

McAvoy says nothing, smiling instead at Manuela, who is gazing mindlessly at her coffee. When McAvoy finally speaks, it's to his girlfriend: "Drink some."

"Do you think that cryptocurrency has genuine potential to become a real borderless form of value transfer?" Cooper says, not sure if McAvoy has comprehended his previous question. "Do you think that it really is the future of finance? Do you think—"

"Sir," McAvoy says, staring suddenly at Cooper, eyes dancing on the thin border between calm billionaire contentment & unhinged Salvadoran warlord madness. "Do you have any idea how easy it is to manipulate cryptocurrency markets? Actually, Sir, let me rephrase that question; do you have any idea how *legal* it is to manipulate cryptocurrency markets? Right now, it's possible to do things that haven't been allowed on Wall Street since the Great Depression. Actually, I was just preparing an example before you arrived here…" McAvoy turns his laptop to face Cooper. The screen is still showing the Medium article on Future Synergy Coin. "Sir, what is your annual salary?"

Cooper hesitates before laughing nervously & attempting to deflect the question: "I'm sure it's a heck of a lot less than the hundred million dollars you sold your software company for."

"Sir, with all due respect, that is not what I asked you. If you'd rather not discuss specifics, I don't blame you for it. I know many people consider it uncouth to discuss personal finance in polite society. But how would you like to double your annual salary in the space of an hour?"

Cooper says nothing.

"Or triple it. Quadruple it. Look." McAvoy turns his laptop back toward himself & narrates as he taps at his keyboard: "See, I just go to this exchange, BitBucks, where you can see from this depth chart, we have people placing sell orders on the coin at intervals running up to one-point-one millionth of a cent. So I buy all the coins up to that amount – here, here, here… and I now control quarter of a trillion Future Synergy Coins, which has cost me the equivalent of a little over three bitcoin – a piddling amount for a billionaire such as myself, Sir. But what I really want is to snap up as much of the available supply as possible for the lowest price possible, so I place a sell order at nine-hundred-ninety-nine thousandths of a cents like this, then I wait for the bot traders to do their magic… yes, Sir, you can see that they're recalibrating… now, I place another buy order… let's says another two trillion, then I drop the price like this, then I buy back in like this…" – the process takes a matter of minutes, McAvoy narrating all the way, Cooper mesmerized by the extent to which the market is dancing to the tune of McAvoy's bitcoin – "and now that I have a suitably large stack, phase one of the market manipulation is complete, and I simply send out a Tweet to my one-point-five million Twitter followers – 'Brief drip in FSC, extremely promising coin, HUGE potential for mooning,' – and – Sir, are you sure you wouldn't like to make a small investment before my acolytes send the price skyrocketing?"

"Umm... I'm not sure... it's... allowed..."

"Suit yourself, Sir. Now I just hit the blue 'Tweet' button, and within the next hour, Sir, my sub-10 Bitcoin investment should be worth somewhere in the region of 100 Bitcoin, netting myself a roughly $700,000 profit."

"Wow." Cooper's not sure whether to believe such an astronomical profit is truly possible in such a short space of time, especially given the source; all his research his told him McAvoy has long had difficulties telling the truth. "That's... incredible... but... isn't it..."

"Illegal? No."

"Immoral?"

McAvoy laughs. "You cannot con an honest man, Sir. Anyone who buys the coins I shill hopes to get rich selling them on to some other schmuck in the near-future. It's just Darwinian Capitalism in action."

"Senor McAvoy." Tiny has reappeared in the doorway, clutching his M16. "Senor Alvarez is here to see you."

"Show him in," McAvoy says, with a regal wave of the hand. "What perfect timing! Now, Sir, during the conversation that follows, you are under no circumstances to reveal that you are a journalist, comprende?"

"Uh..."

"Just keep your mouth shut, Sir, let me do the talking, and I promise I will give you something interesting to write about in your Finance Weekly article."

With Cooper confused & silent, McAvoy directs another command at Manuela: "Eat some more nuts."

As she lifts another handful of nuts from the bowl to her mouth, a portly and heavily-tanned Salvadoran man in a white suit enters the room, removing his hat from his balding head & bowing slightly. "Senor McAvoy," the bald man says. He continues the conversation in Spanish, meaning Cooper can only understand about 15% of it. "I was hoping that we could talk in private."

"Senor Alvarez," McAvoy replies. "My security team made me aware of your intention to visit me today, and I have invited one of my closest associates along to listen to our conversation. This is Matthew Cooper, my accountant. I understand, Senor, that you wish to discuss business matters with me. Therefore, I think that it is only appropriate that my accountant listen to what we have to say to each other."

"Very well. Buenos dias, Senor Cooper."

Confused, Cooper hesitates before awkwardly responding in garbled Spanish: "Buenos noches."

McAvoy smirks, then notices Senor Alvarez looking awkwardly at Manuela, who is staring with disinterest at her half-empty bowl of yogurt.

"The girl does not concern you," McAvoy says.

"Of course," Alvarez flashes an embarrassed smile. "May I sit?"

"You may not."

Senor Alvarez's face tightens, his previously affable demeanour evaporating.

McAvoy: "Speak."

Alvarez: "Well, Senor McAvoy, as you know, the Salvadoran government has been very accommodating of your presence within our humble island community of Joven Belleza. We have turned a blind eye to… certain… indiscretions…"

Alvarez looks pointedly in Manuela's direction; McAvoy bristles.

"…there have been deliveries to this compound from known traffickers of certain substances… there have been numerous reports of disturbances, and missing persons, and many other things that our government would normally be most concerned about… however, we have been pleased with the supplies you have donated to our local police force, and with how you have improved transportation services between our island and the mainland. But, as you may already be aware, a day is fast approaching which will have an enormous impact on the future of our island. As I'm sure you are well aware, I am the current representative for Isla de Joven Belleza in the Salvadoran Senate, and I have been all too happy to represent you, Senor McAvoy, as one of my most important constituents. But, we are in the midst of a fiercely contested election season, and it would go a long way to ensuring our future cooperation if you were to make a small donation to my campaign for re-election…"

"See what I mean?" McAvoy says to Cooper, suddenly switching back to English. "Total corrupt fucking shithole of a country."

"Mr. McAvoy," Senor Alvarez says in English, his face reddening. "I know some American expression. I know when you insult me in American."

"Well get fucking used to it, Sir, because I will not donate a God-damn cent to your campaign."

"Mr. McAvoy, we know you make much money here on our island. Yet you pay much less tax than should be your burden. We know about your deliveries of narcotics, Mr. McAvoy. And we can very easily classify your personal security team as an anti-government guerrilla force."

"Mr. Alvarez," McAvoy says calmly, "I understand exactly what you're saying; you think you can come into my house and push the rich gringo around, correct? You think you can squeeze a few pesos out of the idiot American, correct?"

"Mr. McAvoy…"

"Mr. Alvarez, you can eat my dick, *comprende?*"

Alvarez's face turns bright red. He places his hat back upon his head before speaking again. "I will give you one final chance to apologize and make things right, Mr. McAvoy. You are making a grave mistake."

"You made a grave mistake walking in here today, Senor. With all due respect, get the fuck off my property and go fuck yourself."

"Very well," Alvarez says, staring chillingly at each of McAvoy, Cooper, & Manuela in turn. Cooper shivers under the portly politician's gaze; McAvoy & Manuela are completely unmoved. "You have made a powerful enemy today, Mr. McAvoy. We will be seeing you again very soon."

"Fuck off!" McAvoy says, snatching a handful of nuts out of the bowl in the middle of the table & throwing them in Alvarez's direction.

Alvarez is about to explode with anger & retaliate, but Tiny suddenly appears beside him, flanked by two much larger M16-wielding members of McAvoy's personal security force.

"Very well. Buenos dias, Senor…" Alvarez nods at Manuela – "…Senorita…" – & then at Cooper - "…Senor."

McAvoy throws another handful of nuts at Alvarez as the senator leaves, followed by the two larger members of McAvoy's security team.

"Senor Alvarez is very powerful man," Tiny says. "Are you certain this is good idea?"

McAvoy laughs. "Don't worry about it, Sir."

"But Senor…"

"Sir, do not worry about it!"

Tiny looks into McAvoy's crazed eyes & Cooper perceives a sudden change on Tiny's face; perhaps a flash of future betrayal. Then Tiny turns & leaves the room.

"So, Sir," McAvoy asks Cooper, calm again, as if nothing out of the ordinary had just transpired. "Is there anything else that your readers would like to know about me?"

Cooper tries for several seconds to speak, but trembles & stutters with fear over the potential consequences of what he's just witnessed. He finally manages to squeeze an answer out: "I… think… we're… good…"

"Excellente. Manuela, have you finished your breakfast?"

"Si."

"Then please make your way to the bedroom. I will join you there shortly."

"Si."

Manuela rises from the stool and exits the kitchen.

McAvoy turns to Cooper, & grins at the trembling journalist: "Do you think I'm crazy, Sir?"

"I… n-no… I think…"

"Sometimes I think I'm crazy. Do you know what I'm going to do right now?"

Coopers looks at the door through which Manuela just exited: "I can guess…"

"Really?"

"…yeah…"

"Then what am I going to do right now?"

Cooper stares into McAvoy's crazed blue eyes, then out through the doorway; there seems no point in being coy. "You're going to have sex with her."

McAvoy laughs: "No, Sir. I am not."

"Okay. So… what are you going to do?"

"Above my bed, I have a hammock. Do you know what a hammock is, Sir?"

"…of course…"

"In the center of that hammock, which is suspended above my bed, there is a hole. Manuela will position herself above that hole, and I will position myself beneath it. Why do you think we would do that, Sir?"

"You're… going to… put… your…"

"Come on, out with it!" McAvoy grins, crazed eyes now seeming friendly & conspiratorial.

"…put your penis through it?"

"No, Sir, I am not. Guess again."

"I… don't know."

"I'm going to put my mouth beneath the hole, Sir."

"…okay…"

"And Manuel is going to sit above it. And do you know what Manuela is going to do?"

"…no…"

"She's going to shit directly into my mouth, Sir." McAvoy laughs, then rises from his stool. "Please help yourself to anything you need while I'm in there."

McAvoy strolls confidently out of the kitchen, leaving Matthew Cooper in a total daze. He spends the next minute picturing the bizarre activity McAvoy just described engaging in with Manuela, wondering if it's true, then wondering if it's even possible, then remembering the athletic way in which Manuela sat cross-legged upon her stool during breakfast. With a shudder, Cooper recalls McAvoy's insistence on her drinking coffee & eating digestion-enhancing breakfast foods. Finally, he's hit with full-bodied anxiety as he realizes McAvoy just told a senator to go fuck himself, & that his terrifying head of personal security seemed completely untrustworthy, & that the senator swore vengeance…

In utter panic, Cooper turns McAvoy's laptop toward himself, desperate to send out a plea for help to his editor at Finance Weekly. But when Cooper sees the screen, in spite of his overwhelming anxiety & fear of the mad antivirus billionaire & all the craziness of his Salvadoran island compound, Cooper can't help but notice the current price of Future Synergy Coin: it's now at $0. 000024 – more than doubling McAvoy's investment within minutes, with a continued upward trend seeming inevitable. Cooper steels himself from the panic long enough to make a quick calculation that he's sure will make the perfect final line to his article: *In the time it took Jack McAvoy to tell the senator to go fuck himself, and for him to feed his teenage girlfriend enough to satiate his bizarre coprophiliac desires, that crazy son of a bitch Jack McAvoy made more than $100,000.*

6. THANKSGIVING.

Blandford, Massachusetts. (United States of America.)

06.01.

"So whaddya make of Trump?"

Michael bristles at the mention of the nation's Commander-in-Chief. Larry's been in the house just twenty minutes & barely cracked his first beer open, & he's already gone for the most controversial conversation topic possible.

"It's going about as well as I'd expected," Michael answers diplomatically.

Larry half-laughs, half-snorts. ESPN Sports Center plays on TV, relaying highlights of Russell Westbrook's 34-point performance in a 108-91 Thunder win over the Warriors .

"Whadda you think of Trump?" Larry asks his nephew, Steven.

Steven's sitting in a low chair at the side of the sofa his uncle & father are sharing, holding his phone a few inches from his face, utterly engrossed with whatever he's watching on it.

As soon as Larry poses the question to Steven, Michael's diplomatic instincts are overcome by a desire not to let his brother's views poison the mind of his 14 year-old son. Michael says, "I'd say we're a few months away from either impeachment or World War Three."

"What, because of North Korea?" Larry says. "Come on. If they were gonna do something they'd have done it already. I'd say it's a damn good thing we've got a President who's finally standing up for this country. Not touring the world dishing out apologies like Barack Hussein Obama did."

Michael: "Yeah, and irritating all our allies, embarrassing us on the world stage."

Larry: "Embarrassing us? What are you talking about! I tell you what's embarrassing; us giving up our position as the greatest damn country on Earth to appease all the half-commie European tree-huggers, giving up our industrial base to boost the Chinese economy, letting terrorists run rampant in the Middle East because we're too afraid we'll hurt someone's feelings if we execute our military operations properly."

It's way too early for this, Michael thinks. He focuses on Sports Center's rundown of Shohei Otani's Major League Baseball prospects, answering Larry's statement with calming silence.

Emily enters the room flustered, looking for something.

"How's the food coming?" Larry asks her.

"It'll be another twenty minutes or so," Emily says.

"Well it smells delicious."

"Thank you Larry. Michael, have you seen those Christmas crackers?"

"Christmas crackers?" both brothers say in unison.

"Yes, the ones we brought back from England with us."

Michael: "Oh, those little flash-bang present things with the party hats inside?"

Emily doesn't answer, searching through the various cupboards & drawers within the many items of matching oak furniture within the family's spacious living room: "Found them!"

"Steven, whatta you watching?" Larry asks.

"YouTube."

"YouTube, huh? You ever watch YouTube, Mike?"

"Sure. Sometimes."

"You know, I heard kids today watch something like twenty times more YouTube broadcasts than regular television."

"I can believe it."

"I think it's good for them," Larry says. "There's nobody controlling the narrative on YouTube. People are free to say whatever they want. It's the Fifth Amendment in action. You know who I like? Alex Jones. You ever see Alex Jones on YouTube, Mike?"

"Nope."

"Hey, Steven, you know who Alex Jones is?"

"Yeah."

"You like him?"

"Yeah."

"Adda boy." Larry sips his beer & watches Sports Center. "You know, Mike, you shouldn't believe everything you see on television. The mainstream media's had it in for Trump since day one. He's a total outsider. He doesn't play their game. And the news networks don't like that."

"Oh, come on, Larry," Michael says, finally goaded into expressing himself. "You don't really believe that, do you? He's a billionaire property developer who had his own reality TV series on a major television network for about ten seasons. He's a celebrity first and a politician second. How do you make out he's an outsider?"

"This great country's got a long tradition of outsiders pulling themselves up by their bootstraps and making themselves celebrities, Mike. No offense to Emily, but this ain't Britain. We've not got some rigid class system, unchanged in centuries, where the Queen of England can seize your property any time she damn well pleases. We've not got a thousand layers of aristocracy, Lords and Ladyships, Dukes and Admirals, and all the rest of that crap. Sirs and Madams, Knights of the Round Table. Nope. Not in America. In this country, money talks, and pardon my language, Mike, but money talks, and bullshit walks."

"And Trump's a guy who talks a whole lot of bullshit, Larry."

"But that's as far as the criticism against him goes though, right? He doesn't play the game. He doesn't censor his speech. He says things as they are. And the media doesn't like that one bit. They like to keep things dressed up and hidden. To keep the public dumb and compliant."

"Come on, Larry. He called the leader of North Korea a fat short idiot on Twitter."

"He is a fat short idiot!"

"Yeah, but you're not supposed to say that."

Larry laughs. "That's it, right? I knew it. The only thing you've got against him is he says exactly what needs to be said. A real straight shooter. But that's what this country needs, Mike, after eight years of the snake-oil-salesman-in-chief, Barack Hussein Obama."

"There's a difference between saying it how it is and firing off every half-baked thought you've got to the world on Twitter, Larry. And what's Trump achieved, exactly? He tried to repeal Obamacare, and that failed. He keeps talking about building this stupid wall, but it's never getting built – thank God – and there's no way on Earth that he's going to fool the Mexicans into paying for it."

"Look at the statistics, Mike; the stock market's booming. Jobs are coming back. Eight long years of Obama's economic stagnation is finally over. We're on the road to becoming a truly great country again."

Michael lets the conversation lie there, and instead makes a comment about the likelihood of the Patriots making another Superbowl. Michael's aware of the self-reinforcing belief bubble that he's trapped in, consuming broadcast and social media that reflects his pre-existing opinions, but he also knows his bubble's reinforced with facts. His brother consumes different media, insulating his own bubble with an impenetrable layer of 'alternative facts' & opinions; Michael knows from the messy drunken argument they had about climate change back in August that there's no way either will change their point-of-view. So it's best to change the subject.

Dinner's served, a lavish spread of turkey, cranberry sauce, roast potatoes, mashed potatoes, carrots, peas, parsnips, butternut squash, and bacon-wrapped mini-sausages.

"We call these pigs in blankets," Emily says, after Larry's complimented the bacon-wrapped mini-sausages.

"Pigs in blankets, huh?" Larry smiles. "That's cute. Very British."

"We always have them at Christmas time back at home. Thanksgiving dinner is pretty much the exact same spread as we'd have on Christmas day, except for this butternut squash."

"Well, you make a damn good butternut squash for an English broad."

"Thank you."

Michael frowns at Larry's antiquated use of the term 'broad,' but like most of Larry's most boorish American tendencies, Emily seems to find them foreign enough to be utterly charming.

"Hey, Steven, you don't say a lot," Larry says. "You ought to speak up a little. Get your voice heard. You don't want to end up like your old man, parroting the media without an opinion of your own."

An awkward silence follows, Michael irritated & Steven unmoved. With innate English diplomacy, Emily diffuses the tension: "Larry, have you ever pulled a Christmas cracker?"

"Pulled a Christmas cracker?" Larry repeats, imitating her soft Southern English accent. "That sounds like something a black guy would do uptown on Christmas Eve."

Emily opens the box of Christmas crackers she's been saving all year for just this day; a box of bright Christmassy parcels, with a large middle section & slightly smaller sections at the ends for two people to pull on. She grips the end of a cracker, & holds the other end out for Larry; he gives it a stiff pull, & with a pop it flies open, sending a bottle opener & silver foil crown tumbling out onto the table.

"Hey, would ya look at that! I won a bottle opener!" Larry says.

Emily: "Now you've got to put your Christmas hat on."

"Damn, Mike, would you have ever pictured this?" Larry says, unfolding the silver foil hat and pulling it over his bulbous head. "Three hundred years after the Boston Tea Party, and I got an English broad handing me a crown."

"And read your joke out," Emily tells him.

"Joke?"

"It's inside the cracker."

Larry sticks his fingers inside the middle piece of the Christmas cracker & pulls out a small card with a joke printed on it. Larry guffaws to himself before reading it out: "There's a bird sleeping in your garden in winter. What are you most likely to see?"

Emily & Michael are perplexed, trying to figure the joke out.

Mike: "A bird sleeping in your garden… shoot, I've got no idea."

Emily: "Steven? What do you think?"

Steven shrugs.

Larry: "A couple of blue tits."

Larry laughs whole-heartedly, shaking the dining table.

Emily giggles & smirks: "Oh gosh, I forgot that these are the naughty ones! Cover your ears, Steven!"

Michael: "I don't get it?"

Emily: "'Bird' is a British-English word for a woman. And tits – do you say tits in America?"

Larry: "As often as we can get away with."

Emily: "So a cold woman sleeping in your garden—"

Larry: "A couple of blue tits! Ha, ha, ha!"

Michael frowns & sips his Chardonnay; the wine seems to have gone straight to Emily's head, & with Larry a few beers deep & now throwing wine into the mix, their Thanksgiving Dinner has entered combustible territory.

Emily: "Go on, Michael, you and Steven pull one."

"C'mon, son, let's see what you've got," Michael says, holding a cracker out to Steven.

With minimal effort & the hint of a sigh, Steven half-heartedly pulls at the end of the cracker; Michael pulls thrice as hard, snapping the cracker's end off without a pop, leaving Steven with the winning middle section. Disinterested, Steven places the cracker down next to his plate.

"Go on, Steven," his mother implores him. "What have you won?"

Steven sighs loudly & pulls a mini deck of cards out of the cracker.

"And put your party hat on. Go on. Now read your joke out."

Steven groans & reads with zero emotion: "What legendary hero made many gay men merry?"

Michael shifts awkwardly in his seat, fearing where this is going; Emily & Larry are all smiles, holding their wine glasses in anticipation of the punchline.

Larry: "Beats me."

Emily: "…many gay men merry… Robin Hood… something about Robin Hood…"

Steven: "Throbbing Wood."

Larry laughs ridiculously loudly, wine sloshing over the side of his glass as he slaps his hand on the table top. Emily can't stop giggling.

Michael: "I don't know if Steven ought to be involved in this…"

Emily: "Oh, come on, Michael, the boy's fourteen. I'm sure here's heard worse than that on the Internet."

Steven: "What does 'Throbbing Wood' mean?"

Larry stops laughing just long enough to answer: "Throbbing Cock!"

Emily & Larry burst out laughing, almost falling off their chair, in hysterics.

Michael glugs back wine, thinking Steven really shouldn't be hearing this.

"Come on, Michael," Emily says, red-faced once the laughter's subsided. "You and your brother pull one."

"Come on, chief," Larry says. "Let's see what you got."

Both brothers yank hard at the cracker, snapping it open with a bang; the elder brother, Larry, wins their test of strength. He fishes out a party hat, which he hands to Michael, and a little keyring with a mini-flashlight on it: "Huh, would you look at that!"

Emily: "Go on, Larry. Read your joke out."

Michael: "I really don't think Steven—"

Emily: "Oh, come on, Michael. It's just a little blue humour."

"It'll do the boy some good to hear this kind of talk," Larry says. He reads the joke from inside the cracker, smirks to himself, & then hands the paper to Emily: "You know, I think this would sound a lot funnier read in a British accent."

"OK," Emily says. "What do you call a sweet Japanese dessert with too much white frosting?"

Larry tries to suppress his laughter, belly rippling with the effort. Michael looks nervously at Steven, who seems completely unmoved by all around him.

"I don't know," Michael says with trepidation.

Emily frowns, trying to pronounce the word: "Bu-cake? Bu-cake-uh? Michael, do you know what this says?"

She hands the paper to her husband, who hesitates, knowing damn well what it means, but wanting to preserve his wife & son's innocence. "I've got no idea, honey. Maybe it's a misprint."

Before he can change the topic & stop things from happening, Emily snatches the joke from his hand & gives it to Larry: "Larry, do you know what this says?"

"No idea," Larry says, burying his laughter long enough to fake a look of almost-genuine confusion. He hands the paper to Steven: "Hey, sport, you got any idea what this says?"

"Bukkake," Steven says instantly, pronunciation flawless.

"Bukkake?" his mother repeats. "What does 'bukkake' mean?"

"Look, honey, I really don't think—" Michael says, trying to stop things from escalating.

Larry's whole body's vibrating, face turning red, as he holds a hand to his mouth, trying to stop laughter from completely overcoming him.

"Here," Steven says, as a look of horror floods his father's face. Steven holds his phone up to his mother: "Bukkake."

She screams.

"STEVEN!" Michael shouts, snatching the phone off him. Michael fumbles with it, trying to pause the video, or exit the app, or anything, but as he taps at a screen filled with a dozen naked Japanese men pulling at their cocks, & a poor cum-sodden girl in the middle of it all, Larry in hysterics, Emily shaking with shock, all Michael's efforts just push the volume louder, his horror increasing in step with the poor girl's high-pitched squeals & the odd sound of two dozen hands pumping a dozen cock shafts in concert.

Steven's smirking, the incident having finally broken through his lack of emotion.

"STEVEN!! GO TO YOUR ROOM!!" Michael shouts, having finally got the damn video to stop playing.

"Sure," Steven says, pushing his chair back from the table. "Can I have my phone back?"

"Absolutely not!"

"But—"

"GO TO YOUR ROOM!!"

Steven sighs theatrically & shuffles away from the table.

Larry: "Hey, come on, Mike. The boy was just—"

Michael: "SHUT UP, LARRY!!"

06.02.

"I can't believe it! He's only fourteen years old," Emily says, sobbing as she scrapes gravy-sodden food scraps from dishes, rinses, & loads the dishwasher. "I mean, I'm no old fuddy-duddy, in fact I think I'm pretty with it as far as mums go, but bloody hell, Steven – *bukkake.*" She stops, almost dropping a plate, just about saving it as emotion overcomes her. She brings her free hand to her face to stem the flow of tears.

Michael takes the plate from her, rinses it, & places it into the dishwasher, similarly brimming with emotion, though his is pure unbridled anger.

"I knew this was a mistake," Michael mutters.

"I mean, bloody hell, Michael – all those penises! And that poor girl in the middle of it all! What if Steven thinks… I mean what if he and his friends think that's how you're supposed to .. and what if he…"

Emily's blubbering hard, ready to sink to the floor, into the Earth, her wine-addled mind convinced her whole world's slipping away from her. *My little boy…*

"I'm gonna tell him to leave."

She stops crying and stares at Michael, her face a reddened mess: "What do you mean?"

"This is the final straw," Michael says, voice quivering with anger. "He's been nothing but trouble, and now this – this… this is it. I'm going to tell him to pack his bags and get the hell out of here."

Emily stares at him for a moment, rarely having seen Michael quite this angry. It takes almost a minute of tense staring until she's certain that he's serious. "Oh, for goodness sake, Michael, where's he going to go?"

"What do I care?"

"For pity's sake, Michael, he's only fourteen years old!"

"Fourteen years old… what… no… God no, Emily, not Steven! I mean Larry!"

"Larry?"

"Larry. I'm gonna tell him to get the hell out of our house this instant."

"But… what did Larry do?"

"What do you mean what did Larry do? You saw him! He's been fixing for a fight all day, and then as soon as he got that card, that smirk on his face… He got you to read it out first, remember? And then he gave it to Steven, knowing damn well he'd know what a bukkake was—"

"How the hell would Larry know that Steven would know what a bukkake was? Michael… did you know what a bukkake was?"

Michael sighs, & takes a little too long to summon up a decent answer.

"Oh for God's sake, Michael, what the hell's wrong with you? You bloody men, you're all alike!"

"I mean… come on, Emily, how do you not know what it means?"

"Of course I don't bloody well know what it means! I don't spend my free time debasing myself to filth on the Internet!"

Emily's sadness has evolved into anger. She throws her frustration into action, grabbing another dish & resuming her task of scraping, rinsing, & placing in the dishwasher.

"I'm going to tell Larry to leave," Michael says.

"Don't you bloody well dare!"

"Why not? It's all his fault this has happened! Another family gathering ruined by that jackass!"

"You know what your bloody problem is?!" Emily screams, turning away from the sink. "You and your brother are too much alike."

"Me and that jackass?! Too much alike?!"

"Yes! Exactly! And you're not sending him anywhere. You know what a mess he's been since Barbara left him. He's got nowhere to go, and he drove all this way, and for God's sake, it's Thanksgiving, Michael, and Larry's your brother."

"But—"

"Michael." She stares at her husband, all emotion now coalesced into a tone of supreme finality. "If you tell him to leave, then I'm leaving as well."

"But—"

"Michael."

Michael sighs, defeated.

"So what are we supposed to do? Just sit around drinking beer, and pretend like this never happened?"

"Why don't you go and wank each other off to some Japanese pornography? Since you're both such fucking experts on it."

I hate you, Larry, Michael thinks, leaving the kitchen.

06.03.

"Hey sport, you got a minute?" Larry asks, pushing the door to Steven's room open.

Steven doesn't say anything, sitting on his bed with a Playstation controller in his hand, staring at a television displaying a video game in which he's controlling a soldier in some war-town Middle Eastern hellhole, bullets ringing out in all directions.

Larry pushes the door closed behind him as he moves into the room & sits next to his nephew on the bed. "I brought you a beer."

"Thanks," Steven says, glancing away from the screen long enough to accept the can of Budweiser.

"And I got your phone back."

"Wow! Thanks, Uncle!" Steven drops the controller & gleefully takes the phone.

"Don't tell your old man about this."

"I won't."

Steven cracks the beer open. Larry clanks his can against Steven's: "Salut."

Steven takes a swig & taps frantically at the phone screen.

"So you've discovered Alex Jones already, huh?"

"Uh-huh."

"That's good. Good for you to develop your own opinion on stuff. Not get too influenced by mainstream media. And whaddya think of Trump?"

"He's funny."

"You're God-damn right he's funny. The man's a riot. You think he's doing a good job as President?"

"Uh-huh."

"Better than Obama?"

"Uh-huh."

"That's excellent, kid. Really excellent. Say, whaddaya doing on that thing?"

"I was watching this video earlier, from my favorite YouTuber."

"Alex Jones?"

"No. Dashing Dolph Daggers."

"Dashing Dolph Daggers?"

"Uh-huh. Crypto & a Craft Beer."

"Crypto and a Craft Beer?"

"Uh-huh."

"What the heck does that mean?"

"He drinks craft beer and shills cryptocurrency. Coins always pump as soon as he mentions them, so I wanted to pick some up before the price spiked."

"Before the— hey, kid, you're gonna have to level with me. I'm an old dinosaur. I can barely work the Facebook. What the hell is a cryptocurrency?"

"Like Bitcoin."

"Oh, shoot. You're into Bitcoin?"

"Not really."

"But Bitcoin's a cryptocurrency?"

"Uh-huh."

"And you're into cryptocurrency?"

"Uh-huh."

"You make any money off it?"

"Uh-huh."

"How much?"

"Right now I've got, like, seven hundred and fifty dollars."

"Not bad, kid. Not bad at all."

"I did have more, before I bought the Playstation."

"And how much did that cost ya?"

"Including all the games, it was like six hundred and fifty dollars."

"Shoot. So altogether, you had like… fifteen hundred dollars?"

"Uh-huh. Something like that."

"And how much did you put into it?"

"Like, fifty dollars."

"Fifty dollars?! Are you fucking shitting me?"

"Nope."

"You made fifteen hundred bucks off of fifty fucking dollars?!"

"Uh-huh."

"And how long did that take you?"

"A couple of weeks."

"A couple of weeks? Seriously?"

"Uh-huh."

"How is that even possible?"

"You've just gotta buy whatever Dashing Dolph Daggers buys. The price always pumps just after he mentions it." He holds his phone up to his uncle. "I just bought thirty-two million Future Synergy Coins"

"Thirty-two fucking million… what did that cost you?"

"About fifty-five bucks."

"And you reckon the price'll go up to?"

"Probably. Usually they'll increase by, like, five or six times. Sometimes ten. Sometimes twenty."

"A twenty times increase?!"

"Uh-huh."

"So you're telling me if I gave you a thousand dollars, you could turn it into twenty thousand dollars?"

"Maybe."

"But five thousand dollars minimum?"

"Probably."

"Holy shit. Your old man know how much money you're making?"

"Kind of, but he thinks it's stupid."

"Stupid? He thinks it's stupid his kid made fifteen hundred bucks off of fifty damn dollars?"

"He doesn't know exactly how much I made, but he says that crypto's a bubble. He thinks it'll pop and I'll end up with nothing."

"Hey, kid, let me let you in on a little secret; your old man's a fucking idiot."

"I know."

Larry laughs. "Hey, kid, you're alright. I think you must've got most of your genes off of your mother. Or just the good ones from my side of the family. Maybe they skipped your old man. Say, you know how me and your Aunt Barbara got divorced?"

"Uh-huh."

"You got any idea how expensive a divorce is?"

"Nope."

"Well it's fucking expensive, alright. She's a fully grown woman, but I gotta pay her alimony. You know what alimony is?"

"Nope."

"Alimony means a man's gotta sweat, bust his ass every day, scrimp and save and strive every waking hour of his God-damn life, then give a big chunk of his hard earned cash to his ex-wife because she won the genetic lottery and wound up with a pussy where the penis should be. You understand me?"

"Uh-huh."

"So if I give you five thousand dollars, you think you could buy some of this… what did you say it was again? The thing this Dope Daggers character's shilling?"

"Future Synergy Coin."

"Future Synergy Coin. So if I give you a thousand dollars, you think you could buy me some? I'd throw you twenty bucks for your trouble. Maybe even sneak you a few more beers."

"Sure."

"We gotta a deal?"

"We gotta deal."

Larry laughs & tousles his nephew's hair.

7. BATTLEGROUND.

Incheon, South Korea.

GLOSSARY OF KOREAN WORDS USED IN THIS SECTION:

aish : short for '**ssibal**' (fuck); roughly equivalent to going 'fffffffuuu…' in English.
ajumma (n.) : middle-aged/old woman.
Andae! : 'No!' or 'Don't do that!'.
annyeong : hello (informal).
chamshiman : wait a minute.
daebak : slang expression roughly equivalent to 'Wow!'
dakgalbi (n.) : Korean spicy chicken dish.
Gauza! : Go up!
hagwon (n.) : private afterschool academy for studying English & other subjects.
jaesumhamnida : sorry (v. polite/formal).
Mashiketta! : It looks delicious!
nae : yes.
ng : yes; a grunt of agreement (informal).
noraebang (n.) : lit. 'Singing Room'; Karaoke Room in English.
PC Bang : lit. 'PC Room'; similar to an internet cafe, but expressly aimed at gamers.
SK Wyverns : South Korean baseball team based in Incheon.
somek (n.) : soju + beer ('**mekchu**' in Korean).
Ssibal! : all-purpose swear word, equivalent to 'fuck!' in English.
Ssibal-saeki ya! : similar in meaning to 'You son of a bitch!', though closer to 'You motherfucker!' in severity.

tteokbokki (n.) : a cheap street food popular with students - rice cakes served in spicy sauce.

Yogi-yo! : Here! (Used to get attention of the staff at a restaurant.)

07.01.

"Ssibal-saeki ya!" Jae Seok yells, as a bullet flies from the rifle of some unseen sniper in the building opposite & tears straight through his brain.

"Yaaaa!!" the ajumma at the counter yells across the PC Bang. "Andae!"

"Jaesumhamnida," Jae Seok says loudly, nodding apologetically in the older woman's direction, before muttering Korean swears to the friends sitting either side of him - "Aish… shibal…" – adding a final cuss in Gamer English: "Camping."

Min Ho & Dan Won are silent, keeping their own in-game avatars hidden as they sneak & assassinate their way around Erangel.

"Smoking," Jae Seok says in English, taking his pack of This Plus cigarettes & an SK Wyverns lighter from beside the keyboard & heading to a stuffy ventilated box in the center of the PC Bang. While he smokes, he checks UpBit on his phone, digits in constant flux: Ripple flitting between 300 and 330 Won, Qtum bouncing around between ₩13,125 and ₩14,876, etc., etc. Then he opens a KakaoTalk cryptocurrency chat room, & amidst the constant pleas of 'GAAAUUUUZAAAA!' sees an intriguing conversation:

- Did anyone here hear of FSC?
- No
- On UpBit?
- No
- No Korean exchange
- Only 1 foreign site
- BitBucks
- Get in now, price pumping fast

Jae Seok returns to his seat & follows the anonymous advice, creating an account at BitBucks & transferring 1.5 Ethereum from UpBit to buy FSC with.

"Aiiiishhh…" Dan Won exclaims, his character plummeting to its death after mislanding a bike jump from a clifftop & colliding face-first with the road 100s of meters below. "I'm done. Let's go eat dinner."

"Chamshiman," Min Ho says. "I'm going to win this one."

"You wanna smoke?" Dan Won asks Jae Seok.

"I just did."

Min Ho heads to the smoking booth alone as Jae Seok stares at his phone, transfixed with the ever-fluctuating but upward-trending Korean Won value of his cryptocurrency portfolio.

"Aish!" Min Ho shouts, his character eating a bullet. "What do you want to eat?"

07.02.

"Chicken?" Min Ho asks, reading the menu. "Extra-spicy chicken? Chicken and octopus?"

"Extra-spicy chicken and octopus," Jae Seok says.

"Daebak," Dan Won says.

Min Ho: "And do we want noodles? Rice cake?"

"Combination fixings," Jae Seok says, in strongly-accented English.

Min Ho: "And cheese?"

Jae Seok: "Ng. Cheese."

Dan Won: "Daebak! You're rich!"

Jae Seok: "The coin's are pumping."

Min Ho: "Why isn't fucking Ripple pumping?"

Jae Seok: "Because it's a shitcoin."

Min Ho: "Yaaa… it's not a shit coin. I heard they're making deals with most of the big banks from Europe and America. It'll be the number one coin in the world soon."

Jae Seok: "It's doing nothing while everything else is pumping. It's a shitcoin."

Min Ho: "You're so fucking cocky. You think you're The Wolf of Wall Street."

Dan Won: "The Bitcoin Billionaire of Bupyeong."

Min Ho [to Dan Won]: "How are your coins doing?"

Dan Won: "Neo's pumping pretty hard these days. Qtum's on the verge of a breakout. And fucking Verge isn't doing anything. So what are we drinking? Soju? Beer?"

Jae Seok: "Soju and beer."

Dan Won: "So-mek?

Jae Seok: "Ng."

Dan Won: "So we're ready to order?"

Jae Seok: "Ng."

Dan Won raises his hand & shouts across the packed restaurant at an ajumma: "Yogi-yo!"

"Nae," the ajumma says, side-stepping other groups to reach their table.

Min Ho rattles off the order, Jae Seok reminding him about the cheese; the ajumma notes each item, but pauses after Min Ho mentions the alcohol: "ID?"

Min Ho looks at Jae Seok & Dan Won: "I think I forgot my ID card. Do you have yours?"

They both pretend to check their pockets. Seeing through the ruse, the ajumma tuts & scolds them: "Alcohol is only for adults."

"Daebak," Jae Seok says, once she's left the table. "I wanted soju."

Min Ho: "We can drink somewhere after."

Jae Seok: "Where?"

The ajumma returns & dumps deep-red slices of chicken rib meat & cabbage & rice cake & octopus tentacles into a searing pan in the center of their table. She spreads it across the pan & leaves to attend to other tables, returning intermittently to stir it.

"Cook quickly," Jae Seok implores their meal.

Min Ho: "Are you hungry?"

Jae Seok: "I want to drink alcohol!"

The ajumma throws in the noodles, & finally adds the cheese.

"Mashiketta!"

The trio tuck in voraciously, scooping up noodles & meat with chopsticks & shovelling them into their mouths. The food disappears in ridiculously quick time, the gang not pausing for conversation.

"You want to pan-fry some rice?" Min Ho asks, once the dakgalbi's been devoured.

"Let's drink!" Jae Seok declares.

07.03.

Out on Bupyeong's neon-bathed streets, they're refused entry to a Ho Bar, & then a Woodstock, & a World Beer Market, & various other places, until they're almost at the point of giving up.

"How about a noraebang?" Min Ho suggests.

"But even they won't serve us alcohol," Jae Seok says.

Min Ho: "We can sneak some in."

They go inside a 7/11, Jae Seok gratefully eyeing a pimpled high-schooler playing with his phone behind the counter, assuming he'll be lenient when it comes to drinking age restrictions. They scan the alcohol-laden refrigerators at the back, Dan Won mulling the 4 World Beers for ₩10,000 promotion: "How about this?"

"Let's drink soju," Min Ho says, greedily eyeing the many ₩1000 green bottles in the refrigerator beside the beers.

"Soju and beer," Dan Won replies.

Min Ho: "Yeah, but Korean beer. There's no point using the expensive beer for so-mek."

"How about some of this?" Jae Seok says, looking at the much pricier bottles of imported spirits on the shelves opposite the refrigerators.

"Daebak," Dan Won says. "Your coins must be seriously pumping now."

07.04.

"Annyeong," Jae Seok calls as he enters his family apartment, hoping to move into his bedroom as quickly as possible & avoid arousing his parents' suspicion.

"So he returns," his mother says, moving quickly from the kitchen to the center of the living room to confront him.

His father, on the sofa, hits the button on the remote control to mute the television, then stands up beside his mother: "How was English class?"

"English class… was good," Jae Seok says.

"What did you study today?" his father asks.

"Verbs… and… sentences."

"Grammar?"

"Ng. Grammar."

"Park Jae Seok," his mother scowls, clenched fists at her hips, "do not stand there and lie to me inside my own home."

"You didn't go to the hagwon," his father says. "Why?"

"I… did… go," Jae Seok stutters, face flushing red with a mixture of embarrassment & drunkenness, while his brain freezes before his parents' glare & fails to summon up an excuse.

Sensing something strange in his demeanor, his mother leans toward him, then recoils in horror: "You've been drinking?!"

"Andaaeee," Jae Seok protests, stretching the vowel out to underscore his seriousness.

"Drinking?!" his father erupts. "Fourteen years old and you're drinking!"

Mother: "Who the hell would even serve you alcohol?!"

Father: "First skipping class, now drinking alcohol!"

Mother: "The place that sold it to you should be shut down!"

Father: "Do you hate your parents this much?!"

Mother: "How is it even possible?!"

Father: "Do you want to break your mother's heart?!"

They rant at him for several minutes, taking it in turns to admonish his unbelievable behavior & bemoan the circumstances that allowed it to happen

- "And your friends," his mother asks, horror growing, "Were they drinking too?!"

Jae Seok clutches the single strap of his backpack which is slung over his right shoulder as they speak, hoping for all the world that they don't want to look inside; but with maternal instinct, his mother knows that the bag must be searched, & she takes it from him, unzips, & gasps in horror.

"Shibal!" his father exclaims.

His mother shouts his father's name: "Sung Jae!"

"Sorry," Park Sung Jae says, taking the bottle from his son's bag. "But I thought you'd drank soju. Not this."

"Whiskey?" his mother asks, voice trembling.

"Ng," Sung Jae confirms, turning the quarter-full bottle over in his hands admiringly. "And it's a good one. Johnnie Walker Blue Label." A thought suddenly strikes him: "But how could you afford this? You didn't…"

His mother gasps, staring at her son in disbelief, having reached the same conclusion as her husband: "Stealing!"

"Andae," Jae Seok protests meekly.

"Then how did you afford this?" Sung Jae asks, staring at the inviting liquid within the bottle.

"Because of coins," Jae Seok says.

"Coins?" his mother asks, confused.

"You bought some coins?" Sung Jae asks, his tone softened.

"Ng."

"Coins?" his mother repeats.

"Coins," Sung Jae explains. "Cryptocurrency. Like Bitcoin."

"Bitcoin…" his mother repeats, understanding, but still reeling with shock at the revelation of her son's hidden character.

07.05.

"But it's gambling," Kim Su Min, Sung Jae's wife & Jae Seok's mother, says, once their son has been severely scolded & sent to his room.

"It's kind of investing," Sung Jae says, sipping from a freshly-poured glass of delicious confiscated Johnnie Walker Blue Label.

"But there was a documentary on KBS a few nights ago," Su Min says, fraught with moral panic. "The prices rise quickly, but they fall just the same. Some people re-mortgaged their homes to invest, and lost everything."

"But Jae Seok doesn't have a home to re-mortgage," Sung Jae says. "He's just using our allowance. Would you rather he spent it all on comic books and tteokbokki?"

"And one college student even killed himself, he lost so much," Su Min continues.

"But Jae Seok has more now than he started with. He's fourteen years old and he drinks more premium stuff than I do."

"It isn't funny, Sung Jae! Fourteen years old and drinking alcohol…"

"The alcohol, of course, must stop. And I'm as angry as you are about him skipping English class. That hagwon costs me half my salary! But investing? That actually makes me quite proud of him."

"Proud?! Sung Jae, remember 1997. The IMF crisis. Everything you invested in the stock market evaporated…"

"But he's a boy! He has nothing to lose!"

"And your horse racing habit! Five million won you kept hidden from me, and now your son develops the same tendencies!"

"Ah, come on, Su Min; the horse racing thing was… it was my co-workers, I had to go along with them…"

"For five million won, Sung Jae?!"

"…and it was years ago, these days I never gamble…"

"And beside everything else, the Bible tells us it's a sin to gamble…"

"The Bible!" Sung Jae scoffs, Johnnie Walker emboldening him. Usually he holds his tongue when Su Min starts blathering about Jesus, but he's suddenly determined not to let Jesus stray into this area of their relationship. "The Bible was written thousands of years ago by sheep-herding idiots, Su Min! What did they know about investing?! It also tells you not to eat seafood on Fridays, and to give up your daughters to weary travelers…"

"That's the Old Testament, Sung Jae!! Jesus is quite explicit on which rules we can safely discard from there."

"…and *'thou shalt not covet thy neighbor's ass,'* but every damn time you meet with the other housewives from our building, you're comparing our lifestyle to theirs, and Jae Seok's school grades with their kids…"

"Ah, you just want your son to grow up exactly like you! Gambling, drinking…"

"He's a man, Su Min! And that's just what men do!"

"Jesus was a man. A better man that that."

"Su Min, if you love Jesus so much, why don't you leave me and Jae Seok and run away with him? I'm sure he'll take you – Jesus loves everyone, right?"

Su Min gasps and stares at her husband with greater horror than greeted her discovery of her son's drunkenness.

"Su Min, I'm sorry, I didn't mean…"

Su Min rises silently from the couch and walks to their bedroom, slamming the door shut behind her.

8. YNWA.

Liverpool, England.

McCooley's on Mathew Street is dense with red shirts. Graham edges his way through & finds his Dad at a table with Toby (his Dad's bulbous-gutted co-worker from his days on the Docks) and Graham's old schoolmates Nev & Panzer.

"Y'alright?" Graham says, thinking that Nev looks more like Toby every time he sees him, gaining a pound in weight for every week that passes without them meeting. Panzer was built like a tank since his school days – hence the name – but with his mess of shaggy hair & grey-tinted beard, he's slowly morphing from a battle-ready hefty mass into a bloated war relic left to accumulate plantlife in the Ardennes.

"Y'alright Grah-o, lad," & other such is said back at him, as Graham scans the packed pub for a chair.

"You sitting?" Toby asks, struggling to move his long-booze-reddened face to scan the bar for a seat.

"Yeah, if I can find a chair, I am."

"You eating?" Nev says, scanning the menu.

"Nah, I had dinner 'fore I left," Graham lies. He barely managed to scrape together £10 in change before leaving the house, and with no clue when Dead Bird Press will get around to paying him for the last article, and little else in the way of reliable income, he's loathe to spend £8 on a burger. He finds a chair loaded with coats & bags at a table behind him, and after a bit of tutting and eye-rolling, the middle-aged couple utilizing said chair relinquish it to him & he joins the table with the boys, briefly, before standing up again: "I best get a pint in 'fore the match starts."

"Hey, Grah-o, grab us one while you're up there, la," says Panzer.

"Hey, get us one too, if you don't mind, lad," Nev adds. "And could you order us a Signature Burger? And ask them to leave off the coleslaw and sling a couple more chips on?"

Graham hesitates, knowing there's plenty in his bank account to clear a round, but also aware he's promised Melina not to spend more than the coins in his pocket.

"Here are, Grah-o, get a round in," his Dad says, reaching for his wallet & taking out a crisp £20 note. Everyone throws "Cheers" & "Thanks" in Graham's Dad's direction, before he quickly adds: "Nev, you'd best get your wallet out, lad. I'm not paying for your fookin' burger!"

The teams line up on the television as Graham awaits service at the jam-packed bar. The orchestral UEFA Champions League anthem plays, drowned out as all in McCooley's burst into Liverpool's own footballing anthem, You'll Never Walk Alone, Graham joining them as the chorus reaches its rousing crescendo.

The game's already started by the time Graham's served, and as he carefully brings the first three pints back to the table, the first goal flies in: Firmino getting the ball at the back post on a corner & slamming it into Sevilla's net.

"Yes!"; "Fookin' get in!"; "I told you we'd batter 'em!"; & etc.

"How was Berlin?" Graham's Dad asks once the reaction to the goal's calmed down.

Graham says it was good, and his brother's doing well, and that his little bro Robbie actually helped him get an interview for the piece Dead Bird Press accepted for publication – not mentioning to his Dad that the guy Robbie introduced was a coke dealer – & from there he's explaining cryptocurrency, and how FSC shot up to almost 4x its price after the article he wrote, then increased another 10x this morning after nutcase antivirus billionaire Jack McAvoy tweeted about it.

"Blimey!" Graham's Dad says. "So it's worth about forty times what it was on Sunday?"

"Correct," Graham says, desperately wishing he'd bought some.

"I was never much good at investing," Graham's Dad says. "I had some shares in British Telecom when the Tories privatised it back in the '80s, but I panicked and sold the lot the first time the price dipped. If I'd hung on, they'd be worth a fortune now."

"You getting into crypto, Grah-o?" Panzer asks.

"Crypto?" Toby repeats, perplexed but intrigued.

Graham: "Yeah, kind of. Why, you into it?"

Panzer: "I've been thinking about it. The prices are going mad right now, right?"

Graham: "Yeah. A Bitcoin's worth about eight grand right now, and it were at six at the start of the month. And Ethereum's worth $350, and that were worth less than three-hundred a couple of week back."

"What is this stuff?" Toby asks, always on the look-out for a fresh get-rich-quick scheme. Unlike Graham's Dad, Toby's done reasonably well with stocks; he bought shares in British Petroleum when the price tanked after the Deepwater Horizon oil spill off the Gulf of Mexico back in 2010, and made a tidy profit when the price bounced back a few months later.

Graham tries to explain the concept of digital currency, and blockchain, and distributed ledgers, and trustless transactions, and the proof-of-work mining consensus mechanism, but his Dad – barely able to perform a Google search – is completely lost; though Toby's trying his best to keep up, what Graham's saying might as well be in Chinese.

"Fuck me!" Nev shouts, in sync with similar sentiments from across the bar; all cease discussing crypto to stare at the screen, where a Sevilla forward has just smacked a shot into Liverpool's side-netting.

"I was reading about this one bloke who mined a bunch of Bitcoin years back, when it were only worth pennies," Panzer says, once the shock of the shot's worn off, "and he ended up chucking out an old PC with about ten-thousand coins on the hard drive."

"Shite," Graham winces, calculating the insane amount of money the poor sod lost.

"Yeah," Panzer continues. "He's paid about a hundred grand scouring landfill sites to look for it, but he's still not found it."

"That'd be worth about $80 million," Graham says, eyes glazing over as he imagines the life such a sum of money could bring him Melina & Luis.

"So it's all just stored directly on your computer then?" Toby asks, trying valiantly to understand now he's heard the astronomical figures involved.

Nev's burger arrives as Graham & Panzer struggle to explain what the fuck a bitcoin is and how crypto works. Nev complains loudly that Graham forgot to ask for extra chips instead of coleslaw, but no-one's listening.

Graham & Panzer explain how Satoshi Nakamoto is anonymous & why the Bank of England's quantitative easing measures & Brexit will mean a long-term depreciation in the value of the pound, pausing briefly to react to two more Sevilla chances, until Firmino clips the ball across Sevilla's box into a diving Mane header, making it 2-0 Liverpool, and all attention returns to the football.

The Reds are energised by the second goal & keep pressing forward, Firmino smashing it into an open goal after a saved Mane shot in the 30th minute. 3-0. All talk is then of how Liverpool should definitely top the group, regardless of what happens in the final game vs Spartak Moscow, and how that should put them on a good path to reaching the quarter-finals.

Graham's on his e-cig outside at half-time, as Nev & Panzer smoke real cigs either side of him.

"You want a proper one, la?" Nev asks.

Graham barely hesitates before accepting.

"You actually bought any crypto then?" Panzer asks.

"No," Graham says, before explaining again the quick fortune he could've made on Future Synergy Coin.

"I reckon you've already left it too late," Nev says, understanding the concept with much greater ease than generationally-challenged Toby & Graham's Dad. "There was a thing on BBC News the other day about how Bitcoin's a bubble that's gonna burst and be back to zero before the year's out."

Panzer argues against this, and upon accepting that Nev has a chance of being right, he switches track to say it's still worth a punt, given the huge potential returns on offer, and it's better than buying a lottery ticket.

"You'd have more chance making money betting on Sevilla to make a comeback," Nev replies.

But Graham & Panzer are not discouraged, discussing how to actually buy Bitcoin & other cryptocurrencies after Panzer gifts Graham another cigarette.

"Buy NEO," a pissed young scally in an old '90s Carlsberg-branded green-and-white Liverpool away shirt tells Graham & Panzer upon overhearing their conversation. "It's the fucking Chinese Ethereum, it's gonna go berserk in the next month or two, mark my words. And you can buy me a pint when you've made a mint off it!"

"Look," Nev says, holding his phone up to Graham & Panzer as they move with the other half-time smokers back into McCooley's. "I just stuck ten quid on Sevilla to score three goals or more in the second-half. Twenty-five to one. Two hundred fifty fucking quid, lads! I got more chance of winning that than you've got of not losing your arses betting on Bitcoin."

Graham, Nev, & Panzer are standing at the bar awaiting service when a rush of yells & swears fills McCooly's; they turn to a screen & see Sevilla granted a free-kick at the right edge of Liverpool's penalty area. The free kick is lobbed into a crowded box, where it meets a Sevilla header: 3-1.

Another anguished roar rolls through the bar as the lads carry their pints back to the table: Moreno clipped a white-shirted Sevilla player while clearing the ball in the Liverpool box, and the referee's awarded a clearly-bullshit penalty.

"No way that's a penalty," Toby says, accepting his pint as the trio retake their seats & echo his sentiment.

Banega calmly slots the penalty the wrong side of Karius to make it 3-2. Nev struggles to suppress a celebration of his now-likely £250 winnings as a chorus of 'Fucking hell!'s and 'Fuck's sake!'s rings through McCooley's.

They watch the last half-hour of the game in near-silence, wincing at a barely-saved Sevilla shot in the 62nd minute, groaning at a saved Salah shot in the 70th, & swearing loudly as four minutes' injury time is announced in the 90th.

"Come on," Graham whispers, as Sevilla are awarded a corner in the dying seconds of the game.

Frustrated silence & a mass exodus of red shirts follows Sevilla's last-gasp equaliser.

"Eh, lads," Nev says, breaking a few minutes' depressed silence, "we can still top the group if we beat Spartak. And on the bright side, I just won two-hundred and fifty fucking pounds!"

Nev buys a round of pints & tequila shots to celebrate, then repeatedly suggests having a few more drinks somewhere else. Panzer's keen, but Graham's Dad & Toby say they're too old for that malarkey & are set on taking a taxi back to Toxteth. Feeling half-drunk, Graham's tempted, especially when Nev offers to buy a few more drinks with his winnings, but he thinks of Melina at home with Luis, and says he's got to call it a night, & laughs off the whipcrack motion Nev makes to mock him, which Nev follows with a terrible rendition of the chorus to the Rolling Stone's song Under My Thumb.

A busker at the end of Mathew Street is signing The Beatles' Money Can't Buy Me Love, supported by a gang of pissed-up red-shirted Scousers hopping around in front of him, as a family of bemused Chinese tourists stands to the side filming it all on their phones. Graham's thoughts move from Chinese tourists to Chinese cryptocurrency as he walks from Mathew Street to Lime Street Station, remembering what the young scally said about NEO. Graham takes out his phone as he reaches the station platform and awaits the 22:28 to Rock Ferry. He searches 'how to buy bitcoin' & Investopedia.com recommends Coinbase; he clicks the link to Coinbase & then opens his Barclays online banking; there's £587.63 in his account, with £400 from Dead Bird Press due to go in whenever Terrance gets around to telling someone to pay it, less £185 for Graham's half of the rent ten days from now: *Fuck it,* Graham thinks, beer buzz pushing him towards a purchase as the train pulls up: he thinks *pull the trigger* as he takes a seat, *buy some Bitcoin,* and then use some of that to buy some other cryptos, & he'll surely be better off for doing it: *£50 Bitcoin, £50 Ethereum, £50 NEO,* he tells himself as the doors slide shut & the train rolls out of Lime Street Station; he enters his card details & lets his thumb hover over the final button press, thinking of Nev ballsily sticking £10 on Sevilla scoring 3 goals & getting £250 in return. He hits the button & becomes the instant owner of 0.024 Bitcoin. He next searches 'how to buy ethereum' and mutters "bollocks" aloud as he realises he could've bought it directly through Coinbase; he looks up as the train rolls into Liverpool Central, but the rest of the passengers are too deep in drunken conversation to have cared that he swore. Passengers pile on the train & some barely-noticed bald bloke sits beside Graham as the train rolls on, through Birkenhead Hamilton Square & Birkenhead Central, Graham searching 'how to buy neo'. He finds a bitcointalk.org post from an Australian with the same conundrum, followed by replies recommending buying through Bittrex or Binance; he finds Bittrex through Google, enters his email address & double-enters a password – 19YNWA83 – & after clicking on an email confirmation link, the train's at Rock Ferry, & Graham has a Bittrex account. He wrestles with Bittrex's interface on his phone as he walks past the Rock Station pub, glum red-shirted smokers standing outside discussing the football; he successfully executes a trade as he walks down Grove Street, swapping 0.008652 BTC for 2 NEO. He then scrolls the list of other tokens, scores of unknown three and four letter acronyms, many having shot up in double-digit percentage points over the past 24 hours, many more having fallen by a similar amount; it's all a bit mad & incomprehensible, but Graham feels desperate to understand it & turn this wild & strange new technology into life-changing sums of money. He passes a block of modern flats & looks up enviously at a bloke smoking on a balcony, thinking of how much nicer the interior of those places must be than the place he's now living. Spurred on by envy, he makes trades at random, swapping Bitcoin for 150 XRP, 1000 ADA, & 40 USDT by the time he reaches Mazin's Pizza & the scent of fried chicken & kebabs overpowers him, & he heads in to purchase medium chips with ketchup & mayo with his last remaining two pounds coins.

"Y'alright?" Graham says as he enters the house, a ground-floor flat in a row of modest terraced homes. The chips have soaked up some of his booziness, but Melina still immediately notices alcohol's effect on his speech & demeanour.

"Hola," she says, pausing Narcos on Netflix on the television.

"You've not watched the next episode, have you?" Graham says, sitting beside her on the sofa & drunkenly draping his arm over her.

"You can watch it tomorrow when I'm at work," she says curtly, staring him with angry-beautiful Latin eyes that immediately communicate that he should shut the fuck up.

"Luis in bed?"

"It's almost midnight."

He again immediately senses he should shut-the-fuck-up and move on to another topic.

"You hear what happened in the football? It were a mental match. Liverpool were winning three-nil at half-time, then in the second-half Sevilla pulled back three. But I don't think we've got owt to worry about, we should still top the group if we smash Spartak."

"Graham… I don't know if I should tell you this. You're very drunk, no?"

"No. No. Not at all. Well, a little bit. But I got some chips at Mazin's, and that sobered me up a bit, and—"

"I didn't get the period this month. And it should've come to me three weeks ago. And so today I took the pregnancy test."

Her big brown eyes stare into Graham's; he's drunker than he thought, struggling to piece together the shards of meaning held in her words.

"So… you're… pregnant?"

"Si."

Graham smiles; Melina bursts into tears.

"Eh, what! That's great news! That's amazing! That's…"

"But this house, we are so crowded already, and when another baby comes, we have no room for to give her, and the money we make is not enough for us to get some better place, and…"

"Eh, eh," Graham says, pulling her toward him, hugging her tightly. "It'll be fine, we'll manage," he says. He thinks of the money he just fapped away on stupid cryptocurrencies, thinks *you fucking idiot,* and that Melina would rip his balls off if he told her; but then he thinks of the promise of more, the massive returns, and that maybe it's fate, just like Nev sticking a bet on Sevilla and their improbable comeback prompting his crypto purchase. "It'll be fine," he tells Melina, almost certain he's right.

9. HWAESIK.

Incheon, South Korea.

NEW KOREAN WORDS USED IN THIS SECTION:

-cha (-차) : "round" - a stage in a multi-venue night of drinking *(1-cha, 2-cha…).*
aish : short for '**ssibal**' (fuck); roughly equivalent to going 'fffffffuuu…' in English.
Annyeong hasaeyo! : Hello! (polite/formal).
hwaesik (n.) : after-work drinks.
Keonbae! : Cheers!
nae : yes (polite/formal).
maja : correct (informal).
ng : yes; a grunt of agreement (informal).
noraebang (n.) : lit. 'singing room,' a.k.a. a karaoke room.

1차

"…so now she's angrier with me than our son," Sung Jae says, lips loosened & face reddened by soju.

"Aish," Sung Jae's colleague Jong Gil sighs.

"For one week, I come home from work, and she says nothing. She has me sleeping in Min Seok's room."

"Min Seok is doing military service?" says Nam Soo, the eldest and most senior colleague at the table.

"Nae, Team Leader," Sung Jae answers. "He's almost halfway through."

"It will be good for him," Nam Soo says, leaning back from the table & nodding sagely. "Too many kids in this generation try to commute their service into working with computers or something."

"Nae," Nam Soo's three subordinates say in unison.

"True military service builds character," Nam Soo continues. "It turns a boy into a man. For the next forty years, he'll be at a desk, using a computer. Military service is the one chance most young men today will have to discover their true character."

"Correct, Team Leader," Jong Gil says, raising his soju glass.

The other three at the table clang their glasses together – "Keonbae!" – & then down the clear liquid inside. Hyeong Woo, the youngest of Nam Soo's three subordinates, turns his back from the table as he downs his shot. After the shot, all reach with their chopsticks for pieces of chopped up pork intestine on the grill pan in the center of the table. Hyeong Woo notices none of the other three grimace as hard as he does from the taste of soju, their tongues having long become desensitized to its chemical burn.

"Hyeong Woo-shi, where did you do your military service?" Sung Jae asks.

"At Choijeonbang," the youngest answers.

"The DMZ?" Sung Jae asks, impressed. Sung Jae did his own service in the relative ease & comfort of the southern Jeolla province.

"Nae," Hyung Woo says.

Jong Gil: "Must be fucking cold there?"

"Too cold," Hyung Woo says, before falling into a soju-powered story of shovelling heavy snowfall through the night.

"This is what I mean," Nam Soo says. "Military service builds character! In the city today, who ever shovels snow?"

"But there is something to be said for the young generation and their computers," Jong Gil says, once Nam Soo has finished rambling drunkenly about the character-building nature of hours spent engaged in vigorous manual labor. "You say your son bought Bitcoin?"

"Nae," Sung Jae says, before correcting himself: "Well, not exactly Bitcoin, but coins."

"Coins?" Nam Soo asks, confused.

"Nae, Team Leader, coins," Sung Jae explains. "It's digital money. They buy and sell it through their phones, over the Internet."

"Digital money?" Nam Soo repeats, no less confused.

"Nae," Sung Jae continues. "I don't fully understand it all myself, but the value of our son Jae Seok's coins has increased a lot since he first bought them."

"Enough to buy Johnnie Walker Blue," Jong Gil grunts, refilling the others' soju glasses. "Your boy has good taste."

"Just like his father," Sung Jae quips, taking the soju bottle from Jong Gil so that he can fill Jong Gil's glass.

"So what do they do with this digital money?" Nam Soo asks. "They can spend it on the Internet?"

"I'm not sure, Team Leader," Sung Jae says. "As far as I know, they just buy it and sell it back for real money again later, when the value increases."

"But why does the value increase?" Nam Soo asks.

"I don't know, Team Leader."

"Keonbae!" Jong Gil declares, lifting his soju glass.

They clank glasses together & down them, Hyun Woo turning his back to the others deferentially again as he does so. All then reach for the few pieces of fried pork intestine that remain upon the grill pan.

"Shall we order more?" Nam Soo asks, prompting some grumbling of uncertainty from his subordinates.

"I'm quite full already," Jong Gil says, leaning back & rubbing his bulging stomach.

"Maybe we should move on to 2-cha?" Sung Jae says.

The others "nae" & nod in agreement.

Sung Jae: "Where?"

2차

"I love this song," Nam Soo drunkenly splutters as the slow Sanullim ballad 'Meaning of You' fills the dimly-lit basement LP bar.

"I don't know it," Hyung Woo drunkenly admits.

"You don't know Sanullim?" Nam Soo splutters. "You never heard 'A Flower Blooming in the Haze?' Or 'Spread Silk on My Heart?'"

"I'm sorry, Team Leader," Hyung Woo says, smiling nervously, "I don't."

"Aish, the young generation really knows nothing!" Nam Soo leans in & rants at Hyung Woo about the superior quality & meaningfulness of Sanullim & classic Korean rock groups who played their own instruments & wrote their own songs, compared to modern K-pop, "where the girls dance around wearing next to nothing, and the boys plaster their face in more make-up than a middle-aged prostitute," Hyung Woo nodding deferentially all the while.

Sung Jae scribbles out a song request upon a slip of paper & pushes the paper & pen across the table to Jong Gil; Jong Gil smiles mischievously as he writes his request down, & then holds the paper up for Sung Jae's inspection: "Hey, Sung Jae, in honour of your wife!"

The paper reads R.E.M. – Losing My Religion.

Sung Jae smiles wryly as Jong Gil laughs & calls the barmaid over to collect their request and stares at the twentysomething's ass as she walks away from their table: "Wow," Jong Gil exclaims in heavily-accented English, "that is truly a Gift from God." Then he laughs some more & reaches for his cigarettes in the table's center: "Can we smoke in here?"

"Of course not," Nam Soo snaps, irritated at both the question & being interrupted mid-explanation of Sanullim's supreme & enduring musical talent.

"Sorry, Team Leader," Jong Gil says, bowing his head deferentially. "Sung Jae, you want to join me outside for one?"

It's been almost a week since Sung Jae last smoked a cigarette, & out in the cold of the street the smoke produces a pleasant burning sensation as it brushes the flesh within his throat.

"I don't understand this religious shit," Jong Gil says, waving his cigarette around as he gesticulates. "It's now 2017. 2017! And people still believe all life's answers are in some book written by some idiots in a desert two thousand years ago."

"Ng," Song Jae says, caught between genuinely agreeing & drunkenly regretting the outburst that's made the past few weeks so uncomfortable for him.

"It's fucking stupid. No offense to your wife, but I would've gone crazy too in your situation. It really makes me insane to think that so many people can believe this shit, in this day and age, when we have smartphones in our pockets that can give us all of the world's knowledge in an instant. Do you know what I mean?"

"Ng."

"What does the Bible have to say about the Internet? Or nuclear power? And nuclear weapons? And Chinese pollution fucking up our air quality? You know, the Bible says God created every creature, and that Noah put two of every creature on a fucking boat, and then God flooded the Earth, and every creature that survives today is a descendant of the creatures on Noah's stupid fucking boat. It's ridiculous! Am I wrong?"

"No."

"Of course not! But if you believe that shit, then you believe that no creature can ever go extinct, because every creature exists because God made them a few thousand years ago, and then God asked Noah to put them all on that stupid fucking boat for him. Right?"

"Ng. Maja."

"So if you believe that shit, then it doesn't matter how much we pollute the world, or how many polar bears or rhinoceros or anything we kill, because only God can ever make them extinct, right?"

"Ng. Maja."

"So there's nothing in this world more evil and destructive and harmful to the planet than the stupid fucking Bible, am I right?"

Sung Jae pauses before answering, but Jong Gil's drunken logic is undeniable: "Ng. Maja."

"Anyway," Jong Gil says, tossing his cigarette to the ground & stamping it out, "you think Team Leader will be in any condition to make it to 3-cha?"

3차

Nam Soo stands & sways in the center of the noraebang, eyes closed as he croons into the microphone, his three subordinates lolling back drunkenly in their seats as the boss serenades them with the Sanullim song 'Reminiscence.' Sung Jae's eyes move from his Team Leader to Jong Gil at his right, who's tapping supportively on the song selection remote control, to Hyung Woo on his left, who's struggling to keep his head upright & checking the time on his phone every 30 seconds. Hyun Woo's not looked okay since Sung Jae found him vomiting in the noraebang's toilets. The song ends: Sung Jae & Jong Gil golf-clap & half-heartedly cheer; Hyun Woo tries to lift his arms & open his mouth, but the effort brings him back to the brink of vomiting; Nam Soo falls silent & lets the microphone drop from his hand & clatter to the floor.

4차

"Goodnight, Team Leader," Jong Gil says, holding the taxi door open. "Get home safely."

"Hyun Woo-shi," Nam Soo says, pausing at the open taxi door, "you are of the new generation… and it is my generation which created the world you now inherit… know that you go forth into it as a warrior into a battlefield… know that there is strength in youth, and wisdom in age, and all eternity stretches its fingers into the creases of the present…"

The taxi driver shouts something from inside the cab; Nam Soo turns on him & snaps: "I am talking! Do not interrupt!"

"Aish," Jong Gil mutters, looking at Sung Jae.

"This night is one of many," Nam Soo continues, "in a life of nights and days in which many events will transpire. Live them with all your heart… give your soul to the morning, your mind to the daytime, and your heart to the night… do of these things, and you shall not be disappointed…" Nam Soo sways as he talks, and at one point seems on the brink of tipping over, until he steadies himself upon the opened taxi door. Nam Soo continues speaking, but no-one can make sense of what he's saying, least of all Nam Soo himself.

The taxi honks its horn: Nam Soo turns accusatorily toward the taxi driver, releasing his grip upon the door & almost falling over; Jung Gil steadies him, & helps his silver-haired Team Leader into the backseat: "Get home safely, Team Leader."

Jong Gil slams the door & the taxi speeds off.

"Did you call another taxi?" Sung Jae asks, taking out his phone & opening the KakaoTaxi app.

"I thought maybe we can go to 4-cha," Jong Gil says.

Hyun Woo almost vomits upon hearing the word: "I think I should go home…"

"Maybe we all should go home," Sung Jae says.

Jong Gil: "Go home to what? To stay in your son's bedroom?"

Hyun Woo: "I should go home…"

A taxi appears at the end of the neon-bathed street: Jong Gil throws out his arm to hail it, then says to Hyun Woo: "You take this one."

Hyun Woo bows & bids farewell to his elder colleagues, before his taxi speeds him away into the night.

"4-cha, Sung Jae! What're you saying?"

"4-cha? What 4-cha?"

"I know just the place," Jong Gil says, taking out his wallet and picking through a mess of business cards inside: "Here!"

He thrusts a card out to Sung Jae: upon it is the picture of a lingerie-clad girl in her early-20s, staring at him seductively.

"Aish, women? No way, Jong Gil. It's late enough already. My wife will kill me if she thinks—"

"She won't think anything! You said yourself, she won't even greet you when you get back. She isn't talking to you."

Sung Jae stares into the eyes of the girl in the photo: "…and Jong Gil-shi, you're drunk. Too drunk to do anything."

"I am never too drunk to fuck!" Jong Gil declares.

"Aish…"

***

It's been a quiet night at the Cherry Blossom Love Motel: the usual trickle of high school sweethearts hiding from their parents & other unmarried but clearly-committed couples looking for a safe space to be together outside the family home. At the front desk, Kim Ki Seong is cursing his motel-owning father for having him work the night shift without a single Won in payment: "You have no tuition fees to pay!", his father said, "And no other job to go to! I pay for your clothes, your food, for the home that you live in! And get nothing in return!"; the rant was a long one. Ki Seong bent to his father's will, again, & now spends the night engrossed in his phone screen, alternating between playing games & watching hardcore Japanese pornography.

"Annyong hasaeyo!" the salaryman – (Jong Gil) – shouts, his other salaryman friend – (Sung Jae) – standing sheepishly behind him as he strides toward the counter.

Ki Seong hates the pair the seconds he sees them, not least because they've interrupted him just before the Japanese AV bitch catches her fifth thick load of cum to the face.

"Two rooms, short stay," Jong Gil says, disappointingly handing over a wad of notes & giving Ki Seong no opportunity to see the name printed on his bank card.

As Ki Seong takes the money, he notices with further disappointment that there's no wedding ring upon Jong Gil's finger. He hands Jong Gil the keys to two adjacent rooms, 503 & 507, the latter of which is Ki Seong's favorite, thanks to the camera he's hidden between a crack in the ceiling tiles.

Ki Seong stares at the hand of the other salaryman – (Sung Jae) – as both wait for the elevator, with their backs to him, & sees upon his finger the wedding ring he'd hoped for. But, to add to Ki Seong's troubles, neither man says anything as they wait for the elevator, instead swaying drunkenly in silence, giving him nothing to help work out their identities.

Ki Seong unpauses the video as the salarymen disappear into the elevator. But now he barely pays attention to the pornography, even as the Jap bitch gags on cock almost to the point of vomiting; his attention is instead focused on the CCTV camera footage of the fifth floor corridor, where Jong Gil & Song Jae stand in their respective doorways, each smoking a cigarette, until Song Jae follows Jong Gil into 503. With nothing further to distract him, Ki Seong's attention returns to the pornography, but its staidness & stagedness depresses him. He closes the app & plays the video he filmed earlier, of the high school couple awkwardly undressing each other: the skinny boy climbing on top of his chubby girlfriend & awkwardly flailing around on top of her for all of five minutes.

Two obvious hookers arrive ten minutes later, with overly-teased hair & too-short mini-skirts. They say nothing to Ki Seong as he puts his phone down & watches them. As soon as they enter the elevator, Ki Seong switches his phone to the live camera feed from Room 507. Nothing happens for the longest time; long enough that Ki Seong starts to worry they may have gone for a four-way in 503, or even that his battery or storage space might run out before the good stuff starts; but just as he's on the verge of switching back to the pre-recorded Japanese stuff, the door to Room 507 opens, and the married salaryman leads his hooker inside.

10. 哀 (SORROW) / 樂 (JOY).

Chengdu, China.

哀1.

She wakes with his scent still on the pillow, though as the day overcomes her slumber, she can't help but count the mornings since she last woke up next to him. *What is it now, two weeks?* she asks herself, reaching to switch off the robo-voiced alarm reading the news on the phone he bought her. She thinks of his wife, in some expensive apartment in some central district of Chengdu, far from this block of cramped shoebox apartments on the industrial outskirts. She scolds herself as she gets out of bed & regards her tired face in the mirror. *You should be thankful you're not still in the dormitory.* Staring at her face, she feels her beauty's fading with each day spent here, hope ebbing away with it. She wonders how much makeup to apply: if he's visiting the factory, perhaps she should do everything possible to entice him into visiting her apartment later. But each additional flourish she adds to her face seems to intensify the hatred the other girls have for her. She smirks a little, thinking maybe she ought to make herself prettier than a Disney princess, just to see the jealousy in the eyes of all those simple plain-faced peasant bitches at the factory. They hated her from the second she arrived.

With a little concealer & mascara and the faintest hint of color added to her lips, she's ready to face the day. She walks down five flights of stairs to leave the building, forever afraid the rickety elevator will break & plummet to the depths with her trapped inside. *But would that really be such a bad thing?*

China wasn't supposed to be like this. She'd had big visions of a glittering metropolis filled with newly built skyscrapers, where every building rocketed skyward with the awe & grandeur of Kuala Lumpur's Petronas Towers. Hannah's emails had conjured Chengdu as a place of wonder & riches, where wealthy men would fall instantly in love with a pretty young thing like her: *This customer from the bar I work at bought me so many gifts!!!* French perfume, Italian handbags. And maybe it was true. Maybe Alicia would've stayed with Hannah at the World Class Lounge if Hannah had only warned her what was expected of the girls who worked there. Alicia almost laughs at the naivete of her earlier attitude as she walks toward her workplace. *Is it really any different to how things worked out at the factory?* If she'd stayed at the Lounge, just gone along with it & done what was expected of her, she never would have had to endure those months of sorrow & torment in the dormitory, girls sobbing softly on a dozen beds at either side of her in the darkness of night, familial bonds forming between the emigres from each of China's lesser provinces, she excluded from it all as a Chinese-in-appearance-only foreigner. As things had progressed with the boss, she'd begged him to take her away from it, using the promise of full agency over her body – the thing he clearly desired as much as any of Hannah's gift-buying customers desired hers – to push him into providing a place they could be alone together. Now, it's just a place where she's alone.

Alicia tries to push sorrowful thoughts away & carry herself with dignified defiance as she begins passing the humming factories sharing a street with her workplace. However bad things seem, she consoles herself by remembering she's been promoted above all those plain-face peasant bitches who hate her.

As her workplace comes into focus behind its prison-like metal bars, she sees the girls who hate her standing outside. Dozens, maybe all, of them. Alicia thinks first there's been a fire, but soon sees the police officers standing & talking with them – dozens. Two vans of the kind she's never seen this far from the city center government offices. She freezes. It's common for police to appear without warning, to swoop in & snap up some poor girl who's done something to give them cause to question her paperwork, but this is different. *There's so many of them.* Thoughts fall away, she unable to ascribe the scene any meaning beyond vague existential danger. She turns away from the factory & begins walking back in the direction she came from.

樂 1.

The glass fill splash reflects the ethereal purple glow of the wall-wrapped lighting.

"You been busy?" Wei asks, handing Vincent the g&t.

"Always," Vincent says, swigging the drink.

"This is Hendricks," Wei says. "From London."

"It's good." Purple refracts through the glass as Vincent tips it toward himself.

"It's busy here tonight," Wei says, scanning Venus for attractive females.

"One of the last chances to party before the international crowd goes home for Christmas," Vincent replies.

"I'm gonna be in Hong Kong at Christmas," Wei says. "You go there pretty often, right?"

Morgan – a tall, strikingly-handsome, Harvard-educated dynamo of entrepreneurship – approaches the table with Yu, an almost-equally tall model agglomeration of good genes, flawless skin & high cheekbones, slender frame accentuated with a very expensive sequined halter-top dress. Wei fistbumps Morgan & leans in to give Yu European-styled cheek kisses, then talks with Morgan as Vincent repeats the greeting: "You closed the deal yet?"

"Eh," Morgan says. "I don't know if we'll get it done before New Year."

"Chinese New Year or Western?"

Vincent and Morgan talk about their plans for the holidays as Yu greets a gorgeous girl in a tight white dress that perfectly accentuates a prominent chest & curves to a slender waist.

"Hong Kong!" Morgan says, winning Wei's attention away from the beauty in white. "What are you doing there?"

"This and that."

"Going just to go?"

"Yeah," Wei says. "Pleasure, not business."

"A lot of pleasure to be had in Hong Kong," Morgan laughs. "I just read an article in Vice that called it Disneyland for adults."

A trio of female Swiss students join the table at some point. Wei asks Vincent what he thinks of Hong Kong.

"You know, it looks sort of like Shanghai, but the feeling's different. More concentrated, and more international."

"You know that girl over there?" Wei asks, lounging back in the booth a little while later, pointing his g&t glass at the gorgeous girl in the white dress at the booth's edge, talking to Yu & one of the Swiss girls.

Vincent can't discern from this angle, & with purple saturating everything, whether the girl's pure Chinese or maybe huáyì: "I don't know her."

Someone brushes past the girls and approaches their table, a spectacled acne-flecked guy with unkempt hair in a disheveled but obviously-expensive suit.

"Yo, bro, wassup?" Wei says, rising from his seat to pour the new arrival a drink. "Hey Vincent, did I introduce you to my buddy Justin yet?"

"Hi," Justin says, in awkwardly high-pitched English.

"Morgan," Wei calls across the table as he fills glasses with g&t, "you were telling me about investing in cryptocurrency, right? This is the man to talk to. He's got the third-biggest Bitcoin mining corp in Chengdu."

"Yeah… we're trying to grow it, actually." Justin coughs. "We're aiming for second."

"Oh yeah?" Morgan asks. "What's it called?"

"BitSong. We called it BitSong because Bitcoin is for everyone, just like music. And because we want to build a dynasty. Like the Song dynasty."

"And the Song dynasty invented money, right?" Wei says.

"They were the first world government to introduce paper currency," Justin says, his English-speaking voice strangely unsettling. "And gunpowder. And they made China's first navy. And the population more than doubled under the Song dynasty. And we want to double BitSong every few months. So that's why we called it that."

"Yeah, right, I remember you told me something like that," Wei says, attention diverted as the girl in white moves away from their table without he having given her a drink. "Excuse me one moment, gentlemen."

"So… mining Bitcoin," Morgan muses. "That's pretty much like printing money, right?"

"Yeah. Something like that."

"Of course," the girl in the white dress tells Wei, "I mean, I'm actually moving to America in a few months… I'm going to Princeton… Chemistry…"

She disappears again a short time later, without Wei having asked for her number.

The next morning, the home's strangely quiet. Wei pads around the apartment, heats a bowl of whatever that thing is in the refrigerator, & wonders where his parents are. By mid-afternoon, he's bored of the mystery, & makes plans to meet Vincent & Morgan at Venus again.

"The girl in the white dress…" Morgan ponders, casting his eyes across the purple-hued booth to the spot she'd been standing. "That was Joy."

"That's her English name, right?"

"I don't know," Morgan says. "Is 'Joy' not a typical Chinese name?"

"You think Yu might let me have her number? I wanted to tell her something about the conversation we had yesterday."

哀2.

Why doesn't he answer? He usually sends a message eventually, if only to reduce the risk of his wife seeing her missed calls. Alicia barely leaves the purgatory of her tiny apartment in the days that follow, only venturing to a local mart to stock up on instant noodles. It isn't until Thursday that her repeated internet searches for his & the business's names turn up any results, but when they do, the silence is replaced with an overwhelming chorus of commentary: article upon article reporting on the arrest of a local factory owner & investigation into tax evasion & undocumented workers. Alicia reads it all in numb dumb incomprehension for hours, until thoughts & comprehension finally come to her: *This is his apartment.* However long it's been since he stayed here, it's still registered in his name. Which means – even if she's done nothing wrong, even if she has blame for nothing – she will be ensnared in the investigation if she stays here. The world outside has suddenly become immensely threatening, and her complete isolation all the starker. The apartment is no longer a refuge. *You have to leave this place.* She packs her mercifully few possessions into her tattered suitcase in all of ten minutes, then takes to the chilly winter streets, moving through early evening twilight, wondering if Hannah will forgive her for rejecting the World Class Lounge.

樂 2.

Wei's mother reappears in the home Sunday evening looking gouged of emotion: "They're investigating the accounts. Of the business. One of the policemen said we might learn more tomorrow."

More's not learnt until Tuesday, when Wei's father returns looking emotionally hollower than his mother.

"When you go to Hong Kong, you can take 20,000 RMB in cash," Wei's father tells him. "I will give you the address and phone number for Hyde & Pearce. They are the best people to handle it."

"Come to Hong Kong with me," Wei says to Joy over dinner at The Cathay Room.

"What?!" Joy laughs. "I barely know you."

"So get to know me. Come on! Hong Kong's fun. Do you have anything better to do?"

Her parents are taking to Prague for the holiday; Joy's own plans of drinking heavily with Yoon & Subu are not worth mentioning. "Okay! Sure!"

哀3.

"This is my friend Alicia," Hannah says in perfectly Sichuanese-accented Mandarin, introducing Alicia to a spectacled and acne-flecked guy with unkempt hair and a disheveled but obviously-expensive suit. A bottle of Jaibin baijiu rests on the table in front of them. The acne-flecked guy leans forward & pours Alicia a glass. She takes a delicate sip, smiles demurely, and listens as Hannah lists off his accolades: a computer genius, an entrepreneur making a fortune through Bitcoin mining, and a keen student of history.

"I named the mining company after the Song Dynasty," the Bitcoin guy says. "They were the first government in the world to print paper money. And also I like the double meaning of Song in English. Like Bitcoin, music is for everyone."

"Would you like to hear a song?" Hannah asks, passing the karaoke room's control pad to Alicia. "Alicia has a wonderful voice."

樂 3.

"This place is amazing," Joy says of the room Wei booked at the Mandarin.

"So my Dad's being investigated for tax fraud," Wei says over cocktails at The Nest, twinkling neon skyline filling the dark-lit bar's huge windows. "What even is that? It just sounds so preposterous."

Wei delves into the burden his father charged him with delivering to Hyde & Pearce, only half-joking as he laughs over the realization it would've been useful if he'd asked to Joy carry another 20,000 RMB over the border to Hong Kong.

"How much does he need to move?"

"I think ideally he'd move everything, and I don't know how much everything is, but it's a lot more than 20,000 RMB."

"What happens if he can't move it?"

"I guess the more he has, the more tax they'll try and screw him out of. I don't really get how it all works. So… Chemistry?"

"…the story of Jean Patou," Joy says, gazing dreamily across The Nest at Hong Kong's grand skyline, "who created this fragrance, called Joy, when his business was failing at the start of the Great Depression. And he combined these thousands of flowers – ten thousand jasmine petals, two thousands roses – and created this incredible fragrance, one of the world's greatest. And he went from poverty to the highest end of the luxury fragrance spectrum. And ever since I heard that story, I really thought how cool it would be to make my own fragrance."

"You should totally do that. That'd be awesome! My cousin is a buyer at J'Adore Pacific. If you did it, I'm sure he'd hook you up with an order."

Talk quickly turns to practicalities, and by the time the next cocktail's ordered, a firm plan has been made – shifting Princeton to contingency and going all-in on a dream.

"If you want to move a lot of money out of the country quickly, you could think about moving it into cryptocurrency," Charlie Richards says in the Hyde & Pearce offices. "We'd be able to facilitate a physical cash purchase for conceivably any amount for your father within Shanghai through an intermediary."

"That sounds cool," Wei says. And in front of a Starbucks a few hundred meters from Admiralty Tower, Wei tells Joy. "And actually, I know a guy who's big into Bitcoin mining. Maybe I could sort something out through him." Talk then turns to her philosophy on fragrance, how she'd based it on the artwork of Van Gogh, seen in a trip taken to Amsterdam with her family four years ago: Van Gogh's broad powerful brushstrokes and deep layering of tints from within a highly-restricted palette; it was an artistic strategy she found bled seamlessly into scent production, taking a few robust & unexpected aromas – coriander, rosemary – & layering them with lighter citrus notes and floral weightlessness to create something dynamic & unforgettable.

"That's incredible," Wei says. He forgets all about his father's trouble with the tax investigation as he feeds off the boldness of her ideas. "We could distribute it to all the largest cities in China through my cousin. And we could see about getting a distributor set up here, and in Seoul, Tokyo, Jakarta, Bangkok, maybe I might even be able to speak with someone in New York and get something set up over there –
wow, I'm getting so excited!"

"Me too! Ohmygod! My own fragrance!"

"Yeah! You know who Peter Thiel is? He founded PayPal, with Elon Musk. He's got this thing, the Thiel Fellowship. He'll invest, like, $250 million into your idea – or $250,000, something like that – but you've gotta work on it full-time. No college. Put that shit on hold. And go 110% for something bigger. Something incredible. Something like your fragrance idea. Look – this is going to sound crazy. But… what if you were to do something like that? I mean, I could help you with the money to set it up…"

"Shut up! Are you actually serious? Mygod! I don't know…"

"Look, you don't have to answer me now. Just think about it. As a possibility."

She answers him two weeks later at Venus, he & her in the booth's corner.

"What?!"

"I said let's go with it. The fragrance. Yolo!"

"…and my mother thinks I should get out of the country," Wei tells Joy over dinner at chef André Chiang's The Bridge the following night. "She recommended Korea. She says all you need is $125,000 for an investor's visa. What about launching the fragrance there? Dad's giving me a lot to invest into various ventures, to hopefully keep it hidden from those government fucks and the tax investigation."

When Wei is on his knees holding the ring up in a hotel room later that night, Joy's overcome with her namesake emotion.

哀4.

"I have to go back and get it. It was my grandmother's necklace. My family would never forgive me if I lost it."

What Alicia told Hannah is a half-truth – the necklace had belonged to her grandmother, but it was far from a priceless heirloom or anything of any sentimental significance. It was a nothing piece worth a few Malaysian ringgit that had been in a box of belongings marked for disposal after her grandmother died. Alicia wasn't even sure that she'd brought it to China. But her grandmother's necklace was the first excuse she'd thought of for leaving the small living space she's sharing with Hannah & one other Chinese-Malaysian bar girl.

The bus moves for an hour from the buzz & noise of Chengdu's center to the night-quiet industrial outskirts, Alicia's mind wandering further, from the nearing-zero temperatures of Chengdu night to the balmy tropical warmth of Malaysia. She lets her mind tumble over disconnected images – the factory owner, his (imagined) wife, the Huawei phone he bought her, the cramped apartment she lived in alone, the sofa at the apartment she's living on now, the dormitory at the factory, her dead grandmother's cheap pewter necklace, the pale skin of the Bitcoin mining kingpin & his bush of unkempt pubic hair, the lyrics of the Gavin Chou ballad she'd sung in the karaoke room – *Always be true, Never nothing less than that, Always with you, Never wanting more than that* – : there is no reason or logic or order to any of it. It's just things that happened. A loosely connected series of events, one prompting the other introducing another. Maybe life is this, and nothing more than this. A loosely connected series of events, until your possessions are boxed for disposal by those who come after.

Alicia gets off the bus a few stops earlier than she'd intended, wanting to walk past the factory, almost certainly for the final time, propelled into this endeavor by nothing more than curiosity. And as she walks past the factory, she sees a light inside. She stops & stares at it from the street. She trains her ears & mind to obscure the distant buzz of traffic and focus on the low mechanical hum emanating from inside: it's something new, not the usual frenzied overlapping sounds of garment production. She briefly considers that she may be lost, that she's staring at a different one of the district's dozens of factories, but the frazzled rust edging the metal bars is too particular. *This is the place.* She wonders if he's inside. She wonders if he's visited. She takes her phone from her pocket, looks at the WeChat messages she sent, still unread by him. She stands like this until the cold ceases to bother her, until she feels herself blending into this mess of barely connected narratives forming the second-tier city of Chengdu; her own story, known only to her, losing any sense of meaning amidst the millions of other narratives playing out across the city; the mystery of her manager, his factory, some small fragment of a city & country's development, shifting global capital, the whole confusing epic of human history. *The Song Dynasty was the first world government to print paper currency.* She has something close to 1000 RMB in her purse. Her bank account contains somewhere between 2000 and 3000 more. If she returns to Hannah & the World Class Lounge, that could quickly grow. *Always be true. Never nothing less than that.* She wonders if Gavin Chou actually wrote those words himself. She wonders what he was thinking about if he did. *What are you doing?* She's asking herself the question, but she's not sure who the 'you' refers to – her, Alicia, or he, Taiwanese pop star Gavin Chou, or *him,* her jailed sugar daddy factory owner. In any case, she doesn't know the answer. She taps out a message to him, begging him to call her, to let her know what's happening, to at least let her know if he's safe… then she deletes it all before sending it, and stares at the factory. *What are you doing?*

A door opens. She stares at her phone & starts walking, suddenly conscious of how long she must've been standing out there, likely picked up on CCTV. She gets to the factory's edge before turning back, and sees two figures talking quietly at its door. She snaps a photo, then carries on back to the haggard grey apartment block, climbs five flights of stairs, and realizes she doesn't have her key.

樂 4.

Wei's father looks at his son in incomprehension: "You want to get married?"

A lavish ceremony is impossible, even if the bride's family pays for it. It would be the ultimate show of disrespect to the authorities inspecting him. But as Wei further explains his & Joy's plan for the perfume shop in Myeongdong, Seoul, and an expanding empire of fragrance from there and beyond using the money his father needs sequestered, the concepts become cogs within a much larger apparatus, at least according to the sketch currently being daubed in Wei's father's mind.

"…and Justin told me that me being in Seoul would actually work out amazingly well for getting your money out through BitSong," Wei continues. "He said that the Korean government puts crazy restrictions on capital outflows and cryptocurrency, but the people there are going crazy for Bitcoin, so the price is like fifty percent higher than it is anywhere else. So Justin can send whatever's mined at the factory to me in Seoul, I can cash out through a Korean exchange, and you're making fifty percent extra on everything that's getting filtered through BitSong."

Wei's father smiles. "Son, this girl sounds like she really means a lot to you."

"She does, Dad. She's not like anyone I've ever met before. The connection we have is unreal. I'm truly in love with her."

Fifty percent extra. "Son, your mother and I worried that the day would never come when you told us you were getting married. You know, your mother and I were married before her twenty-first birthday, and we had you soon after. She's told me again and again how your generation waits longer for marriage, that it's become customary to wait until you've established a career for yourself before you seek someone to share your life with. So until your thirtieth birthday, I waited with patience. But, over the past six years, I began to think you'd never marry."

"I hadn't met the right girl, Dad."

"No. I suppose you hadn't. And this girl of yours – what was her name?"

"Joy."

"It sounds like she's really special to you."

"She is, Dad. Just as special as Mom is to you."

"Yes… that must be true… and forgive me for not offering my immediate congratulations. It's just, with the stress of the investigation, and the government watching our every move, it seemed like an impossible time. But… you say the two of you could live in Korea together? And your friend would have no problem in transferring the Bitcoin from the factory to there?"

"I'm telling you, Dad, it's the perfect solution for everyone."

"Then you have my blessing. But with one condition – Joy's parents must be seen to pay for the wedding. You can tell them that we will reimburse them for every yuan once you're settled in Seoul. But the government here cannot see that I'm lavishing money on a ceremony."

"Sure thing, Dad."

Wei holds his arms out and smiles at his father. For the first time since Wei left to study in London, his father hugs him. All the bitter disappointment of Wei's failed studies & decade-plus of listless mediocrity are forgotten as they embrace, and Wei's father thinks of what his son's told him of his plans for Korea –
Fifty percent extra. And his son's genius idea of renting the factory space to his friend at BitSong for use as a Bitcoin mine, at a pitifully low declared rental fee, & concealing the bulk of his wealth in digital currency. Were it not for his son's ingenuity, those treacherous bastards of the government would likely have taken the family's every yuan before locking him up. "Son, I'm proud of you."

"Thank you, Dad. You have no idea how much that means to me."

哀5.

The snoring of the other Chinese-Malaysian girl echoes from within her bedroom & recalls Alicia's mind to the constant soft night-noise of the dormitory as she stares at the photo snapped outside the factory on her phone. She's lying on an imitation leather sofa with most of its covering eroded in patches with a blanket pulled over her. Hannah sleeps in the second of the apartment's two bedrooms. The room Alicia sleeps in is not exactly a living room; more a narrow strip of semi-private hallway. Alicia touches her thumbs to the phone screen's center & slowly slides them apart, the fuzzy outlines of the two figures smoking cigarettes outside the factory growing larger but no clearer. She thinks of those American TV dramas, where some heroic law enforcement agent tells his younger computer-savvy colleagues to enhance the image. If only it were that easy; she sees faintly illuminated facial features in the photograph, but no more than that. She repeats this same useless action each night once the other girl's snoring has begun, & again when Alicia is inevitably woken by the banging of doors & loud conversations in the public hallway beyond the semi-private one that is her home.

She scans the features of each of the World Class Lounge's customers in the days that follow, trying to line them up with the features vaguely seen each night on her phone screen. She knows this is ridiculous – that the odds of any customer matching the blurry image from outside the factory, in a city of 15 million people, is completely preposterous – but she does it anyway. It's something to think about it; a mystery to keep her mind occupied. She's given up on contacting *him* after her last pain-filled messages, where she drunkenly poured her soul into WeChat, drew no response. But she has to keep trying. She has to do something. Something other than just existing, & flitting from loosely-connected event to loosely-connected event with no agency of her own.

Then it all makes sense: he enters again, the Bitcoin mining guy with the spectacles and the acne-flecked face and the unkempt hair and disheveled but obviously-expensive suit and the bush of untamed pubic hair, now mercifully shielded within his suit pants. The messy hair, the slender-to-the-point-of-frailness figure, the contours of his spectacles' frame: all perfectly align with the much-studied photograph. It seems impossible, but…

He sees her staring at him. He looks away shyly, then looks back, she still staring, & he smiles. Without wanting to weight her action with further thought, Alicia strides across the bar & sits next to him. She feels the eyes of another bar girl, whose job it should be to first approach the customer & welcome him joyously & proffer menus, burn into the back of her head. From the corner of her eye, she sees Hannah also watching her, shocked by the uncharacteristic boldness with which she's made her approach.

"Hi!" Alicia says. "Do you remember me?"

"You're the girl who sings. The Gavin Chou song."

"And you're the Bitcoin guy." She immediately regrets these words, so loaded with gold-digging overtones, but he's already been drinking, and if he's bothered by what she says, he doesn't show it.

She's telling him that she's got a song she'd love to sing to him, & he says he'd love to hear her sing it, & the bar girl brings the menu over & looks at Alicia sternly before smiling broadly for the Bitcoin guy & asking what he'd like.

A bottle of Jaibin baijiu is brought to the flashing lights of the karaoke backroom. He pours her a glass & she sings another Gavin Chou song, then one by G.E.M., drinking quickly between bursts of vocals, prompting him to refill her glass repeatedly & increase the rate of his own consumption. She laughs & flirts and duets with him on a Gavin Chou & Joey Huang song about a mermaid, & when they leave the bar, she sees Hannah stare malevolently, as if Alicia has stolen away the affections of the Bitcoin-rich guy just to spite her.

He lives in a plush 14th floor apartment in a tower right beside Tianfu Square, with huge windows providing the sweeping view across the city that finally match her original expectations of China. She flirtatiously pushes him into letting her try glass after glass of exotic European alcohol, he barely able to stand by the time she's guided him through his drinks cabinet. All the alcohol prolongs the inevitable intercourse but she doesn't not enjoy it – the drunkeness banishes much of the bizarre awkwardness with which he'd conducted himself in the bar's backrooms on the last occasion they met. Once it's over, & he passes out, she compares it to her experiences with *him* of the factory & decides the Bitcoin guy has in every way outperformed his meagre efforts – *he* seeming to age with each second spent in the act, until he finally comes & collapses in exhaustion at the end of it. She thinks maybe this could be her true Chengdu destiny, as she gazes again across the skyscraper-filled cityscape, but then reminds herself that this is a business transaction, and she'd be foolish to expect anything more to develop from it. With heavy snoring indicating the Bitcoin guy is now soundly asleep, she takes his phone from a bedside table & delicately uncurls his fingers & presses them to his phone to unlock it. She scans his text messages, then WeChat, finding meme-filled chats with similarly nerdy guys, reams of 10-second clips of his friends fucking girls, but nothing that ties him to *him* from the factory. Frowning, thinking the whole sordid night a failure, she delves through the mass of applications on his phone, so many she has never heard before, until she sees one she guesses might be another messenger app – Telegram. When she opens it, she finds what she's been looking for: messages exchanged with some guy called Wei, scores of them, referencing the factory. She scrolls back through the messages until all mention of the factory disappears & she sees weekly exchanges of plans to meet at Venus in Lan Kwai Fong. From there she moves forward, seeing an explanation of why the Bitcoin guy so perfectly matched the blurry image she spent so long studying: *My dad loved the factory idea! The space is going to waste now anyway, let's talk it over in person soon…* She takes out her own phone & photographs each of the messages, then angles the phone above her head & snaps a selfie with the Bitcoin guy's face & naked hairless chest clearly visible on the bed behind her.

樂 5.

The tension between the two sets of parents at the head table is palpable. Neither has said or done anything to outwardly indicate their displeasure with proceedings, but it's clear from the sullen expression on Joy's father's face what he thinks of this: his daughter being hastily shunted into a marriage, much expense spared on the ceremony, giving up an American Ivy League education for a business funded by a family of such pathetic character. Her mother was more supportive, harping on endlessly to her husband of 'changing times' and 'a woman's right to choose.' "The family has a lot of money," she'd told him, "and only one son to inherit it all." He would have preferred his daughter married some buffoonish American than lowering herself to this. But, drinking glass after glass of baijiu and gorging on beef, duck, & crab in the less-than-five-star banqueting hall, he consoles himself with the bridge-groom's family's promise to reimburse them two-fold for all wedding expenses, just as soon as the couple have set up Joy's long-dreamed-of perfume venture in Seoul.

"Thanks for coming, guys," Wei tells Vincent & Morgan & Yu & Yoon & Subu & other assorted international friends grouped together at one table as the newly-married couple make their rounds of their guests' tables, prompting a chorus of "Of course!" & "We wouldn't miss it!" & comments on how beautiful Joy looks & wry comments from the guys about how well Wei's scrubbed up & how Joy's having a positive influence on him already.

"Huh," Wei says, taking his phone from his pocket & reacting to something on it as they leave the table.

"What?" Joy asks.

"I don't know… someone's trying to get in touch with Dad… they say it's urgent… excuse me one moment." He leaves Joy looking worried between the tables, drawing interested glances from several guests & adding to the ever-deepening disapproval of some of Joy's closest family members. "Dad, I got a message from someone telling you to check your WeChat. They say it's urgent."

"Who is it?" Wei's mother asks.

"They didn't say."

Joy's father looks at Wei's father with undisguised disgust. Wei's father calmly takes his phone from his pocket, holding it as close to his face as possible. No message notification has appeared, but the bubble beside WeChat shows new unseen messages. He knows instantly who the sender is – *that girl,* whose chat he's muted. Trying his best to seem unbothered, Wei's father stands & excuses himself.

"What is it?" Wei's mother asks.

"It's nothing," Wei's father says. "Business. A small thing that someone was taking care of for me."

Wei's father strolls as nonchalantly as possible to the banqueting hall's nearest exit, ignoring staff as he approaches the hotel's entrance, not looking at the phone again until he's a good twenty meters from the building. *That stupid whore,* he thinks. *When will she give up and just get on with her life? Disturbing me on my only son's wedding day…* And contacting Wei! He's only just begun to wonder how she could have got Wei's number when the message opens: the screenshots of Wei & Justin's conversation about setting the Bitcoin mining operation up at the factory, the selfie taken from his bed, vaguely threatening messages about 'a friend' having told her 'something interesting' about the factory and the Bitcoin mining operation…

哀樂.

What do you want?

Alicia stares at the long-awaited WeChat message. So abrupt. So direct. She has no idea how to answer it.

What do I want?

She's walked almost two hours from the cramped apartment, a few blocks south of Jiuyanqiao Bar Street – home to the World Class Lounge - , taking a meandering route along the north side of the river, and then through the ever-growing crowds & concentration of commerce – shops, restaurants, malls; from where she's standing when she receives his message, she can pick out the Bitcoin guy's apartment building from among the towers dotted around Tianfu Square.

What do I want?

She wants all of it: the luxury housing, the upmarket shopping, the quality cuisine, the city & all within it. And why stop at Chengdu? She thinks of Shanghai, with surely five times the amenities & ten times the glamor. *Or Hong Kong.* Maybe even some city further from here, somewhere glittering & glamorous, like Paris, London, New York…

Money is the only thing keeping her in that cramped apartment on the south-side of the river. Money was the only reason she was ever banished to the city's industrial outskirts. Money was what doomed her to live in the dorm with two dozen other girls, and *his* money is what moved her to the modest upgrade of her own one-room living space.

The promptness of his reply & the bluntness of his question – *What do you want?* – tells her that she now has power. While she only vaguely understands his connection to the Bitcoin guy and whatever's now going on at the repurposed garment factory, she knows that she knows enough to exert control over him. *Agency.* Agency over her life & his.

Alicia keeps walking until she reaches a Starbucks, then picks one of the menu's most expensive items – a java chip mocha something something. She sits & waits for her drink, pondering the message. *What do I want?* The rush she felt upon opening the message is quickly fading, replaced by immense fear of the unknown she has now committed herself to. *The moment I reply to him, he's in control again.* He can approve or deny her request. He can do any number of things. But the result will depend on his response. *My future will depend on his response.*

Alicia is called to the counter to collect her drink. She takes it back to her seat, takes a quick sip of the thick cold liquid, then stares again at the ominous text message. *What do you want?*

11. KING OF THE EARTH.

ERR%20%:*('location';=UNDEFINED.)*

LEGAL DISCLAIMER:

In order to make the scenes that follow more interesting, the names of people & places which really exist have been used. However, none of what follows is true. None of what follows has ever – or likely will ever – actually happen(ed). This is a pure work of fiction. Parody. Satire. It is not real. The satirised characters & places that appear in the following chapter (& all previous & later chapters) are in no way a reflection of the real characters & places they share a name with. All that follows should be regarded as fiction/satire/parody & none of it should be taken seriously by anyone ever, least of all any court of law with jurisdiction over regions in which this book is published or sold.

</LEGAL DISCLAIMER.>

The ICO was successfully completed ahead of schedule, 7,500 ETH raised, half of FSC's 10 trillion tokens distributed to investor's Ethereum wallets, & listings on a few minor exchanges secured.

"So now we actually have to do this, right?" Aart says, as Guus gushes to the rest of the frat about their new-found wealth.

"Sure."

A week passes – a week of heavy drinking & missed university classes for all at the frat house, empty bottles of liquor piling up on every surface in the main living area, days ebbing away as the frat lads give themselves up to the night.

"We've got to do this," Aart says. "It's almost two weeks since the ICO now. We can't just keep blowing the money on getting wasted."

"Sure. I'll talk to Nguyen about it."

Days pass, all but Guus curbing their drinking & returning to lectures. Guus spends his evenings with Nguyen in The Three Sisters or Oblomov, drinking glass after glass of Belgian beer – La Chouffe, St. Bernadus, Gulden Draag – & nights in ZO, or Ocean 41, or Kokomo, flaunting their wealth & the enormous confidence it's inspired. Aart cycles to The Three Sisters one afternoon after class & finds Guus & Nguyen sitting at a table with eight blonde German psychology students, a dozen cocktail jugs in front of them, the German girls laughing & smiling & leaning in & listening intently to everything Guus & Nguyen say.

"Aart, you're here!" Guus almost knocks a girl's glass over as he rises & embraces him. "I was just telling the girls about Future Synergy Coin."

"I can't believe you guys are all millionaires!" one girl says.

"This is the genius behind our entire marketing strategy," Guus declares, arm draped over Aart's shoulder, his breath heavy with booze. "If not for him, we would not have made even one cent."

"I thought you wanted to discuss the development roadmap?" Aart says as Guus pours him a rum cocktail.

Guus: "Nguyen, do you want to tell him?"

"We're going to Amsterdam," Nguyen says, grinning stupidly, face flushed red with alcohol.

"Why?"

Guus: "For a conference! This is what you've been telling us, right? We need to make progress. So this is progress. We go to the conference, we network, meet with other projects and investors, and start really making things happen."

Aart rarely sees Guus & Nguyen in the week before the conference, spending hours at the library each day working on university assignments, & coming home to see they're not in the frat house.

Conference day arrives & the entire frat crew move boisterously through the streets of Groningen to the train station, beers in hand, as if they were heading down to Amsterdam for Koningsdag.

Singing & chanting fills the carriage for the next two hours, elderly women throwing disgusted looks at the troupe of half-cut hooligans.

"Guus has to go on stage," Aart confides in Ciara, "in front of all these people, and he's totally wasted…"

"It'll be okay," Ciara lies, trying to reassure Aart. "You know, in England, we call alcohol 'Dutch courage.'"

From Amsterdam Centraal they take a train to Sloterdijk then head to a hotel fifteen-minutes' walk from the station. The frat crew roll through reception, drawing worried looks from the staff, Aart smiling apologetically. They enter the main hall & find little more than twenty people inside.

"Where the fuck is everybody?" Guus asks loudly.

"This is everyone," some nerd in a Bitcoin Cash T-shirt says. "Are you all registered?"

Guus approaches the nerd, still clutching a Grolsch can; Aart steps in front of him & reassures the nerd that, yes, they are registered: "We're here with Future Synergy Coin."

"Okay, then would you mind asking your… team… to keep the noise down?"

Aart tries to shush the rowdy bunch, but they burst into boisterous chatter & laughter as pallid skinny Silicon Valley-style speakers on-stage stutter through boring speeches about blockchain & transformative technological epochs.

"This is fucking everyone?" Guus splutters once his turn to speak arrives.

The nerd in the Bitcoin Cash shirt again assures him that yes, this is everyone; Guus strides on stage & clasps the microphone with supreme confidence: "Goedemiddag, Amsterdam! Hoe gaat het?"

Guus' greeting's met with complete silence & looks of festering disapproval that have built throughout the frat lads' conference antics; even the frat lads themselves are silent, most too drunk to summon up any kind of appropriate response to Guus' opening greeting. After a few moments' awkward silence, Guus feels the alcohol within his bloodstream evaporate. The confidence he gained over the previous few weeks disappears, leaving him a mouth-breathing mess of neuroses, anxiety pricking randomly-distributed nerve endings throughout his body.

"Wooo!" Nguyen yells at the back of the room.

Guus smiles, thinking *you have to do this.* Another wave of anxiety: *I can't remember what I was going to say.* The anxiety becomes him, swallows him whole: *I didn't think once about what I'd say up here…*

His breathing becomes heavier, amplified by the microphone, echoing off the walls, overwhelming the room. Guus stares out at the stone-faced crowd of unwashed crypto enthusiasts, their arms folded, some falling into chatter with the people beside them, others engrossed in phone screens, some lifting their phones to capture his moment of complete capitulation on camera.

Fuck you.

The intrusive thought steels Guus against the anxiety; he licks his lips & tightens his grip on the microphone.

Fuck you. You are not Guus van Hooijdink. *You are Honey Badger.* Be Honey Badger. *Be fucking Honey Badger.*

But then the stupidity of that thought overcomes him, & he crumbles again, & finally, as he sees the nerd in the Bitcoin Cash T-shirt approach, ready to cut him off, Guus pulls his phone from his pocket, desperate to save himself with the text contained within it.

"I am… ahem… I am here today from Future Synergy Coin. On behalf of. To speak for Future Synergy Coin. And vat ve have is ze very interesting products. Ahem. Not… not… products so much. Ve have ze token, of ze Future Synergy. The Coin. Ahem. And… uh… wait… just… one… second… yes… the Future Synergy Coin is…" & from there Guus proceeds to read almost the entire FSC whitepaper, staring into the reassuring white light of his phone, not looking up even once at the audience's bored faces.

The train back to Groningen is a sombre affair, Guus in gloomy silence while Nguyen sleeps in the seat beside him, head lolled back & mouth agape, the others clutching beer cans & making small talk about sports & movies & video games.

"Hey, man, about the speech," Aart says a few days later, entering Guus' room to find Guus lying down on the bed, earphones hooked up to a laptop resting on his stomach.

Guus removes the earphones & turns his glum face toward Aart.

"I know you must be feeling bad about it, but, y'know, it isn't so big of a deal. I mean, I think we can take it as a lesson, y'know? Part of the learning curve. We've got a multi-million dollar project going here. It's crazy that we made it this far, but we can't stop now. It's like Dre says to Kendrick: 'anyone can make it, but what's harder than making it is keeping it, motherfucker.' Do you understand why I'm saying this?"

"I understand."

"So we have to move forward with the roadmap—"

"We are moving forward."

"Oh… did you… speak to Nguyen?"

"I was about to send him a message. You as well."

"…yeah?"

"There's another conference. Next Saturday. In Stockholm."

"Another conference? But—"

"This is bigger than the fucking shit thing in Amsterdam. There will be at least two thousand people there."

"But before we carry on with conferences, shouldn't we—"

"David Sontesebo will be there. From IOTA. Giving the keynote speech."

"Oh… I… don't know… who that is…"

"And this time will not be such a fuck, I promise you."

"But—"

"I fucking swear to you, Aart. I fucking swear to you. I will not let you down again."

"But… don't you think… we need to work on the product? Or something? I mean…"

"Networking is the product, Aart. Conferences are the product. This is a hype game. Think about Tron. Do you even know what Tron's supposed to do?"

"I don't even know what Tron is… I never heard of it…"

"Tron is some fucking shitcoin that some Chinese dickhole made, but this Chinese dickhole goes to every fucking conference, and he's got half-a-million followers on Twitter, and his coin is worth more than eight billion dollars."

"But… you're not Chinese, Guus."

"Does it matter if I'm fucking Chinese or not? Are you fucking racist? No, he's Chinese, but he's charismatic. Charismatic as fuck. And that's what sells the coin. Charisma."

"I mean… it's technology…"

"Yes, it's fucking technology, Aart. And every technology in human history was only adopted because some charismatic kankerautist fooled people into believing in it."

"That's… that… isn't true…"

"Yes it is, Aart. Yes it is. Think about it! Steve Jobs comes along with his black roll-neck sweater and a fucking MP3 player just like a thousand other MP3 players, and the world goes crazy for him. Bill Gates, Mark Zuckerberg, Elon Musk – these are the superstars of our time, Aart. Do you really think Tom Cruise is the all-time greatest actor? Do you think Drake is the most talented rapper? Do you think Donald Trump is qualified to be fucking President? They have charisma, Aart. That's all it is: charisma."

"But… you… don't…"

"There are two kinds of people in this world, Aart: those with a fixed mindset, and those with a growth mindset. If you have a fixed mindset, you think that you are a shit, and you can never do anything, and you will wither and die in a fucking government-provided hovel with six kids who fucking hate you and a failed marriage and a fucking heroin needle hanging out your arm. But if you have a growth mindset, you can do anything. You are the master of your own destiny. Do you think cavemen thought that we would one day walk on the fucking moon?"

"I… what are you talking about?"

"I'm talking about a growth mindset, Aart. I'm talking about being the change I want to see in the world. I'm talking about walking on the fucking moon."

"I… don't…"

"Look at this motherfucker," Guus says, turning the laptop to face Aart. In grainy black & white footage relayed via YouTube, Adolf Hitler is gesticulating wildly, while an enormous crowd of his downtrodden countrymen karate chop the air in crazed approval. "This short, ugly, dumb-moustache-having motherfucker, this piddling little failed artist, conquered half of fucking Europe, Aart. He marched right through this city, through this country. He didn't stop until he got to the fucking Eiffel Tower. He brought the continent to its knees. And when you listen to him speak, you see why; the passion! The fire! The fury!"

"But… Hitler lost the war, Guus…"

"It's not only Hitler, Aart; it's Obama, it's Trump, it's JFK, Reagan, Churchill, Ghandi, Martin Luther King; I've been watching all of them, Aart, all of them; and the comedians! The way they control the crowd! Eddie Murphy, Chris Rock, Dave Chapelle, George Carlin, Louis CK – the way they build around an idea, pull an audience into believing it. The actors, the rock stars, the rappers, the rabbis, the priests, the imams – I've been watching all of them, Aart. All of them! And I promise you, I fucking swear to you, I swear with every fibre of my fucking being – I will not disappoint you again."

Aart stares at Guus, at the mad certainty & wild-eyed intensity of his bed-ridden business partner, & slowly backs out of the door: "Okay… cool…"

A two-hour train ride to Amsterdam & 15-minute transfer to Schiphol Airport & four-hour flight later, Guus, Aart, & Nguyen are in Stockholm, Aart & Nguyen remarking favourably of its brightly-coloured smörgåsbord of architectural styles, Guus as quiet & intense as a death row inmate being conveyed to the execution chamber. Guus spends the whole night in their room at the grand waterfront Elite Hotel pacing & rehearsing his speech, tweaking its pacing & delivery, while Aart & Nguyen recline on the bed & complain about the price of the beers they're drinking.

The next day, the hotel's conference room is alive with activity, a half-dozen crypto teams & expert guest speakers mingling with tall aging bald men in sharp Scandinavian suits who stroke their chins & ponder all the industries blockchain will disrupt, while beautiful blonde Swedish waitresses move through the crowd offering platters of wine & hors d'oeuvres while trying to catch the eye of a crypto millionaire.

Guus is the first on the stage & instantly captures the imaginations of an as-yet unsettled audience, prowling confidently across the stage, staring into the eyes & souls of more than 2000 crypto-curious attendees: "How many of you have ever lost an ID card? A passport, a driver's license… okay, there is quite a few of you. Now how much did it cost you to replace it? Anyone? You? Wow! Sweden's expensive, ja? Oh, you're from Denmark! And how long did it take for you to receive a new document? Wow! That's even worse than the Netherlands! What the heck's gone wrong in Denmark? Okay, now imagine all those documents were securely stored on a decentralised distributed ledger…"

He strides & builds as his speech moves through an easily-digested breakdown of FSC's utility & technology, the audience enraptured. The climax draws a standing ovation from a conquered crowd.

Aart: "That was awesome, man!"

Nguyen: "You fucking killed that shit, bro!"

& Guus smiles & basks in the glory of a job well-done, exchanging small talk with a bevy of Scandinavian tech-experts & finance people, the Swedish waitresses batting eyelashes & exchanging flirtatious looks with Guus as he accepts an unending stream of wine & hors d'oeuvres.

Guus' glory fades through the next four speeches, then dissipates entirely as David Sontesebo takes the stage & delivers a thundering speech, carrying himself like a viking & speaking like a Stephen Hawking-scripted Jordan Belfort. The tangle, directed acyclic graph, the monetisation of data transfer within the Internet of Things: these lofty concepts are relayed with clarity & precision, & when the speech is over, Guus is almost forgotten, until he & Nguyen wangle their way through the conference horde & interface with Team IOTA directly, every single woman in the room & even a few of the married ones forming a circle around them, all angling to flash the best smile at the men of the hour; & when Aart interrupts & reminds Guus & Nguyen they need to leave soon for the airport, Guus is irascible, a junky who's had the finest fix he's ever found snatched away from him.

Guus & Nguyen spend the nights after the conference moving between the pubs & clubs of Groningen, impressing new women at the bar & disappointing them in bed.

"How the fuck is he doing this?" Federico asks one morning, as Guus' fifth new girl of the week leaves the frat house.

Guus' days are spent hungover smoking weed in bed, watching hour after hour of TED Talks & conference speeches & the tubthumping delivery of every despot who's ever been immortalised on YouTube.

"Hey man, don't you think you ought to go to class or something?" Aart asks, hovering in the doorway of Guus' smoke-filled room.

"I don't need to go to BSc Computer Science classes," Guus replies. "FSC is worth more than a fucking PhD."

"Then what about the roadmap? We've made no progress since the ICO."

"Oh, we made progress, Aart. Did you check the price today? We're at six-thousandths of a cents per coin. $60 million market cap. We're ranked at number 132 on CoinMarketCap."

"That's why we've got to work on development, man. The roadmap. People have invested millions of dollars in us. We can't spend all the development budget on partying and conferences."

Guus laughs: "Why not?"

Aart pauses, struggling to think of a reason.

The next conference is in Vienna, in the splendour of the Park Hyatt, a monolithic hotel with grand Greek columns at its entrance & chandeliers dangling from every ceiling in its interior.

"How much did this place cost?" Aart says, going into Guus' rooms after dropping his bag in his own.

"I don't remember."

"We should've stayed somewhere cheaper, man. Or at least shared a room, like in Stockholm."

"We can afford it."

"But we need to use the development budget to actually develop something…"

"Aart, please; I cannot deal with negative energy within 24 hours of a conference speech."

Aart leaves Guus alone to rehearse & tweak his speech, the grandeur of the hotel & the refined cityscape beyond the window seeping into Guus' words & energising them; as he paces & practises, he stops at the window and stares across the city's spires & slanted roofs, hearing the call of history, feeling the same world-conquering firing of the soul this city inspired in a piddling young painter named Adolf.

"What if there's a better way?" Guus pauses for effect, all eyes upon him amid the ornate Viennese refinement of the Park Hyatt's Grand Salon. "What if these documents could be stored securely and immutably within the blockchain? Enter Future Synergy Coin…"

The audience is smaller than Stockholm's, & the applause that greets the speech's end is less thunderous, but the impact of Guus' speech upon all in attendance is in no doubt.

Aart & Nguyen congratulate him on a speech well-delivered, but Guus is left unsatisfied; he craves an audience's total submission to the brilliance of his words & ideas.

The keynote speaker is Sunny Lu of VeChain, & Guus & everyone else in attendance is enraptured by the genius concept of adding tiny RFID chips to all manner of products that can be scanned using any smartphone operating the VeChain app, with consumers having instant-access to the blockchain's full record of the products' origin & movements through the supply chain, ensuring all branded goods are genuine, & all food products safe & sanitary, &etc., & Sunny Lu even has a neat solution to the problem of most crypto coins & tokens being largely useless accessories to an otherwise-neat blockchain-enabled idea: holding VEN will generate another token, THOR, which will then be sold back to businesses looking to buy into VeChain's supply chain solutions; & Guus is mesmerised, but he doesn't move as the audience rises at the end & gives Sunny Lu a standing ovation.

"We need to think bigger," Guus says to Nguyen once Nguyen stops clapping & sits back down. "We need some kind of business-to-business solution. That's where the real money is. And we need some other token that gets created just by holding FSC."

"Yeah, yeah, that's awesome," Nguyen says, nodding enthusiastically to each jargon-loaded sentence.

"But we need to actually have some kind of working product first," Aart says. "We need to make some progress on the main idea FSC's supposed to be based on before we start promising a load of new features. We need to start delivering on the roadmap."

"And what if we created a kind of social network within the FSC ecosystem?" Nguyen suggests. "And instead of just liking or upvoting people's posts, you could give a boost to how much of the other token their FSC generates?"

"Oh my God, that's fantastic!" Guus says. "That's total genius!"

& Aart tries to remind them that if they still haven't even begun working on storing documents on the FSC blockchain, or even creating a blockchain for them to be stored on, and they'll probably never get around to adding all these extra features, but neither Guus nor Nguyen is listening to him.

Aart's struggling to sleep upon the soft king-sized bed within the spacious luxury of his hotel room, rolling over & shifting position, fretting over Guus & Nguyen's sudden obsession with creating a coin that does everything, & the mounting costs of conferences & 5-star hotels, & the tens of millions of dollars riding on them delivering something, & the catastrophic consequences of the whole house of cards falling apart, when he hears a knock at the door, & then a voice outside it: "Hey, Aart, open up. It's Guus."

Aart rolls out of bed & pads across the room, opening the door to see Guus in his underwear & an unbuttoned shirt, pupils dilated, demeanour clearly chemically-altered: "I need condoms."

Aart looks at the shelf above his room's mini-bar, where a box of condoms sits among tubes of toothpaste & other toiletries: "Didn't your room have some?"

"I've used them all already," Guus says, brushing past Aart & moving towards the shelf.

"But it's a pack of six."

"I know," Guus says, snatching up all the miniature bottles of liquor from the shelf, then opening the mini-fridge in search of more alcohol. "These girls are insatiable."

"Wow," Ciara says as Aart enters the frat's kitchen/living room, a dramatic haircut having removed his dreads & imbued him with an air of corporate maturity.

"I'm getting worried," Aart tells her, after bashfully accepting her haircut-based compliments.

"It'll be okay," Ciara lies, trying to reassure him, as she chops some leeks & adds them to the simmering peanut-based Indonesian broth she bought on discount at JUMBO. "You already made a ton of money, right?"

"But we cannot do anything with it," Aart says. "If people see on the Ethereum blockchain that the founders of Future Synergy Coin have moved their coins, they'll lose confidence in our project."

"Yeah," Ciara says, pretending to understand. "I guess that's true."

"That smells good," Wesley says, entering the room a little while later, Aart now helping Ciara prepare the meal. "Can I help you guys with something?"

Ciara's about to tell him no, she's got it under control, when the back door swings open, & Guus & Nguyen enter, carrying JUMBO bags with a dozen bottles of top-shelf alcohol.

"You don't have to cook," Guus announces, depositing his bags directly on top of the onion Aart's half-way through chopping. "I've ordered catering."

"Catering?" Aart says – not takeout, *catering*.

"I spoke to the Indonesian restaurant down the street. They agreed to close for the night and allow us exclusive use of their premises. They're gonna cook for us."

"But… what… why?"

"Because we have a business meeting," Guus says, staring at Aart in bemusement. "Everyone's invited."

"There'll be drugs and hookers," Nguyen says, clearly stoned, grinning ear-to-ear.

Guus: "Not hookers, Nguyen; hostesses."

Aart: "A business meeting with whom?"

"With investors, Aart," Guus says, as if talking to a child. "Like you said a million times – we need to start delivering on the roadmap."

They're soon sat around a long table at Indonesisch Huis, the old woman & her daughter who run the place running from the kitchen to the table to place platters of satay sticks & bowls of salad, Guus filling glasses with Grey Goose & Chivas Regal, nodding approvingly as Nguyen – seated on Guus' right – explains to the business consortium the benefits FSC can bestow upon them: "…your own private blockchain, transactions completely hidden from any government agency – " – *until the advent of quantum computing,* Nguyen just about stops himself from saying – "–allowing you to keep perfect records of all product, all income, all expenditure, without having to keep any kind of unencrypted ledger recording your transactions."

The hulking Jamaican yardie sitting across the table scoffs: "Why we need a blockchain for this, mon? We run our business fine no blockchain, why we gon' start now?"

"I don't think you're quite understanding the magnitude of what my business associate is proposing," Guus says, one eye on the other end of the table, where Federico & Wesley are flirting heavily with the half-dozen heavily made-up girls in micro-cocktail dresses, they wrapping thick hair around fingers as they laugh at the frat lads' jokes. "This is a revolution for your line of business. Imagine if you could expand and supply every Coffee Shop in Gronigen – nee, in Amsterdam – nee, in the country – with cannabis, and know at all times what is where, and how the supply's doing, what's selling…"

"Data," Nguyen says dramatically.

"…exactly, data. Data is the oil of the new digital economy," Guus says, stealing a line from IOTA. "If you can harness data, it is like the English harnessing the power of the combustion engine for to create the Industrial Revolution; the sun will never set on your cartel's empire."

At that reference to England, Guus winks knowingly at Ciara, seated between Aart & the Jamaican on Guus' left.

Aart shifts uncomfortably in his seat, still trying to make sense of what's going on.

"I will to you be honest," says the greasy-haired Dutchman with a big hooped earring on the Jamaican's left, "but my English is not so good, so do you mind if I continue to you in Dutch?"

Guus gives a slight nod: "Lekker."

(In Dutch): "Our business is not a business that requires data; our products sell themselves. There is always more demand than our supply can possibly meet, be our products powder–" the Dutchman gently pushes a silver tray of neatly-racked white lines across the table towards Guus – "–or flesh;–" - he nods gently in the direction of Feredico & Wesley & the girls at the table's end, while Guus takes the rolled-up 20 Euro note from the tray & snorts a line. "I like you, Guus," the Dutchman continues. "We are very impressed by the rate at which your cryptocurrency has increased in value over the past few weeks and months. But I'm just not sure how it could possibly benefit our business model."

Guus gently pushes the silver tray towards Aart; Aart waves a hand to decline; Ciara reaches in & takes the note & snorts.

"The only two paths open to any business," Guus declares, "are progress and decline. Today, you are successful. You operate the largest cannabis distribution network in the Northern Netherlands. More than half the windows in Groningen's Red Light District are operated by your girls. But to stay still is to make your competitors stronger; in five, ten, twenty years, what will your business look like? Do you think men will still wander the Red Light District? Do you think people will still buy narcotics from street dealers? Nee. The most tech-savvy of our generation have already become accustomed to ordering narcotics over the dark web using cryptocurrency. Imagine the possibilities that this opens to you. Imagine every drug user and whorefucker on this continent with an app on their phones that allows them instant access to a catalogue of all your products. Imagine a decentralised rating system, capable of protecting your girls from abusive clients, and your dealers from any police sting operations. Imagine the transactions that take place on this app being completely obscured from any authority, until you've grown rich enough that it is you and your cartel who fund the continent's main political parties. Until you've grown to a size where you are simply too big to fail. When you've become the kingpins of Europe's biggest drug and prostitution network. When you've become akin to Gods."

The Dutchman & Jamaican lean back in their seats, overwhelmed by the grandeur of Guus' vision for their business. Aart looks at Nguyen, who's grinning stupidly, in awe of Guus' grandiose delivery, then at Ciara, who rubs her nose & stares at the lines, clearly contemplating the social acceptability of snorting another. Aart sips from his water to calm his nerves, now regretting having refused a glass of Chivas Regal.

The Dutchman reaches for his cigarettes & asks Guus in English: "Is it okay if I smoke?"

Guus nods.

Within a moment of the Dutchman lighting his cigarette, the elderly Indonesian proprietor returns from the kitchen pushing a trolley laden with the various bowls & dishes of the meal's main course; upon seeing the smoke emanating from the Dutchman, she begins blabbering worriedly at him in Dutch.

"Please!" Guus shouts. "It's lekker."

"It's nee lekker," she says in broken Dutch, before ranting about the strict smoking prohibition her business operates under, while Guus reaches for his wallet. He peels off three crisp 50 Euro notes, then pauses & adds another, & hands them to the woman, who bows her head & falls silent, returning to the task of placing the plates and bowls upon the table.

He just paid 200 Euros to fucking smoke, Aart thinks, staring at the immensely unsavoury characters seated either side of the table, wondering just how huge a disaster their project can possibly become.

"My country once had a man who dreamed of creating such a grand empire," says the huge heavy-browed Croatian on the Dutchman's right. "He united all Yugoslavia, and for a few decades, all was well. Then he died, and his vision crumbled, and Yugoslavia descended into civil war. These grand visions and ambitions may sound attractive, but they almost always lead to disaster. What we have now is safe and stable and in no danger of falling apart; if we reach too far, we risk losing what we already have."

Guus smiles: "Marshall Tito was indeed a great visionary. I have studied his speeches closely. But Yugoslavia did not fall apart because it was too big; it fell apart because it was too small. Bordered on either side by the monoliths of the USSR and NATO, fitting in fully with neither; such a position is similar to that historically occupied by the Netherlands…"

The others pass the tray around & snort as Guus continues, Aart's head spinning from the ludicrousness of the situation & pomposity of Guus' words & the incredible gaping chasm opening up between their original vision and whatever the fuck FSC is turning into; feeling dizzy, Aart excuses himself from the table, though no-one cares, & heads to the toilet, splashing water on his face & looking long into the mirror. As he stares & asks himself *who am I?,* music booms outside the door: it's Honey Badger, asking why everyone calls him King of the Earth, over a pounding Eurodance beat.

Aart exits the bathroom as Honey Badger gives his answer – *because I'm the King of the fucking Earth, bitch* – and sees Nguyen dancing with two of the whores upon the tabletop, kicking satay-loaded dishes everywhere, while the drug kingpins & Wesley & Federico laugh & clap & glug straight from the bottle, Ciara staring at the carnage, mesmerised, while Guus leans back in his seat at the end of the table, hands clasped in front of him, the king smiling regally at the debauchery of his court.

"Neuken in de keuken!" – the chant echoes through Wesley's mind as his eyes blink into wakefulness the following morning. "Neuken in de keuken! Neuken in de keuken!" – as he & who else? – *Federico? Nguyen?* – bent – *who? The hostesses? The Indonesian girl? Ciara?* – over surfaces in Indoensisch Huis' kitchen, rutting like coke-crazed animals. Bleary-eyed & dry-mouthed, desperately craving water, the night a distorted kaleidoscope of fucked-up imagery, some primeval descent into he-knows-not-what… & Wesley looks up, sees the wallpaper of big-boobed blonde models & hears the endlessly-playing Honey Badger track that tells him he passed out at some point on the bathroom floor, back at the frat house… & he moves his eyes down slightly, & sees Aart standing over him.

"We need to stop this."

"Ja," Wesley says, sitting up, utterly frazzled.

"This has gone too far. Guus has completely lost it."

"Ja," Wesley says, rubbing his temples, brain half-destroyed.

"Lost what?" Guus says, emerging from Ciara's bedroom.

Aart stares at Guus; in complete contrast to Wesley, he appears fully sober, utterly in command of himself.

"This… madness," Aart says, struggling to find words for the chaos & debauchery FSC has become. "Those guys you were meeting with are dangerous."

Guus laughs: "They are small little fishes in the ocean. I am the man with the billion-dollar yacht, casting a net into the sea and scooping them up to bring back to shore."

Aart: "We've already made tens of millions… we've already so much to do… and now you're making promises to pimps and drug dealers…"

"To stand still is to die, Aart. Cryptocurrency is a grand zero-sum game of pan-continental warfare. Those who adapt and grow will survive and prosper; those who shrink to protect what they have will wither and die."

The next conference is in Frankfurt, the grand open space of Kap Europa hosting powerbrokers from Germany's largest financial institutions – Commerzbank, Deutsche Bank, UniCredit Bank AG, &etc. – & a few dozen leading crypto teams & expert speakers. A long day begins with a series of roundtable discussions with titles like 'What is blockchain?' and 'What does blockchain mean for banking?', Guus yawning through the dry detail of the sessions, Nguyen doing the heavy-lifting in explaining the mechanics of the blockchain to serious German finance workers.

At a gap between discussions, Guus approaches a beautiful brunette from Commerzbank: "You know, the technology is great and everything, but I don't think that discussion got across the magic Future Synergy Coin is performing."

"Really?" the Commerzbank brunette says, cold & cynical. "And what magic is that?"

Guus boasts of the skyrocketing price, now at $0.0000125, giving FSC a $125 million market cap. The Commerzbank brunette frowns & doesn't even pretend to feign interest, leaving Guus a moment later, all her worst suspicions about nouveau-riche crypto geeks having been confirmed.

Guus downs two cups of free coffee & heads to the bathroom, Aart frowning in his direction while trying to explain to a stern balding Deutsche Bank fund manager just how important & revolutionary FSC's original roadmap as a decentralised storage solution for official documents is, while Nguyen keeps interrupting & talking over him with all the ill-defined mission creep he & Guus have added to the roadmap over the past few weeks: "…and we're gonna be, like, a decentralised social network, Facebook 2.0, and a platform for dApps, blockchain 3.5, and the Dutch Ethereum, and the Netherlandisch NEO, and we'll offer a privacy platform that boasts 10 times the anonymity of Monero, with rewards of FSC Junior for anyone who holds the coin longer than our designated minimum staking period, and we'll provide a better payments solution for established financial firms than Ripple or Stellar, and…"

The Deutsche Bank fund manager nods until there's a gap in Nguyen's rant & excuses himself.

"These fucking dinosaurs," Nguyen snarls. "They know projects like ours are gonna destroy their whole fucking industry. They're terrified. You can smell the fear in their eyes…"

Aart nods a few times, quickly tiring of Nguyen's coke-comedown twitchy cynicism. He watches Guus exit the bathroom & approach two women in sober suits & gesticulate wildly while talking to them, until the women make an excuse & walk away from him, & Guus repeats the same futile routine with the next woman he reaches.

The speeches that follow are detail-heavy & finance-focussed, Guus missing the first as he snorts his way through an entire gram of cocaine while vigorously & seemingly-endlessly pounding his cock while staring into a mirror in the disabled toilets, finally splooshing white gunk over a sink already caked with white-powder residue. Guus cleans himself in the sink & returns to the conference, somewhat calmed.

"Banking is a dying industry," Guus boldly begins a half-hour later, only five minutes' late for his allotted speech. "The days of extortionate fees and tacked-on costs and surcharges are at an end. Every one of you gathered here today is like the band on the Titanic, gamely doing your designated duties while water rises around your ankles. What the speakers from every other cryptocurrency are offering you here today is access to a lifeboat. But as you all clamber from the icy ocean swallowing the banking industry, clawing at the lifeboat's sides, these cryptocurrencies will all capsize and sink to zero. I am not here to offer you a lifeboat. I am here to offer you the gills and temperature-tolerance needed to dive deep into the icy ocean and discover the bountiful treasure hidden in its depths."

As Guus speaks, throwing out wild coke-fuelled gestures & insane proclamations, he feels he's shaken his audience to the core; when he leaves the stage to stony silence, he takes it as confirmation of how completely his world-conquering vision has affected them. When he retreats to his opulent hotel room alone that night, he takes it as a sign the women of the German finance industry are too overawed to spend long in his presence; angels terrified of singeing their wings against the immense heat generated by the Sun.

The price of FSC falls to eight-point-two-thousandths of a cent as word of Guus' overwrought conference performance spreads online, causing Aart to warn it's a sign of their overreach resulting in inevitable collapse; but Aart's silenced as Guus bamboozles a small used car dealership in Zwolle into a vague promise to consider implementing some form of blockchain into their account keeping, which Nguyen hypes on FSC's Twitter as a full partnership with a major automotive industry player, prompting a spike to $0.0000137.

The next conference is in Dubai. Guus spends the 6 & ½ hr flight flicking through The Old Testament in the comfort of his private first class suite, underlining passages where God is particularly grandiose or dramatic, like Chronicles 21:14-15: "Behold, with a great plague will the LORD smite thy people, and thy children, and thy wives, and all thy goods: And thou shalt have great sickness of the bowels, until thy bowels fall out by reason of the sickness day by day," all the while drinking endless red wine & consuming lavish platters of gourmet cuisine, & when they land Guus feels his own bowels are liable to fall out by reason of overstuffing them.

They're greeted in the sleek Arrivals hall by a troupe of white-robed men clutching a sign reading "FUTURE SYNERGY COIN". The white-robed men take Guus, Aart & Nguyen's bags & lead them through the air-conditioned airport to the baking heat & blazing sun outside, where a fleet of shimmering chrome Rolls Royces await.

"Mind if I smoke?" Guus asks the chauffeur.

Aart stares out a closed window at the hulking skyscrapers straddling the sun-kissed boulevard as the Rolls Royce rolls through the desert city, irritated by the smoke wafting around him in the air-conditioned car, but able to distract himself with the strange city outside the window, until the smoke becomes thicker & denser, & Aart turns to see Nguyen puffing on a fat cigar.

The Rolls Royce sweeps along a private highway leading directly from the wide boulevards of downtown Dubai across a golden-sand beach and glistening oceanfront, their hotel overpowering the horizon ahead: the iconic sail-shaped Burj Al Arab Jumeirah.

Aart smiles at first, recognising the place from TV or the Internet or somewhere, excited to be staying there; but then a thought strikes him: "How much did this place cost?"

"Relax," Guus says, lighting another cigarette off the end of his last one, "I got us a shared room to cut down on costs."

They're ushered through a grand gold-plated lobby, with swirling red & yellow weaved through its carpets & brilliant ocean-blue walls all around them, a gigantic staircase rising up at its center; to the elevator, & the 50th floor; & as the doors open, Guus hands the bellhop €100 & apologises for not having withdrawn any of the local currency yet.

The trio are led by red-velvet-suited butlers into a sprawling suite lined with deep royal reds & dotted with black & gold flourishes, all the furniture seemingly antique, windows looking out across the desert city's skyscrapers & over the endless immensity of the shimmering ocean far beneath them.

"Holy shit…" Aart mutters, as Nguyen flops upon the 3-wall-hugging sprawl of sofa at the room's edge, & Guus directs butlers to begin preparing cocktails & hors d'oeuvres, they nodding meekly & promising it won't be a problem when Nguyen declares he wants to eat authentic Vietnamese pho & bun cha.

Aart explores the suite, moving through a cinema room with a giant projector screen & a dozen sizable armchairs in front of it, then back to the main room, & up a central staircase, onto a landing, into a huge study with a giant bookcase & hundreds of foreign language newspapers & the largest globe he's ever seen; Aart pauses at the globe, using both hands to rotate it, gazing at the distance they've travelled, to Dubai from Amsterdam; & he moves through a master bedroom, with four-poster bed, drapes hanging over it; & another room, no less spectacular, with a similarly grandiose four-poster bed in its center; & into a marble-carved bathroom containing a huge hot tub with room for six or seven people, with two completely separate shower & toilet rooms, everything overwrought with opulence & grandiosity fit for a pre-revolution French king.

"How much did this place cost?" Aart asks, heading back downstairs to the suite's main room.

"Care for a Bon Fire?" Guus says, he & Nguyen sipping bright orange cocktails as they recline upon the room's enormous wraparound wall-hugging sofas – a 7-star remake of the frat house's quad-sofa.

"Guus. How much."

Guus sighs. "Ten thousand dollars per night."

"Ten thousand fucking dollars per night?!" Aart flips. "And you booked it for what, three nights?"

"Four."

"Four! So forty thousand dollars?! Why the fuck have you booked the place for four nights?!"

Guus rolls his eyes, leans forward, drains his cocktail, & waves the empty glass at a velvet-suited butler, who rushes across the room to take it from him: "This conference is a fantastic networking opportunity. I thought that it would be prudent to stay another day after the conference ends and try to set up a few deals with major Arab investors."

"Arabs are rich as fuck," Nguyen says, seemingly already drunk from the bright orange cocktail. "They got that oil money."

"That's right, Nguyen," Guus says. "Now, Aart, won't you settle down and have a Bon Fire?"

"A Bon Fire…" Aart mutters, taking a seat at the edge of the hulking sofa; Nguyen is fully reclined on the opposite side, holding his cocktail glass over his stomach as he lies on his back, while Guus sits in the dead center of the wraparound sofa, feet resting on an ornate wooden-legged pouffe, looking every inch the master of global economics in his crisp tie-less Gucci suit.

"The Bon Fire is the signature cocktail of the Burj Al Arab Jumeirah," Guus says. "It is prepared with blazed Havana Maximo aged Cuban rum, to which is added the essence of smoke and aromatic bitters. The fragrance of this potent-but-refined blend is further enhanced with the addition of freshly-picked kaffir lime leaves and authentic orange zest. The delectable final product's understated sweetness is underscored with the addition of select dried fruits and highest-quality brown sugar. The Bon Fire is typically served in the Burj Al Arab Jumeirah's Sky Bar – which I would suggest we visit at some point, given the legendary views it offers across Dubai's distinctive skyline – but as residents of the Burj Al Arab Jumeirah, we have at our beck and call an entire fleet of butlers, who are only too pleased to deliver this potent and refined cocktail directly to our rooms."

Aart hasn't paid much attention to Guus's info-dump, instead watching with disbelief the immense stillness of the two butlers standing with hands behind their backs in the room's kitchen area.

Ten thousand dollars per night, Aart thinks. For four nights. *Plus the first-class flights*… "The cocktails are complimentary, right?"

"Guests of the Burj Al Arab Jumeirah's suites enjoy a range of complimentary cocktails and other drinks and foodstuffs," Guus drones on in a gratingly-fake British accent, all Dutch inflection completely eliminated from his speech, "but the Bon Fire is regarded as a delicacy of supreme rarity and highest quality, and as such there is a surcharge for guests wishing to purchase it; however, as residents of the Royal Suite, we are entitled to a fifteen-percent discount on all purchases from the Burj Al Arab Jumeirah's bars and restaurants."

"How much does the fucking cocktail cost, Guus?"

"Normally, it would be a little over three-and-a-half thousand dirhams," Guus says, "but with our discount, it's closer to three thousand."

"How much is that in a currency I can understand?"

"Aart, part of operating a major financial concern with international aspirations is keeping abreast of exchange rate movements and fluctuations in the global marketplace," Guus explains, as a butler enters with a trolley laden with silver-sheathed platters of food, another butler behind him carrying Guus's cocktail on a silver tray.

"Would sirs like to dine here or in the dining room?" a butler asks, approaching the sofas.

Nguyen groans theatrically before sitting up & draining the last of his cocktail: "Fuck it, let's see the dining room. And bring me another Bon Fire."

"Very good, sir."

"Let's eat," Guus says, belly still bloated from the mass he ate and drank on the plane.

"How much are the cocktails, Guus?" Aart asks again, as Guus accepts the butler's offer of carrying his freshly-made Bon Fire through to the dining room.

"Oh, could you please bring another for my friend here?" Guus tells the butler. "You really must try one, Aart. They simply are divine."

"How much is three thousand fucking dirhams, Guus?" Aart says.

Guus sighs theatrically. "I cannot tell you exactly, Aart. These exchange rates are forever changing. But last I checked, it would be somewhere in the region of a thousand US dollars."

A thousand US dollars. Aart starts to calculate how many Guus & Nguyen have already drunk, but is quickly overcome by the realisation of a four-night stay ahead of them, & endless cocktails to follow; his head spins as the calculation of costs overwhelms him, bringing forth the burning sensation of nausea in his stomach.

"We stand on the precipice of an epoch," Guus declares to a thousands-strong audience in the blue-hued black of the Dubai World Trade Center's Sheik Saeed Theatre. "All that hitherto now hath been known shall be cast aside, dashed upon the rocks by the rising tides of tech and progress. Industries shall be devoured by Artificial Intelligence; economies shall crumble before cryptocurrency; the world and all within it shall be the domain of the blockchain. This grandiose desert-mirage of a city is a miracle of an era that is almost at an end: an age of oil bounties, of international trade and commerce; a world in which gadgets are designed in California, manufactured in Chengdu, and sold here in Dubai; where all the world's economies are interlocked in a delicately weaved web of mutual interdependence. The new epoch shall replace internationalism with true unbridled globalism; a fully decentralised global economy with independent-yet-connected nodes in every city and state upon this planet. He who hath grasped the blockchain shall be unto this new world a master. He who hath grasped not the blockchain shall be but an ant, crushed underfoot in the stampede and panic that follows." Guus's speech is sprawling, mesmerising, but utterly unfocused; when it ends, no-one feels they've understood it, but all have the impression that Guus is a savant with bold, visionary, world-changing ideas, akin to Darwin or Copernicus, & that he'll only be fully understood once the revolution he prophesises has come to pass.

Guus leaves the stage to rapturous applause, & his speech upstages most of those who come before & after; but when Da Hongfei of NEO takes the stage to deliver the keynote speech, Guus's mouth grows dry & palms sweaty as he watches & listens, just as they had done when he'd stammered through that awful first conference speech back in Amsterdam; while Da Hongfei talks of NEO's integrated & regulatory-compliant platform for the future smart economy, and the many dApps that have already been deployed utilising the NEO NEP-5 framework, & the Chinese government institutions already getting on-board with interconnected projects like THE KEY & Ontology, Guus feels dizzy & weak, realising for the first time that what Aart's been saying for weeks – maybe months now – is true; they need to turn their grand words into concrete action.

"You were right, Aart," Guus says, grabbing Aart's arm, light-headed & unsteady, "we need action. Action."

Guus carries on mumbling to himself, feverish, delirious, like a man possessed of some half-divine & half-wicked spirit.

"You okay, man?" Aart says, Guus' pallor frightening him. "You need some water?"

"Yo, Guus, Da Hongfei's speech is over," Nguyen says, strolling toward them at the side of the stage. "Let's get some bitches."

Guus staggers away from them both, mumbling to himself, in search of a bathroom.

"He's looking fucked up," Aart says. "Maybe he should go back to the hotel and rest."

"Guus gets like this when he's not had coke in a while," Nguyen says. "I tried asking a waiter for some but he said you can get in serious shit for even mentioning it here. This country's drier than a camel's asshole."

Nguyen spots two alluringly eye-shadowed women in hijabs standing further into the backstage area, & he walks away from Aart to try his luck with them.

Guus stares at his pallid reflection in the lavish bathroom's mirror, water running down his face, right eye twitching involuntarily. *Be the water-bearer,* a voice within Guus's mind says. *Be He who washes away the sins & wickedness of late-stage capitalism. Be He who ushers in the purity of the Age of Blockchain. Be He who all the world fears & adores – the Alpha & Omega – the Genesis & Revelation…* the voice falls silent as the bathroom door opens & a white-robed Arab enters.

Guus chain-smokes in an asthmatic-nightmare of a hazed ante-room, each dose of nicotine further energising the voices competing for attention within his mind, until he's out of cigarettes, & all voices hath coalesced into one, & he leaves the smoking room & begins a flurry of mingling, talking with representatives of Arab oil consortiums & Emirati government initiatives & power players from Western Fortune 500 companies, dazzling all with his slickness of speech & the limitless potential of the FSC dApps platform & integrated world-changing vision of a blockchain for all Internet-of-Things connected devices & industries & supply chains within the fully global & decentralised smart economy, & as he leaves each with a promise to be in touch very soon about the possibility of collaboration & partnership, Guus moves from conversation to conversation with just one though repeating in his mind: *I'm King of the Earth, bitch.*

That night, Aart sits alone in the suite's lavish study, pouring out glass after glass of cognac as he stares out the window at the impossibly-tall skyscraper lights illuminating the alien darkened desert landscape & taps out messages to Ciara: *I don't know what to do… Guus is having a mental breakdown… Nguyen's turned into a complete asshole… and this trip must've cost us almost $100,000…*

& Ciara says: *But the price is still going up… last time I checked, ur at $150 mil market cap…*

& Aart replies: *but it cant last 4eva, tho… the price is unsustainable… & guus is making all these promiszes…*

Guus & Nguyen's night is a wild blur of bars & clubs & booze & bitches, chauffeured chariots ferrying them between the Islamic-law desert's drink-den oases, running wild in strobe-lit places with names like Sanctuary & Sensation & Catwalk & Boudoir & Alpha, throwing down cash, throwing back drinks, throwing themselves @ women, women throwing themselves @ them, moving, moving, dancefloor, to street, to car, to bar, to dancefloor, to seat, to street, to car, Guus laughing, always grabbing, clutching, pulling closer, meek warnings of "remember where you are," Guus scarcely remembering who he is, & when that thought takes hold, he's standing on a bar, screaming a hellfire-throated freestyle that skids & crashes over a deep house beat: "I am the fucking God of Blockchain / know my name / drink my champagne / and bask in the fantasticness of my accomplishments"; applause is polite, girls smiling, seeing how fucking rich he is, the way he throws down wads & discards bottles, while Nguyen is lost, dancing with two blonde Russians who work for some oil- or energy- or something-company in a club beneath a hotel, while Guus' bizarre performance plays out across Dubai's hottest nightspots, anyone who's anyone of a UAE Saturday night celebration bearing witness, until night is lost to morning, & the driver says to each place Guus rattles off his phone (no care given to overseas data charges) that it's closed already, & finally he's driven to one of the last remaining outposts of night-time entertainment, another club buried beneath a hotel, in a district some distance from the central mirage of the desert city's main street, & Guus enters, & the black girls flock to him, & in one continual blur he's leaving with them, he-knows-not-how-long later, sky weak blue now, commandeering two cabs to take he & his harem back to the Burj Al Arab Jumeirah.

Aart wakes up slumped across the table in the study with a burning desire to piss & an uncertainty over whether he's already emptied his bladder where he sits, followed by an immense wave of confusion at the unfamiliar surroundings, followed by the groaning despair of headache as his eyes find the near-drained cognac bottle on the table next to him, half a glass still remaining in front of it. He stumbles out of the chair & across the room & into the hallway, bumbling through the Royal Suite in search of a bathroom, happening upon a door, throwing it open, seeing Nguyen on the bed rutting a loud-groaning Russian woman, while another lies at his side playing with herself, looking at Aart first with shock & then a smile as the door opens; Aart slams the door shut, & staggers back away from it; finds a staircase, grips the banister, but still almost slips as he descends; & enters the main entrance hall, just as the grand gold-lined door at its center creaks open, the laughing sound of Guus & six African girls growing louder, until Guus is stepping into the hallway, girls behind him, Aart stumbling down the stairs, scarcely able to hold himself upright.

"Aart, you're awake," Guus says, smiling. "Care to join us in the room adjacent for a night cap?"

"These cocktails cost more than a thousand US dollars each," Guus is telling one of the girls, near the center of the giant wraparound wall-hugging sofa, falling into a ludicrous half-British half-French accent as he rattles off the earlier-memorised screed about the Bon Fires that each of the six girls & Guus & Aart are holding one each of, Aart too smashed to bother calculating that each round is now costing them $8,000 US. "It's prepared with Havanius Maxima aged rum and the finest fresh-plucked zaffir leaves and – Tiffany, would you mind removing your dress?"

"Who the fuck's Tiffany?" asks the girl Guus has turned to on his right.

"Yah, that's me," says a girl a few seats away who's been waiting for her chance. She stands up & moves into the center of the room, slow-grinding to the Beethoven Sonata booming through it.

The first-asked girl on the sofa beside Guus stares at the eager exhibitionist with disgust. She stands up: "You not got something with a bit more life in it than this old music?"

"Zaire, would you mind helping Tiffany with her dress?" Guus asks the girl on his left, ignoring the other girls request re: the music.

The girl on Guus' left dutifully gets up & joins the other in the room's center, awkwardly balancing on her high heels to roll the dress down below her waist.

"Garçon," Guus calls to one of the blushing butlers standing guard at the edge of the room. "May we have another round of Bon Fires, post-haste?"

The red-suited butler bows his head & retreats from the room.

"Say, Aart, mon amie, are you not finding this music a little pondiferous?"

Aart says nothing, eyes lolling about in his head as he tries to focus on the massive exposed breasts bouncing around in the middle of the room.

"Say, Melanie, would you do something about this dreadful music? Get some of that lively African stuff we were jiving to in the club on."

Aart's mind is a mess of wh- questions – *where… who… what… why…* – as he awakens face-down upon the carpet of the living room in a pool of vomit. He blinks several times before noticing the congealed mess upon the carpet, then recoils from it & springs to a seated position in a panic, unsure of whether the puke is his own. He then sits & stares at a room that feels wrong somehow for what must be several minutes until he realises; the wraparound sofa has been completely shredded open, its white insides covering almost every inch of wall & carpet. As the sheer confusion of the scene gives way to a realisation of its cost, he screams: "GUUS!!!"

"What the fuck happened here?" Nguyen says, padding into the room in an embroidered hotel-issue dressing gown & slippers sometime later, with Aart spending the intervening period trying to calculate the cost, hyperventilating as he begins to realise the enormity of it:

"I… don't…"

Aart can't finish the sentence, can't think straight, his mind tumbling back through the flashes of shapeless insanity that remain as the previous night's only residue; the only concrete fact among the confusion & new faces being the endless stream of thousand-dollar cocktails that left him face-down, puking on the floor.

"That fucking bitch Tiffany," Guus says, strolling into the room & lighting a cigarette.

"Can we smoke in here?" Nguyen says, fiddling with his dressing gown in vain search of a pack.

"We can do whatever the fuck we want in here," Guus says, throwing the cigarettes across the room; Nguyen catches them. "I've just been settling our bill. It turns out that your little indiscretion has cost us a little shy of eight-hundred-and-fifty thousand dollars."

Aart, still sitting on a carpet strewn with sofa guts, stares at Guus for a moment, then at Nguyen, then returns his eyes to Guus & realises who the comment was directed at: "Me?"

Guus takes a languid drag upon his cigarette & surveys the room's carnage: "At least we managed to subdue her before she finished smashing the kitchen up."

"My indiscretion?" Aart says, standing up.

"Yes, Aart. It's all your fault this bloody mess happened. We were having a lovely time – you seemingly more than most – and then you had to ruin it."

"Guus – what?! What the… You! Did! Everything! This! The girls! The cocktails! It was you! It was…"

"Yes, yes, Aart; I brought six charming young ladies home, provided them with cocktails, one of them took a fancy to you, you whipped your old boy out, one thing led to another, then as she was introducing the tip of said old boy to the inner recesses of her throat, you decided it'd be appropriate to vomit a few thousand dollars' worth of Bon Fire all over the poor girl's head."

"I… what?!"

"Jesus fuck, dude," Nguyen says, shaking his head in disgust.

"WHAT?!"

"Calm down, Aart. It's all taken care of. I told the staff we were good for the money, and I paid the girls to get out of here without making too much of a fuss. But all told, this has been quite the expensive sojourn."

"Would you stop talking like a fucking Harry Potter character!"

Guus sighs as Aart seethes, eyes ablaze with rage; Guus calmly takes a drag from his cigarette & steps back towards the door: "When you've calmed down, Aart, perhaps we could talk about this like adults in the anteroom? Come on, Nguyen; I'd like to go over a few of the business proposals we received on the back of our conference speech."

"Dope."

Nguyen follows Guus out of the room, leaving Aart alone in the debris-strewn site of the previous night's debauched meltdown, Guus' admonishments ringing through his dehydrated brain: *your fault… your fault… your fault…*

The cold of Dutch winter's contrasts with Dubai desert heat the second the plane hits the tarmac at Schiphol, rain lashing the terminal's windows as Aart shuffles miserably through the endless identikit airport bowels to the sphincter of Customs, doing all he can to stare straight ahead & make no pretence of avoiding contact with those cloying shits, Guus & Nguyen. Passport down, eyes in the scanner, & he's into the Baggage Claim area, but as he wills the carousel creaking round empty to hurry up & return his luggage to him, considering abandoning it altogether for the sake of getting away from them, Guus & Nguyen appear, flanked by a nerdy couple in matching Ethereum T-shirts, talking about FSC's unstoppable rise & the future of the blockchain.

"Hey, maybe we should go with these guys into Amsterdam?" Guus says, catching up with Aart as he trundles his suitcase through the cavernous commerce-lined halls of the airport toward its train station.

"Why?"

"I dunno, it might be fun," Guus says, grinning in the direction of Nguyen & the nerdy couple, the glasses-wearing girl twirling thick black hair around her finger as she speaks with Nguyen, who's leaning on the handle of his suitcase, clearly trying to give the impression of being larger than his especially-diminutive-for-the-Netherlands 166cm height. "Decompress from Dubai. Smoke a little weed. What do you think?"

"I think I should get back to Groningen."

Guus shrugs & loudly shouts something at the couple, Aart turning away from them, heading straight to the platform & on to a train, falling asleep almost the moment he leans his head back against the seat.

"Ticket?"

Aart's eyes open to an inspector hovering over him, ticket-checking device in hand.

Aart blinks & pats his pockets, then a realisation hits him: he didn't buy one.

The ticket collector – a stern man of 40-something in a padded jacket bearing the orange logo of the Dutch national rail service – sighs & explains rules & regulations, asks Aart where he's going, & issues a €120 fine.

Sleet is hammering all in Groningen, Aart standing glumly at a bus stop, wondering if he shouldn't just spring for a taxi, eventually yielding to the impulse; the endless expense, spiralling costs, uncontrollability of Guus & Nguyen, the slow-death of all FSC was supposed to achieve & stand for, all gnawing at his sleet-soaked consciousness.

"How was the conference?" Wesley asks.

Aart says nothing, but retires to his room in a depressive funk, one that hangs over him for the next few days, as sleet turns to snow, ice turning the city's streets into a maze of unseen dangers, Guus not returning from Amsterdam until the following weekend.

"Did you see this?" Aart asks Guus soon after his return.

He hands Guus his phone, showing hin an article entitled *'Why FSC is all hype & no product.'*

Guus barely scans the article before smirking & handing the phone back: "It's some idiot spreading FUD. He probably invested heavily in another coin."

"The price is tanking already," Aart says, tapping at his phone to bring up CoinMarketCap. "We're at $68 million market cap and still falling."

"So what? We rose to more than double that in a matter of weeks. This is just a healthy correction. This is good for Future Synergy Coin. We need to consolidate the price and establish a base support price if we want to see real sustainable growth."

The price continues falling through the week that follows, Aart scarcely seeing Guus to discuss their response. Aart's fallen behind on university work, consigning him to long nights in the library attempting to catch up on missed lectures & assignments.

"This is all going to end horribly," Aart tells Ciara in the library one night, when she's working alongside him on an essay. "Our market cap's fallen from over one hundred million to less than fifty in the last three days."

"That's insane!" Ciara says, horrified, but beginning to understand cryptocurrency fundamentals.

"And Guus and Nguyen don't give a shit about it. This whole thing's headed straight to zero. I'm thinking I should cash my coins out before it all collapses."

"You can do that?"

"Yeah." Aart explains to Ciara how his share of FSC tokens are all stored in his private wallet, with a private key allowing only him access, & how movement from a founder's wallet might crash the price completely, but there's nothing inherently illegal in doing it.

"You should do it, Aart."

& Aart can barely concentrate on writing his university report, thinking that with each word he types the price of FSC is dropping further; every wasted moment bringing him closer to crashing from being worth millions to being worth nothing at all. Finally, an hour later, as Ciara disappears to use the bathroom, the impulse overcomes him; he opens his wallet on his phone, stares at his 833.33 billion personal stash of coins, then opens CoinMarketCap to check his stash's dollar value, & sees what he can only describe as an early Christmas miracle: the market cap is suddenly at $202,406,183 & rising. He stares in disbelief at his phone as Ciara returns, tells her what's happened, tells her he doesn't know why, googles 'Future Synergy Coin' & finds dozens of crypto news sites all reporting the same story: 'FUSION SYNERGY COIN ANNOUNCES AMAZON PARTNERSHIP: PRICE SKYROCKETS MORE THAN 4000% IN 2 HOURS.'

"What the fuck…" Aart staggers from the table, saying nothing to Ciara, moving to the library's stairwell, calling Guus as he walks; Guus doesn't answer. He calls again; nothing. He calls Nguyen:

"Yo, dawg, waddup?"

"Nguyen – what the fuck?! You signed a partnership with Amazon?!"

Nguyen laughs: "Yeah, right."

"But… how?! Amazon! The world's biggest online retailer… partnership… how the fuck did that happen?!"

"It's easy, man. I just signed us up for an account."

"An Amazon… account? Like… for buying things through Amazon? For buying books and shit?"

Nguyen laughs again: "Nah, bro. Not, like, books and shit. Amazon Web Services. It's a business-to-business cloud hosting solution."

"But… you just signed up for an account?"

"Uh-huh."

"Like… you paid them to set up an account?"

"Yeah. Relax, dude. It wasn't even that expensive. It'll be, like, less than a hundred bucks a month, US."

"But… the Internet's saying we've gone into partnership with Amazon…"

Nguyen laughs: "Right."

"…why?"

"I mean, we have… kind of." Nguyen hears a doorbell ring behind him. "Oh, shoot, the girls're here. I'll speak to you later. Peace out, homie."

Those fucking idiots, Aart thinks, returning to the library. But as he moves through the hush of studying students & returns to Ciara, he thinks *maybe I'm the idiot* – maybe it really is that easy. Maybe ordering a Domino's pizza is the equivalent of entering into a partnership with a household-name global food distribution company. Maybe taking out an iPhone contract is essentially entering into an exclusive deal to have Apple provide all of your telecommunication infrastructure. Maybe Guus was right all along – maybe all that matters is hype.

Aart barely notices Christmas creep closer, his mind ricocheting between approaching end-of-term assignment deadlines & the implausibly ever-rising value of FSC. He submits the last of his assignments & rides his bicycle back from the library through the icy chill of Groningen's snow-piled wind-struck streets to find Wesley, Federico, Jako, Wander, & Max stapling tinsel to the walls & carefully arranging bottles of booze & platters of finger food around the frat's central living space.

"What's going on?" Aart asks.

"It's the Christmas party," Wesley says, taking a pizza from the oven. "What, you forgot about it?"

"You guys' heads is obsessed with these cryptocurrencies," Federico says, brushing past Aart to extend a line of tinsel across the room.

"Merry Christmas!" a strange figure declares, entering through the front door, wearing the finery of a royal court jester, his face painted with the deep black & reddened lips of a minstrel.

"What the fuck…" Federico says, almost falling off the stool he's stood on to staple tinsel in astonishment.

"I'm Zwarte Piet," Guus-the-minstrel says, strolling through the room & grabbing a Hertog Jan bottle.

"Guus, you're the head of an enterprise worth almost quarter-of-a-billion dollars," Aart says, colour draining from his face & leaving him as white as Guus is black. "You cannot run around in black face!"

"Why not?"

Aart starts listing every reason 'why not' he can think of: the controversy that would ensue were pictures to leak online, the thousands of irate blog posts & boycotts of their token such a thing might inspire.

"Nonsense," Guus says, smiling with recently-treated bright-white teeth & snapping a selfie.

As Wesley, Jako, Wander, & Max speak over each other, defending Guus's decision to black up as an essential part of Dutch Christmas tradition, Aart takes his phone out to check Instagram & sees with horror that Guus's bright white smile & black-caked face is top of his Instagram feed.

"Guus! Delete it!"

"Aart, most of the people who invest in cryptocurrency are libertarians," Guus says, sitting on a stool at the kitchen island. "There is nothing in this world that they hate more than Internet Outrage Culture and the Cultural Marxism of the left-wing liberal Social Justice Warriors who try to police all thought and culture under the banner of 'political correctness.'" Guus continues, explaining at length why it's a form of cultural genocide to eradicate much-loved European traditions like the Dutch practise of blacking up at Christmas while the others try to explain to Federico what relevance Zwarte Piet has to Christmas & why it's definitely not racist.

"Zwarte Piet takes naughty children away with him in a sack to Africa!" Aart shouts, giving up on Guus to argue with the others.

"He takes them to Spain, not Africa," Wesley corrects him.

"And he's literally Santa's slave!" Aart continues. "Santa's African slave who makes toys for all the white European children!"

"How is that any worse than Santa using elves as toy-making slaves?" Jako argues.

"Because elves aren't fucking real! And Europeans didn't spend hundreds of years raiding the coast of fucking elf land to ship elf slaves to their fucking colonies!"

"But elves are just as offensive to short people as Zwarte Piet is to black people," Wander says.

"And I believe J.R.R. Tolkien intended his elves in Lord of the Rings to be based on the stereotype of cunning Far-East Asians," Guus says. "But you still see Hollywood movies being made based on that gross racial stereotype. The hurt feelings of social justice snowflakes and other virtue-signallers should not be the basis for throwing away a centuries-old Dutch tradition."

Ciara enters the room & greets Guus's blacked-up visage with a heartfelt "WHAT THE FUCK?!"; the others speak over each other in a flurry of condemnation & defence of Guus's attire, only stopping when Nguyen appears in the doorway behind Ciara, wearing the exact same minstrel costume & deep-black facepaint.

"Nguyen!" Zwarte Guus exclaims, leaping to his feet to embrace him. "You blacked up!"

Aart spends the next couple of hours sitting on the quad-sofa solemnly sipping Hertog Jan as the party blossoms & swells all around him, the frat house filling with dozens upon dozens of half-recognised students & previously-unseen faces, Guus stumbling around & spouting loud-voiced madness, the white rings around his black nostrils & white dust upon his black chin growing thicker as his loud-voiced madness grows ever louder, until he emerges from the hallway & begins shouting for attention, smashing plates of food & bottles of alcohol to the floor in a final successful attempt to hush the party.

"What the fuck!" Federico shouts, as Guus clambers onto the half-cleared kitchen island.

Aart tightens his grip around his Hertog Jaan bottle, cherishing the thought of cracking it across Guus's head.

"Frat brothers, students, countrymen!" Guus rambles. "This is but the prelude to the Christmas party to end all Christmas parties! The largest celebration of Jesus's birthday since our Almighty Lord arose on Easter Sunday, two-thousands years prior ago. Outside, a fleet of carriages awaits to abscond us to the venue of the real party…" & he continues rambling loudly, jumping back off the kitchen island & placing an arm around an unsteady Nguyen's shoulders, then leading the horde out through the hallway.

"Are you going?" Ciara asks Aart, the room rapidly emptying around them.

Aart sighs & stands & follows her out of the frat house, to the ridiculous sight of a dozen reindeer-drawn sleighs on the street outside. The assembled party-goers laugh & cheer & congratulate Guus on this epic twist in the night, as Aart stands in the doorway, glaring out at his black-faced business partner.

"Ladies and gentleman," Guus yells, drawing the startled attention of passers-by on the street & smokers outside the many nearby pubs. "We are heading to the seaport, 35 kilometers due north-west, where the grandest seafaring vessel you have ever seen awaits the continuation of our celebration! I have purchased for your enjoyment a multi-million dollar superyacht, upon which platters of sushi will be served upon the naked bodies of a hundred A-class models! The original dream and vision of Pussy Sushi Coin tonight collides with the incredible success that Future Synergy Coin has become! And, whatismore, entertainment on-board this grandest of vessels will tonight be provided by none other than the original King of the Earth himself – ladies and gentleman, I have hired for our party tonight none other than Mr. Honey Badger!"

A huge commotion of cheering & football-chanting erupts as the revellers clamber into the reindeer-drawn sleighs.

"Aart, are you going?" Ciara asks.

"No." Aart doesn't even bother to calculate the multi-million dollar cost of a superyacht & reindeer-drawn sleighs & Honey Badger's performance fee; whatever it costs, it's clear whatever was left of FSC's development budget has been wasted on Guus's coke-fuelled blacked-up insanity.

Aart walks away from the door & Ciara follows him back into the mess of the frat house, its floor carpeted with spilled food & broken glass. Aart opens the door to his bedroom & Ciara follows him inside. He opens his drawer & takes out the scrap of paper on which he scribbled the private key for the wallet storing all his Future Synergy Coins.

"I'm withdrawing everything," Aart says, his mood as dark as Guus & Nguyen's make-up. "And then I'm leaving here." He turns & stares into Ciara's deep green eyes. "Come with me."

"Aart," she says, tenderly grasping his wrist.

He drops the paper to the floor & leans in to kiss her; their tongues lap in & out of each other's mouths as the clattering of reindeer hooves & cheers of drunken revellers echo through the streets outside. They're on the bed as the sound dies away, frantically removing each other's clothes, hands exploring each other's bodies with desperate passion.

Ciara wakes in the morning to see Aart sitting in bed beside her, staring at his phone & a YouTube video of Honey Badger performing on the deck of the FSC superyacht, a cascade of fireworks illuminating the night sky in time with the beat.

"Aart," Ciara says softly, kissing his neck as she sits up beside him.

"The price is up," he says, voice aching with misery. "We're closing in on seven hundred million dollars market cap. Goldman Sachs and Price Waterhouse Coopers have expressed an interest in buying up Future Synergy Coins for institutional investors. ING have issued a statement saying they're considering backing FSC as the official cryptocurrency of the Dutch banking industry. Guus was right, Ciara: hype. It's all about hype…"

"Aart…" Ciara says, pulling him toward her & kissing him softly on the lips. "Aart… I really like you… and last night was… it was incredible… but… we have to live together… for the next six months, at least…"

"I understand." It's the final cruel blow; the final confirmation that he's wrong, eternally wrong about everything, and Guus is right; development, partnerships, blackface – none of it matters. All that matters is hype.

She gets dressed quietly, she telling him a few more times that she's sorry, he telling her a few more times he understands, he stealing a final glance at the beauty of her naked form between the gyrations & explosions of Honey Badger's firework-backed superyacht performance.

The frat house empties over Christmas, most returning to family homes for the holidays, a few returning to the house for New Year, while Guus & Nguyen head to Thailand for a four-day beach-based conference called Crypto & Hallucinogens, wild speeches delivered around campfires by thick-bearded true believers, brains bolstered & re-shaped by acid & mushrooms & ayahuasca & strange new Japanese experimental chemicals, Nguyen shedding his clothes & dancing naked in front of the fire on the final night, chanting primevally as Guus – deep within a hallucinogen-cocktail trance – delivers a rambling six-hour speech, climaxing with Guus boldly declaring "I AM BECOME BLOCKCHAIN, DISRUPTOR OF WORLDS," while lightning strikes illuminate the sky from a storm hitting a distant island, all around falling into an almost coma-like state of acceptance of his insane proclamations.

Bitcoin falls from a high above $20.000 a few days before Christmas to as low as $12.000 on Christmas Eve, subreddits & Telegram groups & forums across the Internet full of theories on incoming institutional investment once Wall Street doles out its New Year bonuses & once those who've cashed out for the holidays buy back in. Bitcoin's dollar value bounces sideways into the New Year, but FSC & other alts remain resilient, with FSC's market cap hovering between $800 million and $900 million as 2018 begins.

"Aart," Guus says, he & Nguyen clearly deeply engrossed in important work upon the frat's quad-sofas, as Aart re-enters the home on the evening of January 5. "We've listened to what you said, and you were right about everything: the speculative crypto bull run is nearing its end. Only the projects with real utility and working products will survive. So we've done what you were forever telling us; we've begun working on the real launch of the Future Synergy Coin mainnet."

"Good," Aart says.

"The testnet will go live this week," Nguyen says, before rambling through a lightning-fast & highly-technical breakdown of what they've done & how far along they are & their strategy for allowing existing FSC holders to test their creation before the mainnet launches in Q2 2018.

"Awesome."

"And there will be a 'dry January,'" Guus adds. "Ciara told me that the British do it – " *Ciara;* Aart's heart flutters at the mention of his one-night love's name – "to cleanse the system after the Christmas excess."

Aart nods, hoping but not quite believing what Guus has said will prove true.

"And we're going to Moscow," Nguyen adds.

Aart's hope collapses, a fact Guus senses immediately.

"But this conference will be different," Guus says quickly. "There's strong rumours of government representatives attending, and they'll report back directly to Vladimir Putin himself - "

"Putin." Aart almost spits the name out, so severe is the shock attached to it.

"Putin is obsessed with blockchain," Nguyen says, staring at the screen as he types a thousand keys per minute. "There's reports that he's keeping his advisors up until 3am holding meetings on it. He thinks it's Russia's best chance at skirting sanctions and smashing the US Dollars' control over global finance."

"This is big, Aart," Guus interrupts, seeing Nguyen's rant has made Aart worried. "The keynote speaker is Vitalik Buterin."

"Vitalik Buterin?" Aart repeats. "The guy who made Ethereum?"

"The one and only," Nguyen says.

"And we'll be flying straight from Moscow to Hong Kong," Guus continues. "We're lining up meetings with some of the island's biggest financial firms."

Nguyen: "And after Hong Kong, we're going to Seoul."

Aart: "To Seoul?"

Guus: "South Korea."

Aart: "I know where Seoul is."

Guus: "South Korea is the world's largest per capita cryptocurrency investor. If we get listed on one of their exchanges, there's no telling how far we can go."

Nguyen: "Beyond the moon, beyond Mars…"

Guus: "…beyond the galaxy, Aart."

Nguyen: "To fucking Andromeda."

12. FUD THE WORLD.
(let them know it's crypto's time.)

Liverpool, England.

A poor clearance falls in front of Allen, who tees up a shot at goal the exact second that the stream freezes.

"Fuck's sake!" Graham shouts.

Luis' eyes dart from his iPad to his swearing father.

"¡Oye!" Melina shouts.

"Sorry," Graham says, tapping through tabs on his laptop, trying to find a stream that's still in action. He wants to swear more but holds his tongue, clenching his fists at he stares at the laptop screen: Bitcoin broke $11,000 this afternoon, but it's been slipping ever since, and is now beneath $10,000 – *$9,654* – & seems to be trending down further. His other coins are faring no better.

"It's because you are doing too much on the Internet," Melina says, as Graham clicks through tabs of spinning-circle loading scenes, before returning to the first stream as the commentary kicks in, saying that Allen's shot has gone wide. "Isn't Allen your player?"

"We sold him to Stoke," Graham says, attention now diverted back from the football being Chromecasted to the television to the ever-fluctuating crypto price charts on his laptop. "Poor sod, going from Liverpool to that shithole."

"¿Estás sordo o qué? Do not swear in front of Luis. He will imitate you."

"I'm sorry," Graham says. "Muchos siento. Stoke's a toilet. A Brexit-voting bog-hole."

XRP's trending down with Bitcoin – from 29 cents two days ago, edging fractions-of-a-cent closer to $0.23 every second – while NEO's fallen more dramatically, from $40 at kick-off to $35.16 at 15 mins into the 2nd half. ADA worries Graham most: $0.02 when he bought it, skyrocketing to 13 cents by Wednesday, now at 9.5143 cents, & heading downward. *Should I sell?* he asks himself; *Seal the profits… but squander gains if it reverses…* Meanwhile, ETH – Ethereum, the one coin he failed to buy coming back from the pub after the Liverpool/Sevilla match – went from $350 to $515 yesterday, and has fallen a little since, but is holding its value better than the shite he's invested in, bouncing about inertly between $460 & $450 as Stoke bounce the ball about inertly on the television.

Melina glances up from the Gabriel Garcia Marquez book she's reading every time the commentary gets louder, seeing in these glances a succession of Liverpool players getting yellow carded. Each time she looks up, Graham & Luis are completely fixated on other screens.

"Maybe I will just put on Narcos," Melina says.

"COME ON!!" Graham shouts.

On TV, Mohamed Salah replaces Oxlade-Chamberlain.

"He is good?" she asks.

"What? …oh, Salah, yeah, he's banging," Graham says, beaming now Bitcoin's bounced back above $10,000. But the triumph's short lived, and by the time Salah's swept Liverpool's second goal in, Bitcoin's at $9,604, NEO's hit $31.80, XRP's a slither of a fraction above 23 cents, ADA's $0.090201, & Ethereum's at *fucking* $468.

"Y'know, I was thinking about what we should call him," Graham says, laying his left hand on Melina's barely-perceptibly bloated belly in bed. "My Dad were named after Bill Shankly, and he named me after Graham Souness, and my brother after Robbie Fowler. And we got Little Luis named after Suarez and… well, it's a nice tradition, innit? I were thinking we might name him Steven, after Steven Gerrard."

"It's not a boy," Melina says softly, eyes closed.

"How d'you know?"

"I know."

"We could still call her Stevie. Like Stevie Nicks, off Fleetwood Mac."

"Qué mi esposo más cansón," Melina mutters, keeping her eyes closed. "Our daughter's name will not be Stevie."

Graham removes his hand & picks up his phone, trying to think of a more female-friendly player name as his wife drifts off, those thoughts fading as he taps between price charts, red & green candles indicating positive & negative price movements. Bitcoin ticks upwards – *$10,267, $10,269, $10,271* – its rhythmic upthrusts soothing, like counting sheep; a sleep-inducing lullaby: *$10,274, $10,279…* the price surges upward, spiking Graham's eyes open with adrenaline: *$10,312, $10,308, $10,317, $10,313, $10,345,* battling back & forth, dipping after each new breakthrough, then bounding back higher: *$10,406, $10,444, $10,509…*

In the kitchen, clock ticking towards 2am, Graham watches Bitcoin break $10,600, thinks it must be going back above $11,000, & he should probably buy more next time it dips. He clicks between tabs monitoring the price & tabs loaded with cryptocurrency news & opinion pieces, desperate for the knowledge needed to master the red & green candles, to surf the undulating price charts, to skim across the roaring market's waves…

He opens a new tab & visits a site through which he sells miscellaneous articles for extra income, Constant-Content.com, to see if the three short articles he wrote today on crypto have been approved. When the page loads, he's shocked to see 'This Month's Earnings' have swollen to $125: he submitted three articles late in the afternoon, 4pm at the earliest; he's never sold anything on the site in less than a couple of days of it going active, let alone three articles within a few hours. Sensing opportunity, he clicks between crypto news sites & Wikipedia articles, hastily assembling a few more entry-level crypto texts with questions for titles: 'What's the difference between Bitcoin and Ethereum?'; 'Why does most Bitcoin mining take place in China?'; 'Why does Bitcoin's price keep changing?'. He cracks open a beer midway through the second article, finishes the beer by the end of the third, is now ready to sleep, but checks Bitcoin one last time & sees it's caught in two minds, bouncing erratically between $10,564 & $10,666. He watches the fluctuations, wondering if he should buy more, or if the bubble's bursting. Deciding nothing but feeling invigorated, Graham clicks through more news & background information, piecing together more articles – 'Is Bitcoin a Bubble?'; 'Where will Bitcoin be this time next year?' –

"Graham," Melina's says, startling him, her voice hoarse, not yet fully awake. "¿Por qué estás aquí? It's six-thirty. What are you doing?"

"I couldn't sleep," Graham says. "I've been working."

"You have to take Luis to nursery," she says, awkwardly side-stepping Graham's chair to reach the small kitchen's coffee maker.

"No bother."

"Bloody hell," Graham can't help but exclaim, leaving the nursery school's gates around 9am, checking Constant-Content on his phone: three of the five articles he wrote in the kitchen have sold already, bringing This Month's Earnings to $245. The unsold active one, 'Why does … Bitcoin mining … China?', has already clocked 15 views from potential buyers; the other, 'Where… Bitcoin… this time next year?', has been rejected for some spelling or grammar errors.

Graham hurries home & hammers out nine articles before 4pm, pausing only to brew & pour coffee, not eating lunch, using his e-cig constantly. While crafting a conclusion to 'How can you find undervalued assets in the cryptocurrency space?' he suddenly realizes he's within minutes of being late to pick Luis up.

"Daddy, where do babies come from?"

Graham's shocked. Luis' surely too young to be wondering that. He still believes in Santa. *Melina.* Graham guesses she must've hinted that Luis' sibling's presently gestating. *Or maybe he sensed it,* Graham thinks, half-remembering something Panzer once quoted from a YouTube video about kids having a sixth sense for that type of thing. "Why do you ask?"

"Godzilla says babies come out when girls do a wee. But only if a boy's done a wee in the same place before them. And that's why boys and girls aren't allowed in the same toilets."

Fucking Godzilla. Godzilla is an appropriately-named beast of a child, disgustingly overweight for a four year-old, whose parents are proper Rock Ferry scallies who let him do as he pleases, e.g. watch age-inappropriate movies like Godzilla, his parents so in the little prick's thrall that even his nursery school teachers have been forced into calling him his chosen nom de dickhead, Godzilla, instead of his real name, Adam Tilbury.

"Godzilla don't know what he's on about," Graham says, thinking *at least the little shit's parents haven't let him onto bloody porno yet.* "If that were true, you'd have about twelve brothers and sisters. Me and your Mum use the same toilet all the time."

"And I use it."

"Exactly."

"And then I would be a Daddy to my own brother or sister. But Godzilla says that can't happen because that's called 'insects,' and for humans, doing insects is against the law."

Fucking hell, Godzilla.

Father & son walk a few steps in silence before Luis asks again: "So where do babies come from?"

"It's complicated." Graham's not prepared for this talk & not sure how Melina would react to him nonchalantly shattering Luis' innocence, especially with pregnancy hormones about to wreak havoc on her Latin temperament. But he also doesn't want to feed Luis some obvious bullshit about storks, or deflect the issue like his own Dad did and leave Luis to find out from Godzilla & PornHub.

"Like cooking arepas is complicated? Mummy always says cooking arepas is really complicated. And that's why Daddy can't cook arepas properly."

"What's wrong with my arepas?!"

"Mummy says you don't do them properly."

"Does she? Well… yeah… making a baby is a bit like cooking. You need some… certain ingredients. And when they get mixed together in the right proportion, a baby starts to grow."

"Then what ingredients do you need to make a baby?"

"You need some… well, when boys and girls become big, like Mummy and Daddy, their bodies start producing some ingredients that you're not capable of producing right now."

"Like flowers? Like in arepas?"

"Sort of."

"And is that why babies come out of mummies? Like when Mummy's friend Kayleigh got really, really fat, and then a baby comed out?"

"Yeah… that's pretty much exactly it."

"So when will I be able to make baby flowers?"

"When you're about fourteen."

"Graham!! ¿Por qué you have told Luis that I am embarazada?!"

Graham groans, smashed out of sleep into accusation. The wine & whiskey he drank with his Dad watching Liverpool smash Brighton 5-1 the previous afternoon's caught up with him, along with the bottles he & his parents put away over & after dinner afterwards. At no point during the long-winded Saturday does he recall doing anything of which Melina's accusing him.

"And your parents?! They know?! I fucking told you, Graham! I said say to them that I am working! I do not want to tell anybody until…"

She continues ranting, his head pounding, recalling the calm of the previous afternoon at his parent's house, the goals in the Liverpool game coming often enough to keep Luis distracted from the iPad, he at no point telling his parents nor Luis of her embarazo, their growing second child…

"…the fuck are you on about?"

"In the kitchen, I am with Luis, mixing the flours for to make your fucking Yorkshire fucking Puddings, and he say to me, 'hey, Mummy, Daddy say when I get big, I can make a cooking like that, and then maybe I too can get some fucking girl fucking pregnant… ¿¡WHAT THE FUCK, GRAHAM!?"

Graham stumbles through explanation, sends Melina into tears, gets out of bed, embraces her, apologises for misunderstandings, takes over cooking Sunday dinner, sits with her on the sofa for Country File (still not really understanding what she finds interesting in the turgid minutiae of the British countryside), switching to Narcos once Luis is in bed, Melina gasping as Jorge cuts a deal with the DEA, Graham wondering if the evolution of the narcotics trade in Season 3 after Pablo Escobar's death is mirrored by the move from outsider-niche lawlessness to government-controlled commodity of cryptocurrency, crypto's Pablo Escobar already dead, at least in essence; Bitcoin creator Satoshi Nakamoto, still anonymous, completely silent: & Graham reacts with the same gasp Melina gave Jorge's DEA collaboration to the movement in CoinMarketCap's cryptocurrency rankings, something called IOTA having appeared in the Top 10 with a $5 billion market cap.

"…and it were worth less than a billion a week ago, four billion added to its market cap in a week – *in a week,*" Graham tells Melina, "it's fucking quintupled in value, it's absolutely fucking mental…"

By noon the next day, IOTA's at $8 billion market cap & Graham's written three articles: one on IOTA's price growth; another on the mad Direct Acyclic Graph distributed ledger powering IOTA that allows for instant feeless transactions that'll make it far superior to Bitcoin as a digital currency; and a third on the implications IOTA has for connecting all manner of Internet of Things devices (a growing market expected to be worth trillions within the next decade.) But, happy as he is that This Month's Earnings are at $657 even without the IOTA articles, he's still not figured out how to buy this supernova cryptocurrency, & fears he might've missed his chance.

"RaiBlocks, la," Graham says on his next visit to McCooley's, "there's these two small exchanges you can buy it off, once it hits Binance it's gonna go supernova, it uses that same DAG shite that IOTA uses, so all the transactions are free and instant, it were 25 cents a coin a couple of days ago, and today it's already at 75, I stuck the $700 I got selling them crypto articles

I wrote on it, and that's gone up to more than two grand already, but it ain't slowing down, la, I'm telling you…"

"I should've kept them bloody BT shares," Graham's Dad says. "Might've been able to afford BT Sports on top of Sky Sports then, and we could've all watched this at mine."

"RailBlocks?" Toby repeats. "Ethereal? Toyota? Fusion Energy Coin? How many of these bloody things are there?!"

"There's thousands," Panzer says.

"You two are killing me with all this terminology," Toby says. "I've still not worked out what I'm meant to do with that Bitcoin I bought yet."

"Well, you could leave it on Coinbase," Graham says, "or you could move it your own wallet, or you could shift it to an exchange and start swapping it for other cryptocurrencies."

"RaiBlocks sounds good," Panzer says, "I'll have to have a look at that. You wanna check out TRON, that's another good one. It's only at $150 million market cap at the moment, but it'll be a billion in no time."

"You wanna be careful, lads," Nev says, eyes fixed on the football. "The bubble's gotta burst at some point."

As he finishes speaking, Mohamed Salah smashes Liverpool's seventh goal in. The cheers that ring through McCooley's are almost ironic: it's the 86th minute, Spartak Moscow have long since capitulated, and the Reds' progress to the next round of the Champion's League was a foregone conclusion before the match even started. Watching the muted celebrations on-screen, Graham thinks that might be a metaphor for this surge in cryptocurrency: getting in early, before DAG and all the other wild bleeding-edge technology has had chance to become truly world-changing. It's a guaranteed victory – machine-gunning fish in a barrel.

"Mate, what the fuck were you on about, NEO?" Graham shouts half-jokingly to a scally in an old-school green-and-white Liverpool away kit at the bar whilst getting a round in. The scally stares blankly back at him. Graham elaborates: "Last time I seen you in here, you were recommending NEO. Fucking NEO, mate! It's worth less now than when 'Pool played Sevilla."

"Oh, shit, yeah, sorry, mate. Fucking shite, innit? But have you heard about ZeroX?"

The next morning, after Luis' been taken to nursery, Graham's hunched over a laptop nursing his hangover, feeling the swirl of mixed emotions: Bitcoin's at $16,731 and sliding downward, having hit $18,000 at some point during the night, while NEO & XRP move sideways with a downward tilt, & ADA's back at 10 cents and looking like dropping further, while RaiBlocks has stalled & tumbled back to $0.68. Panzer's recommendation, TRON, has doubled since the Spartak Moscow match. And IOTA – the coin that got away – is now at $15 billion market cap.

$15 billion. From less than a billion less than a week ago. *Fifteen billion.* From a third of that on Sunday.

Fuck it, Graham tells himself, trading his NEO & XRP & ADA at a loss for Bitcoin on Bittrex. *Follow your gut,* sending the Bitcoin from Bittrex to BitBucks to buy Future Synergy Coin, the coin that got him hooked on all this, now dipping to $0.0000076. *The coin that got you into this mess is the coin that will get you out of it.*

Once all transactions are complete, The Beatles' solo stuff Spotify playlist buried behind his laptop's dozen tabs of crypto trading screens reaches John Lennon's Happy XMas (War is Over). Graham realises its December 7th and he's done no Christmas shopping. And he's just thrown $700 into cryptocurrency. And however many articles he sells now, he won't get paid again by Constant-Content until early January. He might become a millionaire in the New Year, but that doesn't help him buy presents before December 25th.

Graham copies & pastes sentence strings from sold articles into Google & finds the websites his articles have been published on: 'Will Crypto Change the Course of Global Finance?' on the LinkedIn feed of a Lebanese Chief Business Development Officer; other articles dispersed across start-up crypto news blogs with names like CoinOClock, BitFeed, Blocktionary, & Cryptopedia. Graham emails all the sites he can find contact emails for, offering his services on an ongoing basis, then searches UpWork for 'blockchain' & 'cryptocurrency,' and spends until 3.55pm sending out pitches & writing samples.

Graham receives word of his first accepted proposal that night, as Jorge and Enrique accuse each other of being the DEA rat in an ominous warehouse on Narcos. The following afternoon, he skims a white paper for Universal Payment Protocol & strings together a Medium post urging crypto investors to look into UPP before it skyrockets, briefly stopping to see three more UpWork proposals have been accepted.

"It's mental," Graham tells his Dad, on the sofa at his parent's Toxteth house watching the Merseyside derby, "that RaiBlocks one I was on about has gone up to a dollar now, and Future Synergy Coin's doubled in a couple of days."

"But they were saying Bitcoin's going down again on the news," Graham's Dad says.

"Yeah, it's up and down like bloody West Brom, but there's a lot of people saying it'll be worth a hundred grand or more a year from now."

"Well, just you be careful," Graham's Dad says, as the referee blows for a soft challenge and gives Everton a ludicrous penalty.

"Come on!" Graham's Mum says, rushing from the kitchen to the living room, she tolerating her husband making the home a Liverpool-supporting household on all but Merseyside derby day.

"It's a shame Melina couldn't come," his Mum says a little while later whilst serving dinner, Rooney's penalty having cancelled out Salah's earlier goal & ended the derby in an amicable 1-1 draw. "It's disgusting having her in work on a Sunday."

"Well it's a restaurant," Graham's Dad says. "They'll be busiest Sundays, won't they?"

"Future Synergy's Coin at two dollars now," Graham tells his Dad & Toby & Panzer & Nev at McCooley's that Wednesday, "and RaiBlocks is up to almost four!"

"TRON's gone fucking mental," Panzer says. "I put five hundred quid on it ten days ago. Almost five grand that's worth now!"

"Bitcoin's going back down again," Toby sighs. "How do you buy all these other ones?"

Graham & Panzer stumble over each other trying to explain the process in the simplest terms possible. At a lull in their speech, Nev pipes in: "Do you reckon it's still worth buying into?"

The football's dull – a 0-0 draw with West Brom – and the night is completely dominated by talk of crypto's unstoppable upward momentum.

"Oyster Pearl," the scally in the green & white away shirt says to Graham at the bar. "It's up four hundred percent this week, la!"

Graham's online banking shows the $834 from the week's UpWork tasks has been deposited as £645.51. While working on a promo piece for Schpoodle Coin – a blockchain-based solution for verifying pedigree dogs within the billion-dollar international upmarket pet industry – Graham finds the perfect gift for Luis, that'll also bring joy to himself: a PS4 bundled with FIFA 18, £270 on Amazon; & he clicks through jewellery, coats, & handbags in search of Melina's gift, eyeing a £2000 Hermes bag he knows she'd love on Ebay, thinking if the coins keep pumping & the writing work keeps piling up, then…

"Gaby was saying today that her father's trying to come to England," Melina says, just after Luis's been put to bed.

"Really?" Graham says, emoting as much shock & interest as possible, happy she seems to have stopped being sour over the £270 he splashed on Luis' gift without consulting her. "Is he gonna move in with them?"

"Sí."

"But her mother and him's divorced, right?"

"Sí. And she has her mother and both her brothers living in Tommy and she's tiny flat. It's almost smaller than this place."

"Christ. Sounds cosy."

"But her father's situación in Venezuela is getting worser and more worse, and he cannot go on with it. He have nothing to eat. Every shop's shelf is empty. Nobody is at work. He's living in a nightmare."

The Prime Minister is on TV, repeating her meaningless mantra, 'Brexit means Brexit,' followed by some bollocks about 'will of the people' & 'upholding democracy.'

"She wants to send him some money to help him to come to England, but she is feeling like this is impossible. She cannot send to a bank account in Venezuela, because the inflación is so crazy, any money will be worthless by when it arrives. And she was thinking to maybe wire money in US Dollar, but her father says that when he goes to the border, the guards will take it. But her father say many people there are these days using Bitcoins for receiving money. This she can send, and the border guard cannot take."

Until today, Melina's reacted to Graham's constant chatter about cryptocurrency with only the pretence of interest. Today, after telling her about the PS4, he showed her Future Synergy Coin was at $220 million market cap, and RaiBlocks had hit $4 per coin, turning his £690 outlay into a portfolio worth almost £2,500. She suddenly became significantly more interested.

"So I say to Gaby, since she do not know almost anything about Bitcoins, and you are now an expert, maybe you can come into the restaurant and explain it her?"

It's the first time Graham's visited Zowee in months, since Melina's boss grew tired of seeing him sup free coffee all day & chatter with the staff whilst working on his laptop. Graham's felt a hole in his day ever since then, home alone, with (until the sudden crypto rush) nothing much to work on. Trying to suppress melded memories of months-long strings of indistinct daytime television & Netflix series, he's happy to see Old Man Jack (the proprietor) isn't in. Graham explains crypto to Gabby in the directest terms: *digital money*. He offers to help her in every step of the Bitcoin-to-Venezuela process. She purchases 0.3456 Bitcoin through Coinbase & sends it to her Dad's wallet address.

After leaving Zowee, Graham wanders around the shops, Christmas shoppers bustling all around him, Graham thinking of how long it's been since Melina was last in Colombia. The interest she took in Gaby's problem with her dad, & the dim glow in her eyes as she talked of families of Colombians in border towns taking in families of Venezuelan refugees… there's clearly no better gift he could give her than a trip home. Graham searches flights on his phone while walking around Foot Locker: £448 per person via Madrid to Bogota in February, 14h 25m flight / 13h 45 coming back. Just shy of a grand for two. *And Luis…* he really ought to see more of his grandparents. He's not been to Colombia, not really, not since he was old enough to remember it. *And what about Mum & Dad?*

Crypto article production cranks up as prices soar improbably: IOTA falling away as Oyster Pearl, RaiBlocks, & TRON thrust up one day to the next. Once RaiBlocks hits $5, Graham shifts some of his profits into other projects – BountyX, Walton, VeChain, Qtum, Quantstamp, Request Network – & with two days to spare before Christmas, his portfolio soars above $10,000. He stares at his Blockfolio crypto-portfolio tracking app in awe as the value of his coins slips & pumps with every second, sometimes gaining or losing the sum of Melina's monthly salary in the time it takes to pour a cup of coffee. He becomes frantic with the loss-cutting & profit-taking & hot-new-coin hunting. He can barely concentrate on the YouTube videos he's watching to turn into articles for crypto news sites, on topics like 'Why Exchange Coins Are the Biggest Guaranteed Win in 2018.' He sleeps at random intervals, crazy price surges occurring at all hours of day & night, Graham desperate not to let a cent of growth escape him. $10,000 becomes $15,000 within three days. New assignments pour into his inbox. He's Community Manager for more coins than he can remember, rattling out articles around the clock, sending out price-moving tweets, every stroke of the keyboard sending one coin or another a percentage point higher. With four days to spare before Christmas, his Blockfolio's broke $20,000, and as that closes in on $22,000, he's resolving to cash out half, to splash it all on a whole family trip to Colombia, taking Robbie as well, thousands pouring into his account from his other ventures for the foreseeable future. To do that, he has turn his scores of altcoins into one of the most fungible – Bitcoin, Ethereum, or Litecoin – & send that to Coinbase, then withdraw from there into his bank account. All are in the ascendancy – with Bitcoin pushing toward $20,000, Ethereum on the way to $900, and Litecoin at almost $330 (from $88 at the start of the month). Wary a knock back could afflict any coin without warning, Graham spends a few hours shuffling his stack around exchanges, eventually depositing 10 LTC, 4 ETH, & 0.2 BTC into his Coinbase account, giving him a total cash-out amount of £7905, with $12,527 left flailing wildly up & down on Blockfolio. A few taps at the laptop later, he's on the verge of depositing the Christmas-making sum into his bank account, when a message pops up, telling him he needs to make an arbitrary £1 deposit into an Estonian bank account to verify his details. He logs into his Barclays Online Banking, realises he needs some silly little device the bank sent him over a year ago to authorise an outgoing transfer, rummages through drawers & in cupboards trying to find it, notices the time's hit 3:57pm, rushes out, to the nursery for Luis, then heads with him to the train station & the 16:14 to Birkenhead Central, sprinting into the Barclays Bank on Grange Road with 5 minutes to spare before they shut at 4.30pm.

"Estonia?" the plump middle-aged woman behind the bank's plexiglass window says, accentuating the vowels in a way that suggests she's never heard of the place. "You want to make a bank transfer of one pounds exactly to an account in Estonia?"

"Yeah."

"Well… we can do it, but there's a fee for over-the-counter transfers."

"S'alright."

"It'll cost you twenty pounds."

"That's fine."

"Twenty pounds. To send a pound. Have you not got online banking?"

"I lost the thing."

"Ah, the… thing. Yeah. Well… if you're sure. But it hardly seems worth it… twenty pounds to send a pound… *to Estonia…*"

Graham rides the train back to Rock Ferry in relative calm, thinking the hard work's been done, and it'll all be sorted by Christmas. He listens to Luis tell him all about their Christmas activities at school, Luis twice making him reiterate his promise to come to the following afternoon's nativity play, and promise three times that Mummy will be coming with him. "Of course! She woul'n't miss it for the world."

"I wish I were playing someone better though."

"What you on about? You're the Innkeeper! You've got the most important part."

"Do you reckon? I hardly say anything."

"Of course! The whole story hinges on the Innkeeper. If it weren't for him, Jesus woul'n't have been born in a barn, would he?"

"But the Innkeeper's a baddie."

"The most fun parts are baddies. And the Innkeeper's one of the all-time greats."

"But Godzilla's got loads more to say than me. And he's on stage for the whole bloomin' thing of it."

"Who's Godzilla playing?"

"Joseph."

Of course he fucking is. "But Joseph's a dry part, that. A proper Tim Banks role, that one. The Innkeeper's an absolute show-stealer. It's the sort of part Gary Oldman or Daniel-Day Lewis would have."

"I'n't he a racing car driver?"

"Nah, nah. You're thinking of Lewis Hamilton. Nah, Daniel-Day Lewis is one of the greatest actors that ever lived. And when he were in his school nativity play, he requested the part of the Innkeeper."

"Did he really? Why?"

"Because the Innkeeper's one of the most fascinating characters in human history."

Luis scrunches his little face up in disbelief as the train rolls into Rock Ferry.

"He might come across as just a greedy so-and-so," Graham continues, strolling calmly past the pub across the street from Rock Ferry station, beer garden already quarter-full of pre-Christmas revellers, "but if it weren't for the Innkeeper, none of what makes the Christmas story so special would've happened. If it weren't for him sending Mary off to Bethlehem without a bed for the night, then they never would've found that barn. And then them Three Wise men woul'n't of known where to find Jesus. Nah, the Innkeeper's the bloke the whole plot hinges upon. It's a much better part than Joseph. Joseph's rubbish. He's just the dumb schmuck God conned into raising His kid after He got his missus pregnant."

The nursery school's hall's packed with parents as Nisha stands at centre-stage, blue shawl wrapped around her head to identify her as Mary, as another kid Graham doesn't know the name of steps towards her, angel wings identifying him as Gabriel: "I've got a message for you from God. He wants you to have his son."

Graham suppresses urge after urge to check his phone & Blockfolio as the nativity play progresses: it's been a bad day for Bitcoin, sliding down from yesterday's high of $17,567 towards $13,000, pulling the rest of the crypto market down with it; ETH tumbling from $816 to $649, Litecoin from $339 to $202, the Christmas-making Colombia trip ebbing away with each downward thrust of godless market volatility…

"We gotta go Bethlehem," Godzilla says, plump little belly bulging beneath his mock zero-AD Palestinian rags. "Augustus wants us to pay him his taxes."

Fucking Godzilla. Graham shoots Melina a glance in the seat beside him; he catches her eyes idling, & they shoot an instant look back telling him to look at the stage. Nisha & Godzilla walk in front of a PowerPoint-projected image of a desert, then a kid hops into centre-stage in a rubber Donald Trump mask: "Hey! Whadda you guys think you're doing?"

Muffled laughter from the assembled parents; Graham looks at Luis' teacher Mr. Mahoney, smiling smugly at the stageside, obviously proud of the parents' reaction to his Nativity's nod to topicality.

"We're going to Bethlehem," Nisha says. "To pay us taxes."

Godzilla does some stupid fucking gurning thing with that fat face of his, and as Graham wonders if it's natural to dislike a small child this much, the guffaws of his bloated mother a few rows ahead encourage Godzilla to contort his face in an ever more ludicrous manner, and confirm to Graham that *yes,* it's perfectly natural to despise the little runt, along with the mutt that spawned him.

A song & dance number follows, the winged angels joining on stage as Nisha & Godzilla & Trump-mask kid sing a tone-deaf 'parody' of a Lady Gaga song: *"There's no other way! Augustus says we have to pay! Gotta go to Bethlehem, so Baby Jesus can be born this way…"*

Trump kid says, "Okay then. But don't you immigrants do any crimes!", drawing more laughs from the grown-ups, and increasing the size of Mr. Mahoney's self-satisfied grin.

Luis' scene starts soon after, Nisha imploring him to let them stay at the inn: "Please, Mr. Innkeeper. I'm carrying God's only baby."

Nisha's put off by the loud guffaws of Godzilla's mother as her demon offspring does more stupid facial expressions. Other parents laugh, even Melina, making Graham wonder if he's not taking the little shit's antics too seriously. But little Nisha looks just as irritated as Graham, and he can't help but laugh as Nisha elbows Godzilla in the ribs to stop the tomfoolery.

"Please, Mr. Innkeeper. Won't you please let us come stay at your Inn?"

"NO!!" Luis yells, loud enough to cause a few gasps among the parents. "THIS INN IS FULL! YOU GO SOMEWHERE ELSE!!"

There's a few murmurs of concern at the gusto Luis's thrown into his performance, but Graham's beaming, his kid pulling off the scene-stealing performance Graham knew he was destined for. The rest of the play totters on, the Three Wise Men arriving with a parody of Ed Sheeran's Shape of You – *"ooh-ahh, ooh-ahh, ooh-ahh, ooh-ahh… we're looking for the Saviour!"* – & then presenting gifts as Graham thinks that if he were Mr. Mahoney, he'd have topically replaced Gold with Bitcoin, Frankincense with Ethereum, & Myrrh with Litecoin. The whole cast – Luis included – return to the stage & give an ear-blasting rendition of Away in a Manager, and then the grand production comes to a merciful end.

Graham takes his phone out the second it's socially acceptable & stares at Blockfolio in horror: *Bitcoin $11,870, Ethereum $540, Litecoin $193…* He's doing sums in his head, converting US Dollars into British Pounds – the ratio was $1=£0.745-something-something-recurring last time he checked, so roughly 0.75, or three-quarters, so he's dividing the dollar figures by 2, then halving again, then multiplying by 3, then dividing or multiplying that by the amount of each crypto he holds: *£4,800,* he concludes. *Bollocks. Fuck.* £4,800. Or something like that. *And what was it before?* £7,905. Almost eight grand. So almost three grand gone. *Fuck.* Bollocks. *Fucking Barclays.* Coinbase. *Wankers.* Fucking *fuck fuck fuck fuck fuck fuck fuck fuck fuck fuck…*

"…and Nisha was amazing!" Melina's gushing to Nisha's parents, the Shahs, first-generation immigrants from Pakistan.

"Have you been watching the Liverpool games?" Mr. Shah asks Graham.

"Aye." Graham likes the Shahs – a damn sight more than Godzilla's mum, anyway – & finds Mr. Shah's habit of talking about football to try & blend in with the locals quite endearing. "Salah's been alright lately, haven't he?"

"Oh, yes! He's quite the player…"

They're cut off as Nisha screams loudly at Godzilla, the pair standing beside Luis a few feet away from Godzilla's mother. Godzilla's mum laughs loudly. A minute later, Melina's talking with her, Graham doing his best to disguise his hatred.

"He were bloody brilliant, weren't he?" Godzilla's mum boasts.

"Oh yes, it was quite the performance," Melina replies.

That night at McCooley's, Liverpool are taking on Arsenal, and the game is a thriller: Mohammad Salah making it 2-0 Liverpool early in the second half, Sanchez & Xhaka pulling two back for Arsenal within the next few minutes, then Ozil making it 3-2 to Arsenal by the 58th minute.

Despite the excitement on-screen, only Graham's Dad's really enjoying it. The others are trying to focus on the football to block out the misery caused by the cryptocurrency price collapse.

"I never should've listened to you bloody idiots," Nev sighs, the sad owner of one-quarter of a Bitcoin, bought for about £3750 when Bitcoin was closing in on $20,000.

"It'll turn around," the scally in the green-and-white away kit tells Graham at the bar. "You wanna look into DeepBrainChain, la. It's a NEO NEP-5 token that'll make a super-computer connecting all the world's artificial intelligence networks. It's gonna be listed on KuCoin right after Christmas. I reckon it'll make you four times your investment before New Year."

Graham wakes up the next morning with a hangover & the grim realization that he still needs to buy Christmas presents. Melina's got work at Zowee, so he takes Luis into Liverpool city centre, gripping his hand the whole day to stop him disappearing into the swirling mass of shoppers that surround them.

"What do you reckon of this?" Graham asks Luis, referring to a £40 handbag in River Island that doesn't look too dissimilar to the multi-grand designer ones he knows Melina would truly love.

Luis scrunches his face up: "Mummy's got loads of handbags."

Graham buys it anyway, telling Luis five or six times to stop trying to kick a floor tile loose as they wait in the interminably long queue to pay.

The next day, Sunday, is Christmas Eve. Robbie returns to England at midday, and sends Graham a text to see if he's up for a pint the second his Dad picks him up at Manchester Airport.

"I'm still feeling it from last night, la," Robbie says, red-lined faced corroborating his wild tale of Berlin clubs & drugs & some Slovakian bird that kept him awake until he took the bus to Berlin's Tegel Airport. "Almost missed my stop, la. I'd be stuck there right now if my bag hadn't fallen off me lap when the bus stopped."

The brothers get hammered together, Panzer joining at 7pm, Robbie's mates Will & Perm bringing a few grams of whizz at 8.30pm, Nev ignoring all texts & phone calls inviting him to join them, Panzer saying: "I hope he's not fucking hung himself. Bitcoin's back above $14,000."

Graham takes the last train home & gets in just after midnight, then finds himself unable to sleep, despite the effect of the two keys of whizz he'd restricted himself to having worn off hours ago. He checks Blockfolio as silently as he can through the night, & watches with great anxiety as Bitcoin bounces between $13,000 and $14,000, the rest of the market erratically bobbing along with it.

Luis walks in their room soon after 5am: "Mummy! Daddy! I just went downstairs, and Santa's been already!"

Melina groans loudly before responding: "Remember what we said about Santa, Luis. If you open the presents too early, Santa's Elves will put a curse onto you, and the presents will disappear again."

"So I still have to wait until 8 o'clock? Maybe he just said eight to be safe. Maybe he's not done dropping the other kids' presents off yet. And his elves must all be mega-busy tonight, d'you really reckon they'll even notice?"

Graham sits up, thinking sleep will now have to wait until Boxing Day. "I s'pose it wouldn't hurt to open them a little bit early."

Melina groans thrice as loud as before, & Graham immediately regrets saying that. But what's said has been said, & he's soon in the kitchen, brewing coffee & preparing toast as a meagre apology. Luis tears Santa's gifts open, the PS4 being by far the star attraction. Graham hooks it up to the TV & Luis almost explodes with frustration as the console starts downloading a multi-gigabyte software update that'll delay his playing it by hours.

"Thank you," Melina says, smiling sweetly at the handbag & a Zara scarf & jacket.

Graham opens his gifts from her & Luis – Luis' gift clearly having been bought by Melina too, causing Graham to curse himself for not doing the same. There's books – Hunter S. Thompson, Bukowski, Kerouac – his three favourite writers, but titles he's never read by them – a bottle of Gentleman Jack & Kraken dark rum, and then the main event: a new laptop to replace the aging model he currently hammers out articles on. "Bloody hell! Thank you! You shoul'n'tve!" & as he hugs kisses wife & child, he feels deep embarrassment at his large haul of presents' clearly superior expensiveness & thoughtfulness to the crap he's gifted Melina.

Once the PS4's updated, Graham easily beats Luis with Arsenal vs Liverpool on FIFA, but then lets the kid trounce his Barcelona & PSG teams as a way of making that up to him.

At 11am, they head over to Graham's parents' house, bringing the PS4 along with them. His Mum's prepared a platter of Iceland mini-bites & a few bottles of prosecco. All assembled are half-pissed by the time Christmas Dinner's served, Graham's Mum burning the brussel sprouts thanks to alcohol-induced forgetfulness, but nobody noticing much difference in their taste. After hefty plates of turkey, lamb, mashed potatoes & other assorted veg, Christmas crackers are pulled, lame jokes read out, then the males of the family (Luis excepted) all fall asleep in the living room while Melina & Graham's Mum chat about the Queen's attire as she delivers her annual speech to the nation. Board games are played, Melina trouncing the family in their first game of the Weakest Link & becoming irritated by being voted out early in the second. Graham, Robbie & Luis stay up later than the others playing FIFA, and Graham & Robbie have a few stiff whiskey & rum-based cocktails and what's left of the previous night's whizz once Luis' been put to bed.

The next morning, Graham wakes up in the guest bedroom a little after 10am, Melina having briefly woken him on leaving the room an hour earlier. He checks his phone: *Bitcoin $15,156, Ethereum $786, Litecoin $284.* Then Coinbase: the payment's been processed! A Christmas miracle! He immediately transfers £6742.38 from Coinbase to his bank account, refreshing Barclays constantly until it appears. Then SkyScanner, quickly deciding on a £483 per-person 13h 47m flight London Heathrow to Medellin via Bogota with Avianca, shelling out just shy of £3,000, still leaving his account healthier than its looked in longer than he can remember.

"Everyone, I got something important to tell yous all," Graham says upon entering the living room. He calls his Mum in from the kitchen, she warning him to make it quick as she's in the midst of preparing the family a fry-up. "Keep your diaries free in May, cos us lot are going to Colombia!"

The adults are thrilled, queueing up to hug & kiss their husband/son/brother, Luis a little bewildered by it all. Melina's even more excited than Graham had hoped, & she barely stops smiling as the New Year approaches. 2018's rung in with a big night out in Liverpool, Graham's parents taking care of Luis for the night, Panzer snogging Gaby at midnight as parties converge. And 2018 begins spectacularly, Graham cranking out more articles than ever before, bank balance constantly in the ascendancy, while his Blockfolio does even better: DeepBrainChain goes from 7 cents on its KuCoin listing to more than $0.50, Oyster Pearl skyrockets from $0.50 to almost $5, RaiBlocks rebrands to NANO & surges from $5 to $35, Ethereum almost doubles to $1,400, and Future Synergy Coin explodes to—

13. STRESS TEST.

Blandford, Massachusetts. (United States of America.)

"Alright me li'l peep-peeps? This is Dalston's own Dashing Dolph Daggers here with another Crypto and a Craft Beer, and today I'm drinking a Wrong 'Un IPA. Now as you all know, these days I am firmly repping me North-East London massive – *Daaaaalstoooonnn!!* – but I'm originally from the North-East of England – Leeds – and that's exactly where today's craft beer comes from. 9% ABV, hoppy as all get out, and just about on the verge of being as tasty as today's 3D Dashing Dolph Daggers' Top Crypto Pick—"

The video freeze-frames on the blond British YouTuber in the ridiculous giant-eyeball/green-monster hat in some 5-star hotel room; a bar appears at the top of the screen: *CALLING - Uncle Larry.*

Steven sighs & taps the bar: "Yeah?"

"Hey, kid, it's your favorite uncle. How you doing? Your parents around?"

"I'm in my room."

"Good, good. How's our little investment looking?"

"It's looking alright."

"Whaddya mean, alright?"

"FSC's at zero-point-zero-zero-zero-zero-eight-three-seven dollars now."

"That's a lot of fucking zeroes, kid. What's the spread?"

"It's about up about five-thousand percent since Thanksgiving."

"Five thousand fucking percent?! Holy shit! So, what, our investment's at five thousand dollars?!"

"Five thousand dollars would be five hundred percent."

"Five hundred… thousand… woah, holy mother of fuck, kid, are you telling me we're at fifty fucking grand?!"

"Something like that."

"Holy shit, kid!! You're a God-damn Wall Street genius!!! You think it's gonna keep on pumping???"

"I think so."

"Hot damn, kid, that's amazing!! Fucking incredible!! So I'm thinking about throwing some more money in… A lot more money. I've freed up as much as I can. You think this FSC shit would be the best use of it?"

"Maybe."

"Why maybe? You got something else in mind?"

"Dolph Daggers just brought out a new video."

"Who's Dolph Daggers?"

"The YouTuber. The one who told me about Future Synergy Coin."

"And this guy's the guy, right? Whatever he picks fucking explodes into the stratosphere?"

"Uh-huh."

"Well, God-damn, kid, what's he pushing?"

"I don't know yet. Your call interrupted the video."

"Whatever it is he's pushing, it's pretty much a sure thing to shoot up in value, right?"

"I guess."

"That's great, kid. Really swell. Because I've just been to the bank, and I spoke with a guy there's who's gonna let me take out a second mortgage on the house. Free up some cash to play around with. You think I should throw it at Dolph Dagger's new coin?"

"Maybe."

"Well are you gonna invest in it?"

"Sure."

"Well alright then. So I got twenty-five thousand dollars available. What's the best way for me to send it to you?"

"I don't know."

"You don't know?! Come on, kid, whaddya want; a bank transfer? You even got a bank account?"

"Sort of."

"What's 'sort of' mean?"

"I got a kid's account."

"So it's, like… accessible by your parents or something?"

"Yeah. Dad keeps an eye on what I spend from it."

"So I don't wanna throw twenty-five thousand dollars into that account, right? Have your old man poking around, asking questions…"

"I guess."

"So what's the best way for me to get this money to you?"

"You could send it in crypto."

"And how would I do that?"

"I don't know… you could buy, like, Ethereum, or Litecoin, or something."

"And how do I do that?"

"Go to Coinbase."

"Coinbase? What's that, like a Home Depot place for cryptocurrency?"

"It's a website."

"Oh, a website… that's good… because there ain't too much around here, kid. We got a Target and a Walmart and not a whole lot else. So it's, what, Coinbase.com?"

"Uh-huh."

"And then I buy some Ebullions or some Life Coins and send them over to you?"

"Uh-huh."

"Okay… alright… I'm gonna get on that. And, hey, kid – thanks a lot. You got no idea how much this is helping me out." Instead of the expected gratitude, all Larry hears is silence on the other end of the phone call. "So, uh, yeah, I'll throw you some more money for your trouble, alright? Fifty dollars sound alright to you?"

"I guess."

"I tell you what, kid, you're doing a great service to me here, and I really appreciate you turning me on to this crypto shit. So I tell you what – how about we call it sixty dollars?"

"Alright."

"That okay with you?"

"Uh-huh."

"But for that much money, I want you to be actively managing this shit for me, alright? I heard there was a bit of a dip in Bitcoin the other day. So if things start to go south, let me know right away, and yank the investment out, okay?"

"Okay."

"Alright then… adda boy. So I'll go to this Coinbase or whatever and send you some Ebullions over, is that right?"

"Uh-huh."

"Alright… thanks, kid. I'll speak to you later."

Larry ends the phone call & Steven resumes the video. Dolph's shilling something called Cattle Onchain Welfare, or COW, an ambitious low-market-cap coin from Australia that aims to track the entire country's enormous cattle industry via a decentralized distributed ledger, allowing consumers to examine the medical records of the cattle from which meat and dairy products have been extracted, to ensure they're not eating an animal that once suffered from some terrible disease or got overloaded with harmful antibiotics.

"…and Australia's beef industry is worth billions of fucking dollars," Dolph explains, as 3D text flashes on-screen saying 'BIG TIME!!'. "They export all over the world – America, Asia, even right here in dear ol' Britain—" Dolph pauses to raise his fist & lower his head patriotically as the opening chords of God Save the Queen play over his video, "—so this has the potential to be absolutely mega-mega-massive. Current market cap is just thirty million dollars, it's nineteen cents per coin, and it's only available on HypeCoinHub and EtherDelta, so you'd better grab this one quick, cause it's gonna fucking *MOOOOOOOOOOOONNN…*"

Steven follows Dolph's advice as soon as the video ends, opening BitBucks on his phone to exchange half his FSC stack into Ethereum & free up some liquid capital for the purchase of COW coin. He trades 600,000 FSC for 0.189942 ETH, then opens HypeCoinHub, selects & copies his Ethereum deposit address, pastes that into BitBucks, & sends his Ethereum

(0.18044 ETH after the withdrawal fee). Then Steven sits on the bed & keeps refreshing, while his deposit slowly gains in transaction confirmations: *0/30, 5/30, 21/30…* and then he stares at his Ethereum balance on HypeCoinHub in bewilderment: *0.36088 ETH.* He reopens BitBucks, and checks how much he sent: 0.189942 ETH, less a 5% withdrawal fee. He clicks back & forth between BitBucks & HypeCoinHub for a few moments, confused, then starts trying to figure out what's happened; he sells another 500,000 FSC on BitBucks for 0.158285 ETH, sends that to his HypeCoinHub wallet, & the same thing happens; 0.308655 ETH added to his HypeCoinHub account – double the amount that he sent. Emboldened, Steven sends 0.5 ETH back to BitBucks, refreshes confirmations – *17/30, 25/30* – & then immediately sends the Ethereum back to HypeCoinHub. *16/30, 21/30,* then the same thing happens – 0.975 ETH added to his HypeCoinHub account, double again, bringing the current total to 1.644535 ETH.

Steven repeats the process, over & over, sending ETH back & forth between BitBucks & HypeCoinHub, BitBucks doubling his withdrawal every time, his total swelling from 1.644 to 3.2 to 12.19 to 23.77 to 46.367 ETH – roughly $41,000 – until his phone screen freezes & a bar appears at the top of the screen: *CALLING – Mom.* She says dinner's ready & he needs to come downstairs.

14. FOMO.

Seoul & Incheon, South Korea.

14.01.

The video appears on Sung Jae's KakaoTalk at the worst possible time: he & Su Min are on the deck of a boat cruising down the Han River, Seoul's towering apartment blocks lining both river banks, the multi-coloured glow of the Rainbow Bridge ahead of them; & then it happens: the 'Kakao!' notification sound; & Su Min asks: "Who's that?", & Sung Jae takes his phone from his pocket, its screen thankfully unseen by her, & reads with horror the message from an unknown: someone with an big-eyed anime schoolgirl avatar as their profile picture & the username MonsterHunter.

Sung Jae says nothing as he stares at the screen: the message contains a video clip, its thumbnail showing a motel room bed filmed from above; & without hitting 'play' on the video, Sung Jae's confusion turns to horror, he recognising it as the room at the motel he went to with Jong Gil months before.

Two 'Kakao!' notification sounds in quick succession announce the arrival of an explanatory message: *Hi!* says MonsterHunter, followed by the grinning face of the KakaoTalk duck emoticon. *Send me 25 million won in the next 24 hours or I send the video to your wife.*

"Who is it?" Su Min asks, turning her attention from the wide flowing river to her husband's worried face.

"It's Jae Seok," Sung Jae lies, turning the screen off at the moment another 'Kakao!' signals the arrival of a picture: Su Min's picture. *From her Instagram?*

"What did he say?" Su Min asks, sensing the falseness with which her husband's trying to parlay his obvious dread into a carefree smile.

"Nothing. It's about the baseball game."

"But I thought the baseball season already finished?"

"American baseball," Sung Jae says, placing the palm of his right hand on Su Min's hip, staring ahead at the multi-coloured jets of water cascading from the Rainbow Bridge across the wide calm surface of the Han River.

Su Min angles her body away from her husband's hand: "We should go inside. It's cold."

She doesn't wait for a response before walking into the indoor seating area. Sung Jae stares at the brightly lit colours of the Rainbow Bridge, cursing himself for being so stupid, wondering who the hell the creep sending the messages is, & feeling immensely pissed off that all the positivity of their 26th Wedding Anniversary – a musical & Italian restaurant in Jamsil, followed by this cruise – has been put at risk.

His mind a mess of stress, confusion, & guilt, Sung Jae thinks for a moment of smoking a cigarette on the deck before re-joining Su Min inside. He quickly realises this will further irritate her & instead turns away & re-enters the indoor area with what his wife instantly senses is a fake & hiding-something smile.

14.02.

*25 million won.** (*The rough equivalent of US$25,000.) Su Min drifts off to sleep beside him, but Sung Jae's eyes stay open, staring at the shadowed ceiling above the bed, calculating the maximum he could possibly yield from his investments & the bank account Su Min doesn't know about before the KakaoTalk creep's 24-hour deadline expires: he concludes he can quickly free about 10 million won, 12 max: & then he wonders if he should even pay it, if he shouldn't instead tell that creep with the anime avatar to go fuck himself. Maybe he could go to the police. It's a clear-cut case of blackmail. *But can you involve the police without Su Min finding out?*

& then he's wondering how the creep traced him – how he got the video in the first place – *maybe the whores were in on it* – or the motel staff – *& Su Min's picture* – from her Instagram… Maybe it was someone he knows – *& Maybe I could borrow the money from someone…* & these two thoughts combine, the friend most likely to lend & prime suspect being one & the same: *Jong Gil.*

Sung Jae gets out of bed as quietly as possible & takes his phone to the bathroom, arguing with himself over whether Jong Gil could really be behind something like this.

As he closes the bathroom door, Sung Jae sees a new message: *If you don't wanna answer me, fine. Maybe I'll send the video to your company, too…*

Who are you? Sung Jae types. He checks the door's locked & the sound is off on his phone, then hits play on the video. It's him in the video, along with the whore Jong Gil suggested… *Jong Gil.*

Think of me like Robin Hood, the creep replies. *I take money from rich assholes and redistribute it to the poor. Of course, if you don't want to help the poor, I can always just send Su Min the video & do some moral good that way…*

"Aish…"

You're asking for too much money, Sung Jae types. *Can we negotiate?*

If you can't get all the money at short notice, I can wait, the creep replies. *But I'm going to need some money by tomorrow to prove you're serious. And I'm going to need that 25 million won eventually.* A bank account number follows.

Sung Jae's phone-holding hand is shaking; he hears Su Min moan & stir in bed in the next room; he unzips & lets a torrent of piss flow into the toilet, as the creep's next message appears: *Send 2 million won. Now. I know you've got your phone with you,* followed by that stupid fucking grinning duck emoticon.

Sung Jae pauses, hands trembling, completely at the mercy of this unknown fuckhead. *What choice do I have?* He opens his banking app & copies & pastes the account number from KakaoTalk. The account name he sent the money to appears as MONSTER HUNTER, giving no clue to the creep's true identity. *I've sent it.*

Cool, the creep replies, followed by that fucking grinning duck. *You've got 1 week. 25 million won.*

Sung Jae's about to turn off the phone screen & exit the bathroom when another message appears: *And the 2 million won you just sent doesn't count. That 2 million is an extension fee. I want an extra 25 million won in my account by this time next week, or I'm sending this video to every person you've ever met. Okay?* & again with the fucking duck.

Sung Jae leaves the room & pushes the door closed behind him as silently as possible.

"Sung Jae, what's wrong with you?" Su Min complains from the bed.

Sung Jae freezes; *does she know?* How could she? *Maybe the bastard sent her the video already…*

"You didn't flush."

"Sorry," Sung Jae says, feeling his heartbeat approach heart-attack speed as he re-opens the bathroom door.

14.03.

Jong Gil's a mess of excess flesh, all middle-aged paunch beneath the tired old suit: his hair cut perfunctorily short, but with odd stray ends & uneven sections, a clear rush job – *he can't have spent more than 5000 won on it* – & his eyes are small beneath the glasses (unstylish thin-rimmed black things, the glass slightly grubby with thumbprints) – & smiling, *always smiling, & what does he have to smile about?* – the more of the day passes, the more convinced Sung Jae is that Jong Gil is the one blackmailing him.

Jong Gil's making jokes all day, as usual – about the government saving money on not heating the place properly, with winter raging outside; & them being part of the Highways Agency, this is always the busiest time of year – how this is a joke Sung Jae doesn't know. But usually he laughs. Today he's faking smiles, but he knows that Jong Gil's hiding something.

& Jong Gil approaches Sung Jae's desk, breath thick with stench of stale coffee & cigarettes: "Everything alright, Sung Jae? You seem distracted."

"I'm busy."

They all eat lunch together, Nam Soo dominating the conversation, Sung Jae & Jong Gil & Hyung Woo nodding & laughing along deferentially as they eat their kimchi jjigae. Then cigarettes & a coffee & it's back to the office, Sung Jae wondering if he ought to bring the money thing up, see if Jong Gil will loan it to him, & see if he can read from Jong Gil's reaction what the bastard's playing at.

I have the bank account details, Sung Jae reminds himself. He isn't sure what use, if any, this is: *Can you tie a bank account back to a person? How?*

"Maybe we should go for a few beers after work, huh?" Jong Gil says. "And something to eat."

"I told Su Min I'd be back early," Sung Jae lies, staring deep into Jong Gil's glass-shielded little eyes until Jong Gil cracks & smiles:

"Okay. Maybe tomorrow."

Does he know I know?

Sung Jae re-reads the KakaoTalk messages as he walks from the office to the underground parking lot; he almost plays the video again, but stops himself. He turns his key in the ignition & the radio starts playing: the news. Something about Bitcoin. About someone in government mooting the idea of doing something to bring the rampant speculation under control. *Bitcoin.* Bitcoin. The rapid rise; the insane profits. *Jae Seok.* He has to speak to his son somehow before he goes home; he cannot dare risk having Su Min overhearing them. No, *if she hears us, she could discover everything…*

And it's Monday – *so what's Jae Seok's schedule?* English hagwon. *Until… 9.30? 10pm?*

Sung Jae taps out a KakaoTalk message to Su Min as his car stops at a red light in the thick evening traffic, saying he has to work late, she shouldn't worry about dinner, but he'll try to get back as quickly as possible. Then he pulls up on the street outside the five-storey hagwon, a fleet of bright orange buses parked in front. *I can't wait here… He's already inside… Just get here before the last class finishes…* So what to do until then? The mounting stress makes Sung Jae want nothing more than to down a bottle of soju, but he instead parks a few streets away from the hagwon outside a Caffe Bene, then nurses an Ice Americano, chain-smoking in the smoking area. The caffeine & nicotine heightens Sung Jae's anxiety but he convinces himself that it's sharpening his mind.

"I'm Jae Seok's father," Sung Jae tells the woman on reception at The English Factory. "He's in Grade 8."

The pale skin of the receptionist's face is overly-taut, perhaps the recipient of too much plastic surgery; nevertheless, Sung Jae finds her attractive; & as he waits on the bright orange sofa in the hagwon's lobby, he scolds himself: *This is how you fucking caused this mess in the first place. Thinking with your dick.* He wants to chop it off, to castrate himself; & then thinks if this all blows up, that might be what's expected of him as penance. *How could you be so stupid… Everything's okay until you get caught.*

"Jae Seok!" Sung Jae says with a smile, catching Jae Seok among the flood of kids & teens rushing in high-spirited laughter to the awaiting fleet of buses. Jae Seok stares at his father in wide-eyed bewilderment; his friends Dan Won

& Min Ho glance nervously at Sung Jae before breaking into a run toward the buses. "I left work late and I figured it was probably about the same time that you'd be getting out of class, so I thought I should come pick you up."

"Why?"

"Why not?"

Sung Jae leads his son to the car & switches the radio off after turning the ignition. "I wanted to talk to you about your coins." Jae Seok shifts in his seat, thinking maybe his mother's convinced his father to lecture him. "They're going well?"

"Yeah."

"Prices rising?"

"Ng."

"I was thinking of investing." Sung Jae delivers the long-winded explanation he perfected in the coffee shop, telling his son how impressed he is with his attitude toward investing & how much forethought he's showing for his age, but Jae Seok is only half-listening, overcome with relief that his father's not trying to make him give up on coins altogether. "So… if I wanted to make a quick profit, what would you recommend?"

"Well… FSC's been doing well for me lately."

"Uh-huh… and what's that?"

"It's… I don't know exactly. But the price has gone up by about five or six times what I paid for it."

"Wow! That much, huh? And you think it's going to keep on increasing?"

"Sure. I think people are only just starting to FOMO into it."

"FO…MO?"

"FOMO. Fear of Missing Out," Jae Seok says in English, before explaining further in Korean. "It's when people see an investment rising really fast and because it's rising really fast they get afraid they'll miss out on making money as the price rises and because they're afraid of missing out they invest and then the price goes higher because people are investing money because they're afraid of missing out and then that makes more people FOMO into it because…"

"Uh-huh," Sung Jae says, running calculations in his mind as his son talks; the price of Jae Seok's FSC coin has gone up five or six times in the time since he's bought. That means Sung Jae can probably double his 12 million won quickly enough to get the creep off his back. "So how do I buy this FSC coin?"

15. KING OF THE UNIVERSE.

ERR%20%:('location';= ***UNDEFINED;[critical.err%20%20%::'location';=ALL:::;;***

LEGAL DISCLAIMER:

Please be advised that the legal disclaimer preceding Chapter 11 ('King of the Earth') applies doubly hard to the chapter that follows. Things start to get a bit fucked from this point onwards. But remember, this is purely intended as a work of satire/parody/fiction. Also, please be advised that what follows contains graphic scenes of sexual violence. Unless you're into that sort of thing, you might want to think about stopping reading here.

</LEGAL DISCLAIMER.>

/ … / dry january :

Dry January' lasts until Federico & Jurate arrive at the frat with three bottles of dry white wine they're sharing with Ciara, which they offer the guys, & which Nguyen quickly accepts, with Guus instantly following. When Aart hears Ciara's name, he asks to join them.

Sometime later they're in The Three Sisters, & sometime after that they're in Kokomo; all are drunk, Guus & Nguyen hunting for girls, boasting about their blockchain billions in the dark of the dancefloor; & Aart ascends stairs to the smoking area & sees Ciara, laughing & leaning toward some muscular jock; & Aart stumbles back downstairs, & out through cold winter streets to the frat house, where he spends little time in the days that follow: always at the library, or on campus, or at cafes, working on essays & assignments & FSC community management, burying himself in work as snow buries Groningen's streets, occasional small talk exchanged with Ciara in the moments before leaving or after returning to the frat house, none of it meaningful: she always having vague plans to go out & meet 'friends,' Aart torturing himself over their identity.

Once January's wet, Guus drowns himself in alcohol, awaking with a vodka & orange juice, then guzzling a litre or two of Stolichnaya vodka every day, neat & in Cosmos & Russian coffees, serving Stolichnaya with refreshing cranberry juice when the excessive alcohol starts drying him out.

Guus eats a diet of pickled herring & boiled potatoes, & splits the hours of each day into alternating 20-minute blocks: 15 mins of deep-dive research into Vitalik Buterin & Ethereum; 15 mins of intensive Russian language study; & 15 mins of free-association drunk Internet wandering; – the five-minute breaks built into each 20 min block being used for mixing drinks, or staring quietly into space & contemplating, or using the toilet, or putting potatoes on & taking potatoes off the boil.

It's during the drunk Internet wandering that Guus goes off-piste into the dark web & spends a good chunk of Ethereum on a bag of white powder that turns up at the frat house a week later; he opens the well-packed envelope & sees the powder inside – "Wonderful!" – & racks up a line on the kitchen island in the frat's main living space, constant drinking having caused him to forget what the powder is.

Guus feels none of the immediate buzz & beauty of the dark web cocaine he's accustomed to & curses his purchase as a dud as he peels potatoes for later boiling, then returns to his intensive schedule of 20-min blocks.

He watches 15 mins of a Vitalik Buterin conference speech in awe of the awkward brilliance of the odd-headed slender prophet on-screen; Vitalik's almost-alien gait & delivery, the density of genius contained within every sentence, the sheer autistic brilliance of the slender pale-white Russian-Canadian who created Ethereum.

Guus mixes a cosmopolitan in the kitchen & spends his 5-min break contemplating the impossibility of competing with Vitalik's other-worldly superhuman genius, then returns to his room for intensive Russian study.

"Kto by ni prisel, menja net doma," Guus repeats – '*Whoever may come, I am not at home*'; "Kto by ni prišël, menja net doma… Кто бы ни пришёл, меня нет дома."

Guus absorbs the use of Russian past tense to express concession with ease, Stolichnaya making all things easier, pronunciation growing more perfect with each repeated utterance: but as he moves on to the fourth sentence, his mouth becomes dry, speech more difficult: "Cto by vy ni resili, on eto sdelaet po svoemu," – '*Whatever you decide, he will do it in his own way*'; "Čto by vy ni rešili, on èto sdelaet po-svoemu… Что бы вы ни решили, он это сделает по-своему."

Guus coughs, & coughs, & coughs again; mouth dry, something in his throat he cannot clear. Guus stutters on through the next two sentences, coughing hoarsely after each, until the 15 mins mercifully ends, & he goes to the kitchen to boil potatoes.

The short walk from his bedroom to the kitchen is unusually difficult: his limbs feel heavy & uncoordinated; heat flushes his cheeks & fevers his mind. Guus sloshes cosmopolitan over the side of his glass as he walks; he swigs, but his dry mouth feels no moister. He fills a kettle at the sink & has to lift the water-filled kettle with both hands, arms weak, to put in on its stand to boil; he awaits the boil, unsteady & dizzy, figuring he's in the throes of full-force hangover; he glugs cosmopolitan to halt the hangover's advance, then sees the white powder on the kitchen island, & racks another line with a bread knife.

He staggers to the stove, rubbing his nose, dizziness growing, & with great effort dumps the potatoes & boiling kettle water into a pan & turns the heat to 6, & then a word occurs to him: *scopolamine.*

"Fuck…"

The details of the dark web purchase rush back, cutting through the fever clouding his mind: sometime in the past, maybe a week or ten days earlier, Guus watched a YouTube documentary on a crazy Colombian mind-control drug that renders its victims helpless zombies, the drug of choice for date-rapists & robbers & kidnappers & other sundry unsavories in South America: *scopolamine.* Scopolamine was what he ordered. Scopolamine was what arrived. Scopolamine is what he just ingested two fat lines of.

"…fuck…"

The walls of the frat house breathe & swell & Guus grins, thinking scopolamine a wild trip; thinking this is some intense South American LSD 3.0 that he will absorb & become more übermensch. With heavy limbs & staggered steps he moves through the breathing walls of the hallway towards his bedroom; but he stops, hearing Honey Badger in the bathroom: & Guus laughs & says aloud: "King of the Earth, you have returned to me!"

But as he throws open the bathroom door & the Honey Badger track plays, Guus stares at the ballooning boobs of the topless blondes papering the walls inside & realises it's just a recording, that Honey Badger isn't present, & some strange fear grips him, something malign in the ballooning boobs & Honey Badger's recorded time-frozen proclamations of kingly dominion over Earth; so Guus slams the door with all the energy he can summon & staggers back from the bathroom, through the hallway, legs growing ever heavier; & grabs his Russian textbook & opens two tabs on Chrome, then plays a Vitalik conference speech & a Russian movie in concert, stuttering over the same textbook sentence as a mantra as the noise grows all around him: "Кто бы ни пришёл, меня нет дома… Kto by ni prišël, menja net doma… Kto by ni prisel, menja net doma… Koto by ni pretzel, makcha dot net domaina… Kotton battered pretzel mad dot net dominance… Kobayashi putzel maddened nethan domino…"

& the words swirl on the page as Guus runs his finger beneath them, trying to maintain his focus, while Vitalik's voice rises, trying to be heard over the loudening angry-growing Russian voices; & Guus gives up on the book, & looks at the laptop screen, & screams as he sees *him* standing on-stage behind Vitalik: Honey Badger, his face emotionless, bald head shining beneath the stage lights, eyes betraying malignant evil, mouthing the words of the sinister Russian conversation: & Guus tries to close the laptop, but his arms are weak – so weak, he can barely lift them to the screen, let alone summon the power to slam the laptop shut; & he shouts at the screen:

"KOTO BIYVI NETZEL MADDANYA! KOVO BITYNI EVETZEL NADAMAYA!", & with one final exertion of effort, forces himself to stand upon his weakened legs, convinced *I need to leave this place immediately.*

/ + 18 days / Москва :

After Guus, Aart, & Nguyen's Aeroflot flight from Amsterdam to Moscow lands at Sheremetyevo airport, they're ushered through bland white airport hallways by a beautiful blonde Aeroflot rep who welcomes them to the country in English. Guus replies in Russian & continues the conversation as they walk through the terminal.

"All my life I have dreamed of visiting this country," Guus tells Anastasia the Aeroflot rep. "I have long harboured an obsession with the masters of Russian literature, from the classics of Tolstoy and Dostoevsky to the more contemporary genii of Bulgakov and Nabokov."

"Your Russian is very well-pronounced for someone who has never been here."

Guus smiles at Anastasia's compliment. There's something so effortless about all he attempts these days that it never occurred to him there was anything unusual in attaining a decent command of the Russian language in a few short weeks. His every waking hour is dedicated to the betterment of self or the pursuit of pleasure; his consciousness has expanded; he hath become truly Übermensch.

As Guus thinks these deep self-congratulatory thoughts, Aart's eyes wander across the souvenir stalls & shops lining the Arrivals area, all loaded with images of the Russian President: T-shirts with bare-chested Vladimir Putin riding on a tiger's back; a commemorative plate showing a bare-chested Putin head-locking a bear. Aart remembers that the country's macho leader will have eyes & ears at the conference reporting back to him. Aart's gaze falls across the stern faces of shaven-headed airport security, sleek black machine guns strapped over their shoulders. Aart shudders.

Anastasia leads them out of the airport, where a waiting chauffeur in a grey suit & cap takes their bags & loads them into a Mercedes-Benz S-Class Maybach, while icy winter wind blasts Aart's not-thick-enough coat & his shuddering intensifies.

Guus gives Anastasia some flowery farewell in Russian & she concludes their dalliance by entering her number into his phone, leaving him with a hard-won Russian smile before he joins the others in the Maybach.

"Yo, can we smoke in here?" Nguyen asks, once the car's moving away from the concrete expanse of the airport.

Guus relays Nguyen's question to the driver in Russian, & gets a negative response: "Nyet. It's against the law."

Nguyen is visibly tense, twitching, body craving nicotine. Guus's initial calm ebbs away as the Benz powers along a motorway, thick forest lining the banks at either side of the road. Guus bites his fingernails & scratches his head & neck, suffering the same nicotine lust as Nguyen. The other two's shifty discomfort deepens Aart's overpowering fear of all things Russian.

The Maybach rolls over two canal-crossing bridges as thick-forested green gives way to the grey of city sprawl, Moscow's austere architecture & snow-piled streets filling Aart with ever-deepening dread. At the journey's end, the spires & domes of the Kremlin & Red Square appear ahead of them. They leave the vehicle and Guus & Nguyen light cigarettes immediately, the chauffeur warning them that they'll not be able to smoke anywhere inside the hotel.

Aart snaps a picture of the Kremlin on his phone, trying to overcome his unease by focusing on how cool this is; here, in the winter cold of Moscow, staying at a 5-star hotel a street away from Red Square, helming a billion dollar tech concern, but as he notices Guus & Nguyen's gaze lingering lustfully on some wealthy & beautiful Russian woman leaving the Ritz-Carlton & entering an awaiting Bentley, Aart's anxiety returns, more all-consuming than ever before.

"You know, this is the same hotel Trump stayed at when Moscow hosted Miss World," Guus says, entering Aart's room.

At Aart's insistence, they've not booked a suite this time, but their individual rooms are beautiful & luxurious, with classic antique decor and the inimitable sensibility of Old Money class.

"Really," Aart says, staring out the window at the majestic-but-terrifying sight of Red Square & the Kremlin below.

"Really." Guus sits on the bed, scrolling through the Ethereum whitepaper on his phone. "It was in the Steele dossier on Trump that got leaked just after his election. Apparently he had a bunch of hookers piss all over the bed in the Presidential Suite because Obama once stayed in it."

Don't get any ideas, Aart thinks.

"Of course, nothing in that dossier was ever verified. And I read that there's only one bedroom in the suite he stayed in, so if Trump really did get a bunch of hookers to piss on the bed, he would've had to have a fold-up bed sent to his room, or else slept on a piss-soaked mattress, which seems ridiculous. Still, it makes for a fun story, no?"

Guus wanders out of the room without waiting for an answer; he's deep in the distraction of the enormity of the event ahead of him. Along with Vitalik Buterin, the Moscow Blockchain Conference is bringing some of the biggest names in crypto to the Russian capital, with many helming projects positioned far ahead of FSC in market cap; success here could be total.

/ -18 days / :

Riding bike. Countryside. Sunshine. Day. Weak winter sun. But dry. Some warm. Road clear. No car. Riding bicycle. Guus. Riding bicycle. In countryside. Guus. Is. Guus is riding his bicycle. In countryside. The countryside. Near Groningen countryside. Countryside just outside the city, heading to or from Haren, a small town a few miles away. Haren. *Why am I going to Haren?*

Guus slows his bicycle & pulls up at the entrance to a cemetery: he recognises it – has cycled this way before – but doesn't know why he's here, or what time it is, or where he's been, or…

He takes his phone from his pocket, notices the screen's cracked, & presses the power button to discover the time & date; but the phone's out of battery, so he returns it to his pocket, & cycles slowly into the cemetery, barren winter trees overhanging the path running through it, realising as he rides that at least one of the bike's tyres has been punctured.

Guus speeds up as he rides the headstone-lined path through the cemetery & emerges onto a tree-lined country road on the opposite side. He takes a left & cycles back towards Groningen, legs growing in strength, speed increasing as he pedals.

Guus is soon back at the frat house, entering the front door to the smell of a tomato-based pasta dish being cooked; he enters the main living area, where Federico's stirring a pot in the kitchen, & Wesley & Ciara are at their laptops on the quad-sofa.

"Hi," Guus says.

Federico: "Yo."

Wesley: "Where the fuck have you been?"

"I…" – Guus has no answer.

"Look, if you want to get fucked up all the time, that's your choice," Wesley says, staring with days of pent-up anger at Guus. "We all know you've got the money. But you need to be more careful. You could've burned the house down."

"I…" – Guus looks at the pot Federico's stirring, & suddenly remembers the potatoes he set to boil just before the scopolamine kicked in.

"And don't leave your shit lying around," Wesley says. "This place isn't your own private fucking drug den."

Guus stares at the kitchen island with horror; its surface is clear.

"I bagged your shit up for you and put it in your room," Wesley says, "but next time, I'll throw it out."

"Or we'll take the shit for ourselves," Federico adds.

"Sorry…" Guus mumbles, backing out of the room, into the hallway, & his own room, where he sees his Russian textbook on his desk, still opened to the page detailing the use of past tense to express concession, a sealed baggie of white powder lying on top of the textbook. Guus lifts the scopolamine & grins at his much remaining powder: "Кто бы ни пришёл, меня нет дома."

/ + 18 days / :

Guus paces his Moscow hotel room, phone in hand, watching Vitalik Buterin's dry detail-rich conference speeches on YouTube. There is none of the flair & panache of the grandiloquent dictators Guus has modelled his stage persona on; Buterin's delivery is that of a man unconcerned with such gimmickry – a man with an autist's focus on the precision with which his ideas are delivered. *And it works,* Guus reminds himself; Ethereum is at $1000 per token, snapping away at Bitcoin's market dominance: BTC sits at just over $11,000, BTC's value falling by almost half since its $20,000 December peak, while ETH stays strong, Vitalik Buterin's genius & awkward otherworldly charisma coming ever closer to eclipsing the creation of anonymous Satoshi Nakamoto.

Guus moves about the room watching hours of Vitalik's speeches, trying to find a flaw, something to exploit; a weakness which he can tear open to weaken the Jesus of cryptocurrency; the Son of the unseen Old Testament Bitcoin God, Satoshi Nakamoto.

Guus does nothing but watch & absorb & seek weakness until a knock at his door some hours later; he opens the door to Nguyen, phone still in Guus' hand, Vitalik's speech at BeyondBlock Taipei still playing.

"Yo, it's getting kind of late," Nguyen says, holding a beer. "I was thinking we could go get loaded, hit a bar or a club, find some bitches…"

"Not tonight. There is much to be done in preparation for tomorrow."

Guus slams the door & returns to pacing & watching Buterin, fully obsessed with conquering this unbeatable foe. As he paces, Nguyen's words prick at his conscience, & Guus suddenly becomes overcome with desire for a cigarette; he remembers the chauffeur's words, the strong admonition against smoking in the room, & for a second thinks *fuck it* – he can easily afford whatever the fine is; but then he remembers that Putin's eyes & ears are all around him, that this is the same hotel where Putin allegedly videotaped the American President enjoying a gaggle of prostitutes' bed-pissing golden shower show, & that any indiscretions here may harm his chance of overthrowing Vitalik Buterin; so Guus drops his phone to the bed & grabs his cigarettes & heads out to the elevator, rides it to the lobby, & steps out into the deep sub-zero Moscow winter cold, barely conscious of the temperature or his lack of a coat, wandering the broad boulevard toward Red Square, staring at the Kremlin as he smokes & smokes, & finishes a cigarette, & lights immediately another; the Kremlin, lit up against the orange glow of mega-city night; the Kremlin, Putin surely sitting somewhere inside;

the Kremlin, the seat of ultimate power in the post-Brexit/post-Trump world; the Kremlin, the place he intends to make his own…

Guus walks back from Red Square, mind unfocused, processing a thousand thoughts per second, a conduit through which some grand world-changing epoch-defining evolution of all that is human is being carried out, some spirit far greater than he controlling all Guus' movements & choices & etc.,

& then he sees him: casually approaching the entrance to the Ritz-Carlton, walking toward it from the opposite direction, wrapped in a thick long coat, eyes focused on the ground…

"Vitalik," Guus says, blocking the man's path at the Ritz-Carlton entrance.

Vitalik's eyes meet Guus's in terror, like an animal staring into the barrel of a hunter's rifle; Vitalik immediately regrets taking the risk of leaving the hotel alone, thinking Guus is at best a journalist, at worst some kidnapping bandit from the Caucasus; but as Guus smiles, Vitalik relaxes slightly, thinking perhaps he's just a fan, in town for the blockchain conference.

"I'm sorry. My name's Guus van Hooijdink. I'm here with Future Synergy Coin. I'm speaking at the conference tomorrow."

Vitalik's guard drops entirely; he's heard of the coin, being omnipotently aware of all tokens issued on the Ethereum blockchain.

"I've been waiting a long time to get a chance to speak with you," Guus says, almost ranting, speaking so quickly, desperate to ensnare his prey: "Are you staying here? I'm staying here. Maybe we could get a drink or something? Have you eaten?"

/ -13 days / :

"I like Federico – a lot – ," Jurate's saying, "it's just… just… I don't know, y'know?"

"I know what you mean." Ciara sips cosmopolitan through a straw & stares across the Grote Markt: shoppers ambling across it, disturbing the pigeons who rise & reposition themselves every few mins with a dumb flutter of feathers; cyclists criss-crossing the Grote Markt & joining & leaving the road running round it, weaving in & out of occasional cars & buses. The serene scene calms Ciara, as it calms Jurate: "I still get the feeling that I don't know how serious he can be, y'know? Like I still have no idea where he is with me… how he really feels… or if it's all a fling."

"With Aart, it's the opposite," Ciara says. "If he wasn't so damn serious, I'd be so much more attracted to him. And I mean, he's nice, kind, friendly—"

Vallya: "Rich."

"Yes," Ciara admits with a laugh. "That he certainly is. And, I guess, thank God he's not gone completely mental since the money came in, like Guus, but… y'know… I just…"

"I know exactly what you mean," Jurate says. "But aren't you the main reason they made so much money anyway? When you wrote that marketing essay for them?"

"The whitepaper?" Ciara frowns; it's not the first time she's thought the same thing.

"Oy, with Russian man is much more easy," Vallya says. "They is always very direct, and tell you exactly what they feel. And with women, they are always the – what is that phrase… *consummate gentleman.*"

"Mmm," Ciara agrees, sipping cosmo again. "I need to find me a Russian man."

Jurate: "Me too."

The girls laugh & clink glasses. Soon only ice remains. Jurate suggests ordering another.

"I don't think I should," Ciara says. "I've got this essay to finish; it's due in Monday…"

Jurate: "What about?"

"It's for this Film Studies module I'm taking," Ciara says, "about the Bechdel test. It's this theory…"

"Ahoy!" – Ciara's cut off as Guus appears beside their table astride his bicycle: "How are you, ladies? I'm meeting Nguyen here. Maybe I'll head in and order a drink first. Can I get you something?"

The girls hesitate a moment before remembering Guus' looseness with the blockchain billions: then they stumble over one another trying to choose the most expensive drink on the menu, Guus grinning all the while; & when they're done, he stares deep into Vallya's hazel eyes & asks in perfectly pronounced Russian if that's everything.

She smiles demurely, Ciara & Jurate both clocking the flirtatious unfolding of her lips before she answers Guus: "Больше ничего не нужно, спасибо."

/ + 13 days / :

Guus glances from the cocktail menu to the colourful swirls of St. Basil's & the hulking Kremlin outside the window, illuminated against the night. He looks across the table at Vitalik, who's turning the menu over, opening & folding it, frowning.

A waiter appears beside their table. Guus orders a vodka-based Red Square from the cocktail menu.

"Would it be possible to get some tea?" Vitalik asks, in perfectly-formed but awkwardly-expressed Russian.

"Certainly, Sir. Would you prefer—"

"Hibiscus. With a lemon wedge on the side, if possible."

"Not a problem."

The waiter takes the menus & disappears. Guus glares out the glass at Red Square, wishing he'd brought the scopolamine outside with him, or that the alien genius sitting across from him would drink something that might make him more malleable than *fucking hibiscus tea with a lemon wedge.*

"This is quite the view, huh?" Guus says.

"Inside is even more impressive," Vitalik says of the Kremlin. "It's very intricate."

"Like a block lattice."

"But completely centralized."

"What's Putin like?"

"He's interesting. He seems to really believe in the power of blockchain."

Guus stares at Vitalik as he speaks, trying to form some impression of the tops of his teeth. Up close, Vitalik's pale skin & acne-brushed cheeks seem stretched across a skull malformed by the superhuman size of the brain contained within it. All he says seems all too earnest, like a peace-seeking alien yet to learn the deceptive ways of alpha homo sapiens like Guus van Hooijdink and Vladimir Putin.

Vitalik talks with low-key intensity of Putin's blockchain awe, & how it possesses the power to transform everything. Vitalik's still talking when the waiter reappears at their table. Guus sips from his Red Square as Vitalik twirls the tea bag's string around the glass handle of his tea cup, Guus wishing the Ritz-Carlton loaded their cocktails with as much vodka as he uses back at the frat house.

"I know what you mean," Guus says, staring out at the Kremlin. "This is a metaphor for the ultimate in centralization, right? Red Square. The Kremlin. Communism. A centrally-planned economy."

"I guess so," Vitalik says, squeezing the lemon wedge over his hibiscus.

"In a way, the whole evolution of Western society – nee, world society – has been this accumulative process of centralization. Disparate groups of hunter-gatherers, all with their own individualistic beliefs and behaviours, coalescing into larger communities. Those communities moving through animism and huge pantheons of deities to monotheism. Centralizing the very essence of being into the one monotheistic God."

"Huh," Vitalik says, sucking the excess juice from the lemon wedge & his fingers, then returning it to the tea cup's saucer.

"And Marx's theory of economics is in essence the first whitepaper. Satoshi 0.1."

"What do you mean?"

Vitalik seems generally interested; Guus smiles at the guileless genius. *Got him.*

"Just as Protestantism was about taking the power from the church, and returning it to the individual worshipper – essentially decentralizing the Catholic God – Communism was intended to decentralize the wealth accumulation mechanisms of Capitalism. The means of production. Distributing profit to the workers who produce things. Proto-Bitcoin mining, in a way."

"Huh. That's an interesting idea."

"I think what Satoshi envisioned – and you refined – is the logical 21st Century technological manifestation of this urge that has gripped all sons of Europe since the polytheistic beliefs of the Romans clashed with the centralization of power in the individual God-Emperor atop the Roman Senate. But then Satoshi's genius – his status as prophet – hinges upon his anonymity. Without that, he is the power-accumulating false prophet of the Roman Senate. The Pseudo-Christ. The Digital Caesar. What I guess I'm saying, Vitalik, is that by being the public face of Blockchain 2.0, are you not in essence the Anti-Satoshi?"

Vitalik's bulbous head is contorted by the slightest of frowns for a half-second before he replies with a smile: "Are you calling me the blockchain Anti-Christ?"

Guus laughs, too loudly, causing turned heads at tables in their vicinity.

Vitalik's answering before Guus has had chance to develop his idea farther: "But all Ethereum was ever meant to do is push the possibilities of blockchain further. If there comes a point where it splinters, forks, whatever… I don't need to be front and center."

"It's an accident."

"…yeah…"

"A happy accident."

"I guess." Vitalik laughs & lifts the half-drained lemon wedge. He pops it into his mouth whole & chews.

проковти́ти.

The act of swallowing the lemon wedge strikes Guus as defiant: defiance of social norms, defiance of the narrative he's trying to lead Vitalik into. "Say, Vitalik… do you maybe want to continue this conversation in my room?"

"In your room?" Vitalik laughs – the high full-faced laugh of the social-outcast boy genius turned billionaire demigod.

"I mean… I don't mean… I just… want to share something… that I'm afraid of other people overhearing."

"Yeah?"

"I have an idea… it'll blow your fucking mind. But I don't want other people overhearing it. It's… I think it could break the blockchain."

"Yeah?" Vitalik ponders for a moment, staring inquisitively into Guus's eyes; Guus stares back, sociopathically adopting the sincerest demeanour possible: two autists sparring over intricacies.

Vitalik breaks the stare first, glancing at his phone to check the time: "I should probably head back to my room now. I have to be up early for the conference, and there's a few things I need to work on tonight."

"It won't take long."

"Umm…"

Guus senses his desperation has repelled Vitalik; he's back where he was months ago, before the ICO and the billions and becoming King of the Earth; back when he was crashing & burning trying to chat up second-rate Dutch sluts in Groningen.

"I really should go. Maybe we can continue this conversation tomorrow." Vitalik slurps his remaining hibiscus & stands up to leave. "But it was good talking to you. And it's interesting what you said about the… religion… and history and stuff. I hadn't thought of it that way before."

And then he leaves, without a farewell, a few heads of those in-the-know turning as Vitalik moves through the lounge.

He didn't even leave me fucking 0.01 ETH for the tea, Guus thinks, sipping Red Square & watching the genius asshole disappear. *Fuck you, Vitalik Buterin. You'll get what you deserve.*

/ -13 days / :

Nguyen never arrives at The Three Sisters, Guus pretending to send him a message & bemoaning his non-appearance when asked by the girls. After their swiftly-drunk second drinks, Ciara says she really has to get back to the frat house to write her essay. Guus asks Vallya & Jurate what their plans are for the evening, effortlessly switching between Russian & English as he addresses them, & suggesting when they tell him "ничто" & "nothing" that they go back to the frat together for pre-drinks & later out to a club.

At the frat house, Guus pours glasses of Stolichnaya & organic farmers' market-bought lemonade, extolling its virtues & health benefits, Vallya's eyes growing wider & lips curving ever upward each time he switches to Russian; & Federico joins them on the quad-sofas for drinks, & then Wesley, then Aart. Ciara finishes her essay by 22.30, with all in the living room growing louder as Stolichnaya flows, & Guus starts racking lines of coke, & all ingest – even Aart, once he sees Ciara take the rolled-up 50 Euro to her nostril, – & two taxis are called to take them to Paradox on the opposite side of the city, Guus talking to the driver in hyper-fast Dutch about the blockchain revolution & how it will go beyond even Uber in disrupting the driver's industry, (though he never quite fully articulates blockchain's relevance to the taxi industry & the driver never quite cares enough to ask), Guus turning to Vallya in the middle-back seat to ask some general get-to-know-you question in perfect Russian every half-minute, while Aart (on Vallya's left) wishes Guus' loud Russian interjections would stop interrupting his attempts to talk to Ciara (on Vallya's right), & the taxis pull up outside Paradox, & all file inside the repurposed grain warehouse in an abandoned industrial swathe of the city: booming techno, strobe-lights whirling round the room; all drink & dance & alternate toilet trips to snort more of the white stuff; & when it comes Guus & Vallya's turn, Guus delicately holds his left hand to her cheek as he lifts his house key to her nostril with the right, then lets the hand linger as he stares into those hazel eyes, until the endorphin rush & tension of chemistry causes their lips to move in sync, tongues lapping gently in & out of the other's mouth, as Guus switches the coke baggie in his left hand with the scopolamine in his pocket, & scoops a hefty key, & lifts his right hand to Vallya's nostril as his face pulls back away from hers: "Приятного аппетита…"

/ + 13 days / :

Does Vitalik Buterin fuck?

The thought keeps Guus awake at night, staring at the blacked-out nothingness of the ceiling from the comfort of an enormous emperor-size bed. *Does the genius engage in the peer-to-peer transaction of bodily fluids?* Does Vitalik experience the bottleneck of horniness that so often swells Guus' cock & drains blood from his brain, leaving him slave to it? Or does Vitalik's bulbous brain do the opposite – pulling blood ever upward, powering the great thoughts of that mind, a million transactions-per-second firing back & forth between the brain's synapses and leaving the genitals barren?

Perhaps he's locked all pleasure up in smart contracts, Guus thinks: releasing hits of dopamine every time a milestone of work is completed. *Maybe my penis is holding me back.* Maybe cutting it off would be the best thing – becoming a tech eunuch; denying oneself the possibility of reproduction, so that all one's legacy becomes concentrated on the betterment of the blockchain.

Blockchain 4.0.

Guus knows his speech must be a blockbuster; he needs to blow every other smug crypto kankerautist to smithereens with the barrage of words he delivers on stage; he needs to be ushered into the Kremlin, to Putin on his hands & knees, begging at the feet of the blockchain master for the key to all the tech evolution that can help Russia supersede America & China & Europe & ascend to the status of sole world superpower.

Fuck Da Hongfei, fuck Sunny Lu, fuck Charlie Lee, fuck Roger Ver, fuck that anonymous cuck coward cunt Satoshi Nakamoto, and especially *fuck Vitalik Buterin.*

The weak winter sun disturbs the room's darkness long before Guus's mind has generated the hash power necessary to ascend to the crypto pinnacle; his dick swells & disturbs his thoughts, summoning images of Anastasia the Aeroflot rep & Vallya & Ciara & Nguyen & all the depravity of scopolamine experimentation; so that he dives out of bed in a rage, 5.20am, on his knees, naked, in the room's center, beating the dick hard as sunlight beats meekly against the curtains, until he's splooshed his seed all over the room's luxurious carpeting. Satiated, he pants, sitting cross-legged on the floor, mind clearing; but genius fails to strike him. He lights a cigarette & showers, flushing the cigarette butt down the toilet when he's done, then puts on his finest Hermes suit, adjusts his delicate black silk tie & styles his hair in the mirror, wraps his Louis Moinet Meteoris around his wrist, then sits suited at the room's desk, staring at the garbled insanity of notes he's produced for his speech; beginning with Blockchain 4.0, then long ellipsis & swirls & indecipherable scribbling, followed by the words *FUCK VITALIK BUTERIN,* over & over again, growing ever-larger, until the final time the words are scrawled, the pen stabs through the paper; he lifts the paper from the desk, stares at it, spits on it, then scrunches it in his hand, throws it across the room, takes a fresh leaf from the stabbed-through notepad, writes the words *Blockchain 4.0,* then stares at the blank sheet until tears fall from his eyes & spot the page.

/ -13 days / :

A short time on the dancefloor's all it takes for Vallya's swaying to become less timed to the music & a far-away look to enter her eyes. Noticing this long before the others do, Guus gently grips her wrist & whispers to her in Russian: "Follow me."

He leads her from the club's crowded dark to the cold empty night outside, not stopping to collect their jackets from the cloakroom. He thinks of calling a taxi, but then considers the possibility of something going wrong, & his phone number tying him to whatever wrong thing might occur, so he leads her instead through the barren silence of the industrial estate on foot.

"Where are we going?" Vallya asks him in Russian, he still leading her by the wrist:

"Nowhere."

Vallya says nothing.

They're soon on a main street with a wide road, though few cars move along it. Guus's sense of geography kicks in as a glance at Vallya confirms she's slipping deeper into scopolamine's embrace; he knows Stadspark is to their right, & he thinks for a moment of leading her inside it & experimenting with the scopolamine's effects before leaving her there, but remembers there's two decent-enough hotels by the Martini Plaza on the other side of the park, & that taking her there would be both less risky & more morally correct.

"You're beautiful," he whispers into her ear as they walk, testing the extent of her scopolamine intoxication. She doesn't react.

Guus grows tense as he enters the hotel lobby, wondering if her limbs may be too scopolamine-afflicted for her to stand freely once he releases her wrist; but his fears prove unfounded as he's required to use both hands to retrieve his wallet & give the front desk staff €310 in cash for a two-night stay (avoiding the use of a debit card, which could quickly link him to whatever might go wrong here, & booking two nights as he's unsure of how long the scopolamine's effects may last.)

He leads Vallya from the elevator to their Privilege Class Suite & regards it with disgust: a sofa & some chairs in one room, a bed in another, all brightly minimalist & functional & sparsely decorated, the entire space less than the size of the third-largest bathroom at his suite in Dubai's Burj Al Arab Jumeirah.

"Go to the bed," he tells Vallya, sensing her standing dumbly in the doorway behind him.

She does exactly as instructed, standing beside the bed, no clear thoughts of her own, as Guus closes the door to the hallway. He moves towards her, grasps both wrists, & stares into her zombied eyes. "What's your name?"

"Vallya."

The name is said without passion or thought; information summoned from within some isolated portion of the brain.

"Get on your knees." She kneels before Guus & he loosens his Armani belt, then lets his Gucci slacks drop, before yanking down his white Calvin Klein trunks. "Open your mouth." He looks at the complete capitulation the scopolamine's caused, remembering his own forgotten bike ride into the countryside as he strokes himself; the bike ride into the countryside, the panic-inducing hallucinations beforehand, all the forgotten time in between; the way Vallya's cheeks curve down into the chin, the perfect straight whiteness of her teeth, an apparent silver filling on the left bicuspid; the coming conference, Moscow, the risk of bringing scopolamine through Customs; Vitalik Buterin, master of Ethereum, his slave, kneeling before him, mouth gaping like that of the girl in front of him now; & he thinks of Vitalik's weird alien head, & whether Vitalik's ever eaten a meal without careful analysis of its nutritional content beforehand, or if perhaps Vitalik's bulbous braincase of a head is so devoted to blockchain he gives no thought to food, & will present to him a mouth full of untreated cavities; & that thought's enough to get Guus off, & send thick white spunk gushing from his dick & ricocheting off Vallya's lips & upper incisors, half the wad landing on her tongue, the other half spilling over her cuspids & dribbling down the right side of her chin. "проглоти́ти."

/ + 13 days / :

Nguyen is clearly hungover, face reddened, as he stands outside the Ritz-Carlton smoking, but there's something about the frazzled instability of Guus's face as he smokes that's far more troubling. Aart stares at Guus, trying to work out what's wrong, until Guus's eyes lock on Aart's with such menace that he's forced to look away, at Red Square & the Kremlin, which Aart stares at until a Bentley pulls up & a chauffeur beckons them inside.

The only sound as the Bentley rolls through the austere grey-lined streets of Moscow toward the conference venue is Nguyen's hungover groans, sounding a few times like he might throw up. Guus stares ahead the entire journey, brain overheating as he tries to force forth some genius Blockchain 4.0 concept, while Aart turns his head from the window to his companions & back again, desperately seeking something to alleviate his sense of impending doom.

Grey Moscow eventually gives way to the thick evergreen forestry of Solinski Park, a monolithic sprawling conference complex eventually appearing at its center. The FSC trio get out & join the scores of other attendees heading inside, where the sounds of thousands engaged in excited conversation about the world-changing possibility of blockchain fills the massive central auditorium.

The trio move between speeches & panels & informal side-meetings in a blur of buzzwords; blockchain, block size, scaling, tx/ps, sharding, concurrent verification models, the benefits of UTXO vs Account/Balance account modelling, Direct Acyclic Graph, removing the coding barrier to issuing smart contracts, the steps needed for mainstream adoption; Nguyen is in his element, explaining how & why FSC will do all these things & more, but Guus is agitated & distracted; each slick futurist fuck with a jargon-loaded vision a competitor, a sworn enemy who must be eliminated; & Aart's the businessman, extolling the benefits of FSC's business-friendly & trust-inducing Netherlands location; & Guus disappears from panels & conversations at random, as if his mind's suddenly slipped out of sync with his surroundings; he frequents the bathroom, but has nothing to sniff, so splashes water over his face & shakes short streams of piss from his cock, coffee after coffee after coffee frequently sending him back to the urinal: & speeches are given, all focused on going forward, moving onward, expanding; decentralization, regulatory compliance, creating a model that works for business, bringing trust to a untrusting world: & finally Guus takes the stage, mind a barren wasteland of blockchain fatigue; he steps to the mic. Applause subsides. Guus slowly opens & closes his lips, tongue drying quick inside. He speaks in a whisper – "...blockchain 4.0..." - then coughs, & coughs, until he's spluttering phlegm over the microphone; he turns his back to the thousands of eyes staring at him, a hacking cough expelling yellow mucus from his chest to the hand clasped over his mouth: & turns to face the audience, eyes staring, his own eyes watering, scanning them for something to hold on to: reducing, shrinking; fear.

& then Guus sees him; back of the room, talking with some presumable Putin stooges in suits: laughing. *Laughing.* At him. *Fuck you, Vitalik Buterin.* And Guus starts to speak, mind whirring into action, his brain's synapses becoming nodes in a decentralized direct acyclic graph distributed ledger of all he knows & all he is: "The future is upon us. And it is a future that will transform us. But as they say here in Moscow, Под лежачий камень вода не течёт – water does not run under a lying stone. It is for us to shape this future; to not Ждать с моря погоды – wait for the weather by the sea. For those who do not act decisively, Игра не стоит свеч – the game is not worth the candles. The candles. Red and green candles, competing, on five-minute price charts on a thousand cryptocurrency exchanges; this is the reality of crypto adoption at this moment. Day-trading speculation; childish dreams of moons and Lamborghinis. This room is full of children for whom У него семь пятниц на неделе – there are seven Fridays in a week. Today is Monday. Our Monday. The day of Future Synergy Coin. The day to synthesize and process and progress, to coalesce all the wasted water vapor of words that have been expelled into this microphone into one crushing tidal wave that will wash over the Sodom and Gomorrah of speculation and wipe this proto crypto civilization out to the sea. You've heard a lot of chatter about distributed this and decentralized that; just words. Vaporware. As ethereal and impermanent as the systems they seek to replace. FSC is the embodiment of something beyond all of this. Of all of you. All you who Брать с потолка – take data from the ceiling, who write nonsense from the stars; you're staring at the builder of the ark that will bear the future of finance, of civilization; a man in direct conference with God." Guus pauses to scan the audience; all faces stare at him with a mixture of car-crash fascination & abject Soviet gulag terror. The famous faces – Jun Hasegawa of OmiseGo, Brendan Blumer of EOS, Charlie Lee of Litecoin – smirk at the stream of nonsense emanating from the stage. *Fuck you. All of you.* Guus' eyes move to the back of the room, where Vitalik was standing, & sees that his principal rival has disappeared. Guus smiles, thinking he must've scared the kankerautist off. "We at FSC are constructing an ark not of wood, but of blockchain. And this is the fashion in which FSC's ark shall be constructed: as long and broad in nodes as there are stars in the sky; each node processing and verifying an endless array of transactions in perfect parallel; a post-blockchain solution that is as scalable as the ocean and faster than the speed of light. A post-blockchain blockchain platform that can be utilized by anyone, from the Wall Street banker and Silicon Valley tech genius to the lowliest African farmer and mentally-handicapped retirement-home-bound geriatric; as decentralized as the indomitable human spirit, as trusted as the word of God Himself; unhackable, unbreakable, unstoppable, limitless, endless; growing, growing, growing, until it consumes all that dare stand in this unstoppable gigantism-inflicted ogre's path. This is the future you have been promised. This is tomorrow. This is today. This is F-S-fuckin'-C." With some difficulty, Guus unfastens the microphone from its stand & slams it to the stage floor, causing the audience to groan & throw hands to their ears as feedback ripples through the auditorium.

Guus leaves the stage before the feedback subsides, most of the audience still wincing as he disappears.

"Did you understand that?" Nguyen asks Aart.

"No." Aart glances at the muttering people all around him, thinking their doom has finally come. He takes his phone from his pocket & opens the official FSC Telegram group: to his horror, the messages that flow through it are fully positive: *'ALL IN on FSC after this!!'; 'Feeling extremely bullish!!'; 'Guus is a fucking genius!!'; 'I wish I could've seen the look on Charlie Lee's face!!'; 'Hahaha this is the future, fuckasses.'* Aart closes the Telegram group & looks at the empty stage, where organizers are conversing in hushed tones, wondering what to do with the twenty-plus minutes that remains of Guus' allotted time. Aart opens Reddit on his phone, seeking the views of those not fully inebriated on the FSC Kool-Aid: a new post, 'Bizarre speech at Cryptopia 2018 by FSC's Guus van Hooijdink,' has already attracted 42 comments. Aart scrolls through them, face twitching involuntarily as all the most upvoted echo the sentiments of the Telegram group –

'Wow! What the fuck have I just witnessed! FSC just blew every other coin out of the water!'; 'FSC was already more than 70% of my portfolio, but after hearing that, I am ALL IN on FSC!!!'; Aart has to scroll to the bottom of the thread, & the most-downvoted comments, to find anyone expressing fear, uncertainty, or doubt: *'Umm did any of you retarded moonboys not notice that he didn't actually say ANYTHING?!'; 'FSC is the most overhyped project in crypto…'; 'I feel like I just had an aneurysm…'*

Guus is flicking through similar responses to his speech on his phone as he wanders without clear direction through the backstage area, everyone he passes lowering their heads to avoid eye contact, until Guus reaches Vitalik Buterin, talking in Russian with the same suits he was standing at the back of the auditorium with. Guus glares at Vitalik & Vitalik smiles back at him awkwardly: "Nice speech."

"Спасибо." *Follow that, you fucking kankerautist.*

/ -11 days / :

"There's something about him that is creepy… that I cannot trust."

"He is… strange," Ciara says.

Jurate 'mmm-hmm's in agreement.

"It's more than strange… there is charm when he talks, but beneath it… there is nothing. Like he hasn't a soul." Silence falls over the three girls outside The Three Sisters beside the Grote Markt. Vallya reaches for the pack of cigarettes in the table's center & lights one. Her mind sweeps back over the blur of Paradox, then awakening in the hotel, Guus gone already. It's the not-knowing that bothers her the most; with a guy like Guus, anything could have happened.

"It's the suddenly-rich syndrome," Jurate says, lighting a cigarette. "He went from nothing to something like that." She snaps her fingers.

"He was always a bit weird," Ciara says. "You're probably better off steering clear of him."

"And you?" Vallya asks.

"What do you mean?"

"You are living with him. I don't know… I feel he's not a safe person to be sharing a house with."

"Why?"

Vallya sighs. "Oy. I don't know. It's just a certain vibe I get."

Vallya's words come to Ciara's mind at moments during the days that follow, but against some instinct within herself, she dismisses the words each time she thinks of them. *He's just a guy,* Ciara assures herself. *Like all the rest.* No different than Federico was to Jurate when they first met. Just a guy looking to score. Especially a guy with suddenly-rich syndrome.

Aart enters the frat house one afternoon after lectures & finds Ciara alone on the quad-sofa, working on an essay on her laptop. His heart flutters when he sees her; the struggle not to fall too deeply into the rush of hormones she engenders within him is failing, constantly, he sinking ever deeper into a unshiftable & unrequited obsession. He thinks of the night they spent together every time he masturbates. "Hey."

"Hey."

"What are you working on?"

& she explains it's an essay for her American Literature class, on Kerouac – On the Road, the Beats: the way the rhythm of his writing is powered by the then-current tech of the typewriter, & infused with the spirit of all the jazz bars he frequented; & Aart shows interest, & asks questions, but Ciara is perceptive enough to note the underlying desperation with which he's talking to her, & it makes her uncomfortable, & when the conversation withers & he asks if she wants to smoke a joint, she says she probably shouldn't, & he leaves the conversation on a note of awkwardness, & enters his room, & rolls a joint to smoke alone.

Wesley's birthday falls on the weekend that follows & by 17:00 the group spread over several tables in front of The Three Sisters is boisterous with free-flowing booze: Wesley, Guus, Aart, Nguyen, Federico, Jurate, Ciara, - (Vallya was invited, but told the girls she'd rather not) – Jako, Wander, Max,

Petr, Norma, Penny, Klint, &etc. &etc., numbering twenty or thirty in total; & when dusk descends over the Grote Markt, Wesley asks those sitting closest to him, "What should we do later? I mean, it's still early, but—"

"That's been arranged," Guus answers.

& they drink continuously until 19:45, when Guus disappears to make a phone call, then announces to all that the taxis are on their way, & Wesley asks: "The taxis to where?"

The fleet of cabs ferry the rowdy revellers across the city to the Martini Plaza, a large modern conference center beside Stadspark, where a line of hundreds is awaiting entry. A cheer ripples through the crowd as Guus steps out of the taxi at the head of the convoy, the blockchain billions having long-since brought him celebrity among the university's students.

"What's going on?" Wesley says, half-drunk, fully-stunned.

"It's for you," Guus says, draping an arm over Wesley's shoulder. "It's your 21st birthday, man! This is a big one! I wanted to pull out all the stops and show you just how much I appreciate you."

"Holy shit," Welsey says, Guus guiding him into the Martini Plaza. "This is insane, man. Thank you. I don't even know what to say."

"You don't have to say anything. Just enjoy your night."

"But the people… where did they come from?"

"I put out the word out on Facebook. Free entry and a free bar all night. No-one's going to turn that down."

"Free booze? For everyone? Shit. How much is this costing you?"

"You don't need to care about that, bro. It's your birthday."

Aart's a few steps behind, between Nguyen & Federico. He shudders when he hears Guus say 'free bar' – another wad of tens of thousands drained from the FSC development budget. *This will all end terribly.*

Ciara's a few steps behind them, besides Jurate, taking in the wildness of the scene & thinking maybe Vallya was wrong about Guus; that he's genuine & generous, & maybe the suddenly-rich syndrome has made him a little wild, but beneath all the bluster, he's truly a kind-hearted & good-natured guy, always looking to take care of his friends.

/ + 7 days / :

"Guus!" Aart is surprised to see him, looking preternaturally calm as he sits in an armchair in the Ritz-Carlton's grandiose lobby, a half-devoured platter of Russian pastries & a tea set spread over the table in front of him. "We were looking for you. What happened?"

"All the talk of blockchain grew tiresome," Guus says, looking straight past Aart & Nguyen to the large entrance doors at the lobby's edge. "I decided to return here for a refreshing afternoon tea."

"You want us to join you?" Nguyen asks, unsettled by the weird intensity with which Guus is staring at the hotel's entrance.

"If you wish."

Aart & Nguyen pause for a moment. Aart speaks first: "I think I'll go to the room for a while."

"As you wish."

"Yeah…" Nguyen says. "You maybe want to get a few drinks and go to a club or something later?"

"Why not."

Aart & Nguyen stand silently for a moment, awaiting more from Guus; when nothing comes, they head to the elevator, leaving him in the lobby, staring at the entrance, taking occasional sips of now-tepid Russian Earl Grey. It's another hour – perhaps two – until Guus finally sees Vitalik Buterin enter. Guus keeps completely still as Vitalik moves through the lobby to the elevator, Guus slighting adjusting the angle of his head to watch as a bellhop beckons Vitalik into the elevator. As the elevator doors slide closed, Guus rotates himself completely to stare as the golden numbers above the elevator tick upwards: 2, 4, 7, 10. Guus stands up the moment the numbers start ticking back down towards 1 again. He moves at brisk pace across the lobby, hands the bellhop a crisp 5000 Rouble note & says in flawless Russian: "To the tenth floor, please." Guus steps out of the elevator and stares at the closed doors lining the lavish creme & wood panelled hallway. He listens for a moment in dead silence for some sign of which room Vitalik entered. "Excuse me," Guus says, again in Russian, returning to the bellhop & the elevator. "I must have been mistaken. My room is on floor six."

/ -7 days / :

"Yo, it's great to be back here in Groningen," Honey Badger says, drawing a roar from the 2000-strong crowd of students packed into the Martini Plaza. "And I'd like to thank the man himself, Mr. Guus van Hooijdink, for bringing me back here." Guus bows his head slightly from the side of the stage as the crowd cheer the mention of his name. "And we're all here tonight for one special boy. Wesley de Gooyer, 21 years-old today." Drunk as hell & high on adrenaline, Wesley grins stupidly beside Guus at the side of the stage, raising his arms in celebration as the crowd cheers his name. "I hope that the King of the Earth can make this a very special birthday for you," Honey Badger says, looking every inch the global superstar in his pristine bright-white suit. "And we gonna make sure tonight, Wesley de Gooyer, you and all us in here's gonna party like we only got six months to live!" The crowd roar as snyth'd strings kick in, followed by an electronic drumbeat & the voices of a half-dozen on-stage backing singers, the crowd going wild & getting down in sync with Honey Badger as he launches into 'P.A.R.T.Y. (like you've got six months to live.)'

Beyond the sprawling crowd clustered at the stage-front, at the long wall-spanning bar at the back of the Martini Plaza, Aart's side-stepping drunk students, seeking another drink to stop himself fretting about how much of the development budget Guus has blown (again) on Honey Badger's performance fees. He stops suddenly a few meters from the bar, subconsciously aware of something soul-destroying before his conscious mind's processed what his eyes have relayed to it: Ciara, at the edge of the bar, a tall muscular blond Dutchman with his hands around her waist, leaning in, smiling, kissing her on the neck; she playfully pushes him back, then grasps his head with both hands, pulls him towards her, & thrusts her tongue into his mouth. Aart pushes his way to a point further along the bar, orders a Long Island Iced Tea, asks for it to be made extra strong, then stares at the stage, despair & aching emptiness filling his soul as glitter cannons explode behind Honey Badger & send golden confetti cascading over the crowd. It takes Aart two songs to drain the Long Island Iced Tea & the best part of another song to be served a second one. As he stares empty-minded at Honey Badger's stage-strutting swagger, a female voice asks him something. "Excuse me?" He turns to the girl, her wide eyes & slight smile mesmerising in the half-dark at the back of the auditorium.

She speaks again: "You're one of the FSC guys, right? With Guus van Hooijdink?"

"Right."

The kiss was fun, but the tall muscular blond Dutch boy was far too quick to get frisky with his hands, & Ciara's soon away from him, scanning the faces she passes, searching for one she recognises. She sees Jurate & Federico some distance away, at one of the reserved tables set up at the auditorium's edge, leaning in to make-out with each other. She sighs & turns & sees Aart, smiling & conversing with another female, & the thought cuts through her drunkenness that *it's him I want.* She fights the thought at first, thinking it simple jealousy – wanting something just because it now appears she can't have it. But as she stares, she finds herself overcome with the realisation that it's more than that. She stares until Aart's eyes slip from the girl in front of him & threaten a glance in her direction, at which point she turns & walks towards the stage, lost in her drunkenness & the swarm of students swaying & shouting along with Honey Badger.

/ + 7 days / :

"Спасибо," Guus tells the bellhop, as he & Nguyen exit the elevator on the 10th floor and move along the carpeted hallway.

"Which room's Vitalik staying in?" Nguyen asks, bubbling with excitement at his first face-to-face meeting with the genius himself.

"Umm…" Guus pauses dramatically in the center of the hallway as the elevator's doors slide shut. "You know – gosh, this is embarrassing – I've actually completely forgotten."

"What do you mean? He just text you, right? Check the message on your phone."

"Yeah," Guus says, stepping carefully along the corridor, listening to what little sound can be heard from within the suites behind the heavy solid oak doors lining the hallway. He pauses almost at the end of the corridor, hearing an almost-imperceptibly soft tapping behind one door: "I think this is it."

"You sure?"

Guus doesn't answer, banging instead with a closed fist upon the door. The tapping inside stops.

"Yeah?" a confused voice shouts from somewhere inside.

"Vitalik! It's Guus. Guus van Hooijdink. From Future Synergy Coin."

A moment later the door opens, Vitalik Buterin appearing, the eyes in the center of his bulbous brain-bloated head staring at Guus in confusion.

"Ohmygod, Vitalik, Mr. Buterin, it's such an honour to meet you," Nguyen gushes.

"Umm… hi…"

"I'm incredibly sorry to disturb you, since you so clearly must be busy right now," Guus says, noting the laptop positioned on a coffee table in front of the suite's chaise lounge in the gap of room visible behind Vitalik's slender frame. "But there's something incredibly important that I would like to talk to you about, and I don't know when we'll next get an opportunity to speak directly face-to-face like this."

Vitalik pauses, scanning Guus & Nguyen for any sign of ill-intention, Seeing Nguyen's stupidly excited fanboy grin, Vitalik relents: "Come in."

/ -7 days / :

"The thing that's fucking great about Honey Badger is that he's straight-up, no pretence, all about the everyday party lifestyle," Nguyen says, speech delivered with speed & confidence that could only be brought about through a near-lethal combination of coke & alcohol.

"Yeah, right," Ciara says in the seat beside him. *He looks cool, exotic,* Ciara's thinking as she talks to him. *Earnest, but not overbearing with it.* "I liked that one song he did with Cheap Ho."

"Fucking no doubt, that was the anthem of the year however many years ago."

She wonders if what they say about Asian guys' penises is true. Losing herself in the red-flushed deep caramel complexion of his skin & alluringly sincere eyes, she figures she wouldn't mind finding out.

"That was quite some set, huh?" Guus says, appearing beside the table with a gigantic bottle of very expensive-looking champagne in one hand & a tray of champagne flutes in the other. "Let me pour you guys a drink," he says, resting the champagne bottle on the table & then removing two scopolamine-loaded glasses from the tray with his freed right hand. "Worth every cent we paid him, as always," Guus says, filling the glasses with champagne, the scopolamine dissolving unseen beneath the dim lighting. He pours a scopolamine-free glass for himself. "Chin-chin," he says, lifting his glass & smiling at Ciara.

"Cheers," Ciara says, lifting the glass to her lips, thinking for a fleeting moment that she sees the soulless malice in Guus's smile that Vallya warned her about.

/ + 7 days / :

"This is one of the finest champagnes ever produced," Guus says, standing in front of the bar in Vitalik's suite's main room, popping the cork & pouring the 1928 Krug into three champagne flutes. "The summer of 1928 was an exceptional one for champagne production: a perfect combination of heat and rain produced grapes with the perfect balance of high sugar content and high acidity, creating perhaps the finest vintage that man hath ever tasted. It is the encapsulation of the spirit of the year in which it was bottled: 11 years on from the Bolshevik Revolution, and 11 years before the outbreak of World War Two; that brief calm moment in the early-to-mid 20th Century where it seemed that peace were achievable in our time, and that the evolution of all peoples and societies were bound to blossom in concert."

"I can't drink," Vitalik says tersely, tapping at his laptop. "I have work to do."

"Of course," Guus says, bowing his head slightly & smiling deferentially, though inside he's raging at the $25,000 he blew securing the bottle from a private collector. He slips the scopolamine out of his pocket. "Nguyen, I trust you'll take a glass?"

"If Vitaik isn't drinking…" Nguyen says, eyes locked in awe on the gangly figure hunched over his laptop on the chaise lounge opposite him.

"Oh, come on. I've popped the cork now." Guus raises his champagne flute to his lips & sips some of the incredibly rich golden liquid inside. "It truly is magnificent."

"Okay. Just one."

"Splendid." Discreetly as possible, Guus cracks the scopolamine baggy open & tips a little white powder into Nguyen's flute. He shakes the glass, watching the specks of powder dissolve among the bubbles. "Perhaps I could order you some tea from room service?" Guus suggests to Vitalik. "Hibiscus with a lemon wedge?"

"I'm fine."

"Perhaps just a glass of water then?"

"I'm fine." Vitalik stops tapping at the laptop & smiles at Guus. "I'm sorry to snap. It's just I really wanted to get this thing finished, and with being at the conference all day, I haven't had chance to work on it, and—"

"I understand," Guus says, moving across the room & handing Nguyen the spiked champagne flute. "No need to explain yourself." Guus sits beside Nguyen on the chaise lounge opposite Vitalik & takes another sip of champagne. "Are you sure you won't try even a sip? The taste is truly incomparable."

Vitalik frowns, not wanting to offend; he lifts his hand from the laptop keys & takes the flute from Guus's outstretched hands.

Fuck, Guus thinks, staring at Nguyen in a panic, having intended to pass Vitalik the spiked glass.

"Wow. Yeah. That's really something," Vitalik says, handing the glass back to Guus.

"It is quite sensational, no? Perhaps you wouldn't mind a glass after all?"

"I really shouldn't."

"Oh. come on. One glass won't hurt you."

"I can't."

"Just a small one? A half-glass? A quarter? A shot?"

"What was it you guys wanted to talk to me about, anyway?"

Guus glances at Nguyen, who is sipping the champagne & staring in awe at Vitalik, beginning to perceive the faintest of ethereal halo glows surrounding him.

"Well…" Guus stalls. *Maybe I could just throw the scopolamine in his face,* Guus thinks. But then it'll be airborne, & affect Guus as well; & in Moscow, with illegal chemicals in his pocket, being strung out for the next two days could effectively be suicide. "We have an idea which will solve Ethereum's scaling issue once and for all."

"What scaling issue?"

"The… scaling issue… with Ethereum."

"We're solving it already. You've heard of sharding, right?"

"Right. But isn't sharding a form of centralization? Concentrating control of the network within a few full nodes?"

"No."

"No?"

"No."

Guus pauses a second, then smiles. "But we have a solution that is truly remarkable. A solution far more elegant than sharding."

"Yeah?"

"Yes. Perhaps you'd like a drink before we begin explaining our idea to you?"

"I'm fine."

"It really is quite an overwhelming idea… even a glass of water will help you process it."

"I said I'm fine."

Guus laughs involuntarily. He glances at Nguyen, whose staring at Vitalik with extreme intensity now, mouth lolling open dumbly; Nguyen leans forward on the chaise lounge, champagne edging towards the rim of the glass.

"Is your friend alright?" Vitalik asks.

"He's fine," Guus says. "He's Asian. They're not genetically equipped to handle alcohol."

Champagne dribbles over the side of Nguyen's glass; Guus leaps up from the chaise lounge & takes it from him. "Nguyen! Careful! This champagne is extremely expensive!"

"I think there might be something wrong with him," Vitalik says, staring with panic into the blank black abyss of Nguyen's glazed eyes.

"He's fine," Guus says, deliberately stepping backward & dramatically thrusting the champagne from the glass toward Vitalik. "Oh, shoot!" he says, missing Vitalik's face as Vitalik leans back; the golden liquid hovers in the air a few nanoseconds, before splashing down onto the laptop keyboard.

"Hey!" Vitalik shouts. "Be careful!"

"I'm sorry, I'm sorry," Guus says, dabbing at the scopolamine-infused liquid on the laptop with his shirt. Once the bottom portion of his Hermes shirt is suitably soaked, he unbuttons the shirt & balls it in his hands, champagne-soaked portion facing outward, prepped to be thrusted into Vitalik's face; but Vitalik is standing already, backing away from the chaise lounge.

"What the hell, man!" Vitalik says, his otherworldly autistic calm finally cracking.

"I'm sorry," Guus says, moving toward Vitalik with the champagne & scopolamine-soaked shirt.

A phone rings at the other side of the room; Vitalik turns from Guus and answers it: "Hello?" Vitalik switches to Russian, cupping the receiver close to his mouth, keeping his speech quiet enough that Guus can't make out what's being said. Guus stands in the room's center, shirt-in-hand, staring with dumb desperation at Vitalik. "I have to go," Vitalik says. "Now. Someone important wants to meet with me."

"But we didn't explain the idea yet," Guus pleads.

"Go. Now."

"But…"

"Now."

Guus stares at Vitalik, & Guus's own shirtless torso reflected against the backdrop of Red Square outside the window behind him. "But…"

Vitalik picks up the phone: "I'm calling security."

"Fine," Guus snarls, grabbing his black Hugo Boss leather satchel from the chaise lounge & snatching Nguyen by the arm & dragging him to his feet. He leads Nguyen unsteadily across the room to the bar, from which he snatches the incredibly expensive bottle of uncorked Krug 1928. "Maybe we can discuss this later?" Guus says, standing by the doorway.

"If you come to my room again, I'm calling the police."

Defeated, Guus throws open the door to the hallway & glugs directly from the bottle. "Come on," he snarls at Nguyen, who stumbles dumbly along the corridor behind him, limbs growing heavier by the second. Guus hits the button to call the elevator, then thrusts two 5000 Rouble notes into the hands of the confused bellhop as the doors slide open.

/ -7 days / :

"Let's go outside." The instruction works, & Nguyen & Ciara are moving through the thick crowd toward the exit, Guus glancing nervously at those he passes.

"Hey, Guus!"; "Great party!"; "Thank you for Honey Badger!"; "King of the Earth!"; "King of the fucking Universe!" & other shit is shouted at him as he passes drunk revellers, Guus smiling & bowing his head modestly.

Aart catches sight of Nguyen staggering through the crowd, 10 meters away, & his mouth opens involuntarily as he sees Ciara follow, clearly drunk as all hell, & then Guus behind them, but before he can add any thought to it, Maureen the big-eyed German girl says something, & Aart leans in & asks her to repeat it, & she clasps the back of his head & pulls his face into hers, & when Aart looks up from the kiss, the three have disappeared, & Aart thinks nothing more of them for the rest of the night.

It's a short walk from the Martini Plaza to the same 4-star hotel Guus took Vallya to. He pays the same €310 for a two-night stay in the Privilege Class Suite, then rides the elevator to the 10th floor, Nguyen & Ciara leaning against the sides as they ride, eyes lolling lazily in their sockets, mouths weakly opening & closing as if trying to speak, moving like the mouths of fish just plucked from the ocean.

They enter the bright sparse minimalist suite. Guus tells Nguyen & Ciara to sit on the sofa. They obey. He fiddles with the mess of phone charging ports on the room's desk to find a C-type to fit his Galaxy Note S9, then sets the camera to record. He takes his iPhone 10 from another pocket, finds the charger for that, then flicks through the list of text-to-voice MP3 files he programmed a few days earlier: *Aart + Ciara, Aart + Federico, Aart… + Vallya, Aart + Wesley, Ciara + Federico, Ciara… + Nguyen.* He smiles & hits play.

"Hello Ciara… Hello Nuh-guy-en," – Guus frowns at the gross robo mispronunciation, hoping it won't fuck the plan up – "I want you to listen very carefully and do exactly as I tell you. Is that okay?"

Ciara & Nguyen stare blankly into the middle-distance, occasional blinking their only movement. Guus lights a cigarette.

"Ciara, place your left hand on Nuh-guy-en's knee." Ciara's arm jerks leftward awkwardly, striking Nguyen's knee, then resting there. Guus feels a stirring in his groin. "Good. Now turn to face him. Good girl. Unbuckle his belt. Nuh-guy-en, help Ciara unbuckle your belt. Good. Now undo the button and pull the zip down." Guus frowns again as Ciara fumbles awkwardly with Nguyen's button-fly jeans; Guus walks to the sofa, brushes Ciara's hand aside, & undoes Nguyen's buttons himself.

Following the robo-voice's instructions, Ciara tries to pull Nguyen's jeans down, but he's sitting awkwardly & doing nothing to help her. Guus pauses the recording & returns to the sofa, pulling Nguyen's jeans off himself, struggling for almost a minute at the ankles until he realises Nguyen still has his shoes on. He flings the brown loafers across the room, striking a framed photograph of the New York City skyline & cracking the glass.

"Ciara, take your dress off," Guus says, wanting to speed things up a bit. "And Nguyen, take off your shirt." Both are soon naked on the sofa, & Guus returns to the desk at the room's edge, flicking through the pre-programmed robo-voice recording to get to the good stuff as he takes the final few drags on his cigarette. Nguyen lies flat on his back across the sofa; Ciara turns her body vertically parallel to his, then lowers herself onto him as per the recorded instructions, opening her mouth to take in his flaccid penis & grinding her genitals over his outstretched tongue. Guus stares at Nguyen's surprisingly-sizable limp dick slipping in & out of Ciara's mouth as her head bobs & the robo-voice praises them ("…good boy… good girl… that's it… that's the good stuff…"): inability to get erect should've been an obviously-foreseen side-effect of scopolamine; Guus thinks *perhaps I should've mixed some viagra in with it.* But regardless of these issues, the scene & his power over it & the thrill of a plan well-executed is enough that Guus's own dick experiences no erectile disfunction, and his slacks are soon bulging from the force of his hardened cock. Guus strips from below the waist & yanks his dick furiously, the ASR of the robo-voice & mechanical monotony of the action on the sofa, plus the realisation of the potential he's unlocked by mastering the power of scopolamine, all getting Guus so excited that he fires spunk out the end of his cock within a minute. He picks one of Nguyen's brown loafers from the floor, wipes his dick off on the insole, then pulls up his underwear & slacks, re-buckles his belt, & heads back out of the Privilege Class Suite to return to the Martini Plaza, leaving the robo-voice to deliver instructions & the S9 to record the scene.

/ + 7 days / :

"YOU FUCKING ASSHOLE!" Guus shouts, throwing Nguyen into his room. Guus glugs hard from the Krug 1928 & wrestles with the zip of his Hugo Boss satchel, pulling out from within it a rubber Vladimir Putin mask. The originally-planned scene briefly plays out in Guus's mind: a scopolamine-controlled Vitalik Buterin, caught on video fucking some unidentified Asian boy in a Putin mask; the scandal that would've surely sunk Ethereum & allowed Future Synergy Coin to ascend to its rightful second place behind Bitcoin at the top of the CoinMarketCap rankings.

"отвали, мудак, бля!" Guus rants, slipping fluidly between languages as he unbuckles his belt, yanks it loose, and whips Nguyen's prone dumbed-out form. "Dome Kutslet! Homofiele kut kanarie! ты чё, сука, охуел, бля?"

Guus drops his Hermes slacks to his ankles & steps out of them, shoes still on his feet, Putin mask in one hand & Krug 1928 in the other. He mounts prone & clueless Nguyen, Guus' knees either side of Nguyen's floored body. Guus tilts the bottle back & drains half of what remains in one giant gulp. Guus drops the bottle to the floor, hundreds of dollars of Krug spilling from it by the second, as he undoes Nguyen's belt & yanks his jeans down.

"Sterf aan kanker, apenkind!"

Guus tears Nguyen's boxers as he yanks at them before pulling his own down, his dick springing loose as the elastic waistband brushes over it. Guus grabs the Krug from the floor & pours what remains it over Nguyen's crotch, lifting his legs to cover Nguyen's asshole in golden liquid. Guus throws the bottle across the room, hearing it hit the wall & shatter. He grasps the Putin mask & pulls it over Nguyen's head with both hands, then shoves his erect cock into Nguyen's champagne-lubed asshole, slamming his insides hard, thrusting furiously, staring at the smiling fake face of Putin, thinking of Vitalik in the Kremlin, and Vladimir, thinking of fucking the hell out of the both of them, dominating them, destroying them, tearing Ethereum & the Russian Federation apart with each thrust, sharding Buterin's asshole, pummeling Putin & Ethereum into nothingness with his unsheathed weapon of mass penetration.

/ -6 days / :

Hot water, gushing from the showerhead… hands run through long hair, shampoo… and then she's there, in the present, steam rising all around as her minds moves out of the fog…

Ciara steps out of the shower in an unfamiliar bathroom. She takes a towel & dries herself. *Where am I?* She sees no clothing in the bathroom, so she wraps the towel around herself, then opens the door & gasps as she sees a figure stirring on the bed.

He sits up, blinking hard into wakefulness, before looking dumbly at Ciara: *Nguyen.*

"What time is it?"

Ciara's too confused, & self-conscious that the towel's all that conceals her body from him. She doesn't answer, & instead scans the bed & floor for some articles of discarded clothing. Finding none, she leaves the bedroom, & finds clothing scattered across the living room of an unknown hotel suite. *Did I…?* A cracked picture frame on the wall displays the New York skyline, & she thinks for a moment she might be in New York City – she could be anywhere, so utterly oblivious & disorientated is she – but after collecting her clothing from the floor & angling the towel off herself as she quickly dresses, she pulls back the curtains; after a moment of pure uncertainty, she realises she's looking down over Groningen's Stadspark. She hears the shower come on in the other room & takes this as her chance to leave, hurrying to the hallway & the lift & hotel lobby, out onto the street, no idea if she might've left her bicycle parked somewhere in the vicinity, instead walking the length of the city back to the frat house.

/ + 6 days / :

Aart knocks on Nguyen's door as the scheduled time for the car to the Solinski Park conference venue draws near. After a few moments, he knocks again. Nothing. Aart knocks on Guus's door next… nothing. He knocks again… nothing. Pause. Knock… nothing. Knock… Guus answers, hair a mess & eyes deeply bloodshot: "What?… Now?… Huh… I'm not going… I have heard enough empty chatter for one trip… You go."

Aart goes to Solinski Park alone & spends the day extolling the virtues of FSC as a dependable blockchain, a bastion of trust, a business-ready solution, a future-proof insurance policy for any business who'll do business with them. Business cards are exchanged, expressions of interest elicited, & the whole day is much smoother & more professional than any conference he's yet taken part in.

Aart returns to the Ritz-Carlton & rides the elevator to the 6th floor & knocks at Nguyen's door. He hears a groan inside, & movement: "Nguyen, it's Aart… open up."

The door opens into a dark curtain-drawn room, Nguyen even more haggard & dishevelled than Guus when he'd knocked in the morning. "What time is it?"

"Almost nine."

"A.M.?"

"P.M."

"Oh… huh… feels like I was sleeping hours, man… I must've only been out, like, what: twenty minutes?"

"You've been out all day. The conference is over."

"The fuck…"

Aart looks at Nguyen's confusion, his bed-creased face & empty eyes telling a story of self-destroying overindulgence. "Have you spoken to Guus?"

"No. He's not with you?"

Aart sighs: "I'll go check on him."

Nguyen shuts the door & flicks a light-switch & stares at the mess of his room; a broken champagne bottle glittering the floor, spots of blood dotting the carpet, streaks of blood on the bed sheets, a rubber mask amidst the mess of glass shards on the blood-specked carpet… He tries to figure out what he last remembers, but all he has is a blur… *conference… Vitalik…* "Fuck…" He recalls being in Vitalik's room, sipping champagne, then slipping into blackout; he shudders, almost vomiting, wondering if he did something stupid, if the blackout is his brain's way of protecting itself from the memory of the hideous embarrassment of whatever shameful episode unfolded in the Ethereum founder's suite. *I've got to stop drinking,* he thinks, stepping carefully barefoot across the carpet, eyes alert for any glimmer of glass. Nguyen touches the dried blood on the bedsheets, wondering what the hell happened, while some burning discomfort in his colon tells him he probably shat blood from all the insanely excessive drinking. He sits on the bed & stares at a mirror, at the tired mess he's degenerated into. He thinks of the last time he blacked out this deep, back in Groningen, after Wesley's birthday; waking up in some unknown hotel room… "What the fuck, man…" – then, as now, imbibing champagne is the last thing he remembers: the champagne lifestyle…. *I guess I'm not cut out for it…*

Each spends the night alone & next day rises to spend morning alone: Aart in Red Square, in awe of the coloured swirls of St. Basil's & snow-piled grandeur, thinking, as other men have stood on the Square & thought, that perhaps he is occupying a special space in history: the dawning of the blockchain era, on the battleground where New Ideas collide with Present Reality; Nguyen slumped in a curtain-drawn depression that can only be lessened with alcohol, & so the mini-bar nurses him through morning & afternoon; while Guus feels strangely blank, absent, thinking for a while of nailing what remains of the scopolamine himself, before flushing it, torn-up baggy with it, & supposing that whatever follows is whatever follows, & while the recent past may be preserved in the irrevocable distributed ledger of eternity, the chain continues, & since the past is irrevocable & the transactions of the future are as yet unspent, all one can do is hodl & await whatever awaits in the pending transactions awaiting the confirmation of reality…

& what follows, in late afternoon, is a Maybach back through snow-buried grey Moscow & the evergreen forest at edge of city & the Aeroflot lounge &

a 9 & ¼ hr flight to Hong Kong: the mad little island town where Asia meets the world;

when a Brit commander negotiated it as settlement for the Empire's expulsion from Mainland China, he was chastised by his superiors for delivering them a deserted hunk of rock as meagre recompense for all the treasure of Ming Dynasty China;

but the British lust for gold & commerce caused a city to arise, a ludicrous accumulation of ludicrously tall towering towers, branded with the big names of international finance: HSBC, Citibank, etc., etc.;

& when the British surrendered it through their surrogate Prince Charles beneath a rainstorm in 1997, it marked the end of all fading glory of Empire & symbolized a descent into obscurity & meaningless that would result 19 yrs later in that historic act of tragicomic national suicide known as Brexit;

or so Aart learns & infers from the exhibits of the Hong Kong History Museum, a fantastic four-floor trek through the island's history, from its geological formation to its present state as quasi-city-state at China's edge;

meanwhile, Guus & Nguyen take a hydrojet to Macau, the ex-Portuguese colony & Asian Vegas island, to gamble away the day at the scale-Eiffel-Tower-flanked Venetian, throwing huge wads of HK Dollars down pursuing 21s at blackjack, completely misunderstanding mahjong & baccarat, fucking around at a poker table too drunk to know what hand they hold or how many chips have flowed to & from them, casino staff on the constant edge of cutting off their alcohol, or kicking them out, but never quite doing it, because the outflow of development budget cash is so damn irrefusable;

& then a hydrojet back to HK, dead of night, to the bars of Lan Kwai Fong, cocaine bought from street-dealing Africans;

& the seedy bars of Wan Chai, full of European ex-pat finance-industry workers & Filipina whores;

& the night continues, much longer than it should, & morning breaks, & as Aart sleeps, Guus & Nguyen wander Causeway Bay, & a huge department store, each buying a Louis Vuitton handbag in fits of giggles, Guus convincing Nguyen it would be truly hilarious to show up for the afternoon's meeting with heavyweight international banking institutions in full haute-couture drag;

& outside one towering mall, an exhibition displays magnificent replicas of Chinese royal headgear produced by revered artisan costume designer Zang Chun Hei for use in Chinese opera:

"These are fucking magnificent," Guus declares, staring in coke-fucked awe at a glass cabinet full of vibrant sequined colour-rich embodiments of the grandeur of Old World pre-Opium War Imperial Chinese majesty. "Imagine turning up wearing one of these things."

"Yeah, that'd be cool," Nguyen says, swaying, can of German lager in his hand.

"Excuse me," Guus says to a security guard in broken Cantonese, "how much would it cost to purchase one of these?"

The bulky security guard looks perplexed for a moment before answering: "These are not for sale. Display only."

"I have money," Guus continues, articulating his thoughts in just-about-passable Cantonese. "I can pay big money for them."

The security guard looks at him, & then his accomplice, Nguyen, swaying, drunk as hell, beer in hand at 11 in the morning, thinking in Cantonese *who the fuck are these idiots?* "Not for sale," the security guard repeats in English.

"One million dollars," Guus says, en Anglais.

The security guard stares, thinking *he must be out of his mind.*

"Not Hong Kong dollars; one million dollars US," Guus says, counting through the dense wad of bills he has remaining from the casino. "I have here about three hundred thousand Hong Kong dollars; I don't know what that's worth, but I think it sufficiently shows I have the means to make good on my proposal. And here," he says, cutting off a quarter of the stack, and handing the security guard a little over HK$80,000, "this is for your trouble. Please call your manager and tell him I am quite serious about making a purchase. Tell him or her that I think the black and gold one in yonder cabinet looks particularly fetching."

The security guard bows sincerely & steps outside to radio the bizarre request up the hierarchy; after repeating it several times, a manger is sent, as Nguyen sways, overcome with fuckedness, & Guus stares with pure capitalist desire at the beautiful black cloth bling-adorned headpiece, floral patterns of gold & jewels stitched into it, a flower of sapphire at its center, lavish yellow tassels hanging off each side.

The manager arrives, a small man in glasses & a barely-designer suit, & bows deeply to Guus, before some transaction is conducted in an overly-long scene that involves Guus showing his tens of millions strong ING account to prove he can afford this insanity, & an international bank transfer is authorized, Nguyen almost falling asleep on his feet as he blinks heavily & sways & waits, & finally the cabinet is opened, & Guus theatrically places the gorgeous headpiece upon his head, & steps out into gorgeously warm midday HK sunshine, the swarms of shoppers & tourists outside all shooting confused glances at the coke-crazed Dutchman with the Emperor's headgear.

Where the fuck are they? Aart thinks, none of his texts or social media messages having been answered, all his calls going straight to voicemail. Aart is on the street outside Eastgate Tower in Admiralty, their scheduled meeting now seven minutes away. He looks from the sun-baked street & squat colonial buildings to the shimmering tower shooting up to the sky, calculating that the elevator to the 32nd floor offices of Hyde & Pearce will take long enough that he is perhaps already late; but as he turns from the street & toward the grand revolving doors of the tower, raised voices sound over the hectic street scene's background noise of foot & auto traffic: "What the fuck, bro! You must've just taken it all already!"; "Nguyen, that African gentleman in LKF sold us six grams of that shitty 'phet-laced coke, and I count precisely four grams thus far ingested by us, and hence, either you imbibed two grams alone, unseen by me, which is impossible, given your genetic inability to process intoxicants, or, the possibility which I consider far more plausible, is that you have lost two fucking grams of my shitty fucking 'phet-laced coke, in which case—"; "Just pay the fucking taxi man, dude! Jesus Fuck, the guy's waiting on you!";

Aart stares in slack-jawed horror at the scene; Guus, taking his wallet out to pay the taxi driver; Nguyen, in jeans & a 'TX/PS & BLOCKCHAIN EXCITES ME' T-shirt, clutching a can of German lager; Guus, turning from the taxi to face him, his meeting-appropriate Saville Row-tailored British suit completely undermined by a ludicrous gold & jewels-adorned yellow & black headdress.

"Guus… this is one of Hong Kong's oldest financial advisory firms… they deal with old-money families, their clients have been steeped in wealth for generations…" The elevator zips through floors too fast, Aart struggling to articulate why wearing that stupid fucking hat is a very bad idea, while Nguyen sways, looks sick, ears popping from pressure as the elevator rockets upward. "…you have to take the hat off, Guus. You have to."

Guus is staring straight ahead, betraying no emotion, until they hit floor 30: "As you wish."

He places the Emperor's hat upon the head of Nguyen, who's too confused to do anything but stumble forward as the doors slide open & they enter Hyde & Pearce's offices.

"The returns are truly remarkable, and quiet unlike anything our clients have ever seen elsewhere…"

"A once-in-a-lifetime opportunity," an elder suited Englishman concurs.

"A once-in-a-lifetime opportunity, indeed," the brutally handsome leader of the meeting says, "and we can see why our clients are very excited to stake a small portion of the money entrusted in us on this type of emerging technology. But with that said, the reason we have thus far been reticent to over-invest in this market is that it has all the classic signs of a bubble…"

"Rapid price rises, irrationality," the greyed elder speaker says.

"…and there is frankly no way of knowing how any of this pans out, long-term," the handsome younger man continues. "I'd say it's likely that ninety, ninety-eight, percent of these cryptocurrencies will crash and disappear and suck whatever's invested in them into the abyss, and that is simply not a risk we can dare take with the funds our clients have entrusted us. So, if I may so bold, I would be delighted if you could answer this question: why is Future Synergy Coin going to be one of the few cryptocurrencies that survives?"

"Well," Aart begins, ready with an answer drawing on the safety of Dutch regulatory compliance & a commitment to expansion & technical excellence.

"I can answer that," Guus interrupts. Aart glares at him for several seconds, as do the conservatively-suited Hyde & Pearce representatives. "Would you mind if I smoke?" Guus asks.

"Absolutely," says the handsome man.

Guus pulls out his cigarettes.

The handsome clarifies: "I meant absolutely, I would mind. You may not smoke in our office."

"I'm sorry," Guus smiles, returning the cigarettes to his pocket. "You know, I find firms like yours quite fascinating. A holdover of a bygone time, when the countries of Western Europe began that magnificent period of global conquest… I'm sorry, does it bother you if I refer to you as European?"

"No," the handsome Englishman says tersely. "Look, is there an answer to the question asked forthcoming? We really have better things to do than—"

"Great Britain, the Netherlands; kindred spirits in an age of global conquest, true pioneers in establishing the necessary conditions for the present era of globalisation," Guus says calmly. "Today, I sit across from you – a Dutchman sitting opposite an Englishman, each commandeering an organisation in the way our forefathers would've commandeered merchant vessels, seeking our fortunes in the golden harbour of Hong Kong."

"I think what he means to say," Aart interrupts, ready to shift the topic to Dutch regulatory compliance.

"…what I mean to say, Mr. Hyde – or is it Mr. Parker?"

"It's Mr. Richards," Mr. Richards the brutally handsome fortysomething Englishman says, quivering upper lip barely concealing seething rage.

"Mr. Richards – as in Keith Richards? The Rolling Stones? Or as in Richard the Third? Shakespeare! The Lionheart!"

"Okay, I think we've listened to quite enough—" Mr. Richards stands, fists clenched.

"Wait!" Guus gasps, standing. He stares Mr. Richards dead in the eyes. He grins. "Mr. Richards, our enterprise is currently valued at 3.6 billion dollars. And that is American dollars, Mr. Richards, not Hong Kongese ones. Six months ago, we were Dutch university students subsiding on a few hundred Euro per month. Today, I purchased this high-end replica of a Chinese Emperor's headdress for one million dollars." Mr. Richards glares at Nguyen in the ridiculous hat. "And again, that is one million American dollars, Mr. Richards. One million dollars to me is play money. Right now, I would happily toss that million US dollar hat out of that 32nd floor window and let the wind take it, so little does the money mean to me. But you want me to guarantee you that our valuation will continue to rise at the same rate?

This I cannot guarantee. But if it does, and you've let this opportunity pass, you'll have done a great disservice to the tradition of cut-throat capitalism on which your firm – and this island – was built. In less than half a year, we've gone from impoverished Dutch students to international billionaire playboys. Such incredible and easily-attained increases in fortune are not normal, Mr. Richards. These are strange times that we are living in, and times which will likely never return again. If you pass up this opportunity to make a return on your clients' investments – returns not of a few percentage points per annum, not some piddling double-digit percentage points return – no, I'm talking hundreds – no, *thousands* – of percentage points. The greatest transfer of wealth in human history, Mr. Richards. A veritable modern-day gold rush. Such a venture is not without risk, of course; nor was the age of colonial expansion that enabled this city to rise up which today welcomes us, Mr. Richards. Great Britain's great adventure of expansion that led to this island's formation was also a venture fraught with risk. But I truly believe the biggest risk is doing nothing. It's letting the future flutter by, like a million dollar hat tossed out of a 32nd floor window."

Mr. Richards & Guus stare into the other's eyes for a moment; Mr. Richards cracks first. "Then let's talk numbers," Mr. Richards says, smiling.

Guus, Nguyen, & Aart leave Eastgate Tower & step into glorious HK sunshine with a Memorandum of Understanding & potential multi-million dollar investment, Guus again adorned with the golden headpiece, smiling broadly as he strides & draws stares from all who pass, Nguyen staggering dead-tired behind him, Aart at a loss for what to feel: the deeper into pure idiocy Guus sinks, the greater his success.

They return to the Mandarin Oriental hotel on foot, Nguyen barely making it to his room before he passes out, Guus exorcising myriad toxic influences from within him through intense exercise – weights, squats, treadmill – then sauna, followed by full-bodied massage, while Aart stares across the harbour-bordered city of super-finance megastructures, wondering what the fuck is wrong with this world, & how Guus seems to have completely mastered it.

Guus takes a 20 minute power nap & then is straight back onto Hong Kong's crowded streets, Emperor's hat atop his head, walking along Queensway to Lan Kwai Fong, in search of more Africans to buy coke from. But the coke dealers seem to be shying away from the sunlight, & Guus instead pounds drinks & rants at a barmaid & an increasingly-irritated red-faced middle-aged British expat about the MoU he just secured, and how incredibly rich he is, & how much his hat cost, & the ex-pat Brit eventually shuffles off to find another bar with less irritating company, while the Cantonese barmaid has no choice but to smile & empty ashtrays & bring fresh beers as Guus blathers on incessantly, until he talks himself out, & begins to drink & chain-smoke in glum silence, eventually leaving the bar &

wandering down to the waterfront, staring at the huge buildings lining the opposite side of the island, thinking nothing, completely numb to all existence, until a thought strikes him of tossing the stupid million-U.S.-dollar Emperor's hat into the ocean; but then he stops himself, finds a 7/11 & downs a can of German lager, & meanders along the waterfront until he finds a place offering helicopter tours, and hands over whatever seemingly-sizable wad of bills is required for the luxury of it, & he's swept up into the sky, to look down on the island & its megatowers from height as the sun sets, & the whole scene around him is so incredibly dull & uninteresting – the purple streaks of sky, the bright lights illuminating all the monolithic skyscrapers – it's just so ghastly dull & boring that he thinks for a moment of slitting the helicopter pilot's throat & letting the helicopter tumble through the air & collide into the crowd of peasants who'd gathered with smartphones to film the helicopter's ascent, or perhaps into the side of a building, or a conference center, with any luck taking at minimum a dozen people out along with him & the pilot – *gosh, that would be something* – but Guus soon realises he possesses no object sharp enough to slit through the flesh of a human male's throat, so the helicopter descends back to its landing spot, the same clamour of peasants record it's landing, & Guus pushes through them, ignoring yells & anger, losing himself in city streets, the swirl of faces & bodies & onset of night & drink & drugs are secured & brazenly blown through until he's lost in the blur, in the swirl of the universe, & some point sometime later, he's fucking two Filipina hookers in some cheap hotel, no idea of how he's got there, but catching sight of himself in a mirror, plowing one from behind, Chinese Emperor's hat atop his head, he slips out & sticks it in the ass, banging hard against panicked groans, the other looking on, cowering, terror-struck, until Guus pulls out & throws the hat down on the bed, & in a frenzy nails two more lines of coke, & whilst racking a third, says with force: "I want you to shit into the Chinese Emperor's hat,";

& she stares at him, stunned silent by the request, & he snorts the third line, & screams his command:

"TAKE A SHIT IN THE CHINESE EMPEROR'S FUCKING HAT!!!"

16. CATASTROPHIC ENGINE FAILURE.

Genoa, Italy.

"Hey, che du coglioni! Giovanni! It fucking stinks in here!" Giovanni doesn't hear Paolo's shouts, so absorbed he is in the grind & the computer screen. "Your body must be rotting. When did you last see sunlight?" Ignored by Giovanni, Paolo strides across the room & throws the curtains open, illuminating his flatmate's heavily-bearded face & stacks of festering take-out containers either side of his keyboard. "You cannot live like this! Hey, putana! I'm talking to you!" Paolo stands behind Giovanni, the stench of deeply-ingrained body odour filling his nostrils. He open-hand slaps the back of Giovanni's head.

"Vaffanculo!" Giovanni yells. "Testa di cazzo!"

"Giovanni, you are losing yourself! Come on, man. What are you doing?"

"There's a problem."

"What do you mean, there's a problem?"

"In the coding… client-side javascript… and an error… double-withdrawal issue… I tried to buy back, buy on Binance, but the price, it keeps on rising…"

"What are you talking about?"

"We have suffered a stolen…"

"What?"

"I've been hacked! BitBucks has been hacked!"

"Shit… how much did they take?"

"I don't know… the Ethereum, the Bitcoin, all on double-withdrawal… the hot wallet's been emptied, but the cold is okay… but the FSC, the Future Synergy Coin… there was an exploit… in the client-side javascript…"

"How much did they take?"

"About one-point-two-five trillion coins."

"How much is that? In Euros?"

"In Euros? I don't know in Euros… but in dollars, American dollars… I don't know, because the price keeps on rising…"

"Giovanni! How much in dollars?"

Giovanni exhales & stares at the current Future Synergy Coin market price on Binance, running calculations in his head: "…about four or five hundred million dollars…"

Paolo steps back from Giovanni: "Holy fuck… che du coglioni…"

"I can make it back… I still have a few hundred million FSC… I can move the price… suppress on BitBucks… arbitrage with Binance…"

"Giovanni… half a billion dollars… you have to go to the police…"

"I cannot go to the police."

"But Giovanni… half a billion dollars… that's insane…"

"If I go to the police, they will take everything! I lose everything, Paolo. Fucking everything! I can make it back… I just have to arbitrage… Binance… and make the S.L.C., the limited-liability company… then I can keep something, I at least do not lose everything…"

"But Giovanni… half a billion fucking dollars… if someone finds out…"

"No-one will find out."

"But Giovanni… someone would kill you for a debt of a thousand Euros… for half a billion…"

"No-one will find out. I'll make it back. Arbitrage… Binance… I can suppress the price…"

"But Giovanni…"

"No-one will find out!" Giovanni snaps, turning from the computer to Paolo, eyes glassy & bloodshot. "Paolo: you cannot tell anyone this."

"But Giovanni…"

"You cannot tell anyone!"

Paolo pushes the air out of his lungs & stares into Giovanni's blood-red eyes: "Okay, I won't tell anyone… but Giovanni… Giovanni… che du coglioni…"

17. TOUCHDOWN.

Blandford, Massachusetts. (United States of America.)

"Are you fucking shitting me?!"

"Larry!" Emily gasps.

"I'm sorry," Larry says, shaking his head.

"They're gonna disallow it," Michael says, eyes focused on the television & the fall-out from the improbable touchdown pass that's put the Eagles in front with 2:22 left on the clock.

"That motherfucking Philly fuck referee!" Larry snarls, on his feet. He glances at his shocked sister-in-law & mumbles an apology as his brother launches into a foul-mouthed tirade of his own:

"Fucking shit-hawk Philly fucks!!"

"Michael! Larry! Language!"

"I'm sorry," both brothers mumble in unison, before each looks at Steven, staring at his phone, paying no attention to the most dramatic Super Bowl finale in history. For Steven, 4chan is aflame with talk of Giovanni Cuomo & the BitBucks scandal; over 1 trillion missing FSC, with a value of around $438 million, depending on when exactly you want to count the loss. Pictures are shared of the frizzy-haired Italian BitBucks founder at a bar with Paolo & other friends, enjoying pasta with his family, hanging out at the beach with Natalia, all accompanied with racially-charged diatribes a thousand times more offensive than anything Steven's mother is hoping to protect her son from hearing in his father & uncle's reaction to the New England Patriots losing the Super Bowl.

"Your boy not into football?" Larry half-grunts, standing & swaying, 15th beer of the day clenched tight in his fist.

"He's always on that God-damn YouTube," Michael says, flashing his son a look of disgust. "And right now I envy him for it."

"We got time," Larry says, focus back on the television.

"We ain't got shit," Michael snaps, prompting his wife to elbow him hard in the ribs: "…sorry…"

Look at the fucking scumbag mook prick's saggy-titted girlfriend, Steven reads from the anonymous green text on 4chan. *I might fuck her,* Steven types, before pausing to think of something appropriately violent to follow it up with.

"Come on, Pats," Larry prays. "Make it Six."

"It's over," Michael says, tears welling up in the corner of his eyes.

"If you don't win, just mind your language, please," Emily pleads with the adults. "I don't want Steven thinking such vile language is acceptable."

"Sure thing, honey," Michael says, eyes glued to the television.

Steven smiles as he taps out the perfect end to his rant: …*but only if I hogtie her greasy spic boyfriend first and jam toothpicks through his eyelids so the mook pajeet cunt has to watch me cuck him with my big black dick.*

"You Philadelphian rapscallions!!" Larry yells theatrically, as Jake Elliott hits a 46-yard field-goal, making it 41-33 & sealing the Super Bowl for Philadelphia.

"Rapscallions?" Emily giggles.

"Hey, you said to tone the language down," Larry says, grinning at Emily with all-too-much meaning.

Michael stares at his brother, then his wife, then his phone-engrossed son, then the crowd belting out 'Fly Eagles Fly!' on the television; he does all he can to suppress an urge to punch every last one of them, including the inanimate television screen, or at the very least scream 'fuck.' Instead, Michael rises slowly to his feet & fixes his son with a look of utter contempt: "Hey, at least you can replay your video games when you lose, huh, Steven?"

"Come on, Mike," Larry says, before draining what little is left of his 15th beer. "Five Super Bowls in eight years ain't that bad." And then in a move which Michael feels is directly calculated to irritate him & charm Emily, Larry bursts into a boisterous drunken rendition of the Philadelphia Fight Song: *"Fly, Eagles, Fly! On the road to victory…"*

"Oh, Larry, what are you like?" Emily laughs, standing up and scooping up some of the many discarded beer cans surrounding their seats.

"…Fight, Eagles, Fight! Score a touchdown, 1, 2, 3!"

"Let me give you a hand taking the trash out," Michael says, pointedly snatching his brother's now-empty 15th Budweiser can before Larry can place it down upon a surface.

So this is the criminal exit-scam cuck mook bitch's home address, Steven is reading on 4chan. *Maybe I'll pay the pajeet nigger cunt a visit next time I'm in Italy…*

"So, hey, sport, how are our investments doing?" Larry asks, sitting down & leaning in conspiratorially as Steven's parents leave the room.

"Not great," Steven says, eyes still fixed on his phone. "The guy running the exchange exit-scammed."

"Exit-scammed? Whadduh that mean?"

Steven hesitates before explaining; he doesn't want Larry to think the loss of his $26,000 investment, plus many tens of thousands more in profit, were in anyway Steven's fault; so he doesn't want to tell Larry that the bulk of his money was only tied up in BitBucks because Steven had discovered the double-withdrawal trick, & had been continually moving his money in & out of the exchange, doubling it each time, until the exchange suddenly shut down all withdrawals & announced they'd been hacked. Instead of all that, Steven simply says: "The guy running the exchange stole everything."

"Whaddya mean, stole everything?" Larry says, smiling at his nephew, not quite comprehending the gravity of what he's telling him. "He stole… everything? Like… everything?"

"Uh-huh."

"Like… everything I gave you?"

"Uh-huh."

"The money I got re-mortgaging the house?"

"Uh-huh."

"Several years of Barbara's future alimony payments?"

"Uh-huh."

"But… that's impossible."

Steven says nothing.

"You said you were buying two different coins… from two different exchanges…"

"They listed the other coin on BitBucks," Steven says, lying effortlessly. "So I thought it would be less trouble than opening another account on a different exchange." He momentarily regrets the perhaps-unnecessary lie, but then guesses correctly that Uncle Larry will have no clear memory of which coins he'd actually invested in, & probably barely even understands what a cryptocurrency exchange is.

"You thought it would be less trouble?"

"Uh-huh."

"But then they… you… lost… everything?"

"I didn't lose everything. The guy running the exchange exit-scammed."

"Exit-scammed?"

"Or he got hacked. But I think he exit-scammed."

"Kid, you're gonna have to be real with me here; you're fucking around with a lot of real money. What the fuck does exit-scammed mean?"

"It means the pajeet mook cunt running the exchange stole everything."

"What?"

"It means the pajeet mook cunt running the exchange—"

"I fucking heard you the first time! But why the fuck are you taking twenty-six thousand fucking dollars of my money and putting it into an exchange run by some fucking pajeet mook cunt who's gonna steal everything?!"

"Larry!" Emily gasps, returning to the doorway.

Michael reappears silently beside his wife.

"Fucking answer me, you little shit!" Larry snarls.

Steven sighs dramatically, sensing that the angrier Larry gets, the more likely his parents are to protect him from any consequences: "It's not my fault the guy stole everything."

"LISTEN HERE, YOU LITTLE FUCK!" Larry snaps, snatching the phone from Steven's hands & throwing it hard against the LCD screen, shattering it with a fizz of gas at the very moment Jeffrey Lurie lifts the Lombardi trophy for the Eagles.

Emily screams; Michael runs across the room & tackles Larry to the floor in a way Patrick Chung should've done to the Eagles attack during the Super Bowl. Emily screams again, as Michael pins Larry's arms at his side & yells into his face: "LARRY!! WHAT THE FUCK'S WRONG WITH YOU!!"

"YOUR KIDS A FUCKING THIEF!!' Larry snarls, face crimson red, spit flying from his mouth to Michael's face as he answers. "HE STOLE TWENTY-SIX FUCKING BIG ONES OFF ME!!"

Michael slams a fist into the side of his brother's head; Emily screams again. "GET THE FUCK OUT OF MY HOUSE!!" Michael screams, standing up & letting his brother struggle back to his feet; he slams a knee into his brother's bulbous gut, grabs what he can of Larry's short hair, drags him on his feet across the living room, slamming another knee into his gut when his brother recovers enough to start struggling.

Emily screams & runs after the brothers, as they disappear from the living room into the hallway. Shouts & accusations ringing out in the background, Steven calmly walks across the room & picks his phone up; he smiles on seeing the television took most of the damage, & that his phone screen is virtually unharmed, save for a slight scuff on the side which took the impact. Steven returns to his seat & stares into 4chan, smiling, thinking *I got away with this,* as he reads the pissed-off screeds of other teenagers who got scammed out of thousands by Giovanni Cuomo & BitBucks. *I got away with this, & Uncle Larry's never even gonna realize I managed to take out about $24,000 out before that pajeet mook cunt exit-scammed.*

18. GAUZA!

Incheon, South Korea.

NEW KOREAN WORDS USED IN THIS SECTION:

ajossi (n) : an older man.

For the first two days, Sung Jae sets notifications on his phone to alert him every time the price of FSC moves +/- 5%. But the vibration is near constant, each small dip & swell in the coin's value bringing forth heart palpitations. By Thursday morning, he's checking the phone twice every few minutes anyway, & turns notifications off.

"So you're into coins too, huh?" Jong Gil says, blasting the back of Sung Jae's neck with his stale cigarettes & coffee breath as sees Sung Jae's phone screen on his way back from the restroom.

"Ng."

"How are they doing?"

"Going up."

Jong Gil talks – *he's always talking* – & Sung Jae grunts whenever appropriate, but his focus is elsewhere.

FSC's value dips & swells & fluctuates minute-by-minute: constant flux, but with an overall upward trajectory. His 12 million initial investment moves between 14 and 15 million throughout Tuesday, then drops to 13 million Wednesday morning, prompting an anxiety attack on the packed subway, but it's recovered to 15 million by lunchtime, hovers between 16 and 18 million through the afternoon, & hits highs of 19.5 million won as he sneakily views the screen while sitting beside Su Min on the sofa watching Infinite Challenge on TV. The pump continues through Thursday, Sung Jae's investment finally breaking the 20 million won barrier by 3pm.

"Maybe tomorrow we should go out for hwaesik," Nam Soo says. "It's Fire Friday, right?"

"Nae, Team Leader," Hyung Woo agrees, his voice betraying none of the dread he feels about another excessive drinking bout with his elder colleagues.

"Sounds great," Jong Gil adds. "Sung Jae, what do you think?"

Sung Jae looks away from the phone, where his FSC holdings are already closing in on 21 million won: "Sure." He smiles as he looks at Jong Gil's big grinning face: *of course he didn't have anything to do with it.* The creep on KakaoTalk uses some Japanese anime schoolgirl as his profile picture; there's no way Jong Gil's into that kind of crap. *No,* Jong Gil is a good & kind-hearted man, & Sung Jae was foolish ever to doubt him. *But then who is this creep messaging me?*

As Sung Jae rides the subway home that evening, standing in the packed carriage & watching the constant flux of FSC's price on UpBit, he receives another KakaoTalk message from MonsterHunter: *Annyeong Sung Jae! 48 hours left* – followed by that fucking grinning duck.

I'll have the money, Sung Jae replies. Feeling emboldened, he adds: *Who are you, anyway?*

I told you already – I'm just a concerned citizen trying to halt the moral degradation of Korean society, followed again by the same stupid grinning duck.

When Sung Jae gets home, he greets Su Min with a kiss on the cheek & pulls her close to him, then kisses her all over her neck, running his hands over her body.

"Sung Jae, stop!" his wife says, giggling girlishly. "Jae Seok will be home soon."

Sung Jae leaves Su Min to prepare dinner in the kitchen & takes to the sofa, letting the news play in the background as he checks his phone again. The day's mad rally seems to have slowed but FSC is still ticking ever upward. His total is now 22,105,324 won. *I might even have some profit left after this,* Sung Jae thinks, grinning as he glances up at his wife, thinking how lucky he is to have married such an enduring beauty, dedicated mother, & skilful cook. Jae Seok enters the apartment & his father is full of questions, taking great interest in how school's going, how things are with his son's friends, what Jae Seok learned in the hagwon, if he's seeing any girls yet…

"Don't worry, you'll have time," Sung Jae reassures his son, when the 'girls' comment seems to have hit a sore point. "A good-looking, intelligent boy like you; you'll have your pick of the girls in no time."

Sung Jae heads to bed that night & resumes showering Su Min with affection, she yielding to the throes of passion, they soon removing each other's clothes & exploring each other's bodies with hands & mouths, before her husband slips inside her & she moans with pleasure as he skilfully & delicately makes love to her, pace quickening after a while, switching position, & going at it & going at it, until Su Min says it's getting really late, & she's really tired, & Sung Jae really ought to sleep soon, & with the last few thrusts she feels the delightful throb & warm explosion of his climax, & they fall asleep in each other's arms, as happy & in love as they were when first making love 26 years ago.

In Jae Seok's room, the couple's offspring is enjoying a far less blissful evening. He had been scrolling through webtoons & Daum Cafes & KakaoTalk chatrooms & was about to finish the night with some pornography, when a sudden flurry of messages in one of his crypto chatrooms jolts him:

- *BitBucks has been hacked* (panicked yellow rabbit emoticon)

- *Daebak!*
- *Really?*

A deluge of worried & crying emoticons, followed by questions – *Really? What? When? Where? How?* – & Jae Seok's searching, finding info as fast as he can. The news is breaking, details scant, but the CEO of BitBucks has announced the exchange is insolvent, that hackers have taken everything; & Jae Seok thinks of waking & warning his father, but remembers his father's biggest concern was his mother finding out about his crypto investment; & so Jae Seok doesn't even send him a KakaoTalk message, deciding instead it's best to wait until morning.

Sung Jae awakes well-rested despite sleeping a little under five hours, his morning & mind bathed in the glory & glow of the night before. He kisses Su Min's neck softly as she stirs beside him, then gets out of bed, puts some coffee to brew, pisses, showers, brushes his teeth, dresses, & checks his phone as he sits in the apartment's kitchen area quick-sipping his morning caffeine fix. He almost spits coffee when he sees it: ₩11,412,305. "Ssibal…" The coffee cup trembles in his hand, liquid sloshing over its sides, as he stares at the value of his FSC, ticking quickly downward… ₩11,405,619… ₩11,386,975… ₩11,358,142… "JAE SEOK!" He leaves his coffee on the counter & storms into his son's room, holding the phone out as his son groggily rubs his eyes & sits up in bed: "What the fuck's going on?!"

"Therewasahack," Jae Seok mumbles.

"A hack?! What do you mean?!"

"Hackkeddd… BitBucks… was hacked…"

"That's why the price crashed?"

"Ng."

"Ssibal… so we need to sell now, huh? Before it falls further?"

"We can't sell."

"Why not?"

"The exchange was hacked. The coins were stolen."

"Our coins?"

"Ng."

"My coins?"

"Ng. All of the coins."

"Everything?"

"Ng."

"EVERYTHING?!"

"Ng."

Sung Jae wants to scream 'ssibal,' but thinks of Su Min & stifles the scream in his throat so that it's emitted as a low whining whimper.

"There's rumours of a class-action lawsuit," Jae Seok says. "Suing the exchange. Maybe everyone can get their money back eventually."

"…eventually?"

"Ng. Maybe in a couple of months… or a year… or two…"

"Aish…"

Sung Jae does nothing that day at work, save for pad back & forth between his desk & the coffee machine & the smoking area, smoking his way through a near-full pack with an hour still left until lunch. Jong Gil's talking & joking, talking & joking – *always talking & joking* – but Sung Jae doesn't hear him; he looks occasionally at his phone, watching the price tumble ever nearer 10 million won, but mostly he just stares into the white of his computer screen, thoughtlessly seeking absolution in the white space of an unwritten report. Sung Jae's barely conscious of eating lunch, auto-piloting responses to Nam Soo's blathering & Jong Gil's jokes. The day's end creeps nearer, Sung Jae smoking most of another pack as the afternoon drags on. Jong Gil reminds him of their plans for hwaesik when the day ends. Sung Jae briefly pretends to have remembered, then a few minutes later makes an elaborate performance of receiving a phone call from Su Min, says her mother's been rushed into hospital & he has to go straight home after work. Riding the subway back through Incheon, staring with neither thought nor hope at the down-trending value of his hacked FSC holdings – *₩9,542,168… ₩9,371,426…* - the call to action grips him: *You cannot do nothing… You have to do something…*

He alights at the next station & walks up & down stairs to reach the platform for trains going back in the direction he just came from.

He stares at the creep's KakaoTalk messages as he stands in the packed subway carriage, trying to divine some clue of MonsterHunter's real identity.

Sung Jae's still staring at the screen as he wanders through twilit streets, passing rowdy restaurants filling with after-work Fire Friday revellers, only returning his phone to his pocket as he reaches his destination & stares up at the pink neon sign of The Cherry Blossom Motel.

Sung Jae pushes through the drapes concealing the license plates of cars within the motel's parking lot & enters the motel lobby through a side door.

"Annyeong hasaeyo," the deeply wrinkled ajossi with the obviously-dyed black hair on reception says.

Sung Jae stares at the ajossi for a moment, completely unsure of what his next move should be. Operating on instinct, he asks for a room, short-stay, then changes his mind – "long stay," meaning overnight – & then takes the elevator to the 7th floor & room 703.

Sung Jae sits on the bed & smokes a cigarette, staring at a mirror angled towards him, wondering if there could be some way of seeing through it from the opposite side, but then he remembers that the video he was sent was filmed from above. Disgust hits him as he stares at the aging face reflected in the mirror. Sung Jae raises from the bed & stubs his cigarette into an ashtray, focusing on the English-language poem written in large curved letters on the light pink wall:

O, for my sake do you with Fortune chide,
The guilty goddess of my harmful deeds…

(Sung Jae's lips moves as he sounds the words out slowly, understanding perhaps two in three of them, though their meaning within the poem is a mystery.)

….public means which public manners breeds…
…And almost thence my nature is subdued…
…Pity me… and wish I were renewed…
…like a willing patient… I will drink…
…No bitterness will I bitter think…
Nor double penance, to correct correction:
Pity me then… I assure ye,
…your pity is enough to cure me.

Sung Jae stares & rereads the poem a few times, its meaning becoming no clearer, but the words nevertheless having some easing effect on his storm-clouded mind; & he reaches for a cigarette, but sees there's just two in the pack, & thinks to get more, but first storms around the room, climbing on the bed, checking the ceiling fan, the air-conditioning unit, behind the television, in search of some sign of a camera, some clue as to the cause of all his misery. Giving up, he rides the lift to reception, sees the ajossi nod slightly to acknowledge his presence, crosses the street to a 7/11, grabs two bottles of soju & a pack of Lucky 7 cigarettes. Back on the bed, Sung Jae chain smokes & shots shot-after-shot of soju, the first bottle & three cigarettes evaporating in a daze. He lies back on the bed, switches on the television, & watches some slow-moving softcore pornography as he glugs the second soju, smoking a fourth cigarette, & a fifth, until he's lost count of cigarettes, & the second soju's half-gone, he half-gone with it, & he rests his head against the pillow, shuts his eyes, &…*What time is it?*

Sung Jae fumbles for his phone on the bed, sees he's spilled soju over himself & his suit – "…aish… ssibal…" – & finds the phone & sees it's 11:42pm & he's received a message on KakaoTalk. Sung Jae knocks back what's left of the soju & lights another cigarette & mutes the soft-moaning of the girl getting her big nipples sucked by some creep on the television, then reads the Kakao creep's new message: *24 hours left Sung Jae! Hope all's well,* followed by that fucking grinning duck.

Sung Jae hurls his phone against the wall, instantly regretting it as he hears the crunching & crack of irreparable damage – "Ssibal." He finishes his cigarette, lights another, opens the refrigerator in search of water, downs a 500ml bottle, then stares at the silent tit-sucking on the television & realizes the only option that makes sense is drinking to oblivion & dealing with the consequences when he sobers up.

Sung Jae rides the elevator back to the first floor, mind moving ahead of him to 7/11 & pondering how many bottles to buy. The elevator doors open

& Sung Jae stares at the counter, expecting to see the ajossi, but seeing instead a strangely familiar younger man, hunched behind the desk, staring down at his phone. The younger man raises his head. His eyes meet Sung Jae's. A look of horror grips his face. Drunk though he may be, Sung Jae *knows*.

"You…"

"Jaesumhamnida," Kim Ki Seong splutters, fumbling with his phone to turn it off, dropping it as his hands & fingers operate at odds to each other, Sung Jae striding toward the counter: "I just started university, and my father's poor, he can't afford the tuition fees, and I desperately needed the money for my education, to make a better life for myself, and—"

19. TOKEN BURN.

< kigali, rwanda >

"8.4 billion dollars. 8.4 billion dollars. The entire gross output of your country's economy. 8.4 billion dollars. I launched Future Synergy Coin in October. It took Future Synergy Coin less than three months to generate half of this country's entire annual economic output. 8.4 billion dollars. For a country of almost 12 million people. Less than 800 dollars per person per year. Many of the speakers at today's Economic Development Forum will tell you that there's reason to be optimistic. They'll say this country is experiencing annual growth of around 10 percent. I don't see that as a positive. I see that as fucking dog shit. 800 dollars per person per year. 800 dollars. Each of my socks cost more than 800 dollars. Falke pure Vicuna socks, costing more than $1,600 a pair. But they tell you that 10 percent annual growth is reason for optimism. 10 percent of 800 is 80. 80 dollars extra per person per year. I've had cups of coffee that cost more than 80 dollars. Esmeralda Geisha 601, grown in Panama and brewed in Los Angeles. $88 a cup. And you're boasting of $80 per person per year. 10 percent of dog shit is still 100 percent dog shit. So why am I telling you this? Why am I speaking with bluntness bordering on rudeness? Because I want to help you. And telling you that dog shit growth is cause for optimism isn't helping you. It's lying to you. And why should I, a blockchain tech genius and crypto billionaire, want to help you? Because I am a humanist. I am a philanthropist. I am a global citizen. I am a benevolent Blockchain God. I don't want your investment. I don't need your investment. You don't have a fucking cent worth investing in me. I didn't fly out to this Third World shithole for an investment that wouldn't even cover my first-class airfare. I flew out here because I believe in you. And I believe in blockchain. And by opening your borders and removing all tax barriers to us benevolent blockchain benefactors, we can together build a better Rwanda. We can together build a better future. A future based on synergy. A future based on Future Synergy Coin."

The reaction's mixed: half the audience greet the end of Guus's speech at the United Nations Development Forum with rapturous applause, the other half with sullen stone-faced disgust.

As Guus steps off stage, he takes his phone from his pocket, & sees he has 12 missed calls from Aart.

< groningen, netherlands >

Another call goes unanswered and Aart is now fully in panic's grip, stumbling through Groningen's streets, not caring where he's going, not noticing where he is, frantically tapping at his phone screen, watching FSC's value plummet & re-reading the idiocy of the email he received from Giovanni Cuomo at BitBucks:

Excuse me sirs & madams, but we have suffered a stolen. We are to be believing this is fully due to the mistake made in the code of the Future Synergy Coin. So it is what i must have to demand is that you must immediately close down the FSC's blockchain and reverse all transactions and recover the stolen monies, elsewise there is no options but for me to declare to all the public that this fault is 100% the fault of the FSC developers and that you offered no help to me in these hours of neediness to help us recover from the stolen we have suffered due to the fault which is completely all your fault.

Thanking for your considerations,

Giovanni 'Gi-Dragon' Cuomo x

There is no reason for Aart to suppose 'the stolen' suffered was anything other than that idiot exchange owner Giovanni's fault, but neither Guus nor Nguyen are answering his calls, & Aart's circling the city in blind panic, watching the long-dreaded collapse of their empire play out: Rome burning while the two idiots fiddle abroad.

< hanoi, vietnam >

"I can't believe it!" Nguyen's mother gasps as the security guard at the gates to Ciputra International City nods & allows their beat-up old car access to the gorgeous tree-lined European-style streets inside.

The contrast to the noise & traffic of the main highway from Noi Bai International Airport, where just 20 minutes ago they collected their son, overwhelms her; she starts to cry, as Nguyen's father suppresses tears in the driver's seat, beaming with pride.

"My baby brother," Nguyen's older sister Trang says softly, while her son Thien bounces excitedly in the seat between them.

"I just wanted to thank you for all you've done for me," Nguyen says, feeling the happiest he's ever felt. "If you hadn't sent me to the Netherlands, this never would have happened."

"That was all you," his mother says through the tears, "winning that scholarship, with your brain and your talent…"

"But I never could have done it if you hadn't bought that computer for me," Nguyen says.

"You're a good boy," his father says, struggling to say the words without bursting into tears of his own. "Where should I go from here?"

Nguyen taps at the map on his phone & directs his father to the new family home, beyond the lake-bordered luxury high-rise condominiums, among the development's most expensive low-rise properties, shrubs lining streets that Nguyen can't help smiling at the authentic Europeanness of. It's even better than it looked on the website.

Nguyen calls the real estate agent & tells her they're close, then tells his father to pull up at a row of homes backing out onto a golf course. The women of the family lose control of their emotions as they hold Nguyen close & thank him a thousand times for this incredible gesture. Nguyen's father is too overwhelmed to speak.

As they await the real estate agent & entry to their new home, Nguyen's phone rings: he answers it, thinking it's the agent; he's surprised when he hears Aart speak: "There's been a hack… BitBucks… he's closed withdrawals already… the idiot's trying to blame it all on the developers – *us* – and the price is falling, word's spreading… we have to do something…"

< johannesburg, south africa >

Guus grips the back of the whore's head & slams it to & from his groin as he thrusts his hips in sync with it, her intense gagging spurring him on, until he hears the phone vibrate on the desk beside the bed, & he releases her, & she sprawls back on the floor, gasping & spitting, & he answers it, expecting to be told the coke's arrived: "Aart?! What… hacked? No… I didn't hear about it… I just took a four-hour flight from Rwanda to Jo'burg, and I've got a few hours' layover until a 16-hour flight to New York JFK, what the fuck do you want me to do?"

"…the price is tanking…"

"So? What am I supposed to do about it? … If you're that worried about it, just pull your coins out… convert them to Ethereum… yeah, of course I did it weeks ago… I bought some EOS, I got a nice little pump off that." Guus's erection fades with every second spent talking & listening. "Look, if you think this BitBucks hack will fuck the price up, pull your coins out; if you don't, then ride it out and solve the problem… look, Aart, I'm busy – you know I've got very important business here in Africa, and you actually interrupted me during a meeting with an extremely important client… yes, then talk to Nguyen about it… then talk to him again." Guus ends the call & looks at his hooker, wiping her mouth, still gasping to get her breath back; his appetite for fellatio is subsiding, but his appetite for cocaine grows stronger by the second: he taps at the phone screen, bringing up the number he received after slipping the reception staff a few hundred Euros, & thinks all this continent's economic troubles are encapsulated in the fact that it takes longer to deliver a little bag of white powder than a human prostitute.

< groningen, netherlands >

After the call with Guus ends, Aart stops walking to take in his surroundings: he's in front of The Dog's Bollocks, a student pub across the street from the university's Academy building. He briefly thinks of going inside & calming his nerves with a strong Belgian beer, but instead decides to be the anti-Guus and face up to his responsibilities as an executive of a multi-billion-dollar enterprise. He re-opens Giovanni Cuomo's idiotic email, & the equally idiotic 'we have suffered a stolen' flurry of Tweets the idiot sent out, causing FSC's price crash; & he thinks of Guus's idiocy, & Nguyen's lesser-but-none-the-less stupid irresponsibility, & figures he may end up regretting this for the rest of his life if he doesn't at least secure some of the fortune he's lucked into with FSC by trading some of his tokens for a more reliable currency, e.g. Ethereum, before the price collapses completely; so he opens his wallet on his phone, waits for it to load, then refreshes, then refreshes again, wondering why it's not working; & on the 5th or 6th attempted refresh, he thinks there might be something wrong with his wallet app, or his Internet connection; whatever it is, his wallet's not loading properly, & his balance is reading zero tokens where 833 billion should be; & as fear, uncertainty, & doubt coalesce in the abyss beneath his conscious mind, he checks the transaction history, & sees with horror the 833.333.333.333 tokens have been moved, in a single transaction, to an unknown address, & almost drops his phone, hands shaking…

< hanoi, vietnam >

"…I can't just reverse the transaction, Aart… it's a blockchain, the whole point is it's immutable," Nguyen says, awkwardly balancing his phone against his ear with his left shoulder as he sits on a box tapping at his laptop, family directing removal men to place boxes about their new home as he speaks, "…all I can do is check the blockchain history… and… yeah, the address it's been sent to… it's been Shapeshifted… it means they switched it for another currency… probably Monero… Monero's untraceable… but – Aart, calm down! – I can check the IP address of…" - Nguyen stops himself from saying "the IP address of whoever made the transaction" when his laptop tells him the IP address represents a location here in Hanoi.

"Aart… maybe I can find something… I don't know… but it's going to take some time… look, I'll call you back as soon as I've done it, okay?"

Nguyen lets his phone slip from his shoulder & clatter to the floor as he stares at the Hanoi-based IP address. He tries to remember if he connected to wifi anywhere since arriving; or maybe someone gained access through the International SIM card he bought… *never should've trusted those assholes,* he thinks, recalling the small stand at the airport he bought the SIM card from. Maybe the SIM card had given them access to everything on his phone? But how would they know to go after Aart's account? And is that even possible? If Nguyen – the architect of the FSC blockchain – knows no obvious way of stealing the funds from Aart's wallet, how could someone else have been smart enough to do it?

< groningen, netherlands >

Aart sits in The Dog's Bollocks for hours, afternoon becoming evening becoming night, working his way through the menu's strongest beers – Guulden Draag, St. Bernadus, La Trappiste Quad – staring at his phone, awaiting some response from Guus or Nguyen, searching his own mind & memories for some explanation of how everything got so irrevocably & unbelievably fucked; and although he tries to stop himself, he can't help but recall in excruciating drunken detail all the awful events that began

: two weeks earlier ;

Federer stretches to hit a forehand return to Seppi, who stands calmly waiting just left of center. Seppi hits a simple forehand return to Federer's left. Federer steps into it & knocks it back to Seppi with a backhand. Seppi fires a rocket cross-court backhand, causing Federer to step to the court's edge to thrust a backhand return. Seppi fires down the line, Federer already right-of-center to return it. Seppi smashes it back from left of center & Federer walks away from it, head down, rapturous applause filling the Rotterdam Ahoy arena as Seppi takes the first game of the decisive 7th set.

"FORZA SEPPI!!" Federico shouts, out of his seat.

"Calm down," Wesley says, "this isn't football."

"I don't know why you are so excited," Jako adds. "He's not even really Italian. He's from South Tyrol – it's 60% German."

"Bullshit," Federico says, grinning like crazy. "He's Italian. You are just salty because your Dutch boy Haase got destroyed by Federer yesterday."

"This is fun, yeah?" Jurate says, turning from the boys' sporting banter to Ciara in the seat beside her.

"Yeah," Ciara says. She hadn't really expected to be so enthralled by it; her only previous tennis-watching experience was catching the end of Andy Murray's last Wimbledon victory, relayed on a big screen in Cardiff's city centre while she was out shopping; but the past two days in Rotterdam have been unbridled fun, Aart's enthusiasm for seeing the Swiss Master Roger Federer being both enlightening & endearing.

"You think Federer might lose this one?" Ciara asks Aart, in the seat to her left.

"No way," Aart says, while Federer & Seppi switch sides on the court for Federer's serve. "He's just lulling Seppi into a false sense of security. You saw how calmly he walked away from the game point."

Federer takes the next game, & another, Federico's hope undiminished, Seppi battling back bravely, taking 3 games, while Federer tallies up 6: then the final point of the final game, Seppi's serve sent straight back by a Federer backhand, diagonal returns from both until Federer sends Seppi far right of center with a powerful forehand; a stretched return, another Federer forehand smash down left of court, Seppi sprinting to send it back; Federer to the net, Seppi dashing cross-court to return; Federer calmly holding the racket upright & letting the ball ricochet off it, dropping far from Seppi, softly into deuce court, to take game, set, & match, & move on to the next day's ABN AMRO World Tennis Tournament final.

"Do you like David Foster Wallace?" Aart asks, over a dinner of sea bream, stewed lamb neck, monkfish, celeriac, & rump roast at their hotel's restaurant.

"Not really," Ciara says. "I got about a hundred pages into Infinite Jest, but I found it too obtuse."

"Well I've not read his novels, but he wrote this amazing piece on Federer, about how watching him play is this kind of transcendent metaphysical experience."

"I can get that," Ciara says, thinking back over the mesmerising movement she's witnessed over two days of the tournament.

They fall into chatter with the others about where to go after dinner, where best to experience Rotterdam's world-class clubbing & nightlife scene.

"I think me and Jurate might head back," Federico tells Aart within the dark of BIRD, midway through Oliver 'N Criss's deep-house set. "You mind if we take the room for a little while?"

"No, it's fine," Aart says, having expected such a situation to arise, despite Federico saying when booking hotels for the weekend that three twin rooms (Jurate/Ciara, Jako/Wesley, Federico/Aart) would be fine.

"They went back? Together?" Ciara says to Aart at the bar a short time later.

"Yeah. I think they will take our twin room," Aart says, before drunkenly stumbling back over the statement's implications: "…but it's fine, I can stay with Wes and Jako, there's plenty of space…"

Ciara leaves a pregnant pause, BIRD's darkness concealing Aart's blushes, until she says what's she's been longing since Friday to suggest: "Stay in my room. We can go back now if you want."

They're in a taxi within minutes, making out in the backseat, pulling hair, biting lips, fumbling as the cab rounds corners, each completely engrossed in the other until the driver shouts "HEY!!" for a fourth or fifth time, & Aart apologises, smiling as he pays, telling the driver to keep the change.

They jog through the lobby, hands at the other's waists; Ciara shoves Aart against the wall as the lift's doors close; he pulls her to him, hands move frantically over each other as they kiss. They realise with a laugh that they've not hit the button for their floor;

& into the room, to the nearest of the twin beds, pulling the other's clothes off as fast as possible;

& fucking & fucking & fucking, until they fall asleep, bodies wrapped around each other;

& Aart wakes & worries that Ciara will again want the night to exist in blissful isolation;

but she wakes, & kisses him softly, & holds him close;

& they fuck, & shower, & fuck again, & dress, & leave their room to find the others.

They hold hands in the stands throughout Federer's final victory over Grigor Dimitrov, the Swiss Master despatching the Bulgarian in straight sets, 6-2/6-2.

Ciara rests her head on Aart's shoulder on the train back to Groningen, where the next days are spent entirely in the other's company, Ciara reading & writing essays as Aart alternatives between university assignments & fretting over the downward trajectory of the cryptocurrency market.

"People were saying it'd pick back up after Chinese New Year," Aart tells her, "but that was last weekend, and Bitcoin's still falling, and dragging everything else down with it."

FSC is among the more resilient alts until a FUD piece titled 'Everything Wrong with Future Synergy Coin' turns market sentiment against them.

"I wouldn't worry about it," Guus tells Aart at The Three Sisters, once Aart's finally managed to get hold of him. "Opinion's fickle. Concentrate on the fundamentals."

"What fucking fundamentals?" Aart says, almost laughing, but stopping at a smirk, thinking of the billions of dollars riding on what Guus says. "We haven't done anything in months. We've just been pumping out hype and watching the price rise. This can't last forever."

"Can't it?" Guus asks, looking away from Aart to some tanned female a few tables over.

"No, it can't. I think this is it, Guus. The bubble is bursting. The last few months were insane – teenagers were making millions of dollars, every project in crypto saw its price multiply at least five times over… and now the market's out of fresh suckers, there's less and less people FOMOing into buying whatever shitcoin's being hyped on Reddit or BitcoinTalk this week, and the only projects that will survive will be the ones with actual working products and real-world use cases."

"Do you think she's Spanish?" Guus asks, still staring at the female. "Spanish or Italian… definitely Mediterranean…"

Aart sighs & snatches his La Chouffe from the table, downing a third in one irritated swig. "Let your billions fall to nothing, Guus, and see how interested in you women are then."

Guus smirks, returning his attention to Aart once the barb's been delivered: "Calm the fuck down, Aart. Things will pick back up. It's a volatile market."

"Not necessarily, Guus. Did the price of tulip bulbs pick back up once that bubble burst?"

"Fucking tulip bulbs, Aart? Jesus Christ. We're building the future of humanity, and you're talking about fucking tulip bulbs."

"It's the same thing—"

"It's not the same fucking thing. Tulip bulbs were purely speculative. They had no utility value."

"And what fucking utility value does Future Synergy Coin have, Guus? It's a fucking coin without a functioning mainnet, without any real-world adoption, without anything other than a community of money-hungry teenage incels who worship you because they think you're a fucking edgelord."

"Edgelord," Guus repeats, smirk growing wider.

"But you're not fucking edgy, are you, Guus? You're not fucking edgy, and you're not a prophet, and you're certainly not a fucking blockchain god."

"Aren't I? What am I, then?"

"You're a useless fucking idiot."

"Really." Guus leans back in his seat, smirk turning into a face-consuming grin. He lifts his Kasteel Rouge from the table & takes a delicate sip. "Please regale me then, Aart. Tell me. How exactly am I a useless fucking idiot?"

Aart stares into Guus's eyes, alive with amusement & thirsting for more; he hesitates awhile before speaking: "There's something wrong with you."

"Is there? Really? What's wrong with me, Aart?"

"…. … … … Vallya… … … …"

"What? Pardon? Excuse me? It sounded like you were trying to tell me something? It sounded like you just said Vallya? You did, didn't you? You did say Vallya. And who's Vallya, Aart? Why did you bring her name up? Gosh, you are being an awfully curious fellow this evening."

"Ciara told me something Vallya told her about you," Aart says, thinking for a second he shouldn't have name-dropped any co-accomplices, but thinking *fuck it,* so sickeningly smug is Guus's expression at this moment, & so overwhelming his desire to punch him in his smug fucking face, that continuing speaking & clasping his La Chouffe in his hands is the only thing

Aart can to do to not dive across the table & batter him. "She said you creeped her out… something about the way you talk, something about your eyes… nothing behind them… like you're capable of anything, like you were born without a soul…"

"Really?" Guus says, grinning & crossing his legs like a mid-century gay literary critic, cradling his drink in the left hand as he takes his phone from his pocket & runs his right thumb along its screen. "It really is quite interesting that a friend of Ciara's would come up with an insight like that," Guus says, staring at his phone. "And equally fascinating that our dear Ciara would think to share such a thing with you. I suppose she's rather a sharp judge of character, this Vallya girl; and Ciara too, by the sound of things. You, though, Aart – unfortunately not. Being a good judge of character wasn't something you were born blessed with." Guus leans forward & turns the phone screen to face Aart.

"What is… what am I looking at?"

"Do you want me to provide a running commentary, Aart? Because I could. Do you like Vietnamese food, Aart? Pork bun cha? Pho? Long stringy noodles, floating about in a bowl of something moist."

"What is… where did you get this?"

"Nguyen sent it to me, Aart. He was boasting about all the things he'd done to this 'insightful judge of character' you're so enamoured with."

"But… fuck…"

"But? But what, Aart? Do you want to ask me another question? Because you really have asked rather a lot of questions already. Would you mind if I asked you one first?" Guus leans forward, eyes locked with delight on Aart, the sordid secretly-recorded scene on the phone screen reflected in the black of Aart's pupils: "How does Nguyen's dick taste?"

Aart stands up & walks straight for the exit, Guus leaning back & smirking as he watches him leave, before reclining in the chair & enjoying the rest of the video, not bothering to hide it when a waitress appears at the side of his table a few moments later asking if he's okay with her clearing the empty bottles.

Where are you? Aart taps into WhatsApp. *We need to talk. Now.*

I'm at the library, Ciara replies a few seconds later. *What's up?*

Aart flies through the city's streets on his bicycle, drawing beeps from annoyed drivers as he veers wildly across the road. He runs upstairs to the library's third floor, finding Ciara on a leather sofa with her laptop & a pile of textbooks on the table in front of her.

"What's happened?"

"Guus showed me the video."

"What video?"

"Of you and Nguyen."

"What video of me and Nguyen?" As Ciara speaks, her mind struggles to piece together what Aart's talking about; & then she's hit with sudden shuddering recollection, of the hotel room beside Stadspark, the blurry forgotten night of Wesley's birthday party, waking beside Nguyen in the morning, no memory of how she got there… *He fucking filmed it?*

Aart watches Ciara's mouth fall open, colour drained from her face, & sees in her expression confirmation: "When."

"I…" *Fuck.* What a fucking creep.

"When."

"I… didn't…"

"There's a fucking video, Ciara. Don't tell me you didn't do it."

"I… don't remember… it was… I don't remember anything…"

"Fucking bullshit."

Shock turns to anger as Aart accosts her; she's furious at that little creep Nguyen, taking advantage of her, *fucking filming it,* showing the video to Guus, Guus showing the video to Aart.

"You fucking fucked him, Ciara. Just admit it."

"Aart… keep your fucking voice down."

Others around them are glancing up from laptops & books, casting discreet glances.

"Was it just once? Or…" – a memory hits Aart, of the wild night of coked-up chaos – *neuken in de keuken* – at the Indonesian restaurant; seeing Guus emerge from Ciara's room the following morning. "Is there anyone in the frat house you haven't fucked? Am I the only one stupid enough to think of you as anything more than an easy fuckbag? Is that what am I to you – a useful idiot, a—"

"Shut the fuck up, Aart!" Ciara says, standing, angry as hell, not caring who turns to watch them. "Yeah I fucked him, and we videoed it, and it was a hundred times better than anything I did with you, and his dick's bigger. Is that what you want to fucking hear?!"

Aart's lips move, wanting to say something, but his mind's gone into shock, situation overwhelming him.

"Go fuck yourself, Aart," she says, no longer able to look at him, closing her laptop, unplugging the charger, & packing the books into her bag. "I don't know how I could've ever been stupid enough to think you were any different than those pricks you hang out with."

</.>

< new york city, united states of america >

"…the price is dipping, dipping, dipping, after months of going up and up and up, and now a lot of those people who were saying before that this is a bubble, their voices are becoming louder, and they're saying that the bubble's popped, and I was wondering if you could tell us your response to that?"

"Well, Michelle, I think really what we have to do first is define what a bubble is," Guus says, staring with deep intensity & sincerity across the desk in the CNBC Money studio at his attractive Asian-American interviewer. "A bubble is simply a globule of one substance which has formed within an exterior shell of another substance, be that a bubble of gas formed within a liquid, or a bubble of money formed within a financial market. And while popular wisdom may claim that all bubbles eventually pop, this is a bit of folksy homespun wisdom that has no basis in real science, where physicists have known since the 1850s that when a bubble acts as the interface between two or more fluids, the surface tension of said bubble actually stabilizes the surfaces of these substances, making the fluid mass more resistant to changes brought about by external pressure than they would have been had the bubble not formed, and I think that this is exactly the kind of Marangoni effect that we're seeing evidenced in the interface between the bubble which consumer and tech-savvy money hath created within the crypto-space as it now ekes toward interfacing with the vast oceanic fluid of institutional investment."

Michelle blinks heavily for a moment, before moving on to her next question: "Right… and so you think that there is still potential for cryptocurrency prices to keep on rising?"

"I think that there is infinite potential for any occurrence within this universe, once one has a full understanding of theoretical physics and string theory."

"And your coin is called the FSC coin, the Future Synergy Coin, and it's kind of supposed to be sort of different to Bitcoin and more similar to Ethereum, right?"

"There is an error of omission in your characterization, but the general thrust of your words have been made toward the correct direction."

& on like this, until the 2mins 30secs allotted for the segment is over, & Michelle thanks Guus for coming on the program & throws to commercial, & he asks her if she'd consider meeting him for dinner tonight, & she says yes, & he takes his phone out of his pocket at the exact moment the screen's seized by a call from Aart, & a production assistant ushers him off-set before he can take Michelle's number, & the ad break is over, & Guus leaves the studio & answers the call, immensely irritated: "What the fuck is it, Aart?! You picked a really fucking shitty time to call me."

"…Guus, the coins, my FSC, Nguyen's stalling, Guus, he said something about the IP address, and the block explorer, and now I can't get through to him, and I need you to check the blockchain for me, see the IP address the transaction was made from…"

Guus sighs theatrically: "Fucking fine, Aart. I'll do it."

< california, usa >

"And here we are," the real estate agent says, her drop-top coupe pulling up at the gates of an extravagant estate rising into the hillsides of Hillsborough, a short drive from the headquarters of Google & Facebook & all the rest of Silicon Valley's world-dominating tech firms.

Guus frowns & nods semi-approvingly as the real estate agent hits a button on her keyfob to swing the gates open, & her car rolls inside, along a paved drive flanked with mature tree cover, to a gargantuan Gilded Age maximalist masterpiece of overblown architectural money-blowing.

"It's cute," Guus says, as the real estate agent pulls up outside his potential new home.

"There's an infinity pool with captivating views across the city and out to the ocean on the far side," the heavily-botoxed fortysomething real estate agent tells him as they exit the car, "but I think the first thing you'll want to see is the main entrance foyer; it is truly breathtaking—"

"Excuse me," Guus says, turning away from her as his phone rings. "Oh, hi, Aart, what's up? … Oh, yeah, I forgot about it… I've been busy, Aart… I've been fucking busy! Christ! I was on MSNBC this morning, straight off a fucking flight from deepest darkest Africa, then a six-hour flight across this fucking continent – can you believe it takes six fucking hours to fly from New York to California? – and I've just gotten to this place I'm thinking about putting an offer in on with the real estate agent… holy fuck, Aart, you are the executive of a fucking billion-dollar blockchain company and you don't know how to check the transaction history on the blockchain explorer using admin privileges to see what fucking IP address a fucking transaction was routed through? Fuck… okay, okay, shut the fuck up, I'm doing it…" Guus glances at the real estate agent & smirks half-apologetically; she smiles back broadly, any offense she may have felt at the vulgarity of his language clearly mitigated by the fucking ludicrous commission she'll secure if she's successful in selling this mansion to him. "Okay, okay, so read out your public key to me… uh-huh, uh-huh, I got it, okay… and there's a big fucking transaction that shows up on here, 833 billion FSC coins, would that be what you're looking for?… Okay, fucking Christ, calm down, no need to shout… okay… so… the transfer was made from an IP address in… Hanoi. Hanoi. Yes, Hanoi, Aart. Hanoi. As in Hanoi in fucking Vietnam, that is correct, Aart… well how in the fuck should I know? … Well then why don't you ask him? … Well… Yes, I suppose if Nguyen stole all your money, he probably wouldn't be answering your calls… Well… Umm, I mean… How the fuck should I know, Aart?! … AART – HOW THE FUCK SHOULD I KNOW?!!?!?… Holy fuck, you're such a little baby… Here, I'll send you the fucking IP address," he shouts, tapping the IP address into a text message, "you fucking deal with it." Guus ends the call & turns to the real estate agent with a smile. "Sorry. Business waits for no man."

"Of course. I've had a few calls like that today myself."

"So, look, let's cut straight through the bullshit – I've not got my green card yet, but I'm figuring if Trump's piece can get an Einstein visa, then a guy like me, with a bank account like mine, I'd imagine I'd be a naturalized citizen before the week's out, right?"

"Uh… sure… I wouldn't imagine you'd have too much trouble securing a—"

"So I'm looking to move into a place here ASAP. What did you say this place was on the market for?"

"Forty-five million dollars."

"Uh-huh. Okay, so say we call it an even fifty, you think they'd let me move in here this evening? I've taken five flights and been on three continents in the past four days, I really don't want the hassle of checking into a hotel."

The real estate agent's heavily-lipstick'd grin stays rigid as mascara'd eyes flutter: "I don't imagine it'll be a problem. I'll call the owner and let you know."

< groningen, netherlands :: hanoi, vietnam >

Hanoi. Nguyen.

Aart's thumbs & fingers hit his phone screen as he sits on the quad-sofa in the frat house, searching for fights: there's an 09.40 Air France flight from Amsterdam, connecting in Paris, arriving in Hanoi 08.05 tomorrow morning. The time now is 02.35. The €2.865 flight's booked, then a €26,60 seat on the day's first train to Amsterdam, leaving 05:05 & arriving at Schiphol Airport 07.25. Aart throws clothes into a suitcase & leaves, boisterous pissed-up students stumbling through otherwise-deserted streets as he moves through the night-swept city to the station, to wait on the platform & chain smoke & drink shop-bought Grolsch to calm his almost-overpowering sense of existential dread. Flat Dutch countryside flies past the window as the train blasts through morning. Aart changes trains at 06.17 in Zwolle & continues to the airport. He shuffles through the check-in line & security & on to the gate. As the flat Netherlands falls away beneath him, he thinks of what he'll do to Nguyen when he gets to Hanoi. *I'll beat the fuck out of him. I'll fucking kill him.* Ciara was one thing. She's a grown woman, & they weren't even dating when it happened. But stealing the coins… Aart moves through Charles de Gaulle in a blur, the 2 hrs between flights quickly evaporating, until he's stuffed into an economy-class seat for an 11-hr onward flight to Hanoi, wishing he'd paid for an upgrade, wondering if he'll ever again afford business class, or if there's legal recourse, some alternative to what he's now doing, the direct confrontation: but Nguyen surely knows enough to deflect attention, to make the hack look genuine; knows much more than that idiot Giovanni Cuomo of BitBucks, whose idiocy was completely to blame for the stolen his exchange suffered; no, *Nguyen's smart,* Aart thinks, *and completely willing to fuck me over.* And maybe Guus is on it. It was Guus that gave Aart the Hanoi IP address. Possibly to deflect blame from himself. Possibly to sow confusion, Guus & Nguyen both working together to fuck him over. *FUCK.* Aart's thoughts swirl above the clouds, ordering endless wine, unable to sleep more than a few minutes in the endless hours between meal services, as others doze off or drift away to the in-flight entertainment service. Aart looks through the endless superhero movies & dumb comedies, none retaining his attention beyond the opening credits; he knows, whatever awaits him in Hanoi, the second he sees Nguyen's expression, Aart will know the truth. Aart fakes a hotel address on his Arrivals Card – the Hanoi Hilton – & enters the swarm of the arrival area in summer-like warmth. *What now?* Taking a taxi is the obvious course of action, *but to where?* He checks Nguyen's social media feeds & sees shots of him with friends & family around the city, but nothing to tell him where Nguyen is at this exact moment. Aart absentmindedly clicks through Instagram, & smiles for the first time in days as he discovers it: a photo of Nguyen & his sister, on Nguyen's sister Tran's feed, beaming smiles, & a caption that mentions Ciputra International City. Aart barks the destination at a taxi driver & almost succumbs to an immense days-long tiredness as the taxi carries him along a highway heaving with traffic, scooters weaving between honking cars; he allows himself a microsleep, until the cab arrives, and Aart realises he has no Vietnamese currency to pay with; after much shouting & confusion, the driver seems to understand, & drives to a bank, an ATM, & finally leaves Aart outside the guarded entrance gates of some sprawling luxury housing development. *Now what?* Aart wanders around the development's perimeter, staring up at the impossibly high walls protecting the wealthy residents inside from the rest of the city. After walking fifteen or twenty minutes in the sweltering heat, he stops & sighs & realises there really is no other option left. He takes his phone from his pocket, turns on data roaming, & taps out a WhatsApp: *I'm in Hanoi. We need to talk.*

"So you can help me out?" Nguyen says (in Vietnamese).

Dao nods, the overhead fluorescent lighting reflecting off the folds of his thick bald forehead. "Bring him here. We serve him some pho. Tell him what he needs to be told. If he tries anything, we'll be waiting."

Further along the sleek steel table, Nguoi Giet cracks the knuckles of his thick meat-slab fists. In the kitchen, Tu Than grasps a hefty meat cleaver & sharpens its blade.

Aart stands at the Quan Chuong gate, entrance to the Old Quarter, never-ending scooters streaming past at either side as he stands & smokes, trying to keep his mind free & clear through nicotine, trying to think no thoughts until Nguyen's arrival. A scooter stops beside him & Aart's instinct is to attack its rider: but he sees its Nguyen & further nicotine keeps further thoughts at bay as Nguyen begins their conservation: "Hey, bro! Welcome to Hanoi. Sucks about the circumstances."

As Nguyen leads Aart through the Old Quarter's bustling streets Nguyen asks if he's eaten, & says he knows the perfect place, & Aart hesitates at the entrance to a basement restaurant and asks why they can't join the dozens of Vietnamese & tourists eating bowls of soup on plastic tables on the street outside. Nguyen says he doesn't want anyone overhearing them. Against his better instincts, Aart descends the steps behind Nguyen, then sits across from him at a steel table in the basement, noting the menacing glances of kitchen staff hacking at unidentified animal corpses with meat cleavers. Aart and Nguyen are the only diners inside.

Nguyen: "You want pho? Bun cha? I guess you've not had chance to try much Vietnamese food yet. How about we get a bunch of stuff to try? I'll pay, of course. And how about a beer? You could probably do with something after that flight, huh?"

Aart says nothing until the order's made & Nguyen brings up the purpose of his visit.

Nguyen: "So, like I told you, I was able to trace the IP address to a location here in Hanoi—"

"You didn't tell me that. Guus told me that."

"Yeah. well I told Guus, who then told you—"

"Guus said he found it out himself. Through the block explorer."

"Well…" Nguyen laughs, thanking Nguoi Giet in Vietnamese as he brings two Hanoi beers to their table. "I'm going to be completely honest with you: I didn't want to tell you what I'd found until I'd had chance to investigate it, but the IP address is just a generic access point for one of the big telecommunications networks here, it hasn't really helped me get any closer to who might be responsible, and for all I can tell, it could've been someone overseas, re-routing their traffic via Hanoi to cover the real source of the theft. And I've got no clue whether they chose Hanoi through pure coincidence, or if—"

"—they wanted to make it look like you stole all my money."

"Uh-huh."

"And who would want that?"

"…well…"

"You think Guus stole my money?"

"No." Nguyen gasps. "Hell no. I mean, Guus has made more money than any of us. Why would he want to—"

"I don't know. I was hoping you could tell me."

Nguyen's silent, trying to read Aart's face. "Look, neither of us have any idea who took your money, but we can all work together to try to find out.

And in the meantime, I'm more than willing to help you out, bro. You got a place to stay here yet? Look, man, you're just as rich as the rest of us, fuck whoever took the tokens. I'm gonna put you up in a good hotel for however long you're here. Fuck staying in some shitty bed-bug ridden hostel here in the Old Quarter. And whatever else you need, name it."

"That's very generous of you."

"Seriously, bro. Don't mention it. I think of this hack as an attack on all of us."

"That's touching."

"Yeah… look… man, you've had a long flight, you must be stressed as fuck… let's eat some food, drink some beers, and forget about this shit until tomorrow, cool?"

Food arrives – steaming bowls of soup & noodles – alongside ice-cold beers. They eat & drink fast, Aart hungrier & more exhausted than he'd realised. They're soon on a 3rd beer, then a 4th, conversation flowing evermore fluidly, Nguyen telling Aart of the place in Ciputra he bought for his family, Aart of the wild cross-continental & panic-ravaged sleepless night that brought him here.

Once their bowls & 5th beer bottles are empty, Nguyen walks to the kitchen to pay, & slyly asks Tu Than if he can follow them to the strip of streetside bars on Ta Hien.

"This is the one place here you can get them good Belgian beers," Nguyen says, as they sit on plastic chairs outside an Irish-style pub at the end of a narrow alleyway loaded with loud foreigners & dozens of small bars.

Aart scans the barely-contained chaos of the street as he sips from the glass of Gulden Draag: he sees Tu Than loitering in a nearby doorway smoking a cigarette, briefly thinking he recognises him; but Tu Than turns away quickly, & Aart's observation is lost to the alcohol.

"That's one thing I really miss about Groningen," Nguyen continues. "The beer. And the weed. And the women. But this is the place in Hanoi to meet white women." Nguyen drunkenly gestures at a table of pale-skinned American girls in shorts & 'I ♥ VIETNAM' vest-tops outside a bar across the alleyway.

Aart looks at the girls until they notice him looking, then quickly stares further down the alleyway, eyes falling across scores of pissed-up white twentysomethings, until he sees her – *Ciara* – he's sure it's her, far down the alleyway, walking toward them…

"Hey, man, cheers," Nguyen says, lifting his glass & pulling Aart's attention away from the girl he thinks is Ciara.

Aart clinks glasses with Nguyen – "cheers" – & turns back toward the girl he'd been looking at. He scans scores of white faces, but cannot find her. After a minute, he gives up, thinking it an apparition brought on by booze and jetlag.

"Guus told me about you and Ciara," Aart says.

"Huh?"

Aart is as shocked as Nguyen; he'd had no intention of bringing that up. But now that it's been said…

"Yeah… he showed me the video you made…"

"…video?" Nguyen's face contorts in confusion, recalling the scant memories he has of awakening in the hotel next to Stadspark, next to Ciara in bed, no memory of the night before…

"Yeah… look, it's cool, we weren't dating or anything at the time. I just thought that you should know."

"…video?"

"Yeah. The video you made. The one you sent to Guus."

"What video?"

"Of you fucking Ciara."

Aart stares at Nguyen: for a moment, his look of pure stunned blankness is convincing. But then logic cuts through the drunkenness, & Aart realises Nguyen must be trying to fool him, & if he's so convincing in denying something of which a video exists – something completely & undeniably correct – then what else is he lying about?

"Guus showed you a video of us?"

"Yes."

Nguyen stares off down the alleyway & glugs Gulden Draag. Both are silent until their beers are almost finished. Then Aart stands up: "I need to take a piss."

As Aart uses the bathroom, Tu Than approaches the table; Nguyen tells him to get them a cab.

"It's late," Nguyen says as Aart returns. "We've both had a long day, right? I'll take you to the hotel. We can talk about this some more tomorrow."

Aart drinks his way through the Hilton's mini-bar until his thoughts become a broken stream of paranoid gurgling & he passes out on the bed. Aart wakes 11 hours later. He showers & dresses & then walks through wild scooter-filled streets to the Old Quarter, passing street restaurants & fake famous brand clothing shops, until he finds a small store selling knives & war-themed paraphernalia. He selects a suitably deadly pocket knife with a dragon on the blade. He sends Nguyen a message: *Just woke up. When & where do you wanna meet today?*

***

A 10th phone call to Guus goes answered, so Nguyen sends a 5th text: *Where u at man? Need to talk w/u asap.* Nguyen takes a moment to stare out the window of the new Ciputra apartment, wondering as he watches the lake &

golf course if Aart is lying about the video, or if Guus somehow recorded them… or maybe Ciara filmed it…

***

Nguyen leads Nguoi Giet & Tu Than into his family's cramped old apartment in the Old Quarter, long-used furniture still in place, most personal items already boxed up & moved to Ciputra. Nguyen tells Nguoi Giet & Tu Than to wait in his parents' former bedroom until told otherwise. Then Nguyen heads outside & smokes several cigarettes, awaiting Aart's arrival. "How you doing, bro? Let's head inside, talk this out," Nguyen says, leading Aart up a narrow staircase to the apartment. He tells Aart to sit on the sofa, then perches atop a coffee table. "Look, I'm confused as hell about what's going on. The video – I've got no idea about it. But something did happen with me and Ciara. But I don't know if Guus filmed it, and showed you, or—"

"Guus filmed it," Aart repeats, nodding slowly.

"Yeah. Or Ciara…"

Aart stops nodding & stares at Nguyen. Aart's eyes are harsh & bloodshot. Nguyen sees malice in them. Nguyen's a second away from calling Nguoi Giet & Tu Than but he composes himself & lets Aart speak.

"I've been thinking about this a lot. All day. All night. It's you, or it's Guus. Those are the only two options. One of you fucked me over and froze me out of the FSC funds. One of you mocked me with this video made with Ciara. One of you – or both of you. And what you seem to be telling me is that it's Guus. Is that correct?"

"Hey, I don't know what Guus showed you, or said to you, but I know what I did and didn't do."

"You didn't steal the money?"

"No."

"So Guus did. And he made it look like the theft came from Vietnam so that I'd blame you. Right?"

"I mean… it's a possibility… but it could also be—"

"—someone else? Bullshit. Who the fuck else could it be?"

"I don't know. Anyone. It's a lot of money, man. People would kill for a thousand dollars. We're talking hundreds of millions. It could be anyone. Hackers, a rival crypto team. That idiot from BitBucks – maybe he's not so stupid. This space is the Wild West of finance, man. It's completely unregulated. There's all kinds of—"

"I don't buy it."

"I'm just saying, bro, it could be—"

"What did you say before?" Aart says, gripping the dragon-bladed knife in his jeans pocket. "People would kill for a fraction of this money? You're probably right about that. And you know what else you're right about? You're right about Guus being behind the hack. Guus is a fucking sociopath. But you're his little fucking sidekick, aren't you? You're the guy he gets to do whatever the fuck he wants done. So Guus doesn't have to get his hands dirty himself."

"What are you—"

Aart draws the knife from his pocket & stands, moving it toward Nguyen's throat, intending solely to threaten him, to force the truth out, having no intention of cutting or going beyond the threat stage; but Nguyen's yell sends the bedroom door flying open, Nguoi Giet & Tu Than rushing out; & in panic, Aart turns to them, slashes in their direction, catches Nguoi Giet's right arm; then he's caught by both of them, thrown to the floor, knife knocked away from him; & boots & fists pummel him, blood & panic gushing out in the moments before he loses consciousness;

& Nguyen stands & stares as they stomp out Aart.

Then Tu Than snatches the knife from the floor…

"STOP!" Nguyen shouts. "Don't. Don't kill him. That's enough."

Disappointed, Tu Than snaps the blade shut & slides it into his own pocket. The trio stand over Aart's bloodied form.

"I can make a phone call," Nguoi Giet says. "I know someone on the police. We can dump him at a hospital. When he wakes up, the police will read out a list of charges. They'll tell him to leave the country before they lock him up. Or, we could take him to the Red River…"

"The hospital," Nguyen says, shaking with adrenaline.

20. ALL-TIME LOW.

Incheon, South Korea.

"My sons!"

Sung Jae smiles weakly, eyes moist, as Min Seok & Jae Seok enter the prison's small visiting room. Sung Jae stands up & grips Jae Seok in a tight hug, then moves to his eldest son.

"Don't," Min Seok says firmly, stepping back from his father's attempted embrace. "Sit."

Sung Jae nods, returning to the metal chair at the room's small table. Jae Seok takes the seat opposite. Min Seok, wearing the combat fatigues of a Korean conscript, remains standing.

"You're looking well," Sung Jae says of Min Seok. "And you're filling out that uniform. The rations they're feeding you aren't too meagre? You look healthier than when you started. Perhaps all that exercise. Outdoors. It's good for your… character…" Sung Jae senses that he's rambling, slipping into the kind of ridiculous lionization of military service he's heard a million times from Nam Soo, his former Team Leader. "You should make the most of your time in the military. It may all seem impossibly hard at the moment, but in ten, twenty, years from now, you'll miss the taste of canteen budae jjigae. Nothing tastes as good as it does when you're half-starved, desperate for something to refuel you after all the training… And Jae Seok," he says, deliberately switching the focus of his ramblings, sensing sheer coldness in his eldest son's face, "you're not letting this whole mess distract from your studies? There is nothing more important than your education. If you knew the effort I put in, the hours I worked, to pay for your hagwons… there is nothing more important to your future than your education."

"Nae, Appa. I know."

"And… your mother? How is she?"

"How do you think," Min Seok says.

Sung Jae's lets his head drop, shamed, before continuing. "I spoke to the lawyer… he thinks that perhaps this won't go so badly as it could have… all that damn soju I drank was the cause of it… I'd never have lost control like that, and lashed out like I did, if I'd been sober… and the boy seems to be recovering well… his face looks almost as good as new, now the surgery's finished… in a few months, he'll probably be prettier than he was before it happened… he really wasn't much of a looker… quite the shifty type you'd expect to be behind this kind of thing. And, of course, everything he did was so completely illegal, and immoral. The lawyer thinks the judge will be understanding."

"You'll be hearing from another lawyer soon," Min Seok says. "Mom's."

Sung Jae stares into Min Seok's hardened face; the puppy fat has dropped off his cheeks in the months he's been in the military. Sung Jae sees in his eldest son the hard angles of taut young manhood. He feels a strange mixture of fear & pride on looking at him.

"That's good," Sung Jae says after a long silence, smiling. "Very good. The more people we have working on this, the better the chances of us putting this all behind us… getting me out of here… forgetting about all this silliness…"

Min Seok rolls his eyes & sighs – a teenage reflex undercutting his newfound military-issue manhood. "The lawyer isn't for the case. Mom's hired a divorce lawyer."

"Oh…"

"And she told me to tell you that she's taking pity on you. She won't press charges for adultery. She doesn't want to make this mess you've made of your life any harder than it needs to be. But in return, she expects you to fully comply with whatever her lawyer suggests. She wants everything resolved with minimal fuss, as quickly as possible."

"I see…"

"And that is all I have to say to you."

As Min Seok's silence spreads through the room, Sung Jae mulls over his words. He'd mistaken Min Seok's brazen informality for the closeness of a father-son relationship; now that he thinks back over what he said, he recognizes something much more troubling about the manner in which his eldest son spoke: a complete erosion of all respect.

"I understand," Sung Jae says calmly, staring at Jae Seok's face, still flushed with the youth now absent in his elder brother. Jae Seok stares back at his father with immense sadness, seemingly on the verge of tears. Sung Jae reaches across the table & grips his youngest son's hand: "You have to be strong, Jae Seok. While your brother is in the service, you will be the man of the house. Take care of your mother. Please."

"Nae, Appa."

"And please don't worry about your old father. I'll be fine. The lawyer is really sure things will all work out. The judge will see the situation I was forced into. Anyone would've lashed out in the same way. I'll be released and this will all be forgotten before you know it."

Jae Seok's fighting against the sadness & guilt raging inside him, but the pitifulness of his father, in prison jumpsuit, the once-commanding father-figure now so cowed & fearful, despite the hope of all his words… it's too much. Tears fall.

"Don't cry, my boy," Sung Jae says, leaning right across the table, hugging his youngest son tight. "Don't cry."

"I should never have told you about the coins," Jae Seok sobs, burying his crying face into his father's prison jumpsuit. "If it hadn't been for the hack, you could've just paid the blackmail, then you never would've had to fight the scammer, and Mom wouldn't have found out, and… it's all my fault, Appa. It's all my fault."

"Ssh, Jae Seok. Ssh. It's not your fault. I've only myself to blame. And there's nothing to worry about. It'll be okay. Everything will be fine."

As Sung Jae holds Jae Seok close & strokes the back of his head, he looks across the room at Min Seok, who stares back with complete contempt. The thought occurs to Sung Jae that one day all-too-soon, Jae Seok will be joining the military & becoming a man, & when does so, he'll look back on this day with the same disgust Min Seok is now staring at him with; disgust at the weak child he once was, & the fool of a father who brought the family so much shame & pain, & when the day comes, if the lawyer's wrong, & the judge lacks pity, Sung Jae might still be stuck here in prison, serving his sentence.

21. 怒 (ANGER) / 喜 (HAPPINESS).

怒 1.

"Have you been here before?"

"Umm… no."

"Okay," the white guy with a European accent says, tapping at laptop keys. "How much do you want to exchange?"

"The limit's five million, right?"

"For Bitcoin to cash, yeah."

"Then I'll exchange five million won for whatever that is in Bitcoin."

"Okay," European white guy says, tapping more keys. "Right now that's gonna be 0.76 BTC."

Wei winces. Yesterday, the European white girl he spoke to gave him 5 million won for 0.62 BTC. "The commission is included in that, right?" Wei asks, unlocking his phone & opening his Bitcoin wallet's QR scanner.

Wei stuffs a thick wad of yellow Korean bank bills into his LV satchel as he descends the stairs from the fourth-floor crypto center, passing the closed black doors of an Irish bar as he calculates how much value his father's funds have lost in the week he's been in Korea. He opens CoinMarketCap on his phone as he walks along Itaewon's main restaurant-lined backstreet. Bitcoin is at $6,552. A week ago, it was over $10,000.

Wei walks down the long escalator into Itaewon Station wondering how pissed his father's going to be when he finds out what a failure his grand idea of Korean arbitrage was. The 50% Kimchi Premium on cryptocurrency prices shrunk to 10% before Wei even arrived in the country. And the Korean government had already banned foreigners from withdrawing cash from Korean crypto exchanges.

Wei rides subway line 6 to Cheonggu, spends another 5 minutes on line 5, exchanges more Bitcoin for 3 million down a back-alley in Dongdaemun, then takes line 2 to Yeongdeungpo-gu Office, gets another 2 million on another backstreet, then gets back on line 2 to Daerim.

"You came here too many times," the old Chinese guy tells Wei in Mandarin.

"Why does it matter how many times I came here? You exchange Bitcoin for cash. That's what your business does. I want to use your services."

"No."

Wei takes line 2 back to Gangnam & finds Joy pawing at her phone screen, reclining on the bed of their 14th floor room at the Novotel.

"The fucking Chinese guy in Daerim cut me off," Wei says. "I got enough to cover the deposit on the apartment but we better make some Korean friends who can convert more of this stuff into cash for us soon. This shit is dropping like crazy."

They meet with the real estate agent that afternoon. Wei hands over most of the past week's withdrawn cash toward key money, transferring the rest from Joy's account.

Joy complains about the arrangement draining the money her parents sent for starting her perfume business, while her father's still waiting for Wei's father to reimburse him for the wedding ceremony, "...and we need to buy so much stuff for the apartment, and we still need to find a place for the perfume store, and a place to make the perfume, and..."

Wei soft-talks her, saying it'll be alright, that he'll withdraw more Bitcoin tomorrow, that they should relax & enjoy their new apartment. Joy's still sullen & irritated until Wei suggests going out for dinner, then hitting a bar to start networking, and maybe stopping at a mall to do a little shopping. And once Joy's mind's moved to malls & Wei's credit card, she smiles at his suggestion of christening the apartment. Joy's dress is soon on the floor, Wei yanking his belt loose as he kisses her neck & rubs her vulva through her underwear. He tries to move her toward a bare mattress, but she pushes him back toward the living room & the sofa instead. Wei bends her over it & slips inside, thrusting back & forth with Bitcoin price-like volatility, until he nuts, whispers, "I love you, baby," then heads to the bathroom to clean up.

"Ohmygod, this is so pretty!" Joy says of a pretty silver-clasped handbag in bumped blue ostrich leather.

"Then get it!" Wei smiles, happy that she's happy.

"But I don't know if it goes with this," Joy says, pouting at the reflection of her figure-accentuating white dress & the jarring blue ostrich bag.

"Then get a new dress, baby. The card's good for it."

After an irritating conversation with a taxi driver who speaks neither English nor Chinese and can't understand the simple instruction of moving them across several lanes of traffic from the department store to their home, Wei & Joy walk back to their Lotte Castle apartment through the subway. After Joy changes into the newly-bought clothes, they take a taxi to Cheongdam. They eat at a French bistro then go to Octagon, a club Wei's booked a table at. They're soon regulars at Octagon, pieces of Joy's perfume plan slowly slotting into place as their social network grows.

 **1.**

I could've asked for more.

The thought gnaws at Alicia as she lies in bed at the Hotel Granvia Osaka, gazing out the window at the city's glowing skyline.

I could've asked for more. He accepted her offer immediately. That means she asked for less than he expected. Less than he would have paid.

She came to Osaka on a whim. It was the soonest flight she could book from Chengdu to a foreign country. She wanted to leave China the moment the money entered her Malaysian account, terrified she would be pulled aside & detained if she'd changed planes at Shanghai or Hong Kong. Osaka was the soonest direct option. She's paying ¥18,900 a night for the room. Alicia calculates that she can afford to stay here a little less than two years, if being alive incurs no other expenses.

I should've asked for more.

But she didn't. She gets out of bed, puts on the dress that she bought downstairs at the Hankyu Department Store, checks her face in the mirror, adds a little eyeliner & lipstick, leaves the room, rides the elevator to the first floor, then exits into the flowing mass of people in Osaka Station's central concourse. She follows the flow of people out of the station's southern-central exit & moves through crowded neon-bathed streets to the dotonbori, an endless covered alleyway of shopping & dining running in a straight line through the city, paying limited attention to her surroundings until hunger occurs to her. She walks into the next ramen place she sees, slides two ¥1000 bills into an automated machine & orders shoyu ramen & a biru. She looks over the other options as coins clatter into the change slot. She picks out her change, slots it back into the machine, & hits the button for a Suntory highball.

Alicia sits at the counter & hands her tickets over. The drinks are placed in front of her. She sips the beer, then downs the highball in four quick gulps. She's almost finished the beer by the time the ramen's served. She asks the guy who serves it for another highball. When she leaves the ramen shop, she's lightheaded & unfocused. She walks through the bright dotonbori, passing chattering groups of smiling Japanese going to or from nights out. She wonders if she should try to gouge more money out of him. *What would he say?* If she tried, she would be breaking their implicit agreement. He would have no reason to believe the next payment would be the last. Asking for more money would escalate things. But she cannot live off this forever. She has to do something else with her life. Move on to the next chain of loosely-connected events.

怒 2.

There's an open store-front on Cheongdam Fashion Street, close to Cartier, Gucci, & Armani.

"This place would be perfect," Joy says, eyes moving over the stylish slim pale Korean women walking past their potential storefront.

But the rent is 240 million Won per month, with a 6 billion deposit, which Wei calculates to be (as of this morning) something like 28 Bitcoin per month & 705 BTC upfront. Less glamorous Cheongdam and Apgujeong backstreets are considered, but rent for all is prohibitively high, and further options have to be considered.

"Y'know, my card is almost at the limit for the month already," Wei says, when Joy suggestively mentions Valentine's Day while gazing in Cartier's window at gem-studded pink & white gold love bracelets. Sullenness & distance colors the rest of the day. The next morning, Wei exchanges 2 BTC for Korean Won at the last exchange that hasn't cut him off yet. He stops by Cheongdam on the way home & surprises Joy with the pink & white gold bracelet.

They fuck immediately, Joy wearing nothing but her new bracelet as they go at it, and she seems receptive when he mentions the many shopping malls at Dongdaemun.

"…it's a perfect place for starting out, tourists go there from all over Asia for the best of Korean fashion and shit, and rent for a little store there will be a fuck lot less than Cheongdam, and once we've built a reputation – which we will, no doubt, when people smell the genius of your fragrance – and once my cousin's got you set up with distributors, the brand will grow, and a year from now, we'll have that flagship store on Cheongdam Fashion Street, baby, I promise you."

Wei's cousin ignores his repeated emails, but Wei assures Joy that his cousin's incredibly busy at J'Adore Pacific, and he'll be in touch soon. Bitcoin is moving upward, back at $10,000 by Friday, hitting $11,000 on Monday as they sign a year's lease on a space on the second floor of one of the multi-storey malls lining the street across from the sleek silver sci-fi style Dongdaemun Design Plaza. The apartment's filled with aromas as Joy struggles through dozens of combinations of essential oils, Wei experimenting with crypto trading as she spends long hours carefully balancing classic base and top notes with experimental mids and bridges. Wei quickly realizes the power his father's Bitcoin stash wields on market movements on varied crypto exchanges, edging prices up & down to maximize margins then offloading random shitcoins in bulk once others pile in chasing the price pump.

Eau de Joy opens March 1, but business is slow, curious Russian & Chinese tourists briefly sniffing at her bottles before moving on to other storefronts loaded with cheap clothing. Each day her frustration grows, the miserable morning commute wedged between bulky salarymen on Line 2 becoming evermore unbearable.

"We need a marketing campaign," Wei says, as they stand outside the mall watching leggy Korean girls in revealing clothing gyrate on a stage to K-pop, shifty men in thick jackets holding their phones up at the stage-front. "Something to let people know how irresistible your scent is."

"What about her?" Wei asks Joy repeatedly from their regular table at Octagon.

Wei leaves Joy playing hostess to Tom and Silvio the American & Brazilian software engineers & Ha Jin the Korean banking guy and some Korean girls they've brought to the table as Wei approaches beautiful girls, sweet talks them to the table, pours drinks, & distributes business cards.

"…but it's a bitch to convert the Bitcoin into cash," Wei tells one of the girls, Soon Ji, over coffee at a Garosugil cafe. "The only way to exchange big amounts into Korean Won is to transfer the Bitcoin to a Korean exchange and then withdraw to a Korean bank account. But the fucking government's blocked foreigners from opening accounts on Korean crypto exchanges."

"My brother invested a lot in Bitcoin," Soon Ji says. "Maybe he could help you out."

Wei's having coffee & macarons with another potential model for the Eau de Joy advertising campaign when Soon Ji sends a KakaoTalk message saying her brother's agreed to help. Plans are made to send one bitcoin to Soon Ji's brother's UpBit account as a trial. Wei meets Soon Ji at a cafe in Gangnam to collect the 10 million Won in cash.

"This is amazing," Wei says. "I can't believe how fucking easy this is! If you knew the shit I've been through exchanging Bitcoin at all these tiny over-the-counter places…"

"Are you hungry?" Soon Ji asks.

Wei suggests a few nearby restaurants, but Soon Ji says she's really craving Chinese-style delivery food. Plans to order it disappear as soon as they enter the elevator at the Novotel, and the conversation shifts from food to whether Wei really thinks Soon Ji is pretty enough to be the face of the marketing campaign.

"I had an idea," Soon Ji says, staring into Wei's eyes as she unzips the back of her dress & slides it to the hotel room's floor. She teasingly clasps the bottle of Eau de Joy against her face, then holds it to her chest & squeezes her breasts around it. "Do you think this might be too suggestive?"

"Fuck no."

"How about this?" Soon Ji crawls along the bed on all fours, then holds the perfume out behind her and sprays it onto the crotch of her black lace underwear. "How does it smell?" she giggles.

Wei almost trips as he storms to the bed & rubs his nose against her moist underwear: "It smells amazing."

He pulls her underwear down & thrusts his tongue between her labia.

"…and we can just put the cash through the business, say we sold X amount in Eau de Joy," Wei explains to Joy that evening. "It's the perfect cover. Money laundering 101."

After two more successful test withdrawals & Novotel trysts, Bitcoin's price decline accelerates. When it drops below $9,000, Wei tells Soon Ji it's time to start moving larger amounts. He transfers 65 BTC into her brother's bitcoin wallet. Then her profile disappears from his KakaoTalk.

"Those motherfuckers! They fucking screwed us! Jesus fucking Christ! You cannot trust these fucking Korean assholes! Fuck!"

"Why don't you call the fucking police?!" Joy screams, furious at her husband's stupidity and the year of packed Line 2 subway rides & pointless days at the shitty mall he's doomed her to.

"I can't," Wei says. He babbles about his father's tax investigation and information-sharing between Korean & Chinese police services, his mind plagued by a story that's dominating Korean news, about a guy who got blackmailed with spy-cam footage and lost a fortune to some shitcoin hack and is in jail for beating the shit out of the motel clerk who filmed him.

喜 2.

"Where are you from?"

"Malaysia. You?"

"England. You don't look very Malaysian."

Alicia stops walking.

"Sorry – I didn't mean… I mean, I thought you were Japanese."

"I'm not." She starts walking. "I'm Chinese-Malaysian."

"You're very pretty."

"Thanks."

He's living in an apartment a few blocks away from the club besides the giant flashing Glico Running Man at the end of the dotonbori that she met him at. She doesn't need to ask what he does to know he's an English teacher. Every white guy at the club was either an English teacher or U.S. military. And she would rather go home with an English English teacher than an American soldier.

"I saw this American guy blow beer in the bartender's face earlier," Alicia says, sitting on his bed as he stands in the center of the room selecting music on his phone.

"Blow beer? How is that even possible?"

"He said there was too much foam. So he blew the foam right in the bartender's face."

"Fucking hell. What a dickhead."

"The bartender didn't even kick him out. He just warned him not to do that."

"It's amazing how calm people can be here."

"Yeah," she says, wondering how calm the Japanese who brutalized Malaysia when they seized it from the British in the 1940s were. "What is this?"

He explains the music, and says he can change it if she wants, but she doesn't care, and the alcohol's getting the better of her, so she says, "Come here," & they're kissing on the bed, & he's undressing her, & it's a blissful blur of bodily sensations. He wakes up as she's getting dressed in the morning.

"I should go. But… I'd like to see you again."

"Absolutely. Here, I'll give you my number."

"Sorry," she says, both standing in the middle of the room, holding their phones. "What was your name again?"

Alicia moves from the Hotel Granvia Osaka to a ¥4,900 a night room a few blocks from Osaka Castle. The room stinks of stale cigarette smoke and has no windows, but it's more comfortable than any place she stayed in Chengdu (the Bitcoin guy's place excluded.) She calculates that, all other expenses aside, she could live here for almost the next decade. At that time, she'll be in her mid-thirties.

"How old are you?" Alicia asks James the English teacher when they meet again at a small fourth floor bar run by an American guy he knows.

"Twenty-nine. You?"

James is interesting, okay looking, reasonably well-dressed (though the old wisdom of looking at a man's shoes to determine his true wealth is not encouraging), and a much more pleasurable experience in bed than anything she experienced in China. Rationalizing the impracticality of living the next ten years in a hotel, she spends her days wandering the castle grounds & the dotonbori, fantasizing about their future life together. He's the only person she knows in Osaka, and as time passes, he becomes her whole world. She calls her mother on Skype twice a week, telling her she got a great job in a bar in Osaka through Hannah, smiling & projecting happiness through her Huawei phone screen. Apart from those calls to her mother, there's only James Keaton. A 29 year-old English teacher from Hull. He introduces her to his friend group – other English teachers, heavy drinkers with names like Scott & Keith from places like Cork & Minnesota, all with impossibly polite & gracious Japanese girlfriends. Everything about her life in Osaka feels unsustainable. She asks James increasingly probing questions – "How long are you going to stay in Japan?", "Do you want to keep teaching English all your life?" His answers are non-commital. The sex becomes less enchanting. One day, she unlocks his phone & sees he's exchanging Tinder messages with some Japanese bitch named Yuki. She doesn't mention her discovery to James. She simply packs her meagre belongings – all old clothes having been discarded for more expensive Japanese ones – & takes her suitcase back to the central concourse of Osaka Station. She stares at the ticket machine until she becomes aware of a man in a business suit behind her, too Japanese to say anything but clearly growing irritated with how long she's taking. She hits the button for Fukuoka. It's far from Osaka, and southern, with a climate as close to Malaysia as exists along Japan's rail-connected main island chain. As the shinkansen roars through Japan at near-airplane speed, she uses her phone to book a room at the Fukuoka Hilton.

怒 3.

Eau de Joy's fortunes rise with Bitcoin's price as spring blooms. Sales are good at a stall at a Cherry Blossom festival on the banks of the Han River in mid-April. Tom the ex-military American software engineer introduces Wei to a Korean guy, Hyeong Min, whom Tom met whilst in the army. Hyeong Min is honest & reliable, regular Bitcoin-to-Won transfers funneled through his accounts pouring seamlessly onto Eau de Joy's balance sheet. Staff are hired to work at the shitty mall in Dongdaemun while Joy devotes her time to a much busier spot in the underground shopping mall at Gangnam Station. Hundreds of bottles are sold every day to the type of well-dressed Korean women Joy always knew would be her core customers. Her dream of the flagship store on Cheongdam Fashion Street is becoming evermore attainable.

"Baby, I've got incredible news," Wei tells her. "My cousin finally got back in touch. He wants us to come meet him in Tokyo!"

More hours are allocated to staff as Joy works constantly on crafting the perfect presentation. As the date of their Tokyo trip nears, Wei's mother arrives in Korea. When Wei meets her at the airport, she seems to have aged a decade since he saw her last.

"Your friend," Wei's mother explains on the taxi ride from Incheon Airport to her Gangnam hotel. "He disappeared."

"Justin? What happened to him?"

Wei's mother places her phone on the seat between them. Wei picks it up and sees some woman in a hotel room, Justin behind her, sleeping on the bed.

"Whoever that woman is in the photograph sent this to your father."

"Who is she?"

"Your father says he has no idea. But he told me to show you this."

"That sneaky bastard motherfucker," Wei tells Joy. "I've known that piece of shit since high school. And he now he's stolen fuck-knows how much money that my father trusted in his Bitcoin mining shit. And he sent this pic of him with some whore to my fucking father, taunting him."

 3.

On a warm Wednesday in mid-April, Alicia is drinking glass after glass of red wine & picking at a loaded plate of buffet seafood in the sun-filled arboretum dining room at the base of the Fukuoka Hilton. This is a habit she's fallen into for she's not sure how long now – a few days, maybe a week. The wine makes the days & nights blur together. But as she sits slowly severing a shrimp's head with a spoon, she notices that today is different; that the normally deathly silent square outside the glass walls of the arboretum is full of people. She hurries her food & bottle and goes outside, joining the swarms of white-shirted Japanese filing into the adjacent Fukuoka Dome. She takes a seat in the upper deck and watches a baseball game unfold, local favorites the SoftBank Hawks' score ticking ever upward. The wine wears off as she watches, the game slowly coming into focus. The scoreboard indicates the game is now on its third innings. The Hawks' opponents are batting. One batter hits the ball. Players rush around the diamond. One makes home plate. The score is now 6-1. Alicia realizes she understands next to nothing about baseball.

The seat to her left is empty. In the seat next to that, a man is leaning forward, greeting Hokkaido Nippon Ham Fighters' point with frustration. The next innings happens, reality overcoming Alicia's earlier wine buzz with each frustrated hit. Nippon Ham Fighters make it 2-6. The man disappears during a break between innings & returns in the fifth with a box of takoyaki & a plastic cup of biru.

"Sumimasen," Alicia says to him, continuing in broken Japanese, "where did you buy that?"

He stares at her in deep confusion, but she's got enough of the residual wine buzz to not be bothered by his appropriate reaction to her deeply stupid question. Instead, she is studying his face; slight lines around the eye indicating he's somewhat older than her, though his blemish-free skin & strong straight bone structure exudes youth & attractiveness. His hair is neatly tussled on top but sensibly short. He wears a plain white shirt & black tie. A quick glance at his shoes shows their reassuringly sheened & pointed – Alicia thinks they may be Italian.

"Inside," he says.

"Gomenasai," Alicia apologizes, quickly tumbling through some horribly broken Japanese spiel about not being from here & not really understanding the game, but going traveling on money her beloved uncle bequeathed to her upon his death, & staying in the adjacent Hilton. He tells her he's staying at the Hilton too, that he's only in Fukuoka on business, that his name is Takahiro, that he's from Kagoshima at the southern end of Fukuoka's Kyushu island, & that he's here in the island capital as a function of his employment as a buyer for a nationwide retail chain. He offers her one of his six takoyaki, which she eats gleefully, before asking for a sip of his biru to wash it down. The fifth innings ends with Fukuoka's SoftBank Hawks leading Hokkaido's Nippon Ham Fighters 8-2. Takahiro says he's going to the bathroom between innings, but returns with two beers & a selection of yakitori.

As they talk, Takahiro makes a brief attempt at conversing in Chinese, before switching to some of the best English Alicia has yet heard from a Japanese. After the game, they drink together at the Hilton's Sky Bar.

Takahiro pays for everything, despite Alicia insisting she contribute. He says he's returning to Kagoshima in the morning, and if Alicia is simply traveling in Japan on the funds she inherited from her uncle, she should maybe consider visiting his city – a beautiful historic place, with a highly-active volcanic island in its bay. She says she'll think about it, and is immensely disappointed when the night ends with a simple exchange of Line IDs, & each returning to their rooms alone.

怒 4.

"So it costs about two-thousand US dollars to mine one bitcoin in China," Wei explains to Joy, on their second bottle of wine in the early hours of Friday morning. "That's for the electricity, without thinking about any other costs, like the equipment, the space you've got your mining rigs in – space which my father was letting that asshole use for free. And right now, you can exchange one bitcoin for a little less than seven thousand US. So that asshole was making about five thousand dollars profit on every bitcoin he mined, right? But then my father was splitting profits on whatever he mined in his old factory 50/50, so that'd leave the asshole with about two-and-a-half thousand dollars profit per bitcoin mined. But the market's jittery as fuck, a lot of people are saying we already bottomed out at just above six thousand, but it was almost twenty thousand dollars for one bitcoin back at Christmas, and then the price started falling, and a lot of people said it would start shooting up again right after Chinese New Year."

Joy sighs. "Why would Chinese New Year affect the price of Bitcoin?"

Wei sighs. "I don't fucking know. Just people were saying it. Like they were saying before that that prices would start going up at the end of January when all the Wall Street bankers got their bonuses. Maybe the rest of the world think us Chinese people start investing in shit immediately after New Year. I don't fucking know. But we're now two months deep into the Year of the Dog and the price is still bouncing between 6K and 10K and no-one knows what the long-term trajectory's gonna be. So maybe that asshole got worried. Maybe he thinks Bitcoin will go lower. Maybe he saw his chance to cash out all the bitcoin he mined with my fucking father's investment and just disappeared with it."

"I still don't understand why he'd send that picture. With the girl. At his apartment."

"Because he's a fucking asshole. I don't know. He's always been an asshole. He's always wanted people to know how fucking well he's doing. In high school, you should've seen him after he aced a fucking math test."

"So all your father's money's gone?"

"I don't know how much is gone. But a lot's gone. My mother barely gets to speak to him. And they're holding him in custody, awaiting sentencing. If he hadn't given his money to that fucking asshole and his fucking Bitcoin mining shit, then maybe he could pay off the officials or something. Pay his tax bill. But now he can't. He wanted to do the right thing, protect the wealth he spent a lifetime accumulating, make sure his family is provided for in the future. And those fucking government assholes are gonna hold that against him. God, China is fucked."

Joy looks away from Wei, out the window, at the fat midsection of the enormous 123-floor Lotte Tower, its lights glowing in the perma-orange sky. "How much bitcoin do you have?"

"I've got a lot of it. And Hyeong Min's helping me turn that into cash. But I think that asshole's got a lot more of it than I do. And if I ever find him, or that whore who took the picture with him, I swear, I'm afraid of what I might do to them."

喜 4.

The shinkansen rockets along Kyushu's western coastline, covering the 281.2km from Fukuoka to Kagoshima in about 2.5 hrs. As Alicia exits Kagoshima Station, she sees smoke billowing out the top of the promised island volcano through an opening between tall buildings & thinks she may have made a mistake. It's 3.21pm on a warm April Friday. She met Takahiro less than 48 hours ago. Thursday was spent in her room & the Hilton's arboretum, thinking of him, thoughts becoming grander & more ridiculous with each glass of wine. Now those thoughts are delicately balanced on the rim of reality. She stares at the distant volcano, letting her thoughts dissipate into Kagoshima's air like the volcano's vapors. Mind clear, she takes her phone & books four nights at a ¥3,450-a-night Airbnb.

She walks through labyrinth sheltered shopping streets until she finds the building entrance, hidden between two clothing stores. She lays on top of a double bed, with two unmade singles across the room, just a sheet atop them. She drifts through vivid half-dreams of the baseball stadium, then standing with Takahiro at the volcano's base, then moving through cityless dotonboris, pursued by *him,* from the factory, & his son, finding shelter at Tianfu Square, the Bitcoin guy brushing past the concierge to usher her into the safety of his apartment...

She wakes to a near-dark room. She grabs her phone: 8.47pm. Her Airbnb host's sent a string of messages, detailing local eating streets & other attractions. Her thumbs hover over Takahiro's Line ID & the handsome professionalism of his profile pic. *It's too late,* she tells herself. *Message tomorrow.*

The shops are all now shuttered, save for the 7/11s & Lawsons convenience stores. A group of young Japanese crouch & sing, one strumming a guitar. She leaves the covered closed-down shopping streets & crosses the road to her host's recommended Bunkadori, a lively street of places to eat & drink. She side-steps promoters thrusting leaflets & imploring in high-pitched Japanese to come inside. She turns a corner to a street full of meandering smoking salarymen & scores of photoshopped photographs of Japanese girls in varying states of undress stamped with hourly rates. The scene so strongly evokes the World Class Lounge that hunger leaves her. She enters a liquor store, grasps as many cans of highball & fruit-flavored Strong Zero as she can carry, then returns to her Airbnb & drifts through drink-fuelled dreams until sunlight fills the room.

Why doesn't he answer me?

More than three hours have passed since she sent the message. She stops in a park along the riverbank & rereads it. *Hi! I came to Kagoshima :) If you're not too busy, maybe we could hang out?,* followed by a grinning emoticon of Cony the Line Friend rabbit. Breezy, unimposing… the tone is perfect. *Maybe he's married?* Maybe that's why he didn't ask her to his room at the Fukuoka Hilton – he's married, & was initially attracted to her, but struck by sudden pangs of conscience…

"Konichiwa."

Alicia looks up at a smiling elderly Japanese man. She bows her head & replies: "Konichiwa."

A string of words she doesn't understand follows. He smiles again & asks simply, "English?"

She nods & smiles: "Hai."

As he talks, she feels the phone vibrate. She answers questions quickly, smiling, wishing the elderly man away. When he leaves, she sees Takahiro's answered: *That's great! I hope you're enjoying it. Did you go see Sakurajima yet?*

She rapidly types out a reply & make plans to go together the next morning to Sakurajima, the volcanic island in Kagoshima's bay.

Sun-filled day becomes neon night. Alicia struggles to sleep for thoughts of the following day. He picks her up at 10am, pulling up beside Temmonkandori Station in a large & tasteful black BMW. He holds the door open to let her into the passenger's side as she greets him with a demure Japanese-style smile & head bow. They talk of his work during the short drive to the ferry terminal (Saturday was busy, which was why it took so long to reply to her message.) On the ferry's upper deck, Sakurajima's broad face fills the horizon, its smoke slowly expanding into the otherwise-clear blue sky.

"People live there? It isn't dangerous?"

"Sometimes. The schoolchildren have to carry hard hats, in case rocks shoot out. But I think it's just for safety. It isn't usually dangerous."

"It doesn't erupt?"

He tells her of eruptions, one in the 1940s, eradicating large swathes of the island's vegetation, and in 1914, completely transforming the island's shape. Then of his grandfather's brother, who disappeared one night while suffering terminal illness. "No one can be sure, but I think he must have jumped inside."

"The volcano?" Alicia thinks of death by molten rock, body melding through immense agony with the violence & heat of the Earth's core. They drive around the island, stopping at tourist spots – lava fields covered in fresh sprouting forest, something of the destruction & renewal of life on Earth speaking to Alicia in a language vaguer to her than Japanese. At the fourth or fifth stop, they ascend stone steps to a modest statue of a woman in a kimono clutching a book. Alicia reads the description of the life of the statue's subject, Hayashi Fumiko (1903-1951): a poet & novelist from Kagoshima. Fumiko moved to Tokyo, dreaming of becoming a writer. There she spent a restless life, flitting between jobs & circumstances – *loosely connected chains of events* – never finding stability, nor happiness, dreaming always of home & Kagoshima, dying at 47 & leaving the world her most poetic couplet: *'The life of a flower is short, but its sufferings are many.'*

Alicia gently takes Takahiro's hand. When she looks away from Fumiko's text, she sees Takahiro is smiling at her with a mix of curiosity & sympathy. She smiles & withdraws her hand.

They take a ferry back to the city in early-evening, sun setting over the bay. He takes her for dinner of Kyushu black pork on a street near her Airbnb. When they leave, he walks her to the Airbnb's entrance. He bows his head & smiles. She asks if he'd like to come inside.

She regrets the invitation the moment they call the elevator, remembering the oddness of the room's three-bed set-up & discarded alcohol cans dotting the room. He laughs when he sees them. She offers him an unopened 9% Tory Highball & opens a lemon Strong Zero for herself. They sit on one of the unmade single beds. Takahiro asks if she was close to her uncle. She pauses a while before she answers: "Sukoshi." She holds her hand up close to Takahiro's face and brings her index finger and thumb close together to illustrate the meaning of 'sukoshi' – *a little* – then giggles as they gaze into the other's eyes. She places her Strong Zero on the floor, then places her hand against his cheek. He places his left hand to her right hip & leans gently forward. They softly kiss, then slowly recline on the unmade single bed. Hands move over the other's body as they kiss. She moans softly then lazes on the bed & undoes the top few buttons of his shirt. He moves across her, lifts her dress, places his left hand upon her right breast. His hands make slow circles over her bra. Her nipples stiffen. She laughs & undoes unseen buttons. "Daijoubu desu ka?" he asks, the laughter throwing him. She grips the back of his head & pulls him toward her, tongues lapping the other's. His right hand slips beneath her bra & softly squeezes. She fiddles hopelessly with his unseen belt until she gives up, laughing. He moves back from her, mirroring her laugh as he unbuckles. She lifts her dress over her head, unhooks her bra, lets it slide from her chest & hit the bed. "Let's move to the double," she says, pointing across the room.

怒 5.

J'Adore Pacific's Tokyo headquarters are on the 21st floor at Gate City Ohsaki, riverbank twin towers a few blocks south of Shinagawa. Joy stands in front of a conference table wearing a white Michael Kors ruffed-sleeve blazer over a simple black knit & double-crepe sable asymmetrical skirt. She speaks first of Jean Patou wandering on the banks of the Seine in Paris in 1929, his business on verge of collapse as the Great Depression ravaged America & its contagions infected all the world's premier luxury businesses. Where others may have shrunk from the turbulence of the times, Patou smelled the roses & jasmine of the riverbanks and let the scents carry him far above the winds of financial misfortune, to craft something not of this earth: pressing 10,600 jasmine & 28 dozen roses with ylang-ylang, tuberose, adelhydes, & darkened iris root. What resulted was a scent not of this world. A platonic ideal of fragrance. A flower of the gods. A scent that touches the skin in an explosion of pungent impact & slowly blossoms into an orchard of deeply-layered notes, whispering of the wearer's interdimensional soul. A scent that endured the trials of France's tragic twentieth-century: jackbooted Nazi oppression, the turmoil of 1968. The scent of Joy overpowered & outlasted the mists of misery. "And now I – Joy – present to you my own fragrance. Eau de Joy. An antidote to the turmoil of our own times. A fragrance to ignite the senses in a time of digital sub-reality. An other-worldly odour in an era of unworldly technological subjugation. A scent to celebrate what it is to be alive."

Samples are passed along the table, each of the seven Japanese men & three Japanese women nodding as they sniff it. Wei's cousin is overtly theatrical as he whiffs the bottle, turning to the woman at his left and proclaiming its greatness. Wei himself is at the laptop, clicking through slides as Joy talks. When her ten-minute pitch is over, the wrinkled grey-haired Japanese man at the opposite end of the table asks each of the women seated for their opinion. Each speaks quietly & deferentially in Japanese, bowing their head & lowering their eyes as they speak, before ending each sentence with a quick glance toward the boss to check his reaction. Once he's listened to the opinions of his underlings, he makes an offer to purchase 20,000 units of Eau de Joy.

Wei spends the 20-minute taxi ride back to Roppongi Hills praising Joy, her poise & delivery, the content of her speech, the size of the order, while Joy's joy falls to worrying about how the hell she can craft 20,000 bottles of the perfume. They return to the towers at Roppongi Hills and ride the elevator to the luxurious apartment Wei's cousin loaned them. Wei's cousin calls & suggests they go out for a meal to celebrate. Joy worries about that too, not having packed something appropriately stylish enough. As she pulls items from her suitcase & holds them up to the master bedroom mirror, she tells Wei she needs a small shopping list of toiletries & cosmetics to transform her power & floral lightness business-style into a for-the-evening elegance. Wei says, "Baby, don't worry, I'll take care of it. I've got it. Don't worry about it.", then leaves the apartment & walks a few hundred meters down Roppongi's main drag until he finds a cosmetics store. He carefully looks over mascaras & powders & other items he has very little knowledge of trying to find exact matches for the items on Joy's list. His eyes move over the pouting & smiling models on the bottles & labels & stickers & stops when he sees a face he recognizes. Wei stands in the store for more than a minute, staring at it. He takes his phone from his pocket. He opens the photo his mother sent him – Justin, the Bitcoin mining prick, asleep on the bed, a woman in front of him. He stares at the image on the shampoo bottle. He looks again at the image on his phone.

喜 5.

"How long will you stay here?"

"In the Airbnb? Or Kagoshima?"

"Kagoshima."

"I don't know."

"And the Airbnb?"

"Until tomorrow."

Takahiro suggests she stay with him. Alicia politely declines twice. An hour later, he's placing her suitcase in the trunk of his car. His apartment is sparse & spacious, elegant interior fittings suggesting modern construction, lack of clutter exhibiting the ideals of Japanese minimalism. On Monday, Alicia walks to the Museum of the Meiji Restoration & wonders what her Japanese-hating grandmother would think of the displays commemorating the local heroes who sparked Japanese industrialism & led the conquest of Hokkaido from the Russians & put in motion the military takeover of half East Asia. In the evenings, they eat & fuck & talk & fall in love. Tuesday, Wednesday, Thursday, she wanders along the riverbank, through an aquarium, another museum, and up a hillside to a park overlooking the smoking volcano in the bay. That weekend, they drive half-an-hour along the bay, past densely forested mountainsides, to Aira, where they visit a temple with a towering tree in its grounds with an incredibly thick trunk that Takahiro tells Alicia is the oldest in Japan. She thinks of the 1,500 years the tree has been alive, predating Hari Merdeka & the Japanese conquest of Malaysia & the British conquest & British re-conquest from the Japanese & the arrival of her ancestors in the country & the arrival of Hindus & Muslims in Malaysia & the Golden Age of Malacca & how one tree can live and stand still as the world rages around it & that night their sex is passionate and intense and transcendent and Takahiro asks her: "How long will you stay here?"

"In Japan? Or Kagoshima?"

Talk turns to practicalities: she's two-thirds through her 90-day tourist visa, and has nothing to return to Malaysia for, but would require some firmness of purpose to stay here longer. She thinks for a moment he's thinking to propose, but instead he tells her that his company is rebranding its cheap own-brand shampoos & rinses and wants a face for the brand to place on its bottles. On Monday, she visits his company's offices. On Tuesday, he takes her to the local immigration office to submit a visa application. On Friday, she officially becomes a Japanese resident.

喜怒 6.

"We need a face for the marketing campaign," Wei says, meat sizzling on the chef's grill in front of them. "Something that truly captures the essence of Eau de Joy. We've been searching really hard for the right person in Korea, haven't we, baby?"

"Yeah," Joy says, faking a smile, not sure why Wei has to be so obtuse about things when talking to his own cousin.

"Korean girls are pretty though," Wei's cousin smirks. "Much prettier than Japanese!"

"Yeah," Wei says, as the chef shouts something in Japanese and places a fresh plate of gourmet yakitori in front of them.

"Gozaimasu," Wei's cousin says. "But not as pretty as Chinese girls."

Joy fakes a smile again.

"But we've been looking everywhere for the right girl, and today Joy sent me out to get some stuff to get ready for going out tonight, and I saw this girl on a bottle that we both thought would be perfect, didn't we, baby?"

"Yeah," Joy says, picking up a yakitori skewer.

Wei pulls the shampoo bottle from his jean's pocket and passes it to his cousin, whose hunched over his plate, tearing chicken gizzards off a stick with his teeth. He laughs when he sees it: "You bought your wife this shit? Holy fuck, Wei, you cheap bastard!"

"That's not the stuff I bought Joy," Wei says. "Is it, baby? I just bought this to show you the girl on it. That's the girl we want for our marketing campaign."

Wei's cousin swallows. "Huh." He studies the bottle. "She's not so pretty, huh?"

"Yeah, but she's got a distinctive look," Wei says. "And the best models look distinctive. You look at supermodels, they're not the prettiest girls in the world – I mean, they're pretty, but not in a conventionally pretty way. They look unique. They capture your imagination."

"Huh," Wei's cousin says, staring at the plain-faced girl on the shampoo bottle. "I think this girl might be Chinese."

"Yeah, that's what we thought, wasn't it, baby? But we really think she'd be perfect for the marketing campaign. And we were thinking, with your connections in the industry, maybe you might be able to find out who she is and set up a meeting with her?"

Wei's cousin calls the next afternoon, when Joy and Wei are arguing over when to leave for the airport: "The girl's living in Kagoshima. I don't know where it is either, apparently it's some shitty little city down south. She's interested, but she's not gonna be in Tokyo until a few days from now."

Wei tries to make Joy understand why it's so important he meets this girl & tracks Justin down through her & retrieves some of her father's money, but all Joy can think of is the 20,000 bottle order from J'Adore Pacific & the enormous workload that Wei is leaving her to complete alone. *Why did I marry this asshole?* She frowns until she leaves the Roppongi Hills apartment, completely ignoring Wei's offer of seeing her into a taxi. That evening, Wei meets his cousin for dinner again. After that, Wei & his cousin go for drinks in some place called Geronimo's, get loaded on shots, hit a club, then respectively fuck a Filipina & African hooker in a nearby brothel.

"Hi! You must be Alicia."

Shit. Alicia recognizes him the second she enters the apartment. *His son.* Wei takes in the look on her face, wondering how much photoshopping they must have done to her on the shampoo bottle. Then he smiles: "Please. Take a seat. You know why I brought you here, right?"

Alicia doesn't say anything.

Wei realizes they both know exactly why he's brought her here. He smiles at her clear discomfort, but then struggles to think of what to say next. He tries to imagine what his father would do in this situation: the wily old businessman, squeezing the best possible deals from clients, crushing competitors… "Would you like something to drink?"

"I'm fine."

"Okay. Well. Maybe I'll take something." He moves quickly to the kitchen, glancing over at her every few seconds as he pours a Hendricks gin & tonic. "You sure you don't want something?"

Alicia says nothing. She thinks how similar his speaking style is to his father's, though the son must be at least 20kg heavier.

"Justin." Wei almost coughs the name out. When he sees her confused reaction to it, he wonders for a moment if he's misjudged the situation; *maybe she doesn't know who he is.* Wei sits down again on the sofa opposite her, sips g&t, and tries another approach. "I have a friend. I think maybe you know him? You look familiar."

Alicia says nothing.

Unsure of how to proceed, Wei swigs off half the g&t as he pulls his phone out & opens the picture. He studies the face on it for a moment & then looks up at her. He finishes the g&t before he's sure that it's her. Then he shows her the phone. "Justin. You know my friend, right?"

Alicia stares at Wei until he's off-put enough that he reaches for his g&t again, but the glass is empty of liquid, and ice clanks against his teeth. He places it down on the coffee table & starts talking: "The guy in this picture stole a lot of money from my father. *A lot* of money. And he sent my father this picture of the two of you together. Do you have any idea why he might have done that?" When Alicia is again silent, trying to figure out why Wei's under the impression that the Bitcoin guy sent the picture, Alicia knowing that it was she who took & sent it to his father, Wei starts speaking more: "I know this guy. I've known him since school. I know what a fucking asshole he is. I know he might have threatened you. I want you to know that we've got no problem with you. If you can help us find him, nothing bad will happen to you."

The more he talks, the more Alicia understands how clueless Wei is. He has no idea about her & his father, the Chengdu apartment, anything behind why that picture was sent to him; and it's clear there's no issue with her & the money she extorted from his father. It's all to do with the Bitcoin guy with the Tianfu Square apartment ripping them off. Once Wei stops speaking, Alicia responds: "I haven't spoken to him in a while. I have no idea who you or your father are. I thought I was coming here for an interview for a modeling job. But if you really want to find Justin, I can help you. I know exactly where he is. But I couldn't betray his trust… without compensation."

Wei tries to think, but thinks of nothing: "What do you want?"

"How much does Justin owe you?"

"He owes us a lot."

"Then I want fifty percent of whatever a lot is."

"Fuck… that's insane. You don't realize how much a lot is."

"Then tell me. And, actually, I wouldn't mind a drink, if you're planning on pouring another one."

Wei smiles: "Absolutely."

Got him.

"Why do you hate Justin so much, anyway?"

Wei explains in excruciating detail about what an asshole Justin was in school, boasting of his superior grades in all subjects, and how he became an even bigger asshole while he was studying Economics at Peking University, and became an absolutely unbearable asshole once he graduated and started his Bitcoin mining company.

"Then why were you friends with him?"

Wei feels tears rise behind his eyes as he stares at an empty spot on the apartment's wall; the gin is causing emotion to overwhelm him. "He was an asshole, but… he was my asshole, you know? We were friends for the longest time."

"I understand." Alicia thanks of Hannah & the World Class Lounge. "I had a friend like that once."

"I thought that we were practically brothers, you know? I thought we'd ride or die, stick together through the best and worst of times, always have each other's backs… then that motherfucker…" Wei can't finish the sentence, holding his g&t to his mouth, scrunching his face in a desperate effort not to explode into tears over the tragedy of it all.

"Hey, it's okay," Alicia says, leaning across the sofa & clasping her hands around Wei's g&t-holding hands. "I'll help you find Justin. I promise. We'll get your father's money back. And that asshole will get exactly what he deserves for screwing his best friend over."

Wei slowly lets the overwhelming emotions dissipate as he stares into the dark pools of Alicia's eyes. She softly takes the g&t from his hands, takes a sip, places it on the coffee table, then touches her hand to his cheek. He reaches his hand to her cheek. He closes his eyes & leans toward her. Alicia holds back her revulsion & kisses him. She tries to think of Takahiro as he fucks her, but that only makes the experience more miserable, so she tries to block out thought altogether. Probably because of the alcohol, the fucking seems to last forever. When he finally comes, she tells Wei how much better he is than Justin, and how tiny Justin's penis is. They laugh together about what an asshole Justin is. Then she tells him she really needs some money, that she thought she was going to get a modeling job out of this Tokyo trip, and that trains in Japan are incredibly expensive compared to those in Malaysia. Wei says he understands, that he'll give her whatever she needs. He helps her set up a Bitcoin wallet on her phone, deliberately averting his eyes as she makes a note of its private key. She watches his phone closely as he transfers her 0.5 BTC. She thanks him, then pours them both another drink. And another. And another, until Wei passes out. Then she grabs both their phones & leaves, transfers the rest of Wei's BTC balance onto the phone wallet he helped her set up, hails a taxi, sets a new wallet up on her phone as the taxi takes her to Narita Airport, transfers the entire BTC balance to the new wallet, tosses his phone into a trashcan at the airport, books a business class flight to New York departing at 09:15 (disappointed no first class seats are available), feels immense anxiety until she's boarded her first flight to Hong Kong & waited another 3 hours in the airport there & finally relaxes as the plane travels over the Pacific, crafting a heartfelt message to Takahiro on her phone about how great the time they spent together was & how unfortunately she has to return to Malaysia to visit a desperately sick relative.

怒 7.

"Wei! You worthless piece of shit!"

Joy is stressed beyond human comprehension. *20,000 fucking bottles.* With no fucking funding. Many perfumes are sourced from ambergris – whale bile. *Bile.* As in what comes out when you puke so much your guts are empty of all other contents. Joy sees how bloated Wei's belly is – *a fucking land whale* – growing larger with every week of their marriage – *with every fucking day* – but she knows if she cut the cunt open the smell would be unbelievably repulsive. *And to lose every last Bitcoin to another fucking scam, after his so-called friend betrayed his father, and getting scammed by the Koreans…*

"It'll be okay, baby," Wei says, exchanging messages with Ha Jin the Korean banker.

"Where's Joy tonight?" Ha Jin asks at their familiar table in Octagon.

"She was feeling sick," Wei lies. "So I need a favor…"

Wei gives some long winded explanation he barely believes himself for why Alicia's bank account needs investigating, but once Wei mentions paying several million won for the help, Ha Jin agrees.

"These smell like fucking shit!" Joy screams when Wei compliments one of the few hundred bottles she's thus far prepared.

Wei plays with manipulating cryptocurrency markets, dicking CPChain around between 0.00018 and 0.0002 BTC, making less profit than is taken from him in trading fees. The meagre amount of Bitcoin he has on exchanges now comprises his entire family's crypto reserves.

Then one day, Wei's browsing the latest cryptocurrency news headlines and sees an article that boils his blood: *Hammurabi Exchange Adds Chinese Bitcoin Mining Guru to its Team.*

Wei clicks. Then recoils.

Hammurabi, the regulatory-compliant New York-based cryptocurrency exchange launched by social media pioneers the Dabrowski twins, has added the head of Chinese Bitcoin mining heavyweights Bitsong, Justin Zhao, to its team. Zhao will work in the capacity of Technological Knowledge Overseer (TKO)…

"Fuck you, Wei! Fuck off to New York! Get scammed out of whatever you have left! See if I give a shit!"

"Baby, he's there," Wei pleads. "We've got him. We can get our bitcoins back."

"I should've gone to New York! I should've gone to Princeton. But instead I had to marry this fat piece of shit!"

Amid the screaming that follows, Wei feels his phone vibrate. He's got a message from Ha Jin the banker: *Alicia Huang just made a card payment for the Midtown Hilton in New York City.*

"Jesus… fuck… Joy! That fucking bitch is there with him! She's stolen the rest of the fucking Bitcoin and taken it to Justin in New York! I told you!"

"Fuck off to New York then, Wei! See if I'm here when you get back!"

22. THE SHILLING MOON.

Medellín, Colombia.

"It's not really what I were expecting," Bill Jones tells his sons.

"No? What were you expecting?"

"I dunno… You hear Colombia, and you just think… I dunno…"

"Drugs and massacres," Robbie helpfully says. "And women that're big in all the right places."

"You've been watching too much Netflix," Graham says, a little irritated on his wife's behalf at the negative image so often painted of her homeland. "It's nowt like that nowadays. Well, apart from the women." He gazes across the hotel swimming pool at Melina, beautiful as ever, baby bump on full display as she teaches Luis how to swim.

Melina's parents had offered to host the family but Graham's parents had insisted on paying for a hotel. Despite what they'd told him, Graham knew it was more about avoiding potential awkwardness with the in-laws than feeling 'it was the least [they] could do after [Graham] paid for the flights.'

Graham's tapping at his laptop as they talk, putting together a piece on the latest downward thrust in the dismal crypto market. "Narcos is a joke anyway," he says, glorious sunshine & a chilled cerveza all making it hard to care that Bitcoin's below $7,400 & Ethereum has lost another 20% over the past 7 days. "Totally unrealistic."

"I wouldn't go that far," Robbie says. "Escobar did run this city, right?"

"Yeah, but the actor they had playing him were a Brazilian. The accents were miles off. They had a Mexican playing his missus and all."

"Do they sound all that different?" their Dad asks. "They all speak Spanish, don't they?"

Robbie: "Brazilians speak Portuguese."

"Imagine a Brookside reboot with Ross Kemp playing Jimmy Corkhill," Graham says. "Or a Beatles biopic with Danny Dyer as John Lennon."

"Fair enough!" his Dad laughs.

Crypto keeps bouncing around, finding new lows then heading briefly back upward, hinting at recovery, an end to the bear market & return to the bull run: but it doesn't matter. Walking through the tourist trap pueblo of Guatape, Graham's mother enamoured by the colourful homes, chatting excitedly with Melina & her mother, while the dads talk football – "That James Rodriguez, he's a helluva player," – Robbie stumbles on a curb & tips his lemon-coconut smoothie over himself, & Graham flashes back to the time his younger brother tipped an ice-cream on himself, when Graham were 10 & Robbie 5, and Graham thinks once laughter's stopped, *fuck it.* It don't matter if crypto's dead, & the market never recovers. Melina kisses him gently on the cheek as he places his arm around her, brushing the palm of his hand against her protruding stomach, little Sarah tucked inside, Luis excitedly telling his grandads how many goals Salah's going to score in the Champions' League final, Robbie wondering aloud where he can get a napkin, Graham thinking *I've already reached my moon.*

The next afternoon, they watch the Champions League final in Patrick's Irish Pub, near the hotel in Poblado. The bar's packed with a mix of American & British gringos, many in the red shirts of Liverpool, and a decent number of locals in Real Madrid shirts with the names of James or Ronaldo on the back.

"I were born the day before Ajax beat us in the '66 Cup final," Graham's Dad tells Melina, she acting as translator between the grandfathers. "And the first game I remember watching were us thrashing Borussia Monchengladbach to win it, three-nil."

On the other side of Graham, Robbie's telling Luis of the magical 2006 final, Liverpool going 3-0 down to AC Milan, only to score three in the second half & win their 5th European Cup on penalties.

But the prospect of another grand European night enjoyed from a balmy Colombian afternoon is thrown into chaos as Sergio Ramos clatters into Mohamed Salah, almost wrenching Salah's arm from its socket, Ramos inexplicably avoiding a red card as Liverpool's star man & little Sarah's semi-namesake leaves the field injured. A tense first-half is followed by a disastrous second: Benzema bundling Real's first goal past Karius, Mane giving Liverpool hope with an equalizer, before a Gareth Bale bicycle kick makes it 2-1 Madrid. Mane almost equalises, all at the table cringing as his shot pings off the crossbar. Another questionable refereeing decision – a clear Real handball, but no Liverpool penalty. Liverpool keep fighting, an equaliser still possible, until Bale pings a shot from far out, Karius gets his hands to it, and it inexplicably ricochets backwards from his gloves, into the net, ending the final & Liverpool's dreams of European Cup #6.

Luis cries when the match is over, Grandad Bill consoling him, though on the verge of tears himself. Robbie starts pounding the drinks and tries to convince his elder brother to help him score some coke: "It can't be that hard, la. We're in Pablo Escobar's hometown!"

Robbie finds some on his own before long, but Graham declines to partake. Even so, lying in bed with Melina that night, Graham's unable to sleep. He briefly considers reaching for the laptop, checking the markets, pounding out another crypto article, but thinks with great profundity *fuck it.* It don't matter. A European Cup final loss, $500 Ethereum, $1 IOTA, 60 cent Oyster Pearl… none of it matters. He watches Melina's stomach gently rise and fall, little Sarah likely latching onto Momia's circadian rhythms & sleeping with her, & thinks how he was once similarly ensconced inside his own mother's womb, & his Dad in his Grandmother's too, in the run-up to the '66 final, and *we've won five European Cups since then,* and *England a World Cup,* and *Man hadn't even walked on the Moon then,* and…

Cryptocurrency doesn't enter Graham's mind in the week that follows their return to Liverpool. Then one afternoon, while working on a piece about the local student housing boom for the Liverpool Echo, he's interrupted by an email from the Technology Editor at The New York Times:

Dear Mr. Graham Jones,

As I'm sure you're aware, the New York Blockchain Week is taking place in New York City next week. I realize that this is incredibly short notice, but our staff writer at The New York Times who usually covers cryptocurrency and blockchain technology has unfortunately become unavailable due to unforeseen circumstances and we need an experienced journalist with an extensive knowledge of the industry to cover the week's conferences. Your work in the area has been brought to my attention and, if you are available, we would like to fly you to New York as soon as possible. We will cover all flights and accommodation and other associated costs and would be willing to offer you payment of…

23. NEW YORK BLOCKCHAIN WEEK.

[all previous legal disclaimers apply.]

Aart's hand reaches through the near darkness to the thinly illuminated silhouette beside him. His hand touches her bare thigh. She moans softly & links her hands with Aart's, pulling him close, on top, kissing, he placing his hands between her thighs as she rolls onto her back. "Ciara," he says, but she says nothing, he feels nothing, and he looks up, at the strange undecorated room, and realises it's a dream. He's in bed. Alone. At the frat house. He hears noises from the corridor. He rises from the bed and opens the door to Guus and Nguyen.

"I thought you guys had left."

"We've tracked down the fuck who stole your money, Aart," Guus says. "We want to bring you to him."

Aart follows Guus & Nguyen through the doors to the patio. Outside, Wesley is chained up, hands suspended above his head, nude, body heavily cut & bruised.

"The fuck…" Aart whispers.

"It was this motherfucker," Nguyen says, handing Aart a saw. "Your so-called frat brother."

"He was jealous of our success," Guus says. "Now he pays the price for treachery."

"No…"

"Fucking ask him, Aart!" Guus shouts. "Ask him yourself if you do not believe us!"

"Is it… is it true?"

"I swear, Aart," Wesley whimpers, tears in his eyes, "I didn't do anything."

"Do it, Aart!" Nguyen shouts. "Kill this motherfucker!"

Aart looks at the saw in his hands, its rusted blade trembling.

"No… I… I can't."

"If you can't, then I will!" Guus shouts, lunging at Aart to snatch the saw away.

Aart grips the saw & runs forward, tumbles down steps, saw slicing through limbs as he falls, splashing down into a bloody pool. He looks up at Guus & Nguyen from the dirty pavement. The earth shakes. The wall behind their house collapses. Bricks fly toward him.

Aart wakes again. At a hotel. This time it's real. He gets up & walks to the bathroom. Inside, Nguyen is fucking Ciara from behind, she moaning & leaning back to grasp his face and tenderly kiss him as Nguyen slams her against the sink. Aart throws the door closed, runs out through the room, into a small dark room with another door, through a door & through another door to another door & through another door & another &...

Aart wakes. He's in the frat house. In his room. Alone. He takes a moment, then realises this is really real reality. He sits up & picks up his phone. Unlocks. Blockfolio is open. Bitcoin is at $9366, Ethereum $775 – around half their mid-January high point. Every other coin is doing even worse, most down 75% or more from the mid-January highs. Future Synergy Coin is now at $1.3 billion market cap & $0.000134 per token. Even with the market retraction, Aart's missing tokens still place his portfolio's tracked value at $108,353,451. $108.3 million. One hundred and eight million dollars. He stares at the sum, tears welling in his eyes. That's fuck you money. That's fuck everyone money. That's money he'll never see again. The police were clueless, but said they'd pass his details along to Europol's serious cybercrimes division. A day later Aart received a phone call. They asked a lot of questions. Promised they'd look into it. He opens his ING banking app. His account balance is €7.612,21. He calculates the difference between what he has and what he had; he's lost one hundred and eight million three hundred and forty four thousand five hundred and sixty four dollars and eighty four cents.

He lets tears roll slowly down his cheeks as he stares at the phone, not wanting to move, do anything else. He touches it occasionally, keeping the screen unlocked. A Blockfolio Signal notification appears at the top of the screen. It's from Future Synergy Coin.

"Just made it to NYC!! Looking forward to meeting all you fiiiine peeps @ the NYC Blockchain Week!! You have our FSC guarantee that this week's conference speech gon be litter than lit boiiiis and ladies. Stream online from 3pm EST, June 6."

He wipes his eyes. *Do something, you fucking pussy. Those pricks stole your money. And your girl.* And they're in New York City, richer than footballers or movie stars. Thoughts of Vietnam & the beating he took flash before him, but he thinks *fuck it;* you cannot give up. *I would rather die than let those pricks get away with this.*

Aart opens SkyScanner. A return flight from Amsterdam to New York leaving tomorrow at 15:00 is €965. After checking the confirmation email, he reopens his ING banking app. His remaining balance is €6647.21.

New York, New York

Midtown Hilton, Room 2705

"Alright, babe? I just checked into the hotel. It's pretty swanky. A lot better than the shite little Travelodge that Dead Bird Press would've set me up with."

"I wish I could be there with you," Melina says on the phone, as Graham stands at the window & stares at the sea of towers spiking skyward.

"I wish you were here too, mi corazón's bello amor."

Melina laughs at his charmingly shit Spanish.

"How're you feeling today?"

"Is okay. Heavy. Very heavy."

"Make sure little Sarah doesn't slip out before I'm back."

"You do not worry about this. I will be like a whale another month. What are you doing today?"

"Nothing much. Might pop out and look about a bit. It's tomorrow when it all kicks off here."

Midtown Hilton, Lobby

The other patrons are not what Alicia had expected of the Midtown Hilton; wearing T-shirts with geek power puns, tapping at laptops, a strange contrast with the upscale minimalist tastefulness of the lobby. As the hotel clerk checks her booking, she thinks they must all be here for some kind of tech conference. Probably wealthy beyond appearances. She wonders what a man who dresses like that behaves like undressed. She thinks of James the English teacher in Osaka. The factory owner. The Bitcoin guy. Takahiro.

"Your room is ready now, madam. If you'd like to follow my colleague…"

"Is there some kind of event here?" Alicia asks the porter as they ride the elevator to the fourth floor.

"Yes, madam. This week our conference rooms are holding events for the New York Blockchain Week."

"Blockchain?"

"Yes, madam. Blockchain. Cryptocurrency. Like Bitcoin."

Deck of the FSC 1, Chelsea Piers Marina

"Have you seen the line-up for Fluidity?"

Guus is shouting orders at the hundreds of staff rushing about the deck of the Future Synergy Coin superyacht, preparing it for the coming party. He doesn't hear Nguyen's question.

"Tim Banks is a special guest speaker. They've got performances from Buggsy Modern and Boujee V. We've got fucking Honey Badger."

"What are you talking about?" Guus asks, before answering a question from a burly longshoreman: "The DJ stuff goes over there."

"Fucking Ethereum! Guus! Their line-up is gonna make us look like amateurs."

"No! That's one of the rear speakers," Guus shouts at the burly longshoreman pushing the amplifier. "That goes on the starboard side."

"That is the starboard side," the longshoreman says, pointing to the lavish DJ booth erected at the front of the yacht.

"Then the other side," Guus says. "The backside."

"The stern?"

"Yes. The back of the boat. The stern."

"Guus! Are you listening? Fuck! They've got Buggsy Modern and Boujee V and Tim fucking Banks doing a speech."

"Who has?"

"Fucking Ethereum!" Nguyen snaps. "While we're in Midtown Manhattan for Consensus, they've got their own conference in Brooklyn, Fluidity. And they've got Buggsy Modern and Boujee V performing."

"Buggsy Modern is shit. And Boujee V is even shittier."

"Yes, but they're much bigger than fucking Honey Badger, Guus. It's 2018. Honey Badger hasn't done shit in four years. He brought out a single with Arriba fucking Venti and it only got to number 40 on the Billboard chart. We're propping that asshole's career up."

"Honey Badger's our homie, Nguyen. He's the FSC mascot. Remember Pussy Sushi?"

"Yeah, and did those Japanese fucks bring the fish for that yet?"

"Nguyen, the party is on Saturday," Guus says. "The fish haven't even been caught yet."

Nguyen sighs aggressively. "This whole thing is turning into a pile of shit already. Have you seen when we're giving the speech at Consensus? We're on at the same time that dickhole Brad Garlinghouse from Ripple is debating the Chairman of the Securities and fucking Exchange Commission."

"Nguyen, I am ten times the public speaker that Brad Garlinghouse is."

"Yeah, but who the fuck's gonna be listening to you? All anyone cares about is the S.E.C. and what they think of regulating crypto in America, and—"

"Nguyen. Calm the fuck down. You are beginning to irritate me."

Nguyen breaks off talking with Guus to accept a phone call.

"It's Darren," Nguyen says, returning to Guus. "His flight just landed. He'll be here in an hour."

"Who's Darren?"

"The fucking screenwriter, Guus! Jesus fucking Christ!"

"Nguyen. Calm the shit down. Smoke a joint or pop a Xanax."

Nguyen walks away, shouting at one of the longshoremen. Guus steps across the deck and lights a cigarette, staring at Manhattan's skyscrapers. The screenwriter. FSC: The Movie. The incredible story of their rise to fortune. The step to a higher level of celebrity. He wonders who'll end playing him. DiCaprio? Ryan Gosling? *No,* both are too old now to pull off the part. Guus takes out his phone, searches 'alberto firenze new york home' and scrolls through an article on the famed director's 19th Century residence on the Upper East Side.

Immigration @ JFK

"How long are you planning to stay here?"

"A week."

"Where?"

"The New York Midtown Hilton," Wei tells the U.S. customs agent. "I wrote it on the landing card."

"I know what you wrote on the landing card. You got a booking you can show me?"

"Yeah, sure, look," Wei says, taking his phone out, unlocking it, and handing it to the thick-jawed Homeland Security officer.

The officer squints as he stares at the screen. "Anything else on this phone I should know about?"

"I don't think so."

The officer glares at Wei. Another rich Chinese prick. *At least this fuck speaks English.* "Okay. Welcome to the land of the free."

Asshole, Wei thinks, continuing into the Arrivals area. *New York, New York.* Alicia and Justin are somewhere in this city.

I will find you, you motherfuckers. I will find you. And I will kill you.

Midtown Hilton, Bridges Bar

The swanky cocktail spot on the Hilton's upper floors is full of the same kind of T-shirt wearing tech geeks Alicia has seen elsewhere in the hotel, many tapping at laptops, untouched beers resting at their side. She sips a honey-kissed grapefruit cosmo and picks at a small plate of olives as she watches the room's only two other women, overdressed for the crowd in tight cocktail dresses, survey the scene from opposite corners. A group at the room's center keeps casting glances at the girls until one skinny pale guy in a 'Bitcoin: Bigger Than Wall Street!' T-shirt leaves his buddies, beer in hand, to approach the blonde in the red dress at the room's edge. He quickly drains off his beer and leaves with her. The other guys laugh for a few moments, the unpicked-up girl casting them occasional glances, until two brown guys leave the table:

one, stick-thin with a mess of frizzed black hair, heads straight for the exit; the other, chubby with short neat black hair and a pink 'Legalize ICOs' T-shirt approaches the brunette in the black dress. She smirks & touches his arm as he talks. He sits next to her and calls the barman over.

"Get a room, you two!" the obese white guy remaining at the otherwise-empty table calls across the bar to them.

"Suck a dick, Sparkle Horse!" the chubby brown guy shouts back.

As Sparkle Horse laughs & starts playing with his phone, Alicia notices the watch wrapped around his swollen wrists: a glimmering high-end timepiece, worth at the very least in the tens of thousands of dollars, completely at odds with his cheap XXXL grey 'Crypto Whale' T-shirt. He sees her stare at it. He smiles. She smiles back.

Immigration @ JFK

"And why would you wait until you arrive to book a hotel?" the Homeland Security officer asks Aart, staring with disgust at the €6583.02 in his ING account.

"I didn't think it would be a problem. I mean, there's a lot of hotels in New York. And you can't always trust the online pictures about how nice it is."

"You smoke any of that Dutch crap in Amsterdam?"

"No. Of course not."

"You're not going to have a problem with me looking through your phone then, are you?"

"No. Go ahead." Aart had the foresight to delete Telegram and Blockfolio and all crypto wallets and all slightly-questionable photographs during the flight. He'd heard of US Customs' aggressiveness and panicked upon landing, paying who-knows-what in roaming charges to log Gmail into his bland @rug.nl university account. Aart's taken into a bright-white side room full of distressed new arrivals, thinking of the huddled masses of European peasants in the Ellis Island scene in The Godfather Part II, except fewer than a fifth of those in this bleak waiting area are white. More than half appear to be Arab or Indian, the rest a mix of Hispanic and black. Aart waits for what feels like hours, each person who approaches one of the Homeland Security officers being told to sit down & shut up.

"Aart Janssen."

Aart approaches the Homeland Security officer who called his name and is led into another room for questioning. Dozens of questions: the purpose of his visit, if he's ever been arrested before, if he has any friends in America. Aart mentions Rick, doing a foreign exchange in Philadelphia, but nobody in New York. Questioning over, he's returned to the bright white room with the other would-be visitors. Time passes, Aart clasping & unclasping hands, shifting in his seat. Anyone who approaches the Homeland Security officers is told to sit down & shut up.

"Aart Janssen."

He's led again into the same room for questioning. The same questions, but in a different order. Aart gives roughly the same answers. When it's over, he's handed his phone and his passport.

"Welcome to America. Don't do anything stupid."

Midtown Hilton, Room 3905

"Wall Street's waking up to crypto," Sparkle Horse says. "The future belongs to us." He locks his three-quarter million dollar watch inside the safe and turns to Alicia. "So… how much are you gonna want for this?"

Thinking of how she should've asked for more from the factory owner, Alicia goes big: "Ten thousand dollars."

Sparkle Horse laughs. "Jesus. That's a little steep. You take Bitcoin?"

"Sure."

He stares at her for a moment, surprised. "How about Monero?"

What's Monero? she wants to ask. Instead, she replies with a simple: "No. Only Bitcoin."

"Huh." Sparkle Horse laughs again. "So even the hookers in New York are Bitcoin maximalists." He reopens the room's safe to retrieve his phone. "Let's do this."

HI NYC Hostel

Aart enters the $50-a-night 12-man dorm on the Upper West Side after dragging his suitcase up and down subway stations during a 1h 20m three-train journey from the airport. Heavy snoring from several bunks echoes through the room. He climbs to his bunk & lays down & wills sleep. He falls through fitful lucid hallucinations of Guus & Nguyen in some lavish five-star suite, surrounded by all the trappings of crypto wealth. Every time Aart succumbs to sleep, snores bring him back to the room.

Old Forge, Upstate NY

Wei drives the rental car until the sun rises over the endless interstate, then on further, until he reaches a hamlet nestled in rolling hillsides. Wei feels sleepier than the hamlet of Old Forge as he pulls in alongside pick-up trucks and SUVs in the parking lot of the Hiltebrant Rec Center, a warehouse-like structure constructed of bolted-together green metal sheets. Inside, American flags cascade from the ceiling above a few dozen vendors with stalls laid out with machine guns, assault rifles, and ammunition. Wei walks a loop through the Old Forge Gun Show, his non-whiteness drawing looks of concern from patrons and vendors. He finds a stall with something less ludicrously oversized than the war-waging machinery most stalls are selling. He picks up a Glock.

"This looks good," Wei says, feeling the weight of it, imagining bashing Alicia or Justin across the face with it before pointing the barrel between their eyes.

"Yessir, that's a heck of a gun you hold in them there hands of yours."

"I don't need a license or anything to buy here, right?"

The heftily-bearded vendor narrows his eyes at Wei. "You ain't a felon or something, now, are you?"

"No, sir."

"And you ain't planning on committing no crimes with that there handgun?"

"Absolutely not. It's for protection."

"And you're sure you a US citizen?"

"Uh… I mean, I haven't got my passport with me, but, yeah, I'm a US citizen."

The vendor smiles. "Then we ain't gonna have a problem."

"Awesome," Wei says, feeling the gun's power surge through his body. "I'll take two."

Midtown Hilton, Grand Ballroom

"Revolutions require rules." Samuel Dabrowski pauses for dramatic effect. "The French Revolution –
the overthrow of the monarchy, the installation of a Republic, the Genesis Block of modern Western democratic liberalism. It was an explosion of centuries of frustration at the unfairness of the European feudal system. But it was a revolution without any rules, and the streets of Paris were soon awash with blood. After the execution of King Louis and Marie Antoinette, all nobles and landowners and small shopkeepers were put to the guillotine, before the revolutionaries turned on themselves, the movement cannibalized itself, and Napoleon Bonaparte seized control as a dictator more brutal than the royalty he replaced."

"The American Revolution," Isaiah Dabrowski continues, "was a revolution that produced a guiding text. Our United States Constitution. And it was a revolution and grand experiment in democracy that continues to flourish to this day. This great city that surrounds you is proof of the success of that rule-bound revolution. It is the proof that a rule-bound revolution is the only revolution that can have long-term success."

"Today's capitalist system is in need of overhaul," Samuel says. "There is great inequality here in our own nation, while many millions across the globe are frozen out of the international banking system entirely."

Isaiah: "Enter Bitcoin."

Samuel: "But cryptocurrency has so far been a revolution without regulation."

"More akin to the French Revolution than the American."

"And that's why we created Hammurabi – the first fully regulatory-compliant cryptocurrency exchange."

Graham is at the back of a packed Grand Ballroom taking notes on what they say & ideas for questions to pose to Da Browski Twins during his later allotted interview slot. Their speech is the star attraction of Day One of NY Blockchain Week's premier event, the Consensus conference. As Da Browkis talk in grand metaphor, Graham scans the rooms other attendees: the chronically over- and under-weight crypto pioneers, wealth well hidden beneath food-stained T-shirts but flaunted with multi-million dollar wristwatches; the suited bankers and Wall Street types, listening with interest to a new way of adding zeroes to the end of their bank accounts; the journalists, like himself, tapping notes on phones or scribbling in notepads, many of the older ones from established media firms looking utterly perplexed by what's being said.

Midtown Hilton, Lobby

"The five-day pass is $2,000," the woman at the counter says.

Aart calculates the devastation that would be wrought upon his bank account. He cannot do it. He walks away & out through the Hilton's grand entrance. Wei moves in the opposite direction, half-crazed from the 12-hour round-trip upstate and a brutal combination of jet lag & near-total lack of sleep. "The five-day pass is $2,000."

"You take cash?" Wei carefully pulls his wallet from his pocket, almost trapping one of the Glocks' butts on it as he pulls it free. He hands the money over and the woman points him toward the security guards and metal detectors blocking entrance to the event. *Fuck.*

"Uhhh… I think I'll go get breakfast and come back later."

Times Square

Aart chows down on a $4 churro & sips a $3 Americano as he stands at Times Square's edge, watching tourists move & pose for pictures & gawp at mimes & other entertainers, wondering how he can achieve anything on this trip. He figures he could stand here, or close to the Hilton, and hand out fliers decrying the lies & bullshit that propelled Future Synergy Coin to a multi-billion dollar market cap. But how much would printing thousands of flyers cost? He thinks of the Homeland Security Officer's warning – "Don't do anything stupid" – and wonders if handing out fliers without a permit might get him arrested & sent back to the Netherlands. *This was a stupid idea.* He could've achieved more posting something on Reddit or Medium, without wasting thousands of his few remaining Euros coming to New York.

Midtown Hilton, Clinton Suite

"All creation comes from chaos. The universe was a swirling mess of primordial gases until the laws of physics gave it order. Cryptocurrency is today a mess of swirling primordial shitcoins – particles flashing briefly like those that can only be formed through nuclear fusion. Some of these cryptocurrency particles will retain mass and become foundational elements of the future financial universe. Others will have a half-life measurable in milliseconds. They'll briefly burn brightly and decay."

Isaiah nods at his brother's grandiose words. "That is what we aim to do with Hammurabi: to allow investors to sort the noble from the ignoble. The Bitcoins from the shitcoins. The future from the fleeting."

"So," Graham asks, "which coins are you planning to list?"

"We're open to any coin with a demonstrable use case and good governance," Isaiah says. "If it has a compelling use case, it can be part of our governed crypto universe."

The Dabrowski twins are more erudite than Graham had expected from their Harvard row team jock reputations. The twin brothers whose idea for a social network was allegedly stolen by another Harvard undergrad who is now an all-powerful tech multi-billionaire, the resulting court case forming the basis of an Academy Award-winning Hollywood motion picture. The twin brothers who built huge wealth anyway getting in early on Bitcoin.

"The initial beauty of Bitcoin was its anarchy," Samuel continues. "A rebel against the established financial system. A new technological epoch without rules or hierarchy."

"But anarchy creates a vacuum," Isaiah adds.

Samuel: "And that anarchy has led to a manipulated market of disreputable ICOs and incredible price volatility."

"A market like that is unsustainable."

"A universe of unstable isotopes is eternal cataclysm."

"Hammurabi is here to bring order to chaos."

"And, like the known universe that surrounds us, once crypto is bound by the physical laws of proper oversight and regulation, it will go on expanding indefinitely."

Graham thinks that such talk would've been cut off a long time ago if Da Browskis had been from Liverpool instead of Connecticut. He thinks of something his Dad once told him – that upper class British public school boys tend to talk in long unbroken streams loaded with rhetorical flourishes, while the working class jabber over each other, cutting off & undercutting the other constantly, trying to get a word in edgeways. The Dabrowskis are the living embodiment of the fact that no-one at their level ever gets told to shut the fuck up & stop talking shite. "But how exactly are you gonna impose rules and regulations on crypto at this point?"

As the Dabrowski Twins talk Securities & Exchange Commission compliance & New York State Finance Department charters, Graham scans the others in the room. A Chinese guy sits behind them playing on his phone, with a wild unkempt mess of black hair. Isaiah pauses to indicate the Chinese guy's relevance to the project – "For instance, Justin here was the head of a major Chinese Bitcoin mining corporation, BitSong. He brings a lot of expertise on how to deftly balance compliance with innovation."

He don't look like his own hair's complying with his head, Graham thinks.

Sheraton New York Times Square, Room 2812

Wei loads & unloads each of his handguns in turn, wondering how quickly he could pull this off in the heat of battle. He stares down at the Midtown Hilton, wondering if he ought to head back upstate & buy a sniper rifle. Maybe he could pick Justin & Alicia off from here if he knew their room number. But he doesn't. He taps the gun against the glass & sighs. He picks up his phone. No message from Joy. He assumes he'll be returning to Seoul to face divorce proceedings. If he even returns to Seoul at all.

Dive Bar, Amsterdam Avenue

"…and I know that one of them stole the money. So here I am."

"That's crazy," the wide-eyed Romanian girl says.

"If it was me," Chad from Idaho says, "I'd kill those motherfuckers. I'd drive upstate to a gun show, grab me a Colt .45, then go wave it in those sons-of-bitches faces until they hand the cash over. Then I'd shoot them both anyway."

"Why don't you go to the police?" the Israeli girl asks.

"I did," Aart says. "they passed it on to some European hi-tech crime force, but I think they have no idea about blockchain."

"How much money was stolen?" the Israeli guy asks.

"The price fluctuates a lot, but last I checked, it was a little over one hundred million dollars." Aart laughs after saying it. The gasps and shocked looks of the others from the hostel confirm the insanity of it.

"Bullshit," Chad laughs. "That's a fucking great story you just told us, but bullshit. Fuck man. I almost believed you! You crazy Dutch motherfucker."

"Yeah," Aart smiles. "Yeah, I was bullshitting you."

The Romanian girl's eyes narrow. The others get into talking about NYC nightlife & how to get to the Meatpacking District from here on the Upper West Side while the Romanian girl stares silently at Aart.

Midtown Hilton, Room 2705

Graham reads through the Wikipedia article on Hammurabi, previously only vaguely aware of the Bablyonian king that the Dabrowski Twins named their new regulatory-compliant crypto exchange after. He reads of the 282 laws comprising Hammurabi's Code: physical punishments, an eye for an eye, a tooth for a tooth, penalties scaled by social status; man over woman, the free over slaves. One line catches his imagination: *'its intended purpose may have been more for the self-glorification of Hammurabi than to act as a modern legal code or constitution.'*

Graham selects & copies this extract and opens the Word doc containing his near-finished article. He hits Ctrl + Z and pastes it in near the end, following it with his own commentary: *'Like the ancient Babylonian laws of Hammurabi their 'regulatory compliant' cryptocurrency exchange is named after, perhaps Da Browskis are more interested in self-glorification (& enrichment) than actually legitimizing Bitcoin and its billion shitcoin offspring.'*

He stares at his articles' pithy conclusion: such a snark-laced denouement would've been perfect were he still writing for Dead Bird, but this piece is for The New York Times. An news organisation which only hired him for his depth of cryptocurrency knowledge. Pissing off the Dabrowskis might exclude him from any future work with them. Other big-time players in the crypto space could join them. If Graham loses access, he loses his usefulness and any future shot at writing for The New York Times. Graham selects what he just pasted & wrote and hits delete. He replaces it with a bland & non-committal closing paragraph on Da Browski's Hammurabi exchange having a 50/50 chance of failure or success. He scans back through the article before emailing it to The NYT's Tech Editor with a note saying he's open to any & all revisions. Work done, he calls Melina.

"Is fine here. And New York?"

Graham tells her of the evening's conference after-parties as he gazes out the window, NYC skyline on the cusp of slipping through sunset to skyscraper-lit night. Block Party at Down & Out in the Meatpacking District. He might go & see if anything happens that's worth writing about.

Midtown Hilton, Room 2706

Alicia looks out at the city's glowing night-time skyline as she scrolls through the events of New York Blockchain week on her phone. She has seven evenings of socially-poor & crypto-rich guys open to her. If all are as eager to use Bitcoin as currency and as quick to climax as Sparkle Horse, she could realistically double the Bitcoin she took from Wei in Tokyo. Eyes flick between her phone and the skyline, then fall on an event that began less than an hour ago: Block Party at Down & Out.

BLOCK PARTY @ DOWN & OUT

The line outside the converted warehouse in the Meatpacking District stretches far & moves slowly.

"This is the spot," Chad from Ohio says. As the others from the hostel debate joining the line, Chad insisting the place is lit & straight fire & worth the wait, Aart notices the 'Block Party' banner hanging over the guardrail blocking the line, 'Official Party of New York Blockchain Week' written beneath it.

The Romanian girl, Elena, sees what Aart sees. She places her hand at his waist & leans in to whisper to him: "You want to go here? Maybe we can just leave them and go somewhere else."

"Eighty," the doorman at the front of the line says.

"Eighty dollars?!" Graham's stunned.

"You're not in Merry Old England now, bitch," a friendly New Yorker says, brushing past Graham to hand the doorman his I.D. & a wad of notes.

Graham turns from the entrance, sure whatever he might see inside is worth less than $80 and spending the night surrounded by arseholes.

Inside, downstairs is bathed in red & blue strobe lights. Upstairs, the dancefloor is rammed with sweating computer-twitchers & NY hipsters. The music is loud EDM, the DJ playing snippets of popular songs before throwing back to blasting warped bass beats. The tables surrounding the dancefloor are taken by the crypto elite, multiple bottles of top-shelf liquor half-drunk on each table.

Wei hands the doorman a hundred and forgets to take his twenty in change as he enters the crowded first floor, scanning each face he passes for Justin and Alicia.

"We need a lot of scenes like this," Guus tells Darren the screenwriter, still frazzled from a rapid drive to LAX Airport & cross-country flight. "We need a montage. Clubbing in Dubai, Paris, Hong Kong."

"And you gotta make sure you show lots of scenes of my character banging hot chicks," Nguyen adds. "And that's not an ego thing, man. It's necessary and it's gonna be real good for getting this script made right now, with all the hashtag-MeToo and Hollywood-so-white stuff. You gotta show an Asian guy banging a lot of white chicks. That'll be big box office in China, bro. An antidote to all those movies where Jackie Chan's this fucking incel karate guy, while Chris Tucker's plowing all the white chicks with his big black dick. We gotta make Hollywood atone for Rambo and present a positive representation of Asian males on-screen."

Wei clutches the Glock in his pocket with a gloved hand as he moves through Down & Out's downstairs. *Maybe they're not here.* Maybe they're upstairs.

Alicia sees Sparkle Horse at an upstairs table with the same brown guys he was with at the Hilton's Bridge Bar. She slips through the dancefloor's crowd, seeking a fresh target. "This time next year, Bitcoin will be one hundred thousand dollars," she hears a loud voice declare. She looks to the source of the claim, speaking from a table loaded with bottles, the speaker surrounded by women. It takes a moment to recognise him as strobe lights flicker across his face. Then… *shit.* It's the Bitcoin guy. The one who ripped Wei's father off. *Justin.*

"If you buy now, you still have a chance of making a fortune," Justin explains to the girls, they twirling hair around fingers as they feign interest.

Wei sees him, at an upstairs table, pouring drinks for hot American bitches, they laughing at whatever stupid shit he's saying. *That snake motherfucker.* Spending Wei's father's cash. Wei's gloved hands grips the Glock. He thinks of taking it out & shooting. *No – that would be retarded.* If he kills him here, on a crowded dancefloor, what happens next? He's never even fired a gun before. What if he misses? *No.* Wei turns away as Justin's head turns toward the dancefloor. *Wait. Wait all night if you have to.* Wei pushes through the dancefloor, back to the stairs. *Just drink & wait.* A beer or a gin & tonic to calm the nerves. Get him when he leaves. *Follow him back to his hotel, or just shoot that motherfucker on the street.* Execute him. Toss the gun and run back to the Sheraton. *This is the way.*

"If you want to get it to Alberto Firenze, I heard he owns a restaurant in Tribeca," Darren the screenwriter tells Guus & Nguyen. "It might be not be a bad idea to go there for dinner one night and respectfully approach him with your pitch."

"And you'll have the script written by Wednesday?"

"Absolutely," Darren tells Guus. "That gives me about thirty-six hours to write ninety-to-one-hundred-twenty pages. That's, what…"

"Three-and-a-third pages per hour," Nguyen says.

"Yeah. I mean, even discounting time for sleep and incorporating your feedback, that's easy. I can jam out twelve pages an hour when I'm in the flow of things."

Guus drops his head to the table to snort another line then lifts it, rubbing his nose, and meets eyes with a beautiful Asian woman in a chic black dress at the dancefloor's edge. She moves toward him.

"You're fucking hot," Guus says.

"Thank you," Alicia smiles.

Beer on beer & bloated feeling, then the gin & tonics; Wei is woozy and forgetting why he came here, what he's waiting for. Bass booms & laser-like hi-hat & staccato sci-fi snare. The chorus to Boujee V 'Silken Discharge.' Wei's bloated bladder screams release. *Focus.* He thought a few would calm his nerves but now he's half-way fucked up. The bloatedness rises within him. He thinks he's going to throw up.

"…and some… fucking… huge guy comes up, and I—" Nguyen struggles to lift his arm, to throw an illustrative punch at the air— "bang, and he goes down, and I… kick him."

"The…," Darren the screenwriter scrolls back through the notes on his phone screen, "hotel bellboy? You punch the bellboy?"

"Yeah, yeah… I punch that fucker right in the…"

"Nguyen," Guus says, leaning across the blonde girl to Nguyen's left to tug at his sleeve. "Cocaine."

Nguyen passes Guus a baggie & continues dictating FSC movie scenes to Darren.

"Malaysia," Guus says, tapping white powder out onto the table & carving it into two thick lines with a credit card. "One of few Asian countries I have not yet visited."

Alicia watches Guus cut the lines & thinks of leaving, never having seen drugs outside of American movies. She looks at the dancefloor, knowing Justin is sitting on the other side of it. Maybe she should just leave the club. That would clearly be the sensible option.

"You know, Malaysia used to belong to the Netherlands," Guus says, rolling a hundred dollar bill.

"I know," Alicia says.

He leans forward to snort the line & passes Alicia the note. She hesitates.

Wei walks back up the stairs, having seen a toilet up there earlier. He stops halfway. A girl irritatedly side-steps him. *What are you doing? What if he sees you?* But the urge to puke is overwhelming. He continues up the stairs, not sure if he'll even make it to the restroom.

"New York City too," Guus says, sitting back & rubbing his nose. "It used to be New Amsterdam."

Alicia leans forward, tightening the hundred's roll between her thumb & forefinger.

"The English stole from us both," Guus continues. "Then the Japanese took from them Malaysia, and the British Empire burned out itself out in World War Two."

She closes her eyes as she sniffs, nostril burning as the powder enters it. She sits back, Guus talking of the inevitable collapse of American global hegemony & rise of China as her eyes open. She sees a guy wearing a baseball cap shoving his way through the dancefloor. His face – *Wei.* The figures blur around him, warp. The music's rhythm shifts & slows.

Wei pushes past dancers, staring in the direction of Justin's table. He reaches a break in the moving mass of people and sees it. Where Justin was sitting earlier. Two girls, staring at phones. Two white guys & two more girls at the table. Justin's spot vacant. *The restroom.*

"Nguyen!" Guus shouts. "Cocaine! You gave to me fucking ketamine!"

Alicia turns to Guus as he turns to her. Her head is heavy & empty, body weak. He leans toward her. She closes her eyes as Guus kisses her.

Wei enters the restroom, thoughts of finally confronting that prick overriding his nausea. Justin is at a urinal, swaying as he pisses, his back to the door. A bathroom attendant stands staring at Wei. Wei backs out swiftly, pushing against a guy & girl in conversation. One drops a glass. It shatters. Wei staggers back from them. The attendant leaves the restroom, telling the guy & girl not to worry, he'll get someone to clean it up. Wei pushes the restroom door open. Justin turns from the urinal, zipping his trousers. His eyes widen. "Wei! Why the fuck are you here—"

Greenwich Village

Recognise them? Graham types in WhatsApp, walking back through the Village's off-grid streets towards 8th Avenue.

Melina's reply to the two pics snapped of apartment buildings appears: *Si! Friends & Sex in the City!! :)*

What time is it there?

2, Graham replies.

Careful. New York must be dangerous at night.

Its ok. Im in the middle of Manhattan. Still lots of people out.

Graham looks up from the phone, sees drunk twentysomethings strolling in animated conversation, couples walking arm-in-arm… homeless people, sure, but this area of NYC feels safer than much of Liverpool or London. *What times it with u?*

6. I just wake up for work. I go take Luis to your parents first.

Ok. Dont work too hard.

I dont. Boss is kind since I get big with embarazo. Pregnancy.

"Weed? Cocaine?"

"Nah, mate, I'm good," Graham says, ignoring the would-be dealer as he passes Jackson Square Park.

"Where you from?" he calls out after him as Graham continues on 8th Avenue.

Graham sees blue & red flashing lights reflected on buildings. He stares down the street – an ambulance, two cop cars, a crowd talking loud & panicked. This is where he was earlier – Down & Out. Block Party. He takes his phone out, films a quick video, walks towards the people, sensing something newsworthy.

New York City

Wei walks streets, following right turns with lefts, distant sirens chilling him. He doesn't know how long he's been walking, and realizing this makes him realize he's lost. He stops and looks up & down the street. It's at once familiar & unfamiliar – the same imposing maze of tall buildings he's been stuck in the last however-long. He cannot tell if he's been here already. As he turns, a homeless guy approaches, hands out, mumbling. Wei turns & walks faster, another corner, feeling his pockets for his phone. *Fuck.* Did he drop it? *No* – the hotel. He left it. *The gun…* dropped in the restroom. His cap, too, thrown off as he joined the screaming mass rushing toward the stairs, people tumbling down them, seeing Alicia below as he reached the top of them…

"Where the fuck am I?" Wei says quietly. Other questions flood his mind: *what the fuck?* & *why?* & *is he dead?* & *did you kill him?* & *what happened?* &

There's no evidence, *right?* No prints on the gun. Gloves. Wei pulls them off as he walks, lets them drop to the sidewalk. *Where are you going?* What if you circle, head back there? *Fuck.*

The baseball cap. DNA, right? *Fuck.* The attendant… *that's why you tossed it. The attendant saw you. Wearing the baseball cap.* But you tossed it. *On the dancefloor.* You fucking idiot.

Did customs take a DNA sample? No… fingerprints. Iris scan. Not DNA. *Of course not fucking DNA. Do you not think you'd remember a fucking blood test?*

Calm down. Slow down. *Fuck.* You killed him. Justin. *What the fuck…*

Alicia… some guy taking her to the exit. *Who?*

Why weren't Justin & her sitting together?

New York is on a grid system. *Look.* West 31st Street. And that's 5th Avenue. *And the hotel is…*

Fuck.

He doesn't remember.

Outdoor patio @ HI NYC Hostel

Aart & Elena talk through the night on the hostel's patio, groups departing for dorms around them, others briefly joining – Chad from Ohio, drunk out of his mind, and the Israeli couple – until it's just them, nursing the last of their wine beneath the lightening pre-dawn sky. Elena studies International Relations in Barcelona and has spent the past semester at Georgetown University in D.C. New York is her last stop before flying back to Europe. She tells Aart her dream job post-graduation is to move to the Far East, Hong Kong or Seoul or Tokyo, and work for a multinational. He tells Elena about the conferences, the chaos, the destroyed million-dollar hotel rooms. At first she's shocked by each debauched episode, but with dawn approaching, she's grown numb to it. She's also developed an intense hatred of Guus & Nguyen: "They are the biggest assholes I ever heard of."

She's sure they worked together to steal Aart's coins. Her certainty makes him certain. "But I don't know what to do about it."

"You came to New York," she says. "You have to confront them."

"I confronted them already. I told you about Vietnam. Nguyen left me in the hospital."

"Then you need to outsmart them. They are fucking idiots. You told me this a thousand times tonight. If they are so stupid, outsmart them."

Elaborate schemes are debated – taking the stage at Consensus; luring them into making a confession on tape. All seem likely to fail.

"When this started," Elena says, swirling the last of the wine round the bottom of its bottle, "with the ICO, the whitepaper, with investors putting their money in, you must have said to people what you will do with this money?"

"There was a plan, yeah."

"And they violated it, no? With a yacht, and global travel, and trashing hotels, and…"

Aart's about to list everything preventing him exploiting this latest attack vector, the vague allocation of funds to 'promotion' and 'marketing' that means their lavish spending of everything invested in FSC was probably legal. But something occurs to him. "What Guus and Nguyen did is no different than what a million other scammy ICOs did," Aart says, "but they're trying to rise above that. They want to be seen as legitimate. And when Guus gives his speech today at Consensus, he'll see it as gaining more power, strengthening his image. But there are hundreds of journalists covering this conference. Guus needs them to pump this image out for him. If we can get to those journalists…"

"…we can destroy Guus and Nguyen."

Aart smiles at Elena. This girl is amazing. He doesn't know what he would've done if he hadn't met her. If he'd stayed in a cheap hotel room instead of a hostel dorm. He probably would've just skulked about on the outskirts on the conference, achieving nothing, sinking deeper into isolation and ineffective depression. He takes his phone from his pocket, connects to the hostel wifi, searches 'New York Blockchain Week.' Dozens of articles from websites big and small, from niche crypto news outlets to mainstream media like The New York Times.

"Woah," Aart says as he scans news articles for journalists' email addresses & Twitter handles. "Somebody got shot at the club we almost went to."

"Did they die?"

Miss Korea

The bowl of samgyetang sits untouched on the table in front of Wei on the third floor of the 24 hour restaurant in Koreatown. He pours out another shot of soju, downs it. See this second bottle now has only a splash in it. Considers ordering another. Drains what's left straight from the bottle. He's replayed the scene in the restroom with Justin a hundred times. The more soju he drinks, the more he's sure he knows what happened. Justin had been belligerent. Aggressive. He'd told Wei to go fuck himself. He laughed about stealing the money. He said if Wei was gonna use the gun, use it fast, or he'd snatch it off him & beat him half to death with it before shooting him through the eyes. *Didn't he? Did he?* Wei calls the ajumma over & orders another soju. She looks at him meanly. *Did I ask your opinion? Get my fucking soju.* He wants to say that but doesn't. A group on another table talk loudly & clank glasses together as they barbecue pork. Wei closes his eyes & tries to imagine Korea. Back with Joy. But instead he thinks of high school. Of Justin. Of the shit they used to say to each other. When he opens his eyes, a fresh bottle of Chamisul soju sits on the table. He unscrews the top. Pours a shot. Downs it. Pours another. *Fuck.* Justin had been a close friend. A near lifelong friend. It was only money. *Fuck.* Wei starts crying, but stops himself, wiping his eyes with tissues, sniffling, spooning the almost-cold samgyetang into his mouth. There's no way anyone knows he's the shooter. When he left the restroom, the place was in chaos. Nobody saw anything. He thinks of rebooking his flight & leaving the country early. *But Alicia…* and the restroom attendant. *He saw you. I am so totally fucked.*

He pours out another shot. Downs it. Closes his eyes from its harshness. Sees Justin fall back against the urinals, clutching his stomach, white shirt exploding red where the bullets hit.

"FUCK!"

The group behind Wei stop talking. He doesn't turn to look at them. He lets them casually fall back into laughing conversation, whispering about what that drunk guy in the corner's problem is.

Why are you even here? In public? *You have no idea how far from the club you are. For all you know, you're a fucking block away.* Police could be searching the area, putting out CCTV footage from the club on news bulletins. *Maybe one of those fucks on the other table will get a notification on their phone.* Breaking news. Click it & see a screenshot of the stupid drunk fuck who's talking to himself at a fucking restaurant.

"What… the fuck…" he mumbles to himself. "You are so fucking stupid."

He pours a shot into the glass, forgetting he filled it already. He stops as soju spreads across the table. Downs the shot. Tries to remember if he wore gloves the whole time he handled the gun; remembers wiping it clean while wearing the gloves in the hotel room.

"How do you…" he stops himself talking out loud, continuing the monologue in his mind: *how are you so fucking stupid?*

He thinks of the impossibility of finding his way back to the hotel without his phone to guide him.

It's a grid system. *How fucking hard can it be? Just pick a fucking street and walk.*

The hotel is at Times Square. Times Square is north of the nightclub. *Just walk north.*

Which fucking direction is north?

Jesus – *how are you so stupid?* West 31st Street, West 32nd Street… *just walk until you find East 32nd Street.* North, East, South, West. *Walk from West until you see East and turn to the fucking North.*

You fucking killed him.

Stop.

He pours another shot, downs it, then glugs straight from the bottle. *Get the fuck out of here. Forget the bottle.* He stands up. But won't that look weird? *What if…*

Fuck. *You're standing already. Just go.*

They've stopped talking. The people barbecuing have stopped talking.

Just fucking go. This is New York City. They see crazy drunk fucks here every day. *Just go.*

And pay! *Fuck.* Pay. *If you get the police called for leaving the restaurant without fucking paying…*

How are you so fucking stupid? How is it possible?

Deck of the FSC 1, Chelsea Piers Marina

"The guy that got shot," Nguyen says, holding his phone up in front of Hrvko, the thick-browed Croat heading up security on the FSC 1 superyacht, "he was working for the Dabrowski Twin's new exchange. This might have been a targeted assassination. Somebody with a grudge against blockchain revolutionaries. If anybody tries to get on the boat, you fucking shoot them, okay?"

Hrvko nods slowly.

"I don't care who it is. Police, ambulance, fire service, Tim fucking Banks – anybody. Shoot them. Okay?"

"Razumije," Hrvko says. "Okay."

"How's the script?" Nguyen asks Darren as he walks back across deck to the hot tub.

"I'm about two-thirds through the first act," Darren says, typing on his laptop as he speaks. "I'm well past the inciting incident, closing in on the turning point."

"Good." Nguyen scoops white powder from a plate with a desert spoon and lays it out on a silver tray, neatly divides it into two enormous lines, sniffs the first, then hands the tray to Darren & rubs his nose: "This should help you work faster."

"Thank you."

"Get the first act done in the next hour and you can come join us and the girls in the hot tub."

"Thanks—" Darren splutters, coughing & rubbing at his nose, wasting most of his line.

"But that first act better be done first, and done good," Nguyen says. "No page thirty, no jacuzzi."

Nguyen continues across the deck to the tub where the two girls from the club are laughing.

"What are you ladies talking about?"

"We were just wondering if it's possible to give a blowjob underwater," one girl answers, looking up at Nguyen coquettishly.

"Only one way to find out!" Nguyen declares, yanking his trunks down.

The girls squeal & clap as he cannonballs nude into the hot tub.

Sheraton New York Times Square, Room 2812

The cold night light of New York's skyline reaches halfway across the room. Wei sits cross-legged beyond where the light reaches, on the bed, tears streaming down his face as school day memories of Justin flood his mind. *What a fuck I am. What a bastard. Piece of shit.* To shoot your best friend at point-blank range. *My best fucking friend.* Over money. And his father, rotting in jail. Never to see daylight. When news hits China from New York of what his son's done, the judge and party officials presiding over the case will treat Wei's father more harshly. All he worked for his entire life will be destroyed. So much senseless waste. *And Joy…* his wife's fury when he told her he was going to New York. When news reaches Asia of what's happened, she'll be the first to accuse him. The plans they had, the business she'd dreamed her whole life of, destroyed. Everything destroyed. The lives of everyone close to him. *My mother…*

Tears spot the bedsheets and the Glock nested atop them in Wei's lap. He lifts it. Clicks the safety off. Pushes his chin up toward the ceiling with it as he whimpers. His sobs increase as his finger trembles above the trigger. He snaps his mouth open, places the gun inside. *Roof of the mouth.* Straight through the brain. *No pain.* Instant redemption. *Bang.*

But he cannot do it. His tears increase. His hopeless sobbing.

"DO IT, YOU FUCKING PIECE OF SHIT!"

He throws the gun across the room, expecting it to fire as it hits the carpeted floor. It doesn't. This latest stupidity causes Wei to buckle over, head in his hands, crying loudly, soaking his sheets.

This continues for several minutes, until his mind focuses in on her. *The real bitch responsible.* The bitch who stole the Bitcoin. Who scammed him & his father. The whore responsible more than anyone else (other than Wei) for Justin's death. Wei lifts his head and stares out the window. The Midtown Hilton. That cunt sleeping soundly inside. *It's too late to atone by killing yourself.*

"You gotta finish this… you have to. You have to. You have to." He rocks back and forth on the bed, repeating the mantra. "You have to. You have to." He has to finish what he's started. He has to kill her. He has to make that cunt pay for what she's caused.

Master Suite of the FSC 1, Chelsea Piers Marina

Alicia thinks of Sparkle Horse at the Midtown Hilton and the 1.573 BTC he was happy to pay for her services. His watch – a three-quarter million dollar timepiece – versus the yacht she's now onboard, which must have cost tens of millions.

"This place is amazing," Alicia says, walking around the four-poster bed and admiring the sprawling master cabin.

"It's a fucking money hole," Guus says on the bed. "If crypto keeps slipping, I might have to sell it."

"I thought you said crypto was the future," she says, gripping the bottom-right post and leaning over him. "That Bitcoin is bringing in the next astrological age."

"Yes, that is true," Guus says, opening a bedside drawer loaded with baggies. "But an astrological age takes some time to get going. Wall Street has just gotten serious about cryptocurrencies. They're suppressing the price so they can accumulate." He takes a large bag of MDMA, snaps off two crystals, wraps them in cigarette paper, then pours a dark rum and downs them. He wraps another for Alicia and passes it to her: she hesitates, mind already flitting on the peripheries of reality from all the other unknown substances she's ingested, but she figures that Guus represents her best chance of short-term refuge from Wei's wrath & a long-term meaningful future of limitless wealth. She turns to the dozen or so bottles on a table behind her. "Is it okay if I pour a drink?"

"Of course."

She grasps a bottle of Krug Grand Cuvee and turns to Guus: "This okay?"

"Gezellig!"

She twists the foil from the bottle & prises it open with a pop. She fills two champagne flutes, downs her bomb of molly with the fizzing liquid, then hands Guus the other glass. She sits on the bed beside him & they clink glasses. He sits up.

"Krug makes an excellent lubricant," he says. "Social lubricant. That is why it is so revered."

She sips more. "It tastes good."

He licks the side of her face: "So do you."

Alicia laughs. Guus spills Krug over the bed as grasps her breasts, licks her neck; she moans softly & carefully holds her flute as she reclines to the bed, letting him clamber on top of her, a drugged-up drunken mess of grasping & licking. She gently pushes him off her & onto his back, rubs at his crotch, feels him swell. She drains the flute & places it on the bedside chest of drawers, then looks at the baggies of powder inside. She takes one of white powder: "This is cocaine?"

"Or ketamine," Guus says, Krug dribbling down his chin as he finishes his flute.

"Ketamine?" Alicia repeats, the word foreign to her.

"Or speed. Maybe 2CB. Or MXE. I don't remember exactly what is all in there."

She opens the baggie & dips her finger inside, then stares him in the eye as she sucks the powder from her finger tip. Her gums become instantly numb, though this gives her no clue as to which of the utterly foreign substances he's mentioned she might have just tasted. She moves toward him & he reaches for the baggie, but she holds it away from him: "Wait one moment." She unbuckles his belt, pulls down his suit pants, grips his swollen member, yanks his boxers down, then pours the powder over his penis. Guus makes some strange grunting noise, like a pig getting fingered. She opens her mouth wide and bobs her head down onto his penis. He grasps the back of her head, forcing her up & down faster. Her head follows his hands guidance, jaw strained fully open, determined to give him more than he's ever had from anyone else. After a dozen or more up-downs, back of her throat numb, his hands release her, he grunts louder, she grips his penis & looks into his eyes: "You like that?"

"Heel lekker." His head drops back onto the bed. "It's fucking gezellig."

She pumps his shaft at speed as her tongue laps the head of his penis. She continues pumping as her tongue moves down to the balls, licking their crevices, gently sucking each testicle, before returning her hyperextended jaw to engulfing & rising, engulfing & rising, faster & faster & faster & faster & faster, pig-like grunting of Guus becoming a farmyard cacophony of guttural sounds; she pours more powder, returns to the motion, minutes pass, more powder, until the baggie's empty, she recoils, gasping for breath, heart racing. He sits up, licks out the baggie, then reaches into the drawer & takes another. Her breath slowing but still far-above normal pace, she watches him pour powder over the bedside chest, lick it up, then take a note from the drawer

& snort the rest. She pulls her dress over her head & sits waiting for him in her underwear.

"This is good shit, no?" Guus says, finished with the powder & grinning pure insanity.

"Heel leeker," she says, imitating his facial & linguistic expressions. "Fucking gezellig."

Guus speeds on all-fours across the bed & snatches the Krug Grand Cuvee from the floor. Guus pours half the bottle over her panties, pulls them down, then rapidly tongues her excitement-and-Krug lubricated vulva. His tongue slips into a rhythm of spelling 'F-S-C' across her labia, followed by a clitoral-flicking rapid up-down, then repeating. Her fingers fondle the shorn back of his head, willing him on faster, then pushing his face deeper, pelvis thrusting upward, he burying his face deeper into her, grasping her ass, until her moans become screams & discharge gushes out at him. Guus dives across the bed, grabs another baggie, tears it open over her, tongues powder & pussy manically. Alicia feels her orgasm extending, rising, vision shaking, ascending to some all-encompassing plain of ecstasy beyond all comprehension, each breath & touch another paroxysm of paralysing pleasure.

"This is the 2CB."

Alicia is gasping, barely realising Guus has ceased licking her.

He laughs at the brightening intensity of the skyline beyond the room's window: "This is fucking gezellig!"

"What?" she says between breaths, still in a dazed state of perpetual orgasm.

"Fucking 2CB," Guus laughs. "Here." He thrusts his fingers through her vulva, coating them in a solution of the powder & their juices, then slides his fingers into her mouth, she licking them clean, bobbing her head in a half-hearted recreation of how she earlier engulfed him. She lets her head fall back to the bed, each breath still prolonging perpetual orgasm, as swirls of moving geometric patterns move across the ceiling above her. Guus grabs the Krug, drains half of what's left of it, and hands her the bottle. She sits up & sips & hands it back to him. Guus downs the rest, throws the bottle at a wall, grabs her thighs, & shoves his penis inside her.

Fluidity @ Pioneer Works, Red Hook, Brooklyn

"…please welcome to the stage, Hollywood's own, TIM BANKS!"

A rousing ovation welcomes the star of countless smash-hits and Oscar-winning pictures to the stage, Tim Banks smiling demurely as he waves to the whoops and cheers that greet him.

"Ladies and gentlemen, before I begin today, I would just like to say a few words about what transpired last night at the Down and Out nightclub." With the poise that has earned him dozens of leading roles and the adoration of generations across the globe, Tim Banks pauses and lets silence fill Pioneer Works' sprawling main hall. "I know many of you were in attendance last night at what should have been a joyous occasion marking the beginning of a very special week in New York City. Many of the brightest minds in one of the world's most exciting new industries were present at the New York Blockchain Week Block Party. It should have been a rare chance to relax amid a busy week of forums and networking. Unfortunately, tragedy struck last night. As I am sure you are all aware, a young man with an extremely bright future in this industry was shot in the bathroom of the nightclub. He was simply enjoying a night of fun amid a busy week, like so many of you here today were. Fortunately, Justin Zhao is currently in a stable condition at one of this great city's finest medical facilities. I am sure you will all join me in wishing him a speedy and complete recovery."

Heartfelt applause and a few cheers greet Tim Banks' poignant words.

"He oughta run for President, huh?" Graham hears a nearby journalist say.

Graham struggles to concentrate as Tim Banks talks about blockchain, Ethereum, smart contracts, all these things that Tim Banks says he never heard of until his youngest son introduced him to them. Graham's night was a long one, rousing the New York Times staff to relay breaking news of the shooting at Down & Out, interviewing attendees, firing out a write-up back in his hotel room. Maybe three hours sleep. Today will be no less busy: Fluidity until it breaks for lunch, then across town to Consensus, for the afternoon's discussion between Ripple CEO Brad Garlinghouse and SEC Chairman Jay Clayton.

He looks down from the stage & Tim Banks to his phone & Melina's WhatsApp message: *I just picked up Luis from school. I read your article. This is crazy!! I told you – New York is too dangerous. Many people have gun.*

Its ok, Graham writes. *I will call you & Louis soon.* He lifts his phone to snap a shot of Tim Banks on stage, Vitalik Buterin smiling proudly in the seat behind him. *Look whos giving the speech.*

A notification of another message appears from a number Graham doesn't recognise.

Hello Mr. Graham Jones. You do not know me but I have a story I think you would be very interested in. My name is Aart Janssen and…

Central Park

Aart & Elena sit on a bench looking over the lake & Bow Bridge, heaving trees featured in a thousand movie backdrops drooping into the water on the opposite shore.

"No word?" she asks, as Aart stares at his phone.

Aart yawns. "Nothing."

"It's funny," Elena says. "You see this place so often on television and films. It feels familiar."

Aart thinks of all the scenes in a thousand sitcoms and romcoms where Ben Stiller or Adam Sandler or some other wisecracking American hero brings a date to the Central Park lake. "In the movies, the guy's always the same. He's somehow fucked up. They want you to think that he's a loser, but he has some huge apartment which must cost three thousand dollars a month to rent. He's chasing some girl who looks much better than him. He gets angry all the time, at all the idiots surrounding him. But in the end, he overcomes them. The loser always wins."

Elena lights a cigarette & offers Aart the packet.

"It would be nice if life was more like in the movies," Elena says, lighting Aart's cigarette.

"If this was a movie, this would be a short scene between us before the big climax happens," Aart says.

"And what would the climax be?"

Aart thinks of interrupting Guus on-stage at Consensus, or dramatically gate-crashing the FSC yacht party. He looks at Elena. She looks at him. He leans forward to kiss her.

"HEY!!" some old woman walking a dog shouts. "You can't smoke in here!"

"Oh, shit," Aart mumbles, taking a final drag before stubbing his cigarette out. "Sorry."

"You're lucky I don't report you," the furious woman says as her chihuahua yaps at them.

Elena waits until the old woman has disappeared & then lifts her cigarette back to her mouth. "Why does she care? We're not sitting anywhere close to her."

Aart picks his crumpled cigarette off the floor and tries to straighten it out. Elena holds the carton out & offers him a fresh one: "That's about a dollar's worth of cigarette you just destroyed."

"The prices here are crazy," Aart says, lighting his fresh cigarette.

"You can pay me back once those bastards give you your hundred million dollars."

"Closer to three hundred million now," Aart says. "The price is rising."

He lifts his head and stares at her, mesmerised by the beauty of her face – the pale skin, big green eyes. He leans towards her as his phone starts to vibrate.

"Oh, shit," Aart says, fumbling to answer it. "I think it's one of the journalists. Hello?"

"Hello? Hey, is this Aart? I got your message. This is Graham. Graham Jones. I'm covering the Blockchain Week for The New York Times. Look,

I'm busy as heck today but if you can meet me at a coffee shop somewhere near the Midtown Hilton in the next twenty minutes, maybe we can talk."

Master Suite of the FSC 1, Chelsea Piers Marina

Alicia wakes in a soft white bed from the deepest of dreamless sleeps. She's alone. She doesn't recognise the room. The previous night returns with a rush of images: Guus, Wei, the club, the Bitcoin guy, gunshots, drugs & chaos. Across the cabin, Guus stands at the window, naked, staring at Manhattan.

"The city's skyline's lined with razorblades," Guus says.

She sits up, tries to make sense of what he's saying. For a long time he's silent. Then he turns to her.

"Great metal spikes, thrusting upward at the belly of the gods. Prodding the stomach, slicing it. Blood and viscera will wash o'er all within her."

Alicia stares at Guus. *What is he saying?* His face is wrought with fear, uncertainty, doubt. *How long has he been standing there?*

"It's… the end is coming. These structures, standing less than a century. Two of the largest, already collapsed. Tidal waves will roar over all… return them to the sea…"

He trails off, licks his lips, looks away from her, seemingly aware his words are madness.

"Come," she begs him.

He walks slowly across the cabin and onto the bed, resting his head against her chest. She holds him close, touching one hand to his cheek, smoothing his hair with the other.

"It's okay," she says softly. "We're safe here. Together."

Did he stay awake the whole night taking drugs? When did she fall asleep?

Guus wraps his arms around her, kisses her between her breasts.

"I'm going fucking crazy," he says.

"You're not," she says. "Last night was crazy. You're not crazy."

"You don't know me. I'm…" he trails off again.

"It's okay," she repeats. "It's okay."

He turns his body around, kneeling between her legs, hands at her sides, staring into her eyes.

"When you look at me," Guus asks, eyes emanating sincere insecurity, "do you think I'm capable of anything?"

She stares deeply into his eyes as she holds her hands against each side of his face. "Of course."

"No." He smiles. Leans back. Their hands fall away from each other. "I mean anything. Really anything. Like… I was born without a soul."

She stares, silent. The question is absurd but she longs to answer it. "Of course not."

They stay perfectly still, staring at each other, neither blinking, breathing becoming slower, falling in sync with each other.

"GUUS!!" Knocking at the door. "It's Nguyen! Open up!"

Guus clambers off the bed, crosses the cabin, & throws the door open.

"Jesus Fuck," Nguyen says, averting his eyes. "Put some fucking clothes on. Look, we need to leave in a hour."

"Leave… leave where?"

"Leave where? Leave this fucking ship! Consensus! The conference! Guus! Your fucking speech, remember?"

Starbucks, 1301 6th Avenue

Aart: "The whole thing's a scam. It was a scam from the start. You know what we called it? We called it Pussy Sushi. No – Guus did. He saw that Honey Badger music video, where he's in the yacht, picking the sushi up off the naked models with platinum chopsticks. We were in the frat house back in Groningen, dreaming of being rich. And he was getting into all these crazy shitcoins with these crazy acronyms, seeing them moon four times in a week. And that's all it ever was - a get-rich quick scheme. There's no development. Nothing. It's just Guus and Nguyen. It was the three of us – but I got frozen out."

"Why?" Graham's conscious of time, coffee helping his tiredness, but he's not in the mood for some long-winded tale that goes nowhere.

Aart sighs & stares across the coffee shop. Its midday clientele are a mix of suited finance types, blissful tourists, & T-shirt wearing tech geeks from the crypto conference across the street at the Midtown Hilton.

"Greed," Aart says. "No. That isn't it. Guus isn't interested in money. He wants to be the guy. The face of blockchain. Satoshi Nakamoto. You should see him talk about Vitalik Buterin from Ethereum. He fucking hates him. Anyone who might take his spotlight."

"And they stole your coins?"

"Yeah."

"How do you know it was them?"

"I confronted Nguyen about it. Flew out to Vietnam. He took me to some abandoned house, had a bunch of thugs beat the shit out of me and left me in the hospital. The Vietnamese police showed up and told me to leave the country." Aart doesn't mention the video, *Ciara,* but he's remembering it. Guus showing it to him, smirking. He wants to get a gun. He wonders how difficult that might be in New York City for a foreigner.

Graham sees the intensity, the unhingedness. He thinks of the club shooting. He glances at the girl sitting next to Aart saying nothing (Elena.) "So what have you been doing since you got to New York?"

"I've been staying in a shitty hostel on the Upper West Side in a twelve-man dorm. While those cunts are on their private yacht, preparing their party."

"You didn't report this to the police?"

"Of course I did! But they don't know…" Aart's dwelling on the party, Honey Badger, platinum-encrusted chopsticks. "This is still new tech. They don't have a clue. I spoke to someone from Europol's serious cybercrimes division, but…"

"And how much was stolen?"

Aart unlocks his phone. "Right now it's about two hundred and ninety three million dollars."

Elena's mouth opens in silent shock.

"And this isn't the only major hack for Future Synergy Coin, right?" Graham asks. "There was BitBucks—"

"Yeah, right. I found out about that at almost the exact same time I saw my tokens were missing."

"You think it's connected?"

"I don't know. It could be."

"BitBucks was run by an Italian guy, right? Giuseppe—"

"Giovanni Cuomo."

"Right." Graham covered the story of the hack and Giovanni's subsequent sudden disappearance for Cointopia or Crypto News Network or one of the other half-dozen sites he was writing for. There was a lot of speculation Giovanni had taken the money and run. Gone to South America or South-East Asia. "In Vietnam, these guys who attacked you – are you sure Nguyen hired them?"

"Absolutely. He brought me to an empty apartment and they were in there waiting for me."

"And Giovanni Cuomo… you think Guus and Nguyen might know something about his disappearance?"

"I don't know… I hadn't thought about it. I guess they could do."

"So the total value of the missing tokens, the ones you say were stolen from you and the ones lost from BitBucks – it's worth over a billion dollars right now?"

"Yeah. Something like that."

Graham imagines penning a multi-page expose on all this for The New York Times, tying it together with the nightclub shooting. *Crypto Mania: Life & Death in Finance's New Wild West.* Maybe they'll make him a permanent staff writer. Maybe he'll move Melina & Luis out to New York City. Maybe Sarah will grow up with an American accent. Maybe he'll win a Pulitzer.

Consensus @ Midtown Hilton

"Guus," Nguyen snaps, "are you fucking crazy?! It is illegal to possess firearms anywhere in the City of New York. Illegal. For American citizens with fucking gun licenses."

"Nguyen," Guus says calmly, "if we speak to them—"

"Speak to who?! What, you think the staff at the fucking Hilton are gonna let you violate federal law because you did too much fucking coke last night and now you're a paranoid fucking mess?"

Graham crosses the street, recognising Guus & Nguyen as they argue at the side of the limousine parked in front of the hotel. Graham looks back across the street at the Starbucks and sees Aart & Elena watching the scene through its windows, Aart keeping his head low, clearly afraid of being spotted by them.

"There are metal detectors at the entrance," Nguyen says. "As soon as Hrvko and the others walk inside they'll be in handcuffs. And we'll be joining them. And there are metal detectors at the entrance! Do you understand? Nobody can bring a fucking gun inside. Nobody is going to shoot you onstage."

Guus thinks back to all the grandiloquent speeches of great dictators he's studied: Park Chung Hee of South Korea; a North Korean spy, rising in the audience, firing at the stage, missing Park, killing his wife. Guus looks at Alicia. She holds his hand and touches her other to his shoulder.

"You are not John fucking Lennon, Guus," Nguyen continues. "You are not going to be assassinated in New York fucking City." *But this bitch you're with might be Yoko Ono, trying to break The Blockchain Beatles up.*

Guus sighs & avoids eye contact: "I am not going onstage without security."

"Then don't go onstage," Nguyen says. "I'll give the speech."

Guus thinks. "You want to give the speech? You've never given a speech before."

"I've seen you do it a thousand times. You've got it written out anyway, right? What difference does it make?" Nguyen lights a cigarette.

Graham takes his vape from his pocket as he watches.

"I have a room here," Alicia says. She shares Guus' fear. Wei is somewhere in this city, surely looking for her. "If you don't feel safe in the conference hall…"

Nguyen stares at Alicia – *who the fuck is this bitch? Fucking whore-ass Yoko cunt.*

Agreement is reached. They move inside. Darren the screenwriter follows them. Hrvko returns to the limousine. It drives off. Graham vapes & thinks. Takes his phone out. Searches for details on the Future Synergy Coin party Aart was talking about. Tomorrow night, Chelsea Piers Marina. Graham looks back across the street at Aart & Elena in the Starbucks, hits his vape a few more times, then walks into the Hilton. He shows his press pass, moves through security, and checks the afternoon's line-up: the Brad Garlinghouse/Jay Clayton debate is at 3.30pm in the Grand Ballroom. Future Synergy Coin's speech is one of the many side-rooms at 3pm.

"Fuck that asshole," Nguyen rants at Darren as they stand to the side of the third-floor Trianon Ballroom. "You got any coke on you?"

"Yeah, I think I brought some," Darren says, taking out his wallet.

"He thinks he's John fucking Lennon," Nguyen says. "Bullshit. Like I can't give a fucking conference speech. There wouldn't even be a Future Synergy Coin if I didn't create this shit. Are you done with that fucking screenplay yet?"

"I'm about a third of the way through the second act," Darren says, passing Nguyen a baggie.

"You can get that shit finished today?"

"I guess."

"Get it done. After the speech, we're going to find Alberto Firenze. I'm gonna hand him the screenplay personally."

Midtown Hilton, Room 2706

"I can smoke here?" Guus asks, turning back from the window to her.

It's prohibited, but how much could the fine be – *$100?* "Sure." Laws become suggestions when you have enough money.

Guus sparks a cigarette & holds the packet up. Alicia nods. He tosses them onto the bed in front of her, takes a drag, leans in to light her cigarette. She wants to ask, tell, to know him, & him her, *but…*

Guus turns again to look at NYC's high-rises. Each smoke in silence, ash creeping further along Alicia's cigarette, she holding it delicately so as not to drop it onto the bedsheets. Guus takes a glass from a table, taps cigarette ash into it, passes it to Alicia.

"You have something to drink?"

"No," Alicia says. "But we can call room service."

"Two bottles of Napa Valley Cabernet Sauvignon," Guus says on the room's telephone, "and one bottle of Maker's Mark."

He sits next to her on the bed & rolls a joint. She rests her head against his shoulder as he taps white powder from a baggie over the weed & tobacco.

Midtown Hilton, The Trianon Ballroom

"A New New World Order." Nguyen's voice booms through the ballroom. "A new astrological age, with the Bitcoin whitepaper as its foundational text."

Graham scans the audience as Nguyen speaks. He recognises the wild blond hair of antivirus pioneer & crypto evangelist Jack McAvoy a few rows ahead.

"The last two millennia were the Age of Pisces," Nguyen says, striding back-and-forth onstage, mic in hand. "The fish, as represents Jesus. And the Christian religion reached its apex with American world dominion. Before that, there were other astrological ages. Ten thousand B.C., the end of the last Ice Age, the Age of Leo."

How old is McAvoy, seventy-something? The head of the young girl sitting next to him barely rises above the back of her seat.

"Eight thousand B.C., the Age of Leo ends, the Age of Cancer begins. The birth of agriculture and dawn of settled human civilization. The convenience trap that's corroded our souls and held our once-nomadic species captive ever since."

Graham glances to the back of the room & spots one of the Dabrowski Twins. He's not sure if it's Isaiah or Samuel.

"Six thousand B.C., the Age of Gemini, the astrological twins. The development of writing and trade and the first far-flung communication networks between the settled agrarian human communities. The written word, developed as a method of bookkeeping. A means of recording trade balance. The first recorded ledger."

The solo Dabrowski seems enraptured with Nguyen's speech. Graham recalls his interview with Da Browskis & the similar stream of grandiose bullshit they spouted.

"Four thousand B.C., the Age of Taurus begins. The rise of the great ancient civilizations – the Egyptians, the Assyrians, the Cretians. Each civilization venerated the bull as god. Two thousand B.C., Moses and monotheism. Chastising the Israelites who venerated the golden calf. The Age of Aries, the ram. The Iron Age. An explosion of creativity in the cultures of Greece, China, Rome, Persia."

Graham thinks of what Aart said, about this all being for self-glorification. He remembers the line he cut from The New York Times piece about the self-glorification of the original Babylonian Hammurabi.

"Zero A.D., birth of Christ, Age of Pisces, slow rise of a global monoculture. Now, the 21st Century. The Internet. Freedom of travel, information, technology."

Maybe crypto truly represents a new era of deluded tech-driven self-aggrandisement. *Maybe these guys truly are the clickbait/instant-gratification/fake-news/post-truth/social-media generation's version of divine prophets.*

"January 9th, 2009. Satoshi Nakamoto's Bitcoin whitepaper was published. The birth of distributed ledger technology. The birth of blockchain. Decentralized trustless bookkeeping. The Age of Aquarius. The emptier of the water pitcher. The destruction of the habitat of the fish. The great threatening global cataclysms of climate change, dying oceans, mass extinction, nuclear winter. But those with understanding and command of the blockchain will for these next two thousand years be gods."

Like Jesus turning a few fish and a loaf of bread into a feast for ten thousand: the pure & untainted anonymous Godhead Satoshi Nakamoto transforming his first disciples' low-level computer processing power into fortunes of hundreds of millions of dollars.

"The death of monotheism, of centralized command structures. The dawn of decentralization. The foundation for interplanetary conquest. A great pantheon of decentralized human gods, eight-billion strong."

Midtown Hilton, Room 2706

Flayed human flesh & featureless faces seep into the walls of another nondescript hotel room. Abscesses bubble o'er skin & disappear with wisps of sulphurous gas. Noise: piano keys played at random, occasional moans distorting into staccato drum beat. Patches of blood creep out across the bedsheet & collapse on themselves, leaving no trace behind. This is that of what Guus sees, hears, & feels which can be coded in words.

Alicia alternates between sleep & nursing him. She sees bright city day beyond the window ebb through afternoon toward dusk. She thinks a thousand thoughts but all fleeting, resolving her life a hundred times just to give it up & gaze without thought over the city a moment later. Each time footsteps & voices pass along the corridor she sits upright, listening, fearing their stopping outside their door.

Chez Firenze Tribeca

"I'm sorry," the waiter says, "but Mr. Firenze isn't here."

"I thought he fucking owned the place!" Nguyen snaps, gesturing at the exposed brickwork and white tablecloths of the restaurant surrounding his table.

"Mr. Firenze is one of the principal owners, but he is not required to be—"

"Just give this to him, okay?" Nguyen says, snatching one of the bound copies of 'BLOCKCHAIN GODS: a Wolf of Wall Street for the Instagram Generation' from the stack piled in front of Darren the red-faced sleep-craving screenwriter, the script still lukewarm from the print shop.

"I'm sorry, Sir, but this is a restaurant, and if you came here without the intention of ordering something—"

"I'm ordering, okay?" Nguyen says, flipping the menu open. "Gimme a Forbidden Black Rice and the Mafaldine."

"And for your friend?"

“My friend?” Nguyen sees Darren's disgusting red face and jabs at the menu for him. "Give him the grilled octopus and the pan-roasted salmon.”

“I'm allergic to seafood,” Darren says.

“Jesus… then give him the Heirloom Tomatoes and a Queso Fundido.”

“Sir, you may be aware of this, but your friend has ordered two starters.”

“Jesus Fuck… Darren, what do you want? The tomatoes or the fundido?”

“What's in the fundido?”

“Give him the tomatoes and a stuffed acorn squash.”

“As you wish, Sir.”

“And a bottle of red.”

“Sir, we carry many varieties of wine. Might I suggest—"

“Give us a bottle of châteauneuf-du-pape,” Nguyen says, pointing to one of the last items on the price-ordered wine list. “And make sure this script gets to Alberto Firenze, okay? There's a huge fucking tip coming if you take this fucking screenplay off me.”

“As you wish—”

“And if you don't give him this script, and Mr. Firenze hears Mr. Nolan or Mr. Spielberg or Mr. Scorsese or Mr. Tarantino bought the rights to the biggest non-franchise movie property of the decade, I don't think I need to tell you what that might do for your waiting career.”

The waiter bows his head & leaves the table with the screenplay.

“Can you believe this shit? Alberto Firenze doesn't even eat at his own fucking restaurant.” Nguyen pats at his shirt and trouser pockets. “Yo, Darren, you got any coke on you?”

Darren takes his wallet out as Nguyen’s phone vibrates on the table.

“Hello?… yeah… what?… what the fuck?… fuck tired! I’m tired. We’re chartering a jet to fly Tickbag from El Scorcho and Whizz from Hotbox Hollywood out from L.A. for this… yeah… and Burt Gale is already in town for… yeah, so, what would wake him up?… Five million dollars… yes. Five million… okay?… he’s okay now?… Not too sleepy?… okay… no, thank you.” Nguyen ends the call & lets the phone drop to the table. “Bom Ceronie’s in. Five million fucking dollars his agent wanted. Five million! For fucking Bom Ceronie! He hasn’t done shit in thirty years.”

“I’m out,” Darren says.

“You’re out? Bom Ceronie’s in, you’re out. What does that mean?”

“Out of coke. We did it all already.”

“Jesus Fuck, Darren! You degenerate fucking cokehead!”

Outdoor patio @ HI NYC Hostel

“You think he believed me?”

Elena says nothing. Aart pours more wine into his glass, then tops up hers.

"You worry very much what people think of you."

Aart sips shiraz. "What do you mean?"

They're alone on the hostel's patio. Elena lights a cigarette. "The money you guys made. It's insane. More than Hollywood film stars, Premier League football players. This type of situation can never exist again. Three guys in a student house in the Netherlands make something on their computer and raise billions of dollars with it. You said many times today, when you talked with that journalist, that Guus wasn't satisfied. That Guus wants to be respected. But I listen and I think you're talking about yourself."

Aart sips shiraz, aware of how annoyed he is by what Elena just said. He wants to argue against it. But. "Maybe you're right. You're perceptive."

"It's a gift."

Aart lifts his eyes to meet her gaze. She stares bullets through him.

"And a curse." She smiles. "What you told, of trying to control them, make them develop the project – why? Why would you care? You made all this money, you're twenty years-old. You see it happen to famous people all the time… They get this success. They go crazy. When they are so young, especially. Like Justin Bieber. But you… no. You're different. It's… interesting."

Aart glugs shiraz & lights a cigarette. "I hope The New York Times thinks so."

"I don't think it's the money that you want. I don't think you care about the money."

Aart laughs. "You don't think I care about hundreds of millions of dollars? Jesus. I don't know what you—"

"I think you want money. Everybody wants money. Needs money. But that is not what motivated you. Everything you said about Guus, lusting for power, respect, control. I think you were talking about yourself."

Aart sips & smokes. "You haven't met Guus, man. Or Nguyen. Or… fuck. Maybe you're right. So…"

"So what?"

"So fucking what." Aart finishes the glass, pours out another. "So fucking what."

"You're upset you didn't see them. You want them to know that you're here. If all you wanted was to talk with a journalist, you could have stayed home in Holland."

"Groningen isn't Holland. Holland is the southern part of Nederlands."

"Groningen is a lot closer to Holland than New York."

Silence.

"So… you think I should confront them? Before I leave New York?"

"It doesn't matter what I think. I think you think you should confront them."

"At their yacht party. Chelsea Piers Marina."

"Uh-huh."

"Huh."

They silently sip shiraz in sync then both take a drag on their cigarettes.

"So tomorrow night," Aart says. "The FSC yacht party."

"Tomorrow night," Elena says.

Aart tops up her glass. "You sure you're majoring in International Relations? Not Psychology?"

She smiles. They clink glasses. He leans toward her. She sips shiraz & kisses him, letting red liquid flow from one mouth to the other.

Midtown Hilton, Room 2705

"I told you," Melina says. "New York is too dangerous. Too many people have guns."

"Yeah, Graham admits, pacing the room as he talks on the phone. "Maybe you were right."

"Of course. I always am right. Eh… it's late here. I should sleep."

"Okay, ¡cuánto te quiero mucho!"

The call ends & Graham sits on the bed, re-opening his phone's web browser. Justin Zhao, the guy shot at the Down & Out nightclub. Graham reads through the Hammurabi press release on his hiring. Justin Zhao's LinkedIn profile,; news updates & New York Times Slack channel discussion on his stable condition & medically-induced coma; a Chinese-language website for the BitSong bitcoin mining corp Justin Zhao used to run. Graham opens a can of IPA & ponders. *Who shot him?* Was it just a random incident? Or something deeper? Graham knows there's a story here. He thinks of Aart, Future Synergy Coin. The disappearance of Giovanni Cuomo. *If these things are somehow connected…*

He copy + pastes the Chinese characters that seem to represent Justin Zhao's name from the BitSong website into Google. Chinese news articles appear. He opens them, Google Translate creating a stilted but semi-understandable story of a government raid, bitcoin mining equipment found in a factory, its owner under investigation for tax fraud. *What if the Chinese government tried to kill him?* Nah – *that's mental.* Killing him in a nightclub. Intelligence services kill people in hotel rooms, not in public. They're experts at making murders look like suicides. They wouldn't have shot him in a crowded nightclub, and definitely wouldn't have let him survive the shooting… *unless they wanted people to know they did it…*

Graham sits up & sips IPA. *Nah. It's crazy. But…* that doesn't mean it's impossible. He thinks of a story that's been big news back in England: the poisoning of a Russian spy & his daughter in Salisbury. The whole thing was so obviously carried out by Russian intelligence services. It was like they wanted everyone to know they did it. And the Prime Minister & her useless government have done bugger all in retaliation. *That was the point of it.* To show that traitors to Putin aren't safe anywhere. That Western powers are powerless against him. Same with Ukraine, Crimea. *And President Trump's just kicked off a trade war with China.* What if this is China playing the same game? The Chinese Communist Party dislikes cryptocurrency. It's a way of facilitating capital outflows from the country. Getting money out & away from the CCP's control. What if the Chinese Communist Party shot Justin Zhou to send a message?

Graham hears something. He stops dreaming up conspiracy theories & stares across the room, at the wall. *Did someone just knock on it?* He waits. He hears it again. He stands up, sips IPA, then walks to the room's far wall. He presses his ear against it. Knock, knock, knock. He stands back. *What the…* He sips more IPA. Then he bangs his knuckles three times against the wall.

Room 2706

Guus presses the glass to the wall & his ear to the glass: "They're talking."

"Saying what?" Alicia sits on the bed, clutching knees to her chest.

"I don't know. I only hear one person. Maybe a phone call."

Fuck. If it's him…

"It stopped. I don't hear anything." Guus drops the glass to the bed, sees Alicia's terror. He drops to his knees, grabs both sides of her face. "I will protect you. If anyone tries to hurt you, I will fucking kill them. I love you."

They kiss, roll on the bed, groping each other, tearing the other's clothes off. Midway undressed, Alicia stops, holds her finger to Guus' mouth: "Do you hear that?"

Both are silent save for heavy breathing.

"I don't hear anything," Guus says.

"I don't know…" Alicia starts to cry.

Guus stands. He hammers on the wall with his fist.

"No! Don't!"

"If he is in there, I will fucking kill this kankerautist! Nobody will hurt you. Nobody!"

Guus bangs his fist against the wall again. Nothing.

He drops back to his knees. Alicia lunges towards him, kissing his neck, his chest, unbuckling his belt. He unhooks her bra, pushes her onto her back, squeezes her tits, licks her nipples, rubs her labia. Her head rolls back, mouth opens & closes, body writhes. Guus' free hand pulls down his trousers & underwear. Sounds, rising colours. Room glows red, orange, purple. A noise. Both hear. Stop. Stare at the door, Guus' finger still inside her. A knock.

"Guus…" Alicia says softly.

Guus stands, kicking free of his trousers & underwear as he strides to the door. He throws it open.

"Who the fuck—"

Room 2705

Shouting from the hallway. Graham drops his phone, walks to the door, stares through the peephole. *What the fuck…*

A naked man from the room next door is shouting at a terrified hotel employee: "Who the fuck sent you?!"

"You did! You ordered room service!"

Graham runs to his phone, opens the camera, presses it to the peephole, starts recording. The voices quieten. The hotel staff hands the naked man two bottles of wine. The naked man turns away from him. It's Guus van Hooijdink. *From Future Synergy Coin.*

What the fuck…

Room 2706

"Did we order these?" Guus asks, a bottle of Cabernet Sauvignon in each hand.

"I… don't remember."

Guus scans the room, sees two empty wine bottles, a half-drunk Maker's Mark. Maybe they ordered it. The glowing hues of the walls start to shift colour again.

"We should get out of here. I don't know if we should drink these. They may be tainted. This Chinese kankerautist, maybe he knows you are here."

Alicia nods, pulling her panties on.

Guus looks at his phone, sees the time, date. "Oh fuck. Now is the banquet. The Plaza Hotel. We should we go there. We will be safe there."

The Plaza Hotel

"You look lonely." Wei looks up from the lobby at the woman hovering over him. "You mind if I join you?"

Wei's in the Rose Room cocktail lounge, jazz musicians playing mournful music on a mezzanine suspended above the hotel's lobby. "I'm waiting for someone."

She smiles & nods & disappears. Wei barely notices anything about her – the faint scent of perfume, a glimpse of blonde hair. He returns his gaze to the lobby below. Suited tech types have been entering for the past twenty minutes. Wei cradles his cocktail as he scans them. The coolness of the glass suddenly prompts him to touch the gun. He closes his eyes as he strokes the steel in his pocket. Aware of himself, he opens them. He's missed some of the crowd coming in – *what if she…* But no. *Why would she come here?* As the stupidity of it dawns on him, he downs what's left in the glass. Then he sees her.

"I fucking knew it..." he whispers to himself as he watches her, walking through the lobby, arm-in-arm with some slender white guy. They move in the same direction as the others who've entered the lobby, toward the Grand Ballroom. The big dinner.

"Would Sir like another?"

"No," Wei tells the waiter. "I'll take the check."

Wei walks out onto 59th Street. The street-lit trees of Central Park are in front of him, dwarfed by surrounding skyscrapers. He touches the gun as he crosses the street. *That bitch...*

Justin hasn't been dead 24 hours & she's already found someone else. He knew it. He knew whatever the biggest, most exclusive event of this whole week of Bitcoin-related bullshit was, she'd find some sucker to bring her to it. He thinks of how effortlessly she made a fool of him in Tokyo. *That fucking whore.* He stares beyond the trees, into the darkness of the park. He thinks of rushing through The Plaza, gun drawn, straight into the Grand Ballroom. Shooting her twice in the chest & once in the face. Turning the gun on himself & blowing his brains out over the tasteful white tablecloths. *No...* make this count. Whoever she's with must be someone important. Wei takes out his phone & taps through conference programs, trying to find him. Without realizing where he's going, he's deep within the park, beside a lake.

"Hey man, you got the time?"

Wei looks at the figure who said it. It's too dark to see him clearly. Wei points the gun at him. "It's time you fuck off."

"Oh, shit, man, fuck..." the would-be mugger blubbers, disappearing quickly, as Wei turns around & heads back toward the park's exit, continuing the search on his phone.

Guus van Hooijdink. Future Synergy Coin.

More searching on his phone as he returns to the exit brings up an opportunity. 'The Official Future Synergy Coin Afterparty.' On a yacht at Chelsea Marina. Tomorrow night, 10pm. Wei stops walking. There's a link – to reserve a ticket. Which requires a name. 'ID must be presented upon arrival.' He walks back to the lake, listening carefully, one hand clutching his phone, the other touching the gun. He moves by conversations – homeless, other shady characters... He hears Chinese. He moves toward the tourists. He asks in Mandarin: "Hey, do you have the time?"

The answers of the small group in the dark betray panic. Wei takes the gun out, holds it so that the lamp light behind him casts its shadow across them: "Give me your wallets."

& Wei's running, alongside the lake, turning through the dark maze, the city's black heart. On the street, he takes the I.D. from one of the wallets. It looks similar enough. *These racist Yank fucks won't know the difference.* He enters the name on the I.D. card, Jin Chunlan, & reserves his place, making the payment with what little Bitcoin is left in one of his exchange wallets.

The Grand Ballroom @ The Plaza Hotel

"Look how far away we are," Nguyen says, gesturing across the chandelier-adorned room beneath the ornate rising arches to the center table, where the heads of the Securities and Exchange Commission & Commodity Futures Trading Commissions are due to sit. "And I'm gonna look such a fucking loser with this asshole as my plus-one."

"Hey," Darren the screenwriter says. "I resemble that remark."

"Shut the fuck up, Darren. The writing gig's done. Don't try to be clever. Hey, Guus, did you bring any coke with you?"

Guus ignores Nguyen's question as he sees Jack McAvoy enter the room, a girl barely half his height walking alongside him. McAvoy glances at Guus and smiles & salutes as he stops by a table & greets Charles Hoskinson from Cardano. McAvoy continues across the room, checking the place settings, before stopping at the table with Guus, Nguyen, Darren the screenwriter, & Alicia.

"Ah, gentlemen! I was hoping that they would sit me beside someone interesting."

Guus rises to shake his hand. "I had the same thought upon seeing your name here."

McAvoy greets each of Nguyen, Darren, Alicia – lingering a little long on staring into Alicia's eyes as he holds her hand – & then introduces the young girl he's brought him with him as Teresa.

"Perhaps we should make the evening a little more interesting," McAvoy says, producing a vial of something after the waiters have poured their first glasses of champagne.

"By all means," Guus replies.

McAvoy tips a little of the liquid into each of their glasses as the heads of the SEC & FTSC enter the room and all rise, clapping.

"Ladies and gentlemen, a toast," SEC Chairman Jay Clayton says. "To an industry that has made my life a heck of a lot more complicated."

Laughter ripples through the room as glasses are raised & clinked & 'cheers' said.

"See, that's how you write a fucking joke," Nguyen snarls at Darren.

Waiters move around the room, placing tastefully-arranged plates on tables & filling champagne glasses.

"Seventy thousand acres," Jack McAvoy says. "One hundred seventy million dollars. The deed is signed. Now the deed must be done. Be a part of it."

"Cryptopia," Guus repeats.

"And everything's legal in Nevada, right?" Nguyen says.

"Yes, Sir," McAvoy confirms. "Legalized gambling, prostitution, no state income taxes, and hundreds of thousands of acres of empty desert just waiting for the next Las Vegas."

Alicia watches auras ebb & glow from each as they talk. McAvoy's aura, a dark, almost black, crimson red. Nguyen's, light red, beating darker as the dream McAvoy's selling them seduces him. Guus, from green to red to green to red, ebbing between the both. She touches his hand as the red glow grows stronger; green in an instant, as he turns to her, smiling. "It sounds gezzelig, no?"

"Gezzelig!" McAvoy laughs, raising a glass.

Teresa, the girl in the chair beside McAvoy, has a sky blue aura that occasionally beats bruised purple. Darren's is a dull yellow grey. Alicia smiles as Guus again looks at her, calming his crimson glow into emerald green. He continues talking with McAvoy about the proposal, a crypto-based wonderland of development & future fusion in the wastelands of the Nevada desert. She wonders what colour her own aura is. She tells Guus she's going to the bathroom. As she walks through the ballroom, she sees the rainbow of auras emanating from each table. At the head table, the Dabrowski's auras pulse silver, the various SEC & FTSC & other government officials a duller grey. Vitalik Buterin's is pure blinding white. She leaves the Main Hall and enters a corridor, the walls breathing. She enters a lavish gold-hued bathroom. The golden colors dance across the mirror like lightning bolts. She stares at herself, examining each feature. No aura is apparent. She splashes water on her face, closes her eyes. *No aura.* The bathroom dims. The gold lightning on the mirror becomes slow-crawling black. Soon her face & arms are all that's distinguishable of her reflection, hair & dress merging with the black. A face: *him.* She screams & turns.

"Excuse me," a startled woman says.

"Sorry," Alicia says, smiling with embarrassment, bowing her head as she passes her & leaves. She walks through the breathing hall, unsure if she's going the right way.

The New York Times Building, 620 8th Avenue

"Four articles a day," the New York Times Technology Editor says, staring across his desk at Graham. "To cover the tech sector in its entirety. For today's four, we've got a piece on how European data privacy laws will affect Facebook, an insider's view on how self-driving cars will impact the automotive industry, a long-form thinkpiece on the long-term profitably of at-a-loss tech start-ups, and your piece on New York Blockchain Week. Everything I commission has to fit within that four-articles-a-day framework. So one crypto piece a day, max. Today's piece is on the SEC Chairman's debate with Brad Garlinghouse. Tomorrow will be an overview of the week. After that, our coverage is complete."

"But this story could be huge," Graham argues, telling the Tech Ed a truncated version of what Aart told him yesterday. "We're talking almost a billion dollars that's gone missing."

"The proven theft of a billion million dollars is a story. A bitter start-up founder ranting in a Starbucks is not."

"But he's gone on record saying the whole project was a scam, that—"

"Ninety-nine percent of cryptocurrency projects are a scam. Yet another scam being uncovered might be worthy of coverage in the blockchain blogs you used to write for, but it isn't worthy of coverage in The New York Times."

Graham leaves The New York Times Building & walks back down 41st Street toward the Midtown Hilton for the last day of the conference, knowing that all the big-hitters have spoken & the debauchery of the after-parties is the only thing likely to add any further colour to his final piece. He thinks back to the thoughts that filled his mind walking back to the Midtown Hilton from the Down & Out nightclub on the night of the Chinese blockchain engineer's shooting: that a bigger story is playing out in the shadows of the conference. All his journalistic instincts tell him there's some common thread that would tie all together. *Four articles a day. Max.* The New York Times' Tech Ed was far more courteous & professional than that dickhead Terrance Kant at Dead Bird Press ever was, but Graham's antagonistic relationship with editors remains. *He weren't saying owt about four articles a day* when Graham broke the news of the nightclub shooting. Graham thinks of the unhinged edge to all Aart said about Future Synergy Coin, then that maniac Guus van Hooijdink screaming at hotel staff, naked in the corridor. The mystery of who shot Justin Zhou. This story isn't over. He takes out his phone & books a ticket to the FSC yacht party as he walks. The last big event of New York Blockchain Week. He can't help but feel this story will end with a violent climax.

The Violent Climax. (Chelsea Piers Marina & the FSC 1.)

Wei walks past the pure white pleasure vessels of the marina, sleek yachts distinguished from each other only by size. Three women talk excitedly of how rich the crypto guys are. Wei follows them, skittering EDM growing louder. The great hull of a yacht casting a moonlit shadow over all overs grows larger. Wei touches the reassuring steel of his remaining gun, wondering if he can get on-board without a security check.

Graham walks along the upper deck of the FSC 1 mega yacht mentally transcribing notes on the scene: crypto YouTubers holding phone's at arm-length & talking to camera with the party's buzz as a backdrop; deceptively rich crypto pioneers with multi-million dollar timepieces & ten dollar T-shirts talking of how Wall Street will soon belong to their unwashed untoned contingent; supermodel-stunning women sauntering & mingling in cocktail dresses or frolicking in the shimmering blue pool in bikinis; New York hipsters marvelling at how much the yacht cost... Graham moves through this disparate mass towards security-guarded steps, where a crowd listens as Future Synergy Coin's Dung Nguyen speaks with one arm draped over the shoulders of hip-pop superstar Honey Badger.

"This man was an inspiration to all of us," Nguyen says, Honey Badger bowing his bald head deferentially. "We were in the Netherlands one afternoon watching your music video, the one with the girls with the sushi on the yacht where you've got the platinum chopsticks, and that's when we thought: fuck, we gotta get rich." Laughter from onlookers spurs Nguyen on. "Watching that video is where this all started for us. So tonight we'd like to pay tribute to that special moment and show that if you work hard enough, and smart enough, and make enough people believe in you, your dreams will come true." Nguyen picks a small silver bell up from a table and rings it. Waiters in white jackets with bow ties stream out from the yacht's interior, pushing long carts draped with black sheets. Dozens come forward, rolling down the ramps at the side of the steps Nguyen & Honey Badger are standing on, crowd manoeuvring to allow their passage, until a hundred waiters with a hundred black carts draped with black cloth cover the seaboard edges of the entire deck. "We would also like to thank chef Shinzo Takahashi and all his staff from Shinzo's on the Upper West Side, Manhattan's only four Michelin-starred sushi restaurant," Nguyen continues. "Shinzo told us he had never catered for an event this large, and would never normally agree to such a thing, but it's amazing what a few millions dollars can do." Laughter, some cheers. "So to thank all of you who've believed in our project and helped turn our humble piece of technology into a multi-billion dollar enterprise, please, enjoy." Nguyen rings the silver bell again and each waiter whips the black cloths from their carts, revealing a hundred naked nyotaimori models, each with a hundred pieces of finest-quality sushi artfully arranged over their multi-ethnic bodies. People move to marvel & snap pictures of the nyotaimori girls and begin delicately removing the sushi with thousands of pairs of platinum diamond-dotted chopsticks. Nguyen leads Honey Badger to the models at the platform at the top of the stairs. "This is so fucking good, right?" Nguyen says, mouth full of rice & raw fish. "Yo, Darren, try some."

"I can't," Darren the screenwriter says. "I'm allergic to seafood."

"Darren, this is no fucking ocean-plucked schlep served for three dollars a plate in some back alley sushi joint. It's gourmet shit from a four Michelin-starred chef served on the naked body of a fucking supermodel. Eat it, you shit."

"I'm allergic."

"Fucking eat it!" Nguyen snarls, grasping a salmon-topped rice clump with his hands & forcing it into Darren's mouth, pushing his jaws up & down to make him chew as on-looking lookers giggle.

"Sir, this is a mighty fine spread that you've put on," Jack McAvoy says.

"Thank you, Sir," Nguyen says, offering McAvoy a handshake.

Aart and Elena board the yacht with no suspicion from the burly East Europeans checking e-tickets. Aart sees a tough-faced man he recognizes among the security, trying to remember where he's seen him before, not connecting Hrvko with that night months ago at the Indonesisch restaurant in Groningen & forgetting about it as he and Elena marvel at the huge crowd on deck and the party's glitz & grandeur.

"What now?" Elena asks quietly as they move through the crowd.

"I guess we find them," Aart replies.

Finding no sign of Alicia among the thousands of faces on deck, Wei stops by the steps at the boat's midpoint and instinctively turns from the burly black-clad security blocking access. Graham, standing beside a nyotaimori table a few meters away, senses something strange in the way Wei stands and looks at nothing. But as Graham's eyes pass over the crowd, he sees Aart with Elena, and instantly switches focus to them, staying still to remain unseen. Wei waits beside the security guards until a group of celebrities passes them – actor Jake Riddervold & rapper Afrodeezeeak with models Isabelle Pelletier & Gabriella Halabi. Others on deck react to the famous faces, snapping pictures, moving toward them, distracting security. Wei slips up the steps & enters a huge chandelier-hung room full of groups of celebrities and stunning females sitting on leather couches around tables covered in champagne bottles and mounds of white powder. Wei recognizes baseball players from the New York Yankees sharing champagne with basketball players from the New York Knicks, a dozen women sitting around them. At another table, shoe designer Bruce Belichick laughs at something music producer Pondlife is saying to actress & model Leanne Bronte. Wei continues through the room & opens a door into a long unpeopled hallway.

"Sir, I wanted to talk to you more about this business proposition."

Nguyen and McAvoy and McAvoy's harem of youthful latinas have moved to a lavish lounge within the yacht's interior labyrinth of rooms.

"As I mentioned last night at dinner, I recently purchased a plot of land in Nevada of about sixty-eight thousand acres. Excuse me – you work in metric, correct?"

"Yeah."

"So sixty-eight thousand acres is…" McAvoy's eyes roll slightly upwards. He leans forward for the silver nose straw and huffs a line of the white stuff off the table. "About one-hundred-six-and-a-quarter square miles." McAvoy blinks. "About a meter shy of one-hundred-seventy-one square kilometers."

"Sounds big," Nguyen says, leaning forward to snort a line.

"Very big, Sir. Very big indeed. This land I bought in Nevada is right outside Reno. Silicon Valley is less than a four-hour drive away. Less than ten minutes by helicopter. And the land I bought is bigger than the city of Reno itself. Just like the mob moved into Vegas in the fifties and replaced the sand dunes with craps tables and roulette wheels, we'll turn a barren desert wasteland into a shimmering blockchain oasis."

Nguyen rubs his nose and blinks. "Sounds cool."

"Yes, Sir. Very cool. And that's why I wanted to talk to you. I've been following the development of your cryptocurrency most closely. Of all the projects in this fledgling industry, none have the gigantic balls of Future Synergy Coin."

Alicia lifts her head as Guus' penis pumps white out at the moment whatever the last white powder was hits and the substance gushing out becomes dancing fractals as her mind shoots at the same as speed as Guus' seed into the stratosphere, far over the yacht and the harbor and the city and the continent and the planet, to some other dimension of outer and inner space where she arrives, some astral form of naked self stripped of the accoutrements of hard-earned ego and identity, to be stared at by strange spectral grey beings who speak and say something in a language more foreign than Japanese but laced with meaning that is comprehensible yet beyond comprehension, alien words that reveal some secret she almost grasps before she returns through the fractal void to the room, and the bed, Guus speaking, head resting on her stomach.

"…the speech I was born to give, to deliver…"

The cheers of the crowd filter through the master suite's walls. The low thud of bass-driven trap beats follows. Guus sits up. "The party has started."

"Nevada has legalized gambling, marijuana, prostitution," McAvoy explains, "but the laws will be of little application in a land where we are the masters. I have a friend who has a private island, far from the prying eyes of any government, where world leaders and British royalty retreat to enjoy the rewards of their position. This is the kind of promised land I plan to build in Nevada."

Nguyen rubs his nose and nods, envisioning McAvoy's wild desert oasis & his own shimmering future of great power and influence. Nguyen closes his eyes & pictures it as a kneeling Latina deepthroats his cock. "Sounds fucking cooool…" The Latina releases Nguyen's cock with a pop, pumping the shaft & moving her tongue to his balls. One big pump follows. Nguyen's cum arcs in the air & splatters the coke mound. "Ah, Jesus Fuck!" Nguyen says, leaning forward, hoping to salvage the splooged powder.

"Not a problem, Sir," McAvoy smiles. "Ivelisse and Teresa are carrying at least a pound of cocaine at all times. Let's clean up, partake in a few more lines, and get back to the party. Your public awaits."

Lil Profit and Lil Boaty hop-scotch back & forth across stage, repeating 'Louis V! Dior, Gucci! Balecianaga, Armaaani' endlessly into microphones, their multi-colored dreads waving wildly as the crowd bounces across the deck, camera phones held aloft. Graham looks through the bouncing mass of people to Aart and Elena, near a nyotaimori table on the opposite side.

"Yo, yo," Lil Profit says as a DJ scratch halts the music. "I gotta say something. I just hit twenty million followers on Instagram!" Big cheer. "And these mu'fuckas who boat we on just hit four billion dollars in market cap." Even bigger cheer. "That ain't no Lil Profit. That's a big fuckin' profit, yo!" Crazed cheers. "Dis shit keep pumping, we all be riding round on yachts, yo! Now, since dey got dat crypto cash, dese mu'fuckas got something special for y'all. Welcome to the stage, the legendary… legendary… LEG-EN-DARY: from Serenades n' Switchblades, mu'fuckas! Mu'fuckin' WHIZZ mu'fuckas!"

Graham looks away from Aart as Whizz strides on stage, wild long black locks falling to his shoulders from beneath his signature bowler hat. Whizz slides the pick down his guitar strings as he finger-fucks the frets. Lil Boaty bounces on the spot and mumble-raps about too many wild parties on too many big boats over a hard rock re-do of one of his hits, crowd bouncing with him. Graham looks back to where Aart and Elena were standing. They've gone.

"Baby, you're going to kill it," Alicia tells Guus as they leave the master bedroom. "Everyone is going to go crazy when they hear your speech."

"No," Guus says, lightly grasping her wrist as she walks down the corridor. "This way. Let's go up."

Wei turns another corner somewhere inside the yacht's maze of hallways & hears voices. He stops & draws his gun. He creeps slowly forward, hearing a man & woman laugh. Another corner. Wei sees a rapper whose name he doesn't remember vigorously fingering a girl he vaguely recognizes from some Netflix series as she leans against the wall, arms around the rapper's neck, laughing. They ignore Wei as he shields the gun from them & continues along the corridor.

Graham moves through the swaying crowd, scanning scores of familiar faces for Aart or Elena or anyone connected to Future Synergy Coin. He sees author Patrick Ward & his millennial boyfriend talking with writer Alan Churchill; ex-footballer Leo Woodward sharing a joke with Russian oligarch Ilyusha Smerdyakov.

"Is that Nguyen?" Elena asks Aart as they stand near the nyotaimori models at the side of the deck.

"No," Aart replies. "That guy's not even Asian."

"Really? I think for sure he is—"

"There!" Aart spots Nguyen but he's moving fast, heading to the stage.

Wei ascends steps to another corridor. He walks along it & turns a corner to another set of stairs leading to a door, which he opens to an outside deck.

Honey Badger's greatest hits medley draws to a close, Whizz thrashing the guitar around as Bom Cernoie turns the final "woooaaaahhh-ohhhhh-wooooooaaaaahhhh-oh-ohh-ohhh" into a spine-tingling final plaintive plea so arresting that Lil Boaty almost walks into Burt Gale's drum kit as he staggers back in awe. Two seconds of silence then all on deck erupt with crazed cheers. Nguyen bounds across the stage and embraces each member of the supergroup, bowing to the audience.

"I just wanna thank this man," Honey Badger says, as the cheering finally quietens, "for all that he and Future Synergy Coin have done for me." Big applause.

No, thank you, Nguyen mouths off-mic, smiling proudly.

"And I just wanna say," says Lil Boaty, "I'm Lil Boaty, but this is a big fucking boat, y'all!" Bigger applause. Cheers. "And you guys are fucking ballers for making this all happen right here."

"Thank you," Nguyen says, taking the mic.

Before he can speak, feedback squeals over the port and starboard-side speakers. A cough follows. Eyes slowly turn to Guus, standing at the top deck's railings.

"Ladies and gentlemen," Guus begins. "Bom Cernoie. Honey Badger. Lil Boaty. Lil Profit. Burt Gale. Tickbag. I want to thank each of you for being a part of what is for us at Future Synergy Coin a very special night." Clapping. Cheering. "And, if I may bother you for a moment of your time, I'd like to speak to you a little a bit about why this is so special. And why everything about what Future Synergy Coin is accomplishing is so essential."

Hush falls across the crowd as the biggest crypto geeks and YouTubers raise their phones to capture Guus' speech.

"I know the Bible is not the most fashionable book these days, but there is one story within it that I think is most apropos for our times. I am sure each and every one of you knows the story of David and Goliath. The little Jewish farmer boy who slayed the great hulking Philistine warrior. Just as the little David of cryptocurrencies launched in bedrooms and frat houses is preparing to slay the mighty Goliath of international banking."

Wei sees Alicia standing at Guus' side. Wei steps slowly across the top deck, Glock in his hands.

"I am sure that most of you think of David and Goliath as the classic underdog story. A little farmer boy armed only with a child's slingshot killing the giant with a meagre pebble. But I think that you and we are not fully understanding the meaning of this story. See, Goliath was a mighty warrior. That is correct. But David's slingshot was not a children's toy. In ancient warfare, the most feared and advanced of each army were its artillery – the archers, the slingshotters. What David picked up from the ground was not a pebble, but a hefty rock. A boulder."

As Graham listens, he remembers a TED Talk he watched from Malcolm Gladwell with almost the exact same content as Guus' speech.

"And when David placed that boulder in the pouch of his sling," Guus continues, "he swung that around his head, six or seven rotations per second—" Guus whips the mic around wildly to illustrate, then thrusts it forward, yanking back quick on the cord to return it to his hand, "—and when it was released, the boulder that struck that giant between the eyes was travelling at perhaps sixty meters per second. That's almost two hundred feet per second, for our metrically-challenged American friends. The slingshotters of Ancient Palestine were accurate enough to strike a bird mid-flight. Goliath stood not a chance. He was killed instantly. But Goliath's death was not due only to David's superior skill and weaponry. When Goliath entered the battlefield, the Bible tells us he lumbered out slowly. He staggered. He did not stride."

Wei freezes as Alicia's head turns slightly in his direction. She looks back over the crowd below and he continues advancing.

"Goliath was a head-and-shoulder taller than even the tallest of the Jewish and Philistine soldiers. He was suffering from a condition that we today call acromegaly, where a tumor develops on the pituitary gland and causes uncontrollable and never-ending release of growth hormones. We know now in our more enlightened times that acromegaly is the cause of gigantism. Acromegaly is what makes giants giant. But acromegaly also has many less beneficial side effects. The tumor which causes acromegaly puts pressure on other nerves and impairs vital bodily functions. Acromegaly causes near-sightedness, slowness of movement, and stupidity. Goliath was too near-sighted to see the boulder flung toward him, and he was too slow and stupid to have reacted even if he had. Just like David, we have not picked up a mere pebble to slay the Goliath of the international banking system. Blockchain is a boulder. A fucking asteroid of dinosaur-extinguishing dimensions. And that boulder is heading straight toward the forehead of the dinosaurs of international finance – institutions so overgrown, so bloated, so stupid, so slow to change, so near-sighted, to be assessed by any physician worth his doctorate as the very textbook example of acromegaly."

Plagiarism and pomposity, Graham thinks. *That's all any of this bullshit is.* A multi-billion dollar empire built on stolen ideas and overhyped proclamations of revolution based on nothing but greed and narcissism.

"When that boulder strikes, the giant will fall. Just as all empires of history have grown so bloated and near-sighted and slow and stupid as to not see the little David's with the boulders flung toward them. Just as this country grounded fighter jets on September 11th, 2001 for a training exercise as the boulders of two airplanes collided with the Goliaths of two twin towers and brought an end to the American Century. Just as the near-sightedness of the British Goliath before it fell to the boulders flung at it from its colonies. Just as the mighty Goliath of the French Maginot Line was powerless when the boulder of German blitzkrieg hit the soft spot of France's Belgian border. Just as the American Goliath of B52 bombers and Agent Orange crumbled to the boulders flung by Vietcong guerrilla warfare, too near-sighted and acromegaly-ridden to realise the Vietnamese simply wanted independence from the French colonisers and communism was no more than a means to an end."

"What the fuck," Nguyen whispers off-mic.

"My point in all this is David was not an underdog. We are not the underdogs. The acromegaly-ridden Goliaths of international finance are the underdogs. The future is now. The future is us. The future is—"

"YOU FUCKING WHORE!!"

Guus stops speaking, wrapping the mic cord around his legs as he turns to face Wei.

Alicia gasps as Wei waves the gun at her, ranting.

"Fucking bitch! This is for my dad and for Justin and for every other—"

BANG.

Wei's finger bumps the trigger too hard as he walks toward her.

Alicia screams.

Guus falls from the deck's railings.

"Fucking hell!" Graham says, fumbling to open his phone's camera app. He rushes across the deck towards the stairs at the back of it, through a crowd stampeding in the opposite direction. The security guards open fire from the bow and the deck becomes pure pandemonium, screaming, running in all directions, nyotaimori models rolling off tables, four-star sushi falling from their naked bodies as they take cover beneath their tables, others diving under after them, seeking cover wherever it exists. Graham keeps moving forward, to the stairs, some of the security team rushing inside, others gathering over the nyotaimori model & table Guus crashed onto & through.

"Guus!" Nguyen shouts, sprinting through the crowd to the stairs.

Graham turns the camera toward him, tracking Nguyen as he races up the steps.

Alicia runs at Wei as he moves toward her. He fires another shot into the air as she collides with him. She claws his face with her nails, throws a knee toward his balls, grasps his arm. Wei's arm breaks free & he smashes the butt of the gun into her nose. She falls.

"Fucking die, whore!"

Alicia's eyes close. Gunshots.

She opens them. Wei stares across the yacht.

Screaming below. More shots.

Wei drops to a crouch, out of view of the fast-advancing security team on the lower deck.

Alicia lunges at him, onto his back, wrapping her arm around his throat.

"Get the fuck off me, bitch!"

Wei falls back, Alicia hitting the floor, tensing her forearm as she struggles to choke him out.

Wei elbows her stomach. She loses her grip.

He spins to face her. She spits in his face.

"Fuck!"

He wipes his eyes with his left hand. She bites his gun-holding right hand.

He drops the gun. Punches her with his left, then the right.

Alicia tastes blood.

Wei's hands grasp her throat. He squeezes hard. He roars. Primeval hatred. Both thumbs squash her larynx, almost tearing through the skin.

She cannot breathe. Becoming light-headed.

Guus. Wei. His father. Takahiro. Malaysia. Her mother, grandmother, sister.

Images. Her life. Ending.

It stops.

She rolls onto her stomach, Wei's weight lifted off her. She clutches her throat, sucking whatever air she can into her lungs. She looks across the deck at his gun. Onto her knees. Hears choking. Turns. Wei being dragged backwards to the door, being dragged inside, one of the security team pulling on a chain wrapped around Wei's throat, a second security guy holding the door open.

Aart & Elena are already standing there when Nguyen reaches Guus.

"What the fuck are you doing here?!" Nguyen looks from Aart to the upper deck, source of the first gunshots. "Did you fucking do this?!"

"I—"

"You motherfucker!" Nguyen snarls. Then he drops to his knees, smoothing Guus' hair as he lies atop the twitching nyotaimori model.

Guus' eyes open. "What… the fuck just happened…"

Darren the screenwriter stumbles across the area at the top of the stairs clutching his stomach, his throat swelling up, stomach somersaulting. As he reaches Nguyen & Guus & the crushed nyotaimori model, a torrent of salmon & rice & wine & stuffed acorn squash & stomach acid erupts from his mouth.

After the After-Party.

This is incredible, the Tech Ed replies in the New York Times Slack Channel.

Graham turns from West 23rd Street to Fifth Avenue, still trying to hail a cab.

How fast can you get something written? the Tech Ed's next message asks.

New York City

Aart & Elena ride the A train back to 103 Street Station in silence. Emerging from the subway, Aart holds his hand out to Elena. She ignores him, stuffing her hands into the pockets of her leather jacket.

"What are you going to do now?" Elena asks as they wait for the hostel's elevator.

"Sleep."

They enter the elevator. Aart watches her mouth slowly open, her tongue touch the top of the lower lip. She speaks as her floor approaches: "Aart… good luck. I hope you get your money back."

She exits the elevator. He opens his mouth to speak as the doors close. They ping open again for the floor above. He enters his dorm to the sound of heavy snoring. His phone lights the path to his bunk. He climbs the ladder, hears the person beneath him stir. Aart lies on top of his sheets and stares at the ceiling. He stares until the room slowly lightens at dawn.

CRYPTO CHAOS IN NYC: Bullets & Bloodshed in Finance's New Wild West

New York Blockchain Week was supposed to celebrate cryptocurrency's transition from rebellious outsider to mainstream financial asset. Instead it proved the truism that all revolutions eventually descend into bloodshed.

By Graham Jones

June 9, 2018. Updated 10:20am ET.

NEW YORK – The first shots of the blockchain revolution rang out in the bathroom of a New York City nightclub. Three days later, cryptocurrency's attempted takeover of New York City erupted into all-out warfare on the Hudson River.

The extravagant party aboard a superyacht moored at Chelsea Piers Marina always seemed likely to end New York's first Blockchain Week with a bang. But as bullets flew over the heads of terrified revelers in the early hours of Saturday morning, there were almost as many bangs as host Future Synergy Coin has made bucks.

"It was a scam from the start," said Aart Janssen, one of three students from the University of Groningen in the Netherlands who created Future Synergy Coin. Together with co-founders Dung Nguyen and Guus van Hooijdink, Janssen dreamed of yacht-purchasing wealth as he watched hip-hop music videos from the couch of the trio's shared fraternity house.

The entrepreneurial students were more successful than they could possibly have anticipated. Within a year of Future Synergy Coin's creation, their dream had become a multi-billion dollar reality. By allocating 25 percent of the project's coins to each of its three creators, Janssen and his fraternity brothers had amassed personal fortunes of hundreds of millions of dollars.

But Janssen's dream-come-true soon became a nightmare. As he attempted to exchange some of his personal tokens for a more stable currency during one of this volatile market's frequent downturns, Janssen discovered that his entire fortune had disappeared.

Janssen booked a flight to Vietnam to speak with co-creator Nguyen about the hundreds of millions of dollars he was no longer able to access. The violent conclusion to Janssen's brief stay in Hanoi convinced him that his co-founders had deliberately exorcised him from Future Synergy Coin's success.

Are you a New York Times subscriber?

Continue reading this article by logging in or creating an account.

CONTINUE

Independent journalism matters.
View our subscription options to support us in our work.

24. DOXX'D.

;%:ERR;%;%:

</.>.

Giovanni's elbows touch those of the passengers at either side of him as he grips the middle seat's armrests. He wants to scream as the plane hurtles over tarmac, hundreds of kmph, the surge so much more intense than he expected. The plane tilts upward, the rolling runway out the window to his right falling, the airport and its surroundings getting smaller. White clouds of water vapor seep from overhead baggage compartments. *What the fuck?! Is that normal?!* Landing gear retracts with a mechanical whir. Giovanni leans into the aisle to see flight attendants at the front, facing the passengers, faces bored with the monotony of another standard take-off. *If they don't panic, then it's normal.* Giovanni's never flown before. He left Italy a few times, but always close enough to the center of Central Europe to travel by car or bus. His heart beats hard & fast. All sound is submerged by changes in altitude & air pressure. The middle-aged woman in a sari to his right clasps both hands before her face & bows her head slightly. *Can you not fucking do that?* Giovanni wants to shout at her. *This is the safest way to travel,* he tries to convince himself. *Hurtling thousands of meters above the ground in a gigantic metal husk.* The plane dips & twists through the sky, heading ever upward. The orange seatbelt sign blinks off. Giovanni hits the button to call a stewardess & asks for a straight whiskey. He orders another soon after. The alcohol calms his nerves but he desperately craves a cigarette. He never used to smoke – an occasional cigarette with drinks at Santino's, nothing regular – but since BitBucks imploded he's smoked two packs a day. Trapped within the terrifying physics-defying aeroplane, he's brutally aware of how nicotine-dependent he's become.

The terminal in Delhi doesn't look dissimilar to the one in Milan, save for brown people now being in the majority instead of white. He follows signs guiding him to domestic transfers, joins a long line, shows his passport, smokes, wanders shops, smokes, sits, smokes, thinks, smokes, boards another plane, hurtles back into the air, panics as turbulence rattles the cabin, lands in Jaipur, gets a tourist visa stamp at Customs, waits for his bags, then exits into Departures and sees a stout Indian man with a thick black moustache in a white shirt and suit pants holding up a sign that says 'Bryan Gale' – the fake name he chose to be picked up under.

"How was your flight, Sir?" the Indian guy asks as he drives, Giovanni too fucked-up & jet-lagged & focused on his cigarette to answer.

"So," a similarly mustachioed doctor says inside the hospital, "you want to be dead!"

Giovanni flinches; the doctor laughs.

"It's okay. I know. We have many people in situations similar to yourself. It is not a problem. My nurses will perform on you first a quick health check, so that we can give correct details when anybody will ask what state we found your body in. Things like height and weight are very important to record accurately to give you the most legitimate death certificate possible. So we will run a few tests, then we will issue your death certificate, and within maybe one hour from now, you will officially be a dead man. That sounds all to your liking, Sir?"

Giovanni nods. Nurses lead him through physical examinations that seem mostly pointless – holding something in front of each of his eyes and reading numbers to test his vision, sitting in a booth and tapping a button when he hears sounds in his left or right ear to test his hearing, getting weighed, his height measured, a strap wrapped around his arm for the taking of a blood sample.

"Blood type is a very important component of verifying your identity," the doctor says. "Please, just relax. And if needles are to you unpleasant, please look away."

Giovanni looks away as the nurse taps at a vein with a swab and then slides a needle into it, piercing his skin.

What's happening? and *Is this normal?* Giovanni tries to ask, the nurse pixelating then fading in front of him in the seconds before he loses consciousness.

24.01.

(Nguyen.)

"Have you fucking seen this shit?!" Nguyen says, smashing fingers at his phone screen, wishing it was still the 20th Century and he had a physical newspaper to slap down dramatically on the desk.

Guus stands in the center of the rapidly-assembling Future Synergy Coin Global Headquarters on a tree-lined street in sunny Palo Alto, California, smoking a joint. Nguyen hands Guus his phone and accepts the joint in return. All around them, workmen wheel in equipment and furniture, electricians fit overhead lights, carpenters smooth desks, and painters decorate walls. Guus smiles, slowly scrolling through the article. He hands Nguyen's phone back. Nguyen takes two final big drags from the spliff and exchanges it.

"Yes, I read it this morning," Guus says. "Pretty incredible, no?"

"Pretty fucking fucked up! That fucking prick's screwed us! It's not our fault that stupid idiot can't take the first fucking steps towards keeping his stupid fucking money safe. The moron probably entered his private key over a public wifi network or some shit." Nguyen continues ranting, but sees Guus is paying no attention, instead lazily eyeing the organized chaos of their headquarters' quick construction. "And the asshole who wrote it did no research. Look, the third fucking paragraph, he writes that we were all in the frat together. I was never in the fucking frat, bro—"

"This is like in Wolf of Wall Street," Guus says, "when that journalist does that piece on Stratton-Oakmont, and the next day every wannabe Wall Street stockbroker wants to join their company."

Nguyen looks back at The New York Times article on his phone. "Have you actually fucking read this thing?! It says the whole thing is a scam. Was a scam from the start. No development, no product, no nothing, just a get rich quick scheme—"

"—which went from zero to four billion dollars in less than a year. With no development, no product, nothing."

Nguyen takes the spliff from Guus and walks outside to the parking lot to finish it. Standing between his & Guus' FSC-yellow Lamborghini Aventadors, he thinks of Aart. That bitter little prick, trying to fuck everything up for them. He should never have shown the snake motherfucker mercy in Hanoi. Should have let Tu Than & Nguoi Giet kill him. Tossed his body in Ho Tay lake to bloat and rot. Nguyen tosses the spliff end and gets into his Lamborghini Aventador then tears through Palo Alto's sun-kissed streets to the Hi-Tech Highs marijuana dispensary & picks up a half-ounce each of Twatter and Facekush. As he sits in the driver's seat of his Aventador rolling a joint, his phone vibrates. He stops rolling to answer it.

"Hello? Is this Dung Nguyen? I'm calling from the office of Alberto Firenze at Subterrania Productions—"

24.02.

(Alicia.)

"...and Olly Amsterdam wants to spend a week shadowing me to get into the part," Guus says as his knife slices through the romesco-encrusted lamb loin.

"That's amazing," Alicia says, gently swirling her wine glass, charred eggplant soca growing cold on the table in front of her. Olly Amsterdam. The name floats amid her Xanax & Santa Cruz Mountains Monte Bello Cabernet Sauvignon-induced high. Olly Amsterdam. "Who's Olly Amsterdam?"

"Insect Boy," Guus says. "From the Protectors of the Planet movies. You want to try this?"

He cuts her a piece of lamb and delicately lifts the fork to her mouth. She chews slowly, savouring it. He knocks his wine back. The sommelier reappears beside their table to pour him another glass. They've dined most days for however many weeks it's been in Silicon Valley at Michelin-starred restaurants. Alicia wonders how many are left to sample.

Guus is talking: Alberto Firenze, Olly Amsterdam, a Hollywood movie. Alicia drifts in & out of listening, eyeing diners at other tables, dolled-up white & Asian women with suit-wearing venture capitalists and other business and finance types, most middle-aged, almost all white. Guus is talking about how this will be the spark that sets the fire that etc., knife slicing through lightly-seared lamb flesh as he speaks.

<--->.

Giovanni has no idea how long he's been out; no idea where he is. His eyes open and his brain runs through all the unfamiliarity of the past day (or days): Genoa to Milan, Milan to Delhi, Delhi to Jaipur, Jaipur to the hospital; but none of it squares with what he sees in front of him. He tries to bring his hands to his eyes, to rub them, but he cannot move them; they're suspended above his head. He pulls hard; his hands are shackled to the ceiling. He looks at battered brick walls. This is not the pure-white tiling of the hospital he last remembers. He hears talking behind him. A moment later, two men appear in front of him, one black, one white.

"You woke up," the black man says with a Jamaican accent.

"Welcome to India," the white man says with a less distinct accent from somewhere in Eastern Europe. "Do you speak English?" the white man continues, before switching to Italian in an accent Giovanni instantly identifies as Croatian: "Or would you rather I speak to you in Italian?"

"What's happening?" Giovanni asks, in Italian.

"You're being faced with the consequences of your actions," the white Croat says. "I'll get the big man," the Croat tells the Jamaican in English.

The Jamaican gives Giovanni some English-language scene-setting exposition: "You a clever boy, Giovanni. It was very clever to come Jaipur to get you a death certificate. Disappear forever with all your stolen coins. But that's a lot of money that you planned on disappearing with. Problem is, that money never belonged to you. You was simply watching over it. And them people you was s'posed to watch over it for got eyes and ears everywhere. Them people been watching over you."

"I see our guest has arrived," a slightly-off British accent calls out.

Giovanni hears footsteps behind him. The man with the slightly-off British accent appears in front of him. Giovanni recognizes him: one of Future Synergy Coin's founders. Guus van Hooijdink.

24.03.

(Alicia.)

Alicia's eyes move to the reflection of Alessandro's eyes in the rear-view mirror as Guus shoves his hand beneath her dress and rubs at crotch, breathing heavy on her neck, Alessandro making no pretence of looking at the road as the Rolls Royce Phantom VIII rolls down California Avenue to I-280. Alicia's eyes close as Alessandro accelerates on the highway, Guus' mouth moving from her neck to her lips as the feel of his hand grows heavier, pushing her panties inside her with his fingers. The engine roars louder as Guus leans into her, pushing down against the leather seat, free hand slipping her dress straps from her shoulders.

"Don't," she says, moving her mouth from his, eyes opening to see Alessandro staring in the rear-view as the Rolls accelerates.

Her words do nothing to deter Guus so she kisses him, trying to keep him placated and prevent progression until they're home, alone in the master bedroom, away from Guus' live-in assistant Alessandro's impassive stare.

Guus' hands work Alicia's underwear deeper inside her as the car moves, she drifting away from thoughts of Alessandro, Xan & Cab Sav calm becoming her.

Guus' hand slips free & he almost falls from the seat as the Rolls makes a sharp turn off I-280 into Hillsborough, Alicia tilting her head back to see the grand Gilded Age mansions flash by the window half-illuminated.

Alessandro opens the back door on Guus' side upon their arrival, so that Alicia has to slide awkwardly across the seat and exit through his side, trailing behind as Alessandro asks Guus softly what his needs are & etc., her thoughts drifting away from what she hears and dissipating into nothingness as they walk across the white flagstones to the entrance.

Alessandro swears loudly in Italian as they enter: the chimp's on the curving central staircase, shattered picture frames carpeting the marble staircase leading up to him, the beast holding an original Warhol sketch in his hands, shrieking maniacally, as Rosa the maid cries helplessly in Spanish. Alessandro storms to the center of the entrance hall, throwing his arms out as he berates the animal in Italian. The chimp leaps from the staircase's bannister to a chandelier, half its glasswork yet to be repaired from the last time this happened.

"Raskolnikoff!" Guus shouts.

The chimp ceases tearing glass bulbs from the chandelier and drops, hanging from one arm by it as he stares at his master.

"Raskolnikoff! СТОП!"

Raskolnikoff the chimp releases the chandelier and drops to the floor, then slowly approaches Guus, head lowered in shame.

"How many times must I tell you?" Guus says in flowery 19thC Russian, stern but loving.

After a moment spent staring shamed at the marble floor, Raskolnikoff the chimp leaps into Guus' arms. Guus walks through the entrance hall, speaking softly to his chimpanzee, Alessandro and Rosa following, Alessandro admonishing Rosa in a mix of English and broken Spanish, leaving Alicia alone. She ascends the marble staircase and walks the corridor to the master bedroom. She sits at the dresser and takes the Xanax from a drawer. She finds a bottle of half-drunk Krug Grande Cuvee amid the bottles on the bar, places two triangular green pills upon her tongue and knocks them back with the flat champagne. She stands and steps slowly toward the bed as she selects a Gavin Chou song on her phone: Uncommon Emerald Flower. As the soft piano is joined by swelling strings, she rolls onto the four poster bed and closes her eyes. As Gavin Chou softly sings in Mandarin of summertime sparrows outside the window & memories of the girl he kissed beneath the summer rain, Alicia sinks into the bed & what she knows to be a dream, sinking through the bed, through the floor, floating above the first floor of the home, over the entrance hall, to Alessandro's room, where Guus' assistant is fellating Raskolnikoff the chimpanzee as Guus vigorously pumps Rosa's plump Mexican backside, she bent over the bed, the four of them naked. Gavin Chou's words narrate the scene as Uncommon Emerald Flower shifts to Sufferer of the Princess Disease: *You say my words defile you, and my actions make you break. / You say that I betray you, when you're not awake. / You say you saw me in your dreams, and my heart's one truth is fake…*

The room swirls slowly, Alicia sinking lower, passing through each of the four participants in the bizarre interspecies orgy, feeling their sensations, until the whole room blurs and shakes, four become one, and she's aware she's no longer dreaming, Guus is on top of her, rubbing her panties, fingers slipping past them, she not yet wet, kissing, hands grasping, he unbuckling, pausing to snort white powder from a silver tray laid upon the bed beside them, and Alicia sits up & accepts the platinum nosestraw, hoovers a line, strangeness of all accentuated, Gavin Chou's voice slowing, slipping out of sync with the music, as Guus guides himself inside her, enters with a push, she falls back, waves of intoxicating energy coursing from him through her, opening & closing her eyes slowly, and for one brief second, she sees Wei on top of her, but when her eyes open & close again, it's Guus, and

<...>.

Guus stands back and smiles at Giovanni. "It's okay. Please. Calm down. I believe you. You were hacked. Some bastard hacked into your exchange and stole all of the Future Synergy Coin tokens that were stored on it. And you have no idea who that hacker was, do you?"

"No, no, I swear, I don't, I know nothing, nothing—"

"So you have no access to any of our missing currency, and no idea where to find it, and that means that you are of absolutely no further use to us, correct?"

"I… fuck… I… I… I…"

"Yes, yes, you, you, you. You are as much use to us as a corpse as you are a living man, correct?"

"No… I… I…"

"Then you do know?"

"I… FUCK! I can help you! I will find this bastard that fucking stole your money." Giovanni is spluttering blood as his speech becomes more animated.

Guus steps back further, frowning at the flecks of blood that have spotted his white Armani dress shirt. "Giovanni, please. Control yourself. You are not making any sense. And you are making a mess of my fucking shirt. The way I see it, there are two possibilities: you are telling me the truth, and you know nothing, so your constant squealing and pleading that is beginning to cause me a fucking headache is all for nothing, and the most sensible thing to do would be to cut your fucking tongue out so that you'll maybe shut the fuck up."

Giovanni gasps, hyperventilating, trying to control his speech, falling into a negative rhapsody of high-pitched half-whistling.

"The second possibility is that you are lying. That you have stolen our money. That you are pulling an exit scam."

"I… no! Fuck no! I swear! I swear!"

"You swear a lot, Giovanni, and it is almost as irritating as your squealing. Now, if you have been lying to us up to this point, I would have no reason whatsoever to trust anything you may say to me from this point forward. And I believe that it is Proverbs 10:31 where The Bible tells us that the tongue of the righteous man brings forth wisdom, and the tongue of the perverse is best removed."

"I… I... please… please…"

Guus steps toward Giovanni. "And since this shirt is already ruined, I may as well proceed to the next step in our inquiry."

Giovanni's mouth opens & closes rapidly as Guus selects a Wüsthof meat saw from the metal cutting implements laid upon a wooden table.

"…please… don't… please…"

Giovanni's breaths grow sharper & shallower as Guus touches the meat saw to the lower right side of Giovanni's face. He then drags the saw over flesh & bone, Giovanni screaming as it slices with ease through face & jaw & gum, severing cranial nerves, blood gushing out in thick rivulets. Hrvko the Croat dry-heaves and turns away as the Jamaican registers his disgust with a low: "…oh man…"

Guus turns to them, holding the perfectly-sliced lower half of Giovanni's upper jaw in one hand & the meat saw in the other, laughing: "What?! Come on, boys! The fun is just getting started!"

"…hhhease… hhhease…" Giovanni splutters, bloody spraying the back of Guus' shirt & neck.

Guus places the blood-smeared Wüsthof meat saw back upon the table & selects a Yoshihiro Shiroko sushi knife.

"…hhhease… hhhease…"

Guus grasps Giovanni's slippery blood-slickened tongue, Giovanni ineffectively trying to manoeuvre it away, to impossibly clasp his dissected jaw closed, until Guus holds Giovanni's head steady enough to slice the sushi knife through the tongue in one fluid thrust, & Giovanni's noises become a gargling of viscous red bodily fluid.

24.04.

(Nguyen.)

Nguyen stands and sweats and surveys the desert stretching endlessly over the horizon, trying to picture what will soon be erected here. The only building is the metal shed behind him, burly Latin American guards strapped with assault weapons pacing across the sand in front of it.

"It looks like another world to our own," Jack McAvoy says. "Like you're the first human to set foot on Mars before the colonies are built. But the colony will be built, Sir. And it will be glorious. Our blockchain Las Vegas. Cryptopia. You and Future Synergy Coin providing the casino chips to power it all."

"Neat," is all Nguyen can think to say. He lifts his phone to take a picture, sees the time is 3.35pm. "I need to get back to the office. I've had those idiots working around the clock on getting the mainnet ready. We're supposed to be going live in a week."

"I understand," Jack McAvoy says, placing a hand on Nguyen's shoulder. "You're a busy man. You have much to accomplish. Sir, I admire that. That's why I choose you out of all the thousands of projects and coins in existence. But before you leave, please, step inside Casa McAvoy for uno momento."

McAvoy keeps his arm on Nguyen's shoulder as he guides him back across the sand, past the guards and the helicopter, into the giant metal shed. From the outside, it looks like an airplane hangar. Inside, Nguyen's led into a grand Weimar Berlin banqueting hall, beautiful women & girls of various ethnicities & ages staring at their phones on long red leather sofas or at tables. Each raises their eyes and smiles as they enter.

"Would you care for a drink, Sir?" McAvoy says, guiding Nguyen to a seat at a table with three of the prettiest of his substantial harem. "A cocktail? Tea?"

"Tea," Nguyen says, transfixed by the big brown eyes of one of the girls staring across the table at him.

"Ayahuasca okay?"

"Sure."

"Madame barkeep!" McAvoy shouts across the lavish room, following it with a string of Spanish containing the words 'ayahuasca' and 'mi amigo.'

24.05.

(Olly Tulip.)

The chartered Gulfstream GIV from Hollywood's Bob Hope Airport touches down smoothly at Palo Alto Airport as Olly's manager Elizabeth Duvante confirms that Guus van Hooijdink is expecting them at The Sip + Splurge lounge at Hotel Ethereal in Downtown Palo Alto.

"Amazing," Olly says, rising from his seat and following Elizabeth to the exit as Olly's assistant Darnell gathers their bags.

Elizabeth guides Olly down the steps to an awaiting stretch limousine, Olly telling her excitedly how this is his first time this far north in California. Elizabeth encourages his enthusiasm as they await Darnell and the chauffeur to load the bags and enter the limousine, sharing Olly's excitement about what a leading role in a gritty Alberto Firenze movie may do for her client's future career prospects. But she's also cautious of the chaos her assistants' research has told her so often surrounds Guus van Hooijdink.

The drive to Downtown Palo Alto is a straight twenty-minute shot down Route 101, Olly telling Elizabeth what she already knows about Guus' rise to fortune: "…and they were just a bunch of university lads living together, and overnight they made this multi-billion-dollar empire, it's absolutely incredible, I am absolutely chuffed to bits to be meeting him…"

They leave the limousine with Darnell trailing behind them, concierge guiding them to the elevator, and the cocktail lounge, and a private room at the back of it, where Guus van Hooijdink sits with an impassive twentysomething Italian with slicked back black hair, looking like a particularly handsome extra from one of Firenze's mafia flicks. Elizabeth notices the bottle of Barrel Bourbon on the table, a third of it already drained, as Guus rises and shakes Olly's hand, tells him how happy he is that Insect Boy wants to play him in the Firenze movie, and Olly reciprocates the excitement, and Guus introduces his assistant, Alessandro (the impassive twentysomething Italian), and Guus asks Alessandro to please take care of

Elizabeth and Darnell and make sure they have whatever they want at the main bar as he and Olly talk in private.

"It's okay," Olly tells Elizabeth as she tries to argue.

Alessandro leads her and Darnell away, saying nothing as they walk to a table at the farthest side of the room, the few middle-aged white men in suits within the lounge on a weekday afternoon turning to look at them discreetly as they walk. Elizabeth looks back across the bar to the closed door of Guus' private booth, fearing what may be said inside.

24.06.

(Nguyen.)

All of Silicon Valley sprawls from the Pacific Ocean and the mountains to the San Francisco Bay beneath them as the helicopter moves from Nevada to California. Nguyen suddenly becomes conscious of the movement of the helicopter, and the movement of the girl on her knees in front of him, mouth sliding over his penis, and then McAvoy sitting across from him, smiling, a girl at either side of him: "You've come back to us."

"I… saw… God…" Nguyen says, trying to articulate what has happened, where he has been, while still uncertain of where he is now. He looks out the window at Silicon Valley's sprawl and the shimmering waters at either side of it.

"And what did He say to you?" McAvoy asks.

"She," Nguyen corrects him. Nguyen's silent, thoughts drifting across each other, not yet crystallizing into full grammatical utterances. Nguyen becomes more aware of his body, and what the girl on her knees is doing to it. It feels good. He thinks maybe it was her that spoke to him. "She told me to keep on the path I'm going… that I'm on the pathway to greatness… for all humanity…"

McAvoy smiles & nods & says no more as the helicopter swoops lower, Nguyen's eyes returning to the window, drifting away again beyond it, only returning to the helicopter's cabin once it has touched down in the parking lot outside the FSC building. Unsure of if he ejaculated or said goodbye to McAvoy or the brown-eyed God Girl, Nguyen enters the building, dozens of developers at computers, some sleeping, others nudging them to wake up as Nguyen walks into the room and Caroline the MD who is in love with him rushes across the office, panic wrought across her pretty face.

"There are two men here to see you," Caroline says, "I think they're government agents, maybe SEC, or FBI, CIA, shoot, I don't know, they wouldn't tell me, they said they had to speak to you about something important. I told them to wait in the conference room."

"Okay," Nguyen says, entirely unbothered, but aware he is no state to converse with them. "Could you make me some coffee?"

"Okay," Caroline says, rushing off to do as instructed as Nguyen avoids walking past the glass-walled conference room and takes a long route through the back labyrinth hallway beyond the main open area with all the developers and enters his own private office and locks the door. The room swells and shrinks as his mind adjusts to it. Nguyen hears the whispering from the God Girl and is transfixed by it, then returns to the reality of what must be done now. He must speak with these agents, whomever they are. Nguyen rummages through drawers, papers, trying to find some coke. He pulls a powder-smeared tray from inside a cabinet and scratches at it with a credit card, vaguely aware of some low-level drumbeat & the God Girl rhythmically whispering. The scraping of the tray produces a thick line that stretches across its entire length. Nguyen hacks the long line into sections, finds a $100 bill in his wallet, and snorts the first. The drumbeat grows louder. He hears the God Girl's voice again. The cocaine isn't balancing out the vestiges of the ayahuasca yet. He snorts a second line, rubs his nose. The drumming is louder. The God Girl says his name. He snorts a third.

"Nguyen! It's Caroline!"

He opens the door to her; she hands him his coffee. He thanks her, returns to the desk, and alternates between giant gulps of coffee and snorting of the final four lines carved out on the tray. Then he leaves his office, walks through the corridor, and enters the glass-walled conference room where two mean-looking All-American white guys in suits are sitting waiting for him. Introductions & questions pass in a blur. Nguyen is talking, explaining, possibly answering: "Aart is a fucking moron. Do you know how stupid you have to be to be the marketing director of a fucking billion-dollar blockchain company and you can't even access the fucking public Ethereum block explorer to track what happened to your fucking tokens? Fuck."

"Mr. Nguyen," one of the agents of whatever agency says.

"Please," Nguyen cuts him off. "Call me Dung. No, call me Nguyen. Everybody calls me Nguyen. Because when I was learning English at school, my teacher told me Dung means poop in English, and I didn't wanna make an English name, like, I thought about it, but nothing stuck, y'know? And when I got to the Netherlands, I needed one, and I wasn't gonna go around saying my name was Dung, and most of the professors didn't know shit about Vietnamese naming conventions anyway and called me Nguyen, so I just introduced myself to everybody as Nguyen, so that's what everyone calls me, so please, just call me Nguyen, not Mr. Nguyen, because Mr. Nguyen sounds fucking weird to me."

"Nguyen," the agent continues, "I am sure you are aware of a New York Times article that—"

"Yeah, that fucking rat bastard Aart tried to fuck us over going to the press about bullshit that isn't true and is complete fucking fabricated bullshit, like, he said that we were just doing this for the money, and it's bullshit, how many fucking developers do you see outside in that room?! If this was a scam, would we be renting this office space, in fucking Palo Alto, heart of Silicon Valley, next to Facebook and Google and the rest of the fucking big shots, do you know how much money this office costs?! And we are allocating every fucking cent our whitepaper promised for development to fucking development. Aart is just a bitter fucking asshole whose own fucking stupidity is the reason that he—"

"Nguyen," the second agent interrupts, "do you know who Wei Liu – or Liu Wei – is?"

"Wei Lui… Lui Wei… is that, like, some Hawaiian thing? Like a Hawaiian party or something?"

"That's a luau," the first agent says.

"Wei Lui," the second agent explains, "or Lui Wei, was a gentleman who attended your company's party aboard your yacht in New York City's Chelsea Piers Marina on the 8th of June of this year. I believe he made something of a scene onboard and many witnesses have corroborated his being there."

"Wei Lui Wei Lui Wei Lui Wei Lui Wei Lui," Nguyen repeats, trying to connect something to the name, suddenly stopping himself as the name echoes independently of his speech, becoming the wailing of police sirens, making him suddenly aware that these are two government agents, and why the fuck is he speaking to two government agents?! And he should definitely not be speaking to two government agents without a lawyer present, least of all whilst under the influence of cocaine and caffeine and ayahuasca, and he drifts away as the sirens subside, thinking this insight another gift from the God Girl.

<.\>.

The ice pack held within Giovanni's mouth with the roll of tape wrapped around his head keeps his severed tongue from bleeding out while the suspension of his enchained legs behind him keeps his body angled forward, preventing blood building up in his throat & drowning him. After the sushi knife sliced through each eyeball, he's unable to see what is happening, and the severed & savaged nerves running the length of his body overwhelm his brain with signals of total pain. His ears are his only untouched body part & Giovanni wishes, second only to a wish for death to finally come, that he could no longer listen.

"Whaddadafuckman?" the Jamaican says.

"IN THE ASS!!" Guus says, gorerificuly gleeful. "The penis goes into the ass! And you fuck yourself! And youfuckyourself, Giovanni, and you—"

Hrvko vomits again.

"Hey, Hrvko," Guus shouts, blood smeared across his face, heaviest over the lips, "you hungry? I can save you some!"

Hrvko's vomiting intensifies until he leaves the room.

"That's fucked up!" the Jamaican says definitively. "Kill this fucking rasclat already!"

"Uno momento," Guus says, ripping the tape from around Giovanni's head, letting the ice pack fall to the stained concrete floor, blood deluging out after it. Guus stuffs the severed penis into the donor's own mouth & snaps Giovanni's neck back, then pulls at the chains to drop the legs so that his posture shifts a full 180, & Giovanni swallows it.

The Jamaican draws his gun: "Kill this fuckin' bumboclaat! The fuck, mon!"

"As you wish," Guus says, holding Giovanni's head back by the exposed teeth of the remaining upper half of his jaw. A swift slash across the throat with the sushi knife, slicing through the larynx. Guus releases Giovanni's head. It drops forward. Unsure of if he's dead yet, Guus rams the sushi knife's blade into the back of Giovanni's skull.

24.07.

(Olly Tulip.)

"Go slowly," Guus tells the Uber driver. "They won't let us smoke on the helicopter."

Olly feels his mouth open in shock as Guus takes a lighter to a silver pipe: "Is that…"

Guus inhales deeply, closes his eyes, falls back against the seat.

Olly sees the driver watching the scene with interest in the rear-view.

Guus hands Olly the pipe. Olly holds it awkwardly in his mouth & brings the lighter to it, hands shaking. Then steady, calm, rush. The driver shouting something, Guus shouting something back, as Guus reaches to the floor at Olly's feet & picks the pipe up, leaving a burn hole on the carpeting. They talk with each other in anger, Guus flinging more money at the driver, the driver saying something about TMZ & getting a lot of money for a story like this, Guus saying who the fuck would believe you, words occurring away from Olly, world a dream, a beautiful dream, eyes opening & closing slowly as pure pleasure overcomes him, thoughts an empty rush of serotonin as the helicopter ascends above Oakland & swoops over the shimmering Bay & the Lamborghini tears through Palo Alto. When it stops at a red light, Olly's suddenly aware that he's able to think full thoughts again. He looks at Guus. "Was that crack?"

24.08.

(Alicia.)

Alicia hates the parties. Each of the many rooms at the Hillsborough mansion fills with smoke & chaos. Each party is more debauched & senseless than the last. It was the housewarming party when she first saw Guus fuck someone else. *No,* she corrects herself, walking across the upstairs landing, conversation echoing from the entrance hall below. At the housewarming party, she had opened the door to the gentleman's parlour to see Guus, Alessandro, others, standing in a circle, masturbating, a skinny girl lying in the parlour's center, a guy twice her size fucking her.

"Hey baby," some creep Google software engineer says as Alicia reaches the bottom of the staircase. "You ever been fucked by an Indian?"

Alicia knows the Indian software creep works for Google because he told her, at some previous party, when he'd made a similar attempt at wooing her. She ignores him & continues through the hall to the kitchen, recalling the actual first time she saw Guus fuck someone else.

"Hey, baby!" the Indian Google creep calls after. "They say once you've banged a man from Bangalore, you won't fuck American guys no more!"

The Indian Google creep's creep colleagues & acquaintances laugh. In the kitchen, a group of low-level Facebook employees are nailing lines of coke with a couple of suited hotshots from Sand Hill Road venture capital firms.

The third party was the first time she saw Guus fuck someone else. The third or the fourth. In the sitting room, in the servants' quarters. The door from there to the kitchen had been left ajar. She was – as she is now – pouring a glass of wine in the kitchen. She'd heard high-pitched squealing and glanced to her left. Through the gap in the doorway she saw Guus, wearing one of his white Armani dress shirts, hands clasped around the naked waist of some only half-seen other, thrusting. From where she stood, she couldn't tell if the recipient of his thrusts was male or female. She glugs wine & supposes it doesn't much matter.

"Wanna get nailed?" asks a smirking Sand Hill Road VC type.

She stares at his face without truly looking as the wine interacts with the Xanax & her mind contrasts it with the cold look Alessandro had given her through the gap at that third or fourth party before he slammed the door shut. "Sure," she says, taking a rolled-up banknote from the VC type's hand.

He leans in to whisper into her ear as she touches the tip of the banknote to the end of a white line: "I wasn't just talking about coca-cola, baby."

She lets the banknote drop to the floor as she rubs her nose & walks through large French doors to the poolside, mixed groups of males and females laughing & recording on their phones as Raskolnikoff staggers & downs beer from discarded bottles, the chimp tossing them across the lawn each time he finishes. It is a scene Alicia has seen play out too many times to take much interest in it. She continues past the pool, where buxom naked black girls frolic with pasty white software developers in the water, across flagstones to the pagoda in the Japanese peace garden. This is the life she always dreamed of, or so she tries to convince herself.

(Olly.)

The Warhol sketches & splattered Pollock canvases jump from the library's walls with vibrant colour as Olly Tulip stares at them, sucking smoke from the pipe end.

"No, nigga, not like that," the bearded white boy in the durag says, taking the pipe from Olly's hands. "You gotta dissolve that shit."

A black guy with bloodshot eyes grins with a mouth half full of gold teeth & giggles like Muttley off Wacky Races – "Shiiit, we poppin' Insect Boy's rock cherry!"

Olly smiles & imitates the bloodshot eyes guy's giggle. Durag guy hands him the pipe back, shouting: "Now! Now! Hit it! Hit it! Hit it!"

Olly sucks & coughs, mind thrown like paint across the walls' Jackson Pollock paintings, durag guy's throaty snicker layered over bloodshot eyes guy's Muttley giggle, neither real, nothing corporeal, floating like the wild sax jazz Peter Brötzmann's playing in front of stoned Silicon Valley dev types on chaise lounges at the other end of the room. Olly's only thought is how fucking good this feels, the massaging hands of one of the Oakland crew's bitches upon his shoulders & her soft whispers of "That feel good, baby?" heightening Olly's ecstasy.

"I told ya, nigga," the bearded white durag guy's saying, followed by streams of slang and sentences Olly doesn't quite comprehend, "I ain't purping about nuttin', nigga! In'rnational Bou-lay-vard is the fucking Hollywood of international sex trafficking, yadada? The Silicon Valley of teenaged titties, nigga, and I don't purp, nigga, ya boy never puprpin', nigga, never."

Brötzmann's manic sax becomes him, Olly staring without thought at the gruff bearded German sectagenarian saxophonist as the heavily manicured hands massage his shoulders & he sinks back deeper into the chaise lounge, barely aware of the durag guy standing, or durag guy's shouting, gesticulating, bloodshot eyes guy standing, clutching a bottle, until the massaging stops, and the sweet crack rush fades.

"—this nigga my nigga, nigga!" the bloodshot eyes guys shouting, at some tubby white software developer, another black guy behind the white guy, imploring him – "Don't!"

"You might be okay with his use of racial slurs, but others are not," tubby white software guy says.

Olly's eyes roll over the room. More of the Oakland boys gather behind the white tubby software developer and his leaner black boyfriend.

"I was at Freemont High with this nigga," the bloodshot eyes guy's saying. "He got a nigga pass."

"Whatever he or you want to say to each other is one thing," the tubby software guy continues, "but when you start rattling off racial slurs loud enough for others to hear you, then it becomes unacceptable. Unacceptable."

"Nigga, you steppin' to me in front of my niggas is unaccep'ble, yaddada?" white durag guy snarls.

Emboldened by Heineken, the tubby software guy doesn't back down, even as his boyfriend pulls at his arm.

Talk quickly becomes action. A bottle smashes over the tubby guy's head. The Oakland guys set upon both, a cacophony of fists & kicks & hollering as Brötzmann's sax playing grows more frantic, drowning out shouts & screams, soundtracking a symphony of sudden violence.

I have to do something, Olly thinks, staring wide-eyed at the carnage, feeling crack's warm high completely leave him. He's no longer Olly Tulip, mild-mannered movie actor, but Insect Boy, world-saving superhero. He leaps from the sofa to an antique Venetian coffee table & flies into the brawling mass with what he imagines as a spinning roundhouse kick. His foot trails behind him, striking the girl who'd been massaging his shoulders in the jaw, before he hits heavy oak flooring, winding himself, before the boots & kicks of the crazed Oakland crew descend upon him & his ribs & face & limbs.

Somewhere amid his pain & squeals, Olly hears the click-clack of a shotgun being racked, then a blast that causes the pummeling to cease. Olly struggles to his knees, coughing blood. The Oakland crew around him stare to the door to the library, Brötzmann's wild sax continuing unaffected. Guus stands brandishing the shotgun, screaming something about 'decorum' and 'guests in this house.' The Oakland crews' heads drop, apologies are mumbled. Olly scans the room to see if anything was hit & sees a smouldering hole blasted through a paint-splattered Pollock canvas. Blood from the tubby software guy's head similarly splatters the soft magnolia fabric of the chaise lounge.

(Alicia.)

Water trickles gently over rock into the koi pond as Alicia sits on the edge of the pagoda, smoking, sipping wine, the two tech guys on the bench a few meters away occasionally chancing glances as they talk.

"Jobs. Gates. Page. Brin. Bezos."

"That's a basic bitch Tech Rushmore. And it's one too many."

"How many's a Rushmore? I thought it was top five?"

"Mount Rushmore is four. Four presidents. It's more selective than a top five."

"Then cut Page or Brin. Whichever is least responsible for making Google. No – scratch it. Go corporate. Corporate logos carved in rock. Microsoft, Google, Apple, Amazon."

"That's still a basic bitch Tech Rushmore."

"Those are the ones, dude."

"Where's Zuckerberg?"

"Oh shoot… well, you want Internet Age Rushmore? It's gotta have Facebook."

"I was joking, you cretin. Why don't you put Tom from Myspace on there?"

"Then who've you got on your Tech Rushmore?"

The guy who's been asked pauses to smoke the joint & ponder before answering & passing the joint: "Babbage. Gutenberg. Turing. Berners-Lee."

"That's such a hipster Rushmore."

"How is that a hipster Rushmore? It spans centuries. It has it all, it's got—"

As he justifies his choices, Alicia ponders the topic: her Rushmore. Guus. Takahiro. Liu Feng the factory owner. James the English teacher. Carved in rock, for all eternity. The sufferings of a flower.

"Who's even on the real one?"

"I don't know… Washington, Lincoln… Kennedy…"

"Kennedy! Holy moly…"

"No, it's older, right? Roosevelt!"

"Which Roosevelt?"

"Teddy."

"Yeah. And…"

"And?"

"Four. That's three."

"You know?"

"Of course I know."

"The other Roosevelt. Franklin."

"Rushmore's older than that. Holy guac, did you even do AP history class?"

"Jackson?"

"Jackson! Andrew Jackson?! He's, like, the worst fucking pre-Trump President."

"Hey," Alicia says to the pale stoned tech geeks, "could I smoke a little of that?"

(Olly.)

"He was already a pet," Guus is telling the Sand Hill Road venture capitalists & Facebook contingent in the kitchen, "some old Hollywood producer owned him and he died of a heart attack."

"So it's illegal to bring a new chimp to California from fucking Brazil or wherever," one of the Sand Hill Road VCs clarifies, as Guus leans to the kitchen island to hoover another line, "but if he's already in captivity here…"

"Yeah, that's what he just said," another VC says, taking the silver nose straw from Guus & hitting a line.

"Yeah, I fucking know, I'm making conversation, dick."

"Stupid fucking conversation," the other VC says, line finished.

He holds the straw out to Olly; Olly hesitates, then reminds himself of the sacred oath he's sworn to mirror Guus, to method act; the debt he owes De Niro, Brando, Stravinsky.

"Chimpanzees don't come from Brazil," one of the coke-emboldened Facebook geeks says.

"Yes they fucking do," the VC says. "Chimps come from the Amazon."

"You don't order pet chimps on fucking Amazon," the most wasted of the Facebook dweebs laughs.

"Not fucking Amazon," the VC snarls, "the fucking Amazon. The fucking rainforest."

"They don't come from the fucking rainforest either," says coke-emboldened Facebook geek. "They come from Africa."

"Raskolnikoff is neither Brazilian nor African," Guus says. "He's Russian."

"There are no fucking chimps in Russia either," the coke-blasted VC says.

"There's shitloads of chimps in Russia," says the wasted Facebook dweeb. "They used them for the space program."

"Yeah, captive fucking chimps—"

"And what's this fucking chimp if he's not fucking captive?" chimes in coke-emboldened FB geek. "He's not in the fucking rainforest or the savannah. He's captive."

"Russians sent chimps into space," says wasted FB dweeb.

"No they didn't," says coke-emboldened FB geek.

"They did," says wasted FB dweeb. "America, too."

"Yo, Insect Boy," the second VC smirks. "You gonna hit a line or just stand around listening to these idiots talk about monkeys all night?"

"Chimpanzees are not monkeys," says wasted FB dweeb.

"Exactly my point!" says coke-emboldened FB geek. "Russia didn't send chimps into space, and neither did America, and nor did France. They sent rhesus macaques."

Olly snorts a line & lifts his head from the kitchen island feeling rejuvenated, sharper, more alert.

"I bet you hit a lot of that shit on set with Bobby Maverick, huh?" the second VC smirks.

"Oh, no, man," Olly says, "Bobby is cool, really cool, he was wild once, but these days, he's just super cool, super chilled, so fucking cool…"

"There's the fucking monkey we've been talking about!" the first VC says, as Olly sees a furred hand clasp the silver nose straw.

"Hey, hey!" Guus says to Raskolnikoff, cradling the chimp in his arms. "Папа первый!"

Raskolnikoff's head droops as he pushes the straw into Guus' left nostril. Guus uses his free hand to move the straw to the right & leans down to the kitchen unit.

"So the monkey really is fucking Russian," laughs the first VC.

"He's not a monkey," says wasted FB dweeb.

"Now watch this," Guus says, passing Raskolnikoff the silver straw.

Guus leans toward the table so Raskolnikoff can reach the line. Both VCs pull their phones out to record a video, laughing, as Raskolnikoff imitates his master perfectly, holding the straw steady in his left nostril with one hand and pressing his right nostril closed with his right index finger. Raskolnikoff snorts the line, throws his head back, and goes, "hoooo, hooooooo, hoooooooooo, pant hooooooooooooo!", the VCs almost dropping their phones they're laughing so hard, and Raskolnikoff leaps from Guus' arms to the kitchen counter & frantically snorts the remaining lines, then grasps the mound of white powder, coke-emboldened FB geek protesting "That's my shit!", the VCs laughing harder, then "Fuck off, you little Russian monkey bastard!", and Raskolnikoff is screaming pure rage at coke-emboldened FB geek, and second VC manages to say through the laughing fit "You do not want to fight that fucking monkey, dude!", and Raskolnikoff is screaming, and all in the kitchen are staring & recording, a dozen phones pointed at Raskolnikoff from all directions, & Raskolnikoff leaps from the counter onto a blonde girl, she screaming, others a mix of coke-up laughing & panicked "ohmygod!"s, Olly staring at it all dumbfounded, as Raskolnikoff grips the blonde hair & thrusts, the girl screaming, throwing her head around, trying to get him off, as the chimp's erect penis prods her face & eyes, and Guus shouts: "Alessandro! ALEEEESSSAAAANDROOO!!"

And his Italian assistant rushes into the kitchen from wherever he was, & Guus points at the commotion and says simply: "Raskolnikoff."

And Alessandro sighs, mutters "vaffanculo," and steps towards the chaos, shouting at the chimp in a mixture of English & Italian.

And Guus grabs Olly's wrist and leads him from the kitchen to the entrance hall and through the enfilade.

"There is something that I would like to share with you," Guus says, leading Olly by the wrist through darkened rooms, "but I would like for you to be in the right mind first."

Guus opens a door to a descending staircase.

"Where are we going?" Olly says, insect sense tingling at the sudden shift in atmosphere.

Guus says nothing as he leads Olly down the stairs to a grand wine cellar, thousands of bottles racked all around them. Guus grabs a bottle of red, slams it down on a wooden table, picks up a corkscrew, & opens a drawer.

"Here," Guus says, sliding a small silver platter across the table towards Olly.

Olly looks at the tray & the neat white line racked upon it.

"More coke?" Olly asks.

"Better." Guus drops a silver nose straw next to the tray: "This is primo shit."

"I'm… kind of… already… high as shit…"

"I promise. You won't regret this." Guus pulls the cork out awkwardly from the wine bottle, red liquid splattering over the wooden tabletop.

"Alright, I guess one more won't make much difference," Olly says, leaning forward to snort the line of scopolamine.

(Alicia.)

"I'm Chinese-Malaysian."

"Okay," the tech geek says, "the Malaysian Rushmore then."

She thinks about it. She realises she doesn't care. "I don't know."

"Okay, then…"

"This is stupid," the other interjects. "This is a boring topic of conversation." He laughs, stoned.

Alicia smiles. She smokes the joint.

"What's the capital of Malaysia?" the first tech geek asks. "Kuala Lumpur?"

"Uh-huh."

"They have those two big towers there, right?"

"The Petronas Towers."

"Uh… yeah."

"Yeah."

"…cool…"

"So how long have you been here in America?" the other asks.

Groaning, growing closer; a figure stumbling through the bushes at the other end of the peace garden. All three stare across the koi pond toward it. The figure moves into the soft light of the moon and the lanterns at the koi pond's edge.

"Is that Insect Boy?" one of the tech geek asks.

Olly Tulip staggers to the koi pond's edge, stares at his reflection, shaking, seemingly about to vomit, then falls forward, body rigid, with a splash.

(Olly.)

Guus pulls out a wine bottle. The rack slowly rotates, opening a dark stone-walled room, steps beneath it. He follows Guus down them. A voice. Whimpering. As they get closer, it says kill me. Please kill me. Kill me. Just kill me. Kill me. And Olly follows Guus toward it, numb to all thought, any reaction. And when they reach it, the immense horror of it, the abject terror of the scene, the poor chained sod with sawn-off jaw…

The images dissipate in the dream. When Olly wakes, they're gone forever. He doesn't know what he saw. Doesn't know where he is. At all. Nothing of any of the past 24 hours comes to him, and then it does, in a torrent of half-remembered flashes. He briefly sees the face of the Chinese prisoner as he sits in an unknown place, panting, but it vanishes, never to be recalled again.

A woman sleeps beside him. She stirs as Olly pants. She sits up slowly. Olly recognises her, but it takes several minutes to realise from where: Guus introduced her, when they first came to the house. Alicia.

"What happened?" Olly asks as she opens her eyes.

(Alicia.)

"You fell in the pond," Alicia says sleepily. She brought him into the tea house & removed his wet clothes, apart from his boxers. Laid him out on the futon. Opened a bottle of sake and smoked the rest of the tech geeks' spliff and popped a Xanax and fell asleep beside him.

"There was a pond…" Olly Tulip doesn't sound it quite as a question; more an admission of a fact previously unknown to him. He absorbs the information then looks at Alicia, his eyes wide and innocent. "Did we…"

"No." She pauses, watching his soft face grow softer, calmer. "Do you want to?"

He frowns and looks away from her. She regrets the question. He stares at the shoji screen shielding the window, glowing with sunlight. She tries to guess what he's thinking: perhaps weighing up whatever friendship or loyalty has developed with Guus against a desire to become Guus, to truly method act. An astrological age seems to pass before he again looks at her.

(Olly.)

"Okay."

25. BLOCKCHAIN GODS.

Extract from Graham Jones, BLOCKCHAIN GODS (FletcherWilliams, 2019):

Every religion has its creation myth. The religion of cryptocurrency begins in January 2009 with the mining of the first block on the Bitcoin blockchain. With suitably biblical overtones, this first block was called the genesis block. There are now on average 144 blocks mined per day, with each yielding its miner 12.5 bitcoins. At the start of 2017, each bitcoin was worth less than $1000. By mid-December 2017, their value had soared close to $20,000. By mid-December 2018, this had collapsed to less than $4000. At the time of writing, it's back above $10,000, but the next twist in its trajectory is as much a mystery as Bitcoin's origin.

As with most religions, Bitcoin's creation myth is an enigma shrouded in speculation and metaphor. Nobody knows the true identity of its Creator: a man, woman, group, or alien lifeform who published a whitepaper outlining the concept of Bitcoin under the name Satoshi Nakamoto in October 2008. There has been constant speculation and repeated claims surrounding the identity of cryptocurrency's Creator. Some suspect Satoshi's early acolytes, computer scientist Hal Finney and software developer Gavin Andresen, who like Moses of the Old Testament communicated with the Creator and were charged with spreading His message to the world. A Newsweek article published in 2014 identified Japanese-American computer engineer Dorian Prentice Satoshi Nakamoto as The Creator. Dorian Nakamoto had an impressive resume of advanced systems and computer engineering work on classified U.S. government defense projects and at major financial firms such as Citibank. Dorian Nakamoto was also a libertarian, a political stance opposed to government regulation which aligns neatly with Bitcoin's ethos of a one world currency beyond any central bank or government's control. And – well – his name is Dorian Prentice *Satoshi Nakamoto.* But when confronted by reporters, Dorian Nakamoto claimed to have no knowledge of Bitcoin's creation. Few now believe Dorian Prentice Satoshi Nakamoto to be the One True Satoshi Nakamoto. Others have claimed to be The Creator but few have been convinced by their arguments. The mystery of The Creator endures.

Over time, all religions splinter into distinct sects and antagonist belief systems. There exists Mahayana, Theravada, and Vajrayana Buddhism; Vaishnavist, Shaivist, Shaktist, and Smartist Hinduism; Reform, Conservative, and Orthodox Judaism; Catholic, Protestant, and Orthodox Christianity; Sunni, Shia, and Kharijite Islam. And most of these major branches have splintered into further offshoots and subsects. Yet most claim to be the One True Interpretation of The Creator's intent.

In July 2017, disagreement among disciples of the Bitcoin faith over the sacred rules governing the Bitcoin blockchain led to a hard fork and the creation of a new form of Bitcoin: Bitcoin Cash. In November 2018, another schism occurred as Australian computer scientist Craig Steven Wright claimed he was the One True Satoshi Nakamoto and splintered Bitcoin Cash into another form of Bitcoin, inelegantly dubbed Bitcoin Cash Satoshi's Vision. Just as Christianity has supplanted traditional Pagan festivals with Easter and Christmas, both Bitcoin Cash and Bitcoin Cash Satoshi's Vision incorporated the existing status quo of the Bitcoin blockchain into their new religions, gifting followers of the old networks the new cryptocurrency tokens at a 1:1 ratio.

Great Prophets such as Jesus and Mohammed have forged new religions from updated stances on existing sacred texts. Many consider Russian-Canadian computer programming wunderkind Vitaik Buterin to be the Crypto Jesus to Satoshi's God. Just as Jesus was raised Jewish and overwrote Old Testament prohibitions on eating pork and shellfish, Vitalik Buterin's Ethereum is seen by its True Believers as the Blockchain New Testament: replacing Bitcoin's rigid focus on facilitating simple value transfers with complex smart contracts that allow more advanced use of blockchain and cryptocurrency technology.

And just as new religions such as Scientology are derided as cultish cash grabs based on the documented beliefs of their False Prophet founders, the third largest cryptocurrency XRP is seen by many cryptocurrency believers as an antithetical attempt to subvert all that is good and true in Satoshi Nakamoto's foundational whitepaper. XRP was created by San Francisco tech company Ripple Labs Inc. to provide banks and other financial institutions with a faster and more efficient way of processing payments. Critics point to the huge amount of the XRP cryptocurrency held by Ripple Labs Inc. as proof of their heretical intentions. Ripple releases batches of the XRP token to the market at regular intervals, generating huge sums for Ripple Labs to fund its operations. A Forbes article published in January 2018 claimed that XRP's success has made Ripple CEO Brad Garlinghouse and other executives multi-billionaires.

Token sales, or Initial Coin Offerings (ICOs), have allowed new cryptocurrencies to generate huge funds before development has even begun. The most successful of these ICOs was EOS, which generated over $4 billion through a year-long ICO. After the token sale was completed, the total value of EOS tokens rose even further, reaching an all-time high above $17 billion in April 2019. The value ascribed to these tokens compares favourably with the sums raised through Initial Public Offerings (IPOs) of shares in household name tech companies. Spotify raised $9.2 billion in the biggest tech IPO of 2018, while Uber's IPO in 2019 saw the sale of $8.1 billion worth of shares. Over 10 million trips are taken by Uber users every day, while Spotify has over 100 million paid users of its Premium service. In contrast, the most popular apps on the EOS blockchain have only around 6,000 users.

Many other religions and cryptocurrencies have risen and fallen in prominence since Bitcoin's genesis block, attracting varying masses of disciples and true believers. Some, such as Tezos and Nano, have attracted followers who believe that an ascetic focus on supreme technological superiority is the only path to crypto enlightenment. Disciples of Monero have an unyieldingly orthodox stance on privacy and decentralization. Others, such as IOTA and Stellar, have earned their followers' faith through touted partnerships with major companies. TRON, like Scientology, has risen to prominence with endorsements from American celebrities.

The line between a cult and a religion is difficult to define. Those who consider themselves truly enlightened after bingeing Richard Dawkins and Ricky Gervais videos on YouTube say that all religions are cults. Others point to lack of transparency in belief systems and a focus on profit generation as separating cults from true faiths. When a mass of followers die after drinking the Kool-Aid, most would agree the dead have been deceived by a cult.

Cryptocurrency is full of exposed scams akin to Kool-Aid drinking cults. Oyster Pearl was created by the pseudonymous Bruno Block. Its whitepaper claimed it would allow websites to generate revenue by users contributing computer resources instead of viewing advertisements. In January 2018, the total value of Oyster Pearl tokens was more than $120 million. In less than a year, this dropped to around $5 million. After the value of tokens made a brief return to levels above $20 million, it emerged that Bruno Block had built a vulnerability into the Oyster Pearl smart contract that allowed him to create millions of new tokens, sell them, and disappear forever into anonymity, leaving the price to collapse back into the nothingness from which it arose.

Some believe that every cryptocurrency from Bitcoin onward is nothing but a cultish scam designed to separate greedy fools from their real-world fiat currency. Others believe there is a distinction between genuine cryptocurrency projects and outright scams. Where any of the thousands of cryptocurrencies created over the last ten years fall on the line between scam and real project depends on who you ask. One cryptocurrency which has danced carefree across this line between crypto legitimacy and cultish fraud is Future Synergy Coin.

</extract.>

Genoa, Italy.

"Giovanni was the most brilliant student in class, always. We met when we was only eleven years old. The first year of *media* school – how you call it in English? Middle school?"

"Comprehensive," Natalia says. "Americans say middle school. British says comprehensive."

"Is right?"

"Yeah," Graham says. He's sitting opposite Paolo and Natalia in a red velvet and wood-clad Italian imitation of a classic British pub. Graham's phone sits on the table, recording the conversation.

"From the first time of comprehenza school, Giovanni was the best student," Paolo continues. "Giovanni was best at everything – matematica, lingua, scienza. We used to make websites, we both. Is funny, one time he hacked into my website. Is not special thing, just talking about football and pretty girls, but he change it to say that I am gay man and I am supporter from Roma, and I am fucking the Americano at the Colosseo. Is just funny children's thing. When it happen, I am fucking angry, you know? I spend much time to making the website. But now… is just funny. He always one of the best friends for me. And we come together from Napoli to Genova, we both studying Computer Scienza, and he telling me about these cryptocurrency, I must buy, will be worth very much money, and he say we make even more making the cryptocurrency exchange. But I know nothing, you know? Giovanni know everything. He make the website for the cryptocurrency exchange, and everything changing."

"How so?"

"He becoming more distance, no more interest in *calcio* – football; no more interest in girls…"

"Giovanni was very fun to be around," Natalia says, her hand sliding over Paolo's on top of the table as he trails off. "But in year two of the university, he changed. He stopped coming to class, or coming here or another bar for hanging out with us."

"He was making so much money," Paolo says, staring at Graham with sudden passion. "So much money. Is completely crazy how much. But is too much, you know? The exchange is just him, in his room, some servers. He at his computer, twenty-four hours of the day. And then one day, I walk in, and he talk me he been hacked. I say, Giovanni, how much is there stolen? And he tell me one half billion in dollars. So fucking crazy, no? For him, alone in this room, to be having so much money. And then he lose it. And I think many people must very angry from this. Very angry. I say to him, I say, Giovanni, a man will kill you for one thousand euro. For half of one billion…"

"What you think happened to him?" Melina asks when Graham meets her and Luis & Sarah at a cafe on the harbour.

"I don't know," Graham says, staring at the yachts in the harbour, thinking of the Future Synergy Coin yacht party in New York, Lui Wei the Chinese gunman; the chaos that follows in Guus van Hooijdink & Dung Nguyen's wake. The year since New York Blockchain Week has been good to Graham. Sarah Maureen Carmella Jones was born on the 4th of July 2018, her mother induced into labour amid the stress of an England vs Colombia World Cup match. Her birth weight of 9.7lbs beautifully mirrored the £972 of cryptocurrency Graham had left after the market's steep decline. Off the back of his work for The New York Times, Graham landed regular writing jobs with the Liverpool Echo and occasional freelance bits with bigger publications, including a piece on the plight of Syrian refugees in Berlin published by The Guardian. Then news broke that Alberto Firenze was directing a movie on the rise of Future Synergy Coin. Graham hastily sent proposals for a book on the true story behind the movie to every major publisher in London and New York. FletcherWilliams responded with an offer that included a £250,000 advance. A deposit was put down on a plush new house in the upper middle-class Liverpool suburb of Gateacre. He bought an Audi. And Liverpool won their 6th European title after losing the first leg of the semi-final 3-0 to Barcelona. On the same day he learned of the FletcherWilliams book deal, he watched Liverpool thrash Barca 4-0 in the semi-final return leg with his Dad & Toby & Panzer & Nev at McCooley's. Luis stayed with his grandmother for the night to watch it. When Graham got home, Sarah was asleep upstairs in her crib. One thing led to another with Melina on the sofa and she is now pregnant with their third child. They've decided to keep the Liverpool FC-inspired naming tradition of the Jones family alive & name their next-born child in honour of semi-final goalscoring hero Divock Origi: Oliver if it's a boy & Olivia if it's a girl.

Extract from BLOCKCHAIN GODS:

Future Synergy Coin's ascent stalled after Giovanni Cuomo's tweet announcing the BitBucks hack. This sudden loss of altitude turned out to be nothing but turbulence and FSC was soon soaring to new highs, but not without severe injury to some of those onboard with the project.

Choi Sung Jae, a 45 year-old local government worker from Incheon, South Korea, was sentenced to four years in prison after severely assaulting a teenage motel clerk. The clerk had reportedly secretly filmed Choi having extramarital relations with a prostitute at the motel and attempted to blackmail him with the footage. Choi testified in court that he had invested in Future Synergy Coin a week prior to the BitBucks hack in an attempt to raise the funds to pay off the clerk. The funds intended for paying off the blackmail were lost to the hack. Choi returned to the motel and beat the clerk so badly he needed facial reconstruction surgery.

Larry Sullivan, a 52 year-old hot tub salesman from Massachusetts, USA, committed suicide after losing $25,000 in the BitBucks hack. His 14 year-old nephew Steven posted an emotive account of the Sullivan family's emotional turmoil following the suicide to the /r/cryptocurrency subforum on Reddit.

During our conversation at Santino's Pub in Genoa, Paolo Matteo and Natalia Ottonello told me in harrowing detail of the death threats and abuse they received after their social media accounts were posted to the notorious internet forum 4chan. But the effect of these threats pale in comparison to the pain Paolo feels over the disappearance of his friend.

"Giovanni was my best friend since middle school," Paolo told me, his expression pained. "I just wish he could be there at my and Natalia's wedding. I want him to be my best man."

</extract.>

Liverpool, England.

"How'd it go?" Bill says, opening the door to Graham and Melina.

"Everything's great," Graham says.

"It's a girl!" Melina adds.

Bill hugs her as Margaret rushes out to the hallway, thrilled, hugging & kissing her son and pregnant daughter-in-law.

"We're gonna call her Olivia," Graham says, sitting next to Melina on the sofa, "after Origi."

Talk between father and son quickly turns to football, both alive with excitement at Liverpool's run so far, five points above Man City at the top of the league with maximum points from their first five matches.

"Not five minutes you've spent talking about your new granddaughter before you start banging on about the bloody football," Margaret says.

"How are Everton getting on?" Graham asks, smiling wryly.

"Oh, give over!"

Margaret steers talk back to Melina's growing baby bump and how the third-time mother-to-be is feeling. Graham feels his phone vibrate. An unknown number. He stands and walks across the room as he answers it.

"Yo, Graham? This is Nguyen. I heard you're writing a book about us."

Graham slides open the door to his parents' patio.

"How was the pasta in Italy?"

"It were grand," Graham says, stepping outside and sliding the door closed.

"How were the prawns at Ostaietta?"

"They were good. You been there?"

"No."

Fuck. This creepy little shit, Graham thinks, *trying to intimidate me with specifics of what I ordered in a fucking restaurant. He probably wants me to ask him how he knows. Well, I don't give a shit.* "How are you doing, Nguyen? Y'alright?"

"I'm good. Better for finally speaking to you. You know, it isn't nice to talk about people behind their backs."

"Yeah, you're right, it isn't. That's why I've sent so many emails asking to interview you."

"Well… I guess this is our interview then."

"Right. Grand. Well… how's the mainnet launch coming along?"

"You didn't send any emails."

Graham smirks. *Idiot.* "I did, mate. Shitloads. To your office in Palo Alto."

"Asking to interview me?"

"Yeah. Well, not *you* specifically—"

"Guus."

"Yeah."

"Yeah, well… I'm the lead developer. Co-founder. Future Synergy Coin is my project. From the ICO onwards. Anything you want to know about it—"

"Is there some tension between you and Guus?"

"I'm asking the fucking questions, *mate.*"

"Are ya? Thought this was an interview."

"It's a conversation. You find what you were looking for in Genoa?"

"I did, yeah. Got a whole chapter out of it."

"I know. I've seen it."

"This is on the record, is it?"

"What do you mean? Am I recording you?"

You daft bastard. "No. I mean, am I alright to report all the details of what you're telling me right now in the book I'm writing?"

"Those two fuckwits you talked to, they're nobodies. Giovanni Cuomo was a nobody."

"Was?"

"Was. Is. Whatever. Wherever the fuck he is, he's not important. Some two-bit fucking exchange, some footnote—"

"So, hold on, let me get this straight: you're saying you've hacked my Google Drive, or emails, or hard drive, and you've read what I've written for the book, yeah?"

"I didn't say that."

"You heavily implied it."

"Listen, you little fuck. You came at us after New York, and what happened? We got a fucking movie deal. Come at us. Do your fucking worst, you low-class Liverpool Echo fucking hack. Enjoy selling your book off the back of what we've built, make your money, but you put one word in there that's not verifiable—"

"Like this conversation?"

"This fucking conversation is between me and you, dickhead."

"You said it were on the record."

"*You're* on the record. You're on *my* record."

"What, with Giovanni Cuomo? And Liu Wei?"

"You… …. …. on the record, like a figure of speech, right? Like, this is allowed to be reported on? Are you recording this? Because it's illegal in the United States of America to record a conversation without both parties' knowledge."

"That depends on which state you're in, mate."

"Are you recording me?"

"I might be." Graham winces after saying it, stops pacing about the patio. *Stupid thing to say.*

"Are you fucking recording me?"

"No, I'm not, no. You just fucking called me, mate. I'm at my parents' house. How am I gonna be recording you?! You think I've got all calls set to auto-record or what?"

"Well then… this is between the two of us? Off the record?"

"Yeah. Absolutely. Unless you want—"

"So you better be fucking careful, is what I'm telling you."

Graham looks in through the glass doors to the living room. Melina is staring at him as the others watch TV, Sarah in her lap. "Careful about what?"

"Careful of who you're fucking with. If you try and fuck us, then we're going to fuck you. We're going to turn you into fucking mincemeat. Literally."

"Like you did Giovanni?"

"Listen here, you fuck. That idiot lost half a billion dollars of other idiots' money who don't know better than to not store their coins on some shitty fuck Italian exchange run by some shitty Italian fuck idiot. Maybe he fucking ran off to India to get a fake death certificate, maybe some pissed off investor hunted him down, I don't fucking know. It has nothing to do with me, and nothing to do with Future Synergy Coin. But if you step out of line… you're at your parents' house, right? Melina there with you? Sarah? Luis?"

Graham sees Melina react to the change in his expression; he turns his back to the living room.

"Are you drunk?" Graham asks.

"What fucking difference does that make?"

"You are, aren't ya?" Graham's pacing again, smiling, gesticulating, wresting back control of the conversation. "And you're fucking high. Are you coked up, Nguyen?"

"Fuck you."

"Look, I'm writing a book on Future Synergy Coin, and if you'd like to have some input on it, I'd be more than happy to have a proper chat with you about—"

"Just fucking watch yourself. Because we're watching you."

The phone call ends. Graham walks to the end of the garden, out of view of the living room. He takes out his e-cig, wishing as he vapes that he had a real cigarette.

Extract from BLOCKCHAIN GODS:

Of all the wild shooting stars pulled into crypto's orbit, none have burned as bright nor flown as erratically as Jack McAvoy. McAvoy is a relic of the time before the dotcom boom, a man who made his fortune in the early days of the Internet as prolific inventor of computer software. There is a good chance that your computer at home or work still runs some of McAvoy Industries' programs, though the man himself is no longer associated with the products bearing his name. Jack McAvoy sold his software empire in 1996 for a reported sum of $100 million. The story of what McAvoy did before and after this could fill many volumes. The truncated version is that he was a gifted computer programmer with an impressive resume that included stints at government departments and major companies before he started McAvoy Industries. His life after the sale included stints as a cultish yoga guru in the Australian Outback and a quasi-warlord in El Salvador.

After selling his stake in his software company, McAvoy invested in other tech start-ups and built an extensive global real estate portfolio. The crown jewel of his real estate empire was an 120,000-acre ranch in Australia where McAvoy established a yoga retreat. A later Netflix documentary features testimonies from more than a dozen attendees who claim to have been forced into partaking in bizarre sexual rituals during their stay at the McAvoy Ranch.

McAvoy's fortunes fell in line with the global economy when the subprime mortgage crisis hit in 2007. He sold his ranch and most of his other real estate holdings and moved to the Central American nation of El Salvador. McAvoy's attempts to cultivate new medicinal plants in El Salvador were unsuccessful, but it was during this time that he began rebuilding his fortune as an early investor in Bitcoin. McAvoy also made international headlines while in El Salvador when a ferocious gun battle at Casa McAvoy resulted in the deaths of several of his personal security team and members of El Savador's National Guard. McAvoy and the El Salvadoran authorities have given conflicting explanations of what caused the bloody battle at Casa McAvoy. Finance Weekly journalist Matthew Cooper believes McAvoy's claims that it was linked to a heated argument which Cooper witnessed between McAvoy and Senator Jose Alvarez over campaign contributions.

</extract.>

Liverpool, England.

"This guy's a fucking nut," Graham says, scrolling back through his lengthy chapter on the exploits of Jack McAvoy.

"How someone can eat human shit?!" Melina replies, recalling one of the many salacious episodes in Jack McAvoy's wild media interviews that Graham has told her about. "Is not just disgusting, but it must be unhealthy for your stomach."

Graham frowns and grows quiet as he reads back over McAvoy's links to Future Synergy Coin: the recent trips to Venezuela, North Korea, and Iran made by Dung Nguyen, rumours of the pair working together to expand their operations into countries frozen out of the international financial order by the United States; and visits by both Nguyen and McAvoy to countries like Cambodia, Myanmar, South Sudan, and Eritrea: nations with limited law and order, corrupt officials, and malleable legislative processes. Dynamics of power, geopolitics, danger. Graham hasn't told Melina what Nguyen said during the phone call, but he thinks about it constantly. He writes exclusively on an air-gapped computer, using his second Internet-connected laptop for research. Deaths and disappearances: every time Graham hears a noise on the street at night, he thinks of Giovanni Cuomo and Lui Wei and the dead among El Salvador's National Guard and McAvoy's personal security team.

But the benefits of writing the book far outweigh Graham's fears. He reminds himself of the Audi and the house in Gateacre. They're leaving the cramped home in Rock Ferry on the 3rd of next month.

It's early September and Luis has just started back at school from the summer break. He'll have one more month at the primary in Rock Ferry before moving to a new school closer to their new home. This morning, Luis' class is going on a school trip to the Barnstable activity centre. The coach is parked in front of the school, slowly filling with kids, when Graham arrives in the new Audi to drop Luis off. He shares a few words with Nisha's father Mr. Shah about Liverpool's perfect start to the season and the Jones family's upcoming move.

"I will miss these little chats with you," Mr. Shah says.

"Me too," Graham says, keeping eye contact with Mr. Shah as he sees Godzilla's mother approaching in his peripheral vision.

"You're moving to Gateacre?!" she splutters. "Bloody hell! What, have you won the lottery or summin'?"

Graham explains the book deal as vaguely and concisely as possible before he drives off in his Audi, thinking he'll not miss seeing Godzilla's mum, or having Luis hanging around with her little twat devil child. He wonders what the kids at the new school will be like. Probably all the offspring of lawyers and doctors. He hopes it doesn't make Luis grow up too cossetted and middle class. Graham thinks of what his Dad says about the upper classes waffling on at length with unwarranted confidence; that twat Boris Johnson in Number 10, and all his Eton school chums in the cabinet; Graham's interview in New York with the Dabrowski Twins. It's a strange thing, the relationship between money and class and expectations from life and personal identity. Years ago, a guy from a background like Graham's would never have gone to university in London, or wound up a writer with The Guardian and New York Times on his résumé. He remembers Panzer telling him how Panzer's Dad had done brilliantly on his final exams at school and had ambitions of going to Manchester University to study economics; but Panzer's Grandad had laughed at his son's pretensions and told him he would be starting work Monday at the Ogden's Imperial Tobacco factory. When he gets back home to Melina, Graham is full of happy thoughts of how blessed his life is, feeling all the happier on seeing his heavily pregnant wife watching This Morning on the sofa, little Sarah playing on the floor in front of her, Sarah and Luis' little sister Olivia due any day now.

Extract from BLOCKCHAIN GODS:

Alicia Huang and Guus van Hooijdink met just moments before Lui Wei shot his old school friend in the Down & Out club's restroom. Huang and van Hooijdink left together and stayed together over the months that followed. Huang was living with van Hooijdink in his grand Gilded Age mansion in Hillsborough when actor Olly Tulip arrived in Silicon Valley to shadow van Hooijdink in preparation for his role in Moon Boys. Before principal photography on Moon Boys had even begun, British tabloid newspapers were printing pictures of Alicia Huang and Olly Tulip together in Tulip's English hometown of Thames Ditton. Huang and Tulip arrived together for the London launch of Huang's fashion label Sufferings of a Flower in May 2019. In June 2019, they announced their engagement.

</extract.>

Liverpool, England.

Graham looks back over what he's just written. It bothers him that he's missing some illuminating piece of information. Liu Wei's attempted murder of Justin Zhou during New York Blockhain Week is one thing: he knows they went to school together, that Justin was operating a bitcoin mining operation out of a factory owned by Liu Wei's father; some disagreement over the profits from the operation was surely what prompted Liu Wei to travel to New York and shoot his old classmate. But why did Wei try to shoot

Guus van Hooijdink during the Future Synergy Coin yacht party? The more he stares at the screen, the more it bothers him. There is some clear link between Justin and Wei, an obvious potential for motive to form. Which would mean Wei is not some crazed gunman looking to take out anyone in the cryptocurrency scene. Which would mean he must have had a reason for what he did on the yacht.

As he's staring at the screen, hoping for some eureka flash that brings these disconnected fragments of story together, he feels his phone vibrate.

"Hello?"

"Hi, Mr. Jones? I'm so sorry to have to call you like this, but during the class trip—"

All thoughts of Liu Wei & the yacht & Future Synergy Coin evaporate as Graham stares at the screen and listens. Luis. Missing. Come. Barnstable Centre. He can't remember what's said to Melina about it as he drives off. As his car reaches leafy countryside road, he pulls his phone from his pocket & calls his Dad: says what he can about what he's heard, asks if he & his Mum can go over and make sure Melina's alright. Graham says he'll let them know when he finds out what's happening.

"And what did you say these gentlemen's names were?"

"Guus van Hooijdink, Jack McAvoy, Dung Nguyen."

"Could you spell those for me?"

The police officer writes the names down. He tells Graham that it's incredibly unlikely his son would have been kidnapped but he's grateful for the information. Graham walks back across the car park to Godzilla's mum Sheryl and Godzilla & Luis' teacher Mrs. Ryland. They stop talking as Graham approaches. Tears stream down Sheryl's face as she stands, arms crossed, smoking. Mrs. Ryland looks at Graham pitifully and apologetically, on the verge of tears herself. Sheryl splutters out smoke between sobs.

"Could I have one of your cigarettes?" Graham asks.

Extract from BLOCKCHAIN GODS:

I ask our translator to ask her why she's in London. After the question has been rephrased in Mandarin, Lui Wei's mother looks at me like it is a question with an answer so obvious that it need not have been asked.

"I will go anywhere if it might help me find my son."

</extract.>

Liverpool, England.

"This is the last one," Sheryl says. "I can give you twos on it if you want."

"No, you have it," Graham says, feeling his pockets for the e-cig that he quickly realises he's left at home. "I've had enough off you." He's lost count of how many cigarettes he's smoked. *How long have we been waiting here now?* And *why won't the police just let us get into the forest and help find them?* Surely the more people looking for them the better.

"Mr. Jones," says a balding man in a beige jacket, a non-uniformed police officer. "Could I speak to you a moment?" He leads Graham away from Sheryl and Mrs. Ryland. "Now first, I want you to know that there's no need to jump to conclusions at this point. Your son and his friend almost certainly will have just wandered off on their own and will be found. But just so that we can act as quickly as possible in all circumstances, I'd like to confirm a few details about what you told one of my colleagues earlier."

The non-uniformed officer asks Graham questions about van Hooijdink and Nguyen and McAvoy, what contact he's had with each of them, when Nguyen called him, if he knows where he was calling from. Graham's phone vibrates in his pocket as the officer speaks. The questions are followed with more words of reassurance. Graham turns back to look at Mrs. Ryland and Sheryl. *Godzilla's mum.* What a prick he's been to that woman. The thoughts he's had. Now, his *stupid fucking greed and ambition and… Luis…*

Graham looks away, trying to control the thoughts swirling, dread deepening. He remembers his phone vibrated. He takes it from his pocket. A missed call from Dad. Graham rings him back.

"Any news?"

"No," Graham says. "They're out searching all around the Centre. Said they reckon him and his friend will just have ran off somewhere. But… no. No news. Is Melina doing alright?"

"Yeah, well, me and your Mum are with her now. That's why I was ringing you. We've just called an ambulance. We think she's gone into labour."

BLOCKCHAIN GODS:

As Aart Janssen lay recovering from the attack in a Hanoi hospital bed, two police officers visited and told him to leave the country as soon as possible. Janssen is convinced the two police officers had been sent by Dung Nguyen. Money, power, and influence are a dangerous cocktail that grows stronger as its ingredients ferment.

</extract.>

Liverpool.

The coach has taken the other schoolkids from the Barnstable Centre's car park, leaving a half-dozen police cars, vehicles belonging to Mrs. Ryland and the school principal Mr. Cornelius, two other cars belonging to Barnstable Centre staff, and Graham's Audi. Graham curses the car, the stupidity of putting money over his family's safety. Mr. Cornelius talks alternately with stressed Barnstable Centre staff members and police officers, trying to make a show of doing something where nothing can be done. The police have turned down repeated offers of help in the search for Luis and Adam Tilbury. They say it's better for their officers to cover the area unassisted. But it's been hours now. Sheryl Tilbury paces slowly over the tarmac, arms still folded across her chest, shaking her head, face reddened from regular crying fits. Graham sees Sheryl looking at cigarette butts on the floor. She's probably wishing she had another left to smoke. He does too. But he wishes more than anything to leave here with Luis. If they find him, he promises never to smoke again.

Was it Nguyen? Nguyen and McAvoy? Nguyen, McAvoy, and van Hooijdink? Working together? A warning, not to continue with the book; or worse, punishment for writing it. But *are they that insane?* It's illogical. But during the phone call, Nguyen was wild. *Clearly coked up.* And McAvoy, van Hooijdink; both no doubt have ingested enough chemicals to fuck their brains beyond all standard logic. The trail of missing that surrounds them… *But if they did what you think they did, that would be so fucked, so crazy. They'd be jailed for years, life, in any country. Would lose everything. But only if they were caught.*

And that last thought is too much for Graham; he has to turn again from Sheryl and Mrs. Ryland, walk to the car park's edge, stare through the trees to the forest, thoughts now with Luis, with Adam; are they still in there somewhere? *They have to be.* They couldn't have been kidnapped. *Could they?* But… *if all they wanted to do was send a message, then…* would they even need to take them from the woods?

And that thought forces Graham to turn from the forest, and walk back across the car park, trying not to look at anything, anyone, trying to think of Melina, Olivia, in the hospital: his daughter's birth. *Her brother…*

BLOCKCHAIN GODS:

Spent bullet casings and the bodies of their targets lay inside and outside the palatial Casa McAvoy. The dead included El Salvador National Guard members Pvt. Marlon Ayala, 18; Pvt. Oscar Pacheco, 18; Pvt. Hugo Siguenza, 19; Pvt. Emerson Zometa, 19; and Cpl. Vitor Rajo, 21. From those believed to be part of McAvoy's private security detail, the dead included Alcides Avalos, 16; Atilio Garcia, 17; Zenon Castillo, 24; and Hugo "Tiny" Mattias, 25.

McAvoy claims the raid on his home was ordered directly by Senator Alvarez as punishment for McAvoy's refusal to contribute to Alvarez's re-election fund. The El Salvadoran authorities claim the raid was ordered after they uncovered evidence that illegal narcotics were being produced in the McAvoy compound.

The government of El Salvador demanded Jack McAvoy be returned to the country to stand trial over the allegations of narcotic production and also for his alleged role in the gun battle. Despite a bilateral extradition treaty signed by the United States and El Salvador in 1911, President Trump refused to send McAvoy back to El Salvador. Trump called the charges against McAvoy "total bullshit" and characterized the raid on Casa McAvoy as an illegal attempt to extort money from an American citizen over invented crimes. Trump also called his counterparts in El Salvador's government "totally corrupt." Between 2018 and 2019, Jack McAvoy made three donations totalling $7 million to groups supporting Trump's bid for re-election.

Money. Power. Influence.

Liverpool.

"They've found him."

Bill Jones' intake of breath can be heard through the phone.

A moment of silence.

"Is he… he's…"

"He's with me now, yeah," Graham says, "I'm fucking fuming at him. How's Melina doing?"

"Where were he?"

"Him and his dickhead mate Godzilla ran off from the fucking Centre together. Into the woods. Said they wanted to go on an adventure, seeing as it's their last fucking week at school together. I don't know which one of them I'm more pissed off at."

"So he's with you now?"

"Yeah, he's in the backseat. I'm driving over to the hospital now. How's Melina?"

"She's doing alright, considering. Well, she's in excruciating pain and she's worried sick about Luis."

"Well go tell her we're on our way."

"Yeah. Will do. See you in a bit, son."

Graham sees Luis in the backseat in the rear view mirror, tears trickling down his cheeks, shoulders hunched, shaking. Graham is hit with guilt for the rage with which he shouted at him. But *if he does ever anything that stupid again…*

"We're here," Graham says, switching the engine off.

"Is Mummy mad at me?"

Graham sighs. He turns to look at his son. "No. Look, I'm sorry for shouting at you. But you don't know how worried we were. That was so bloody stupid of you. Running off like that, without telling anyone."

"Godzilla said it wouldn't matter. We could go explore in the woods, then come back before everyone had finished. But then we got lost. And I fell and hurt my knee. And—"

Fucking Godzilla. "It's alright. But Luis, mate, don't you ever fucking do something like that again. Okay?"

"I won't. I'm sorry."

Olivia Valentina Antonella Jones enters the world at just after midnight on the 19th of September, 2019, weighing 6.4lbs. As Graham holds his daughter, he looks from her face, full of wonder at the world, to her mother's: drained, exhausted, but content. The scare with Luis makes Graham question whether to submit the final draft of Blockchain Gods or cancel the project. Melina reminds him of the house in Gateacre. He sends the final draft to FletcherWilliams. They move into the new home in Gateacre. While unpacking, Graham's new literary agent Mark Elmore phones to give him details of the launch event, scheduled for London in November, to coincide with the screening of the Alberto Firenze film Moon Boys at the London Film Festival. The whole family head to London for the book launch, Robbie flying in from Berlin just for the occasion, all put up in rooms at The Savoy by FletcherWilliams. The book rockets up the non-fiction bestseller list off the back of the movie hype. Liverpool remain at the top of the Premier League, winning every game until the leap year day of 29th February, 2020. But as Graham leaves McCooley's half-drunk, turning down Nev & Panzer's suggestion of another pub, the 3-0 loss to Watford doesn't bother him. He has a beautiful family, a beautiful wife, two beautiful daughters, a son whose settled in well to the new school and thankfully won't be spending any more time with that little shit Adam 'Godzilla' Tilbury. His writing career is hitting an all-time high, big-name publications more than happy to commission his articles after the success of Blockchain Gods. He pitches FletcherWilliams his idea for a follow-up, looking at where the Gen Zs and Millennials hungry for a get-rich-quick scheme have moved since the cryptocurrency bubble burst: a book on the self-proclaimed autists of reddit.com/r/wallstreetbets, whose outlandish punts on puts and calls have made some riches and seen many others share screenshots of colossal losses. And Liverpool are safe at the top of the league, 22 points ahead of Manchester City with 28 games played. A near-perfect season, a near-perfect life. The grand home in Gateacre, an incredible improvement on the cramped place they were renting in Rock Ferry. Liverpool about to win their first league title in 30 years, the first since 1990, since the Premier League was created. Three beautiful healthy children named after Liverpool heroes. A wife he loves more than anything but the kids. The world slips into lockdown as the COVID-19 pandemic replaces Brexit and Trump's impeachment hearing as the dominant story in the news cycle. The lockdown life suits Graham and Melina and the kids well, their big garden providing plenty of space to live a comfortable life without venturing far from home. As the lockdown restrictions ease in summer, Graham invites his mother and father to the house and the family watch Liverpool lift the Premier League trophy together. And as news reaches Graham of Guus van Hooijdink's death, it's an opportunity to write a follow-up to Blockchain Gods. He sends a pitch to FletcherWilliams and receives another six-figure advance on his next project, The Death of a Shitcoin Billionaire.

26. THE LAST MAN ON EARTH.

Groningen, Netherlands.
& London, England.

The others are drunk & intense, draping arms over shoulders & staring into each other's eyes as they tell with sodden-livered intensity of how they'll keep in touch, whatever happens, and the past three years have been formative, & unforgettable, & nothing can top this - the brotherhood, the camaraderie, the…

They run into Vallya & Jurate at Kokomo. Aart chain smokes as he talks with Vallya about Ciara; Vallya hasn't seen her or heard from her. Ciara has deleted her Facebook, her Instagram. Aart thought she'd blocked him specifically. But she's blocked everyone. The conversation ends an uncountable number of cigarettes later, when Federico & Jurate spill into the smoking area, touching each other constantly.

"You look out of it," Wesley says beside Aart at the urinal in Warhol.

"Yeah." Aart shakes & stares at piss-splashed steel. He has no words to share. No feelings left.

"Look," Wes says, "I meant what I said earlier."

Aart looks at Wesley. He has no recollection of what he's referring to.

"Give it a try, man. This job in London, they'll definitely hire you. You were the co-founder of a multi-billion dollar company! The only work experience I have is a summer internship at Rabobank and they hired me. It could be your last chance to work in England before Brexit happens. London is awesome, man. It's such a cool city. And what else are you gonna do? Stay with your parents in Drachten? Try for some corporate job in Amsterdam or Rotterdam?"

Aart stays with his parents in Drachten, in a two-up two-down on the suburban outskirts. It rains every day. He watches a lot of Netflix and plays a lot of Civilization and spends a lot of time browsing Reddit.

His mother cooks stamppot for dinner and says Randstad are hiring and that Philips, which just employed their neighbour's boy, is still actively hiring from the latest crop of graduates. And that if Aart doesn't act fast, he'll be a year behind, and the next batch of graduates will be taking all the best positions. Aart's father says he should move away from here; go anywhere. Amsterdam. Berlin. London. Asia. Aart's seen a lot of the world already, his father reasons. He came close to doing something very special with that little tech start-up. But he has to build on it. Quickly. The same conversations surround every dinner. His parents' concern grows as graduation grows more distant. He calls Wesley.

"You left it late! I'm flying to London on Thursday. But I'll email the recruiter, maybe they still have some openings."

Aart speaks to the recruiter on Skype two hours later. He appears on the laptop screen, a twentysomething with a slick pompadour and a neatly-trimmed beard. He's impressed with Aart's resume. He says there's a lot of money to be made in direct marketing. Footballer money. He tells Aart he can start with Wes on Monday if he books the flight.

The flight from Schiphol that Sunday is fast, barely hurtling over runway & tilting up towards sky & skimming clouds before it's down. Aart clears Customs quickly with a passport & iris scan, Brexit still yet to have any effect on his entry as an EU citizen. As he moves through the modest airport, he thinks of all the airports & wildness of the FSC conferences. He withdraws British Pounds at an ATM & buys a ticket for the Underground. Liverpool Street Station, grander than Luton Airport, getting the feel of one of the few great cities of Europe he's not previously visited. Then Hammersmith & City line to Stepney Green, struggling to find a wifi connection, finally contacting Wesley via the wifi at a Co-op supermarket, Wes appearing five minutes later & leading Aart to a block of flats on a grassy lawn surrounded by taller blocks in worse condition than the one they're living in, dodgy-looking London teenagers smoking weed & staring at them from the edge of the lawn.

"Those guys are good to have around," Wesley says, opening the door to Aart's new shared home. "You ever want to buy weed, they're always outside."

Aart takes the suitcase to his room, the smallest of three upstairs in the house. Wes knocks the door of another room & introduces Aart to his new flatmate, an Australian from Adelaide named Andy.

"How ya doin', mate? Another fuckin' Dutchie in the house! Christ, we've been gekoloniseerd! Better get to the kitchen and hide me fuckin' spices! You bring any wacky baccy with you from Amsterdam?"

They're soon smoking a spliff on the living room sofa, London skunk far stronger than Aart expected. The TV in the corner's tuned to BBC News.

"Democratic Presidential frontrunner Joe Biden has accused Donald Trump of overwhelming abuse of power… British tour operator Thomas Cook is seeking a financial rescue deal of £250 million… Houthi rebels in Yemen have offered to end their attacks on Saudi Arabia if the Saudis halt their bombing campaign…"

Aart zones out on the drip of headlines, heavy British skunk overpowering the brain with greater force than the stuff he normally smokes back in the Netherlands. In bed, skunk thoughts fly from London to New York & California and Guus & Nguyen and over the world in search of Ciara. Aart interrupts these thoughts by checking the time on his phone, finally drifting into semi-sleep after 5am, sunlight beating against the bedside curtains. A little over two hours later, the alarm wakes him from some weird

& quickly forgotten dream. A little under two hours after that, Aart and Wes emerge from Oxford Circus tube station with hundreds of other shuffling commuters on an overcast Monday morning and move along the great shopping thoroughfare of Oxford Street. They take several right and left turns and ascend a staircase into a room with other early-twentysomethings in cheap suits, all chattering excitedly. A slightly older woman in a power-suit stands in the centre of the room. When the clock affixed to the wall behind her strikes 9, she begins.

"Good morning. Today is the first day of the week and we have many new faces among us." She talks practicalities, assigning the new hires to the sales force vets, putting a chunky blonde British girl in charge of Aart & Wes. They're soon back onto the street, Aart & Wes listening and nodding as Amanda the blonde British girl leads them back to the Tube, telling of how much money they can make doing this if they just stay persistent, etc., Aart long bored of listening to her by the time the Northern Line reaches Archway.

Amanda leads them along a street lined with three-storey Victorian terraced houses, knocking at several doors without an answer. An old man finally opens the door to the fourth or fifth.

"Hiya! Good morning! We're just here collecting money for a naked fun run."

The old guy's confused. Amanda continues, laughing and smiling, saying she's just joking, they're actually gathering on-going donations to the British Red Cross. Her tone becomes sombre as she explains the important work the charity is doing helping victims of wars in Syria & Yemen and injured British troops and those who've had their lives destroyed by other recent disasters. The old man offers her a fiver, but she says they can only accept on-going monthly contributions paid via card or direct debit. He offers five pounds a month. She says the lowest they can go is £8. He says, "Go on then," and jots his card details down on her clipboard.

"That's the thing," Amanda says, leading the way to the next home on the street, "we don't start to earn any commission until they've pledged over eight pounds a month." She delivers her same well-rehearsed speech to the woman in a dressing gown that answers the next door. She isn't interested. Nobody answers at the next few houses. Then those that do answer aren't interested either.

"Maybe you guys can try the next one."

Wes perfectly imitates Amanda's spiel about the war-ravaged and the disaster-afflicted and the injured soldiers. The gruff bloke who answered the door snaps when he hears soldiers mentioned: "They shouldn't be over there in the first place! And it should be the government that's paying for them, not expecting normal citizens to foot the bill out of their own pockets."

Hundreds of doors are knocked throughout the day. Aart and Wes each manage a single sign-up. Amanda gets around a dozen.

As they turn off the main street to one of the many other streets surrounding it, a group of kids in tracksuits lob rocks at them.

"Hey!" Aart shouts. The kids run off laughing.

"This is shit," Wes says, sucking on a cigarette as they wait for Amanda to go to the toilet inside a pub.

"Yeah," Aart agrees, wondering how much money they could possibly make doing this shit all day every day, in all weathers, earning no base salary, commission only.

When they return to the office, Yasagi the owner gives a motivational speech about how difficult this job can be, but how important perseverance is, and how she earns half-a-million a year, within eighteen months of starting where they all are now, and that could be them, &etc. Then the group stand in a circle and clap as each of their team leaders hits a gong to represent how many sign-ups they got. The group counts each hit out loud. The guy who goes before Amanda, a bulky lad from Birmingham with bad acne, strikes the gong ten times. Amanda strikes fourteen.

"Fuck," Birmingham acne guy mutters.

"So," Yasagi says. "We like to make this fun."

Each of the team leaders has been competing against another. Those with the least sign-ups have to apologise. Birmingham acne guy awkwardly gets onto his knees in front of Amanda, apologising.

Yasagi wants more. "Grovel! She beat you. Show your appreciation."

"I'm sorry," he says, cheeks blushing as red as the spots adorning them. "I'm really sorry."

"Tell her how much better she is at this than you. How much better of a salesman."

"Yeah, what the fuck was that?" Wes says, when Aart brings up the ridiculousness of the grovelled apologies as they sink pints with Andy from Adelaide in a student pub on Whitechapel Road.

"Sales is a harsh mistress," Andy says. "You ever seen that movie, The Boiler Room?"

Andy goes on about co-workers doing coke off their desks and losing their mind at customers in the call centre he works at. Wes scans the pub for girls. They're soon talking with a group of art students from Central Saint Martins. Aart's tired from traipsing around North London all day and the booze has quickly got the better of him. He struggles and fails to make interesting conversation. All but one of the girls go home after the bell's rung for last orders. The remaining girl walks a few paces behind Aart & Andy, laughing at whatever Wes is saying to her, as Andy tells Aart how much he hates how fucking cold London is, both in climate and character. Aart tries to watch a Netflix documentary on the dirty money laundered by international crime syndicates through London's financial giants as Wes & the girl's laughing and moans and creaking bed springs sound over the electro house mix Wes is playing and overpower the max volume setting on Aart's laptop.

"So since today is the first time most of you will be making sales of your own," Yasagi says during the morning's motivational speech, "I thought it might be fun to end the day with some entertainment. So, each of you who gets fewer sales than your opponent will be singing a song of my choice when you get back to the office."

"This is fucking bullshit," Wesley says when he meets up with Aart again at the end of the street somewhere in Streatham.

"No luck?" Aart asks.

"No one fucking answered. And I can't believe we pay our own fucking transport for this shit." He lights a cigarette. "Let's do one more street and go for a beer."

Aart manages three sign-ups, Wesley none. Wes sings I Kissed a Girl & I Liked It to a clearly-uncomfortable girl in a hijab at Yasagi's instruction back at the office. The plump acne-riddled Birmingham boy stands in front of Aart and looks close to tears as he sings I'm Bringing Sexy Back.

"Come on," Yasagi demands as Birmingham boy mumbles all words but the title.

"I don't know the lyrics!" Birmingham boy pleads.

Yasagi sighs and lets the performance end. Then she tells a lad from South London to regale a half-Japanese girl from Guilford with Wonderwall.

Daily drink and smoking breaks escalate more rapidly than sign-up success. Aart gets four sign-ups on Wednesday, but this drops to two on Thursday against Amanda's twelve and Aart has to drink a shot glass of Worcestershire sauce while Wes downs one of Colman's extra-strength English mustard.

On Friday morning, Yasagi's usual motivational speech and outlay of punishments is replaced by a conference call that she tells her salesforce is being simulcast to five hundred Hydra-affiliated teams across Europe.

"When I started what would become Hydra, I literally had less than nothing," Hydra Group Ltd. founder Chris Diakos says, unseen in an audio-only speech relayed to the surround sound speakers affixed to each corner of the room.

Aart scans the room's many motivational posters as the group stands and listens.

'Every champion was once a contender who refused to quit.' - Sylvester Stallone as Rocky Balboa.

"I came to London in 2015 with little more than a suitcase of tattered old T-shirts and a single pair of dress shoes. I walked my arse up-and-down the dusty streets of this great metropolis banging on doors of businesses, but no-one would hire me."

'Every failure brings you one step closer to success. Every rejection brings you one step closer to a yes.'

"After wandering every street in Central London, I found myself in an industrial estate near Lewisham. There was a security systems company operating out of a battered old warehouse. The guy running the place gave me a shot."

'We are what we do repeatedly. Excellence is not a quality but a habit.' - Aristotle.

"He said if I went door-to-door selling his security systems, he'd give me fifty percent of whatever profit I made for him."

'Persistence + Perspiration = Progress.'

"That week, I made my first sale on one of the most expensive streets in North London. By Saturday, I'd sold over a thousand burglar alarms."

Aart zones out on the motivational bullshit tacked to the walls and pouring out from the speakers. He thinks of crypto conferences, Guus' wild rants, the cult-like following surrounding FSC on subreddits and Telegram groups.

"There's hundreds of these fucking places," Aart tells Wes as they smoke on a street somewhere in New Cross. "Every city in the UK has them. All with different names but all feeding back to the main Hydra group. And they're in Greece, Italy, Spain. That cunt Chris Diakos is a billionaire."

"Who?"

"That pestkop giving the speech earlier. The prick who owns this company." Aart rants about what Amanda's said to them about her dream of following Yasagi's path to the top, moving from team leader to branch owner, earning half-a-million a year. "It's a fucking pyramid scheme."

Aart gets no sales all day. Same for Wesley. Back at the office, Yasagi cackles as the girl in the hijab and the half-Japanese girl hit them each with shaving foam pies.

"It's bullshit," Wes says over a pint of ale at a pub near Tottenham Court Road.

"Are you gonna go in tomorrow?" Fatima (the girl in the hijab) asks.

"Fuck no."

"Tim said they make more on Saturdays," Emily (the half-Japanese girl) says.

"How much do you think we made this week?" Aart asks.

Wesley says: "Barely enough for two pints in this fucking city."

"They said Saturday's optional, right?" Fatima asks.

"I'm not working there tomorrow," Aart says, slouched in his seat, staring at his £6 pint.

"Exactly," Wes says. "It's Friday. Let's get fucked up. Enjoy it."

"Cheers," Fatima says, lifting her glass. The others clink theirs against hers.

"I'm not going back Monday either," Aart says, leaning forward. "This is bullshit. It's a fucking pyramid scene."

By mid-way through the next pint, the girls & Wes have agreed with him. Not wanting to waste more of a salary they've yet to earn, the group moves to Soho Square Gardens with cans of lager and a bottle of cheap High Commissioner whisky bought at Sainsburys. The buzz of the surrounding streets grows as they drink, workers becoming revellers at the dawn of the weekend. In an alcohol blur they move to a club in Shoreditch. Fatima makes a phone call & they stop at a cash machine for Aart & Wes to take out more funds which are then given to a shifty looking homeless guy who reappears a few minutes later with a baggie of MDMA. The music gets better & Aart's mind clearer until the music gets really good & everything's sharp but fuzzy. The club closes at 3am and talk is of the next place. They take a taxi back to the flat, Aart & Wes giving the driver a tenner each. More booze is bought at a nearby off-license & one of the local boys is called & meets Wes in the grassy patch outside to hand the weed over.

"I'm feeling tired," Emily says.

Wes hurries her upstairs. Aart & Fatima talk on the sofa a little more. Aart asks if she wants to go upstairs. She says that the Tube's open & she'll head back home. Aart smokes another joint in bed, listening to Wes & Emily & creaking bed springs, trying to calculate the cost of the night & how long he can survive without stable income & what the fuck happened to his FSC multi-millions. Wes' creaking bed springs stop long before Aart falls asleep.

Aart walks into the living room on Saturday afternoon. Andy from Adelaide's talking about his wild night with the lads from work, some crazy club in South London & a German girl who sucked him off in the smoking area. Aart & Wes get bread & hummus & smoothies from the Co-op and eat & smoke in a stoned haze on the sofa, BBC News on TV relaying reports of the recall of the US envoy to Ukraine & a subpoena to hand over documents to President Trump's impeachment inquiry & a Hong Kong rally to mark the 5th anniversary of the yellow umbrella protests & Japan's shock victory over Ireland in the Rugby World Cup. Andy suggests getting cans & they're soon on the second round, each eight cans deep by the time they leave, walking Whitechapel Road to Brick Lane & smuggling shop-bought cans into Cafe 1001, zonking out on ketamine at 93 Feet East, Aart losing all sense of self to a hefty dose & returning to reality to see Wes & Andy making out with two girls on the dancefloor, night continuing into the blur & brightness of morning, hummus & smoothies & spliffs on the sofa, Andy swearing incessantly as Wales edge out a Rugby World Cup win over Australia. Aart silently wills Wales on, wondering if Ciara is watching her country's victory.

He sleeps from mid-morning until evening and dreams that he's with her aboard the FSC superyacht in a New York City harbor.

"I spent too much this weekend," Aart tells Wes on Monday afternoon, staring at the €2219.52 balance on his ING banking app. The £500 he transferred to his newly-opened UK account's gone. He sends €1000 more. His UK Barclays banking app balance now shows £890. Aart checks it compulsively after spending £6.50 on a curry, £5 on beers at Co-op, & withdrawing £20 for a bag of weed from one of the local boys. On Tuesday afternoon, he & Wes walk to a larger supermarket to stock up with pasta, tinned tomatoes, vegetables & chicken breasts. On Tuesday night, they take a bus with Andy to The Roxy on Tottenham Court Road. £4 entry with a flyer. They quickly lose track of £9 cocktail pitchers & 2-for-£3.90 bottles of Kronenbourg. Aart stares at the £774.23 in his Barclays account as he smokes a spliff in bed & tries to ignore creaking bed springs & other sounds from the Greek girl Wes brought back. Wednesday night Scream pub, Thursday Koko in Camden, Friday techno at Lightbox in Vauxhall, Saturday free party in a dilapidated building in Hackney, £206.11 left by Sunday afternoon. £179.46 after buying rolling tobacco, a couple of pints & a pub Sunday roast.

"I need a fucking job, man," Aart tells Wes on Monday, transferring what's left of his ING balance to Barclays, topping the account up to £1412.88, that sum due to be halved in a week when rent's due.

BBC News tells of tens of thousands of climate protesters in Central London & protestors disobeying face mask bans in Hong Kong & troubled Brexit talks between the UK and EU & President Trump's refusal to cooperate with impeachment proceedings as they eat cheap & smoke rollies and spliffs & drink shop-bought beers Monday through Wednesday, emailing applications to everything on Indeed.com & Monster.co.uk & provisional inquiries to every London-based marketing firm they can find contact details for. By Wednesday, Andy's raring to get out & drink & talks them into sticking to shop-bought cans and going to Brick Lane. Thursday night a few pubs in Central. Friday bar-hopping in Dalston. Saturday warehouse rave in Hackney Wick. Home at midday on Sunday. Wake up close to midnight emotionally & physically drained, £989.01 remaining.

Monday afternoon, spliffs with Wes on the sofa. BBC News tells of Boris' plans for Britain after Brexit being outlined to Parliament in the Queen's speech.

"Oh, shit," Wes says, scrolling on his phone. "I've got an interview."

Wednesday, Aart's alone at home. BBC News talks Brexit talks, Hong Kong chaos, US Democratic Presidential candidates debating spending plans & taxing of billionaires. Aart thinks of his stolen fortune. Wes gets the job. Celebration drinks near Spitalfields market. Thursday evening, drinks in Central. Friday, rent. £486.81. Dalston bars. Saturday, early wake up to Andy screaming at the TV as England smash Australia out of the Rugby World

Cup. Free entry to the Tate Modern in the afternoon. Drinks on the South Bank in the evening. Club in South East in the night. Sunday, £321.40 remains.

Monday, BBC News talks of Parliament voting down Boris' Brexit deal, forcing the PM to send a letter to the EU asking for another delay. Aart leaves the house in mid-afternoon and walks. Whitechapel Road, Tower Bridge, the South Bank, Houses of Parliament, Buckingham Palace, St. James Park, Trafalgar Square. Bus. Home before Wes & Andy return from after-work drinks with co-workers.

Tuesday, BBC Breakfast. A special guest – movie director Alberto Firenze. Aart lets the TV's words fall over him as he smokes.

"These guys made billions!" Firenze says. "Before they even finished university! It's really crazy the amount of money involved."

Something compels Aart to rise from the sofa & open the back door, stepping into the weak mid-autumn sunshine in the compact overgrown back garden. He puffs at his spliff until he hears voices beyond the fence in an adjacent garden. He goes back inside & locks the door. BBC Breakfast is discussing the just-announced snap general election, an attempt to overcome the Brexit impasse. Without turning off the TV, Aart grabs his weed & rolling tobacco & phone & walks out the front door, turns onto Whitechapel Road, continues to Tower Bridge, crosses it, stopping to stare at the powerful water flow beneath & the grand city on its banks. Along the South Bank, tourists and street entertainers, a guy painted silver with a hat full of coins and banknotes. Aart stops to roll a cigarette outside the British Film Institute. He stares at Olly Tulip's face on a billboard as he smokes. *Moon Boys. The new film from Alberto Firenze. Bulls make money. Pigs get slaughtered. Wolf of Wall Street for the Instagram generation.* Aart crosses another bridge, walks along The Strand, through Covent Garden, Leicester Square, more movie billboards affixed to the cinemas on the square making him think of the Alberto Firenze/Olly Tulip film as he rolls another cigarette. Moon Boys. *Pigs get slaughtered.* He wonders if he can get away with smoking a joint on the grass covering Leicester Square. He looks at the business people eating a quick lunch on the benches & the scores of tourists snapping pictures. He can't. He stops in McDonalds for a £1.29 double cheeseburger and continues his walk to Piccadilly Circus and Oxford Street, thinking of going back to his old workplace, wondering if Fatima or Emily are still working there & if Amanda will ever get her half-million a year. *Pigs get slaughtered.* He thinks of New York & Emilia. He thinks of Guus & Nguyen in California. They've probably hung out at parties with celebrities like Olly Tulip. Aart side-steps shoppers & tourists along Oxford Street's entire bustling length until he reaches Hyde Park. He wanders off the path, finds a quiet spot beneath a tree & rolls a spliff. Once it's smoked, he leaves the park, finds a Tesco Metro, looks over the beers & settles on 3 large bottles –

Cobra, San Miguel, Staropramen – for £5. Back in the park, he prises the Cobra's cap off with his lighter, swigs, rolls another spliff, checks Barclays: £308.21. He's mid-way through the San Miguel when dusk descends. He walks through the park, finishes the bottle by the exit, dumps it in a bin, briefly wonders if any laws prohibit street drinking here, thinks *fuck it,* pops the Staropramen open & continues on through Kensington, the classy part of the city, wealth emanating from every storefront and suited dick on the street, Aart thinking he was briefly richer than all of them. *Pigs. Slaughtered.* Alberto Firenze & Olly Tulip. He walks past Harrods, continues until his second beer's drained, then goes back and walks through it, plush old-world grandeur department store, Arab businessman eyeing luxury watches, perfectly-attired middle-aged white women perusing handbags…

"Where've you been?" Andy asks.

"Out."

"Yeah, well…" Andy continues what he was explaining to Wes: their bills for gas, electricity, and council tax have arrived. Total £225.66 for the month. Split three-ways, it's £75.22 each. Aart holds the bills without focusing on their content. He transfers £75.22 to Andy's account. £232.99 remaining.

Andy & Wes have long left for work when Aart walks downstairs to the living room the following morning. He finds a half-tub of hummus and two pita breads in the fridge. He sits on the sofa, wraps a spliff, smokes, then eats, bored of BBC News' unrelenting focus on Brexit talks & delays & the snap election to come in December, switching to ITV & British actress Joanna Lumley in Japan, wandering Kyoto in search of a cherry blossom tree. Aart recognises her. He wonders from where. It strikes him: *the Wolf of Wall Street.* She was Margot Robbie's auntie. The Wolf of Wall Street. Moon Boys. *Wolf of Wall Street for the Instagram generation.* Slaughtered pigs. Aart picks up his phone to search for details on the movie, clearly connected somehow to cryptocurrency, but mid-way through typing, he realises he has no interest in a bullshit movie version of something he has painful first-hand experience of. Aart goes to Co-op & returns with more hummus & pita bread & four cans of Stella Artois, along with £20 from the cash machine for weed. £204.49. Suddenly aware it's dark outside and TV is deathly dull & he's re-watching the same looped BBC News report on Brexit delay & Trump impeachment, he checks the time on his phone: 18.35. He sees the date: 31 October. Halloween. He thinks of messaging Wes, or Andy, but figures they've gone for drinks with workmates, and he'd have been invited if they wanted him there. *But Halloween…* Aart stands. He cannot waste it. He checks the cans on the table: half of one remains. He drinks it as he paces the room, stopping to roll another spliff. He searches for London Halloween parties on his phone. He stops at Co-op for an £11.69 pack of Camel Blue cigarettes & a big bottle of Cobra then walks Whitechapel Road to Brick Lane, buying two cans of Red Stripe at an off-license, stuffing one into his pocket as he sneakily opens the other at a bench outside Cafe 1001, eyeing a conversation to angle his way into too. Aart finishes his can & slips inside & slips out the second can, moves around, eyeing groups on couches upstairs, sitting alone, sipping until the can's half-done, then onto the street, lighting a Camel, into some bar with overpriced pints and shitty paintings on the wall, more overheard conversations, snippets of living London, a club in Hoxton or Shoreditch that's full of teenagers, then another that's full of pervy guys in their 40s, and on, until the nights a blur & all pretty much indistinguishable, and he's walking across Tower Bridge, and stops along it, beneath the great iconic towering Towers, great gushing waterflow of the Thames beneath, and he thinks if he threw himself off, he'd probably die instantly, and if not, he's heard somewhere that drowning is a pretty good way to go, that once you've given up struggling some strange serenity descends over the brain like dusk, and his hands are on the centuries-old brickwork, ready to propel himself forward & down, but voices of a chattering group in suits crossing the bridge interrupt him, and he carries on walking, to London Bridge station & a night bus home.

BBC News talks of the Brexit party's offer of an election pact with the Conservatives. Aart's stomach rumbles. He takes a shit. He watches the news. He returns to the toilet. He thinks of what he ate yesterday, remembers only pita bread & hummus. Checks Barclays: £105.75. *Fuck*. He checks the fridge & cupboards, walks to the supermarket, returns with £2 of vegetables & £5 of beer, chops & cooks a vegetarian pasta dish, eyes the blade, wonders how long it would take to bleed out if he sliced his wrists with it.

"Hey! You have smoke?" Wes asks on returning. Wes slumps on the sofa in his suit as Aart wraps a spliff.

Andy's back soon after.

"Nah, man," Andy says when Wes asks if he went out last night. "Well yeah, but not out out. Went with a girl from work to that film festival down on the South Bank. Frigid bitch was on the next bus home once it was over. Film was alright though."

"What did you see?"

"That Olly Tulip film. Moon Cowboys or whatever the fuck it's called. Yeah, it's pretty decent. You boys would like it. Olly Tulip's playing one of your lot."

"Olly Tulip's character's Dutch?" Aart asks.

"Yeah. Ironic, right? A guy called Tulip playing a Dutch cunt. Fucking Goose or something his name is. Some stupid Dutch shit. Pretty fun flick though. Fair few titties on display, lot of drug taking."

"Guus?" Aart asks, hand shaking, spilling weed & tobacco over the sides of the Rizla. "Olly Tulip plays Guus?"

"Yeah, Guus, Goose. Something like that."

"What are you guys talking about?" Wes asks, the room's weird atmosphere ending his stoned fixation on the television.

"This fucking movie, mate. Christ, you deaf or something?" Andy recounts the plot, weed prompting an over-explanation of every detail, Wes & Aart's interest spurring him through it.

"Holy fuck, man," Wes says. "That's our story!"

"What… the… fuck…"

"What are you two cunts going on about?"

Wes explains as Aart sinks to a cross-legged position beside the coffee table, unaware of weed & tobacco spilling over his lap. "Am I in it?" Aart asks once Wes is quiet.

"Are you in it?!" Andy scoffs. "Nah, mate, it's about this fucking Dutch bloke and some dopey Chinaman."

Wes is at his phone: "Fuck, man! It's all sold out. The film festival is like an advance fucking screening or something. It's not on general release until December."

Aart smokes spliff after spliff in bed, reading review after review of Moon Boys and watching interview after interview with Firenze & Tulip & the rest of the cast, until sunlight's bothering the curtains, and he tries to sleep, but his heart is pounding, and he feels it, heart rate intensifying, until he's out of bed, on Whitechapel Road, walking into the A&E department of a hospital. The doctor runs an ECG. He asks Aart if he's taken any drugs. Aart says no. "Well, I smoked some weed." The doctor sends Aart away with assurance it's just an anxiety attack, and he should smoke less cannabis. He returns home and lies on the bed. He hears Wes and Andy wake and walk downstairs and some muffled conversations from the kitchen and living room. The front door opening and closing twice. He falls asleep. When Aart wakes its dark.

"Yo! Aart! You home?!" His bedroom door opens. Wes. "Yo, fuck man, you been asleep all day?"

"Uh-huh."

"Look man, get the fuck up. It's Friday. Let's do something."

Aart sits up. Mumbles something about not having money. Wes says not to worry about it, he just got paid. An hour later they're in Central, in some centuries-old pub near Chancery Lane, Wes telling his suited co-workers every minute detail of Future Synergy Coin, the story behind the new movie: the wild rise, the money-splurging insanity, the birthday party Guus threw in his honour. His co-workers are immensely impressed. Aart drinks and drinks and smokes a spliff every time they go out for cigarettes, Wes' workmates chatting a hundred questions at him. Someone buys coke. They're in a cab, then a club. Ketamine. MDMA. Some girl tells Wes in the smoking area that she's an actress. Aart looks at her: she looks like an actress. Pretty. Slim. Blonde. The kind of girl who would play the lead role in some cheesy London-set rom-com. Her favourite actress is Jodie Foster. She tells Wes about Foster's roles, how much she loves Children of Men, Magnolia, Cab Stand. *Firenze.* Wes is off, and she's heard of Moon Boys, and is looking forward to seeing it, then she's speaking with Aart, and he tells her everything: the stolen money, Hanoi, the hospital, the video of Ciara and Nguyen…

"Fucking hell, mate. That's insane."

They take a bomb of MDMA together and a dance quickly becomes passionate making out on the dancefloor and then the club's closing and one of Wes's workmates suggests an afterparty at his place in Canary Wharf & Ally the pretty blonde actress tells Aart to come back to her place instead. She lives in an upstairs single-room flat near Old Street station. Aart pays the £12.20 taxi fare with his card, thankful when it isn't declined. She pours glasses of white wine & Aart rolls a spliff and they drink & smoke & make out on the bed listening to Tame Impala. As sun beats against the curtains, Ally gently pushes Aart away and says she wants to slip into something more comfortable. With her back to him, she opens the wardrobe, unzips the back of her dress & pulls it over her head, unhooks her bra, drops it to the floor, and pulls on a T-shirt. She returns to the bed. They make out more, he grasping her breasts under the T-shirt. She rubs her hand against his crotch, undoes his belt. Feels it skin on skin. Maybe because of the drugs, the late hour, the alcohol, or likely a combination of all, it only half swells. They make out more, Aart removing her T-shirt, she removing his, he kicking his jeans off, it still not fully rising. He apologises. She says don't worry about it. She falls asleep resting her head on his chest. He drifts into dreams of Guus & Nguyen & parties with Olly Tulip, they all taking it in turns with Jack McAvoy & Justin Sun & Vitalik Buterin & Satoshi Nakamoto to fuck Ally & Fatima & Elena & Ciara as Aart stands naked on the yacht deck, furiously tugging at his penis, desperate for an erection, the others laughing as they switch partners frequently and the girls groan and Aart stands tugging at his flaccid dick.

When they wake in mid-afternoon, Ally says she has to meet someone, but she wants to see him again, and he takes her number, and leaves, and sees he has missed calls & messages from Wes, and talks as he walks toward Old Street Tube station, and goes to meet Wes & Andy at the Wetherspoons on Leicester Square. As they drink, Aart types & deletes a half-dozen draft messages to Ally. They move to another pub, and another, and one of Wes's workmates joins them, then two of Andy's, and they move to a club near Notting Hill, and Aart blacks out at some point, vague recollections of trying to impress some girl in the smoking area by saying there's a movie based on him, and her boyfriend wanting to punch him, and Wes trying to calm things and Andy threatening the girl's boyfriend until Andy got punched, and Sunday's lost to the bed, everyone out of the house already when Aart goes down to the sofa just before midday on Monday, Britain's upcoming election

& the mounting evidence of the Trump impeachment inquiry dominating BBC News over the next two days.

"It's Guy Fawkes night," Wes says on the phone.

Aart doesn't know what it is but agrees to join Wes & some co-workers at the South Bank to drink beer and watch fireworks fill the sky. He messages Ally asking if she's watching the fireworks. No reply comes. He pauses each time he chops vegetables in the kitchen, considering taking the knife to his wrist.

"It's Friday," Wes says.

Wes wants to go out. Aart's bank balance is nearing zero.

"Don't worry, man, you'll make some money soon. I know you'd do the same for me."

Dingwalls, a small music venue in Camden. Goodbye Mr McKenzie, some grey-haired Scottish rock group who sound American. Chatting to beautiful East European girls drinking cans outside an off-license. Hours and hours of house at Egg, MDMA making music ever better in the strobe-lit Victorian warehouse's interior. Conversations quickly forgotten.

Aart lies in bed mid-afternoon Monday, staring at the messages he's sent Ally, wondering why she's ghosted him. He makes a mini-spliff with weed & tobacco debris from the living room table as BBC News discusses Thursday's election. Aart has £11.21 left in his Barclays account. He owes Wes many times that for what was spent over the weekend. He stands & turns off the TV as his phone vibrates with a message. He lifts it, expecting Ally; disappointed, he sees it's Wes. Moon Boys is out now on general release. Does he want to go see it tonight? Aart doesn't reply. He leaves the house. He walks Whitechapel Road through light rain to Tower Bridge, the daytime bustle across it too hectic to entertain ideas of throwing himself off. He continues along the north bank of the river, the dour grey buildings and skies of overcast London inducing deep melancholy. *Pigs get slaughtered.* Seeing the movie is the last thing he wants to do. Rain gets heavier, umbrellaless pedestrians dashing for cover as Aart continues along the Strand, past Trafalgar Square, the Mall, Buckingham Palace, St. James Park, Hyde Park, Kensington. Amid the calm residential streets and embassies of posh West London, Aart stops to stare at hoarding outside a conference center. *Future of FinTech 2019. Exploring blockchain's impact on the next generation of finance.* Rain falls ever harder as he stands and stares. Then his mind clears as the rain lessens. He thinks of the fucked status of his own financial future and walks toward the venue.

Security guy: "You got a ticket, mate?"

Aart walks away from the venue. A few minutes later he's in a pub, paying most of what remains in his account for a second-rate IPA. He stares at Wes' message on his phone. *Do you want to see the movie?* The time's 5.25pm. Wes will finish work in five minutes.

"It's a fucking cracking film, mate, you gotta go see it," Aart hears someone in a group a few tables away say. "And it goes to show, marketing's everything in this game. Just like you saw with Boris in the election. We've gotta make marketing the top priority before we roll out anything. That coin what the movie's based on, they've still not sorted a working product out, but it's pumping like hell with that bloke who plays Insect Boy and Alberto Firenze making a bloody two-and-a-half hour infomercial for them."

"Yeah," another voice at the table reasons, "but we're not bloody likely to get a Hollywood motion picture based on us, are we?"

"Yeah, no, but long before that, them lads put everything into marketing. That's all they had was marketing."

"Excuse me." The three mid-30s blokes at the table turn to look at Aart. "I'm sorry, but were you guys talking about Moon Boys?"

"Yeah," says the conversation leader, a bald bloke in a Ralph Lauren polo shirt. "Why's that?"

"I heard you guys talking about the marketing behind Future Synergy Coin. Well, I actually used to be their marketing manager."

Where do u wanna watch it?

7.10pm, the Vue on Regent Street.

The theatre darkens.

FADE IN.

White dots appear on screen, flashing for half-seconds, faint, like the forming of a universe.

A beat passes, and the stars begin lasting on screen longer; links start forming between them - a VISUAL REPRESENTATION of the BLOCKCHAIN.

As the star-like white dots & their interconnected links fill the screen, we HEAR our narrator, OLLY TULIP, playing the role of GUUS VAN HOOIJDINK, begin to SPEAK:

OLLY TULIP as GUUS VAN HOOIJDINK:

I've seen the best minds of my generation enriched by blockchain: coding hysterical tokens, dragging themselves to white-collar conferences at dawn, looking for investment capital; angelheaded hipsters programming a new ancient heavenly connection to the starry dynamo in the machinery of night, whose billion-dollar marketcaps shoot up, rocketing from supernatural darkness to moon landings across the tops of cities struggling with regulatory-incompliant finance fuckery; who built their blockchains to Heaven with distributed ledgers and saw the great huddled masses grow wings & become angel investors, pouring their souls into a hundred million billion-dollar ICOs…

MOON BOYS.

An Alberto Firenze Film.

MUSIC: Honey Badger ft. Lil Profit & Lil Boaty – Crypto Cats Eat Pussy Sushi.

Credits play over a MONTAGE SEQUENCE: Olly Tulip as Guus addressing conference halls, plazas, jump cuts between locations, words.

OLLY TULIP as GUUS VAN HOOIJDINK:

…like the band, playing on the Titanic as water rises around your ankles…

…replacing crude internationalism with pure globalism, a fully decentralized economy with independent nodes in every city and state upon this planet…

…a post-blockchain blockchain platform for all, from the wealthiest Wall Street banker to the poorest African subsistence farmer…

…death to monotheism, to centralized command structures…

…I AM BECOME BLOCKCHAIN, DISRUPTOR OF WORLDS…

…those who master the blockchain will for the next two thousand years be gods.

EXTERIOR SHOT: a yellow Lamborghini Aventador races through sunny Californian streets.

A cute bit of meta commentary as the scene FREEZE FRAMEs;

OLLY TULIP as GUUS VAN HOOIJDINK:

That's me, Guus van Hooijdink. Creator of Future Synergy Coin. Billionaire. Blockchain God. And that's Olly Tulip in the seat next to me. He's the actor who portrays me in this movie. He's come to California to shadow me in preparation for this role. The poor kankerautist doesn't know what the fuck he's letting himself in for.

UNFREEZE: the Lamborghini roars off, the pulsing Californian punk of Agent Orange – Bloodstains blasting from the car stereo & over the movie's soundtrack.

INTERIOR - THE FRAT HOUSE:

Olly Tulip as Guus & the sort-of vaguely Asian-looking Yuval Mendes as Nguyen sit on quad sofas in a near-perfect replica of the frat house, Honey Badger music video playing on the television as they share a joint & stare at laptops & discuss the price trajectories of various cryptocurrencies.

A FRAT-MATE (unnamed) enters, complaining about the mess & debris covering the room from the previous night's party.

Yuval Mendes as Nguyen leaves the sofa to join Unnamed Frat-Mate #1 in grabbing cans, stuffing them into trash bags, while Olly Tulip as Guus keeps smoking weed & staring at the laptop screen.

Unnamed Frat-Mate #1 stands over Olly Tulip as Guus, shouting his frustration.

A doorbell rings.

UNNAMED FRAT-MATE #1:

Fuck! She's here!

Unnamed Frat-Mate #1 drops the trash bag & exits the room.

Olly Tulip as Guus keeps smoking the joint & staring at the laptop. He slowly turns his head to the television as Honey Badger's music video reaches the bit with the naked big-titted blonde girl, her body covered in sushi.

Unnamed Frate-Mate #1 returns.

UNNAMED FRAT-MATE #1:

Yo Guus, this is Kendra.

ELLEN CHAPMAN as KENDRA:

Hi!

The movie continues as a twisted alternate dimension rendering of the truth: Ellen Chapman as Kendra standing in for Ciara, helping with the whitepaper, she falling for Olly Tulip as Guus as she works on it; the first disastrous conference speech in Amsterdam, the growing swagger & confidence through those that follow; a celebratory Christmas party, Olly Tulip in blackface as Guus as Zwarte Piet, Ellen Chapman as Kendra drunkenly making out with Yuval Mendes as Nguyen, a love triangle causing conflict between the leads. The trashed suite of the Burj Al Arab Jumeirah. A fist-fight in the Moscow hotel suite of Jesse Eisenberg as Vitalik Buterin. Terse conversation between Olly/Guus and Yuval/Nguyen in a Groningen pub as the price collapses. New York Blockchain Week. Yang Yu as Alice approaching Olly/Guus & Yuval/Nguyen's table at a nightclub moments before gunfire erupts from somewhere inside. An intimate love scene between Olly/Guus & Yu/Alice in her hotel room, Olly as Guus making the whole theatre except Aart & Wes laugh as he throws the door open naked to the employee bringing their ordered room service. Honey Badger & Lil Profit & Lil Boaty performing Crypto Cats Eat Pussy Sushi aboard the FSC superyacht against a New York City skyline backdrop, Olly as Guus interrupting them from the upper deck, his speech cut short by an assassination attempt. Reconciliation between Olly as Guus & Yuval as Nguyen at the new Future Synergy Coin offices in Palo Alto. Closing monologue over a wild party scene at Olly as Guus' Hillsborough mansion, Olly Tulip as Olly Tulip drawing huge laughs as he stumbles fucked up through the chaos.

"Tha's wild," Shanise says. "So they just straight up stole your money? And you don't get no movie royalties or nothing?"

"Nope," Aart says.

"What a pair of fucking arseholes," says Laura.

Aart & Wes & Wes' two co-workers - Shanice from South London & Laura from Glasgow – are in Foundation on Covent Garden drinking £10 cocktails. A few rounds later, they're in a taxi, then Stepney Green, spliff on the sofa, then Shanice is in Aart's bedroom, gushing as he tongues her, screaming as he thrusts inside her, their noise far drowning out that from the next room.

Aart arrives at Holborn station around 10.30 the next morning and stares with satisfaction at the slick steel-and-glass office complex, smoking a rollie made from tobacco borrowed from Wes. He enters the building at 10.42 & rides the elevator to SharkFin's 10th floor office.

"Good morning!" Luke the bald SharkFin chief says, reintroducing Aart to Mark, a pompadoured hip urbanite in a checked shirt who was also at the pub yesterday & now is busy at his computer, and Damian, a previously-unseen computer programmer with long greasy black hair and a Dimmu Bogir T-shirt furiously working on lines of code, the back of his computer monitor touching Mark's. Aart glances out the window over the bustle of Central London before sitting opposite Luke at the only other desk in the compact office space.

"So you've heard of payday loans, yeah? Someone needs cash quick, maybe their boiler's sprung a leak, or their cupboards are bare, and they don't get paid for another week, so they take out a small loan to tide them over.

Few questions asked, little in the way of credit checks, but exorbitant rates of interest."

"Yeah, sure," Aart says, not having heard of payday loans, but thinking he should give them a google if he doesn't get the job.

"It's become a hot topic these days because what they are is glorified loan sharks. You take out one hundred pounds today and if you pay it back next week, all's fine and dandy. But you're buggered if there's a balls up. Two thousand percent APR. You borrow a hundred quid today, you might be paying off twenty grand before you've got a handle on it. That's where SharkFin comes in. We're finishing these loan sharks – disrupting the little buggers' swimming patterns and drowning the whole sordid industry. Peer-to-peer lending through a mobile app. You wanna borrow some cash pronto, just whip out your phone, say how much you need, another user sends the cash to you, you pay them back with five percent interest per month. Lovely stuff. And our Great Whites, as we call them, throw whatever cash they fancy into the pot and get a guaranteed return of three percent per month, leaving us a fair two percent take. Now, three percent per month might not sound a lot to a blockchain moon boy like yourself, but let me tell you, that is three percent guaranteed per month, which, compounded interest over the course of a year, gives you about a forty-two-point-five-seven-six percent interest rate. Absolutely shits on any high street savings account. Shits on stocks, shits on real estate. Heck, that kind of return shits on anything you could stick your money in, other than cryptocurrency. Invest a hundred grand today, get almost a hundred fifty back this time next year. Sounds pucker, yeah?"

"Yeah. It does."

As Aart's wondering what 'pucker' means, Luke's explaining how the app's in beta, they've onboarded a few early sign-ups, but with Christmas around the corner, now's the perfect time to go big with a killer marketing campaign to capitalise on the silly amounts of money people will be pissing away on parties and presents. "So what do you reckon?"

"Yeah, it sounds good. Great."

"I mean, what do you reckon for the marketing campaign? We need to get working on this pronto. We gave you a google, we know you're legit. Future Synergy Coin went from a penny stock to a four billion dollar market cap in what, four months? Look, how about you have a think about it today, pop back in tomorrow and tell us what you've come up with? Have a play around on the app first…"

With total trust in Aart's marketing acumen, Luke helps him install the app on his phone, shows him the £4,500 a month salary he'll be getting, and personally approves a £2,000 SharkFin app-enabled advance on it to prove how easy it all is.

"Holy shit," Aart says, walking along Kingsway, staring at the £2,001.21 balance in his Barclays account. He thinks of Shanice. Moon Boys. £4,500 a month. Fucking a fit black girl. He stops outside a pub, thinking of taking a celebratory drink, but carries on, thinking of the need for a marketing idea. He buys a packet of Camel Blue, smokes two, then goes into a Caffe Nero and spends £8 on a panini and a grande Americano. £1,981.75 remaining.

Sharks. Sharks are elasmobranch fish with cartilaginous skeletons, gill slits, and pectoral fins. Loan sharks are informal microfinanciers often associated with the criminal underworld. Shark finning is the practice of removing sharks fins at sea, increasing the maximum load obtainable by a single fishing vessel. Sharks first appeared in Earth's oceans 450 to 250 million years ago and have since diversified into over 500 distinct species. Payday loan providers in the UK saw business grow by 400% between 2006 and 2009. Finned sharks are returned to the ocean where, unable to swim, they sink to the bottom and drown. The UK payday loan industry peaked at £2 billion in 2013 and has since sunk to around £228 million due to increased regulation & compensation claims. Though the global shark product trade is thought to be approaching $1 billion per year, comprehensive knowledge of the trade remains elusive.

"Fucking sharks," Andy says between gulps of the big bottle of beer Aart gifted him. "Nasty cunts, sharks. Boy I was at school with had his fucking left ankle bitten off by one of them fishy fuckers."

"Remember what you told me when you were first starting with the shitcoin?" Wes says, wrapping a spliff with fresh-bought skunk. "About mouthwash? They didn't have a use for it, they thought it might be industrial cleaner or something. Then the marketing guys invented a use."

Aart stares at the television. The magicians and music and comedy performances of the bizarrely British birthday celebration for Prince Charles comes to a commercial break. Andy lifts the remote.

"Don't," Aart says. "I need to see how people advertise here."

"This poncey pom royal shit is the only thing on anyway," Andy says, standing up to go take a piss.

Ads play. Usain Bolt as James Bond for Virgin Media. Natalie Portman diving into the ocean for some fragrance. Night Nurse Day & Night for colds & flu. A sad orangutan & plastic-filled oceans for the World Wildlife Fund.

Wes rants about charities, the bullshit rip-off, the sad orangutan reminding him of their sad week going door-to-door.

Relieve the feeling of foot fatigue with Scholl Gel Active Insoles. The Dirty Louisiana is back, only at KFC. An excitable gay voiceover narrates a girl spilling crisps on the sofa as her mum enjoys her daily free play on the Sky Bingo app. *I used to be a smoker… now I'm a Dad. When your baby feels hip, you can feel hip too with Hipp – the organic baby food company.* A cute computer-animated meerkat telling his identical but Russian computer-animated meerkat cousin how much money he could save on car insurance.

When Andy & Wes go to bed, Aart stays on the sofa, chain smoking and scribbling notes and ideas, looking up at each ad break, searching through channels for them. He enters the 10th floor office the next morning and tells Luke his marketing plan: a TV spot with a sunny beach, sunbathers rushing in panic after spotting a shark fin. SharkFin dude emerging, saying *don't worry, this shark's on your side!* Promo staff at busy Tube stations, shark fins strapped to their back, handing out flyers. A free fiver when you install the app, slogan: *lunch is on us – eat like a shark!*

"Good stuff, mate! Good stuff. But… well, we're not gonna find a sunny beach to film on in England any time soon, and shooting overseas at short notice is a bit of a potch, and a fiver's a bit steep… maybe two quid? Have a nibble on us?"

Aart's soon on the phone to costume makers and graphic designers. The week passes in a blur of activity. Wes is paid back what he's owed. Ally messages. She'd lost her phone, now restored WhatsApp. Friday few beers with the SharkFin guys, then Aart joins Wes & his co-workers at another bar in Central, they all sharing opinions on Boris Johnson's landslide election victory. He makes out with Shanice when others leave the smoking area. Back to her place in New Cross. Fuck again in the morning. Meet Wes and Andy in Camden for beers at the Wetherspoons on the Canal. Bar-hopping and a club in Dalston. Back to some fashion student from Sheffield's place in Stoke Newington. Her tongue probes Aart's inner ear as her finger slips inside his rectum. Morning wake to a text from Ally: *How's your weekend going? Fine,* Aart replies, balls still cupped in the sleeping fashion student's hands. *How's yours?* Meets her at some dimly-lit cocktail bar near her place where the drinks are based on movies. Ally follows a La La Land with a Moulin Rouge, Aart drinking a Raging Bull & a Wolf of Wall Street. To her home, lines of ketamine, she telling of a part she's up for in a BBC spy series, showing him a clip of Oishin Byrne awkwardly licking her nipples from the one independently-produced feature film she made a brief appearance in. Aart's soon recreating the scene, she laughing, more keys of ketamine before he enters her, Monday morning slowly arriving through a haze of K snorting, white wine sipping, fucking & napping. To the office in the same clothes he left work Friday in. Getting quotes from TFL for Tube & bus ads. Meeting Wes & Shanice & others of Wes' co-workers at a pub. Bringing Shanice back to Stepney, making her squirt through cunnilingus & then drilling her hard as a follow-up. Tuesday, dash to work, no time for a shower. Returning home, smoking one spliff on the sofa, heading to bed & passing out immediately. Wake up 5am Wednesday. Lie in bed until 7. Finally shower the days of filth & fucking away. Clean the nose out with cupped hands of water, clotted blood-snot hitting the sink. Delivery at the office of a shark costume, a dozen fins, and several thousand flyers. Candidates file in for interviews to stand around London hotspots handing flyers out. Shock at Fatima & Emily, the hijab-wearing and half-Japanese girls Aart & Wes briefly worked with on the shitty door-to-door job, arriving for an interview. Aart tells them they start tomorrow then makes sure to assign them to a patch he will have direct oversight of. Beers with Wes & Andy at the house after work then back into Central & Tottenham Court Road & The Roxy, then back home again with two Swedish girls, Aart drunkenly pushing the black-haired girl's legs back at such an awkward angle that she sours on fucking & finishes him off with a handjob. The next day's spent bothering shoppers on Oxford Street with Fatima & Emily & a purple-haired Czech girl whose name Aart soon forgets. Aart invites the three of them to the flat in Stepney Green. Somewhere between the third and fourth bottle of wine, Andy drops a deck of cards on the coffee table & suggests a game of strip shithead. Fatima's soon in nothing but the hijab, unwrapping the bottom of it to cover other parts of herself. She refuses to let the hijab be part of the game, conceding defeat. Wes, Aart, & Andy strip to boxers to encourage Emily & the Czech girl to keep playing. The living room is soon an orgy of rotating partnerships, Aart heading to the bathroom to clean off after giving the Czech girl an Eiffel tower with Wes to find Fatima scrubbing at her hijab, furious Andy got cum on it. Friday, plans for the post-Christmas period & review of progress made thus far discussed at the office. With Wes & Shanice & others of Wes' co-workers to a pub then club near Piccadilly Circus. Message from Ally asking if he's busy. Blowjob from Shanice down an alleyway. Disappearing mid-way through the night to Old Street & bombing MDMA, chain smoking cigarettes, telling Ally she'll find a role that suits her & watching her recite Julia Stiles' 10 Things I Hate About You soliloquy to Heath Ledger & fucking softly while kissing side-by-side & falling asleep in each other's arms & waking Saturday to Ally saying her parents are in London for the day & she has to go meet them & heading back to Stepney to pick up weed, the most dependable local boys not answering, eventually contacting one lad who passed Aart his number months ago & meeting him down some secluded alleyway half-way to Bethnal Green & two much bigger lads saying "Blud, the fuck you playing at, buying off teenagers?", Aart's heart palpitating as he anticipates a beating & mugging but leaving instead with the number of a new weed dealer, leaving the skinny Indian-British teen to argue with the bigger lads as he walks home with his 20 bag. Wes asks where he went last night & says Shanice seemed pissed off. They meet her & Laura the Scottish girl Wes works with for drinks in Central & Shanice is distant & they leave soon after and Wes & Aart go meet Andy & his co-workers & watch Manchester City thrash Leicester 3-1 & pick up several grams of coke & head to Fabric for a long night of German-style house & techno. Recovery Sunday, smoking weed at home & watching Goodfellas. On Monday the 23rd, Aart & Wes fly together from Stansted to Schiphol and head into Amsterdam for a frat reunion before returning to their families for Christmas.

"I's crazy, their stupid fuck idea became this Hollywood movie," Federico says as they sit drinking Belgian beers on a pavement cafe at Rembrandtplein, "and the name is what I told them, FSC, the fucking shitcoin. I should be paid some of the monies from all of this."

"Don't mention the monies around Aart!" Jako says, playfully slapping Aart on the shoulder.

"They really stole from you everything, huh?" asks Wander.

Aart sighs. "I don't know." He's done with it. He's long given up on the investigations of Europol's hi-tech crime task force & their American counterparts turning up anything.

"I tried to get in touch with Guus while I was in the States," Rick says, "but I never heard back from him."

"He's gone," Max says. "Rich beyond us fucks' wildest dreams."

Conversation flits to other topics through the evening but always comes back to the unlikely star of their frat alumni.

"When I see Olly Tulip playing him in this movie, I think, how can I be like this?" Federico says as they smoke spliffs in a coffee shop off Dam Square. "The girls. Is crazy, no? You must miss this shit of when you were going around the world with them."

"Yeah," Aart admits. "It's funny; before we made the coin, we were talking about how we could be more like you. You had girls back all the time. Me and Guus… not so much."

"But then I become like a shit comparing to you," Federico says. "Once you become rich."

They drink & smoke through the night at their overcrowded Airbnb, Aart thinking how he's begun imitating Guus without realising it. And it's working.

The next day, the group splinters on train rides back to their home provinces. Aart's younger sister Marjolijn returns to Drachten from her university in Madrid. Together with their parents & grandmother they enjoy a traditional Dutch Christmas: appelbeignets, advocaat, kruidnoten, kerststol, & speculaas. Aart refreshes his banking app constantly, wondering why SharkFin's payment still hasn't appeared. He keeps refreshing through Saturday & Sunday as the family play board games & watch television, but knows it's unlikely to be processed on a weekend. On the train back to Schiphol Airport on Monday, his concern at the non-payment grows.

"Don't worry," Wes says back at their flat in Stepney Green. "It's probably just delayed because of the holiday."

On New Year's Eve, Aart messages Ally & Shanice & Emily & Fatima & the Swedish girl from The Roxy & the art student from New Cross asking how their Christmas was. None of them reply. Andy complains of how boring Christmas was alone in London and how fucking cold it is as they drink through to the evening, then head into Central, ring in New Year in a pub, Aart's drunken attempts to get a midnight kiss from any of the women inside rejected. Drugs on drugs at a Hackney squat rave. Wednesday 1st January, brutal combination of hangover & comedown leaves Aart bedridden until close to 8pm. Then he joins Andy & Wes smoking spliffs in the living room. 2020. A new decade has begun.

Thursday 2nd January, Aart rides the Tube to Holborn with other bleary-eyed work returnees. He rides the elevator to SharkFin's 10th floor office. The door is locked. He knocks. No answer. He calls Luke. It rings through to answerphone. He calls Mark. It doesn't even ring. Aart stands outside the locked door feeling his world collapse. Maybe he stands there five minutes, maybe it's an hour. But it becomes clear nobody's coming. Follow up calls to Luke ring without being answered. Calls to Mark don't even ring.

Back on the street, Aart walks a few steps toward Holborn Station then turns back, wanting to lose himself in London. He walks into the next pub that he passes. He sees Damian, SharkFin's metalhead computer whizz, sitting at a table with a pint.

"Oh, bloody hell," Damian says glumly on noticing him. "I guess you're just as fucked as I am?"

By the fourth pint, Aart is fully convinced by Damian's theory: that SharkFin failed to make anything much in their first week of operation & owed a ton to those who'd invested start-up capital. Luke and Mark had cut their losses. Possibly left the country.

Aart barely leaves the flat in the weeks that follow. By mid-January, Wes has given up on asking him out for drinks. Aart watches his bank balance creep slowly back toward zero as he spends days smoking heavy spliff after heavy spliff, eating pitta bread & hummus, BBC News painting a picture from morning until night of a world slipping ever closer to calamity: American airstrikes killing an Iranian general, wildfires roaring through Australia, huge crowds & stampedes & a hefty death toll at the Iranian general's funeral, smoke-filled orange skies over Oceania, Iranian strikes on US bases in Iraq, a 6.4-magnitude earthquake in Puerto Rico, a passenger jet crashing after take-off in Tehran, a volcano erupting in Mexico, Iranian authorities admitting they downed the passenger jet accidentally, the march to an American-Iran war coinciding perfectly with the build-up to Trump's impeachment hearing, a strange new virus passing person-to-person in China…

"Man, you have to do something. When did you even shower last?"

Aart doesn't remember.

"Come on," Wes continues. "You have to do something."

"What?" is all Aart can think to answer.

"Find a job. Leave the house. Live your life. Come on."

"Why?"

Wes doesn't have an answer. BBC News fills the silence, reporting of a full lockdown of the city of Wuhan in China, nobody allowed in or out of the city of 11 million people – a city larger in population than London.

"I cannot afford to pay your rent again," Wesley warns.

Aart says nothing, watching the crowds in facemasks in China on the television.

He lies in bed at night staring at the ceiling, wondering if his time in London is over. 2020. A new decade. *Pigs get slaughtered.* Australia in flames. Wuhan in lockdown. America's President on trial. He cannot continue to drift and sink. Light fills the curtains before sleep comes. He listens to Wes and Andy leave for work. He walks downstairs. He doesn't touch the television. He opens the laptop. He searches: london, cryptocurrency, blockchain, marketing, finance. He submits CVs. He receives a phone call. He travels to Canary Wharf, an enclave of sleek high-rise finance towers floating on the Thames, connected to the rest of the city by a futuristic monorail. The interview goes well, the woman and man interviewing him having seen Moon Boys. Another phone call, an offer. February, the decade looks bright, busy days in the bustle of Canary Wharf's financial district, thoughts of moving out from Stepney Green & finding a place of his own, moving onward & upward, leaving all that happened in the 2010s behind.

"Aart."

Aart turns from his co-workers. *Ciara.*

He says something to his co-workers, maybe, he's not sure. He forgets his lunch and walks with her to the Starbucks in front of the tower he now works at.

"You look good."

"Yeah. You too."

"How long have you been in London?"

He doesn't even know the answer. Ciara continues talking – explaining she's seen his picture on the website, a press release about the bank he's working for's new blockchain initiative.

"Look… Aart. I know what happened to your coins. I have them." She explains: his secret key, written on a scrap of paper in his room at the frat house. She transferred it all to another wallet, then shapeshifted it to other cryptocurrencies. She was so angry at him after their argument. And so fucked up over finding out Nguyen made a video. She flew to South-East Asia after she did it. And she felt fucking terrible but too scared to go back.

"I have to go back to work," Aart tells her. "We'll talk later."

Aart can't concentrate on anything through the afternoon. When he leaves, she's standing outside waiting for him. They make small talk as they walk to the nearest bar and each order a Peroni.

"Ciara… what the fuck. I don't understand. Explain it to me again. Slowly."

She does.

"So… you have the coins? All of the coins?"

"Yeah. Most of it. It's in Bitcoin and Monero and Ethereum and some other cryptocurrencies. I didn't know what to do with it… I regretted it so fucking much, but… once it was done… I didn't know what to do. I couldn't go back… I panicked. It drove me crazy. Aart. I don't know… I'm so sorry." She starts to cry. He doesn't know what to say, think, feel. Relief, anger, joy, fury, sorrow. All at once. She says she's staying at a Premier Inn next to the London Eye on the South Bank. They ride a crowded Jubilee line train to Waterloo, saying little until they're in the room & the door is closed.

"So… how much is left?"

"All of it. I mean… the value is less than when I took it, because of the market crash, but I spent, like, a few thousand dollars. I'm sorry. It's fucking shitty of me, and crazy. I wanted to find you, and tell you. But I went back to Groningen, and it was too late. You'd gone. I couldn't tell anyone else. I didn't want to message you and tell you… I had to find you… and tell you face to face…"

Why? Aart doesn't ask her this. He considers the possibilities. Maybe she genuinely felt this had to be communicated face-to-face. Maybe she was afraid of admitting the theft in writing.

There are practical matters: contacting the authorities, telling them the funds have been recovered, to call off the investigation. Arranging a large OTC sale of all the cryptocurrency, transferring what remains of the fortune into fiat currency. Lawyers are needed. Tax expert accountants. But he's sure to have tens of millions of dollars, however complex and costly the process of legitimising the recovered funds.

"You must hate me," she says.

He tells her that he doesn't; he's just relieved. Not just for the money; to see her again. He isn't sure if he means it.

"The video… with Nguyen… I was so drunk that night… all I remember is waking up in a hotel room with him, and I had no idea he filmed anything… or even what we'd done together… and I'm sorry, Aart… I'm so fucking sorry… I was so angry at him, and you, and all of you… but… it wasn't your fault… and I acted like an idiot… *fuck*… I am so sorry, Aart…"

They drink two bottles of wine and talk endlessly and she falls asleep in his arms on his bed, he looking out at the London Eye, thinking of the months he's spent in this city. He supposes there's little point in returning to work. Remaining in London. He can do anything. Buy a boat. Cruise the Med. Stop off at cities along the coastlines of Spain, Italy, Morocco, Algeria, Greece, Cyprus… keep going, circling the waters. Together. Live like that forever. Or talk it over one more time. Record her confession. Hand the evidence to the authorities. A lawyer. Lock her up. Or take the boat to the Med, slit her throat, throw her body overboard. Or forgive. And love. Live together forever. He stares out the window at the London Eye, illuminated against the hazy semi-dark of London night, listening to her breathe, feeling the weight of her head on his chest.

What would Guus do?

27. LIFE ON MARS.

…& fireworks explode over Silicon Valley, the new decade begins, partygoers kissing, cheering, happy new years in all directions, & Guus grabs Caroline the FSC MD he knows Nguyen's fucking & asks for a midnight kiss & she hesitates before leaning toward him cheek-first, & Guus sees Nguyen watching him & smirks & takes another champagne flute & hors d'oeuvres and shouts across the Hotel Valhalla rooftop bar "WHO'S GOT COKE?!" & rails lines with software devs & asks the Chinese-American if his name is 'Who' & coked-up suck-up software devs adopt it as inside joke & shout "Who's got coke!" each time Guus passes them & he stops to nail another few lines, & he sees Nguyen leave with Caroline & Jack McAvoy & McAvoy's harem of surely-not-21-yet latinas, & there's more lines & drinks & things said & things done, an altercation, an Irish pub, a bar fight, kicked out onto the street, into the blur of chaos, the Bay Area, phone lost, wallet, January 1st, walking for hours through San Jose, Santa Clara, Mountain View, to Palo Alto, all the buzz & energy drained from him, but he reaches the Future Synergy Coin headquarters, bangs at the door, realizes he's locked out & no-one's inside, & he's only half-way to his home in Hillsborough, & the thought of more hours walking defeats him, & he passes out in the parking lot, & police wake him, & he mumbles about the lost phone & wallet & keys to the office, the police officers verify his story, their demeanour changes on seeing he belongs here in Silicon Valley, he's not some vagabond who makes a habit of sleeping rough, & they drive him the rest of the way home, & Alessandro opens the door to the mansion, &

that rat Olly Tulip wins Best Actor for his portrayal of Guus @ the Golden Globes, & Guus sees Alicia at the table with Olly Tulip & Alberto Firenze & Yuval Mendes & Ellen Chapman & Yang Yu as he drinks Glenglassaugh 1967 & watches the ceremony in his home theater, & Guus calls numbers of people who can bring stuff, tells Alessandro he's having a party, & girls arrive, & men bearing drugs, & Raskolnikoff bites one of the hookers, & Guus flings thousands of dollars at her when she threatens to call the police, then waves a shotgun around & tells all his guests to fuck off, & passes out in Alessandro's bed, & wakes & moans at it all, the sordidness of Silicon Valley & hollow new-world old-money wealth of Hillsborough, this fucking dead Gilded Age town of cossetted cunts living among the ghosts of once-great American newspaper tycoons & railroad barons, & Alessandro speaks softly & reassures Guus all will be okay as he strokes & sucks Guus' flaccid penis, minutes passing before it reaches erection, far longer still until Alessandro's moist Italianate lips tease out faint mist reminiscent of cum, & Guus rises & uses Alessandro's en suite shower & walks naked through the servants quarters & kitchen & half-dozen rooms of the enfilade surveying the debris of the night before's chaos, & shouts for Rosa, & Alessandro rushes to Guus & removes the toothbrush from his mouth to tell Guus she left after what the two Google guys did to her, & Guus doesn't ask what they did, & doesn't much care, but wants to leave Hillsborough, & go where the stars are, & tells Alessandro they're going to Los Angeles, &

the second night in L.A. is when the craziness escalates: drinking endless Jack Cokes with two Australian tourist girls in a booth at the Rainbow Room on the Sunset Strip, Guus boasting of knowing Wizz & Tickbag & Bom Ceronie & showing videos on his phone to prove it when the girls call bullshit, & Alessandro returns having procured the requested acid tabs, & Guus spends the next hour or so ranting about how primitive humans discovered mushrooms & ingesting them caused us to formulate consciousness, giving our species the edge over neanderthals & denisovans; & the '60s was a second revolution of consciousness sparked by LSD, the Californian counterculture & the Beats & the hippies & Steve Jobs in India, acid firing the imagination & fuelling the Information Age, the Internet, the smartphone, social media, all Silicon Valley's fertile tech soil enriched by Lysergic Acid Diethylamide backwashed across the San Francisco Bay, & all are tripping hard when his rant turns to astrological ages & Aquarius, water carrier to the gods, & the Australian girls get scared or bored or both & leave, &

argument with security outside the Viper Room, Alessandro drags Guus away, Sunset Strip to Hollywood Boulevard, Guus determined to piss on Olly Tulip's star on the Hollywood Walk of Fame, & Alessandro distracts with promises of escorts brought to their room at the Roosevelt, & Guus says get them or I do it, fuck the police, & he's rapping it loudly as he walks, black homeless guy laughs & joins in & Guus takes him to their suite @ the Roosevelt, Guus masturbating on a plush velvet seat at the glass dining table as the homeless guy fucks the Latina escort with the vigour of a starving man, &

"THREE MILLION DOLLARS, ALESSANDRO, YOU SLUT WHORE RENTBOY PIECE OF SHIT FUCK!"

& Alessandro mumbles apologies as the paramedics tend to him & the police say please calm down sir & the Lamborghini Aventador's wrecked, rolled, shattered, crumpled, pieces of its FSC yellow chassis strewn across I-5, & Guus refuses medical attention until the police say you're going with them or you're coming with us, & after stitches & payment he leaves Scripps Memorial Hospital & takes an Uber to the Mexican border, &

what he's asked for is peyote but what he's got is meth & days bleed into nights & nights into days amid the stupid fat Yank tourists posing for pictures with donkeys painted like zebras on Avenida Revolución & meth-fuelled ravaging of the prostitutes of Zona Norte & more meth purchases & shake downs by the Federales & $500 fines & phone & wallet & passport disappearing from the $20 a night motel room taken when too fucked-up and confused to find his way back to the Palacio Azteca after watching Olly Tulip collect the Oscar for portraying him & Alicia on-screen beside Olly & money wired via Western Union & hours of tweaking comedown at the U.S. Consulate &

disorientation on the flight,

Uber @ San Jose Airport,

home in Hillsborough; most rooms of the mansion fucked, Raskolnikoff thin & weak, maybe weeks unfed; food ordered in excessive quantities, feast of pizza & Indian & Chinese & Mexican, flies filling kitchen & swarming over it as it decomposes;

& drugs & wine & rare whiskies, & smell of the shackled corpse beyond the wine cellar becomes revolting: dragged through garden at night, Guus' stomach churning, dry heaving, trying not to look at him; decomposing corpse doused with bottle of Macallan No. 6 & set alight in the tea house in the Japanese Peace Garden,

& walk across garden becomes a run, fear of the flames engulfing the tea house & police reports, fire fighters, investigation, charred corpse identified by dental records;

& extinguisher found, tea house interior sprayed, &

California under stay at home order, no life left in the state beyond the mansion,

fear of inviting guests for the state of it, & the growing stench & insect infestation in the kitchen, & fear of entering garden for what state the tea house has succumbed to;

& more drugs & sometimes food ordered to the front door, & injecting Raskolnikoff with heroin when the chimp gets wild & restless,

& drifting across deep careless highs above Hillsborough, & when the heroin runs out, there's weed, & coke, & other powders & pills washed down with wines & whiskies,

& energy comes, furious need for fucking, for life beyond this Gilded Age prison as it rots & is reclaimed by rampaging nature, &

Guus' own rampaging nature, furious half-hourly masturbation staring at the fading features of his sallowing complexion,

Krug Grand Cuvée taken from the wine cellar, Raskolnikoff found picking through the rotting foodstuffs abuzz with insect life in the kitchen & led to the salon, the least fucked room of the enfilade, & plied with drink until the chimp topples back, squeaking softly as he lolls on the carpeting,

& Guus unfastens his belt & let his trousers drop, drops to his knees, knocks back Krug Grand Cuvée, pours over Raskolnikoff's genitals & anus & stuffs his erect penis up his chimpanzee,

& thrusts & grunts, faster, harder; Raskolnikoff's squeals grow louder, angrier,

& his hips snap away from Guus, & teeth clamp upon forehead & rip,

& blood blinds Guus, & pain, &

.

$hitcoin.

ABOUT THE AUTHOR

Haydn Wilks was the first writer to enter the Dead Bird Press Aviary with his novel The Death of Danny Daggers, published in 2015. Wilks is from the Welsh valleys town of Caerphilly. He studied English and Film at King's College London. After graduation, he bounced between dead-end jobs on the Cardiff call centre circuit before moving to South Korea to teach English. Wilks' time in Cardiff call centres inspired his first two Cardiff-set novels. The Death of Danny Daggers is a wild tale, a murder mystery with a twist rooted in gritty contemporary British reality. Follow-up Cold Calling is something far more twisted and macabre, a horrific and often sickeningly humorous tale of a call centre drone gone rogue.

Wilks has since lived in Korea, Japan, and the Netherlands. The Death of Danny Daggers was published while Wilks lived in Seoul, South Korea. Cold Calling was written in Groningen, the Netherlands and Tokyo, Japan. Wilks was inspired to write $hitcoin while juggling a teaching job at a university in Gwangju, South Korea with freelance writing work for cryptocurrency news websites.

For more information on Haydn Wilks, head to
deadbirdpress.com/haydn-wilks

COLD CALLING by Haydn Wilks.

"American Psycho meets Crime & Punishment on the Cardiff call centre circuit."

You spend your days staring into a computer screen, trying to sell life insurance to young couples with new babies. You spend your nights staring into a computer screen, extracting filth from and injecting bile into the internet. You still live with the same dickhead housemate you went to university with. Your only respite from computer screens are nights spent getting smashed with your dickhead housemate at student bars, watching him prance around, trying to pull much younger girls. Your life sucks and you suck at it. One drunken night, you try something new. Something terrible. But something that brings you new energy, new drive, new desires. You start eating the young.

READER REVIEWS

"This is hands down, one of the best Horror/Psychological Thrillers I've read in quite some time." – *William Bitner Jr., Goodreads.*

"Haydn's writing is brilliant, he effectively expresses the mind-set of the depraved, the dialogue is realistic and raw, the pacing compelling and perfectly crafted, and whilst the story is pretty damn sick I had to continue reading." – *Spencer, Goodreads.*

"The prose is tight, edgy and authentic. Prepare to be shocked. If you are tired of the very safe and predictable style of so much modern literature go on this journey to the margins of life in Cardiff." – *Thomas Harte, Goodreads.*

"This is a beautifully crafted descent into darkness, a measured deterioration of all that is right. So much new literature is poorly written, but this uses language to draw you in and spit you back out again. Something it accomplishes in the blink of an eye, impossible to put down." – *Tony, Goodreads.*

THE DEATH OF DANNY DAGGERS by Haydn Wilks.

Cardiff. The last few days of summer. Danny Daggers is about to die. He just doesn't realise it yet. A Leeds University student with a very popular YouTube channel, Danny Daggers is taking his alcohol-downing stunts on tour. He's about to find out that not everyone's a fan. Ji Eun is a Korean student doing work experience at the South Wales Post. Rory Gallagher is the alcoholic veteran journo who's mentoring her. Carnage in Cardiff might be just what they need to begin and revive their respective careers. Tom and Joseph work at one of Cardiff's many call centres. Tom is fed up of working boring jobs and living for the weekend. Joseph is just happy to have a job. Then there's the Amstell brothers. Simon's just escaped from prison. And he happens to be the father of Joseph's girlfriend's son. And his brothers happen to be psychopaths. These stories collide and intersect over a frantic few days of heavy drinking, drugs and ultraviolence, set against a backdrop of dystopian modern Britain.

READER REVIEWS

"This is an excellently vulgar small-scale catastrophic story that you just need to read to believe." – *Sam, Goodreads.*

"If you're into dark humor such as that of Chuck Palahniuk, Irvine Welsh, and the like, I highly, highly recommend reading The Death of Danny Daggers. I loved this book. A lot. It was truly a treat to read, and I'm quite looking forward to reading more by Haydn Wilks." – *Kelliann Gomez, Goodreads.*

"Gritty and frighteningly real. I would describe this as a mirror of modern society if they weren't already using the mirror to cut another line. The narrative is an authentic voice of wide experience and the writing is clever without being detached. This is a (very) contemporary who-done-it, a mystery for today's world." – *Tim, Goodreads.*

"Well-paced, very cleverly plotted, with many twists and turns but which all tie up satisfactorily at the end, this is a very fine piece of writing indeed. The descriptions are vivid, the dialogue – often in the vernacular – is convincing, and the characters realistic." – *Mandy, Goodreads.*

"I bloody loved this novel, it held me in a way that only certain novels do. It's dark, foreboding and chilling, it has angst, terrifying characters and real life stories told in a way that transports you to the gritty ketamine fuelled streets of Cardiff." – *Lizzy Baldwin, Goodreads.*

Lightning Source UK Ltd.
Milton Keynes UK
UKHW021032080720
366204UK00005B/76